UPGRADE SOUL

DEDICATED TO MY DAD, DARYL, WHO
GAVE ME SCIENCE FICTION.

AND MY GRANDPA, LEON. MY BEST FRIEND
AND MY INSPIRATION FOR HANK.

YOU'LL BOTH BE FOREVER MISSED.

EZRA CLAYTAN DANIELS

UPGRADE SOUL

A GRAPHIC NOVEL

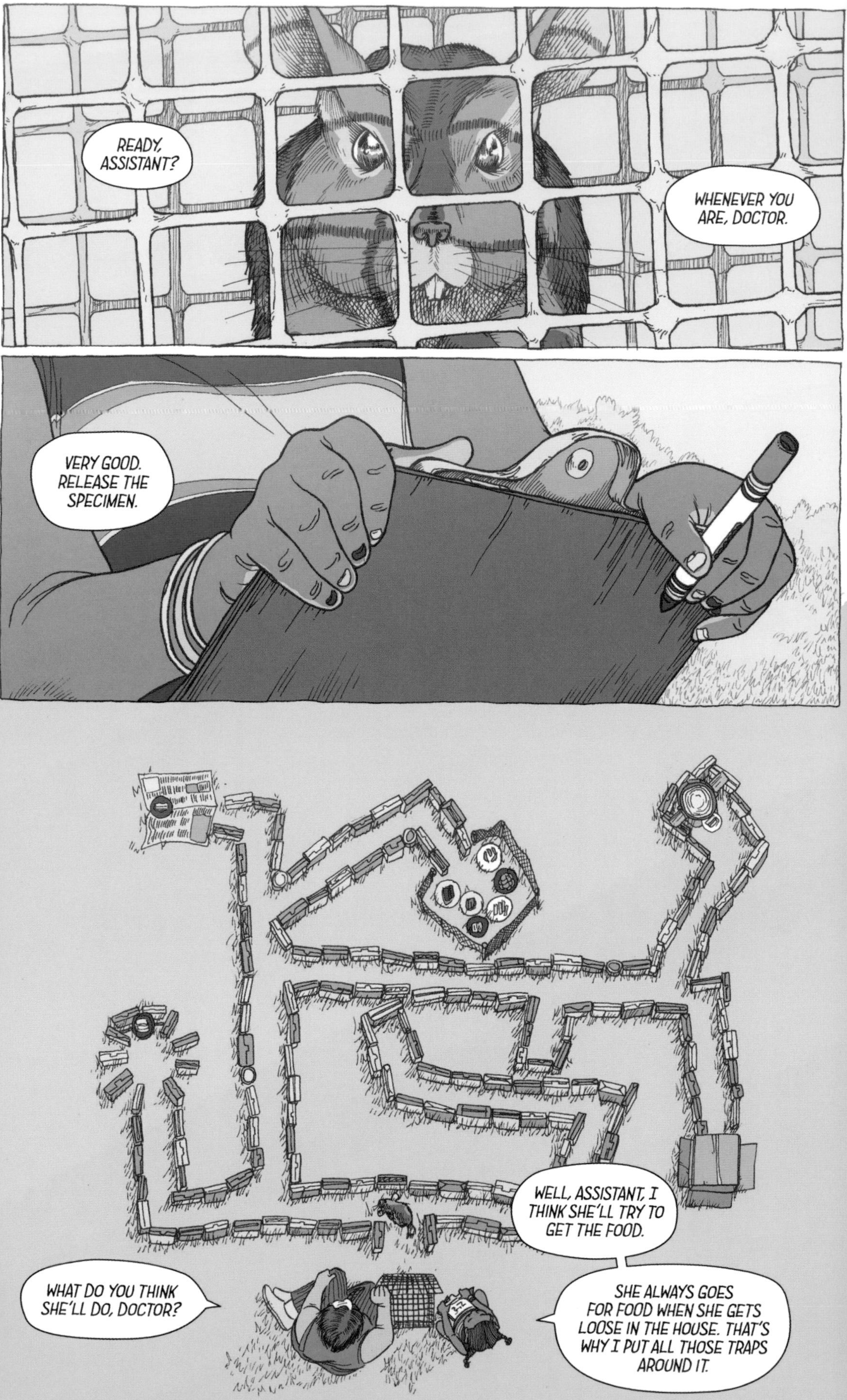
READY, ASSISTANT?
WHENEVER YOU ARE, DOCTOR.
VERY GOOD. RELEASE THE SPECIMEN.
WHAT DO YOU THINK SHE'LL DO, DOCTOR?
WELL, ASSISTANT, I THINK SHE'LL TRY TO GET THE FOOD.
SHE ALWAYS GOES FOR FOOD WHEN SHE GETS LOOSE IN THE HOUSE. THAT'S WHY I PUT ALL THOSE TRAPS AROUND IT.

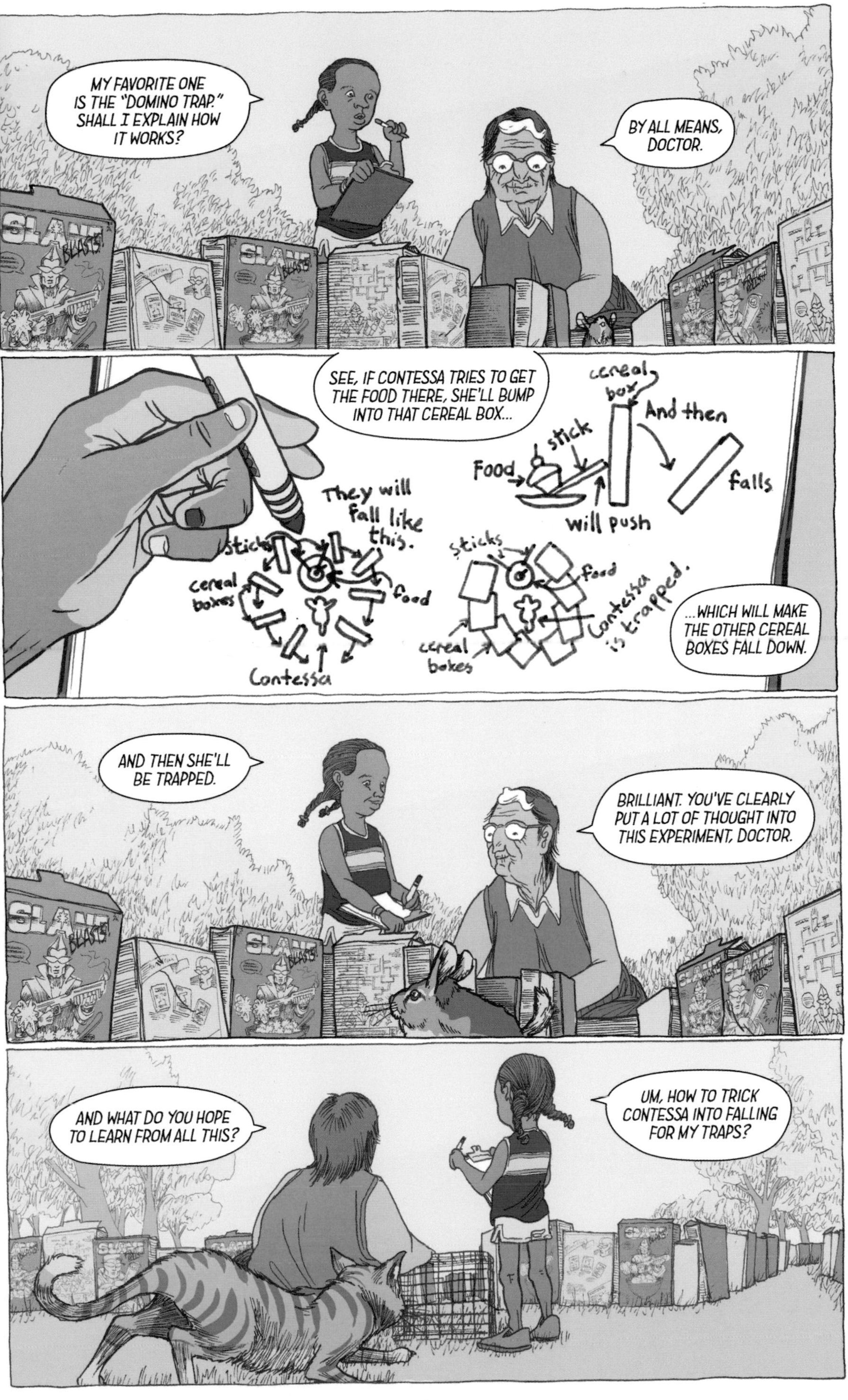

MY FAVORITE ONE IS THE "DOMINO TRAP." SHALL I EXPLAIN HOW IT WORKS?
BY ALL MEANS, DOCTOR.
SEE, IF CONTESSA TRIES TO GET THE FOOD THERE, SHE'LL BUMP INTO THAT CEREAL BOX...
cereal box
And then
stick
Food
falls
will push
They will fall like this.
sticks
cereal boxes
food
Contessa
sticks
food
cereal boxes
Contessa is trapped.
...WHICH WILL MAKE THE OTHER CEREAL BOXES FALL DOWN.
AND THEN SHE'LL BE TRAPPED.
BRILLIANT. YOU'VE CLEARLY PUT A LOT OF THOUGHT INTO THIS EXPERIMENT, DOCTOR.
AND WHAT DO YOU HOPE TO LEARN FROM ALL THIS?
UM, HOW TO TRICK CONTESSA INTO FALLING FOR MY TRAPS?

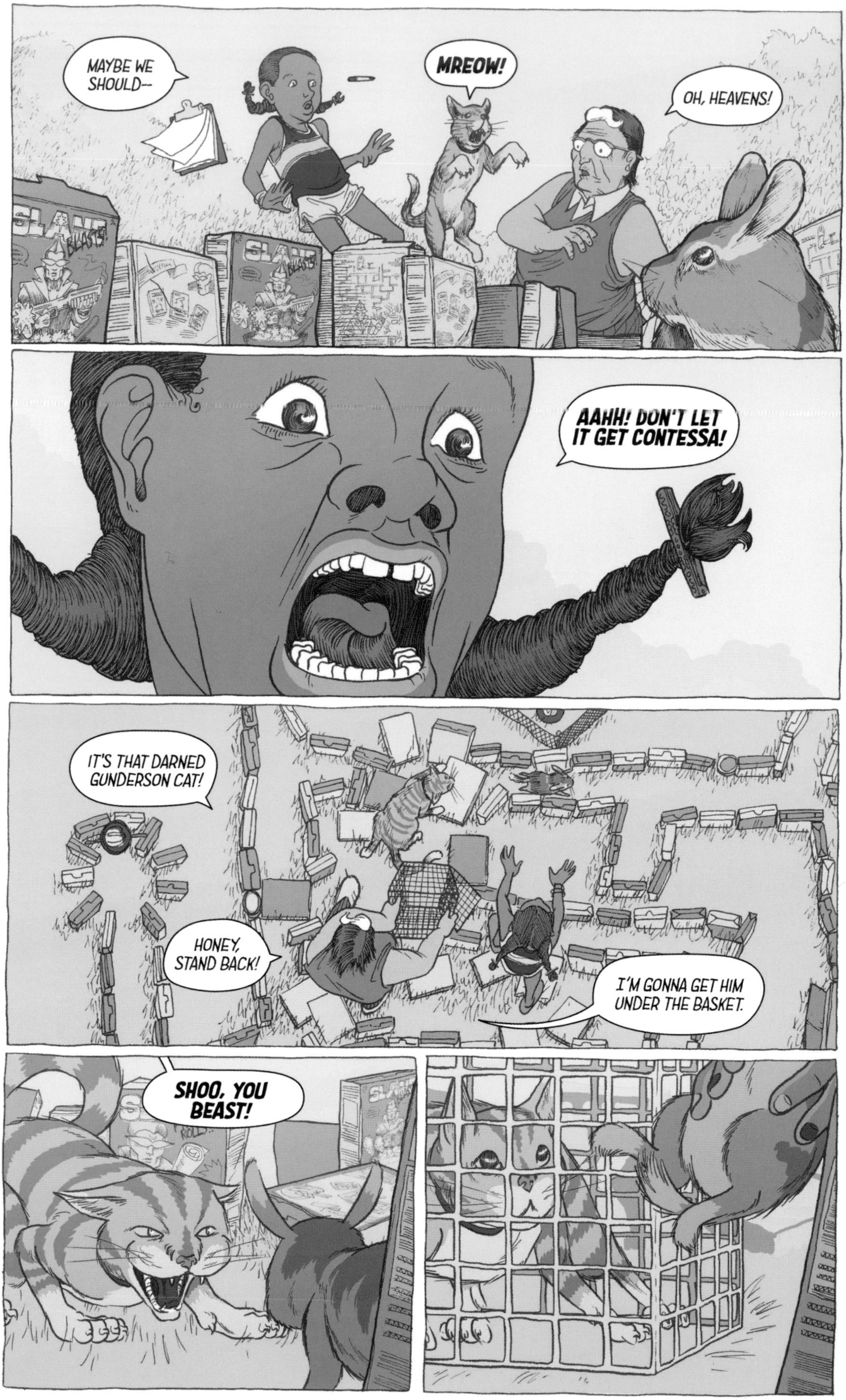
MAYBE WE SHOULD--
MREOW!
OH, HEAVENS!
AAHH! DON'T LET IT GET CONTESSA!
IT'S THAT DARNED GUNDERSON CAT!
HONEY, STAND BACK!
I'M GONNA GET HIM UNDER THE BASKET.
SHOO, YOU BEAST!

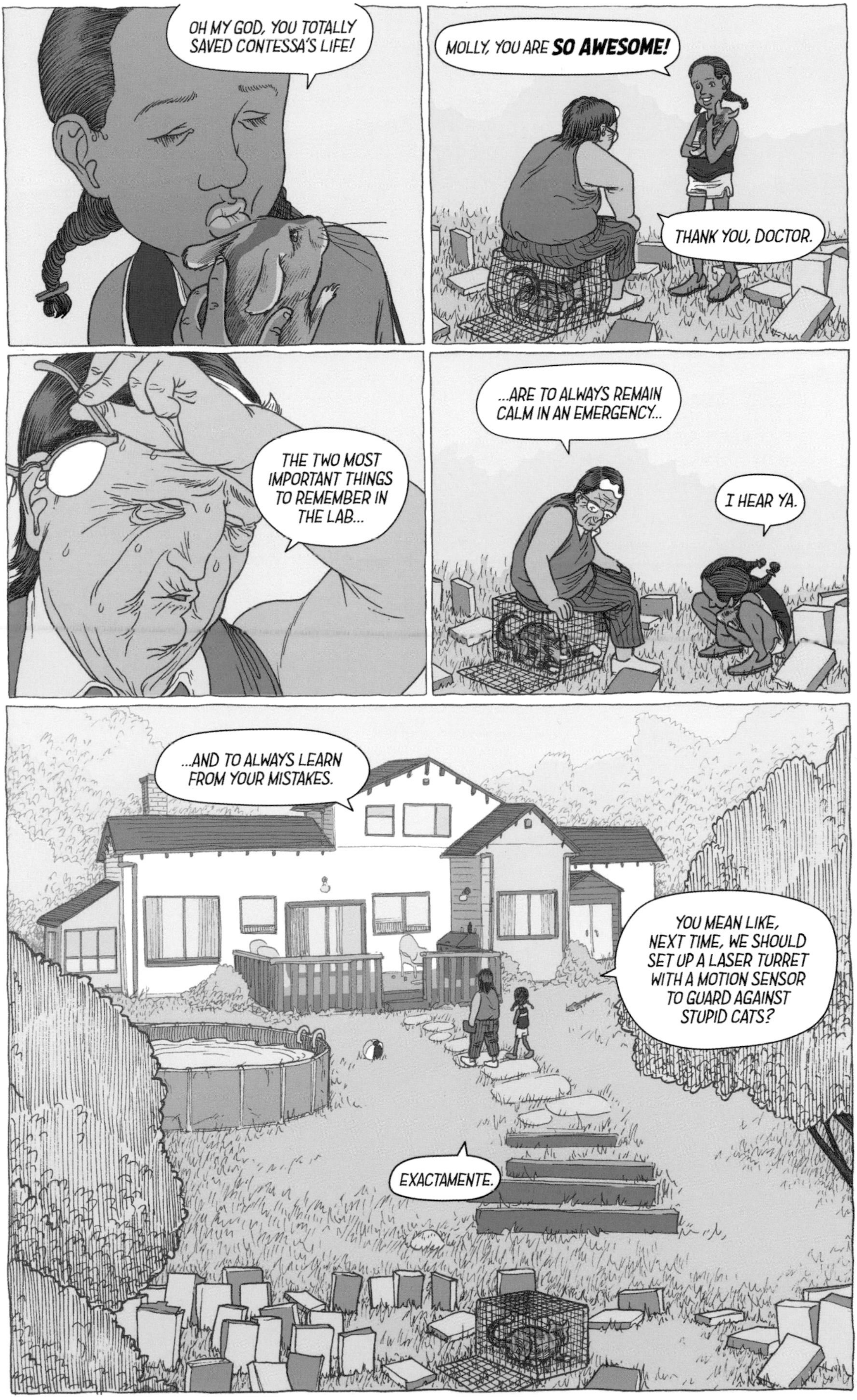
OH MY GOD, YOU TOTALLY SAVED CONTESSA'S LIFE!
MOLLY, YOU ARE SO AWESOME!
THANK YOU, DOCTOR.
THE TWO MOST IMPORTANT THINGS TO REMEMBER IN THE LAB...
...ARE TO ALWAYS REMAIN CALM IN AN EMERGENCY...
I HEAR YA.
...AND TO ALWAYS LEARN FROM YOUR MISTAKES.
YOU MEAN LIKE, NEXT TIME, WE SHOULD SET UP A LASER TURRET WITH A MOTION SENSOR TO GUARD AGAINST STUPID CATS?
EXACTAMENTE.

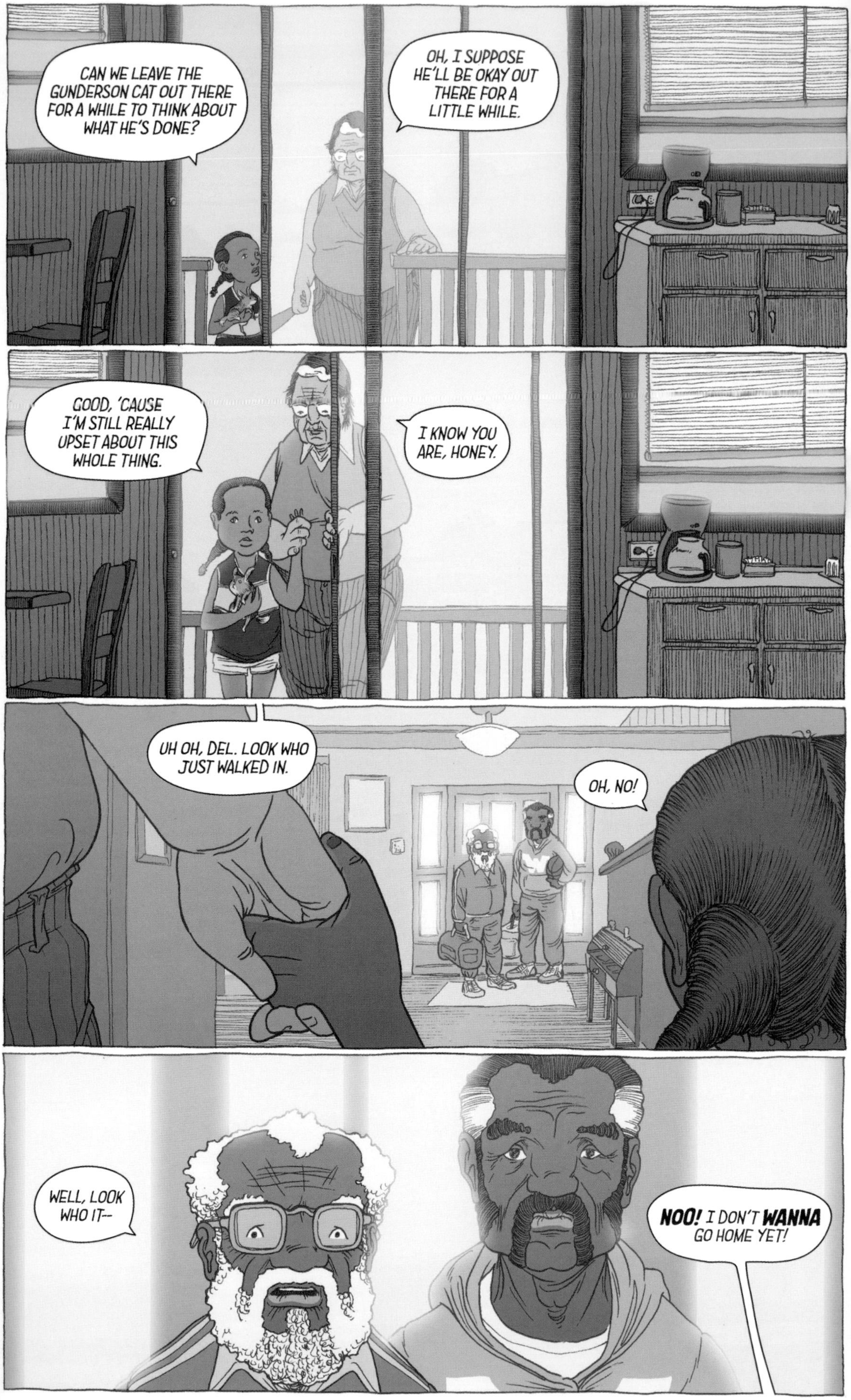
CAN WE LEAVE THE GUNDERSON CAT OUT THERE FOR A WHILE TO THINK ABOUT WHAT HE'S DONE?
OH, I SUPPOSE HE'LL BE OKAY OUT THERE FOR A LITTLE WHILE.
GOOD, 'CAUSE I'M STILL REALLY UPSET ABOUT THIS WHOLE THING.
I KNOW YOU ARE, HONEY.
UH OH, DEL. LOOK WHO JUST WALKED IN.
OH, NO!
WELL, LOOK WHO IT--
NOO! I DON'T WANNA GO HOME YET!

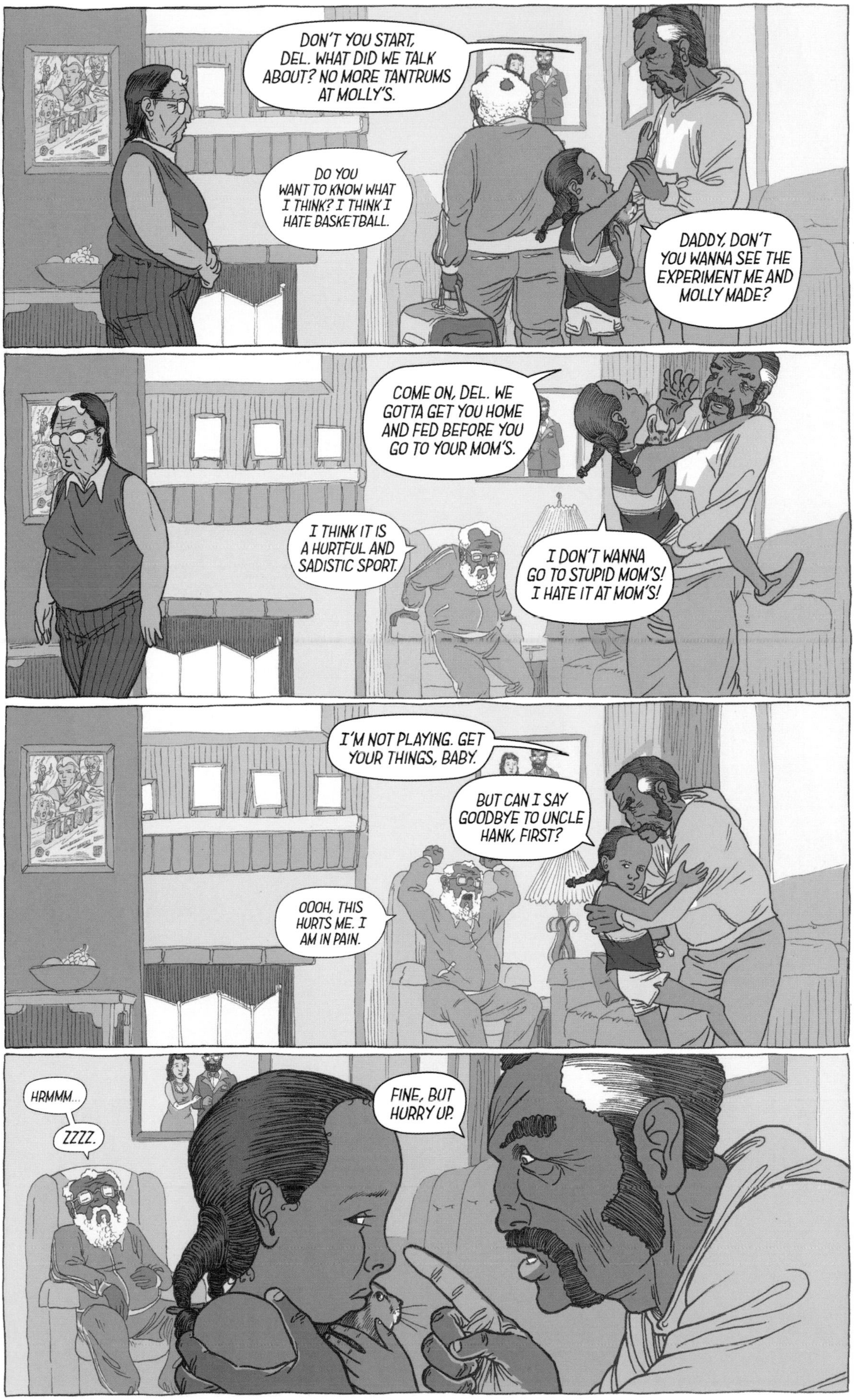
DON'T YOU START, DEL. WHAT DID WE TALK ABOUT? NO MORE TANTRUMS AT MOLLY'S.
DO YOU WANT TO KNOW WHAT I THINK? I THINK I HATE BASKETBALL.
DADDY, DON'T YOU WANNA SEE THE EXPERIMENT ME AND MOLLY MADE?
COME ON, DEL. WE GOTTA GET YOU HOME AND FED BEFORE YOU GO TO YOUR MOM'S.
I THINK IT IS A HURTFUL AND SADISTIC SPORT.
I DON'T WANNA GO TO STUPID MOM'S! I HATE IT AT MOM'S!
I'M NOT PLAYING. GET YOUR THINGS, BABY.
BUT CAN I SAY GOODBYE TO UNCLE HANK, FIRST?
OOOH, THIS HURTS ME. I AM IN PAIN.
HRMMM...
ZZZZ.
FINE, BUT HURRY UP.

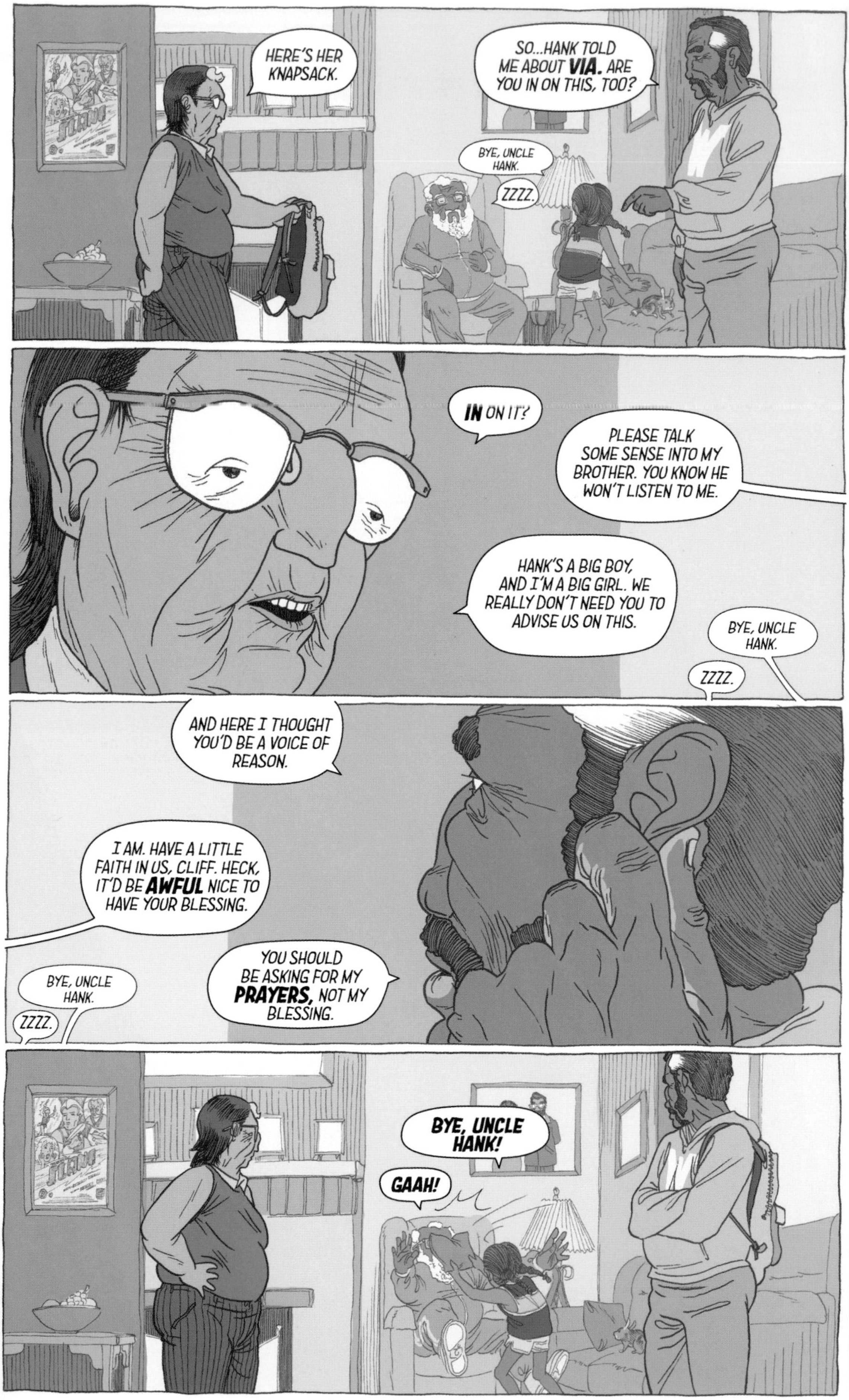
HERE'S HER KNAPSACK.
SO...HANK TOLD ME ABOUT VIA. ARE YOU IN ON THIS, TOO?
BYE, UNCLE HANK.
ZZZZ.
IN ON IT?
PLEASE TALK SOME SENSE INTO MY BROTHER. YOU KNOW HE WON'T LISTEN TO ME.
HANK'S A BIG BOY, AND I'M A BIG GIRL. WE REALLY DON'T NEED YOU TO ADVISE US ON THIS.
BYE, UNCLE HANK.
ZZZZ.
AND HERE I THOUGHT YOU'D BE A VOICE OF REASON.
I AM. HAVE A LITTLE FAITH IN US, CLIFF. HECK, IT'D BE AWFUL NICE TO HAVE YOUR BLESSING.
YOU SHOULD BE ASKING FOR MY PRAYERS, NOT MY BLESSING.
BYE, UNCLE HANK.
ZZZZ.
BYE, UNCLE HANK!
GAAH!

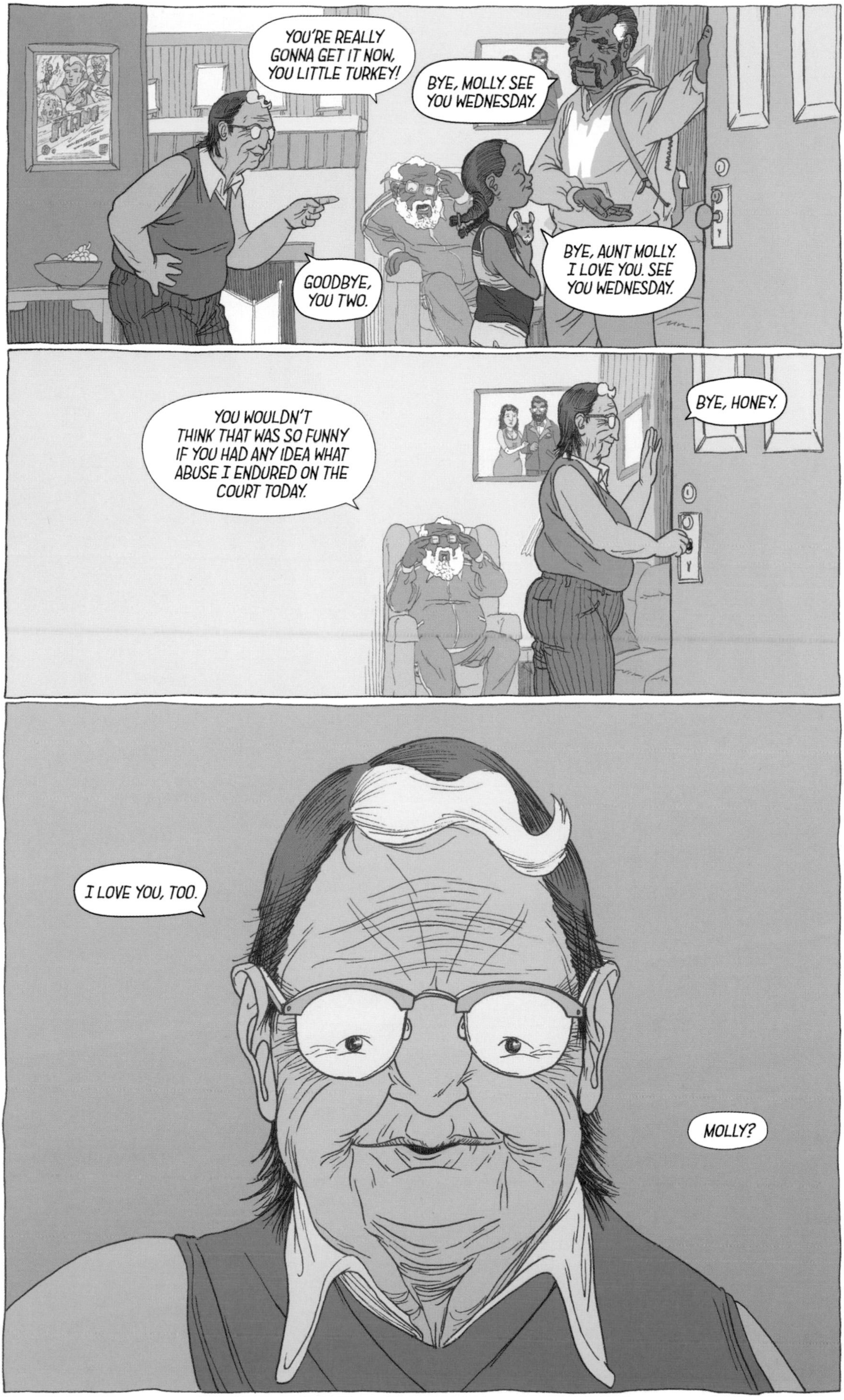
YOU'RE REALLY GONNA GET IT NOW, YOU LITTLE TURKEY!
BYE, MOLLY. SEE YOU WEDNESDAY.
GOODBYE, YOU TWO.
BYE, AUNT MOLLY. I LOVE YOU. SEE YOU WEDNESDAY.
YOU WOULDN'T THINK THAT WAS SO FUNNY IF YOU HAD ANY IDEA WHAT ABUSE I ENDURED ON THE COURT TODAY.
BYE, HONEY.
I LOVE YOU, TOO.
MOLLY?

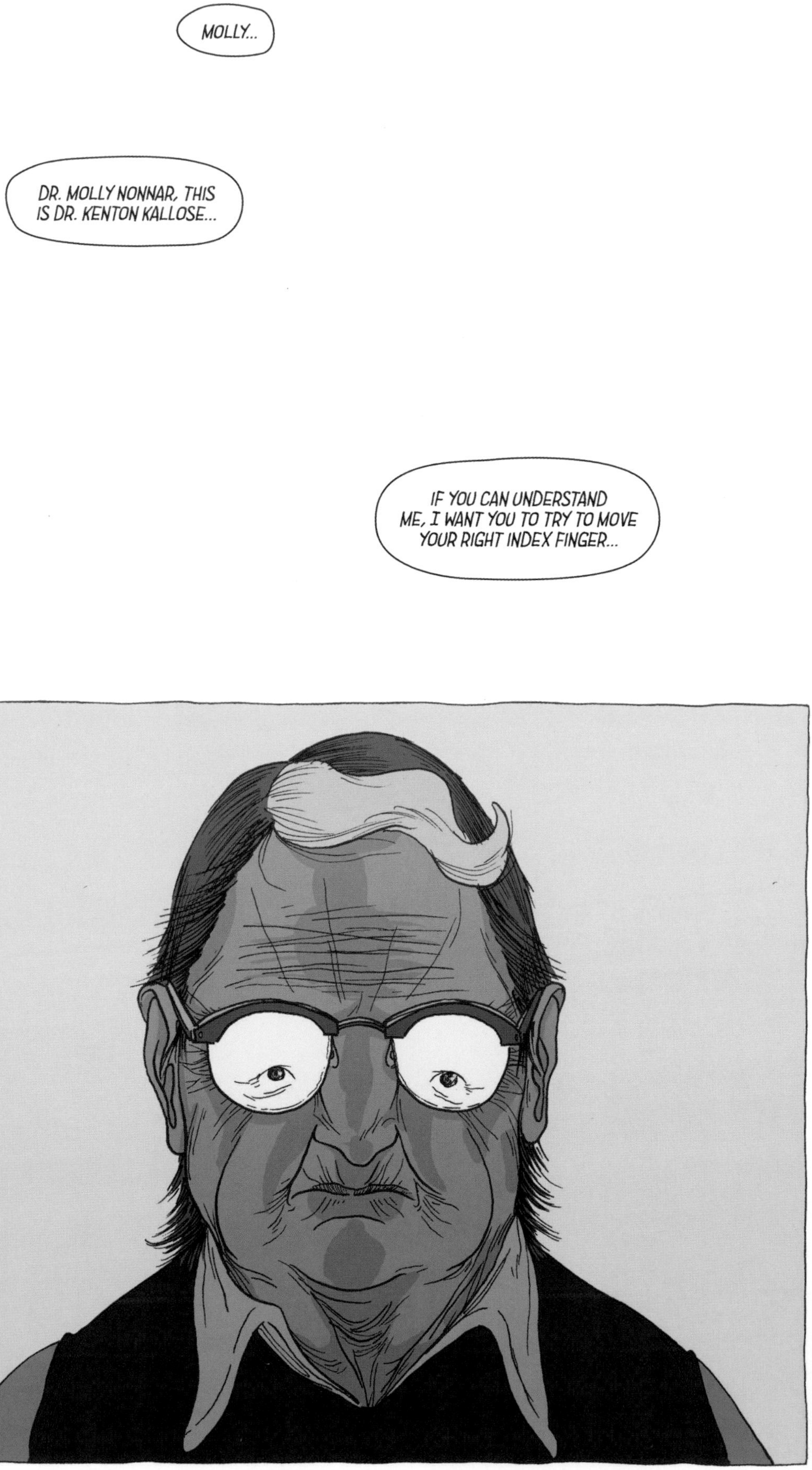
MOLLY...
DR. MOLLY NONNAR, THIS IS DR. KENTON KALLOSE...
IF YOU CAN UNDERSTAND ME, I WANT YOU TO TRY TO MOVE YOUR RIGHT INDEX FINGER...

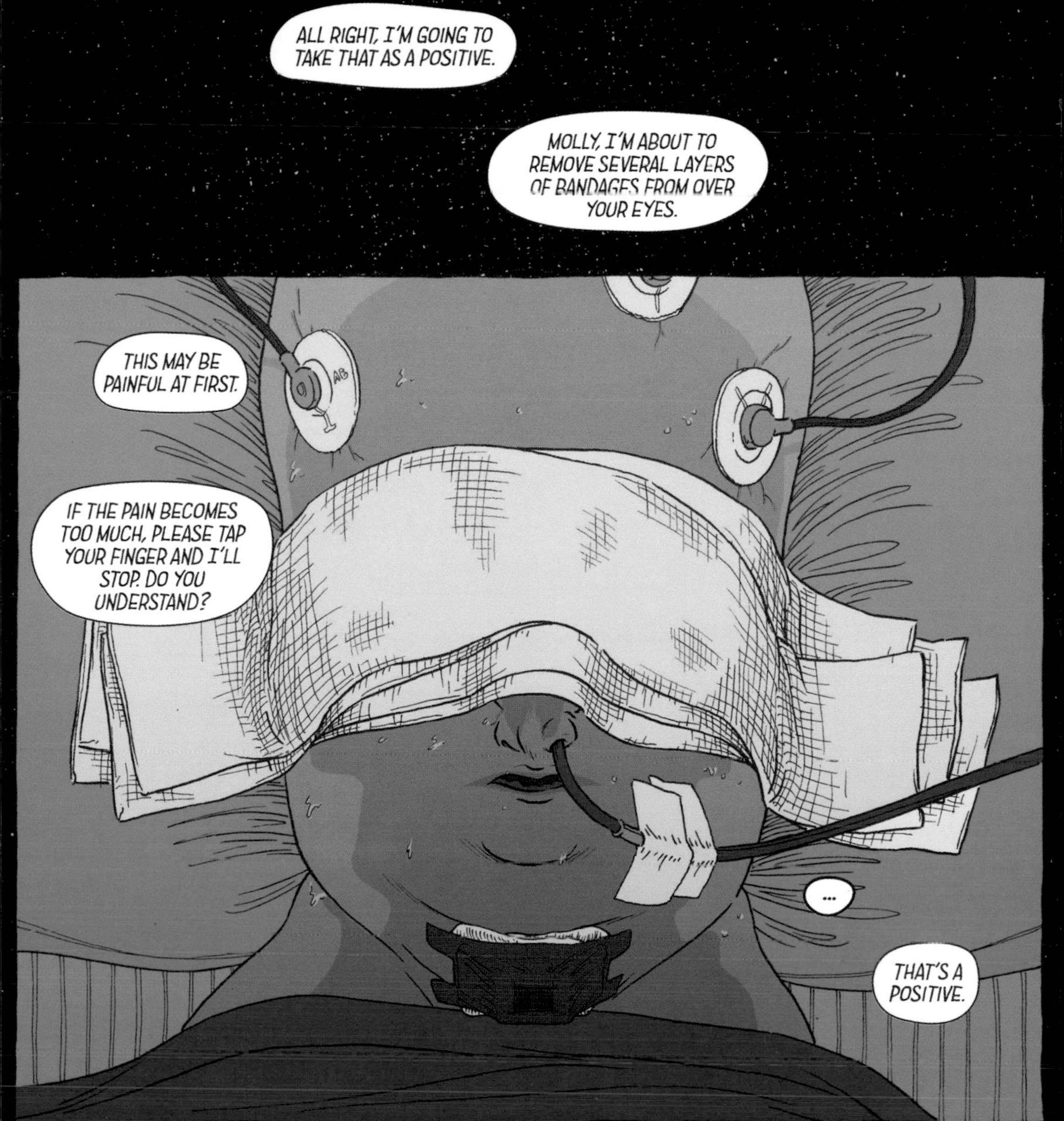
ALL RIGHT, I'M GOING TO TAKE THAT AS A POSITIVE.
MOLLY, I'M ABOUT TO REMOVE SEVERAL LAYERS OF BANDAGES FROM OVER YOUR EYES.
THIS MAY BE PAINFUL AT FIRST.
IF THE PAIN BECOMES TOO MUCH, PLEASE TAP YOUR FINGER AND I'LL STOP. DO YOU UNDERSTAND?
...
THAT'S A POSITIVE.

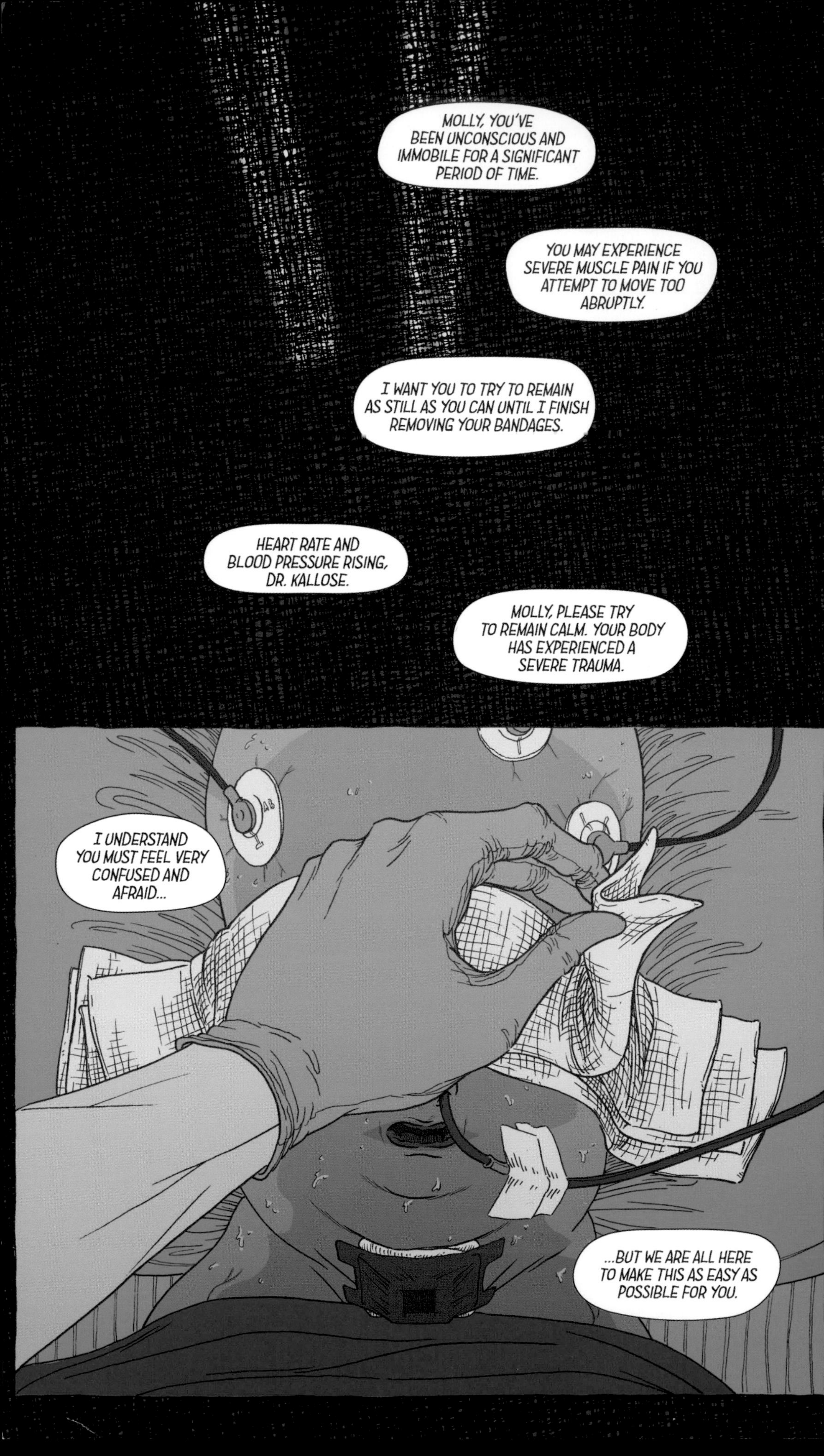
MOLLY, YOU'VE BEEN UNCONSCIOUS AND IMMOBILE FOR A SIGNIFICANT PERIOD OF TIME.
YOU MAY EXPERIENCE SEVERE MUSCLE PAIN IF YOU ATTEMPT TO MOVE TOO ABRUPTLY.
I WANT YOU TO TRY TO REMAIN AS STILL AS YOU CAN UNTIL I FINISH REMOVING YOUR BANDAGES.
HEART RATE AND BLOOD PRESSURE RISING, DR. KALLOSE.
MOLLY, PLEASE TRY TO REMAIN CALM. YOUR BODY HAS EXPERIENCED A SEVERE TRAUMA.
I UNDERSTAND YOU MUST FEEL VERY CONFUSED AND AFRAID...
...BUT WE ARE ALL HERE TO MAKE THIS AS EASY AS POSSIBLE FOR YOU.

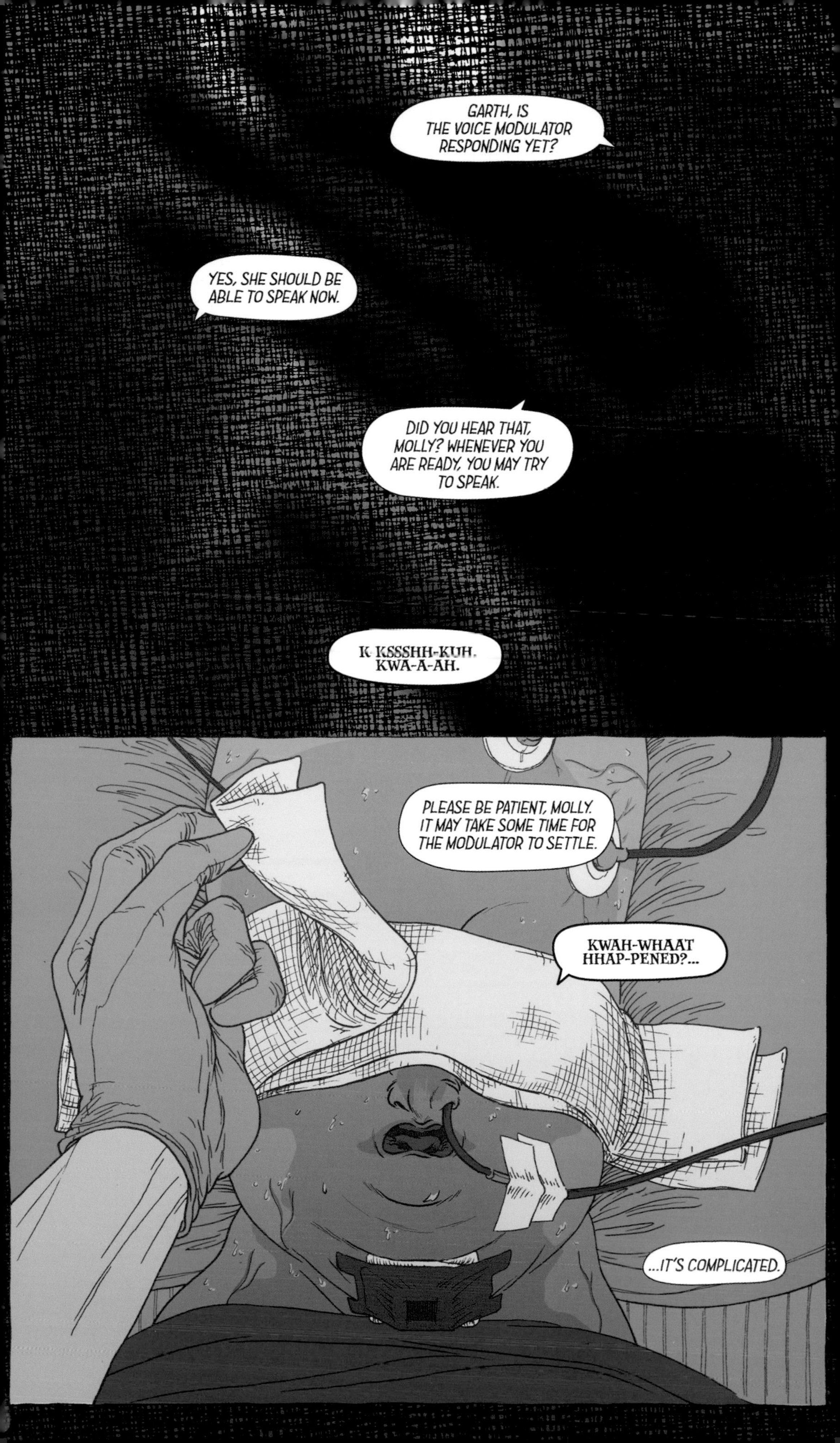
GARTH, IS THE VOICE MODULATOR RESPONDING YET?
YES, SHE SHOULD BE ABLE TO SPEAK NOW.
DID YOU HEAR THAT, MOLLY? WHENEVER YOU ARE READY, YOU MAY TRY TO SPEAK.
K-KSSSHH-KUH. KWA-A-AH.
PLEASE BE PATIENT, MOLLY. IT MAY TAKE SOME TIME FOR THE MODULATOR TO SETTLE.
KWAH-WHAAT HHAP-PENED?...
...IT'S COMPLICATED.

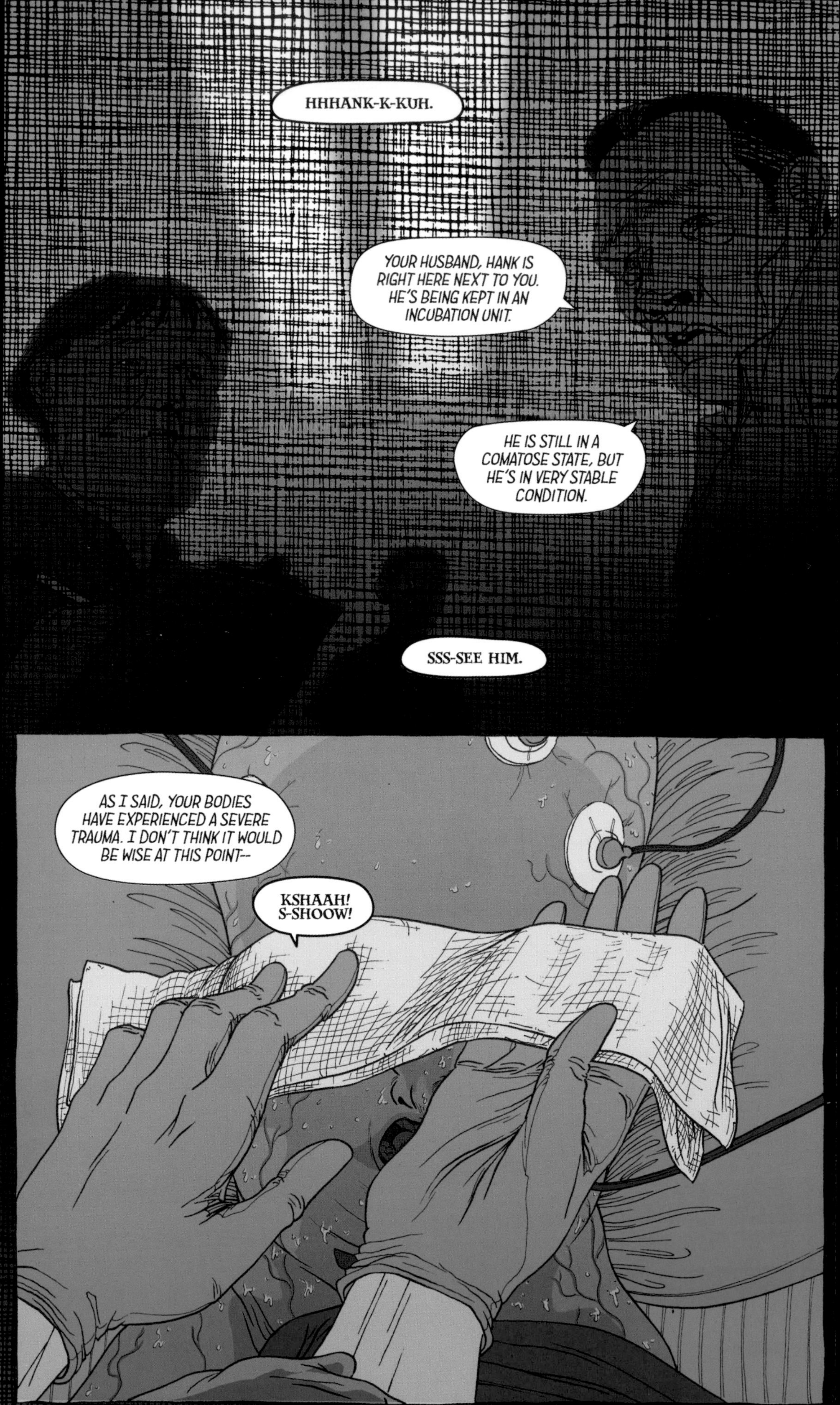
HHHANK-K-KUH.
YOUR HUSBAND, HANK IS RIGHT HERE NEXT TO YOU. HE'S BEING KEPT IN AN INCUBATION UNIT.
HE IS STILL IN A COMATOSE STATE, BUT HE'S IN VERY STABLE CONDITION.
SSS-SEE HIM.
AS I SAID, YOUR BODIES HAVE EXPERIENCED A SEVERE TRAUMA. I DON'T THINK IT WOULD BE WISE AT THIS POINT--
KSHAAH! S-SHOOW!

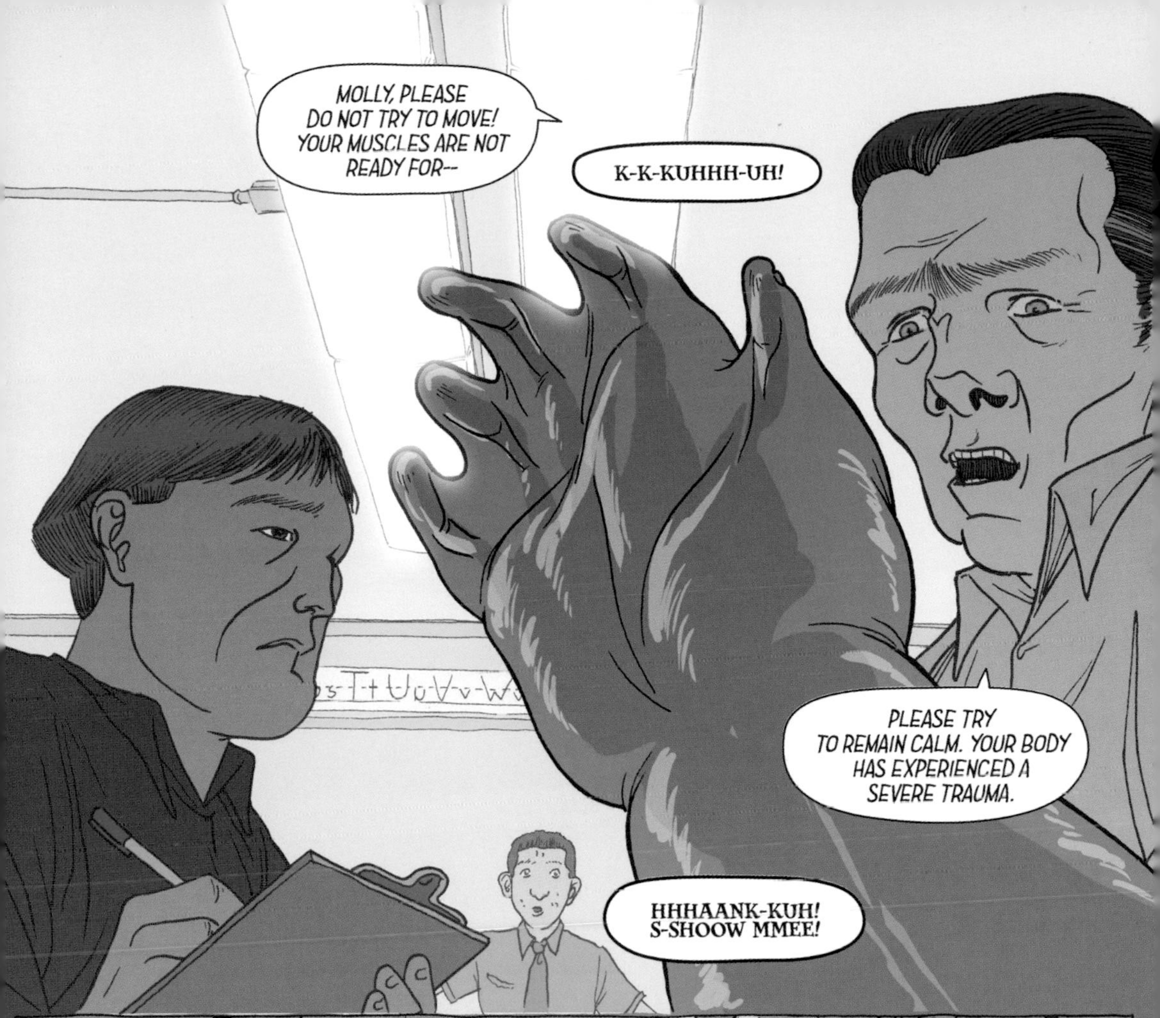
MOLLY, PLEASE DO NOT TRY TO MOVE! YOUR MUSCLES ARE NOT READY FOR--
K-K-KUHHH-UH!
PLEASE TRY TO REMAIN CALM. YOUR BODY HAS EXPERIENCED A SEVERE TRAUMA.
HHHAANK-KUH! S-SHOOW MMEE!

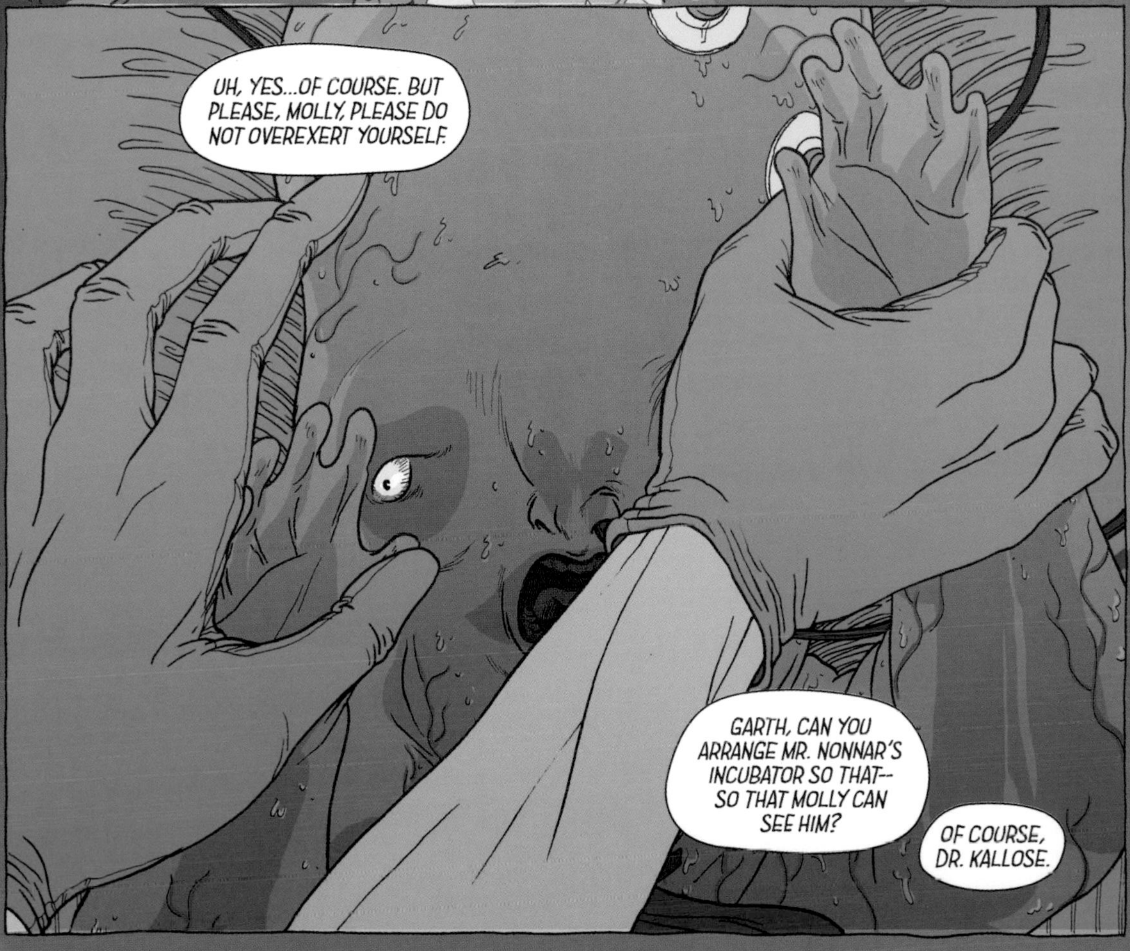
UH, YES...OF COURSE. BUT PLEASE, MOLLY, PLEASE DO NOT OVEREXERT YOURSELF.
GARTH, CAN YOU ARRANGE MR. NONNAR'S INCUBATOR SO THAT-- SO THAT MOLLY CAN SEE HIM?
OF COURSE, DR. KALLOSE.

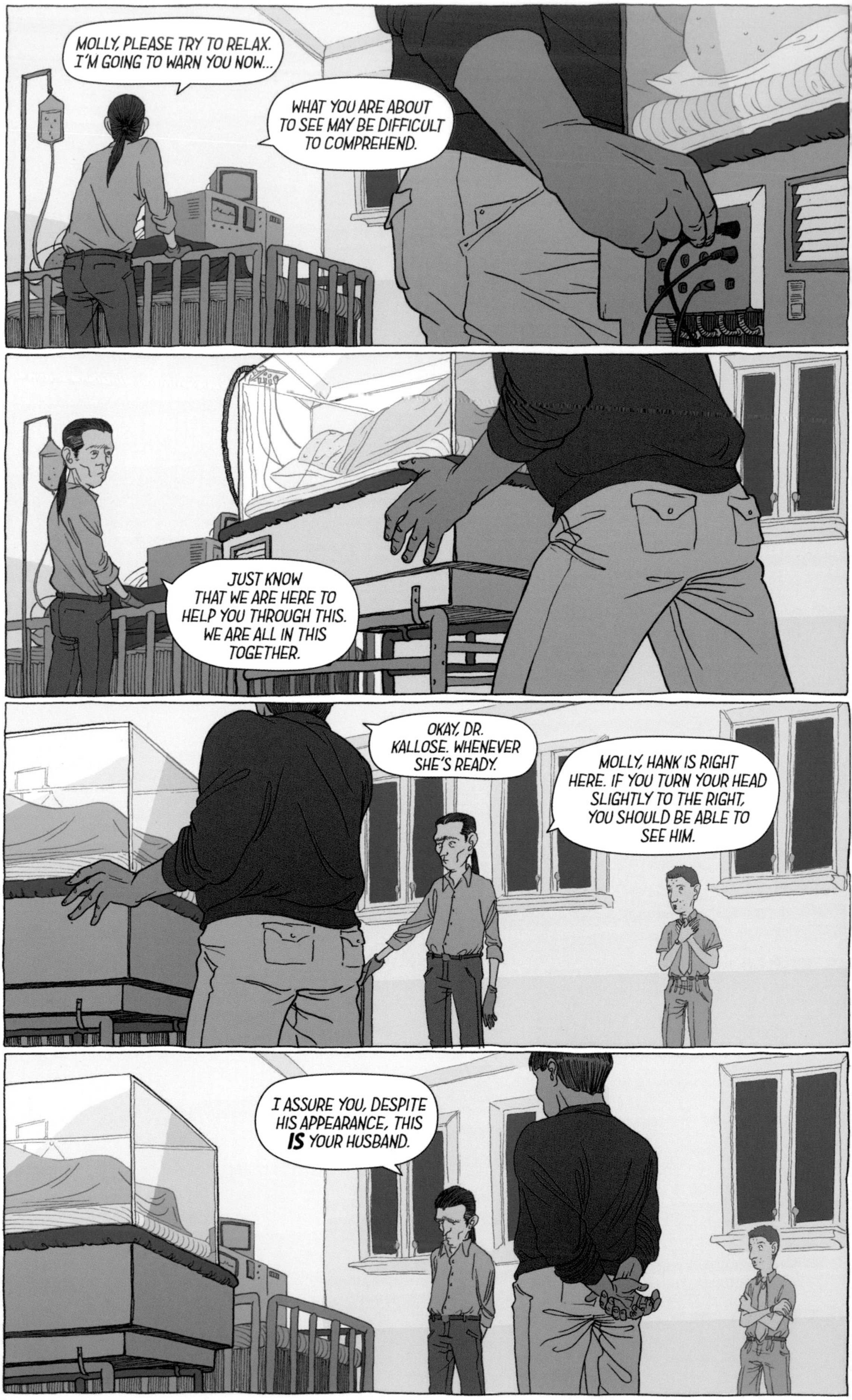
MOLLY, PLEASE TRY TO RELAX. I'M GOING TO WARN YOU NOW...
WHAT YOU ARE ABOUT TO SEE MAY BE DIFFICULT TO COMPREHEND.
JUST KNOW THAT WE ARE HERE TO HELP YOU THROUGH THIS. WE ARE ALL IN THIS TOGETHER.
OKAY, DR. KALLOSE. WHENEVER SHE'S READY.
MOLLY, HANK IS RIGHT HERE. IF YOU TURN YOUR HEAD SLIGHTLY TO THE RIGHT, YOU SHOULD BE ABLE TO SEE HIM.
I ASSURE YOU, DESPITE HIS APPEARANCE, THIS **IS** YOUR HUSBAND.

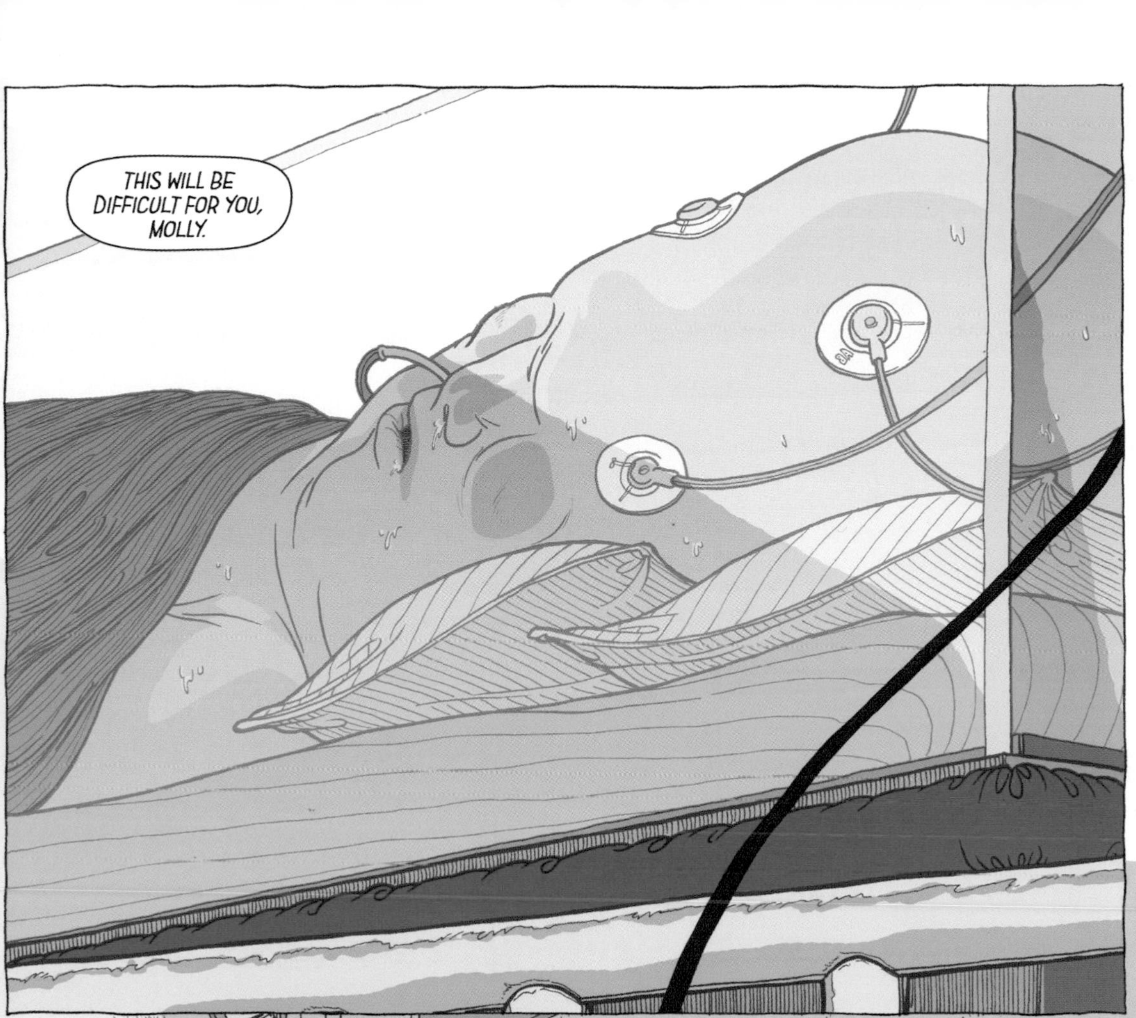
THIS WILL BE DIFFICULT FOR YOU, MOLLY.

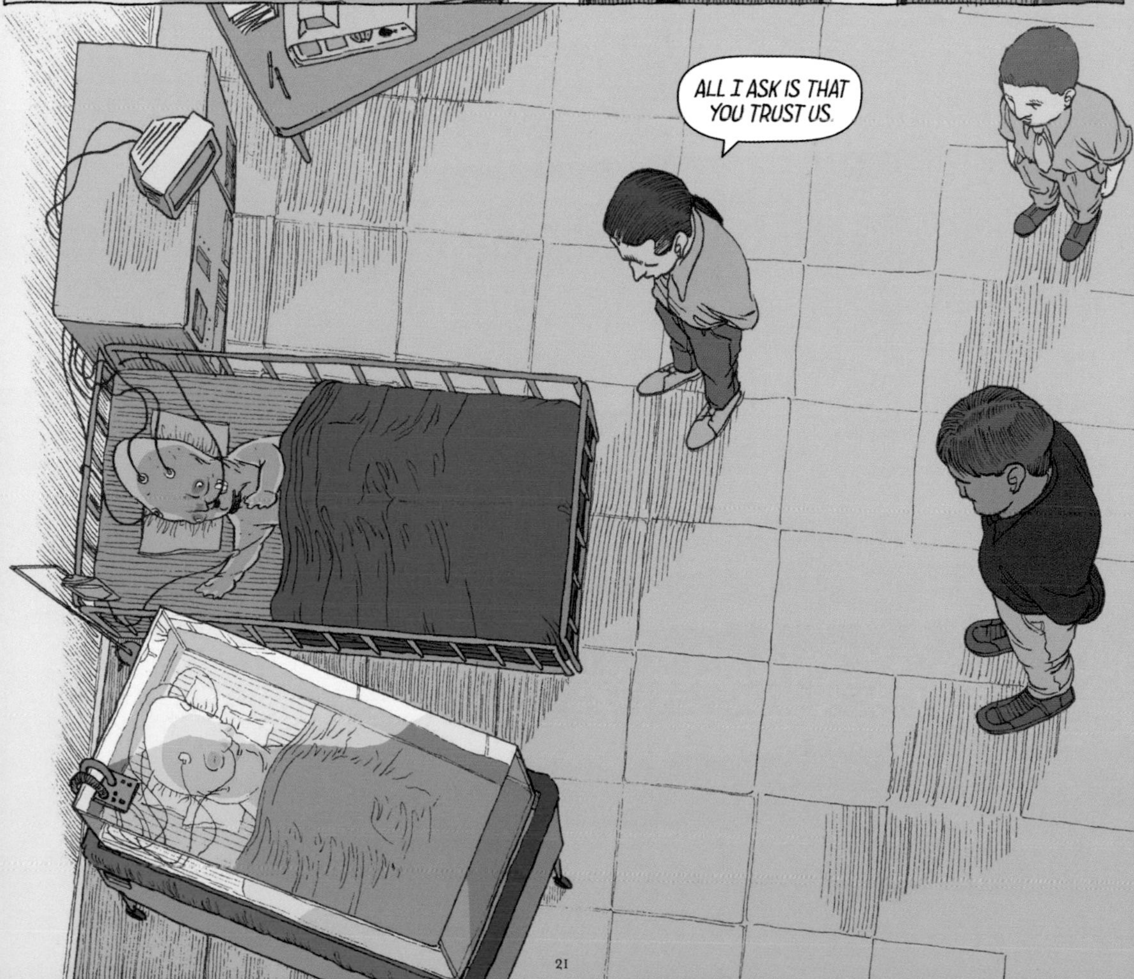
ALL I ASK IS THAT YOU TRUST US.

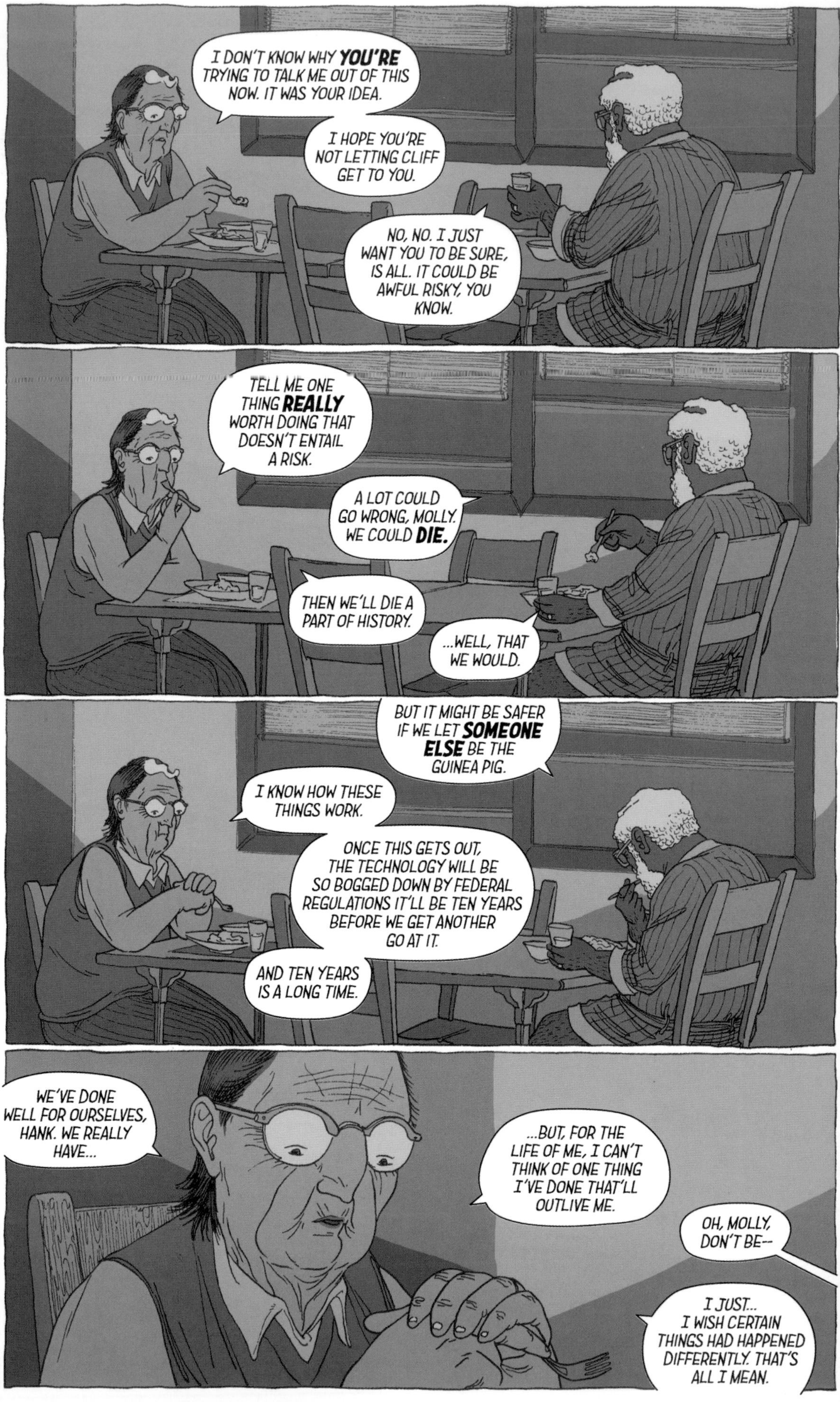
I DON'T KNOW WHY **YOU'RE** TRYING TO TALK ME OUT OF THIS NOW. IT WAS YOUR IDEA.
I HOPE YOU'RE NOT LETTING CLIFF GET TO YOU.
NO, NO. I JUST WANT YOU TO BE SURE, IS ALL. IT COULD BE AWFUL RISKY, YOU KNOW.
TELL ME ONE THING **REALLY** WORTH DOING THAT DOESN'T ENTAIL A RISK.
A LOT COULD GO WRONG, MOLLY. WE COULD **DIE.**
THEN WE'LL DIE A PART OF HISTORY.
...WELL, THAT WE WOULD.
BUT IT MIGHT BE SAFER IF WE LET **SOMEONE ELSE** BE THE GUINEA PIG.
I KNOW HOW THESE THINGS WORK.
ONCE THIS GETS OUT, THE TECHNOLOGY WILL BE SO BOGGED DOWN BY FEDERAL REGULATIONS IT'LL BE TEN YEARS BEFORE WE GET ANOTHER GO AT IT.
AND TEN YEARS IS A LONG TIME.
WE'VE DONE WELL FOR OURSELVES, HANK. WE REALLY HAVE...
...BUT, FOR THE LIFE OF ME, I CAN'T THINK OF ONE THING I'VE DONE THAT'LL OUTLIVE ME.
OH, MOLLY, DON'T BE--
I JUST... I WISH CERTAIN THINGS HAD HAPPENED DIFFERENTLY. THAT'S ALL I MEAN.

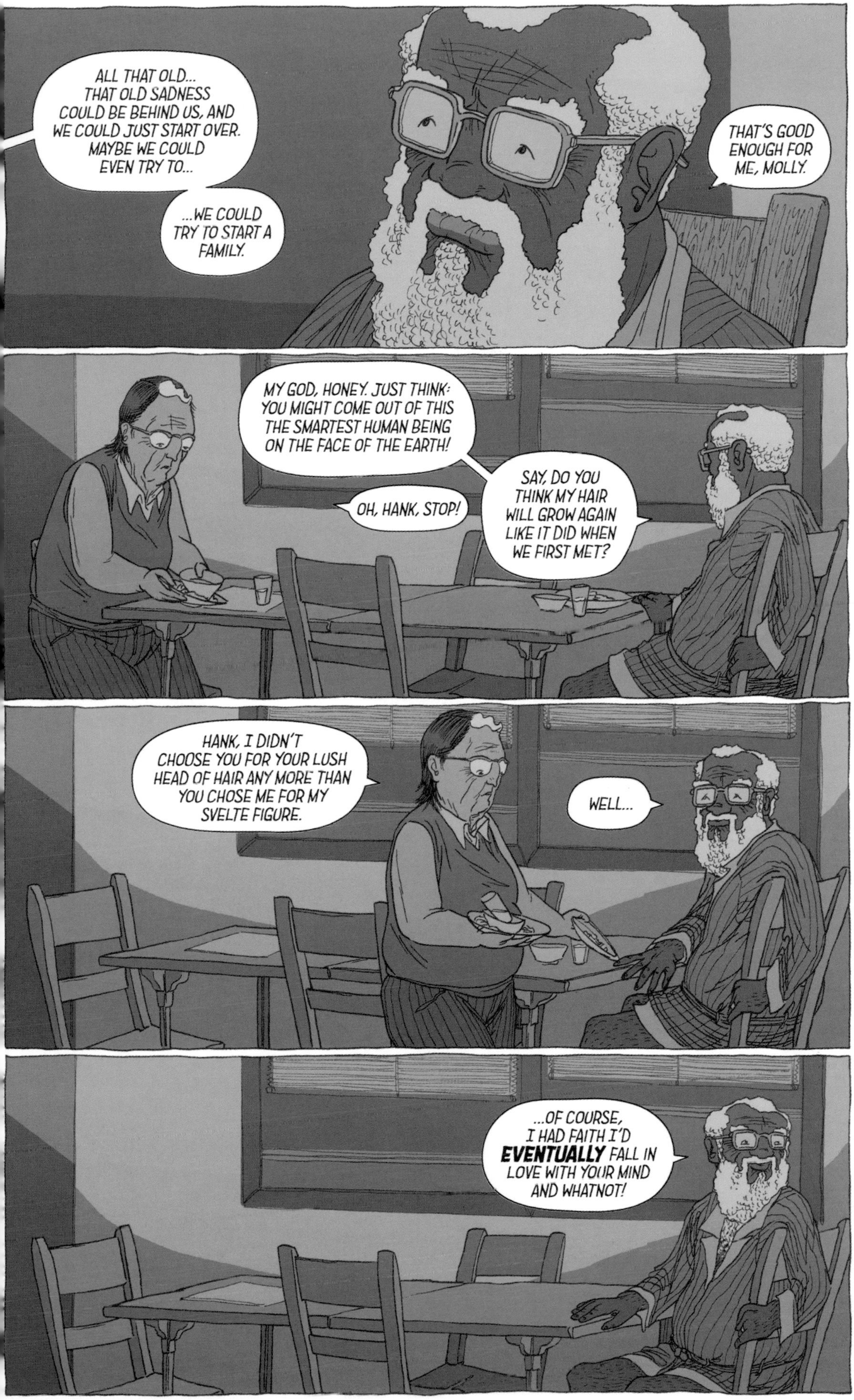
ALL THAT OLD... THAT OLD SADNESS COULD BE BEHIND US, AND WE COULD JUST START OVER. MAYBE WE COULD EVEN TRY TO...
...WE COULD TRY TO START A FAMILY.
THAT'S GOOD ENOUGH FOR ME, MOLLY.
MY GOD, HONEY. JUST THINK: YOU MIGHT COME OUT OF THIS THE SMARTEST HUMAN BEING ON THE FACE OF THE EARTH!
OH, HANK, STOP!
SAY, DO YOU THINK MY HAIR WILL GROW AGAIN LIKE IT DID WHEN WE FIRST MET?
HANK, I DIDN'T CHOOSE YOU FOR YOUR LUSH HEAD OF HAIR ANY MORE THAN YOU CHOSE ME FOR MY SVELTE FIGURE.
WELL...
...OF COURSE, I HAD FAITH I'D **EVENTUALLY** FALL IN LOVE WITH YOUR MIND AND WHATNOT!

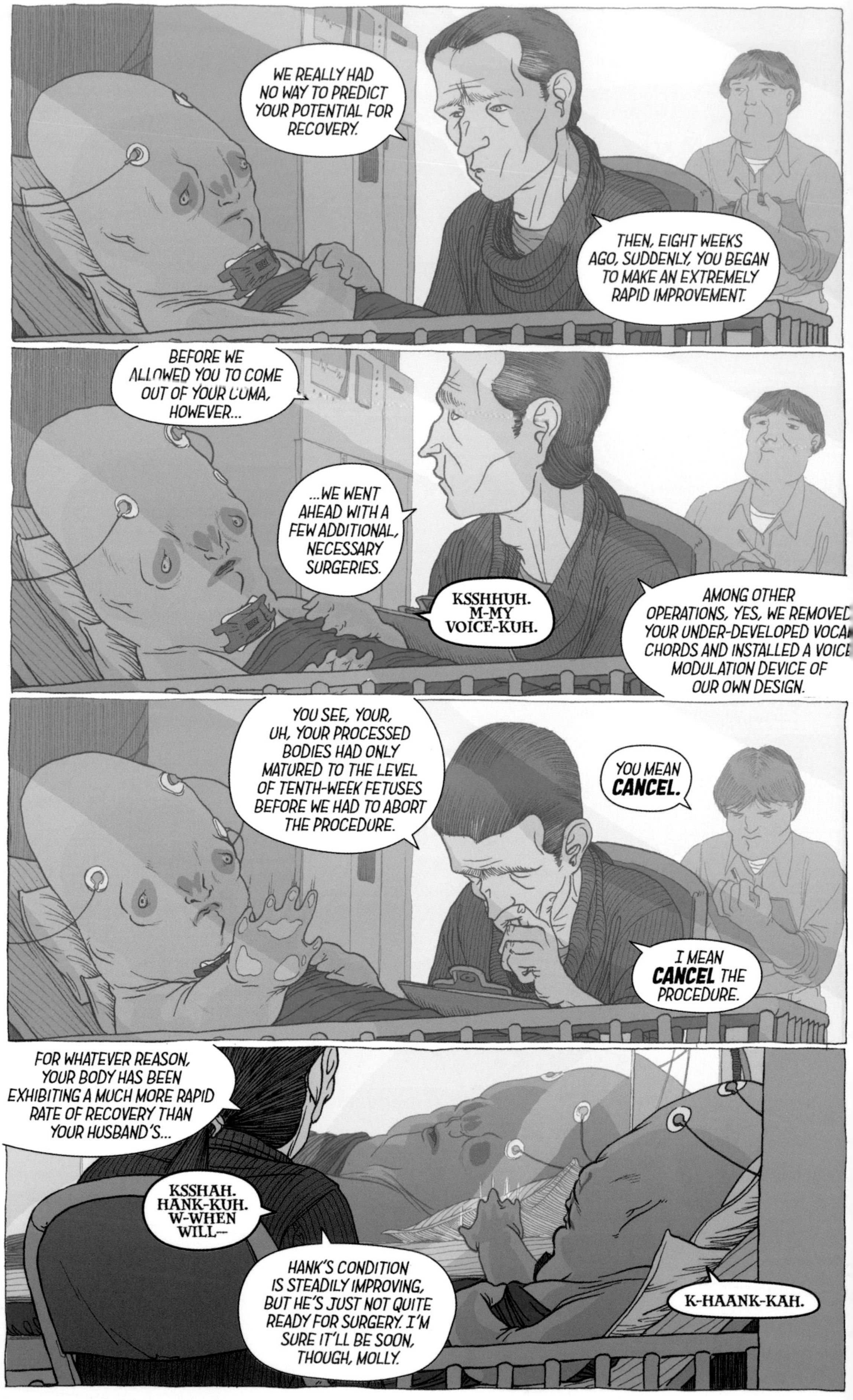

WE REALLY HAD NO WAY TO PREDICT YOUR POTENTIAL FOR RECOVERY.
THEN, EIGHT WEEKS AGO, SUDDENLY, YOU BEGAN TO MAKE AN EXTREMELY RAPID IMPROVEMENT.
BEFORE WE ALLOWED YOU TO COME OUT OF YOUR COMA, HOWEVER...
...WE WENT AHEAD WITH A FEW ADDITIONAL, NECESSARY SURGERIES.
KSSHHUH. M-MY VOICE-KUH.
AMONG OTHER OPERATIONS, YES, WE REMOVED YOUR UNDER-DEVELOPED VOCAL CHORDS AND INSTALLED A VOICE MODULATION DEVICE OF OUR OWN DESIGN.
YOU SEE, YOUR, UH, YOUR PROCESSED BODIES HAD ONLY MATURED TO THE LEVEL OF TENTH-WEEK FETUSES BEFORE WE HAD TO ABORT THE PROCEDURE.
YOU MEAN CANCEL.
I MEAN CANCEL THE PROCEDURE.
FOR WHATEVER REASON, YOUR BODY HAS BEEN EXHIBITING A MUCH MORE RAPID RATE OF RECOVERY THAN YOUR HUSBAND'S...
KSSHAH. HANK-KUH. W-WHEN WILL---
HANK'S CONDITION IS STEADILY IMPROVING, BUT HE'S JUST NOT QUITE READY FOR SURGERY. I'M SURE IT'LL BE SOON, THOUGH, MOLLY.
K-HAANK-KAH.

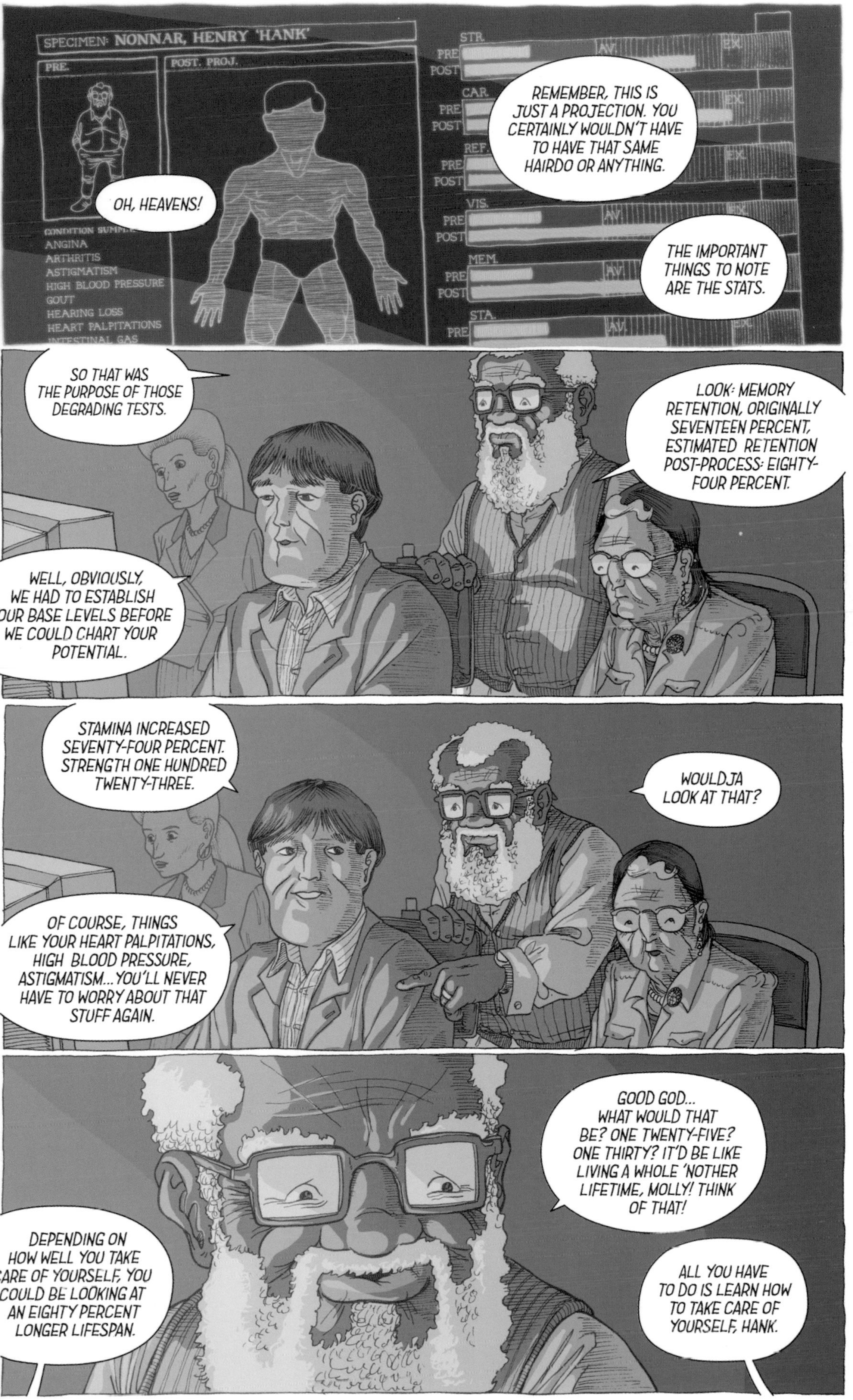
SPECIMEN: NONNAR, HENRY 'HANK'
PRE.
POST. PROJ.
ANGINA
ARTHRITIS
ASTIGMATISM
HIGH BLOOD PRESSURE
GOUT
HEARING LOSS
HEART PALPITATIONS
STR.
CAR.
REF.
VIS.
MEM.
STA.
PRE
POST
AV.
EX.
OH, HEAVENS!
REMEMBER, THIS IS JUST A PROJECTION. YOU CERTAINLY WOULDN'T HAVE TO HAVE THAT SAME HAIRDO OR ANYTHING.
THE IMPORTANT THINGS TO NOTE ARE THE STATS.
SO THAT WAS THE PURPOSE OF THOSE DEGRADING TESTS.
WELL, OBVIOUSLY, WE HAD TO ESTABLISH OUR BASE LEVELS BEFORE WE COULD CHART YOUR POTENTIAL.
LOOK: MEMORY RETENTION, ORIGINALLY SEVENTEEN PERCENT, ESTIMATED RETENTION POST-PROCESS: EIGHTY-FOUR PERCENT.
STAMINA INCREASED SEVENTY-FOUR PERCENT. STRENGTH ONE HUNDRED TWENTY-THREE.
OF COURSE, THINGS LIKE YOUR HEART PALPITATIONS, HIGH BLOOD PRESSURE, ASTIGMATISM... YOU'LL NEVER HAVE TO WORRY ABOUT THAT STUFF AGAIN.
WOULDJA LOOK AT THAT?
DEPENDING ON HOW WELL YOU TAKE CARE OF YOURSELF, YOU COULD BE LOOKING AT AN EIGHTY PERCENT LONGER LIFESPAN.
GOOD GOD... WHAT WOULD THAT BE? ONE TWENTY-FIVE? ONE THIRTY? IT'D BE LIKE LIVING A WHOLE 'NOTHER LIFETIME, MOLLY! THINK OF THAT!
ALL YOU HAVE TO DO IS LEARN HOW TO TAKE CARE OF YOURSELF, HANK.

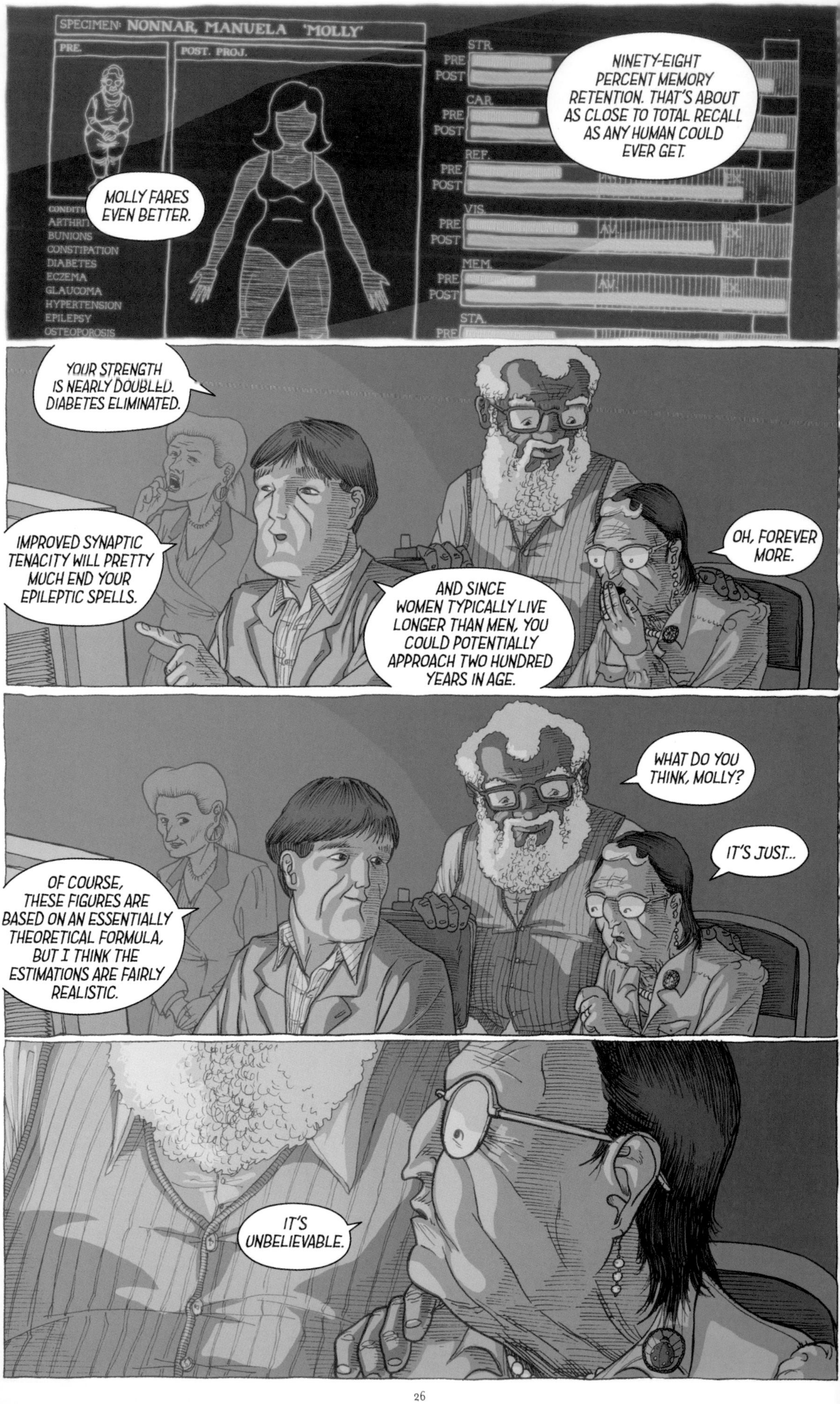
SPECIMEN: NONNAR, MANUELA 'MOLLY'
PRE.
POST. PROJ.
STR.
PRE
POST
CAR.
PRE
POST
REF.
PRE
POST
VIS.
PRE
POST
MEM.
PRE
POST
STA.
PRE
NINETY-EIGHT PERCENT MEMORY RETENTION. THAT'S ABOUT AS CLOSE TO TOTAL RECALL AS ANY HUMAN COULD EVER GET.
MOLLY FARES EVEN BETTER.
ARTHRITI
BUNIONS
CONSTIPATION
DIABETES
ECZEMA
GLAUCOMA
HYPERTENSION
EPILEPSY
OSTEOPOROSIS
YOUR STRENGTH IS NEARLY DOUBLED. DIABETES ELIMINATED.
IMPROVED SYNAPTIC TENACITY WILL PRETTY MUCH END YOUR EPILEPTIC SPELLS.
AND SINCE WOMEN TYPICALLY LIVE LONGER THAN MEN, YOU COULD POTENTIALLY APPROACH TWO HUNDRED YEARS IN AGE.
OH, FOREVER MORE.
OF COURSE, THESE FIGURES ARE BASED ON AN ESSENTIALLY THEORETICAL FORMULA, BUT I THINK THE ESTIMATIONS ARE FAIRLY REALISTIC.
WHAT DO YOU THINK, MOLLY?
IT'S JUST...
IT'S UNBELIEVABLE.

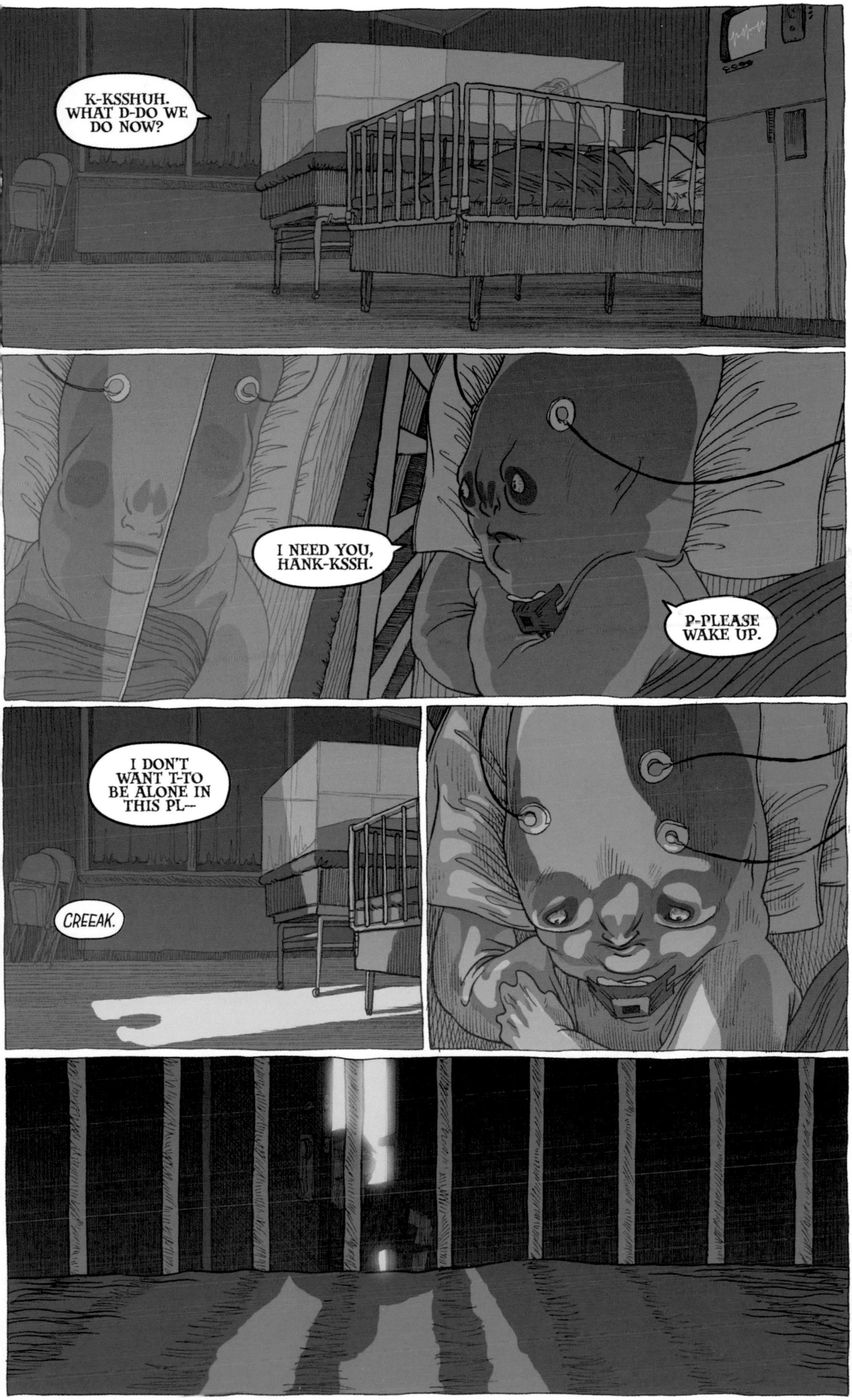
K-KSSHUH. WHAT D-DO WE DO NOW?
I NEED YOU, HANK-KSSH.
P-PLEASE WAKE UP.
I DON'T WANT T-TO BE ALONE IN THIS PL--
CREEAK.

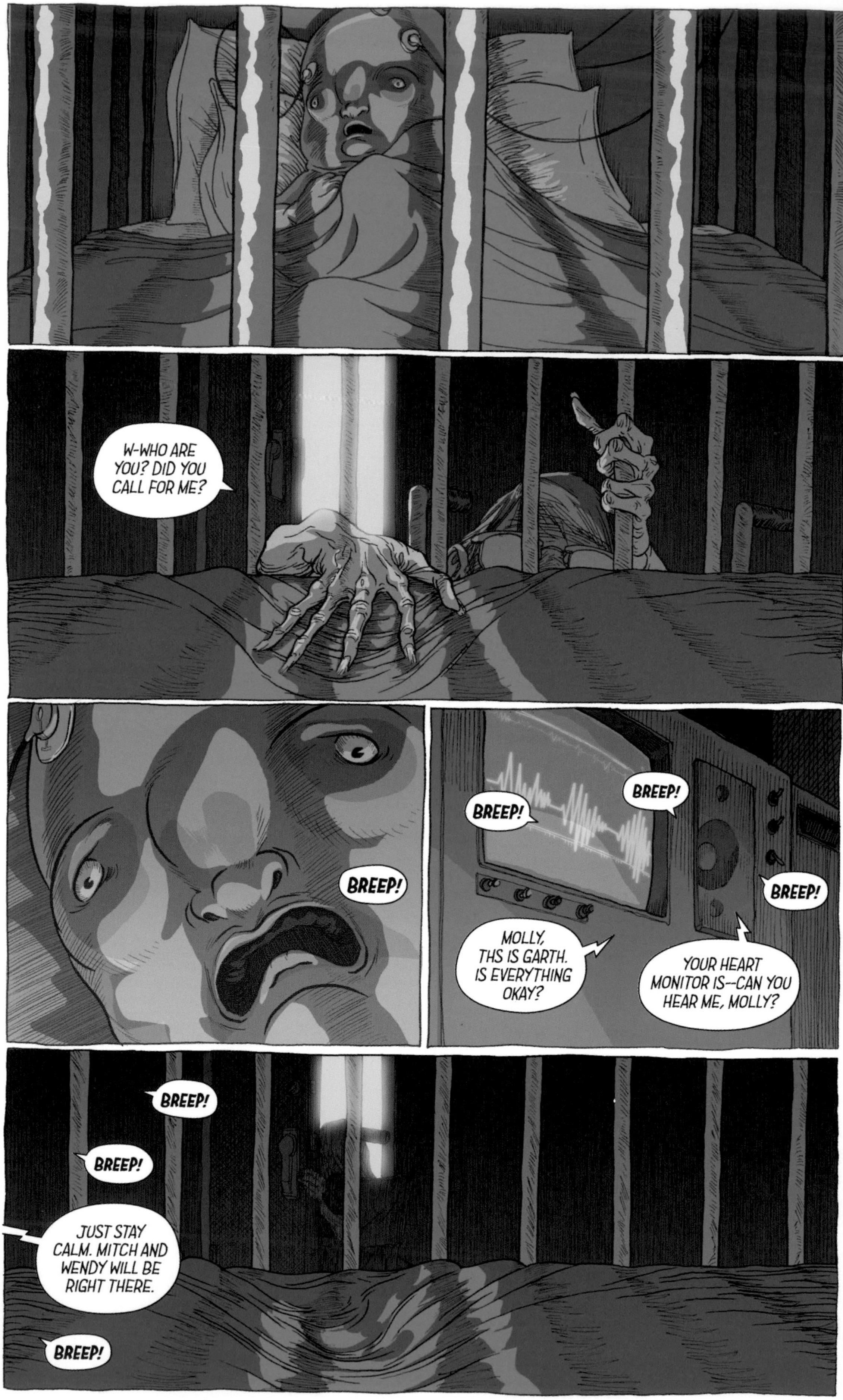
W-WHO ARE YOU? DID YOU CALL FOR ME?
BREEP!
BREEP!
BREEP!
MOLLY, THS IS GARTH. IS EVERYTHING OKAY?
BREEP!
YOUR HEART MONITOR IS--CAN YOU HEAR ME, MOLLY?
BREEP!
BREEP!
JUST STAY CALM. MITCH AND WENDY WILL BE RIGHT THERE.
BREEP!

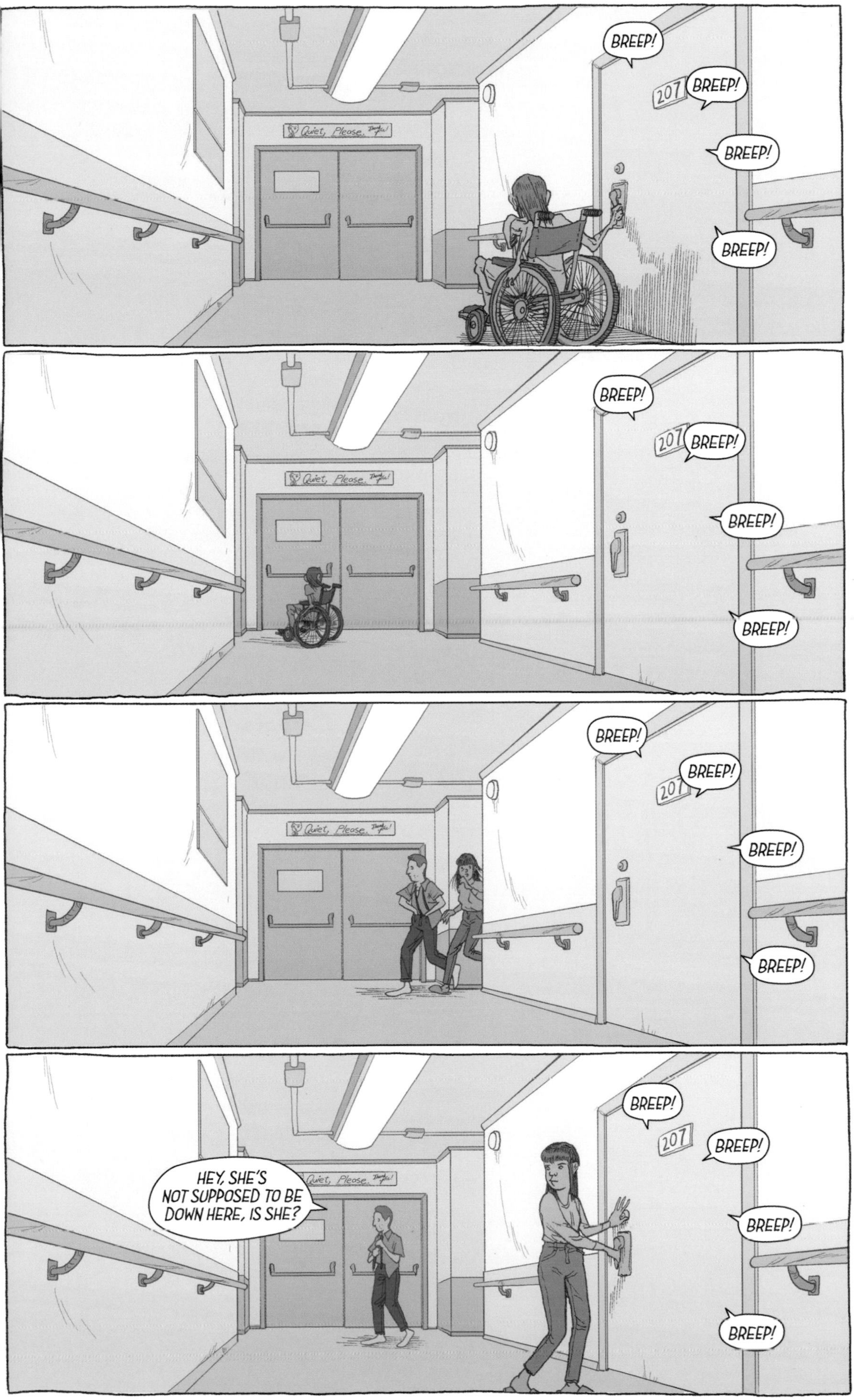
Quiet, Please.
207
BREEP!
BREEP!
BREEP!
BREEP!
Quiet, Please.
207
BREEP!
BREEP!
BREEP!
BREEP!
Quiet, Please.
207
BREEP!
BREEP!
BREEP!
BREEP!
HEY, SHE'S NOT SUPPOSED TO BE DOWN HERE, IS SHE?
Quiet, Please.
207
BREEP!
BREEP!
BREEP!
BREEP!

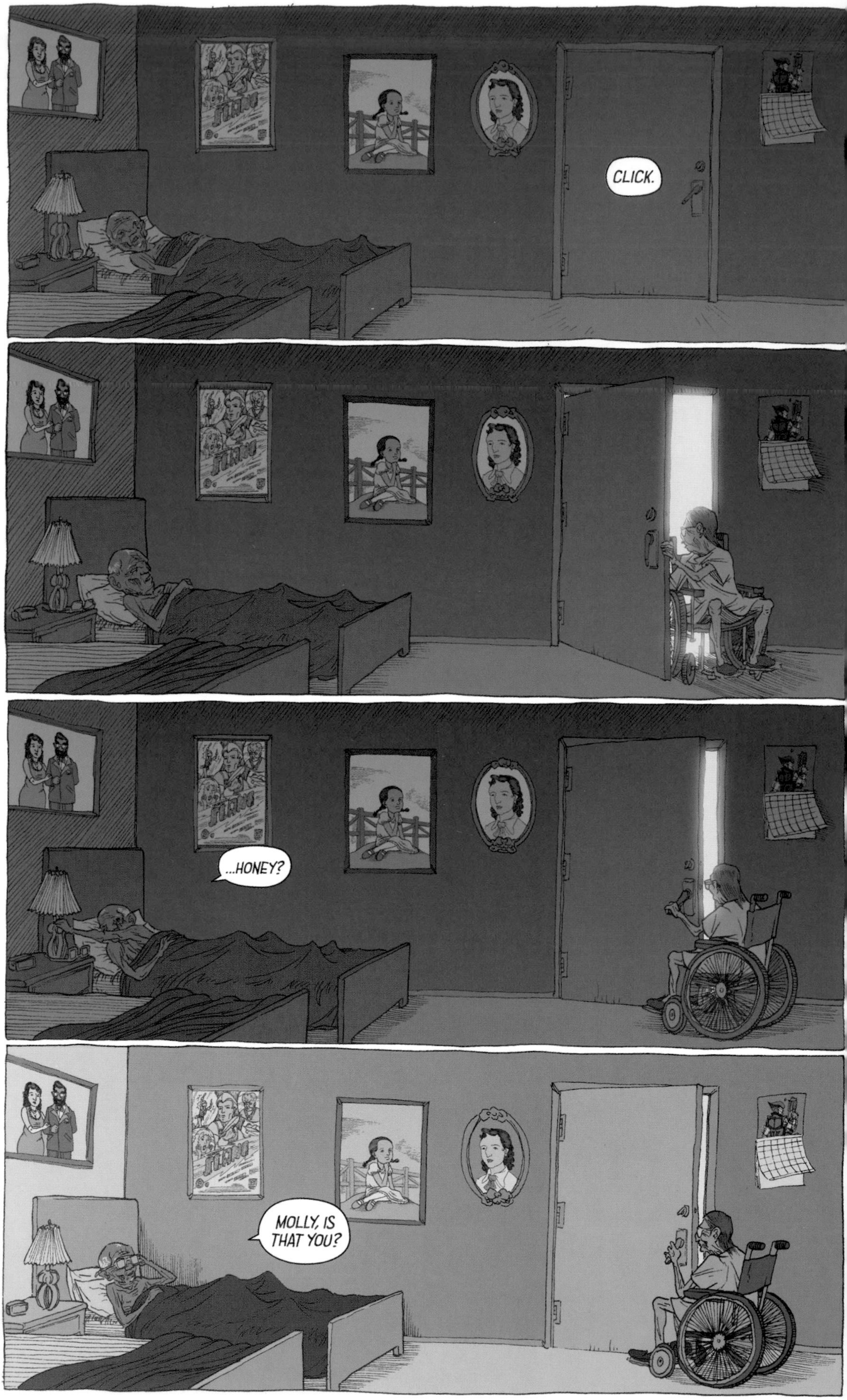
CLICK.
...HONEY?
MOLLY, IS THAT YOU?

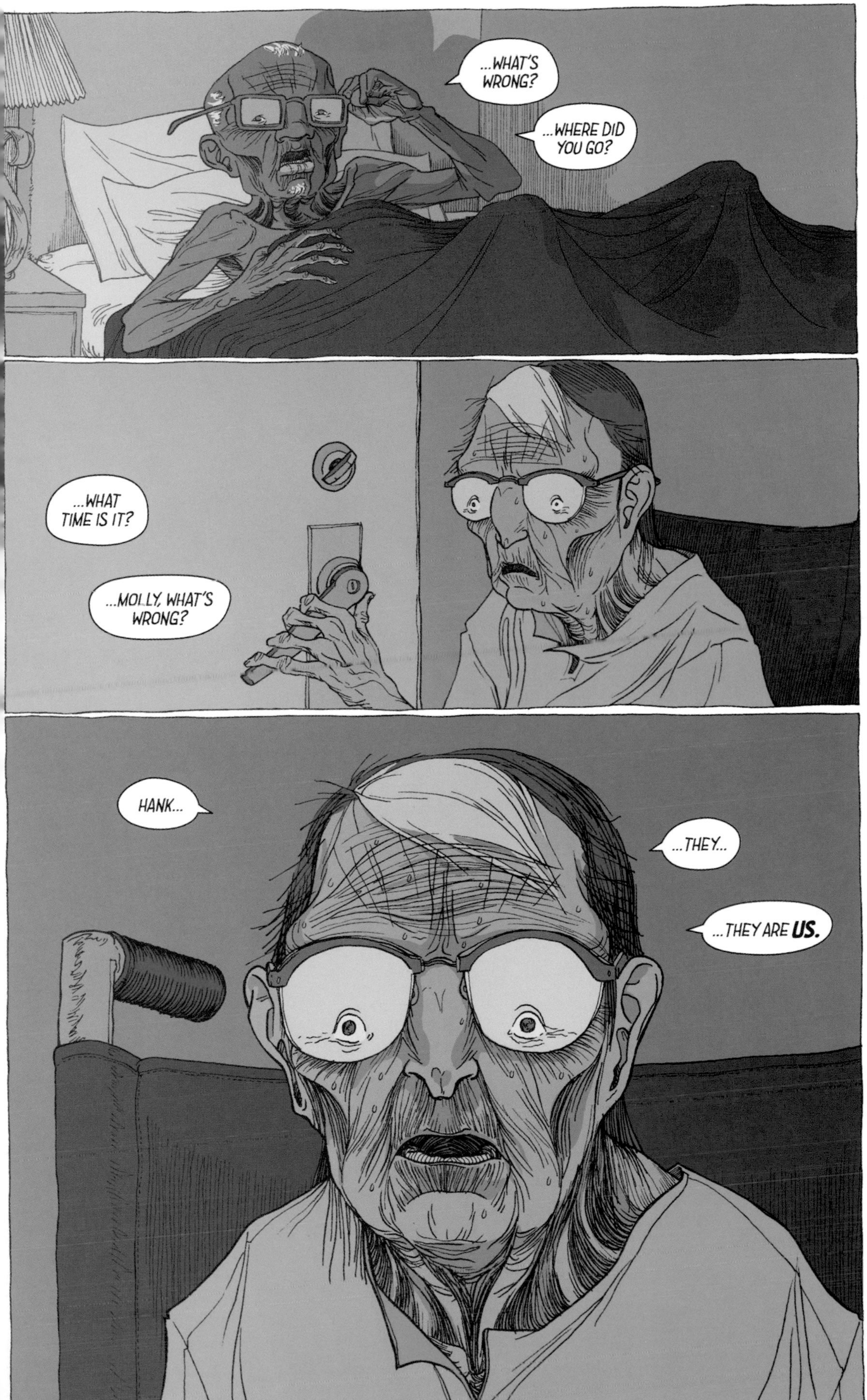

...WHAT'S WRONG?
...WHERE DID YOU GO?
...WHAT TIME IS IT?
...MOLLY, WHAT'S WRONG?
HANK...
...THEY...
...THEY ARE **US.**

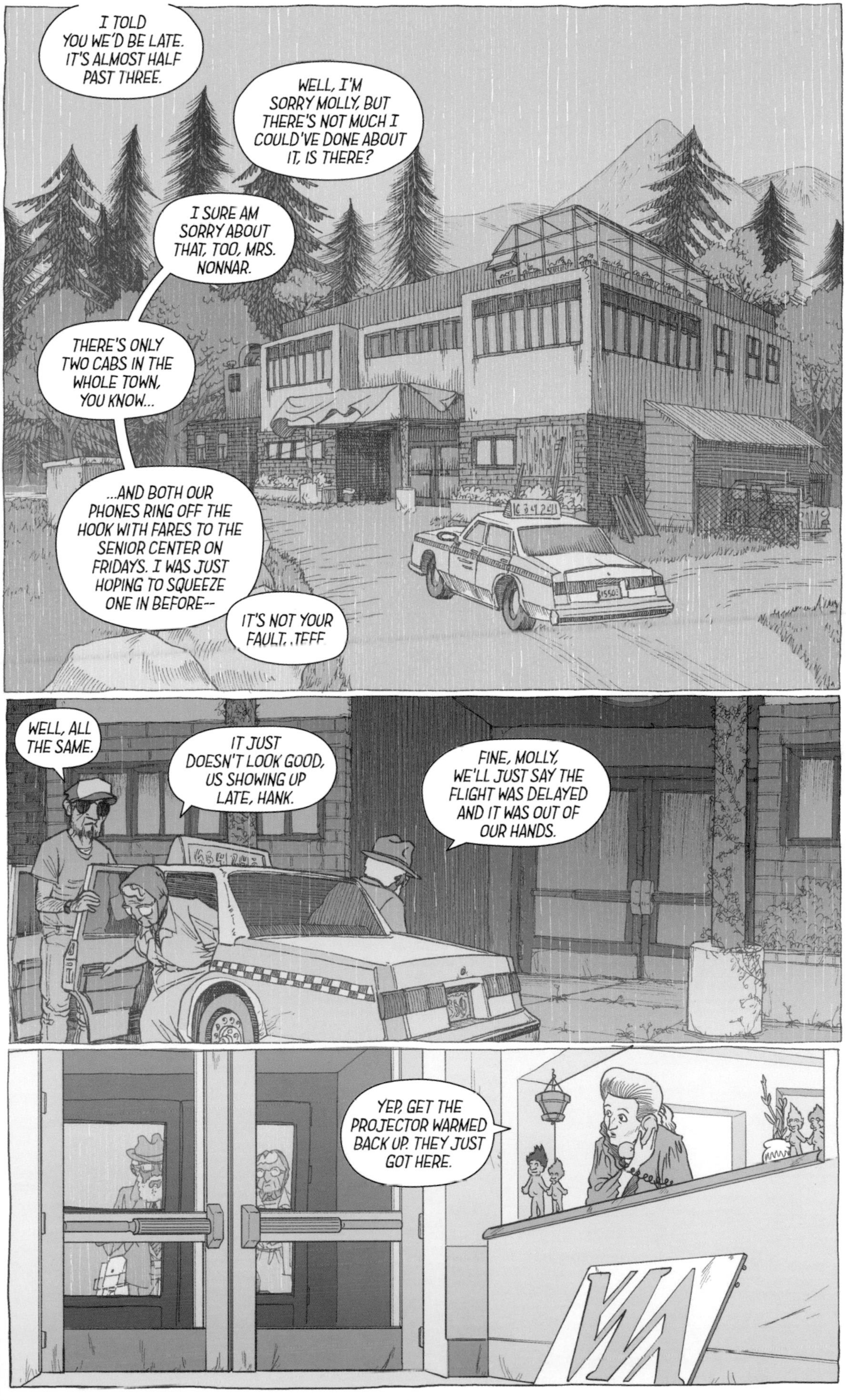
I TOLD YOU WE'D BE LATE. IT'S ALMOST HALF PAST THREE.
WELL, I'M SORRY MOLLY, BUT THERE'S NOT MUCH I COULD'VE DONE ABOUT IT, IS THERE?
I SURE AM SORRY ABOUT THAT, TOO, MRS. NONNAR.
THERE'S ONLY TWO CABS IN THE WHOLE TOWN, YOU KNOW...
...AND BOTH OUR PHONES RING OFF THE HOOK WITH FARES TO THE SENIOR CENTER ON FRIDAYS. I WAS JUST HOPING TO SQUEEZE ONE IN BEFORE--
IT'S NOT YOUR FAULT, JEFF.
WELL, ALL THE SAME.
IT JUST DOESN'T LOOK GOOD, US SHOWING UP LATE, HANK.
FINE, MOLLY, WE'LL JUST SAY THE FLIGHT WAS DELAYED AND IT WAS OUT OF OUR HANDS.
YEP, GET THE PROJECTOR WARMED BACK UP. THEY JUST GOT HERE.

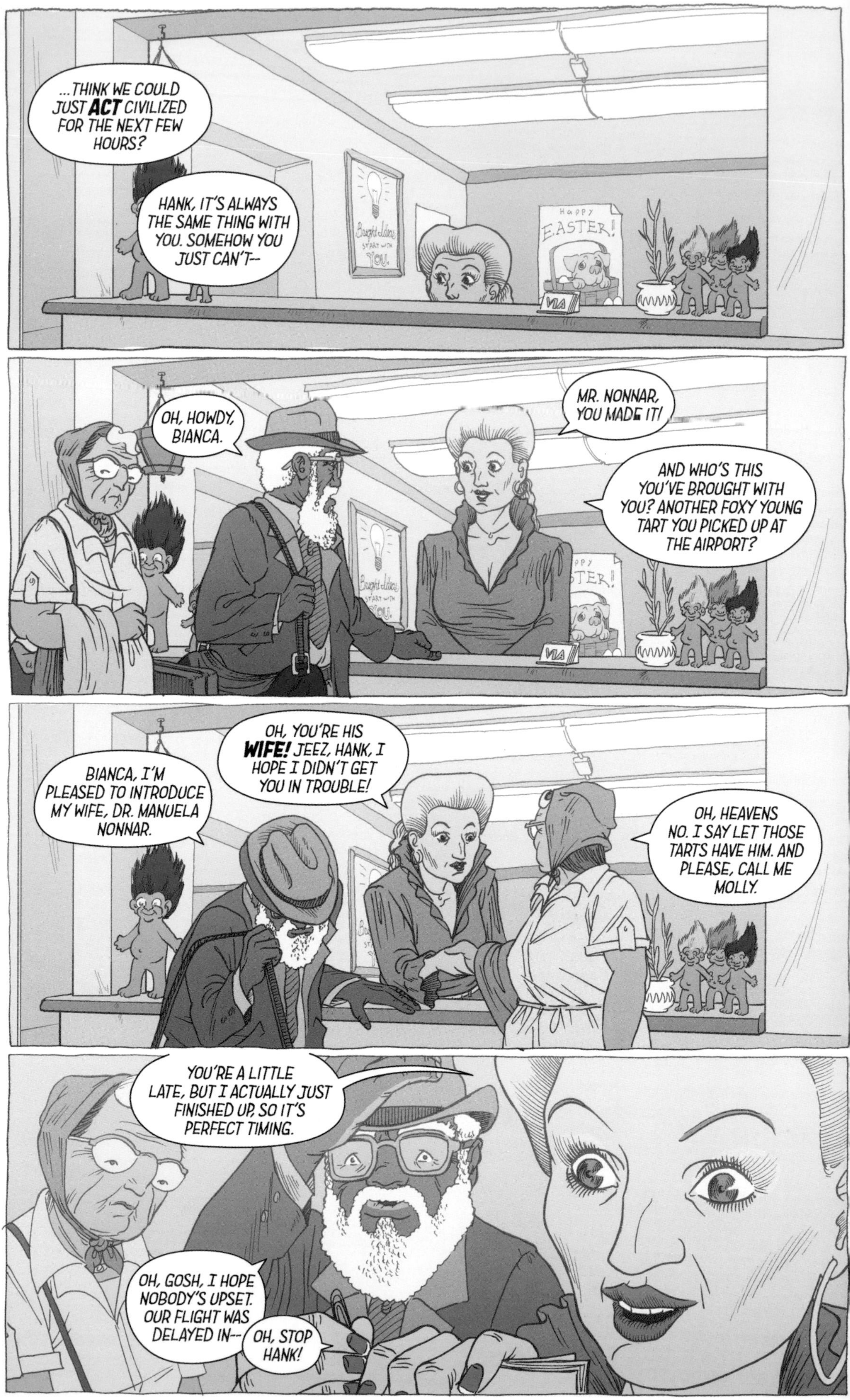

...THINK WE COULD JUST **ACT** CIVILIZED FOR THE NEXT FEW HOURS?
HANK, IT'S ALWAYS THE SAME THING WITH YOU. SOMEHOW YOU JUST CAN'T--
Happy EASTER!
OH, HOWDY, BIANCA.
MR. NONNAR, YOU MADE IT!
AND WHO'S THIS YOU'VE BROUGHT WITH YOU? ANOTHER FOXY YOUNG TART YOU PICKED UP AT THE AIRPORT?
BIANCA, I'M PLEASED TO INTRODUCE MY WIFE, DR. MANUELA NONNAR.
OH, YOU'RE HIS **WIFE!** JEEZ, HANK, I HOPE I DIDN'T GET YOU IN TROUBLE!
OH, HEAVENS NO. I SAY LET THOSE TARTS HAVE HIM. AND PLEASE, CALL ME MOLLY.
YOU'RE A LITTLE LATE, BUT I ACTUALLY JUST FINISHED UP, SO IT'S PERFECT TIMING.
OH, GOSH, I HOPE NOBODY'S UPSET. OUR FLIGHT WAS DELAYED IN--
OH, STOP HANK!

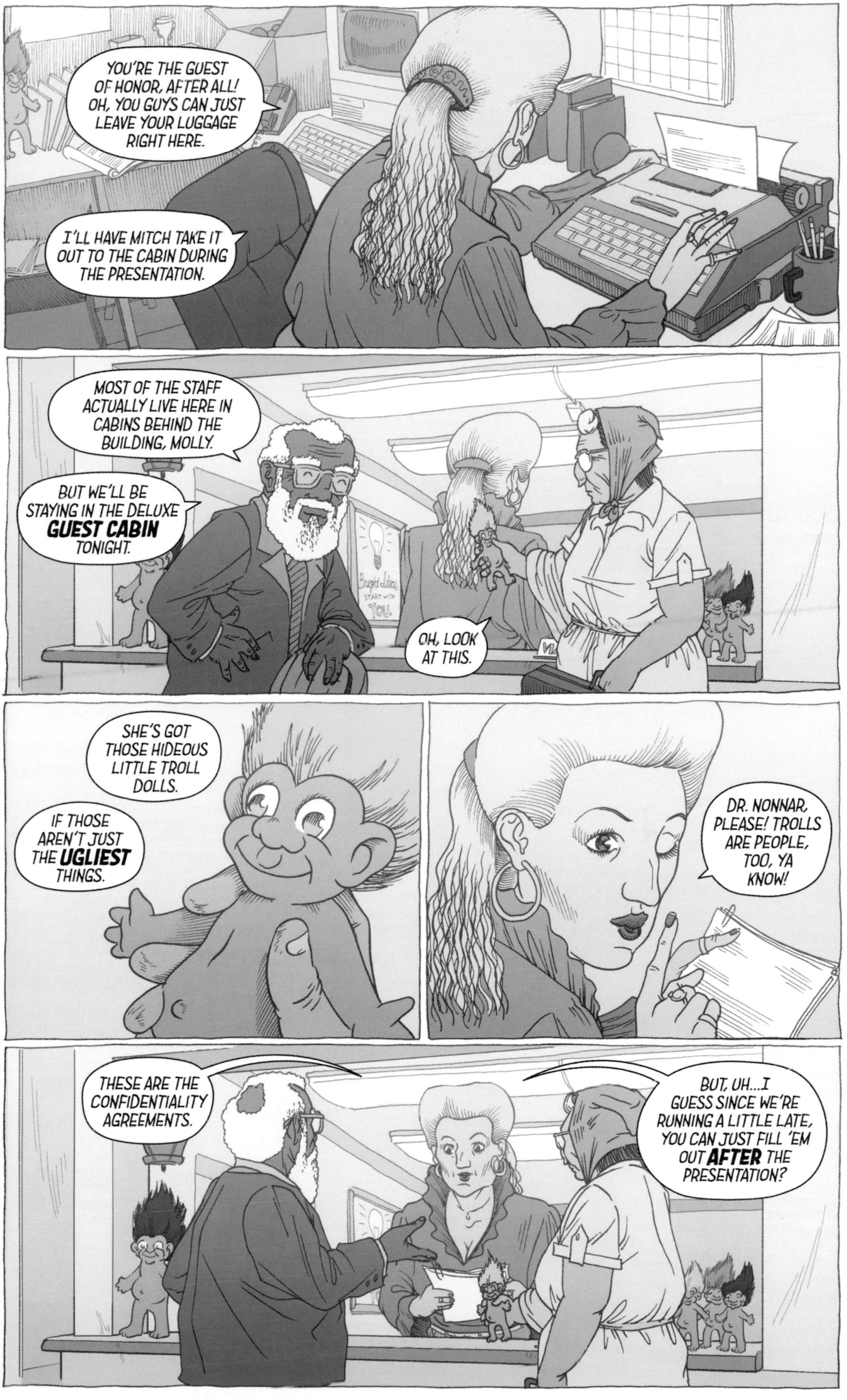

YOU'RE THE GUEST OF HONOR, AFTER ALL! OH, YOU GUYS CAN JUST LEAVE YOUR LUGGAGE RIGHT HERE.
I'LL HAVE MITCH TAKE IT OUT TO THE CABIN DURING THE PRESENTATION.
MOST OF THE STAFF ACTUALLY LIVE HERE IN CABINS BEHIND THE BUILDING, MOLLY.
BUT WE'LL BE STAYING IN THE DELUXE **GUEST CABIN** TONIGHT.
Bright Ideas START WITH YOU.
OH, LOOK AT THIS.
SHE'S GOT THOSE HIDEOUS LITTLE TROLL DOLLS.
IF THOSE AREN'T JUST THE **UGLIEST** THINGS.
DR. NONNAR, PLEASE! TROLLS ARE PEOPLE, TOO, YA KNOW!
THESE ARE THE CONFIDENTIALITY AGREEMENTS.
BUT, UH...I GUESS SINCE WE'RE RUNNING A LITTLE LATE, YOU CAN JUST FILL 'EM OUT **AFTER** THE PRESENTATION?

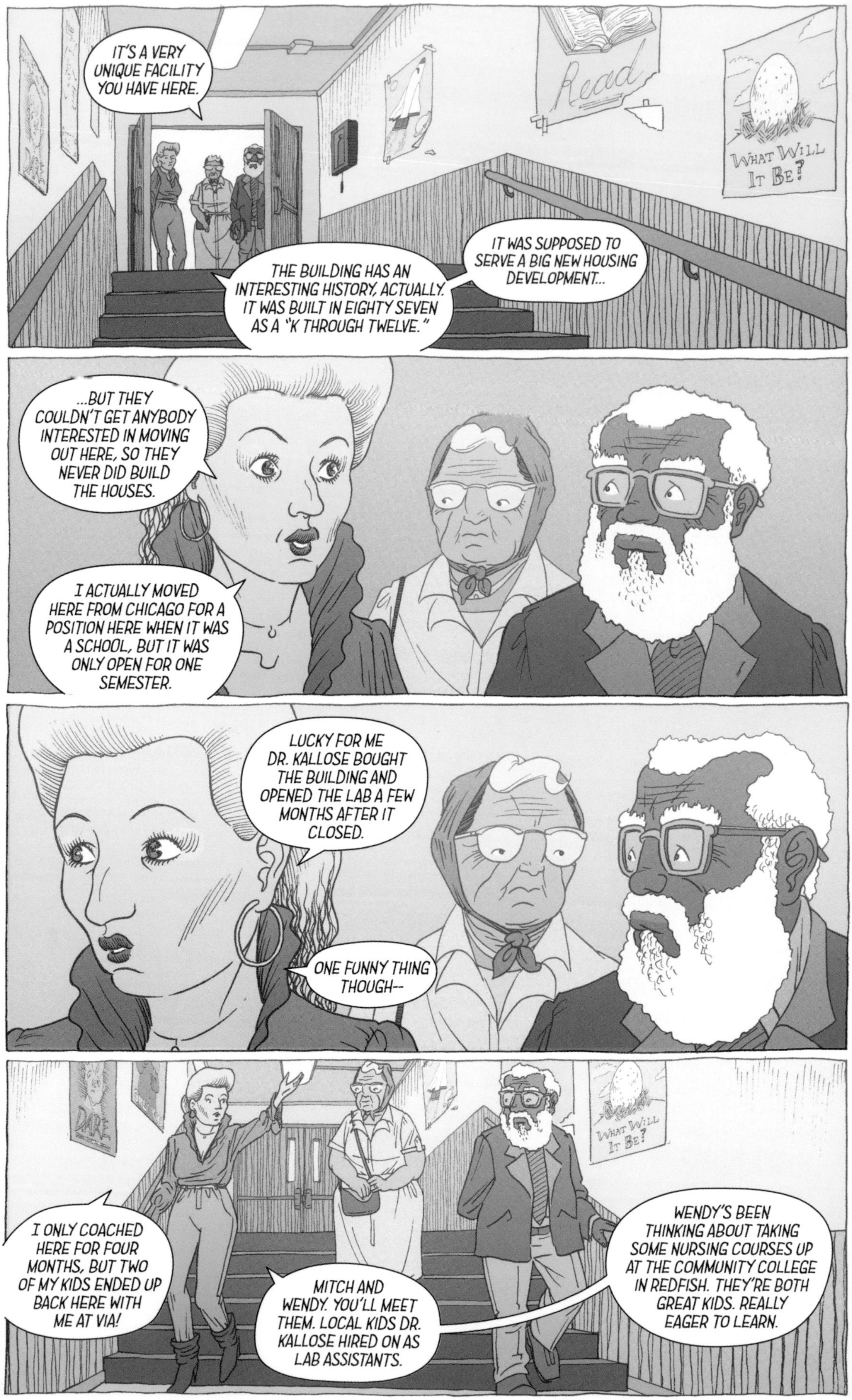
IT'S A VERY UNIQUE FACILITY YOU HAVE HERE.
DARE
Read
WHAT WILL IT BE?
THE BUILDING HAS AN INTERESTING HISTORY, ACTUALLY. IT WAS BUILT IN EIGHTY SEVEN AS A "K THROUGH TWELVE."
IT WAS SUPPOSED TO SERVE A BIG NEW HOUSING DEVELOPMENT...
...BUT THEY COULDN'T GET ANYBODY INTERESTED IN MOVING OUT HERE, SO THEY NEVER DID BUILD THE HOUSES.
I ACTUALLY MOVED HERE FROM CHICAGO FOR A POSITION HERE WHEN IT WAS A SCHOOL, BUT IT WAS ONLY OPEN FOR ONE SEMESTER.
LUCKY FOR ME DR. KALLOSE BOUGHT THE BUILDING AND OPENED THE LAB A FEW MONTHS AFTER IT CLOSED.
ONE FUNNY THING THOUGH--
DARE
WHAT WILL IT BE?
I ONLY COACHED HERE FOR FOUR MONTHS, BUT TWO OF MY KIDS ENDED UP BACK HERE WITH ME AT VIA!
MITCH AND WENDY. YOU'LL MEET THEM. LOCAL KIDS DR. KALLOSE HIRED ON AS LAB ASSISTANTS.
WENDY'S BEEN THINKING ABOUT TAKING SOME NURSING COURSES UP AT THE COMMUNITY COLLEGE IN REDFISH. THEY'RE BOTH GREAT KIDS. REALLY EAGER TO LEARN.

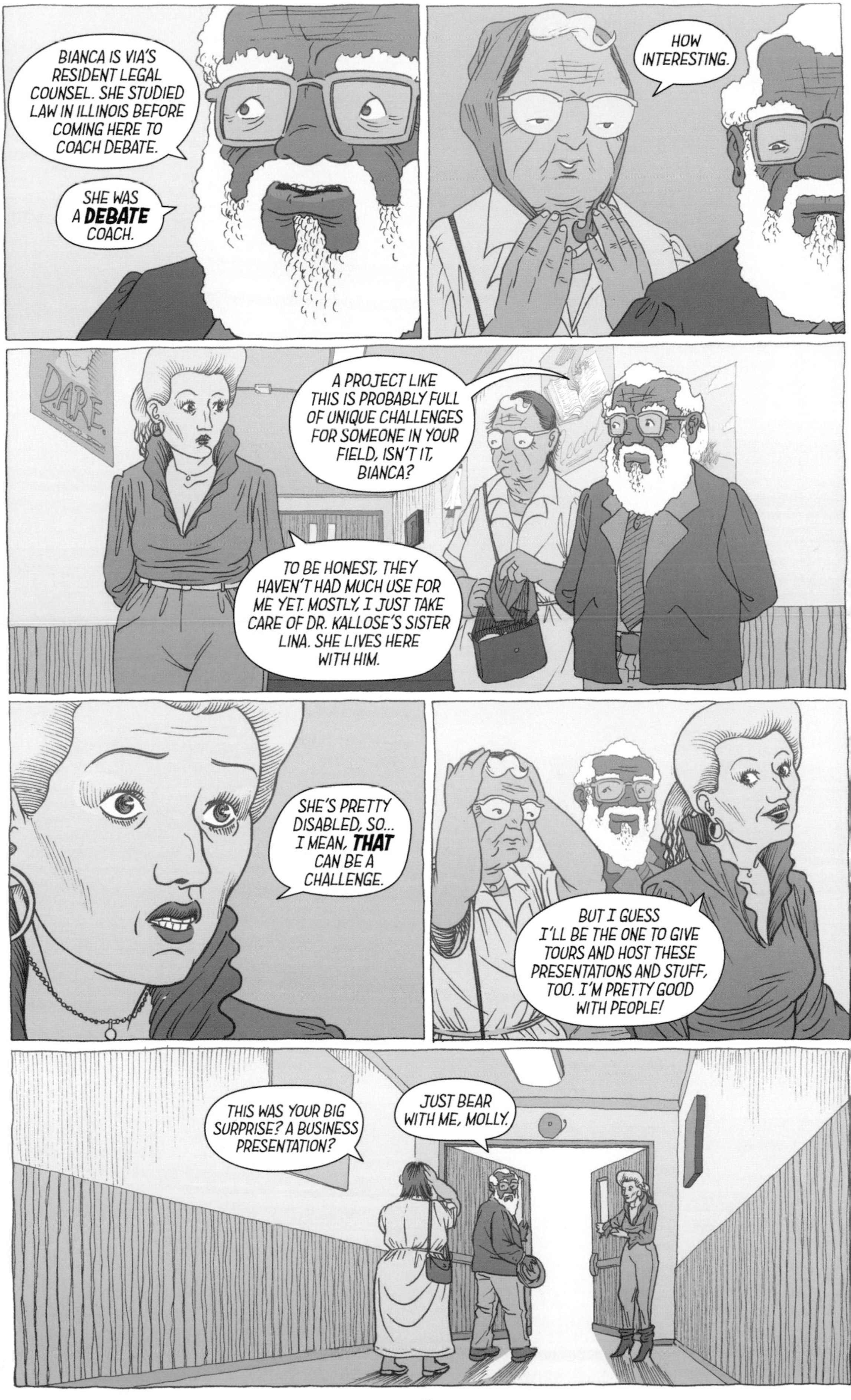

BIANCA IS VIA'S RESIDENT LEGAL COUNSEL. SHE STUDIED LAW IN ILLINOIS BEFORE COMING HERE TO COACH DEBATE.
SHE WAS A **DEBATE** COACH.
HOW INTERESTING.
A PROJECT LIKE THIS IS PROBABLY FULL OF UNIQUE CHALLENGES FOR SOMEONE IN YOUR FIELD, ISN'T IT, BIANCA?
TO BE HONEST, THEY HAVEN'T HAD MUCH USE FOR ME YET. MOSTLY, I JUST TAKE CARE OF DR. KALLOSE'S SISTER LINA. SHE LIVES HERE WITH HIM.
SHE'S PRETTY DISABLED, SO... I MEAN, **THAT** CAN BE A CHALLENGE.
BUT I GUESS I'LL BE THE ONE TO GIVE TOURS AND HOST THESE PRESENTATIONS AND STUFF, TOO. I'M PRETTY GOOD WITH PEOPLE!
THIS WAS YOUR BIG SURPRISE? A BUSINESS PRESENTATION?
JUST BEAR WITH ME, MOLLY.

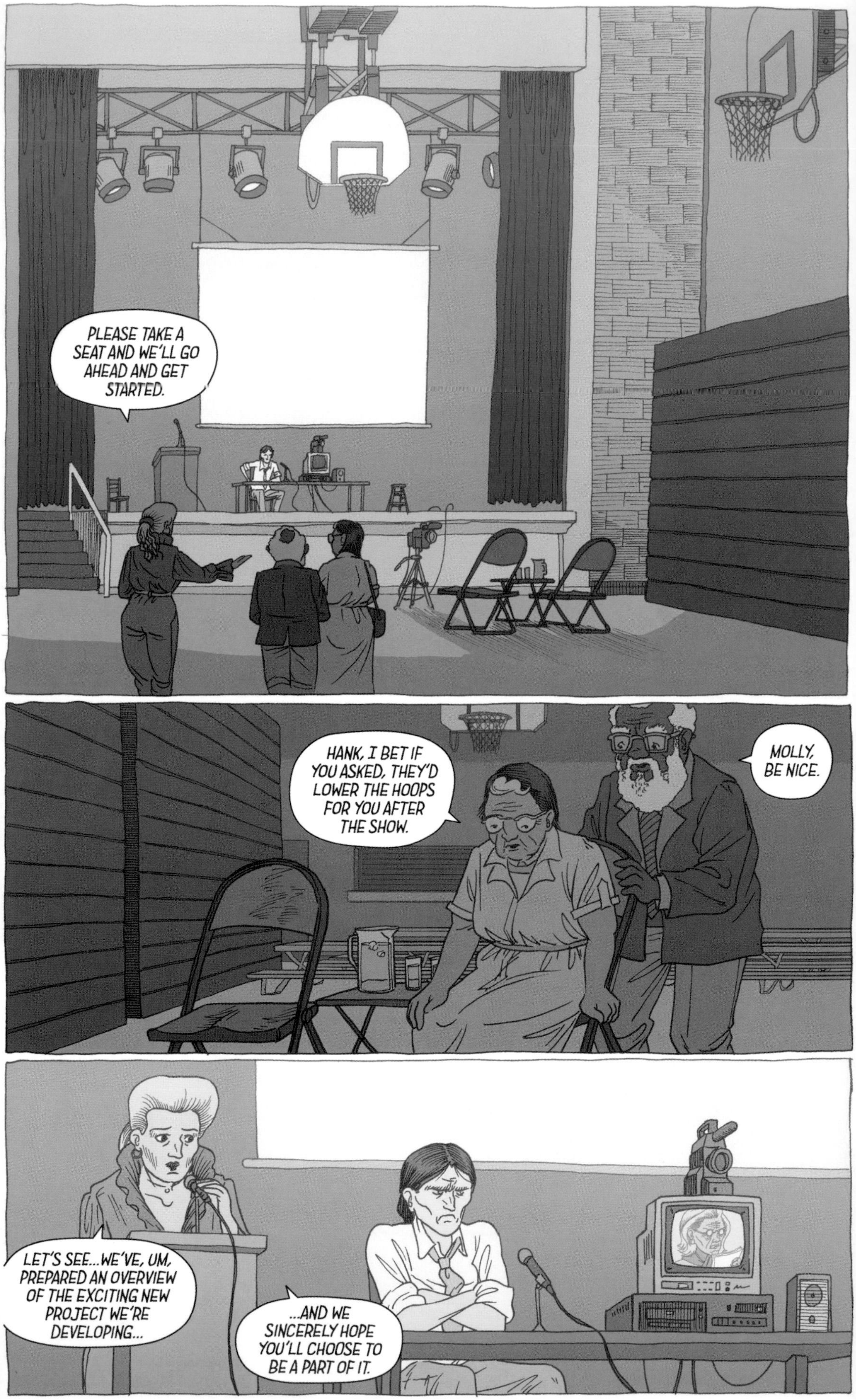
PLEASE TAKE A SEAT AND WE'LL GO AHEAD AND GET STARTED.
HANK, I BET IF YOU ASKED, THEY'D LOWER THE HOOPS FOR YOU AFTER THE SHOW.
MOLLY, BE NICE.
LET'S SEE...WE'VE, UM, PREPARED AN OVERVIEW OF THE EXCITING NEW PROJECT WE'RE DEVELOPING...
...AND WE SINCERELY HOPE YOU'LL CHOOSE TO BE A PART OF IT.

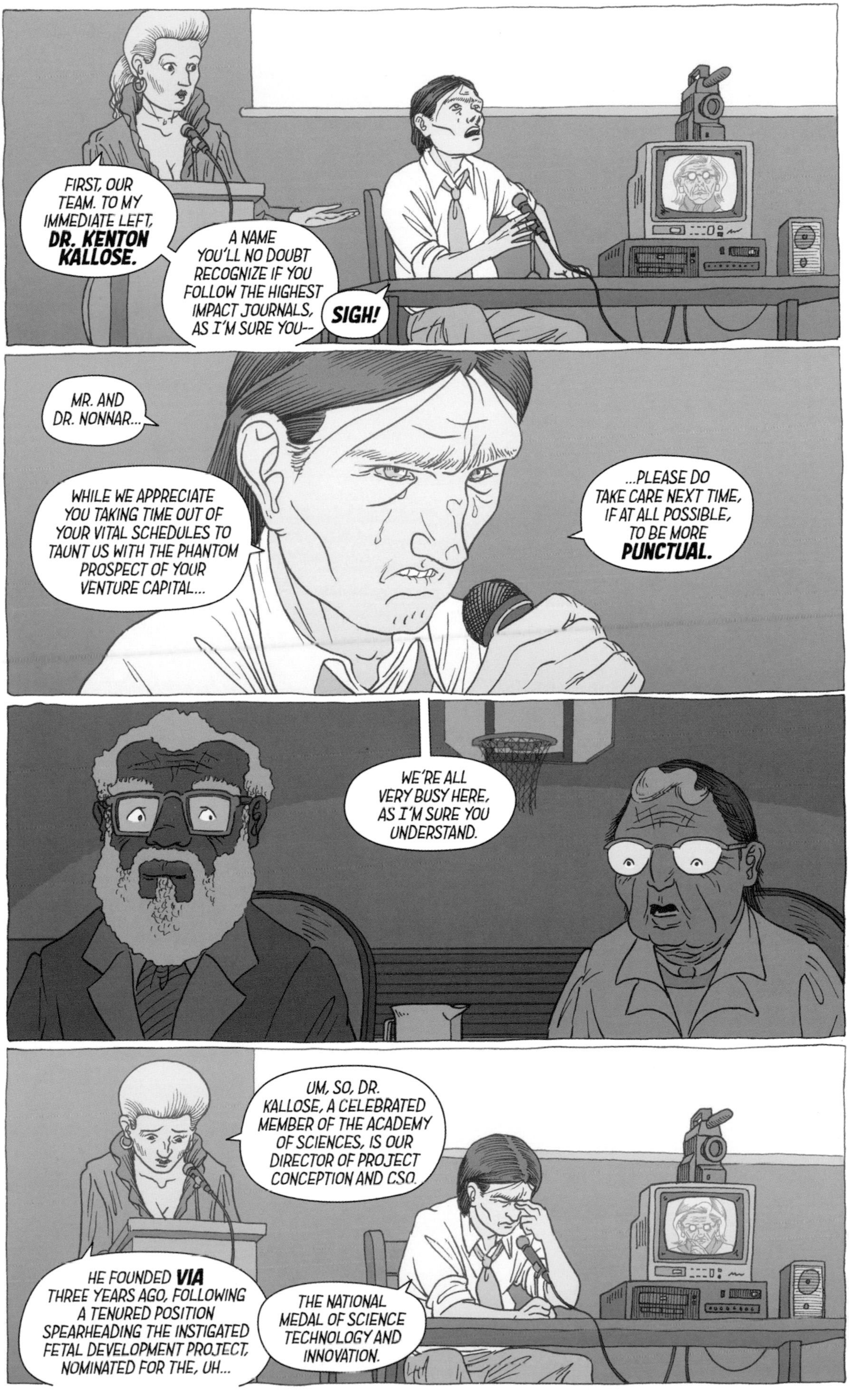
FIRST, OUR TEAM. TO MY IMMEDIATE LEFT, **DR. KENTON KALLOSE.**
A NAME YOU'LL NO DOUBT RECOGNIZE IF YOU FOLLOW THE HIGHEST IMPACT JOURNALS, AS I'M SURE YOU--
SIGH!
MR. AND DR. NONNAR...
WHILE WE APPRECIATE YOU TAKING TIME OUT OF YOUR VITAL SCHEDULES TO TAUNT US WITH THE PHANTOM PROSPECT OF YOUR VENTURE CAPITAL...
...PLEASE DO TAKE CARE NEXT TIME, IF AT ALL POSSIBLE, TO BE MORE **PUNCTUAL.**
WE'RE ALL VERY BUSY HERE, AS I'M SURE YOU UNDERSTAND.
UM, SO, DR. KALLOSE, A CELEBRATED MEMBER OF THE ACADEMY OF SCIENCES, IS OUR DIRECTOR OF PROJECT CONCEPTION AND CSO.
HE FOUNDED **VIA** THREE YEARS AGO, FOLLOWING A TENURED POSITION SPEARHEADING THE INSTIGATED FETAL DEVELOPMENT PROJECT, NOMINATED FOR THE, UH...
THE NATIONAL MEDAL OF SCIENCE TECHNOLOGY AND INNOVATION.

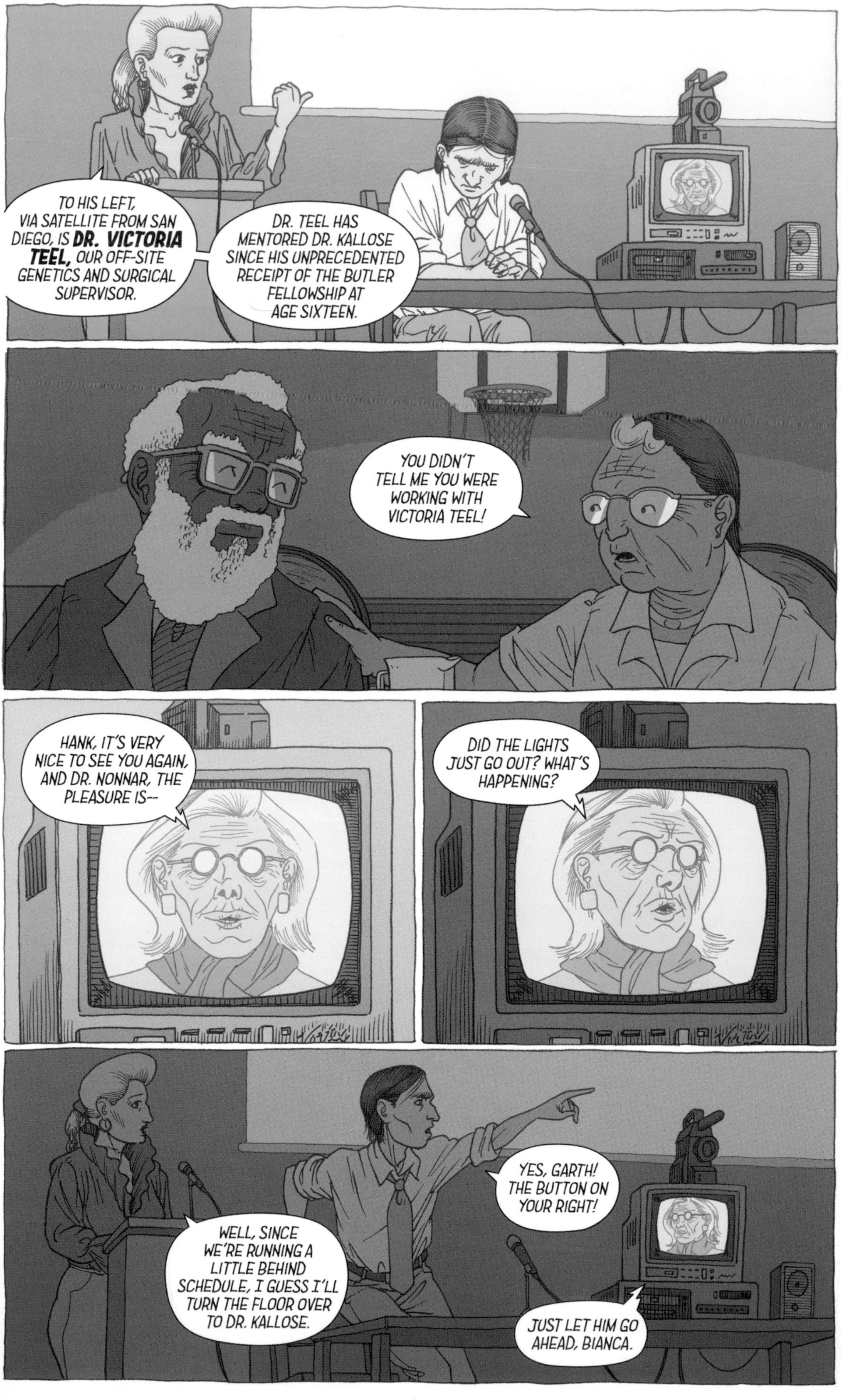
TO HIS LEFT, VIA SATELLITE FROM SAN DIEGO, IS **DR. VICTORIA TEEL,** OUR OFF-SITE GENETICS AND SURGICAL SUPERVISOR.
DR. TEEL HAS MENTORED DR. KALLOSE SINCE HIS UNPRECEDENTED RECEIPT OF THE BUTLER FELLOWSHIP AT AGE SIXTEEN.
YOU DIDN'T TELL ME YOU WERE WORKING WITH VICTORIA TEEL!
HANK, IT'S VERY NICE TO SEE YOU AGAIN, AND DR. NONNAR, THE PLEASURE IS--
DID THE LIGHTS JUST GO OUT? WHAT'S HAPPENING?
YES, GARTH! THE BUTTON ON YOUR RIGHT!
WELL, SINCE WE'RE RUNNING A LITTLE BEHIND SCHEDULE, I GUESS I'LL TURN THE FLOOR OVER TO DR. KALLOSE.
JUST LET HIM GO AHEAD, BIANCA.

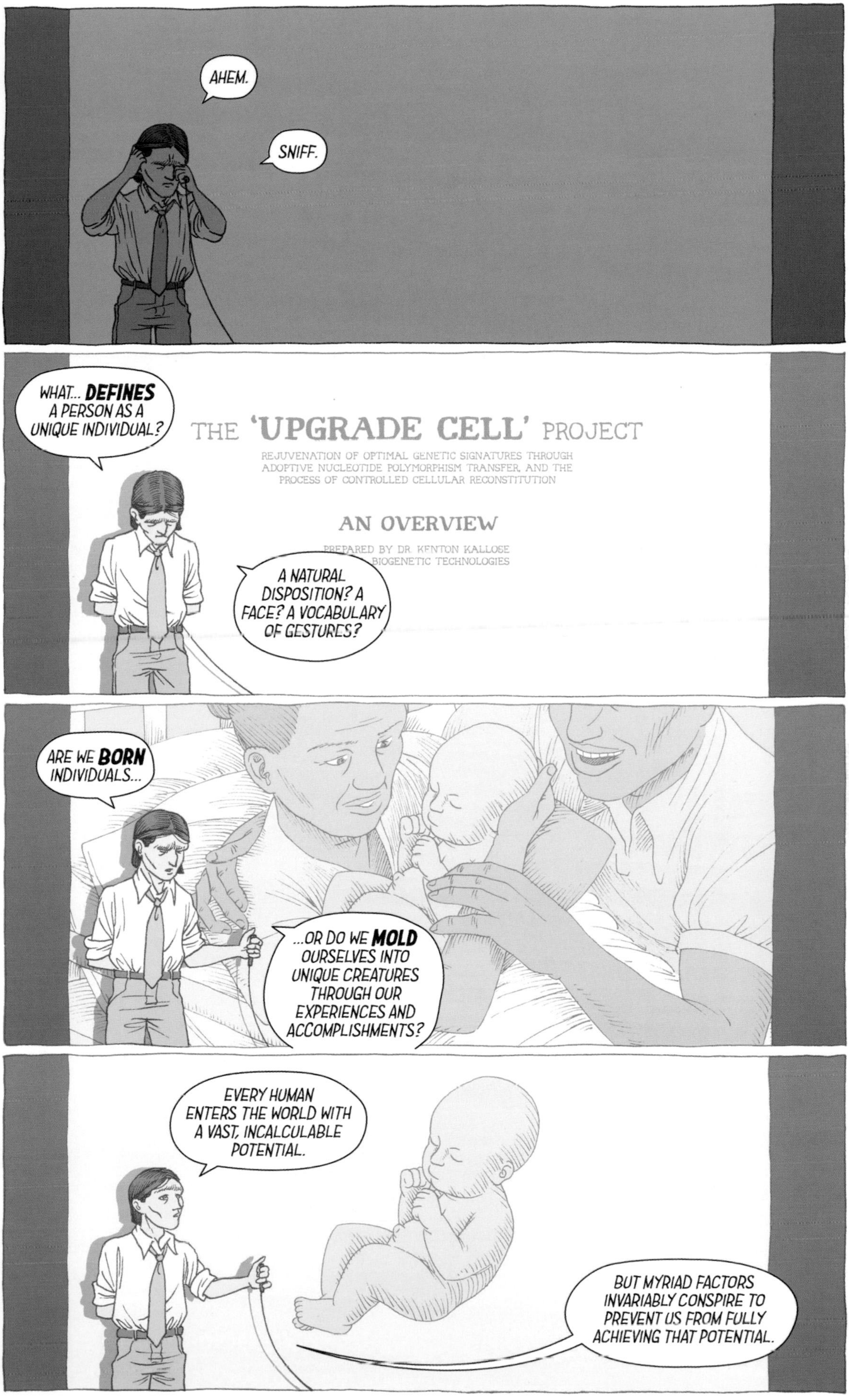
AHEM.
SNIFF.
WHAT... DEFINES A PERSON AS A UNIQUE INDIVIDUAL?
THE 'UPGRADE CELL' PROJECT
REJUVENATION OF OPTIMAL GENETIC SIGNATURES THROUGH ADOPTIVE NUCLEOTIDE POLYMORPHISM TRANSFER, AND THE PROCESS OF CONTROLLED CELLULAR RECONSTITUTION
AN OVERVIEW
PREPARED BY DR. KENTON KALLOSE
BIOGENETIC TECHNOLOGIES
A NATURAL DISPOSITION? A FACE? A VOCABULARY OF GESTURES?
ARE WE BORN INDIVIDUALS...
...OR DO WE MOLD OURSELVES INTO UNIQUE CREATURES THROUGH OUR EXPERIENCES AND ACCOMPLISHMENTS?
EVERY HUMAN ENTERS THE WORLD WITH A VAST, INCALCULABLE POTENTIAL.
BUT MYRIAD FACTORS INVARIABLY CONSPIRE TO PREVENT US FROM FULLY ACHIEVING THAT POTENTIAL.

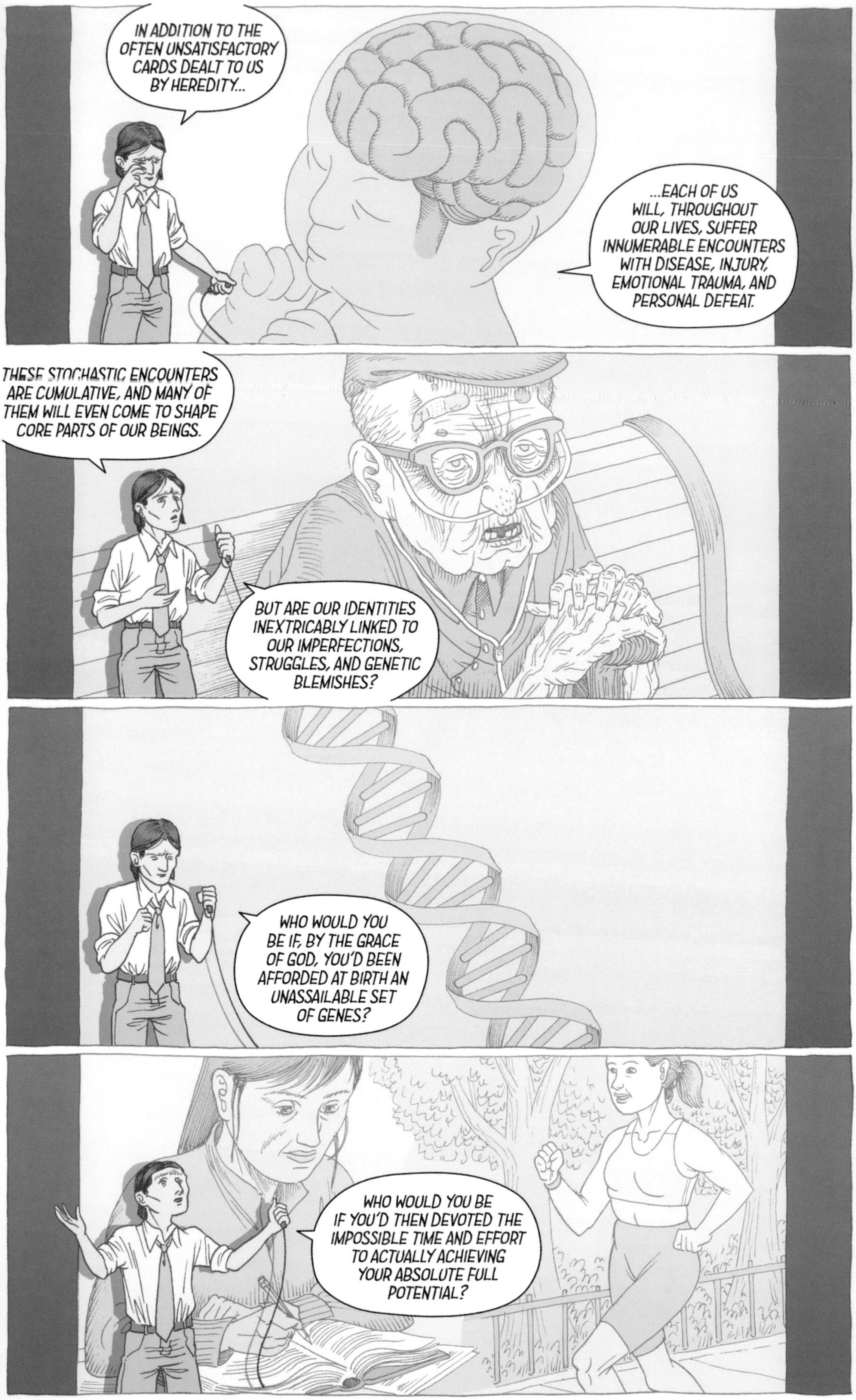
IN ADDITION TO THE OFTEN UNSATISFACTORY CARDS DEALT TO US BY HEREDITY...
...EACH OF US WILL, THROUGHOUT OUR LIVES, SUFFER INNUMERABLE ENCOUNTERS WITH DISEASE, INJURY, EMOTIONAL TRAUMA, AND PERSONAL DEFEAT.
THESE STOCHASTIC ENCOUNTERS ARE CUMULATIVE, AND MANY OF THEM WILL EVEN COME TO SHAPE CORE PARTS OF OUR BEINGS.
BUT ARE OUR IDENTITIES INEXTRICABLY LINKED TO OUR IMPERFECTIONS, STRUGGLES, AND GENETIC BLEMISHES?
WHO WOULD YOU BE IF, BY THE GRACE OF GOD, YOU'D BEEN AFFORDED AT BIRTH AN UNASSAILABLE SET OF GENES?
WHO WOULD YOU BE IF YOU'D THEN DEVOTED THE IMPOSSIBLE TIME AND EFFORT TO ACTUALLY ACHIEVING YOUR ABSOLUTE FULL POTENTIAL?

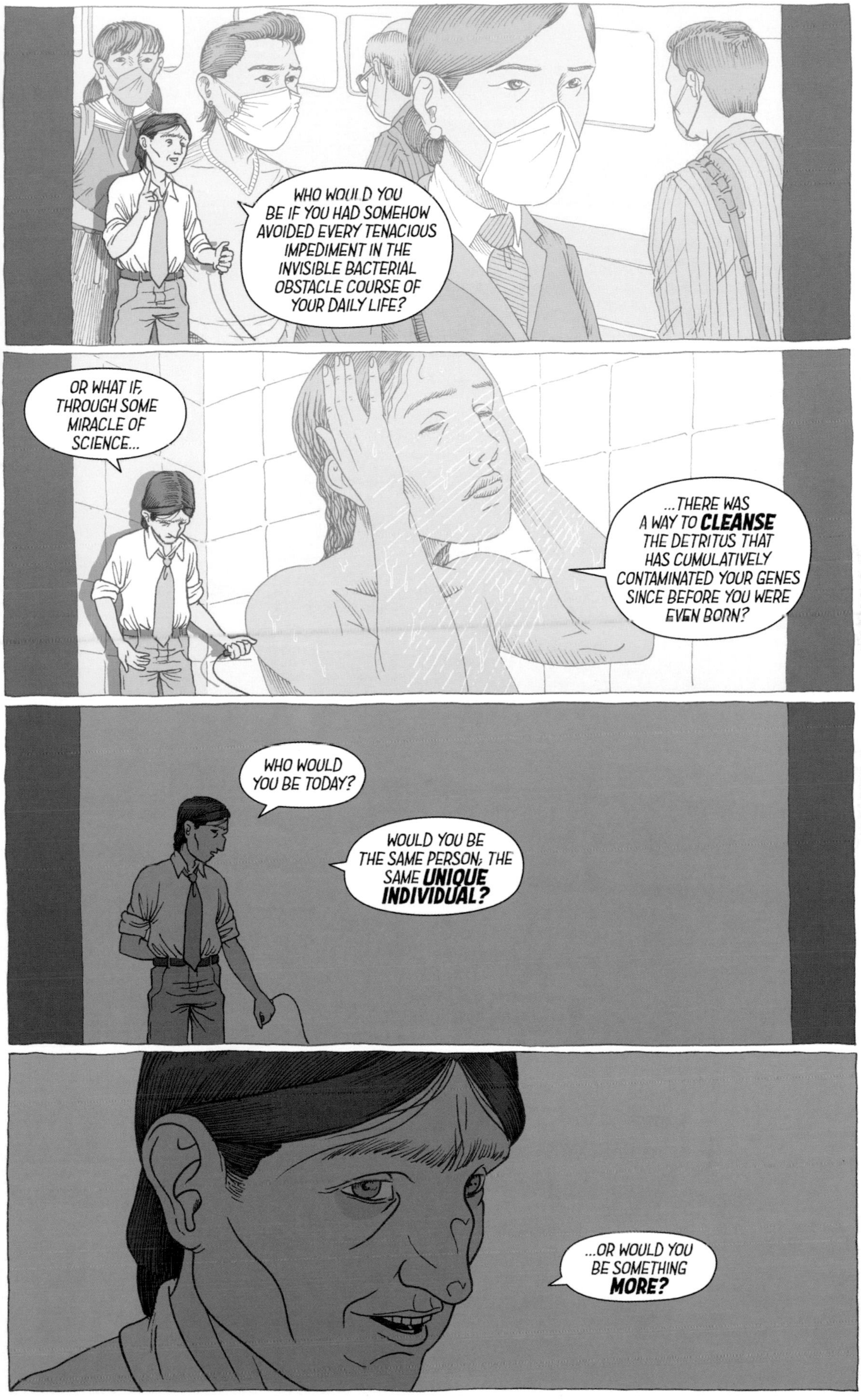
WHO WOULD YOU BE IF YOU HAD SOMEHOW AVOIDED EVERY TENACIOUS IMPEDIMENT IN THE INVISIBLE BACTERIAL OBSTACLE COURSE OF YOUR DAILY LIFE?
OR WHAT IF, THROUGH SOME MIRACLE OF SCIENCE...
...THERE WAS A WAY TO **CLEANSE** THE DETRITUS THAT HAS CUMULATIVELY CONTAMINATED YOUR GENES SINCE BEFORE YOU WERE EVEN BORN?
WHO WOULD YOU BE TODAY?
WOULD YOU BE THE SAME PERSON; THE SAME **UNIQUE INDIVIDUAL?**
...OR WOULD YOU BE SOMETHING **MORE?**

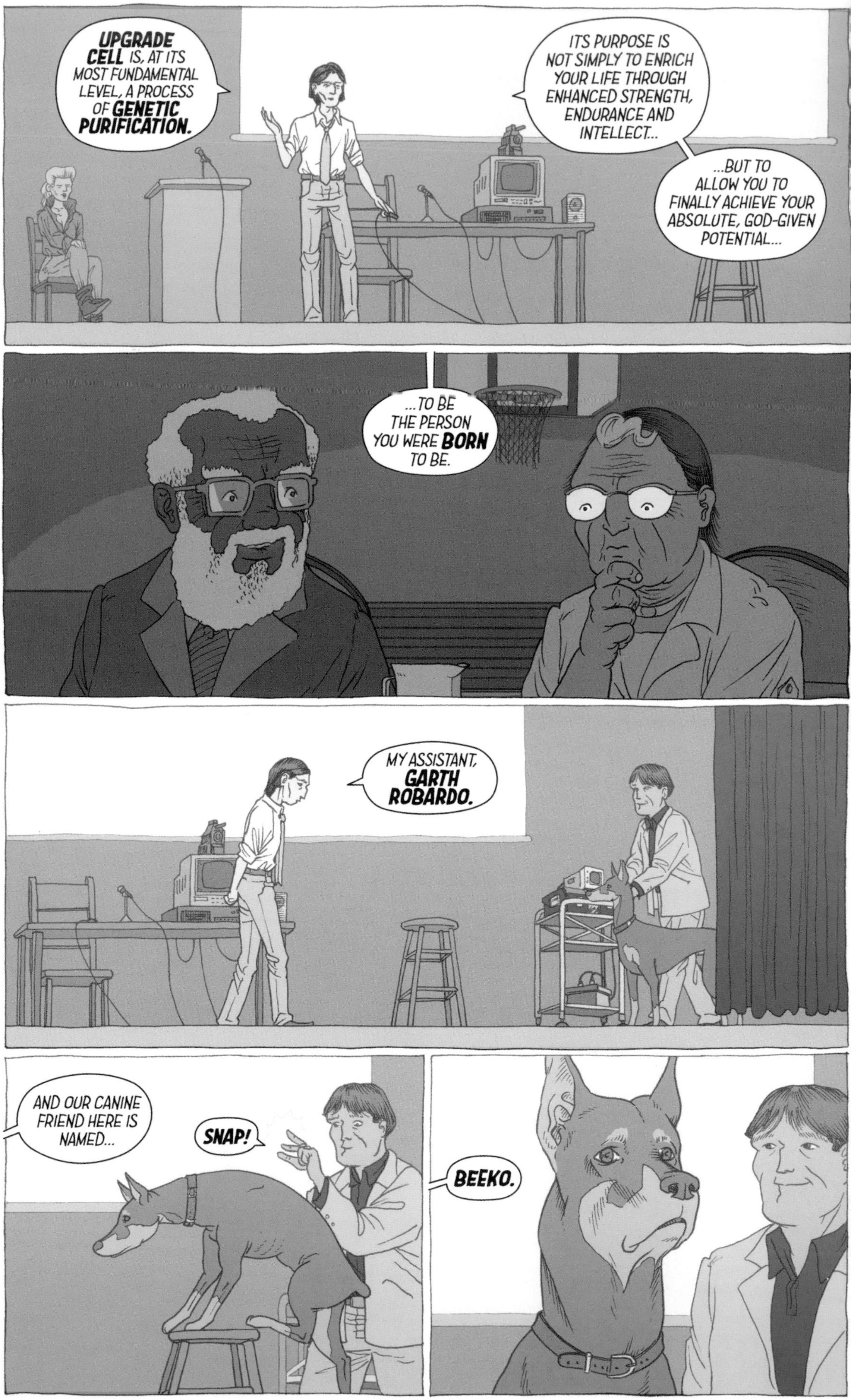
UPGRADE CELL IS, AT ITS MOST FUNDAMENTAL LEVEL, A PROCESS OF GENETIC PURIFICATION.
ITS PURPOSE IS NOT SIMPLY TO ENRICH YOUR LIFE THROUGH ENHANCED STRENGTH, ENDURANCE AND INTELLECT...
...BUT TO ALLOW YOU TO FINALLY ACHIEVE YOUR ABSOLUTE, GOD-GIVEN POTENTIAL...
...TO BE THE PERSON YOU WERE BORN TO BE.
MY ASSISTANT, GARTH ROBARDO.
AND OUR CANINE FRIEND HERE IS NAMED...
SNAP!
BEEKO.

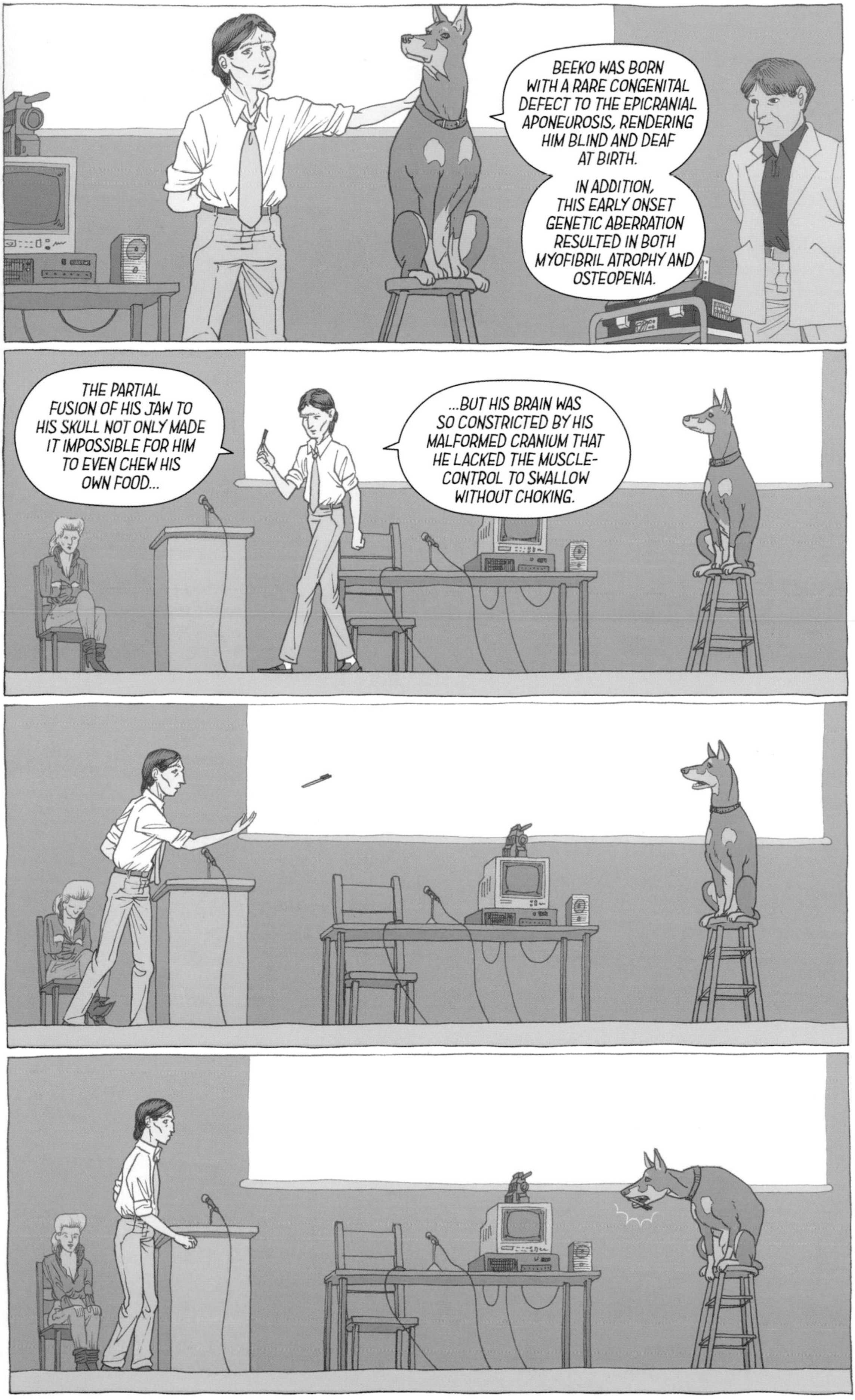
BEEKO WAS BORN WITH A RARE CONGENITAL DEFECT TO THE EPICRANIAL APONEUROSIS, RENDERING HIM BLIND AND DEAF AT BIRTH.
IN ADDITION, THIS EARLY ONSET GENETIC ABERRATION RESULTED IN BOTH MYOFIBRIL ATROPHY AND OSTEOPENIA.
THE PARTIAL FUSION OF HIS JAW TO HIS SKULL NOT ONLY MADE IT IMPOSSIBLE FOR HIM TO EVEN CHEW HIS OWN FOOD...
...BUT HIS BRAIN WAS SO CONSTRICTED BY HIS MALFORMED CRANIUM THAT HE LACKED THE MUSCLE-CONTROL TO SWALLOW WITHOUT CHOKING.

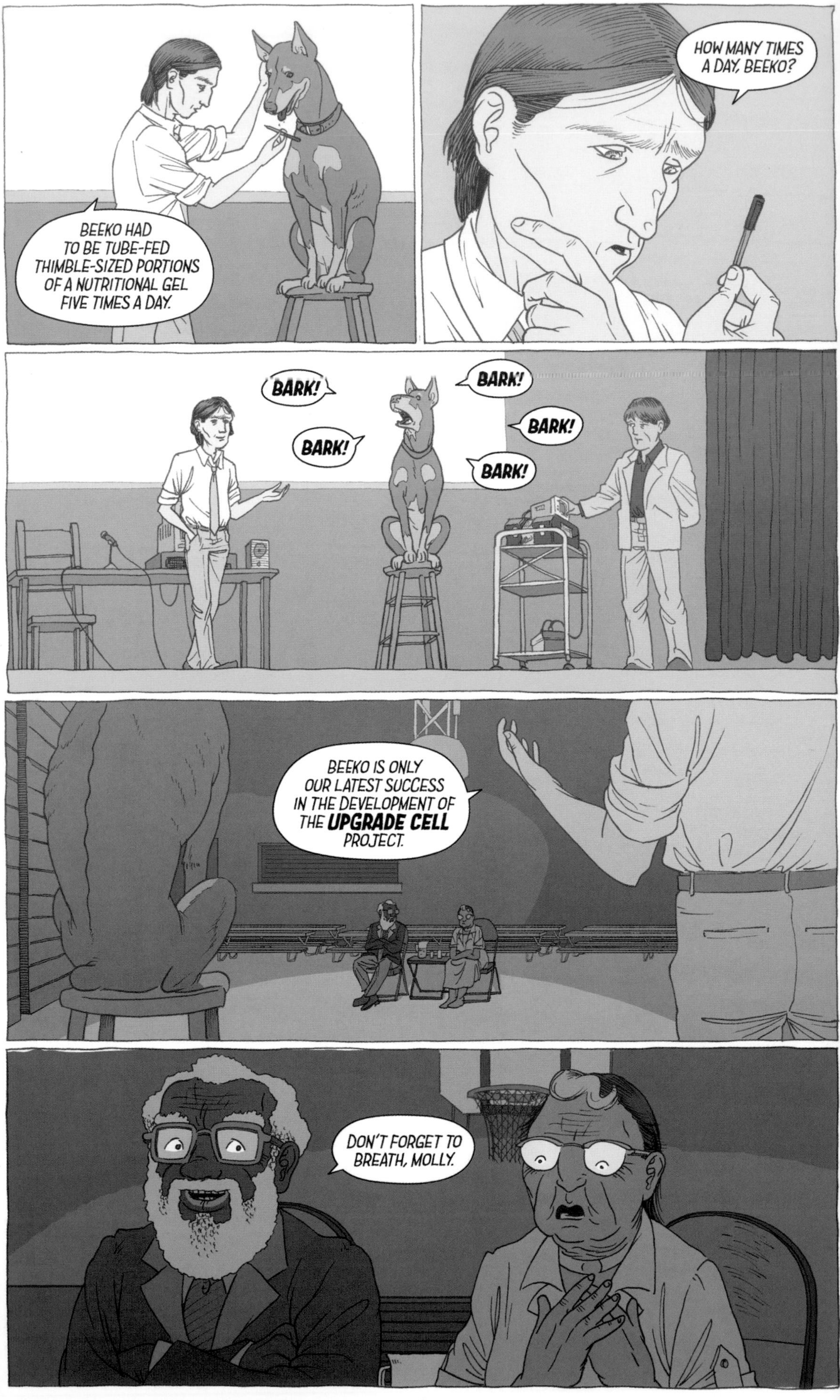
BEEKO HAD TO BE TUBE-FED THIMBLE-SIZED PORTIONS OF A NUTRITIONAL GEL FIVE TIMES A DAY.
HOW MANY TIMES A DAY, BEEKO?
BARK!
BARK!
BARK!
BARK!
BARK!
BEEKO IS ONLY OUR LATEST SUCCESS IN THE DEVELOPMENT OF THE UPGRADE CELL PROJECT.
DON'T FORGET TO BREATH, MOLLY.

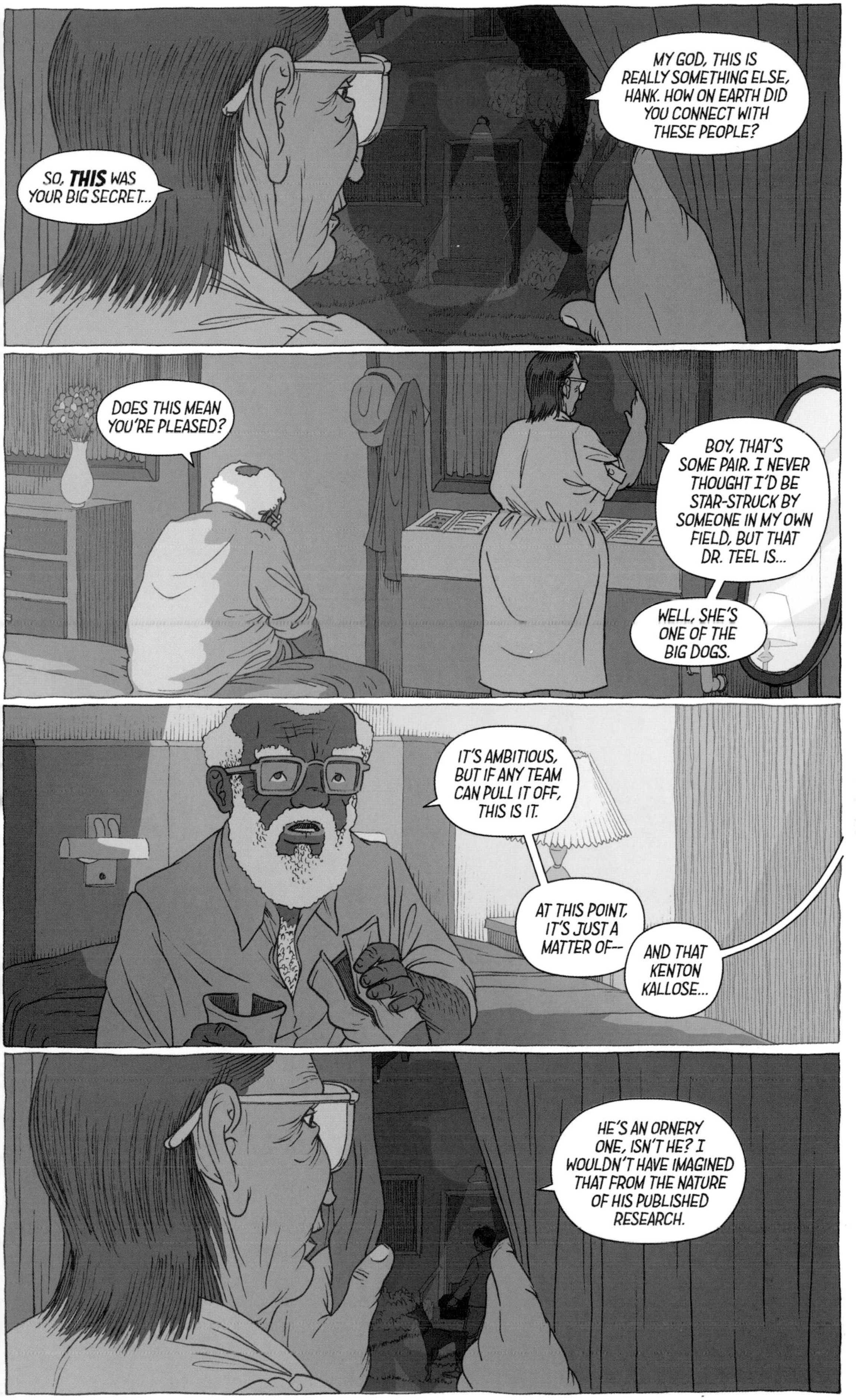

SO, THIS WAS YOUR BIG SECRET...
MY GOD, THIS IS REALLY SOMETHING ELSE, HANK. HOW ON EARTH DID YOU CONNECT WITH THESE PEOPLE?
DOES THIS MEAN YOU'RE PLEASED?
BOY, THAT'S SOME PAIR. I NEVER THOUGHT I'D BE STAR-STRUCK BY SOMEONE IN MY OWN FIELD, BUT THAT DR. TEEL IS...
WELL, SHE'S ONE OF THE BIG DOGS.
IT'S AMBITIOUS, BUT IF ANY TEAM CAN PULL IT OFF, THIS IS IT.
AT THIS POINT, IT'S JUST A MATTER OF--
AND THAT KENTON KALLOSE...
HE'S AN ORNERY ONE, ISN'T HE? I WOULDN'T HAVE IMAGINED THAT FROM THE NATURE OF HIS PUBLISHED RESEARCH.

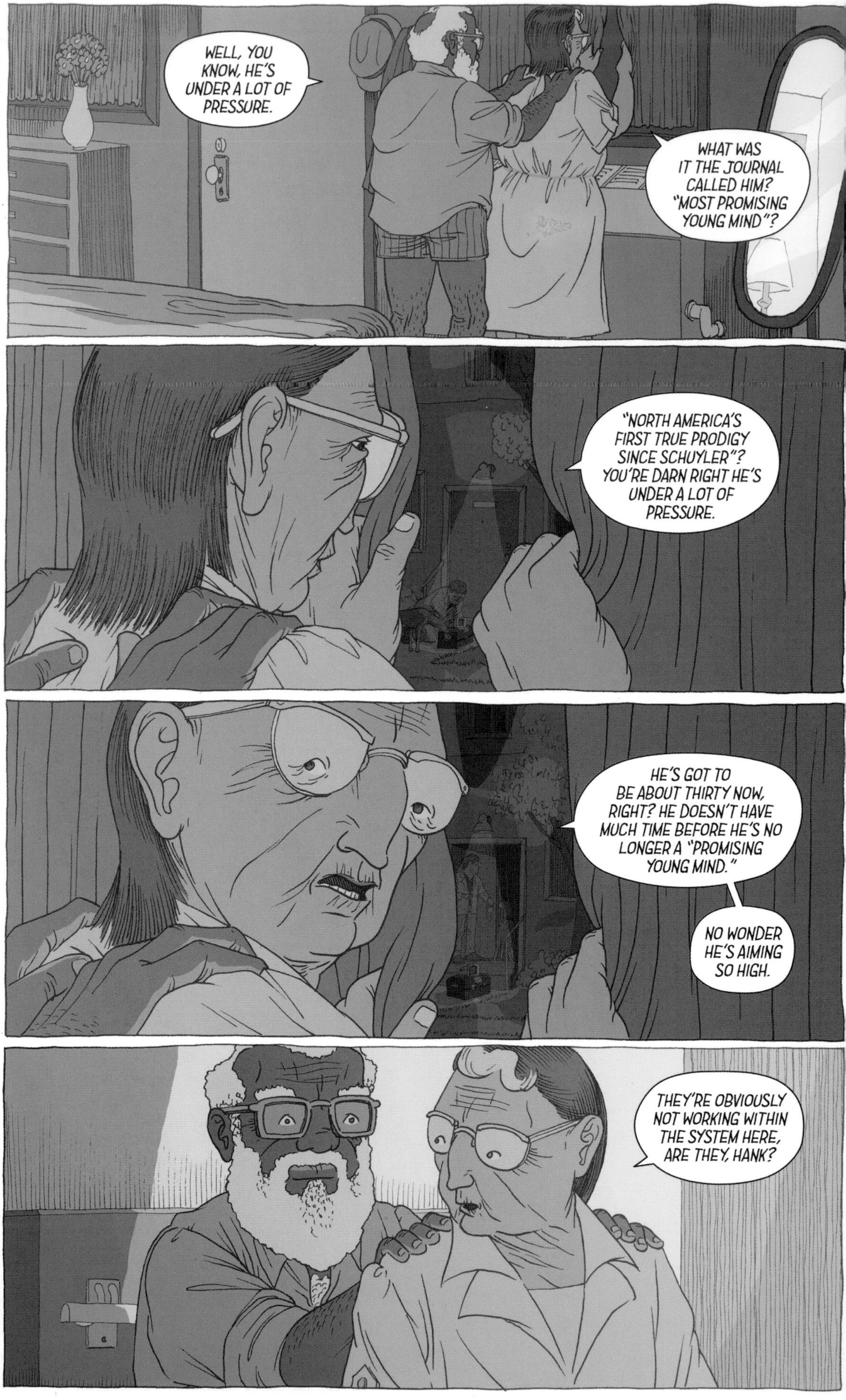
WELL, YOU KNOW, HE'S UNDER A LOT OF PRESSURE.
WHAT WAS IT THE JOURNAL CALLED HIM? "MOST PROMISING YOUNG MIND"?
"NORTH AMERICA'S FIRST TRUE PRODIGY SINCE SCHUYLER"? YOU'RE DARN RIGHT HE'S UNDER A LOT OF PRESSURE.
HE'S GOT TO BE ABOUT THIRTY NOW, RIGHT? HE DOESN'T HAVE MUCH TIME BEFORE HE'S NO LONGER A "PROMISING YOUNG MIND."
NO WONDER HE'S AIMING SO HIGH.
THEY'RE OBVIOUSLY NOT WORKING WITHIN THE SYSTEM HERE, ARE THEY, HANK?

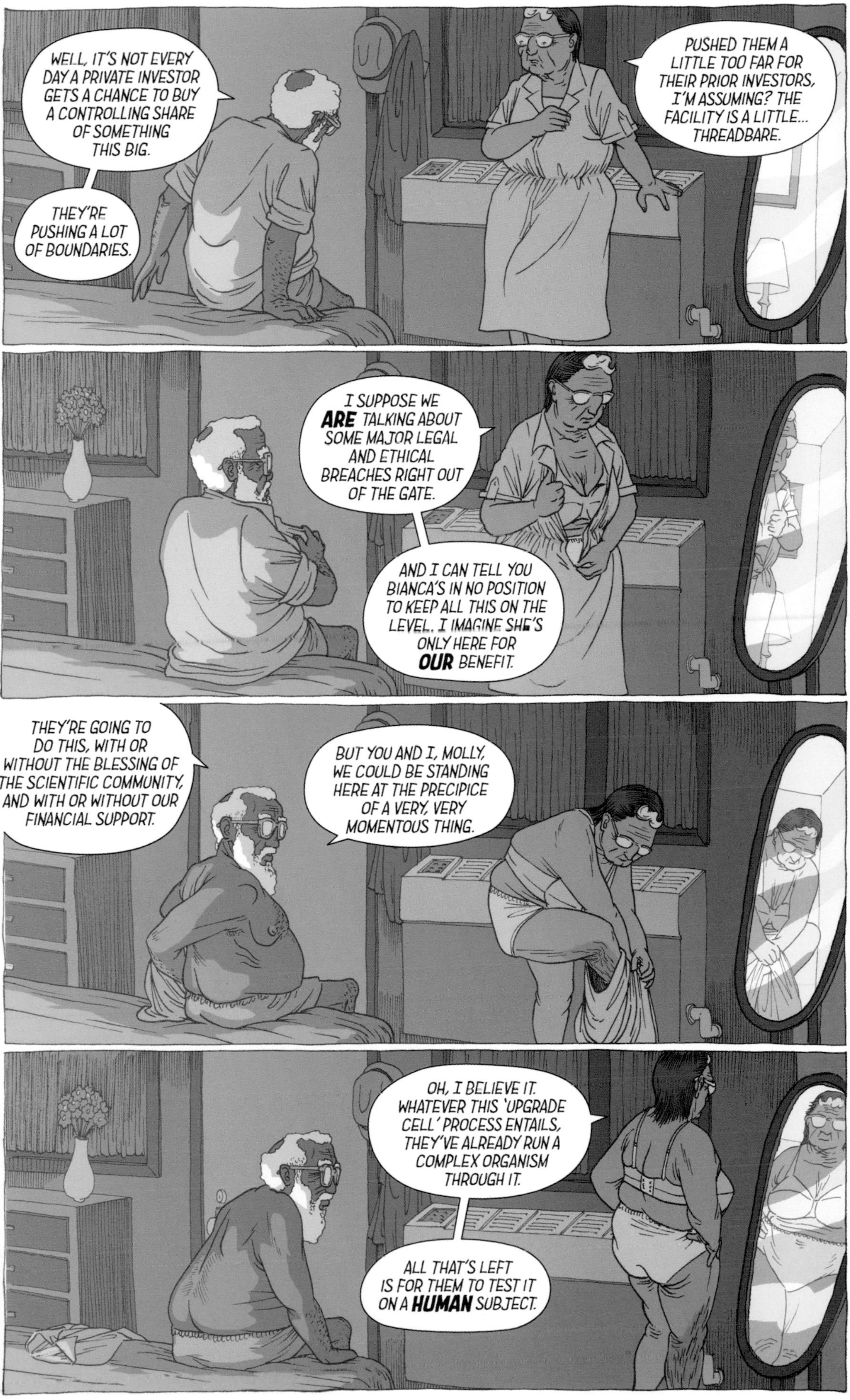
WELL, IT'S NOT EVERY DAY A PRIVATE INVESTOR GETS A CHANCE TO BUY A CONTROLLING SHARE OF SOMETHING THIS BIG.
THEY'RE PUSHING A LOT OF BOUNDARIES.
PUSHED THEM A LITTLE TOO FAR FOR THEIR PRIOR INVESTORS, I'M ASSUMING? THE FACILITY IS A LITTLE... THREADBARE.
I SUPPOSE WE **ARE** TALKING ABOUT SOME MAJOR LEGAL AND ETHICAL BREACHES RIGHT OUT OF THE GATE.
AND I CAN TELL YOU BIANCA'S IN NO POSITION TO KEEP ALL THIS ON THE LEVEL. I IMAGINE SHE'S ONLY HERE FOR **OUR** BENEFIT.
THEY'RE GOING TO DO THIS, WITH OR WITHOUT THE BLESSING OF THE SCIENTIFIC COMMUNITY, AND WITH OR WITHOUT OUR FINANCIAL SUPPORT.
BUT YOU AND I, MOLLY, WE COULD BE STANDING HERE AT THE PRECIPICE OF A VERY, VERY MOMENTOUS THING.
OH, I BELIEVE IT. WHATEVER THIS 'UPGRADE CELL' PROCESS ENTAILS, THEY'VE ALREADY RUN A COMPLEX ORGANISM THROUGH IT.
ALL THAT'S LEFT IS FOR THEM TO TEST IT ON A **HUMAN** SUBJECT.

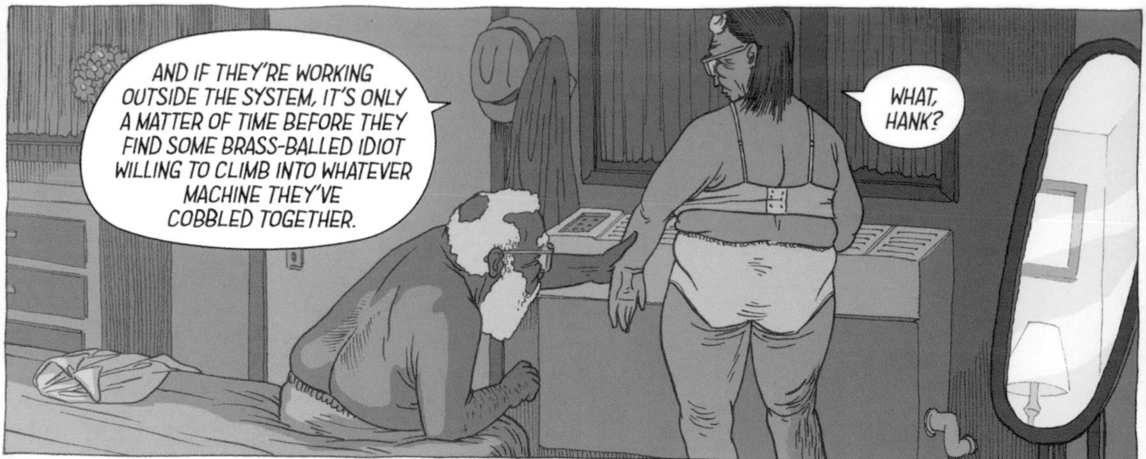
AND IF THEY'RE WORKING OUTSIDE THE SYSTEM, IT'S ONLY A MATTER OF TIME BEFORE THEY FIND SOME BRASS-BALLED IDIOT WILLING TO CLIMB INTO WHATEVER MACHINE THEY'VE COBBLED TOGETHER.
WHAT, HANK?

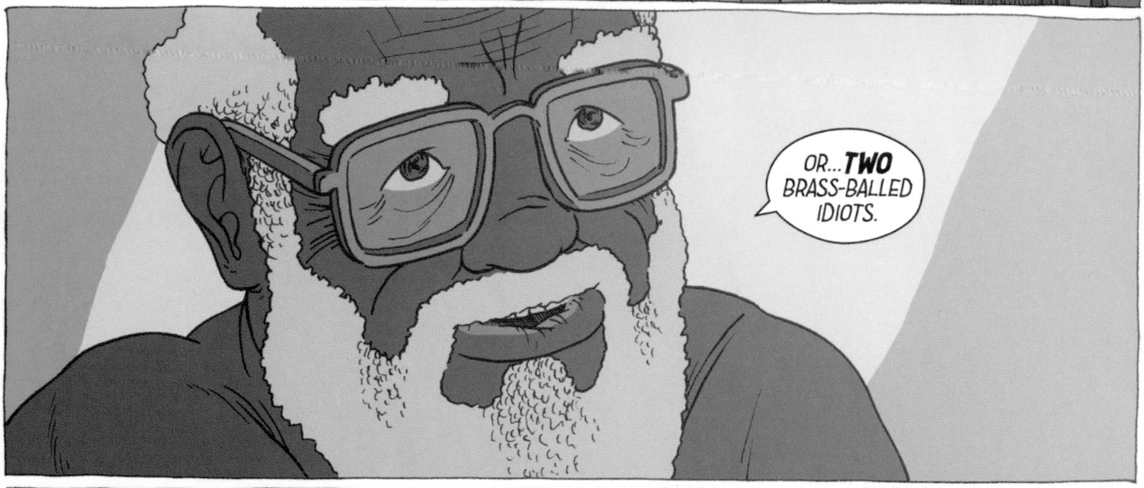
OR... **TWO** BRASS-BALLED IDIOTS.

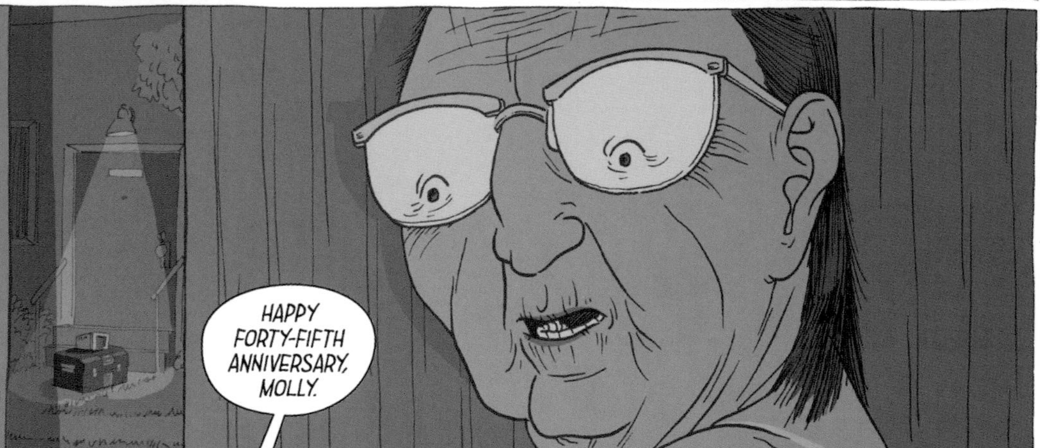
HAPPY FORTY-FIFTH ANNIVERSARY, MOLLY.

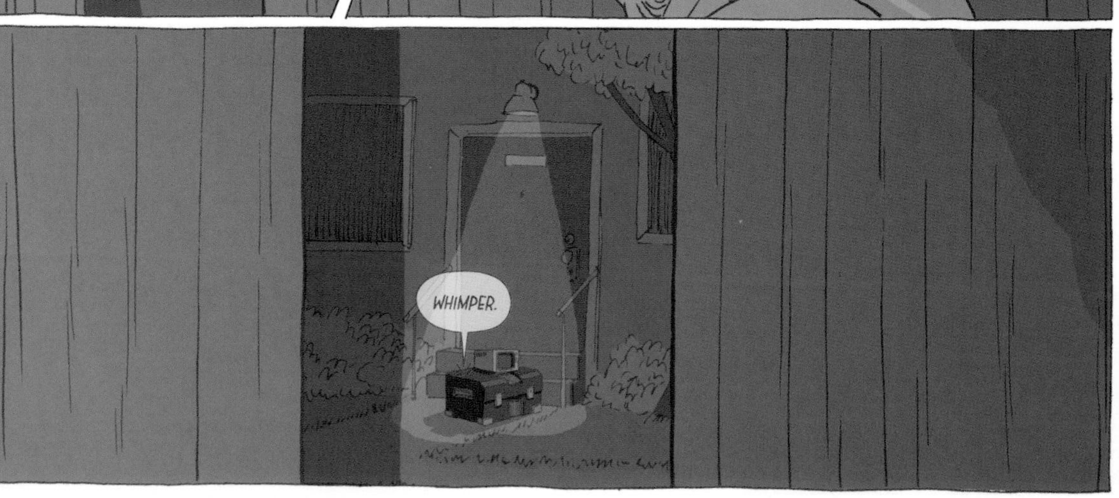
WHIMPER.

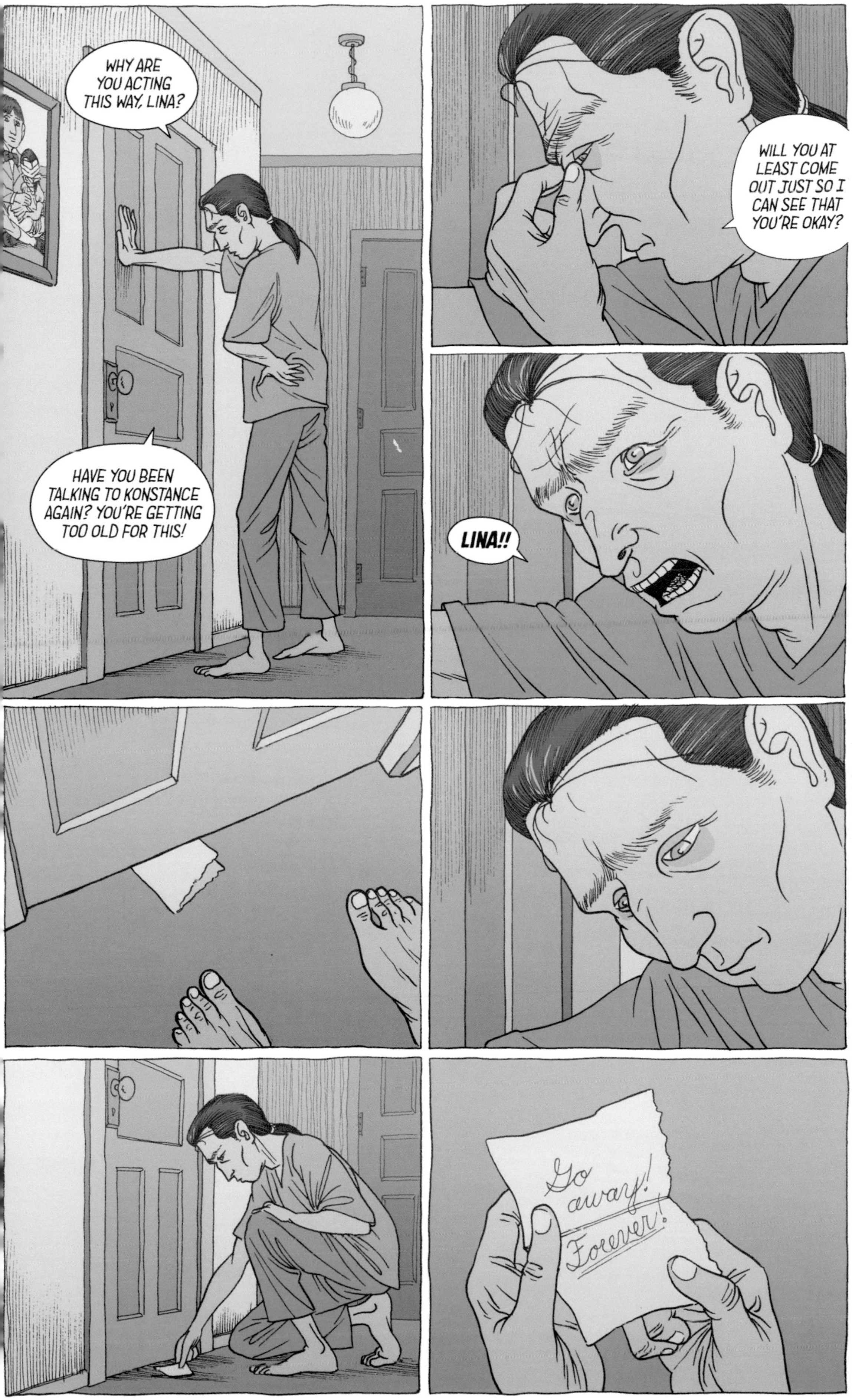
WHY ARE YOU ACTING THIS WAY, LINA?
HAVE YOU BEEN TALKING TO KONSTANCE AGAIN? YOU'RE GETTING TOO OLD FOR THIS!
WILL YOU AT LEAST COME OUT JUST SO I CAN SEE THAT YOU'RE OKAY?
LINA!!
Go away! Forever!

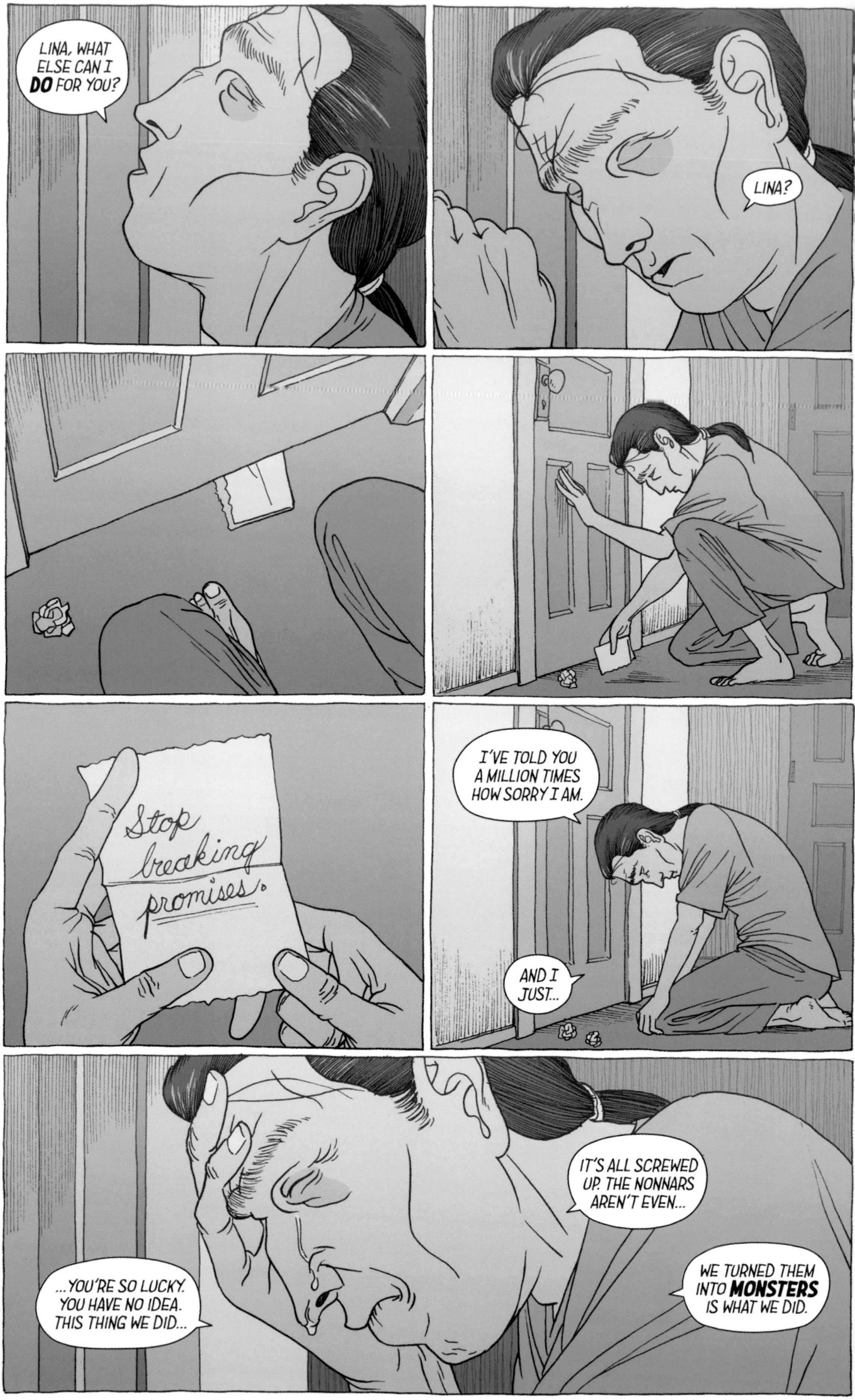
LINA, WHAT ELSE CAN I **DO** FOR YOU?
LINA?
Stop breaking promises.
I'VE TOLD YOU A MILLION TIMES HOW SORRY I AM.
AND I JUST...
IT'S ALL SCREWED UP. THE NONNARS AREN'T EVEN...
...YOU'RE SO LUCKY. YOU HAVE NO IDEA. THIS THING WE DID...
WE TURNED THEM INTO **MONSTERS** IS WHAT WE DID.

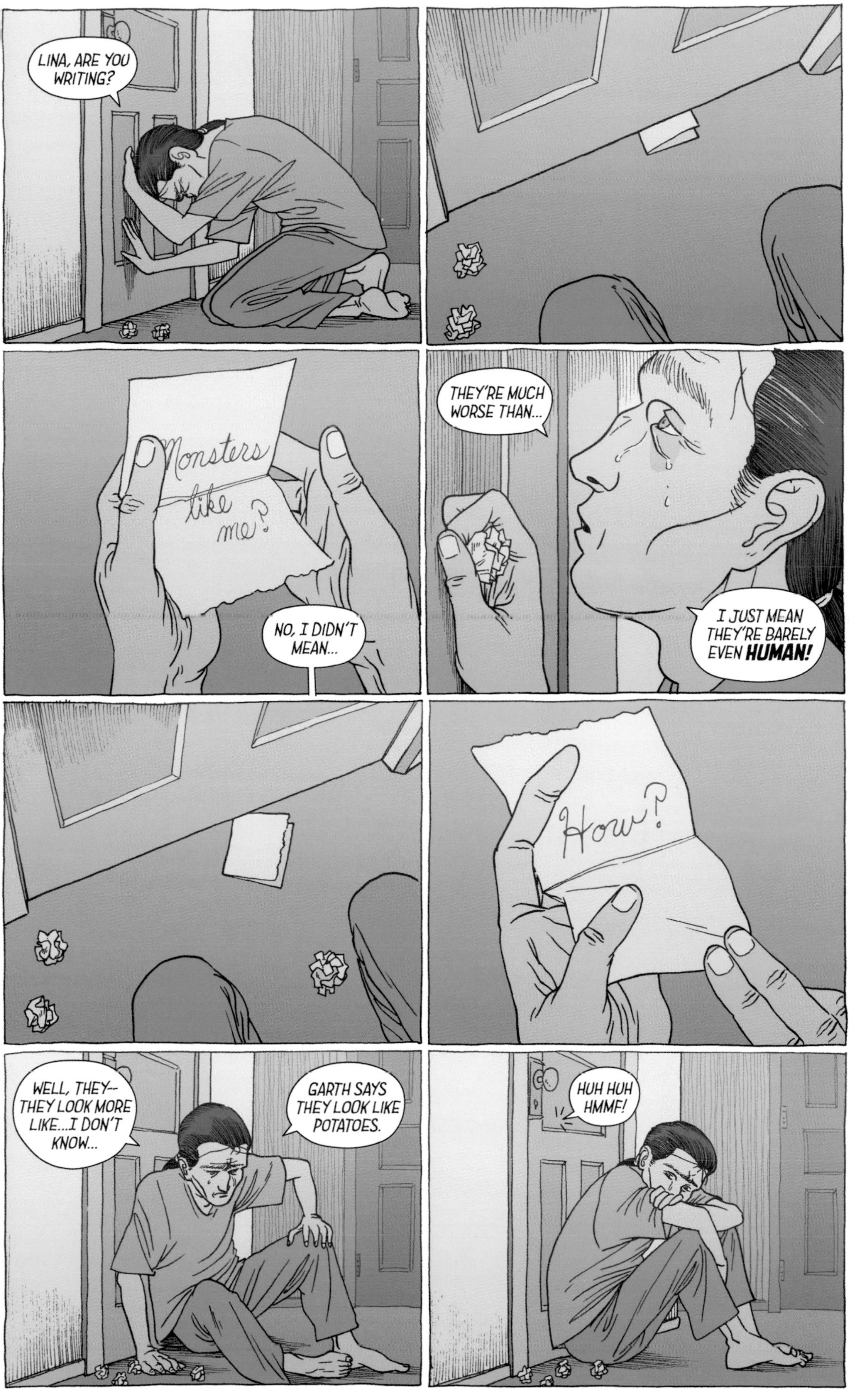
LINA, ARE YOU WRITING?
Monsters like me?
NO, I DIDN'T MEAN...
THEY'RE MUCH WORSE THAN...
I JUST MEAN THEY'RE BARELY EVEN **HUMAN!**
How?
WELL, THEY-- THEY LOOK MORE LIKE...I DON'T KNOW...
GARTH SAYS THEY LOOK LIKE POTATOES.
HUH HUH HMMF!

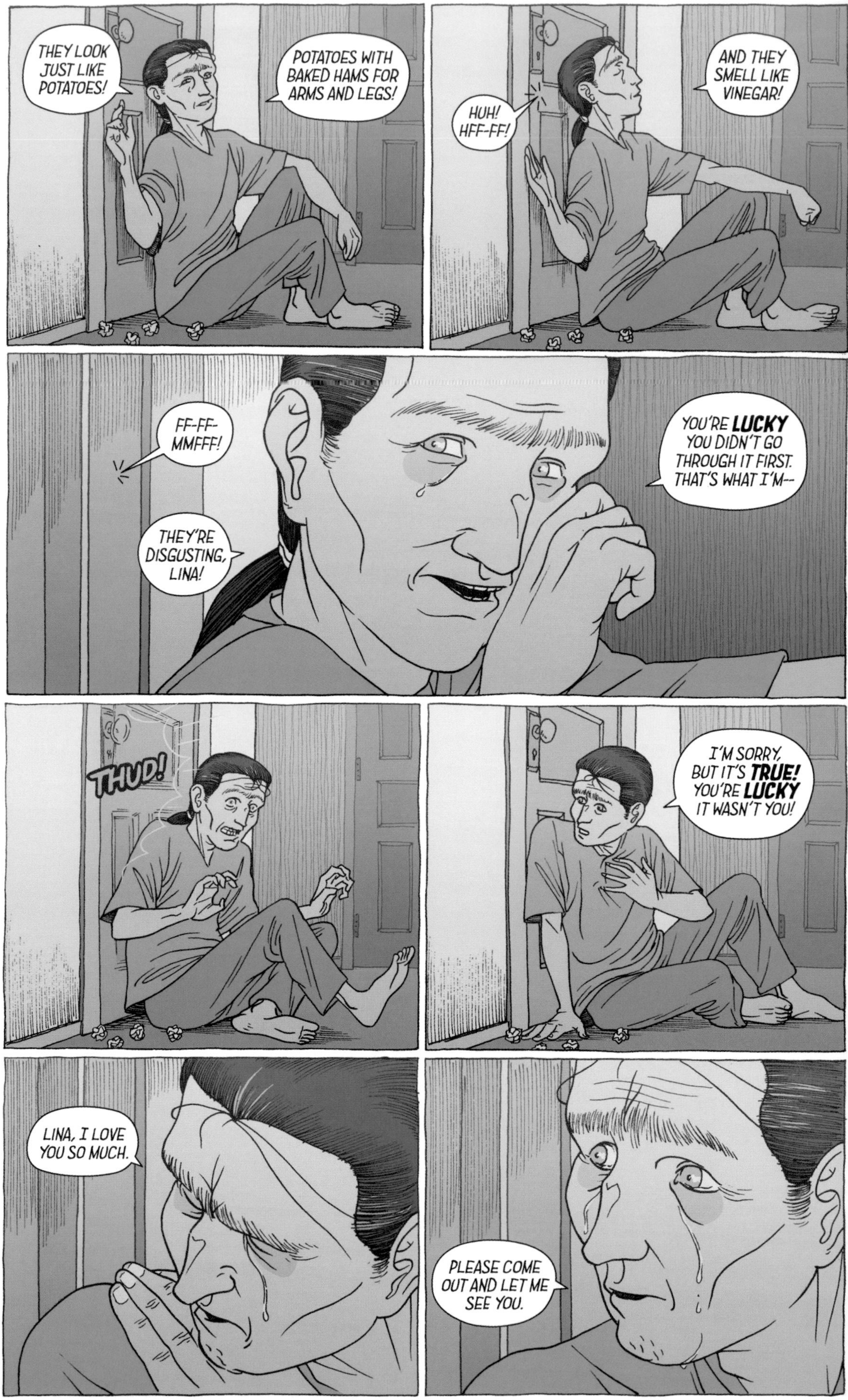
THEY LOOK JUST LIKE POTATOES!
POTATOES WITH BAKED HAMS FOR ARMS AND LEGS!
HUH! HFF-FF!
AND THEY SMELL LIKE VINEGAR!
FF-FF-MMFFF!
THEY'RE DISGUSTING, LINA!
YOU'RE **LUCKY** YOU DIDN'T GO THROUGH IT FIRST. THAT'S WHAT I'M--
THUD!
I'M SORRY, BUT IT'S **TRUE!** YOU'RE **LUCKY** IT WASN'T YOU!
LINA, I LOVE YOU SO MUCH.
PLEASE COME OUT AND LET ME SEE YOU.

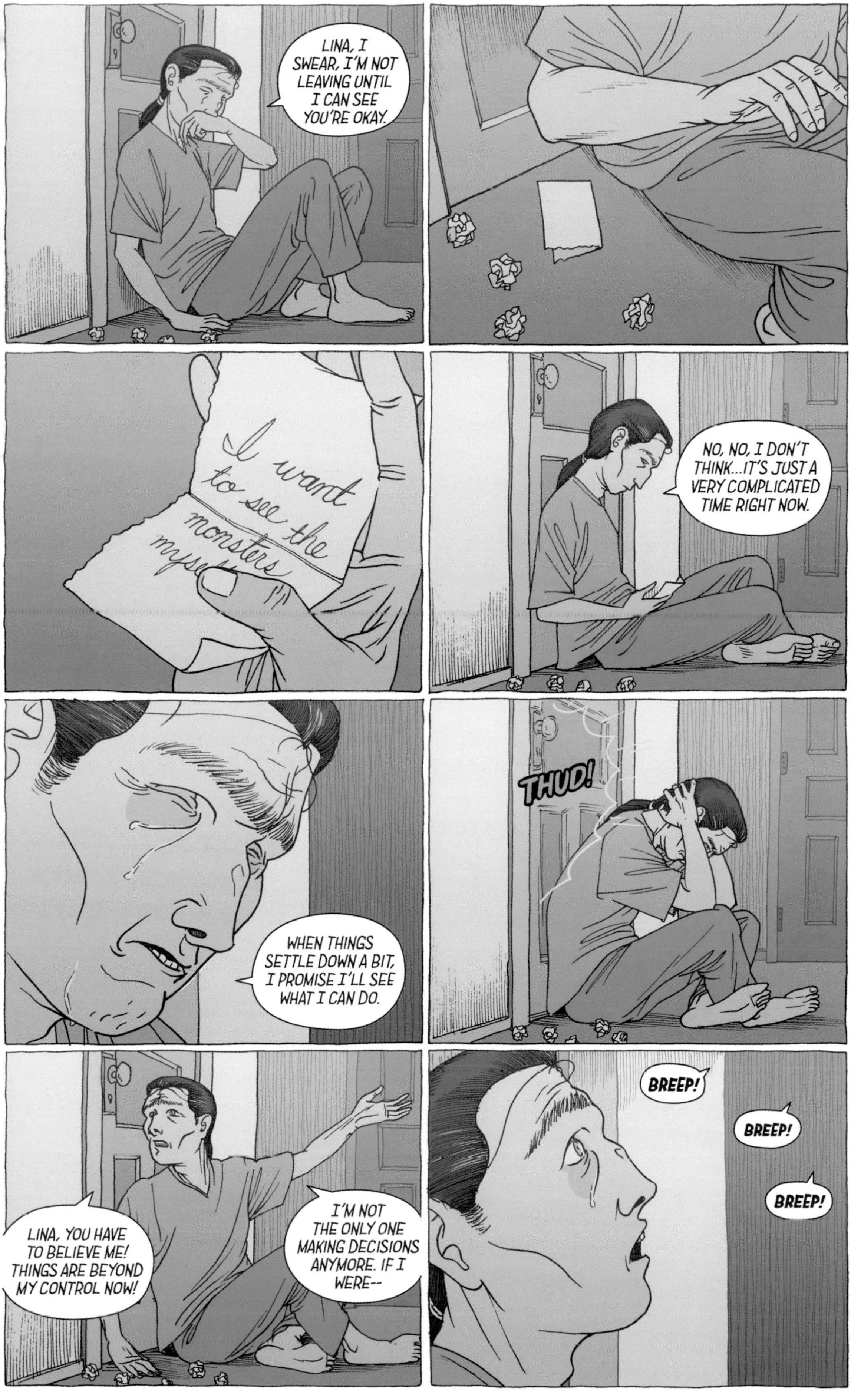
LINA, I SWEAR, I'M NOT LEAVING UNTIL I CAN SEE YOU'RE OKAY.
I want to see the monsters the myse
NO, NO, I DON'T THINK...IT'S JUST A VERY COMPLICATED TIME RIGHT NOW.
WHEN THINGS SETTLE DOWN A BIT, I PROMISE I'LL SEE WHAT I CAN DO.
THUD!
LINA, YOU HAVE TO BELIEVE ME! THINGS ARE BEYOND MY CONTROL NOW!
I'M NOT THE ONLY ONE MAKING DECISIONS ANYMORE. IF I WERE--
BREEP!
BREEP!
BREEP!

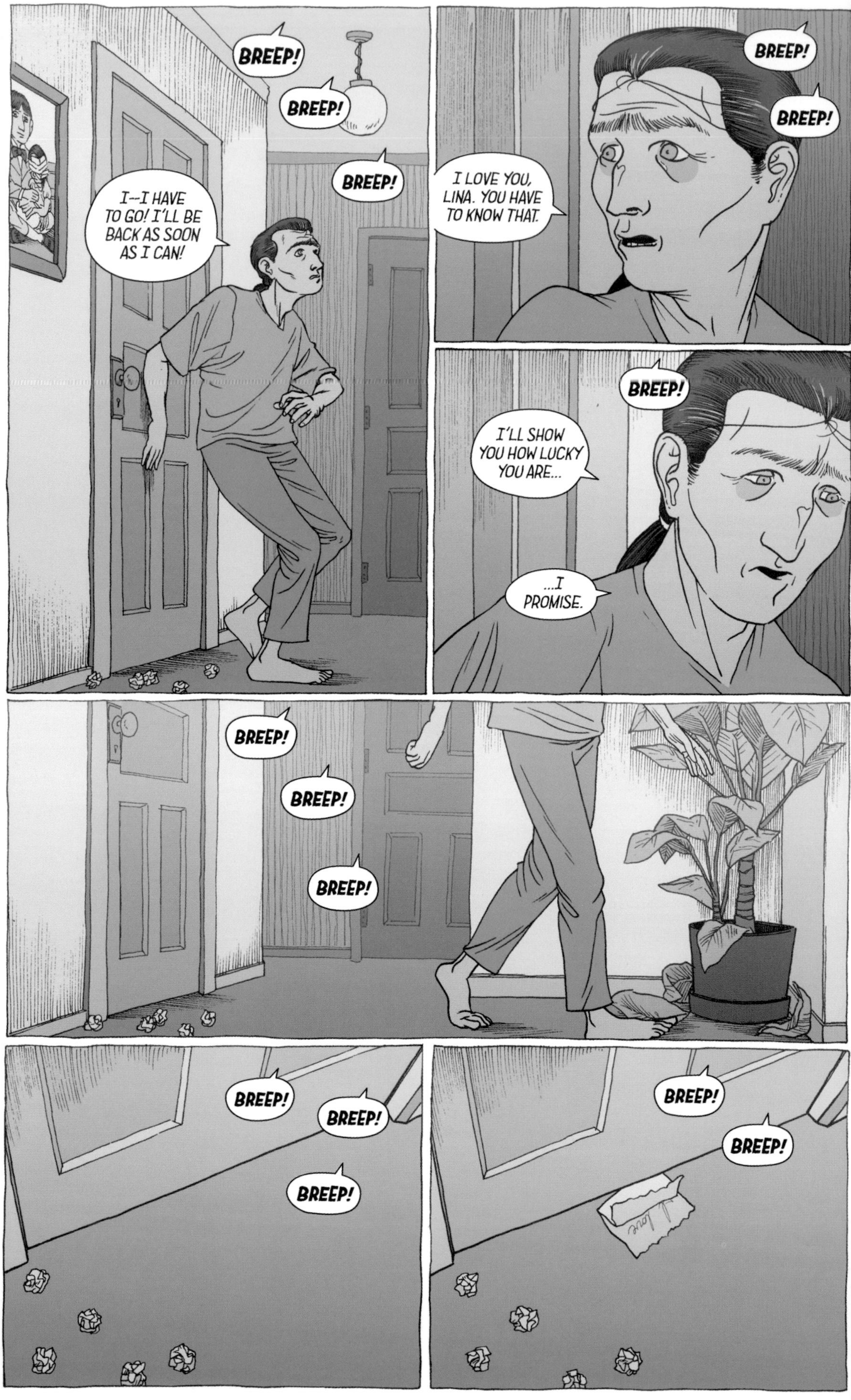
BREEP!
BREEP!
BREEP!
I--I HAVE TO GO! I'LL BE BACK AS SOON AS I CAN!
BREEP!
BREEP!
I LOVE YOU, LINA. YOU HAVE TO KNOW THAT.
BREEP!
I'LL SHOW YOU HOW LUCKY YOU ARE...
...I PROMISE.
BREEP!
BREEP!
BREEP!
BREEP!
BREEP!
BREEP!
BREEP!
BREEP!

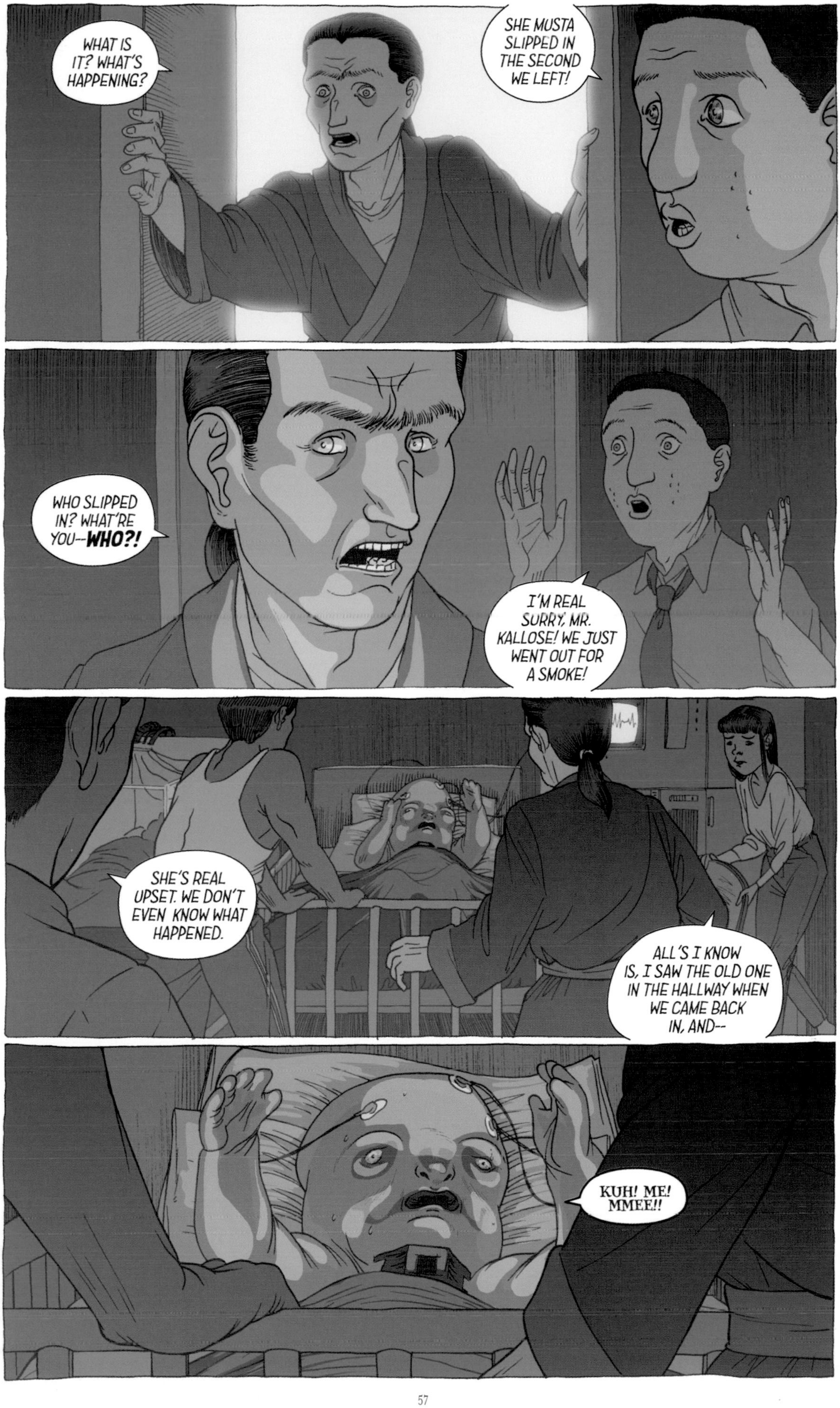
WHAT IS IT? WHAT'S HAPPENING?
SHE MUSTA SLIPPED IN THE SECOND WE LEFT!
WHO SLIPPED IN? WHAT'RE YOU--**WHO?!**
I'M REAL SORRY, MR. KALLOSE! WE JUST WENT OUT FOR A SMOKE!
SHE'S REAL UPSET. WE DON'T EVEN KNOW WHAT HAPPENED.
ALL'S I KNOW IS, I SAW THE OLD ONE IN THE HALLWAY WHEN WE CAME BACK IN, AND--
KUH! ME! MMEE!!

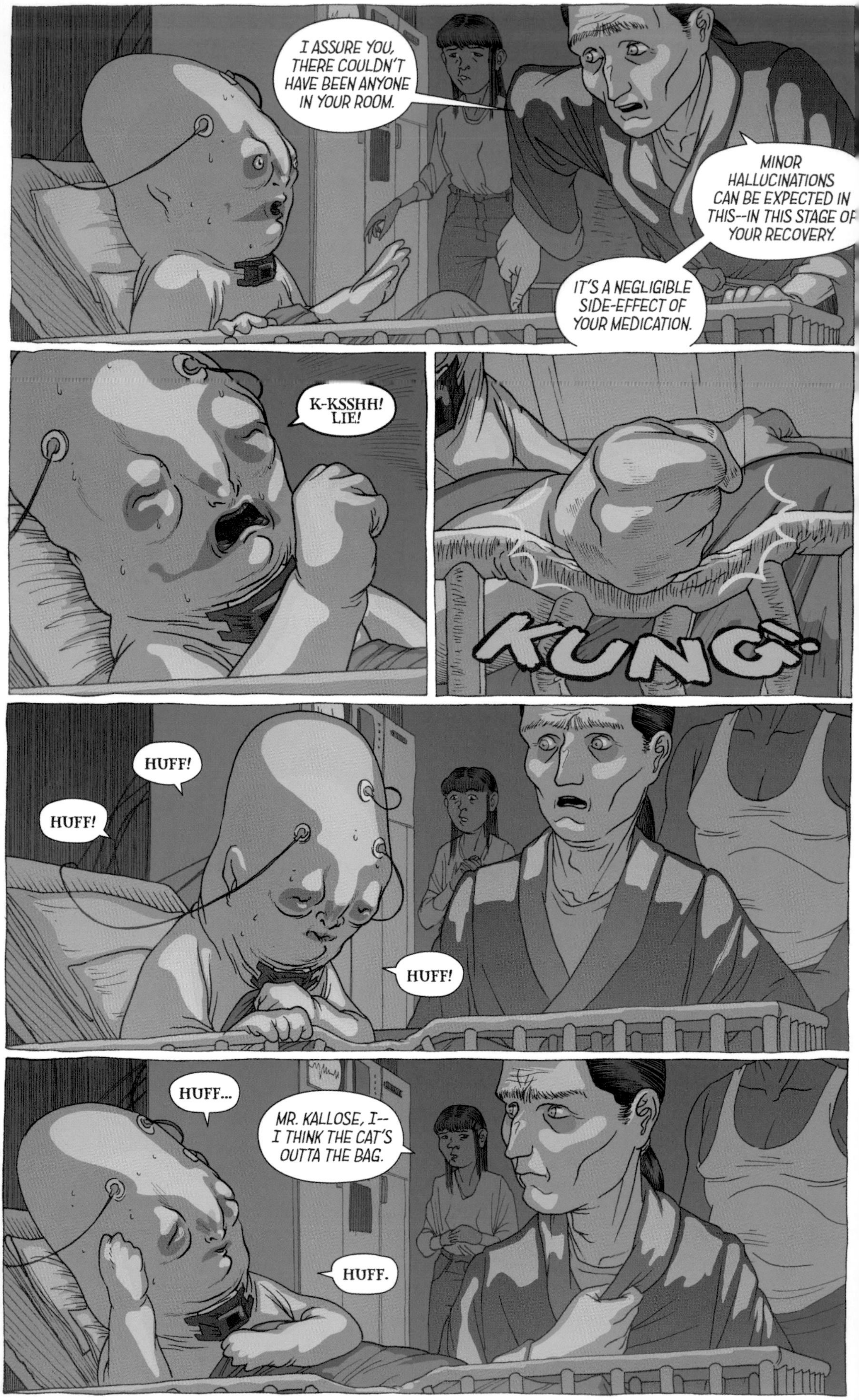
I ASSURE YOU, THERE COULDN'T HAVE BEEN ANYONE IN YOUR ROOM.
MINOR HALLUCINATIONS CAN BE EXPECTED IN THIS--IN THIS STAGE OF YOUR RECOVERY.
IT'S A NEGLIGIBLE SIDE-EFFECT OF YOUR MEDICATION.
K-KSSHH! LIE!
KUNG!
HUFF!
HUFF!
HUFF!
HUFF...
MR. KALLOSE, I-- I THINK THE CAT'S OUTTA THE BAG.
HUFF.

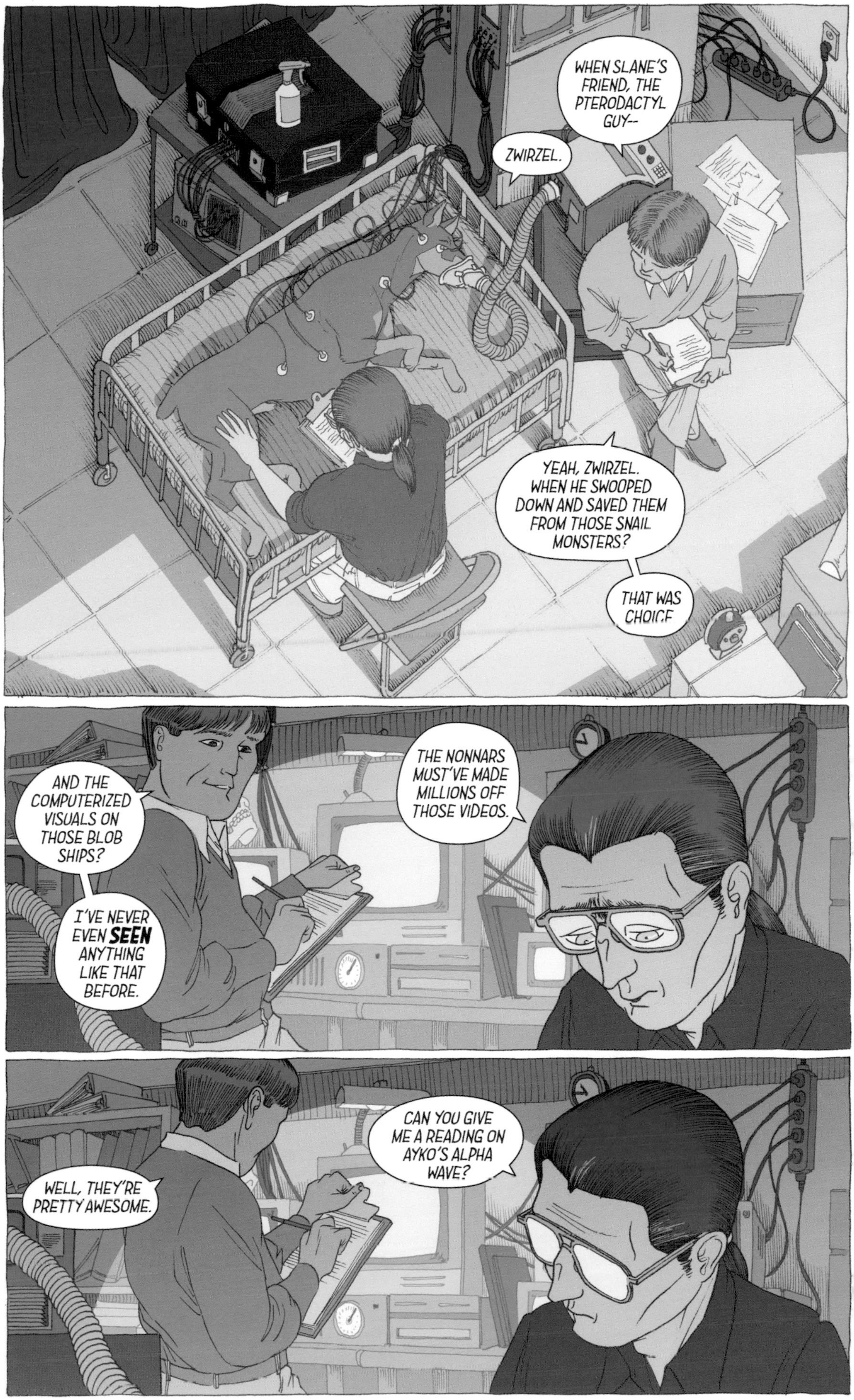
WHEN SLANE'S FRIEND, THE PTERODACTYL GUY--
ZWIRZEL.
YEAH, ZWIRZEL. WHEN HE SWOOPED DOWN AND SAVED THEM FROM THOSE SNAIL MONSTERS?
THAT WAS CHOICE
AND THE COMPUTERIZED VISUALS ON THOSE BLOB SHIPS?
I'VE NEVER EVEN **SEEN** ANYTHING LIKE THAT BEFORE.
THE NONNARS MUST'VE MADE MILLIONS OFF THOSE VIDEOS.
WELL, THEY'RE PRETTY AWESOME.
CAN YOU GIVE ME A READING ON AYKO'S ALPHA WAVE?

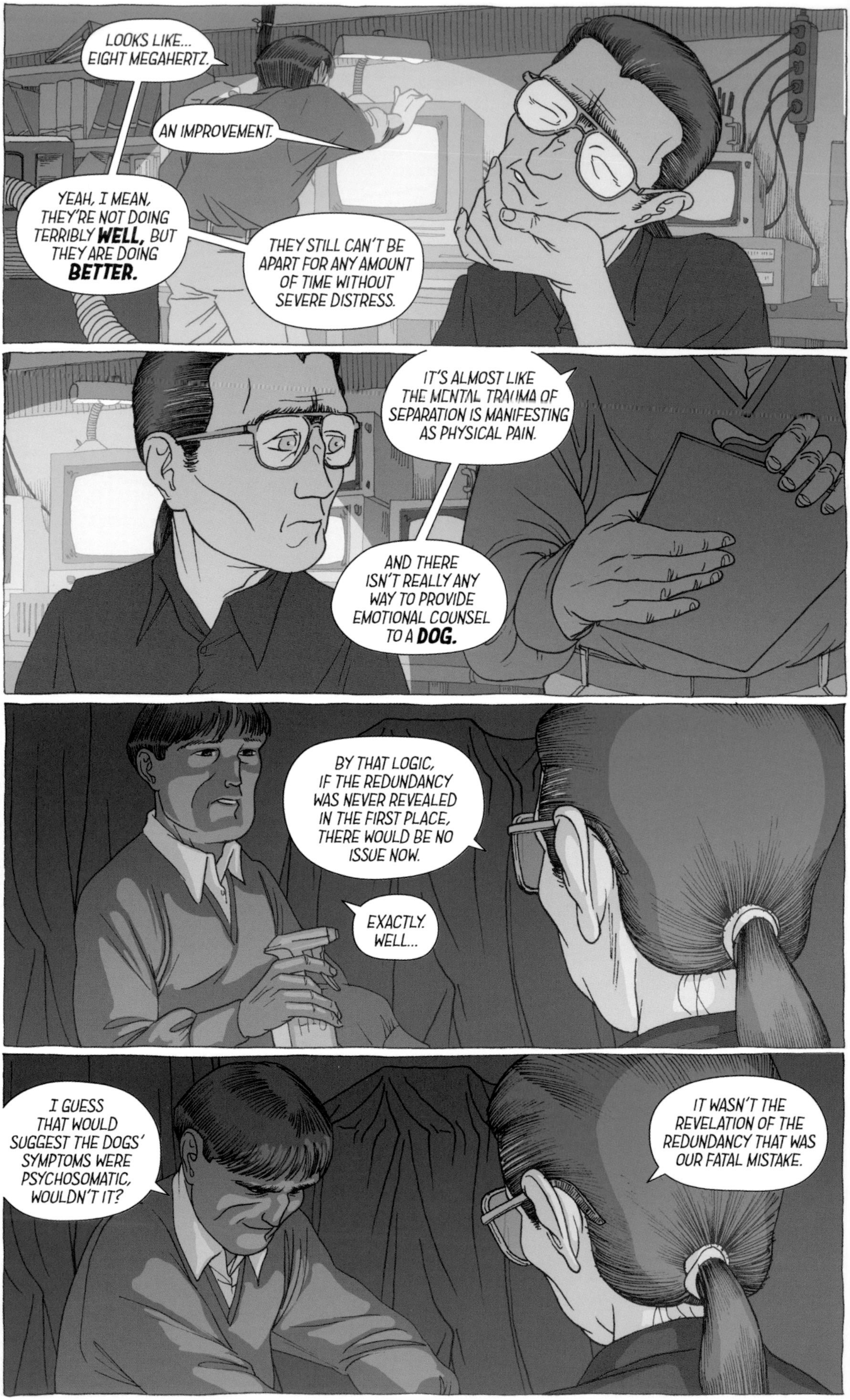
LOOKS LIKE... EIGHT MEGAHERTZ.
AN IMPROVEMENT.
YEAH, I MEAN, THEY'RE NOT DOING TERRIBLY **WELL,** BUT THEY ARE DOING **BETTER.**
THEY STILL CAN'T BE APART FOR ANY AMOUNT OF TIME WITHOUT SEVERE DISTRESS.
IT'S ALMOST LIKE THE MENTAL TRAUMA OF SEPARATION IS MANIFESTING AS PHYSICAL PAIN.
AND THERE ISN'T REALLY ANY WAY TO PROVIDE EMOTIONAL COUNSEL TO A **DOG.**
BY THAT LOGIC, IF THE REDUNDANCY WAS NEVER REVEALED IN THE FIRST PLACE, THERE WOULD BE NO ISSUE NOW.
EXACTLY. WELL...
I GUESS THAT WOULD SUGGEST THE DOGS' SYMPTOMS WERE PSYCHOSOMATIC, WOULDN'T IT?
IT WASN'T THE REVELATION OF THE REDUNDANCY THAT WAS OUR FATAL MISTAKE.

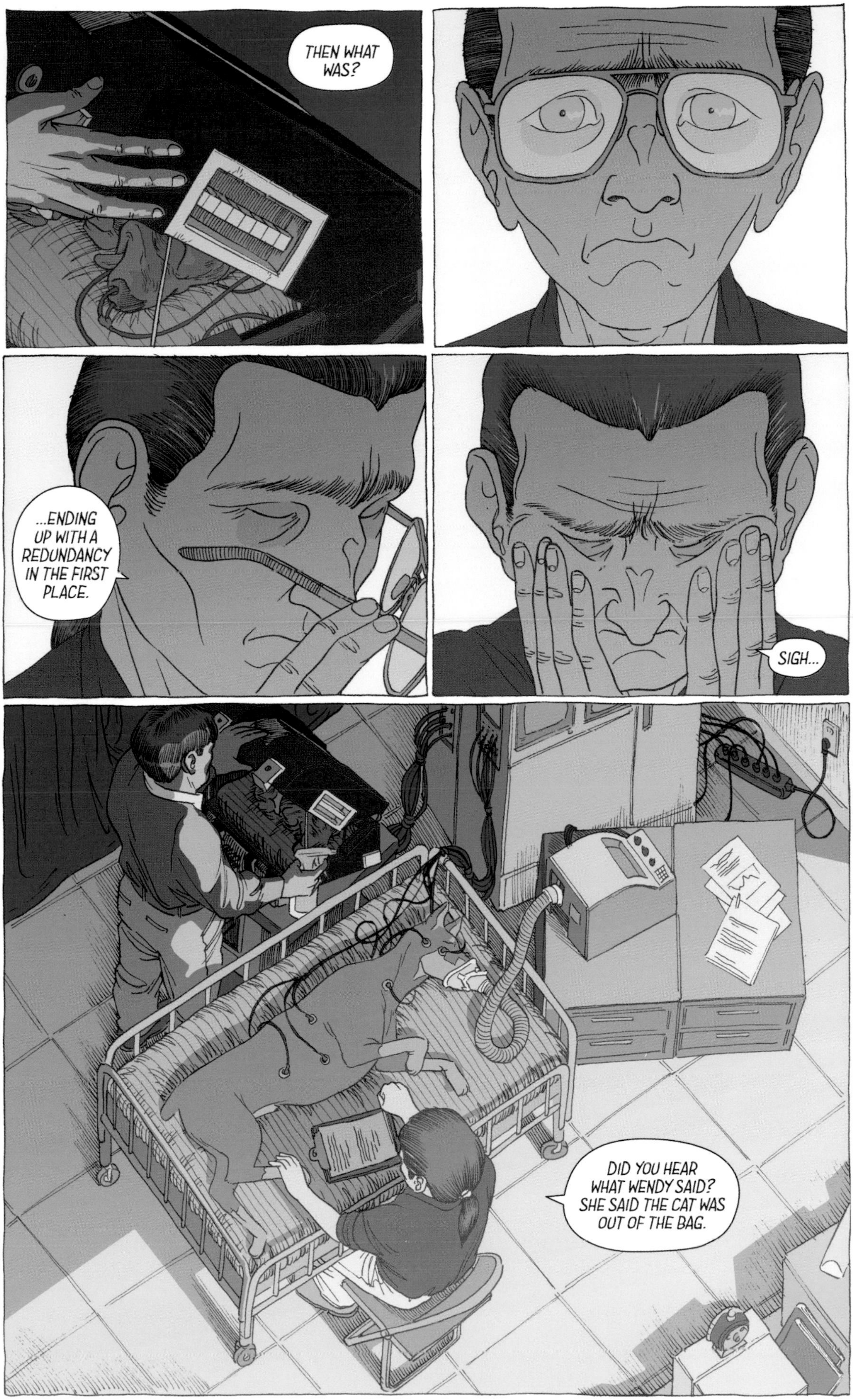
THEN WHAT WAS?
...ENDING UP WITH A REDUNDANCY IN THE FIRST PLACE.
SIGH...
DID YOU HEAR WHAT WENDY SAID? SHE SAID THE CAT WAS OUT OF THE BAG.

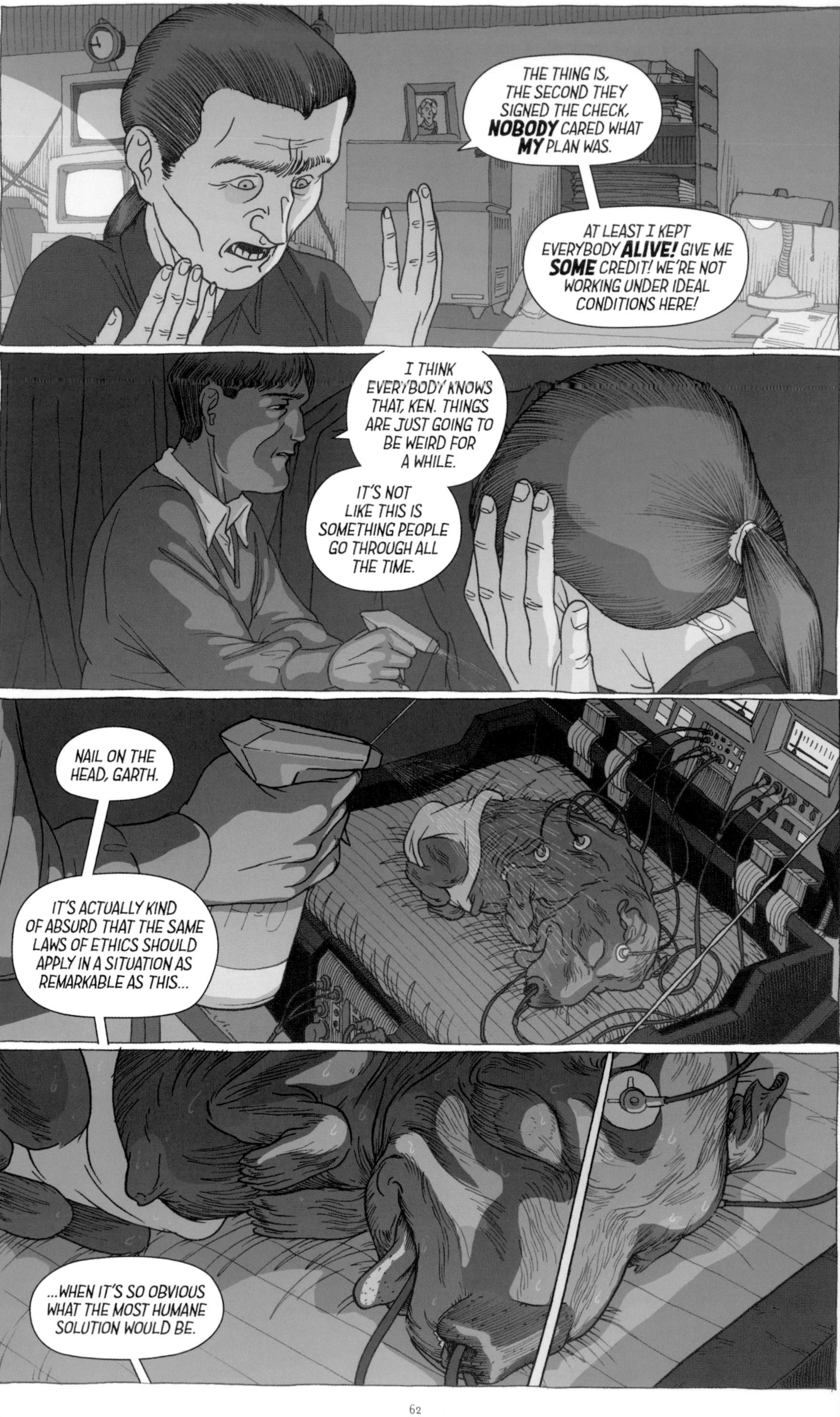
THE THING IS, THE SECOND THEY SIGNED THE CHECK, NOBODY CARED WHAT MY PLAN WAS.
AT LEAST I KEPT EVERYBODY ALIVE! GIVE ME SOME CREDIT! WE'RE NOT WORKING UNDER IDEAL CONDITIONS HERE!
I THINK EVERYBODY KNOWS THAT, KEN. THINGS ARE JUST GOING TO BE WEIRD FOR A WHILE.
IT'S NOT LIKE THIS IS SOMETHING PEOPLE GO THROUGH ALL THE TIME.
NAIL ON THE HEAD, GARTH.
IT'S ACTUALLY KIND OF ABSURD THAT THE SAME LAWS OF ETHICS SHOULD APPLY IN A SITUATION AS REMARKABLE AS THIS...
...WHEN IT'S SO OBVIOUS WHAT THE MOST HUMANE SOLUTION WOULD BE.

3

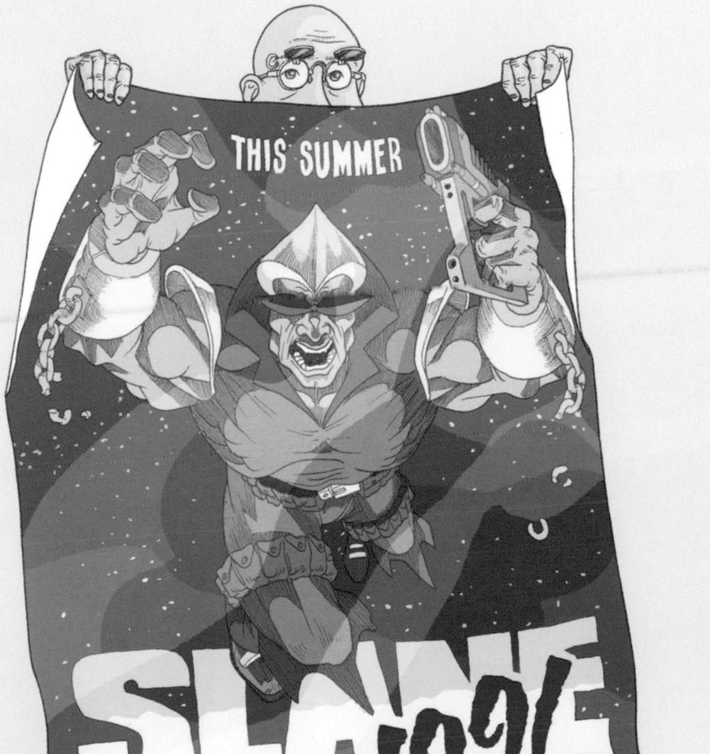
THIS SUMMER
SLAINE
1991

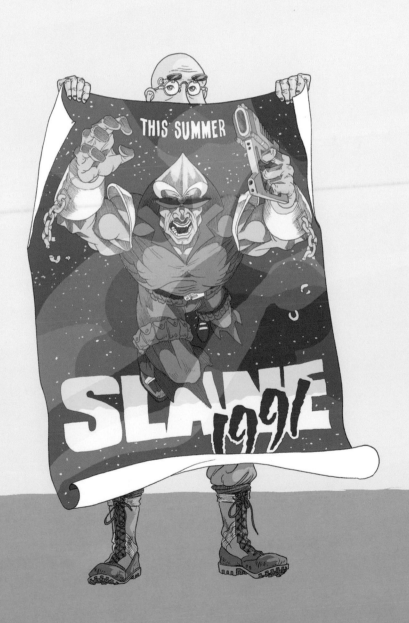

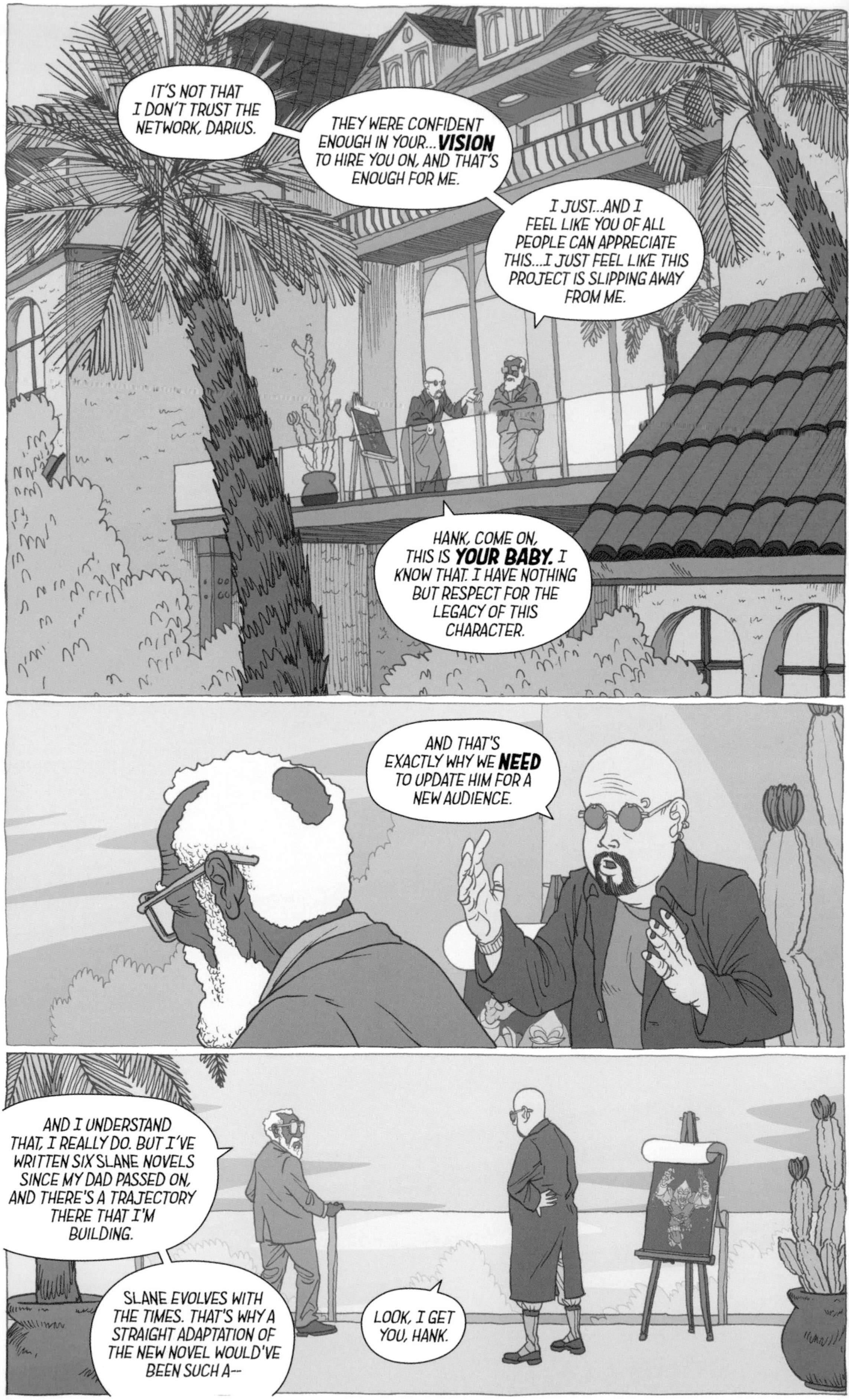
IT'S NOT THAT I DON'T TRUST THE NETWORK, DARIUS.
THEY WERE CONFIDENT ENOUGH IN YOUR... **VISION** TO HIRE YOU ON, AND THAT'S ENOUGH FOR ME.
I JUST...AND I FEEL LIKE YOU OF ALL PEOPLE CAN APPRECIATE THIS...I JUST FEEL LIKE THIS PROJECT IS SLIPPING AWAY FROM ME.
HANK, COME ON, THIS IS **YOUR BABY.** I KNOW THAT. I HAVE NOTHING BUT RESPECT FOR THE LEGACY OF THIS CHARACTER.
AND THAT'S EXACTLY WHY WE **NEED** TO UPDATE HIM FOR A NEW AUDIENCE.
AND I UNDERSTAND THAT, I REALLY DO. BUT I'VE WRITTEN SIX SLANE NOVELS SINCE MY DAD PASSED ON, AND THERE'S A TRAJECTORY THERE THAT I'M BUILDING.
SLANE EVOLVES WITH THE TIMES. THAT'S WHY A STRAIGHT ADAPTATION OF THE NEW NOVEL WOULD'VE BEEN SUCH A--
LOOK, I GET YOU, HANK.

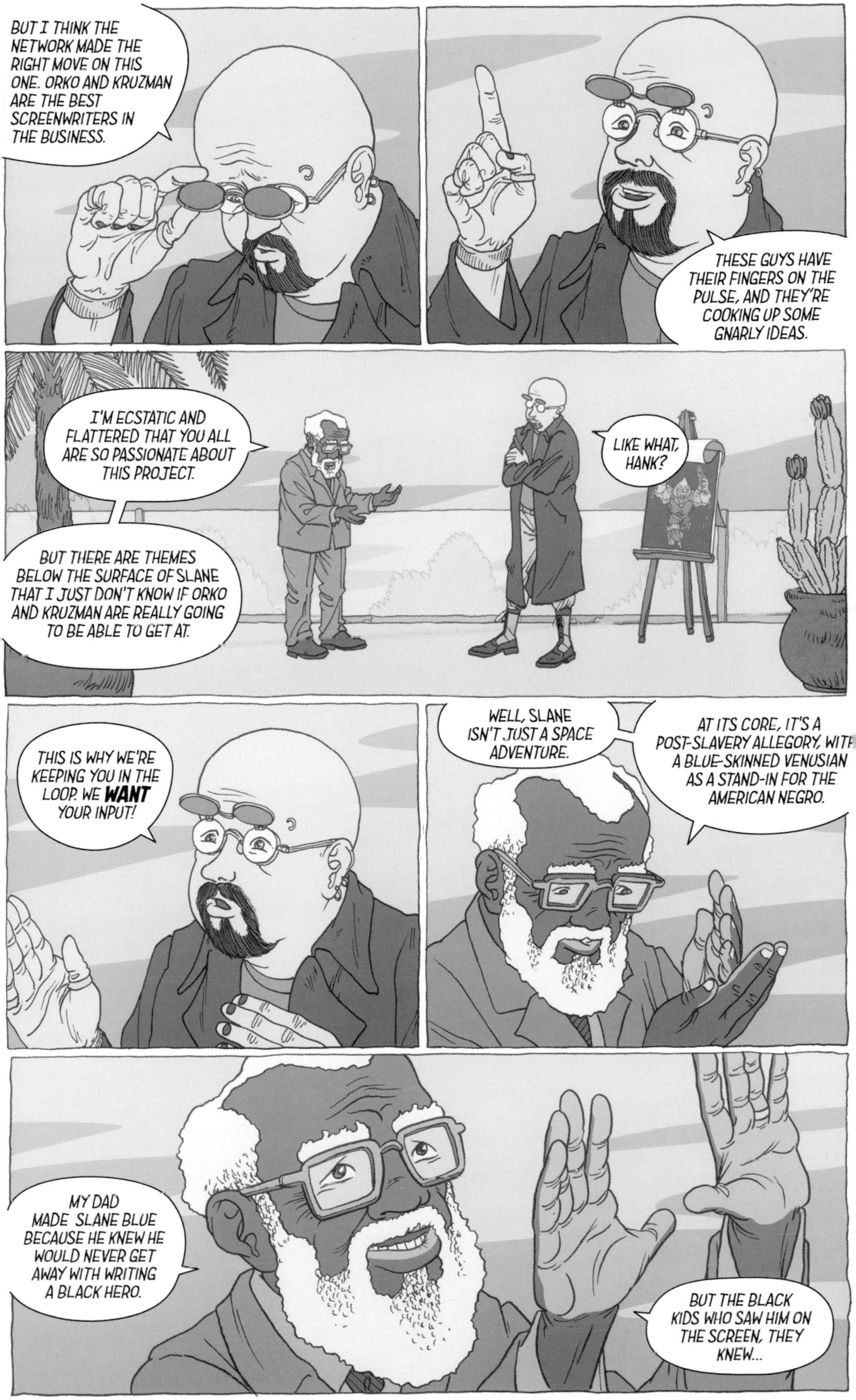

BUT I THINK THE NETWORK MADE THE RIGHT MOVE ON THIS ONE. ORKO AND KRUZMAN ARE THE BEST SCREENWRITERS IN THE BUSINESS.
THESE GUYS HAVE THEIR FINGERS ON THE PULSE, AND THEY'RE COOKING UP SOME GNARLY IDEAS.
I'M ECSTATIC AND FLATTERED THAT YOU ALL ARE SO PASSIONATE ABOUT THIS PROJECT.
BUT THERE ARE THEMES BELOW THE SURFACE OF SLANE THAT I JUST DON'T KNOW IF ORKO AND KRUZMAN ARE REALLY GOING TO BE ABLE TO GET AT.
LIKE WHAT, HANK?
THIS IS WHY WE'RE KEEPING YOU IN THE LOOP. WE **WANT** YOUR INPUT!
WELL, SLANE ISN'T JUST A SPACE ADVENTURE.
AT ITS CORE, IT'S A POST-SLAVERY ALLEGORY, WITH A BLUE-SKINNED VENUSIAN AS A STAND-IN FOR THE AMERICAN NEGRO.
MY DAD MADE SLANE BLUE BECAUSE HE KNEW HE WOULD NEVER GET AWAY WITH WRITING A BLACK HERO.
BUT THE BLACK KIDS WHO SAW HIM ON THE SCREEN, THEY KNEW...

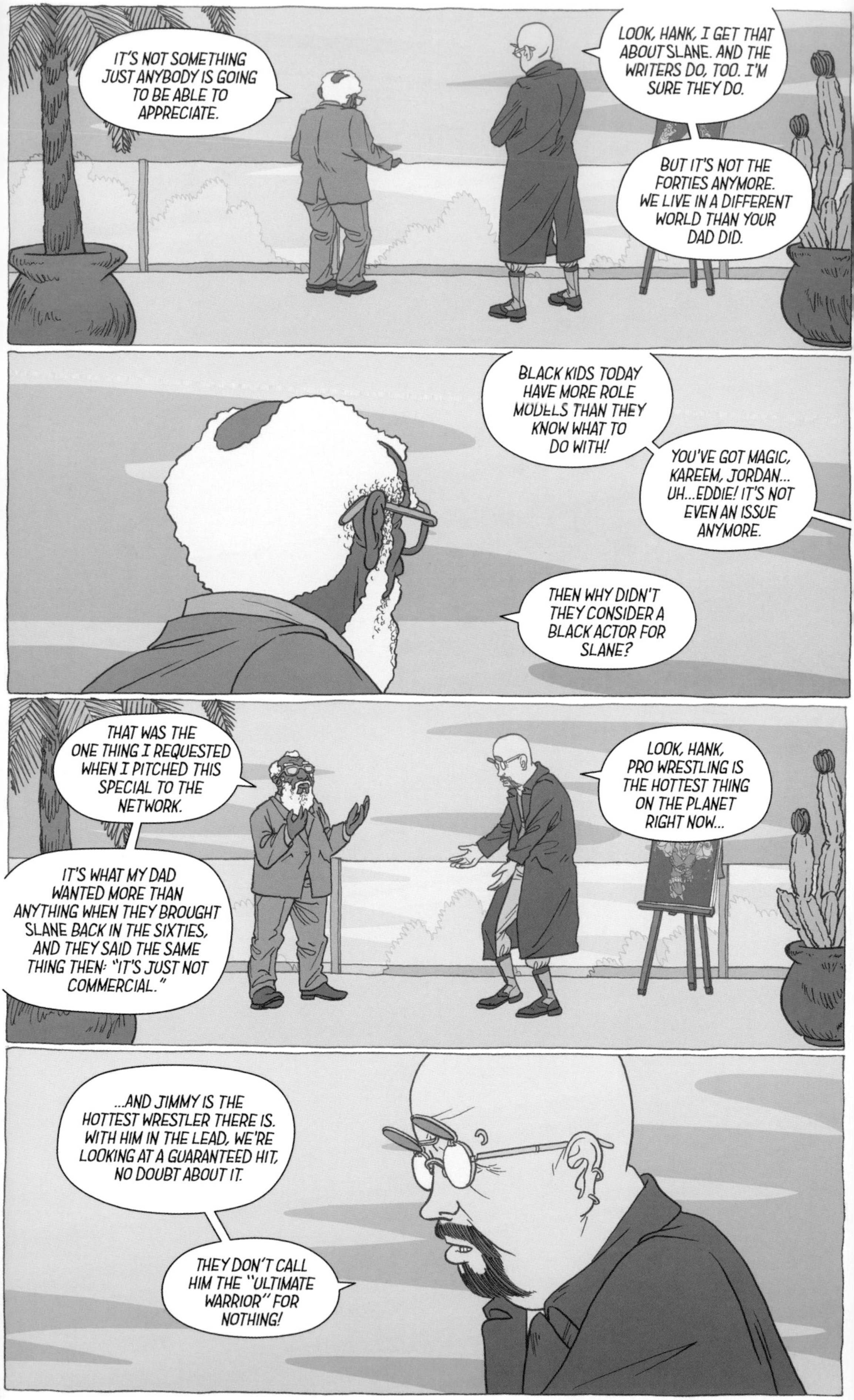
IT'S NOT SOMETHING JUST ANYBODY IS GOING TO BE ABLE TO APPRECIATE.
LOOK, HANK, I GET THAT ABOUT SLANE. AND THE WRITERS DO, TOO. I'M SURE THEY DO.
BUT IT'S NOT THE FORTIES ANYMORE. WE LIVE IN A DIFFERENT WORLD THAN YOUR DAD DID.
BLACK KIDS TODAY HAVE MORE ROLE MODELS THAN THEY KNOW WHAT TO DO WITH!
YOU'VE GOT MAGIC, KAREEM, JORDAN... UH...EDDIE! IT'S NOT EVEN AN ISSUE ANYMORE.
THEN WHY DIDN'T THEY CONSIDER A BLACK ACTOR FOR SLANE?
THAT WAS THE ONE THING I REQUESTED WHEN I PITCHED THIS SPECIAL TO THE NETWORK.
IT'S WHAT MY DAD WANTED MORE THAN ANYTHING WHEN THEY BROUGHT SLANE BACK IN THE SIXTIES, AND THEY SAID THE SAME THING THEN: "IT'S JUST NOT COMMERCIAL."
LOOK, HANK, PRO WRESTLING IS THE HOTTEST THING ON THE PLANET RIGHT NOW...
...AND JIMMY IS THE HOTTEST WRESTLER THERE IS. WITH HIM IN THE LEAD, WE'RE LOOKING AT A GUARANTEED HIT, NO DOUBT ABOUT IT.
THEY DON'T CALL HIM THE "ULTIMATE WARRIOR" FOR NOTHING!

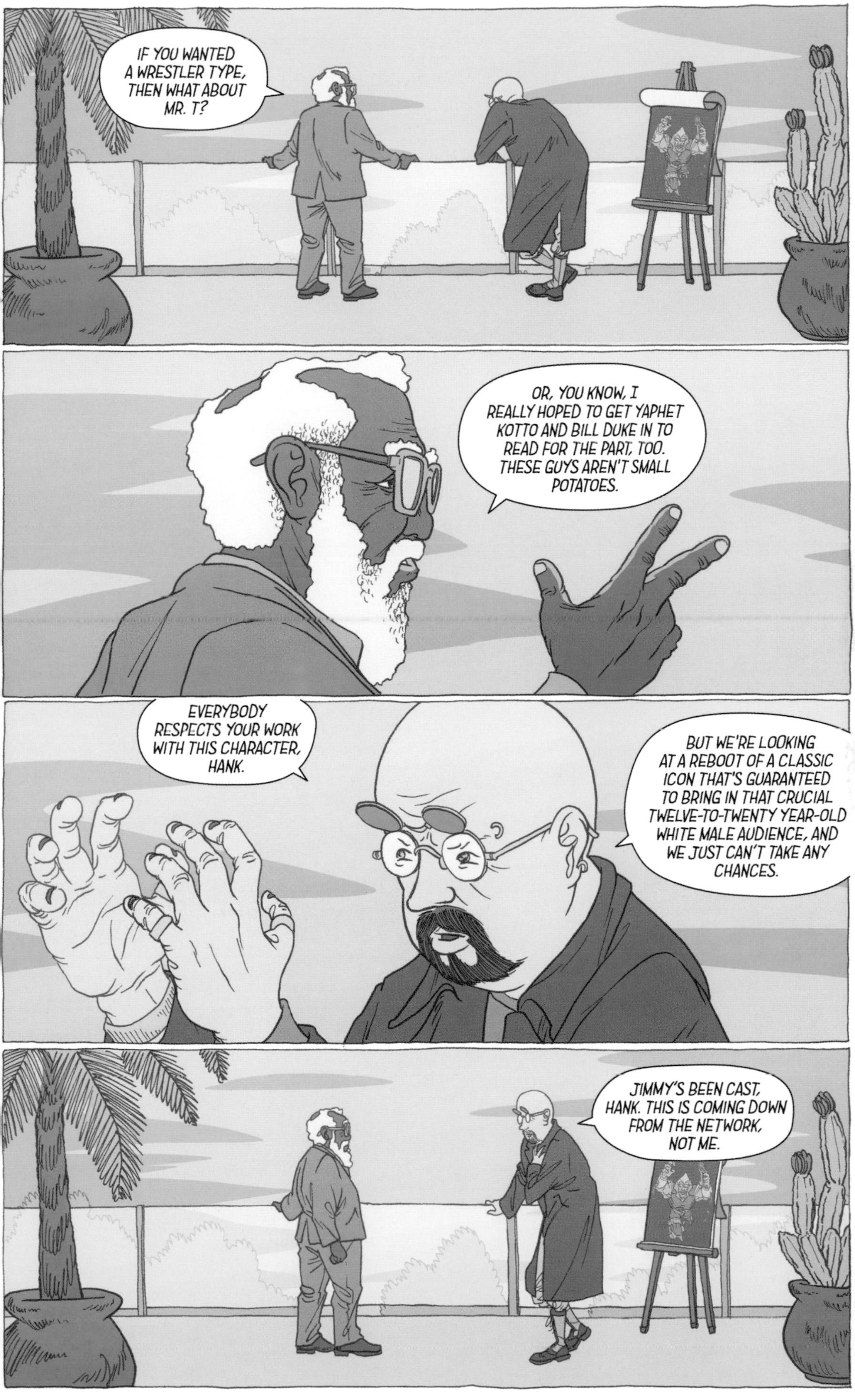
IF YOU WANTED A WRESTLER TYPE, THEN WHAT ABOUT MR. T?
OR, YOU KNOW, I REALLY HOPED TO GET YAPHET KOTTO AND BILL DUKE IN TO READ FOR THE PART, TOO. THESE GUYS AREN'T SMALL POTATOES.
EVERYBODY RESPECTS YOUR WORK WITH THIS CHARACTER, HANK.
BUT WE'RE LOOKING AT A REBOOT OF A CLASSIC ICON THAT'S GUARANTEED TO BRING IN THAT CRUCIAL TWELVE-TO-TWENTY YEAR-OLD WHITE MALE AUDIENCE, AND WE JUST CAN'T TAKE ANY CHANCES.
JIMMY'S BEEN CAST, HANK. THIS IS COMING DOWN FROM THE NETWORK, NOT ME.

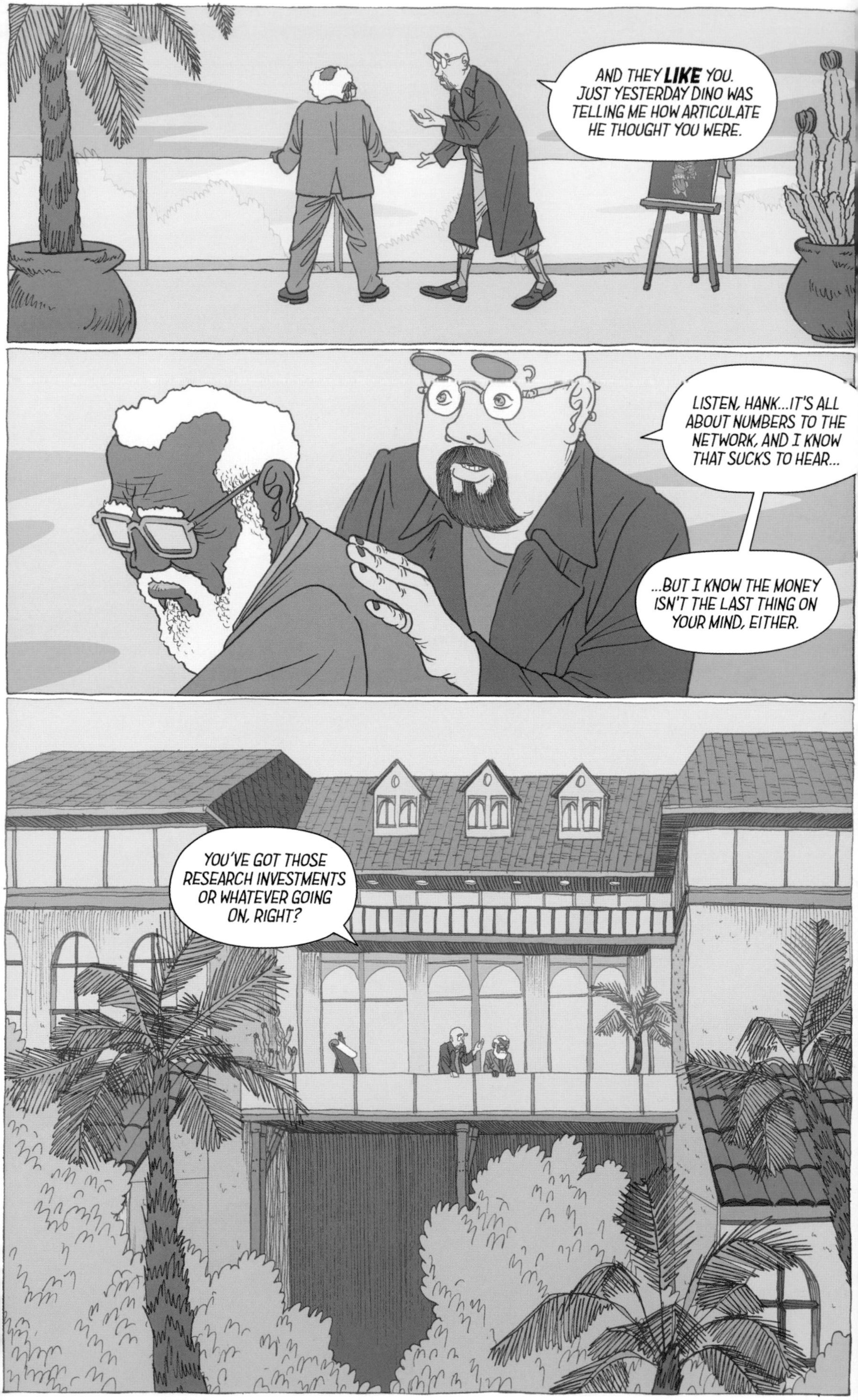
AND THEY LIKE YOU. JUST YESTERDAY DINO WAS TELLING ME HOW ARTICULATE HE THOUGHT YOU WERE.
LISTEN, HANK...IT'S ALL ABOUT NUMBERS TO THE NETWORK, AND I KNOW THAT SUCKS TO HEAR...
...BUT I KNOW THE MONEY ISN'T THE LAST THING ON YOUR MIND, EITHER.
YOU'VE GOT THOSE RESEARCH INVESTMENTS OR WHATEVER GOING ON, RIGHT?

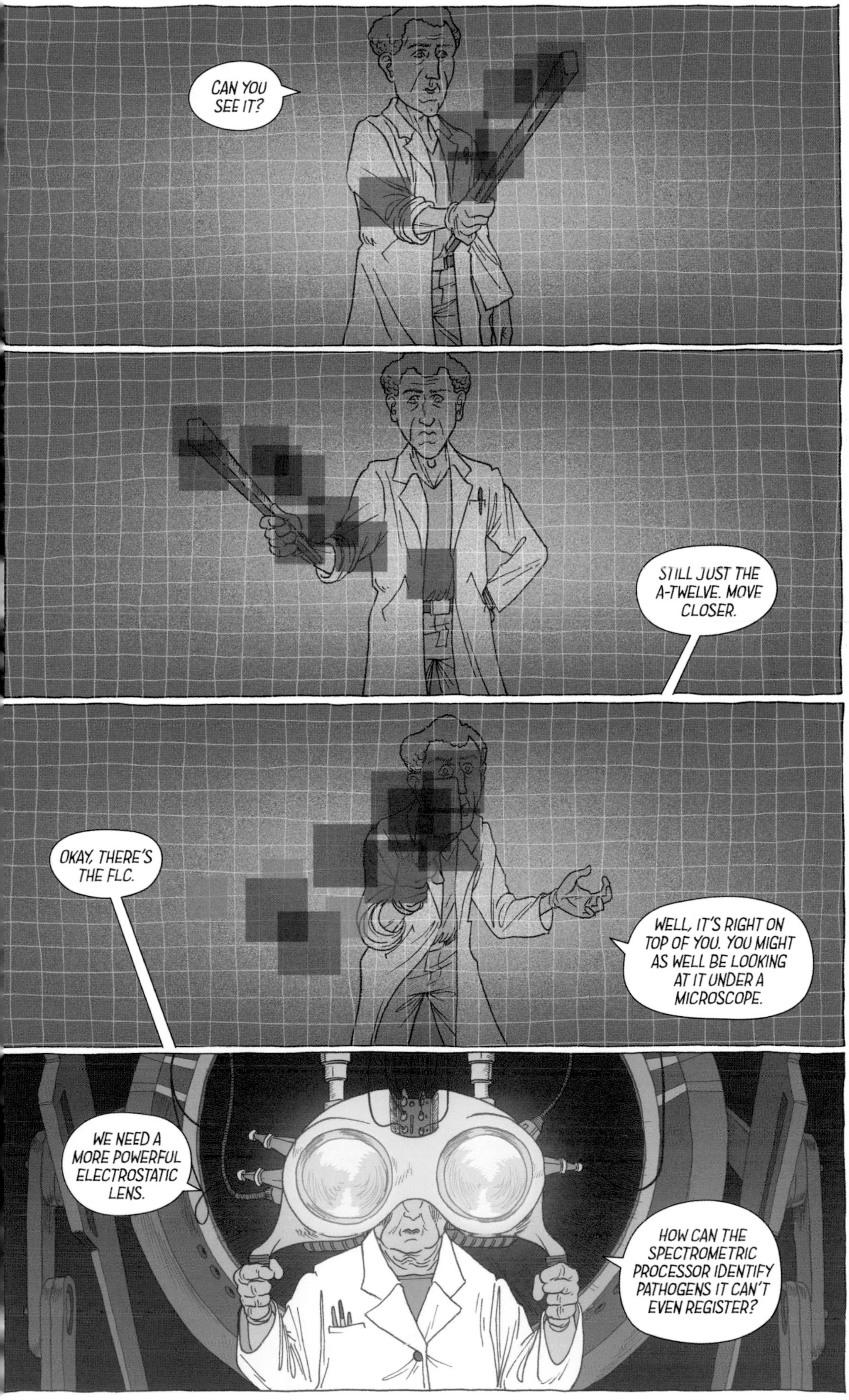
CAN YOU SEE IT?
STILL JUST THE A-TWELVE. MOVE CLOSER.
OKAY, THERE'S THE FLC.
WELL, IT'S RIGHT ON TOP OF YOU. YOU MIGHT AS WELL BE LOOKING AT IT UNDER A MICROSCOPE.
WE NEED A MORE POWERFUL ELECTROSTATIC LENS.
HOW CAN THE SPECTROMETRIC PROCESSOR IDENTIFY PATHOGENS IT CAN'T EVEN REGISTER?

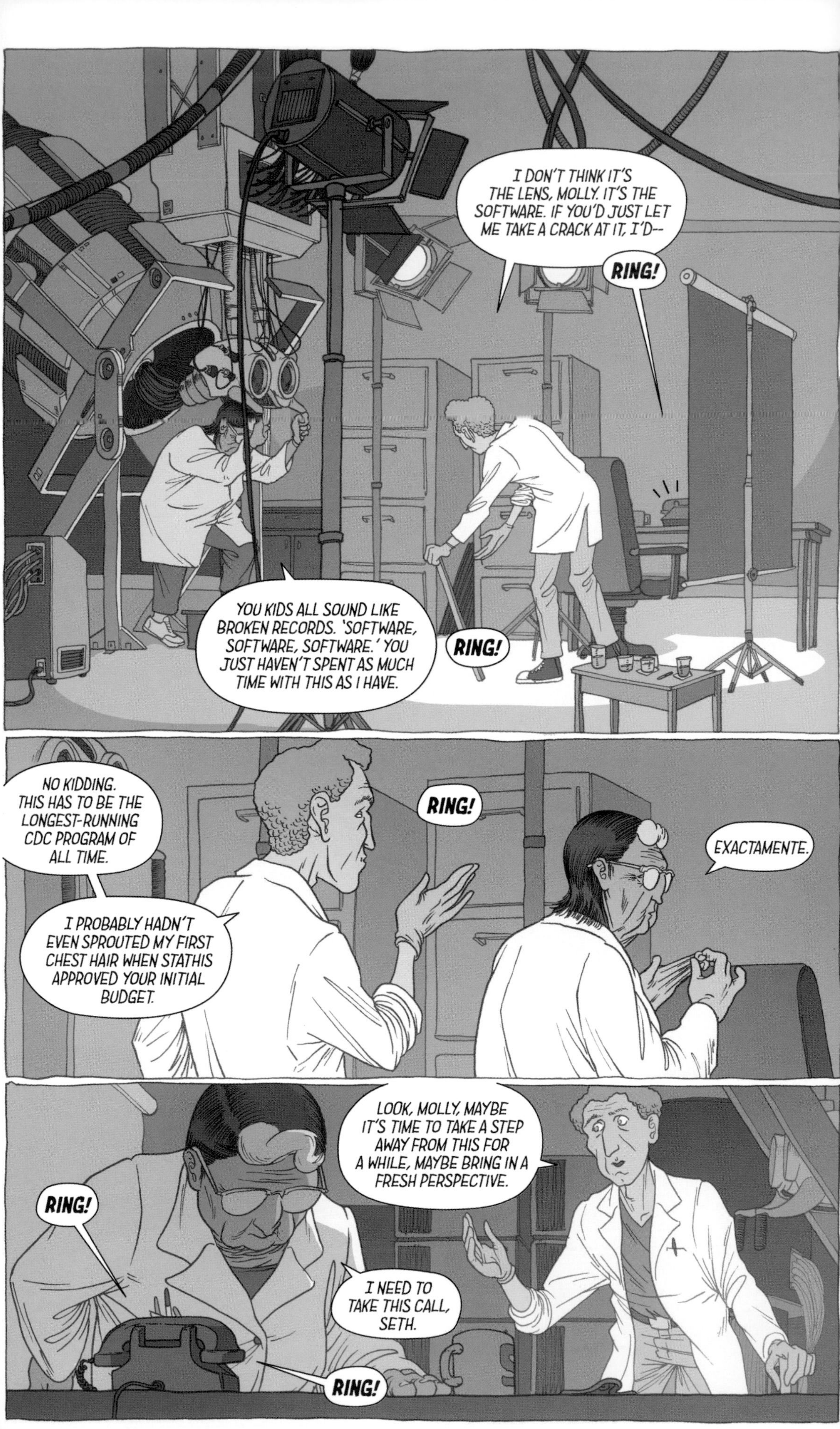

I DON'T THINK IT'S THE LENS, MOLLY. IT'S THE SOFTWARE. IF YOU'D JUST LET ME TAKE A CRACK AT IT, I'D--
RING!
YOU KIDS ALL SOUND LIKE BROKEN RECORDS. 'SOFTWARE, SOFTWARE, SOFTWARE.' YOU JUST HAVEN'T SPENT AS MUCH TIME WITH THIS AS I HAVE.
RING!
NO KIDDING. THIS HAS TO BE THE LONGEST-RUNNING CDC PROGRAM OF ALL TIME.
I PROBABLY HADN'T EVEN SPROUTED MY FIRST CHEST HAIR WHEN STATHIS APPROVED YOUR INITIAL BUDGET.
RING!
EXACTAMENTE.
LOOK, MOLLY, MAYBE IT'S TIME TO TAKE A STEP AWAY FROM THIS FOR A WHILE, MAYBE BRING IN A FRESH PERSPECTIVE.
RING!
I NEED TO TAKE THIS CALL, SETH.
RING!

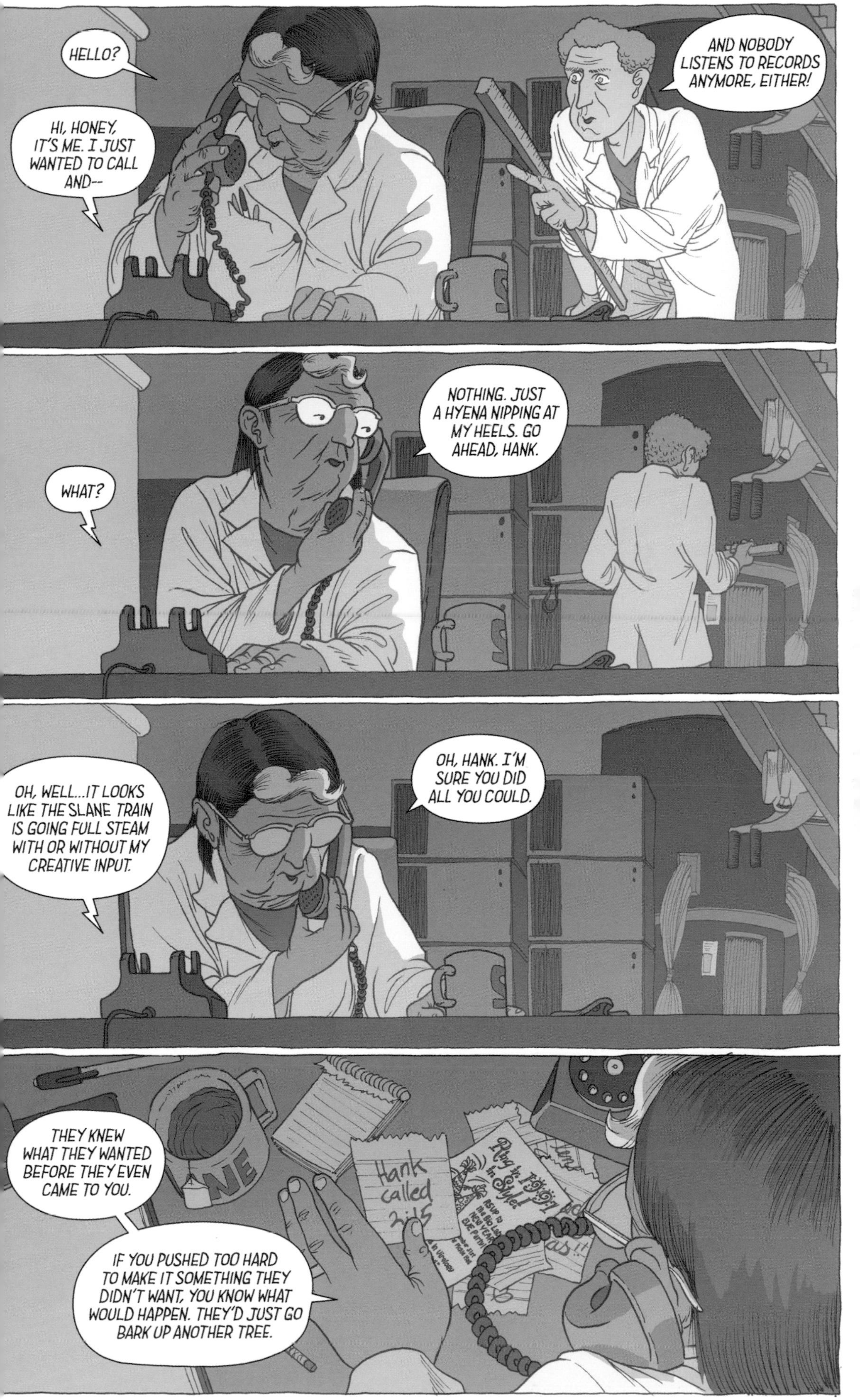
HELLO?
AND NOBODY LISTENS TO RECORDS ANYMORE, EITHER!
HI, HONEY, IT'S ME. I JUST WANTED TO CALL AND--
WHAT?
NOTHING. JUST A HYENA NIPPING AT MY HEELS. GO AHEAD, HANK.
OH, WELL...IT LOOKS LIKE THE SLANE TRAIN IS GOING FULL STEAM WITH OR WITHOUT MY CREATIVE INPUT.
OH, HANK. I'M SURE YOU DID ALL YOU COULD.
THEY KNEW WHAT THEY WANTED BEFORE THEY EVEN CAME TO YOU.
Hank called 2:15
IF YOU PUSHED TOO HARD TO MAKE IT SOMETHING THEY DIDN'T WANT, YOU KNOW WHAT WOULD HAPPEN. THEY'D JUST GO BARK UP ANOTHER TREE.

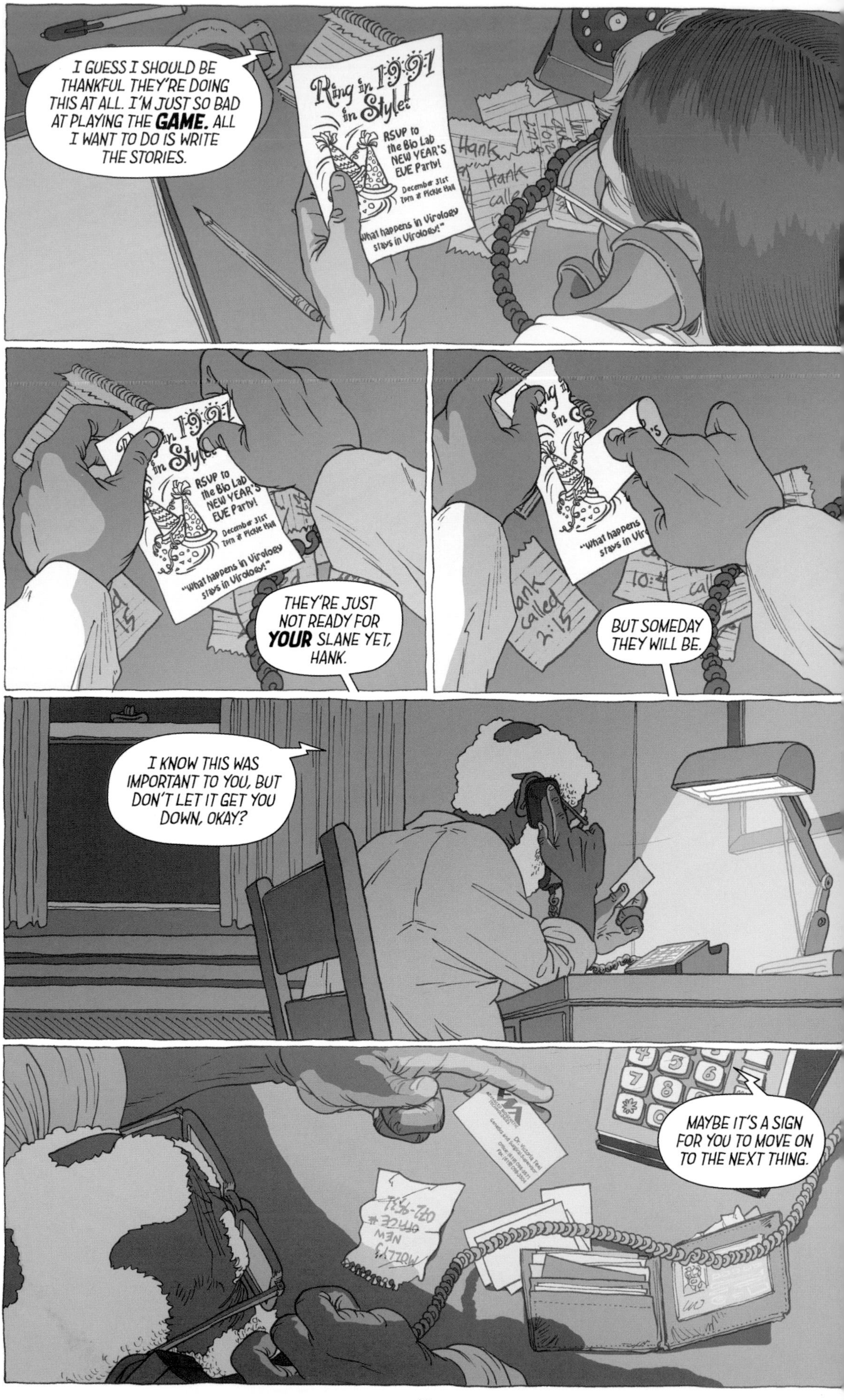
I GUESS I SHOULD BE THANKFUL THEY'RE DOING THIS AT ALL. I'M JUST SO BAD AT PLAYING THE GAME. ALL I WANT TO DO IS WRITE THE STORIES.
Ring in 1991 in Style!
RSVP to the Bio Lab NEW YEAR'S EVE Party!
December 31st 7pm @ Pickle Hall
"What happens in Virology stays in Virology!"
Hank
Hank called
THEY'RE JUST NOT READY FOR YOUR SLANE YET, HANK.
Hank called 2:15
BUT SOMEDAY THEY WILL BE.
I KNOW THIS WAS IMPORTANT TO YOU, BUT DON'T LET IT GET YOU DOWN, OKAY?
MAYBE IT'S A SIGN FOR YOU TO MOVE ON TO THE NEXT THING.

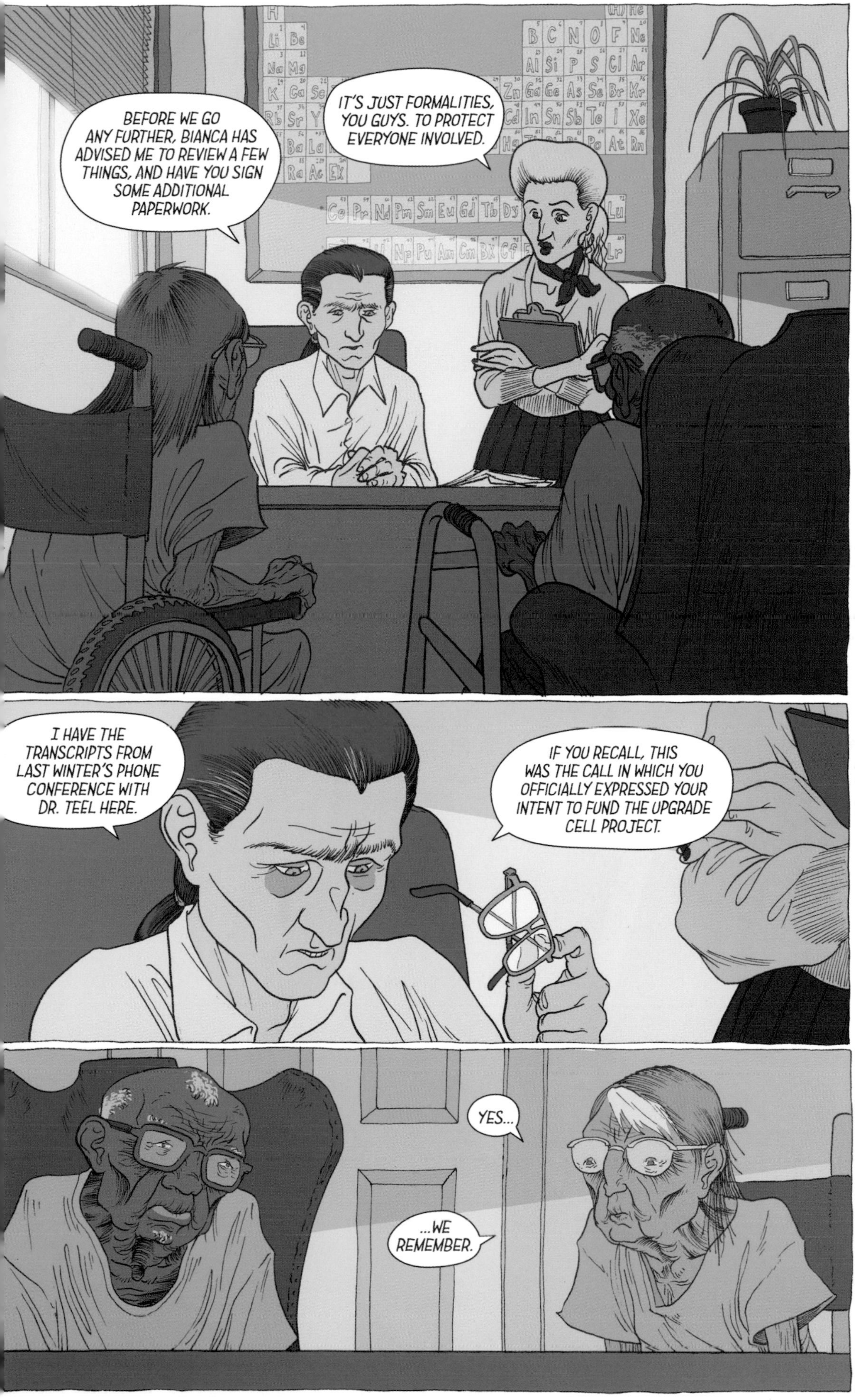
BEFORE WE GO ANY FURTHER, BIANCA HAS ADVISED ME TO REVIEW A FEW THINGS, AND HAVE YOU SIGN SOME ADDITIONAL PAPERWORK.
IT'S JUST FORMALITIES, YOU GUYS. TO PROTECT EVERYONE INVOLVED.
I HAVE THE TRANSCRIPTS FROM LAST WINTER'S PHONE CONFERENCE WITH DR. TEEL HERE.
IF YOU RECALL, THIS WAS THE CALL IN WHICH YOU OFFICIALLY EXPRESSED YOUR INTENT TO FUND THE UPGRADE CELL PROJECT.
YES...
...WE REMEMBER.

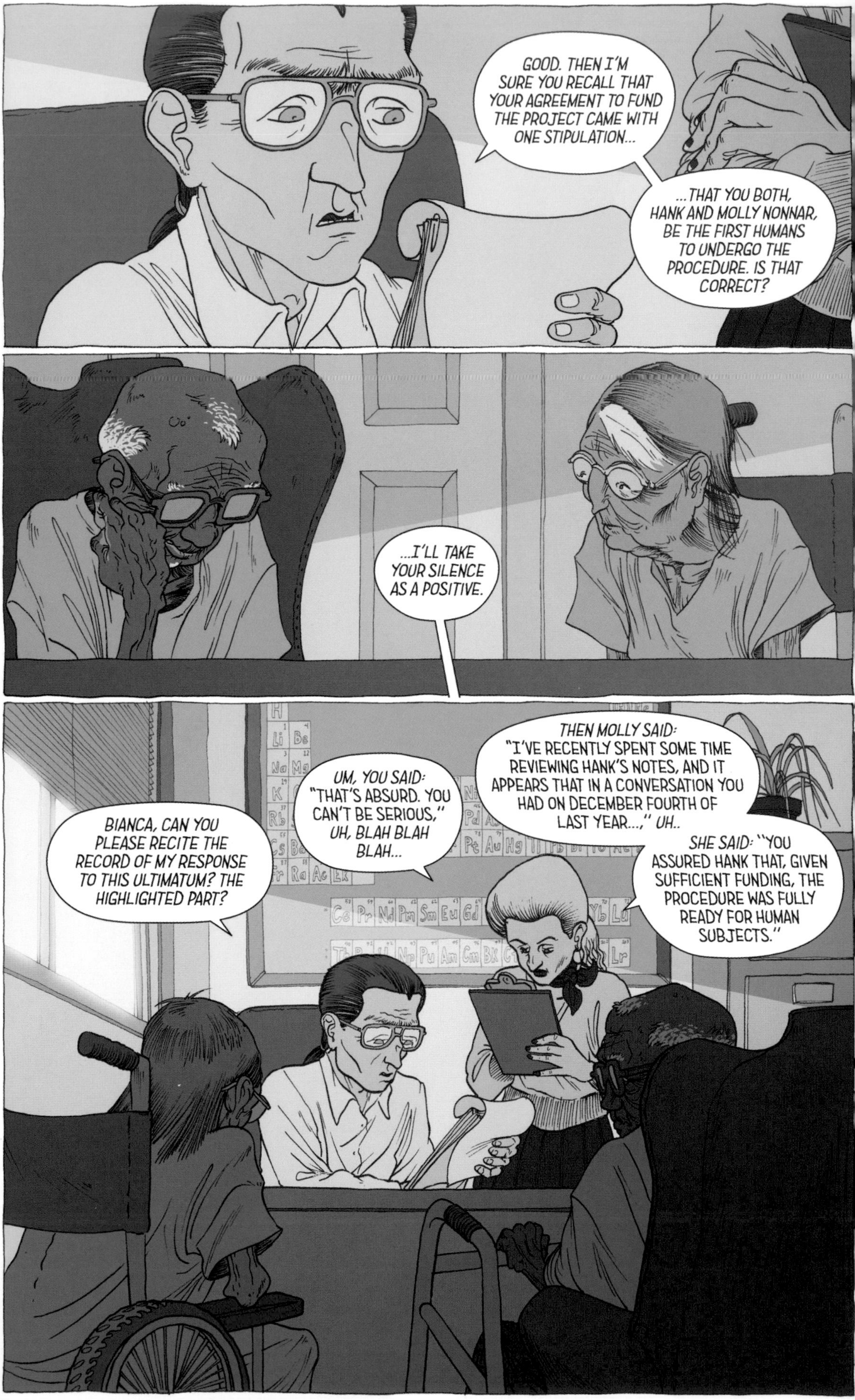
GOOD. THEN I'M SURE YOU RECALL THAT YOUR AGREEMENT TO FUND THE PROJECT CAME WITH ONE STIPULATION...
...THAT YOU BOTH, HANK AND MOLLY NONNAR, BE THE FIRST HUMANS TO UNDERGO THE PROCEDURE. IS THAT CORRECT?
...I'LL TAKE YOUR SILENCE AS A POSITIVE.
BIANCA, CAN YOU PLEASE RECITE THE RECORD OF MY RESPONSE TO THIS ULTIMATUM? THE HIGHLIGHTED PART?
UM, YOU SAID: "THAT'S ABSURD. YOU CAN'T BE SERIOUS," UH, BLAH BLAH BLAH...
THEN MOLLY SAID: "I'VE RECENTLY SPENT SOME TIME REVIEWING HANK'S NOTES, AND IT APPEARS THAT IN A CONVERSATION YOU HAD ON DECEMBER FOURTH OF LAST YEAR...," UH..
SHE SAID: "YOU ASSURED HANK THAT, GIVEN SUFFICIENT FUNDING, THE PROCEDURE WAS FULLY READY FOR HUMAN SUBJECTS."

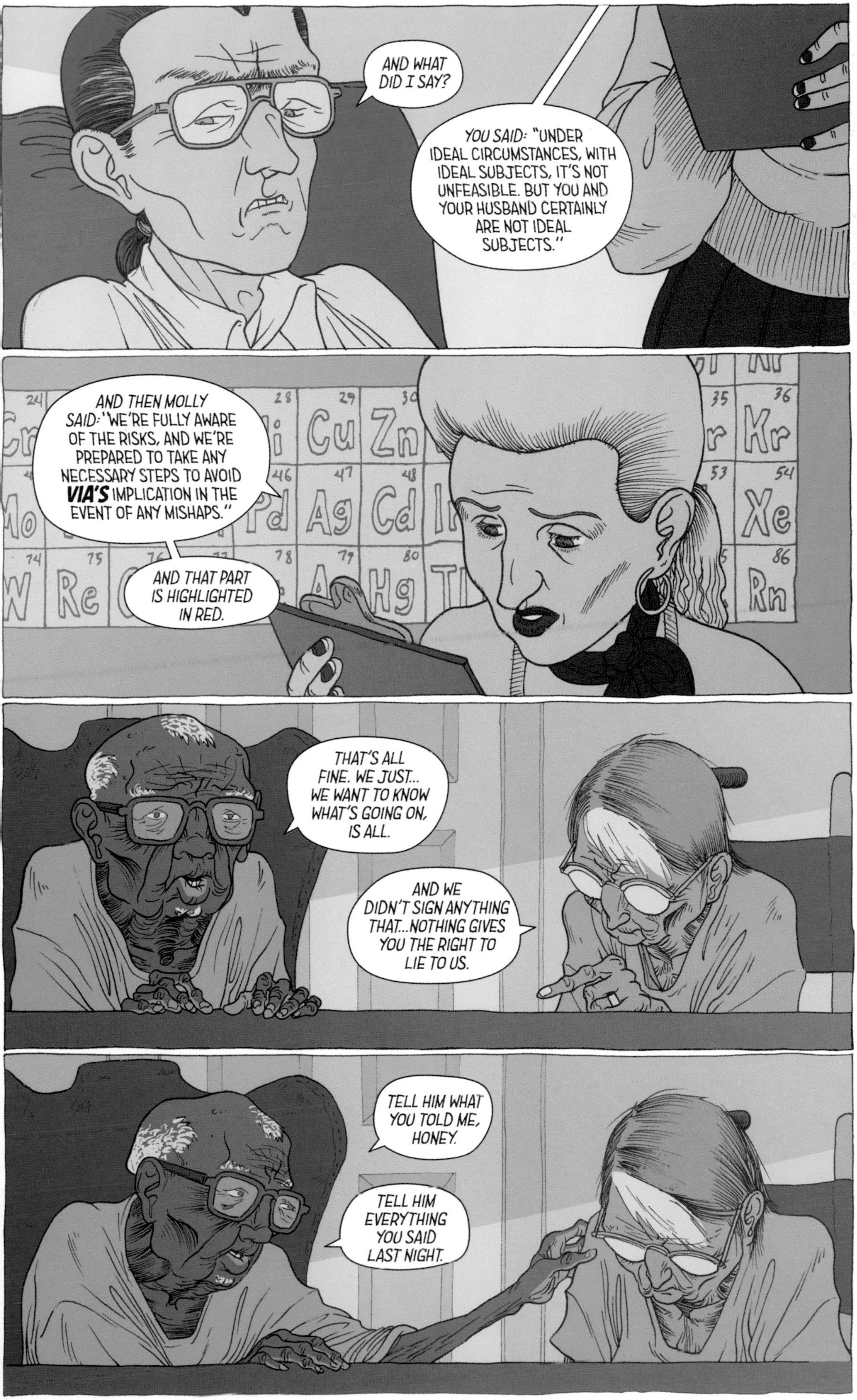
AND WHAT DID I SAY?
YOU SAID: "UNDER IDEAL CIRCUMSTANCES, WITH IDEAL SUBJECTS, IT'S NOT UNFEASIBLE. BUT YOU AND YOUR HUSBAND CERTAINLY ARE NOT IDEAL SUBJECTS."
AND THEN MOLLY SAID: "WE'RE FULLY AWARE OF THE RISKS, AND WE'RE PREPARED TO TAKE ANY NECESSARY STEPS TO AVOID VIA'S IMPLICATION IN THE EVENT OF ANY MISHAPS."
AND THAT PART IS HIGHLIGHTED IN RED.
THAT'S ALL FINE. WE JUST... WE WANT TO KNOW WHAT'S GOING ON, IS ALL.
AND WE DIDN'T SIGN ANYTHING THAT...NOTHING GIVES YOU THE RIGHT TO LIE TO US.
TELL HIM WHAT YOU TOLD ME, HONEY.
TELL HIM EVERYTHING YOU SAID LAST NIGHT.

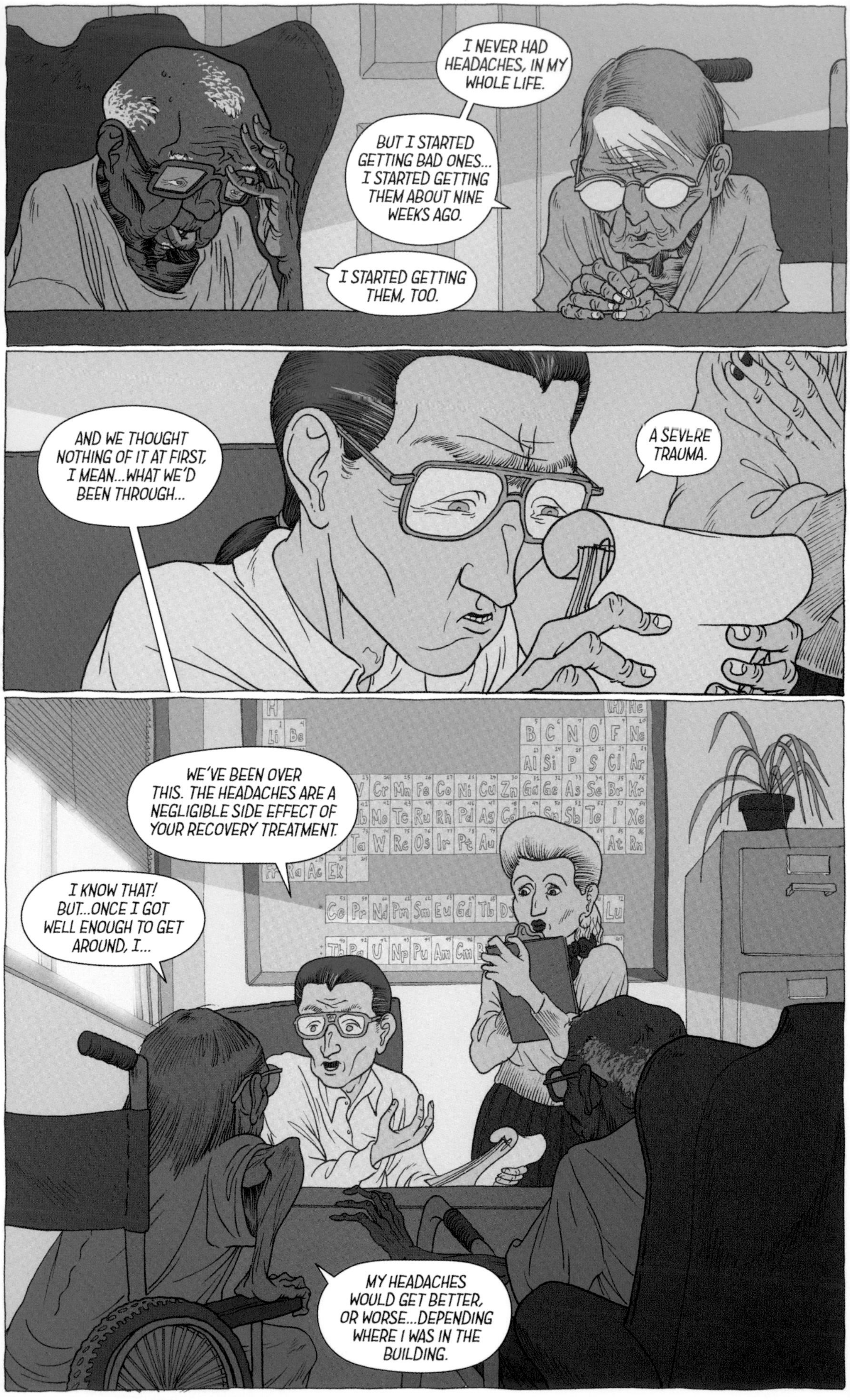
I NEVER HAD HEADACHES, IN MY WHOLE LIFE.
BUT I STARTED GETTING BAD ONES... I STARTED GETTING THEM ABOUT NINE WEEKS AGO.
I STARTED GETTING THEM, TOO.
AND WE THOUGHT NOTHING OF IT AT FIRST, I MEAN...WHAT WE'D BEEN THROUGH...
A SEVERE TRAUMA.
WE'VE BEEN OVER THIS. THE HEADACHES ARE A NEGLIGIBLE SIDE EFFECT OF YOUR RECOVERY TREATMENT.
I KNOW THAT! BUT...ONCE I GOT WELL ENOUGH TO GET AROUND, I...
MY HEADACHES WOULD GET BETTER, OR WORSE...DEPENDING WHERE I WAS IN THE BUILDING.

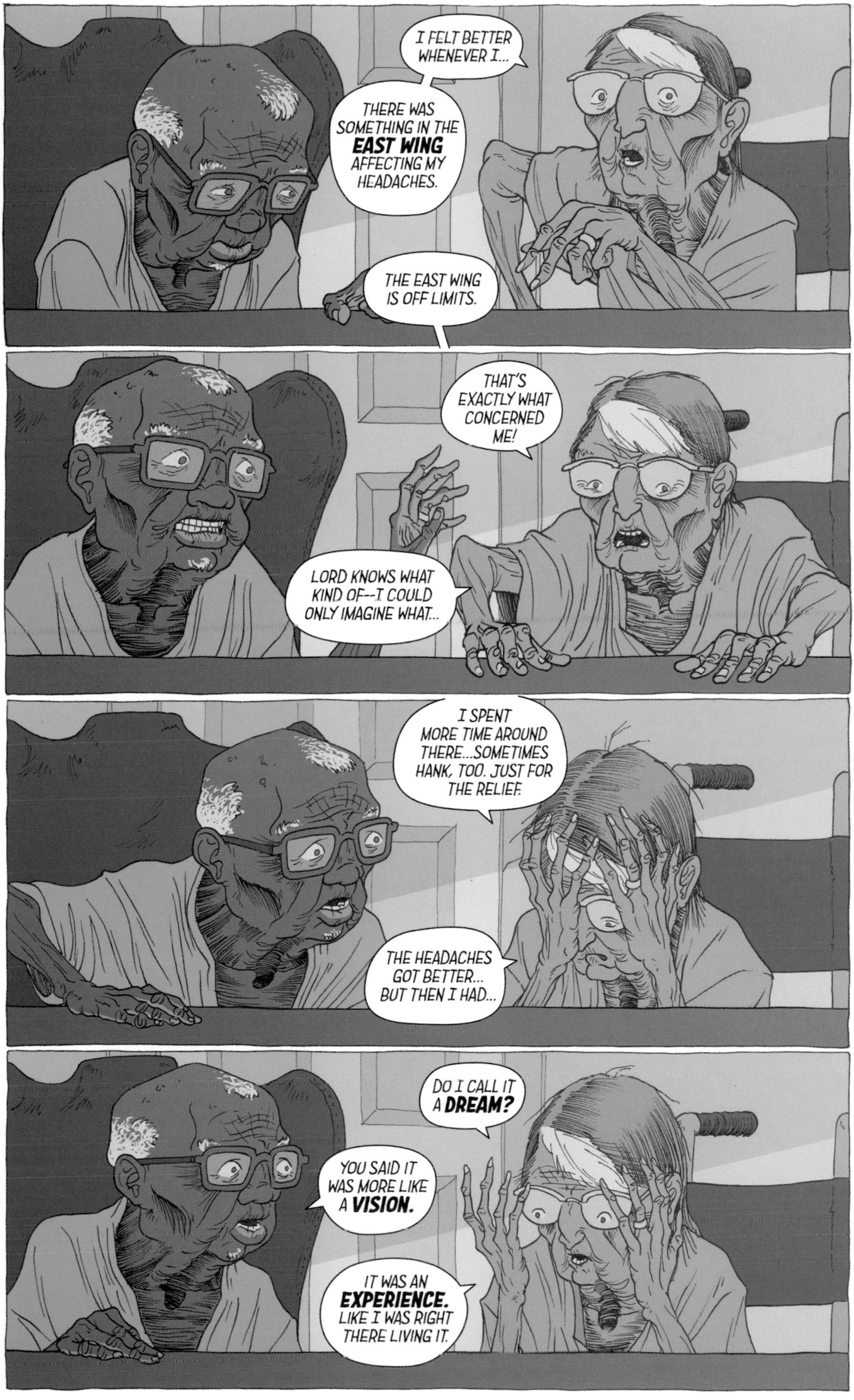
I FELT BETTER WHENEVER I...
THERE WAS SOMETHING IN THE **EAST WING** AFFECTING MY HEADACHES.
THE EAST WING IS OFF LIMITS.
THAT'S EXACTLY WHAT CONCERNED ME!
LORD KNOWS WHAT KIND OF--I COULD ONLY IMAGINE WHAT...
I SPENT MORE TIME AROUND THERE...SOMETIMES HANK, TOO. JUST FOR THE RELIEF.
THE HEADACHES GOT BETTER... BUT THEN I HAD...
DO I CALL IT A **DREAM?**
YOU SAID IT WAS MORE LIKE A **VISION.**
IT WAS AN **EXPERIENCE.** LIKE I WAS RIGHT THERE LIVING IT.

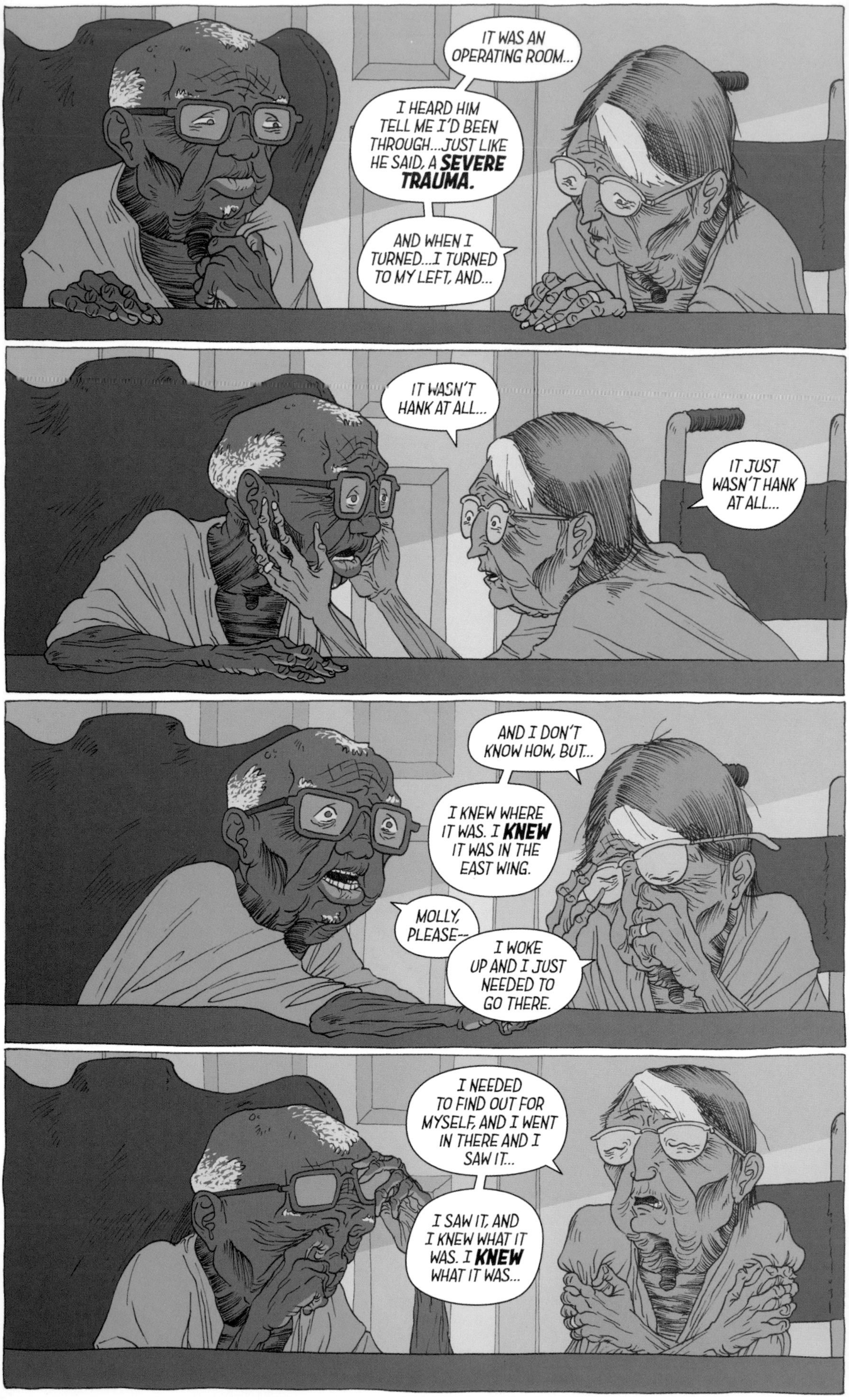

IT WAS AN OPERATING ROOM...
I HEARD HIM TELL ME I'D BEEN THROUGH...JUST LIKE HE SAID, A **SEVERE TRAUMA.**
AND WHEN I TURNED...I TURNED TO MY LEFT, AND...
IT WASN'T HANK AT ALL...
IT JUST WASN'T HANK AT ALL...
AND I DON'T KNOW HOW, BUT...
I KNEW WHERE IT WAS. I **KNEW** IT WAS IN THE EAST WING.
MOLLY, PLEASE--
I WOKE UP AND I JUST NEEDED TO GO THERE.
I NEEDED TO FIND OUT FOR MYSELF, AND I WENT IN THERE AND I SAW IT...
I SAW IT, AND I KNEW WHAT IT WAS. I **KNEW** WHAT IT WAS...

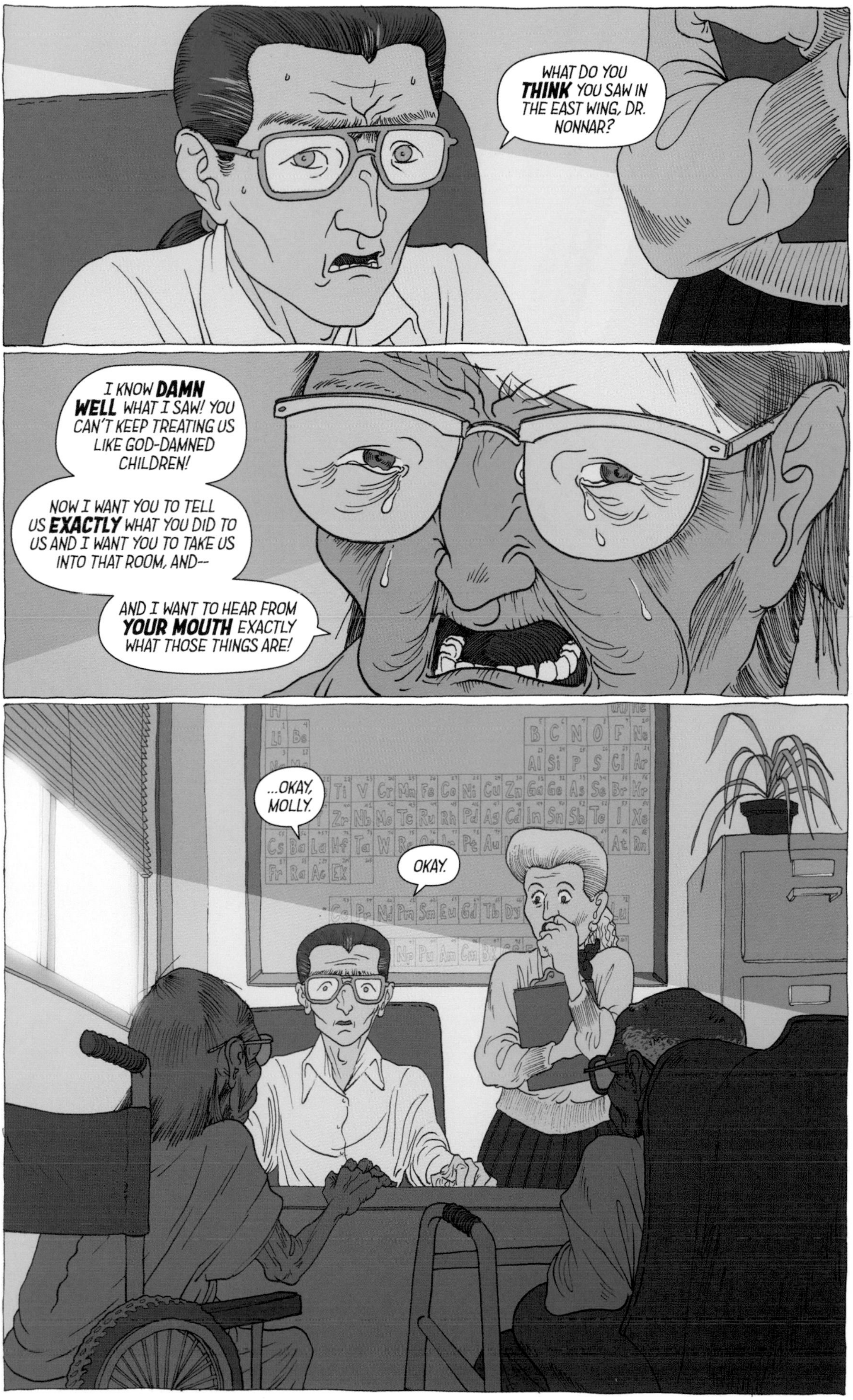
WHAT DO YOU THINK YOU SAW IN THE EAST WING, DR. NONNAR?
I KNOW DAMN WELL WHAT I SAW! YOU CAN'T KEEP TREATING US LIKE GOD-DAMNED CHILDREN!
NOW I WANT YOU TO TELL US EXACTLY WHAT YOU DID TO US AND I WANT YOU TO TAKE US INTO THAT ROOM, AND--
AND I WANT TO HEAR FROM YOUR MOUTH EXACTLY WHAT THOSE THINGS ARE!
...OKAY, MOLLY.
OKAY.

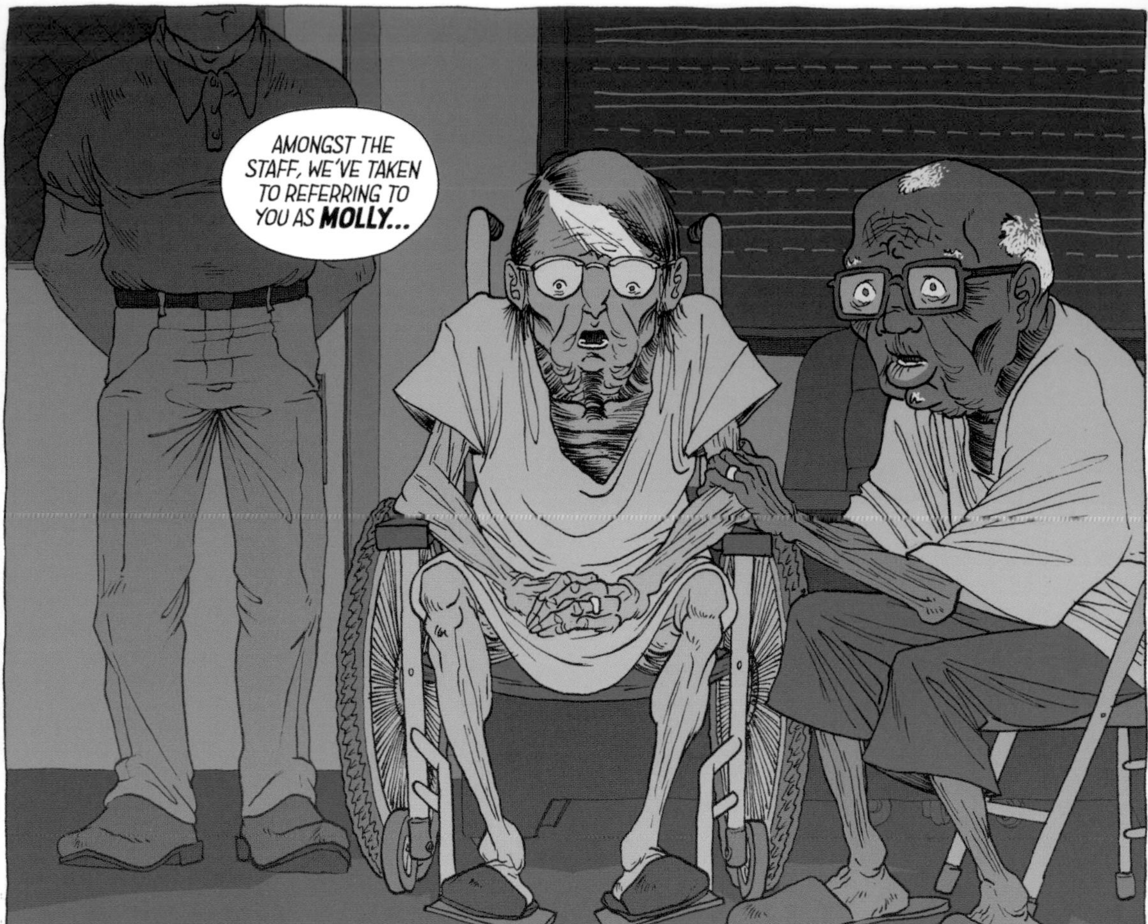
AMONGST THE STAFF, WE'VE TAKEN TO REFERRING TO YOU AS **MOLLY...**

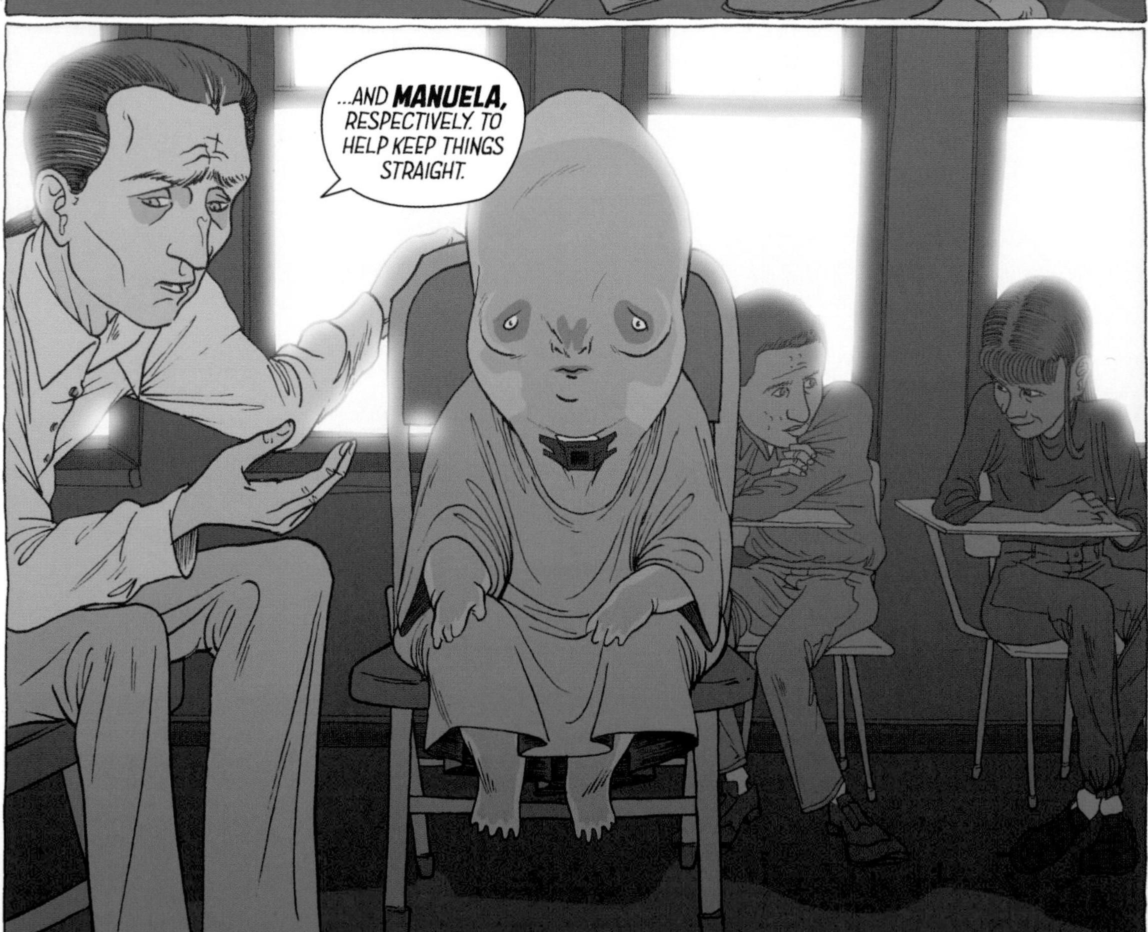
...AND **MANUELA,** RESPECTIVELY. TO HELP KEEP THINGS STRAIGHT.

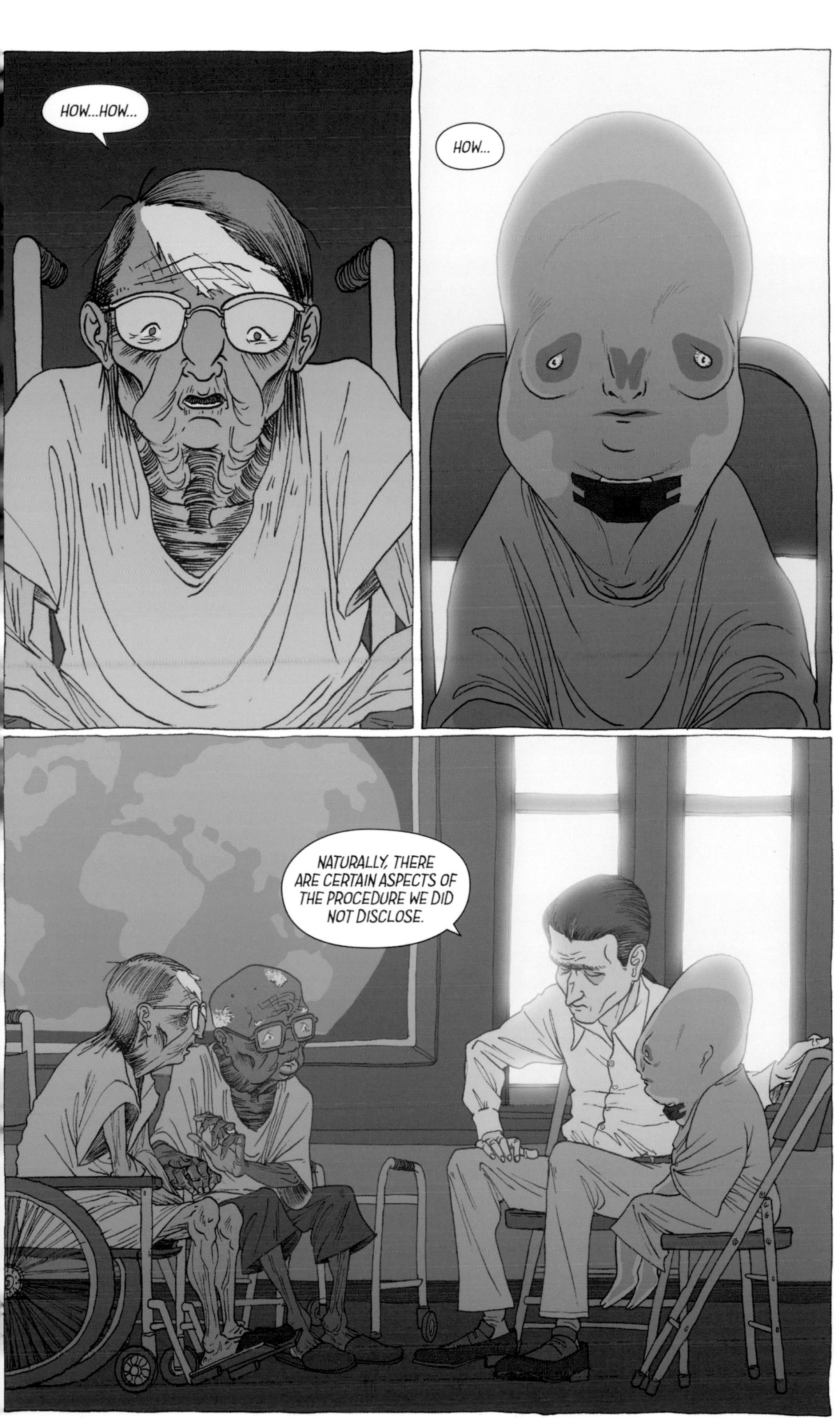
HOW...HOW...
HOW...
NATURALLY, THERE ARE CERTAIN ASPECTS OF THE PROCEDURE WE DID NOT DISCLOSE.

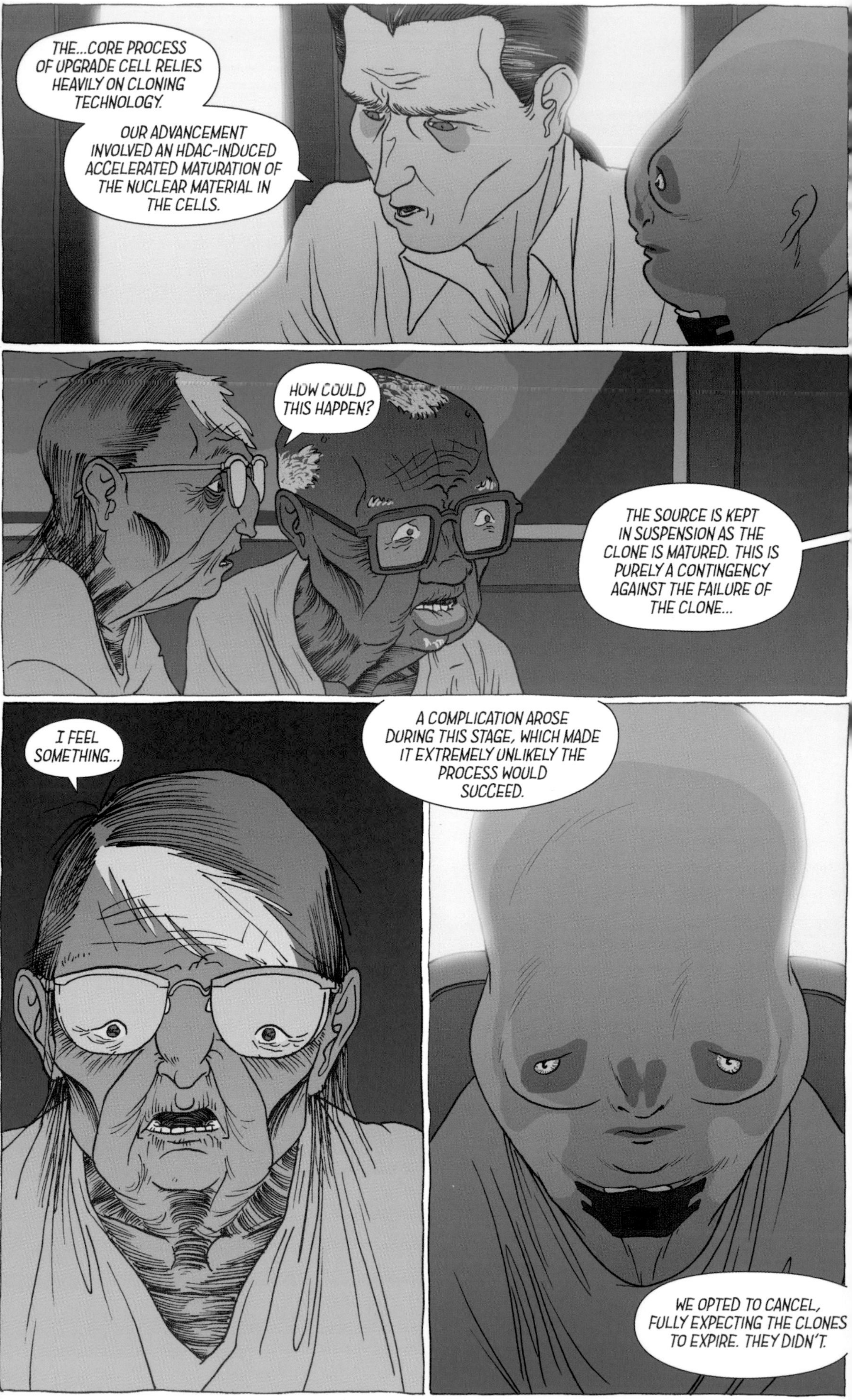
THE...CORE PROCESS OF UPGRADE CELL RELIES HEAVILY ON CLONING TECHNOLOGY.
OUR ADVANCEMENT INVOLVED AN HDAC-INDUCED ACCELERATED MATURATION OF THE NUCLEAR MATERIAL IN THE CELLS.
HOW COULD THIS HAPPEN?
THE SOURCE IS KEPT IN SUSPENSION AS THE CLONE IS MATURED. THIS IS PURELY A CONTINGENCY AGAINST THE FAILURE OF THE CLONE...
I FEEL SOMETHING...
A COMPLICATION AROSE DURING THIS STAGE, WHICH MADE IT EXTREMELY UNLIKELY THE PROCESS WOULD SUCCEED.
WE OPTED TO CANCEL, FULLY EXPECTING THE CLONES TO EXPIRE. THEY DIDN'T.

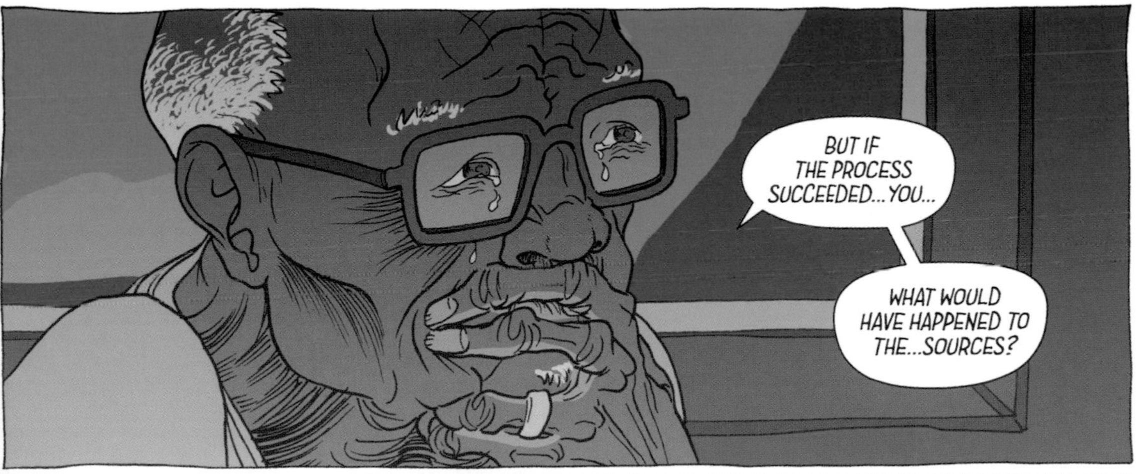
BUT IF THE PROCESS SUCCEEDED...YOU...
WHAT WOULD HAVE HAPPENED TO THE...SOURCES?

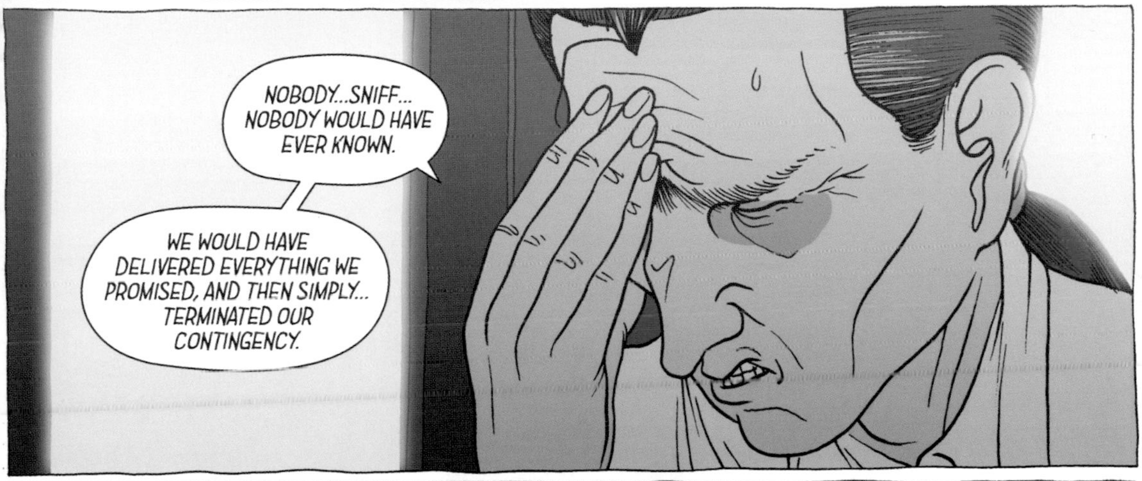
NOBODY...SNIFF... NOBODY WOULD HAVE EVER KNOWN.
WE WOULD HAVE DELIVERED EVERYTHING WE PROMISED, AND THEN SIMPLY... TERMINATED OUR CONTINGENCY.

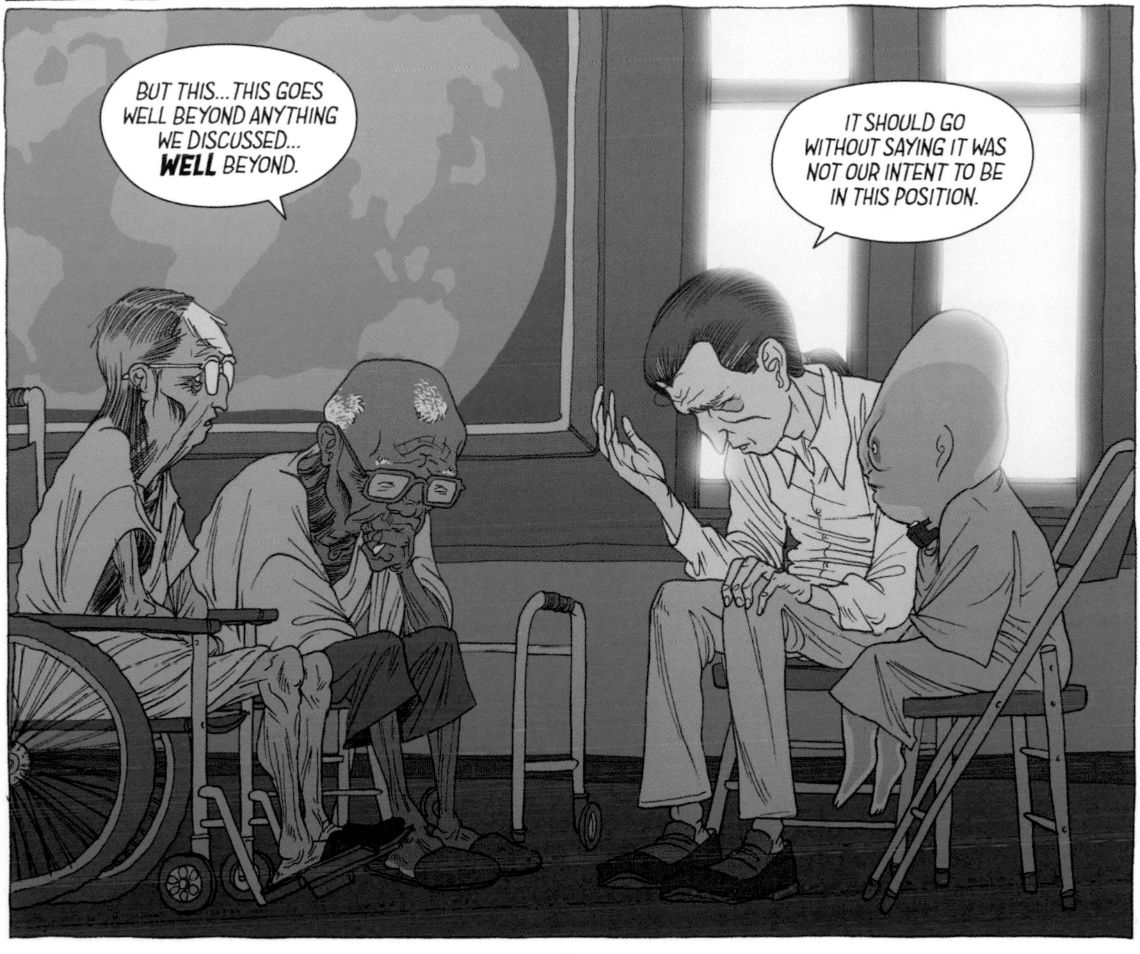
BUT THIS...THIS GOES WELL BEYOND ANYTHING WE DISCUSSED... WELL BEYOND.
IT SHOULD GO WITHOUT SAYING IT WAS NOT OUR INTENT TO BE IN THIS POSITION.

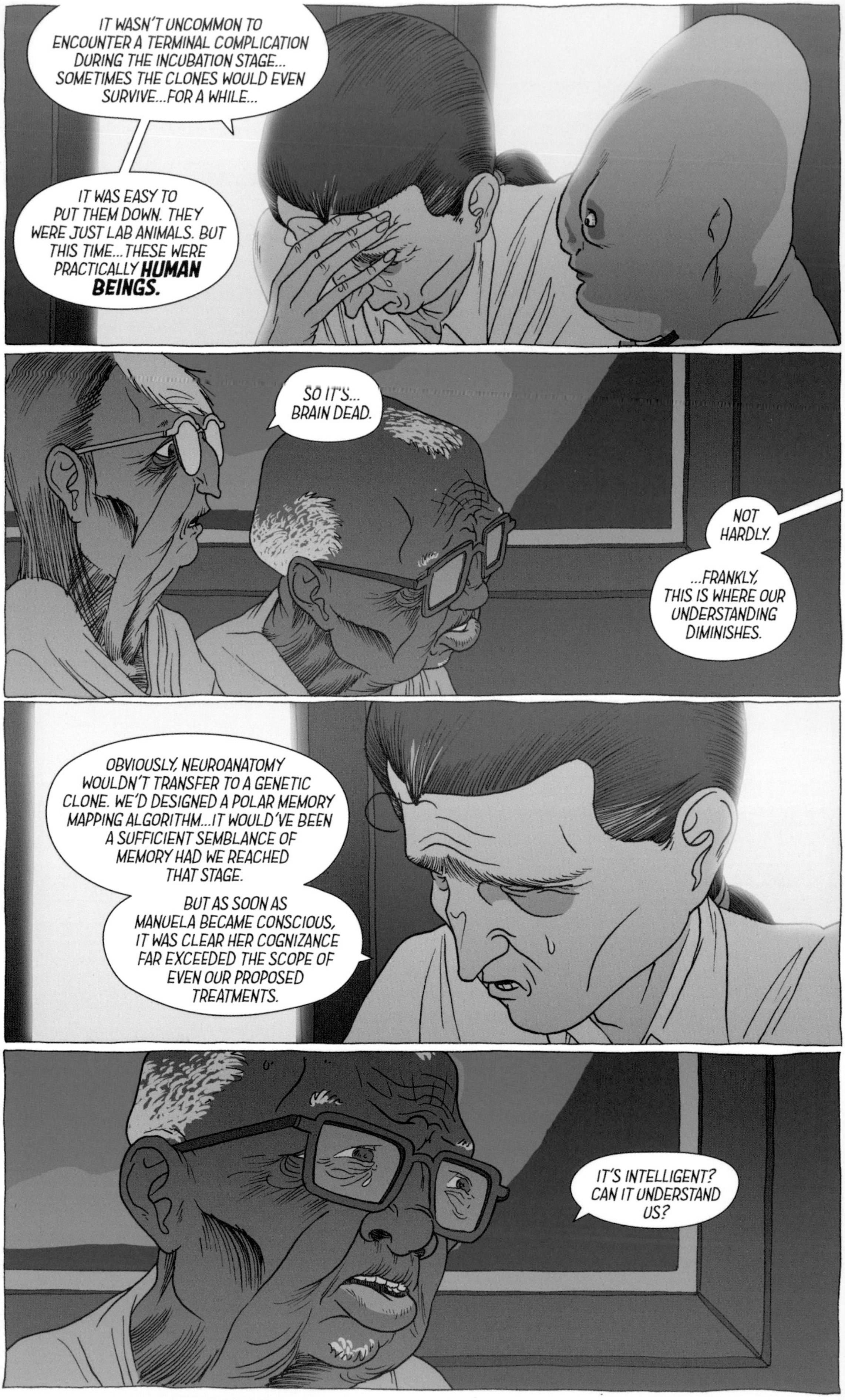
IT WASN'T UNCOMMON TO ENCOUNTER A TERMINAL COMPLICATION DURING THE INCUBATION STAGE... SOMETIMES THE CLONES WOULD EVEN SURVIVE...FOR A WHILE...
IT WAS EASY TO PUT THEM DOWN. THEY WERE JUST LAB ANIMALS. BUT THIS TIME...THESE WERE PRACTICALLY **HUMAN BEINGS.**
SO IT'S... BRAIN DEAD.
NOT HARDLY.
...FRANKLY, THIS IS WHERE OUR UNDERSTANDING DIMINISHES.
OBVIOUSLY, NEUROANATOMY WOULDN'T TRANSFER TO A GENETIC CLONE. WE'D DESIGNED A POLAR MEMORY MAPPING ALGORITHM...IT WOULD'VE BEEN A SUFFICIENT SEMBLANCE OF MEMORY HAD WE REACHED THAT STAGE.
BUT AS SOON AS MANUELA BECAME CONSCIOUS, IT WAS CLEAR HER COGNIZANCE FAR EXCEEDED THE SCOPE OF EVEN OUR PROPOSED TREATMENTS.
IT'S INTELLIGENT? CAN IT UNDERSTAND US?

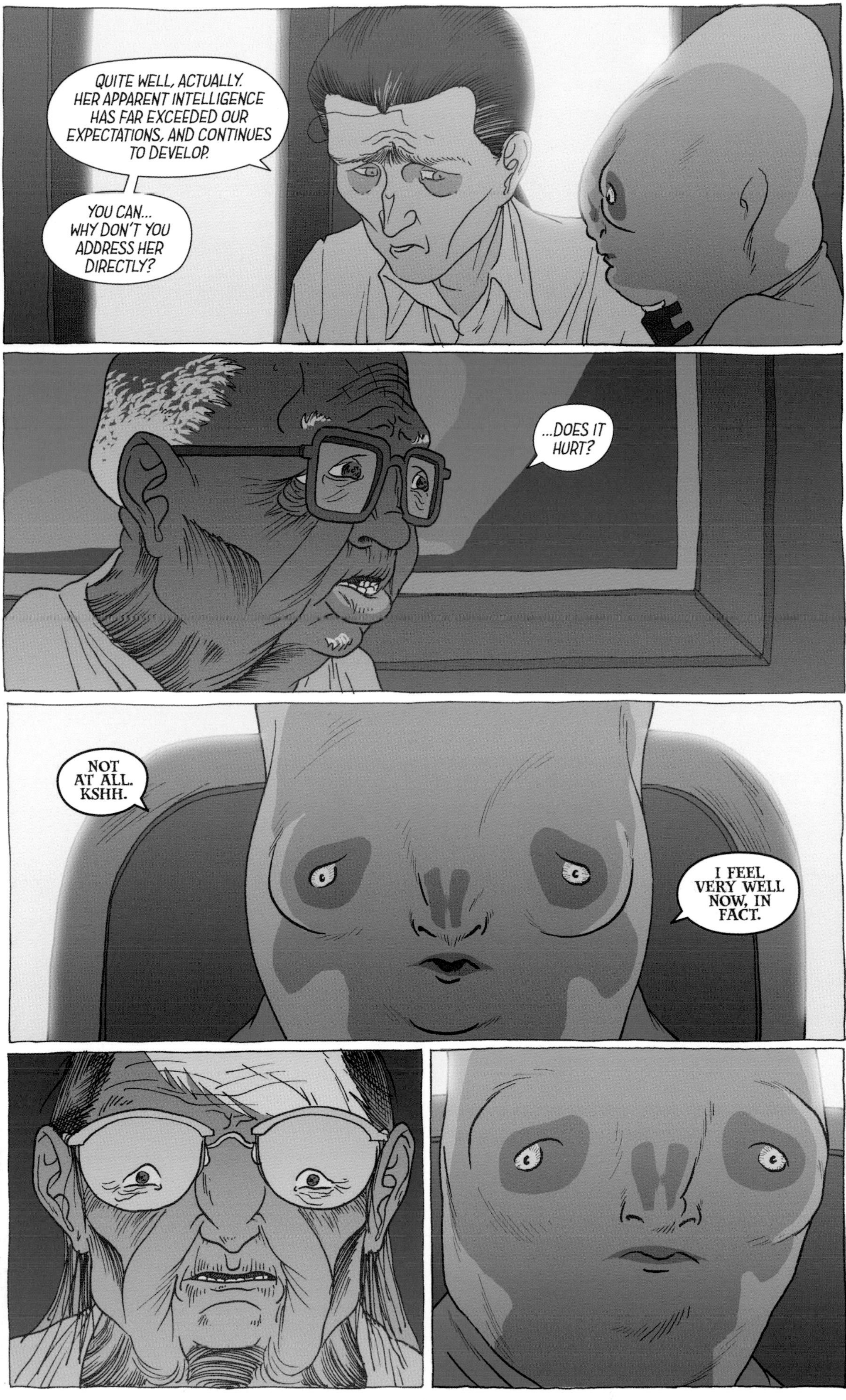
QUITE WELL, ACTUALLY. HER APPARENT INTELLIGENCE HAS FAR EXCEEDED OUR EXPECTATIONS, AND CONTINUES TO DEVELOP.
YOU CAN... WHY DON'T YOU ADDRESS HER DIRECTLY?
...DOES IT HURT?
NOT AT ALL. KSHH.
I FEEL VERY WELL NOW, IN FACT.

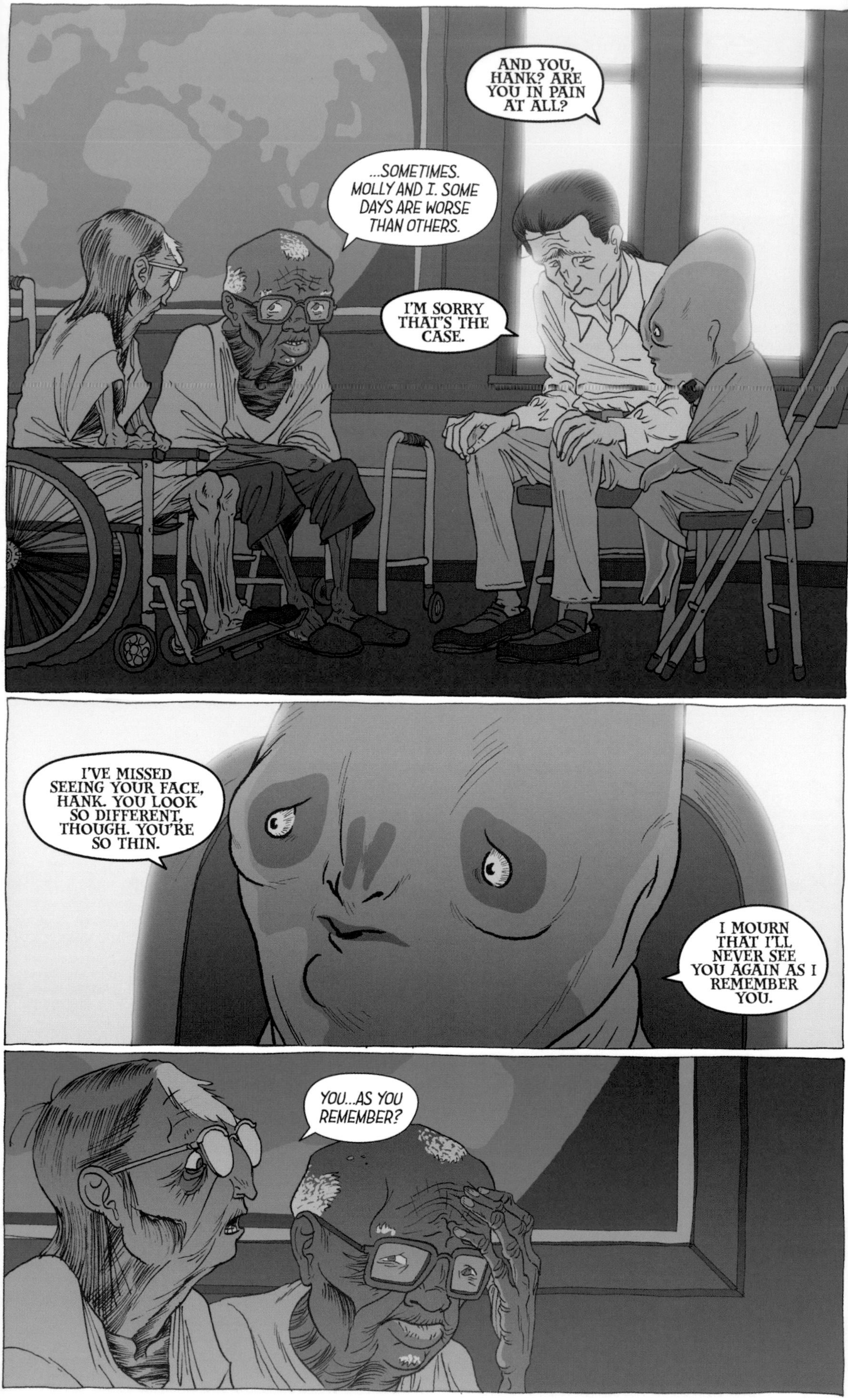
AND YOU, HANK? ARE YOU IN PAIN AT ALL?
...SOMETIMES. MOLLY AND I. SOME DAYS ARE WORSE THAN OTHERS.
I'M SORRY THAT'S THE CASE.
I'VE MISSED SEEING YOUR FACE, HANK. YOU LOOK SO DIFFERENT, THOUGH. YOU'RE SO THIN.
I MOURN THAT I'LL NEVER SEE YOU AGAIN AS I REMEMBER YOU.
YOU...AS YOU REMEMBER?

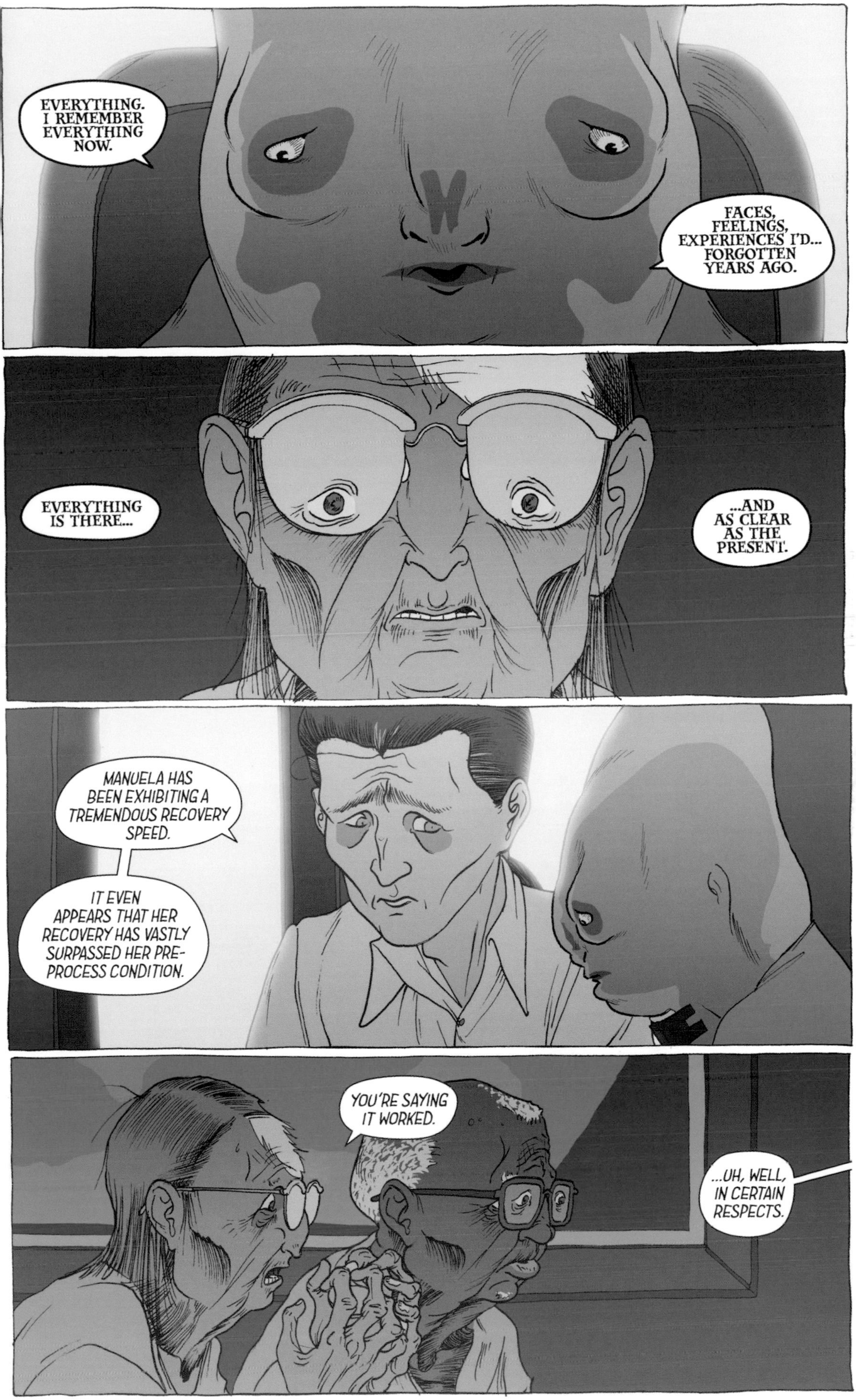
EVERYTHING. I REMEMBER EVERYTHING NOW.
FACES, FEELINGS, EXPERIENCES I'D... FORGOTTEN YEARS AGO.
EVERYTHING IS THERE...
...AND AS CLEAR AS THE PRESENT.
MANUELA HAS BEEN EXHIBITING A TREMENDOUS RECOVERY SPEED.
IT EVEN APPEARS THAT HER RECOVERY HAS VASTLY SURPASSED HER PRE-PROCESS CONDITION.
YOU'RE SAYING IT WORKED.
...UH, WELL, IN CERTAIN RESPECTS.

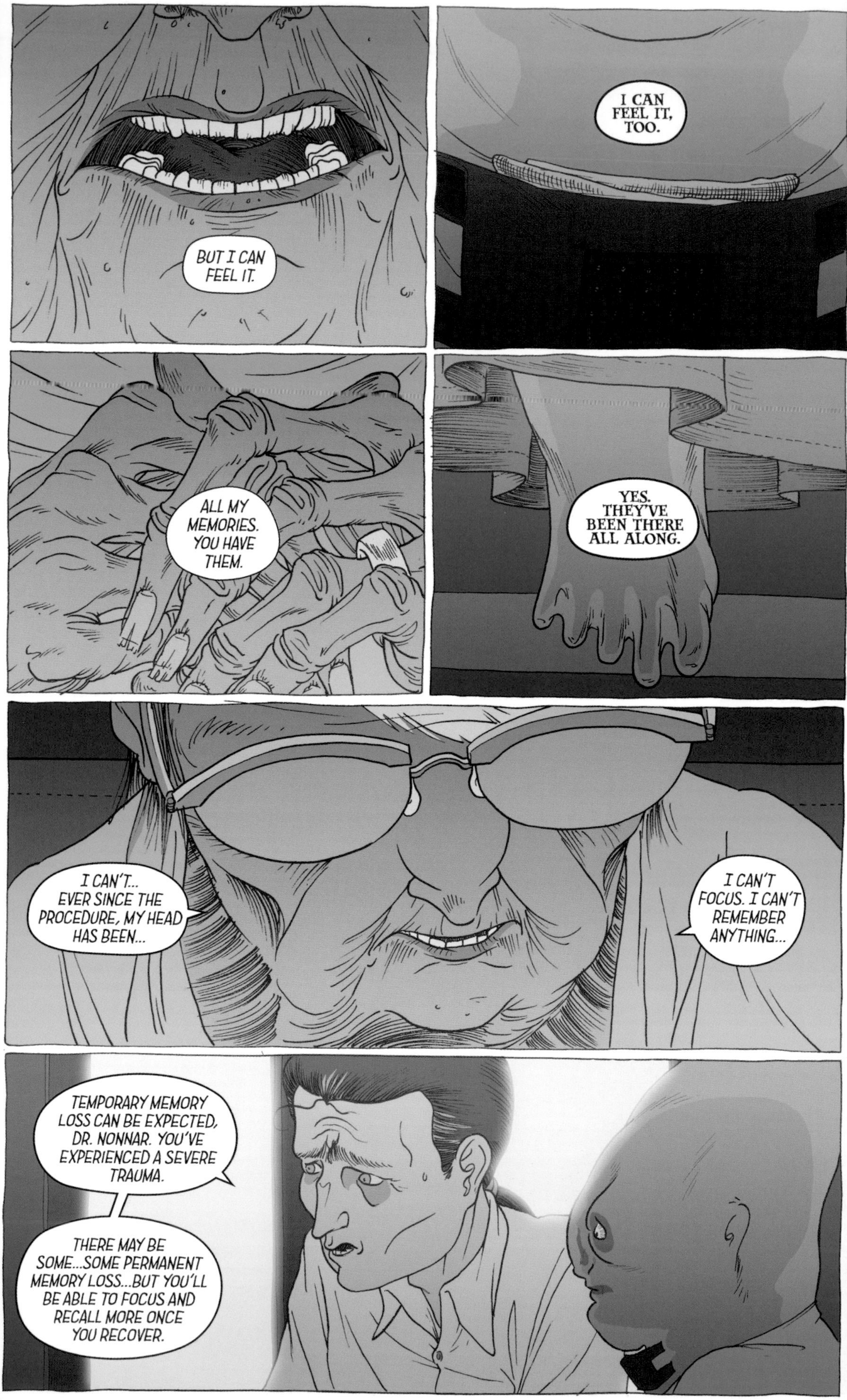
BUT I CAN FEEL IT.
I CAN FEEL IT, TOO.
ALL MY MEMORIES. YOU HAVE THEM.
YES. THEY'VE BEEN THERE ALL ALONG.
I CAN'T... EVER SINCE THE PROCEDURE, MY HEAD HAS BEEN...
I CAN'T FOCUS. I CAN'T REMEMBER ANYTHING...
TEMPORARY MEMORY LOSS CAN BE EXPECTED, DR. NONNAR. YOU'VE EXPERIENCED A SEVERE TRAUMA.
THERE MAY BE SOME...SOME PERMANENT MEMORY LOSS...BUT YOU'LL BE ABLE TO FOCUS AND RECALL MORE ONCE YOU RECOVER.

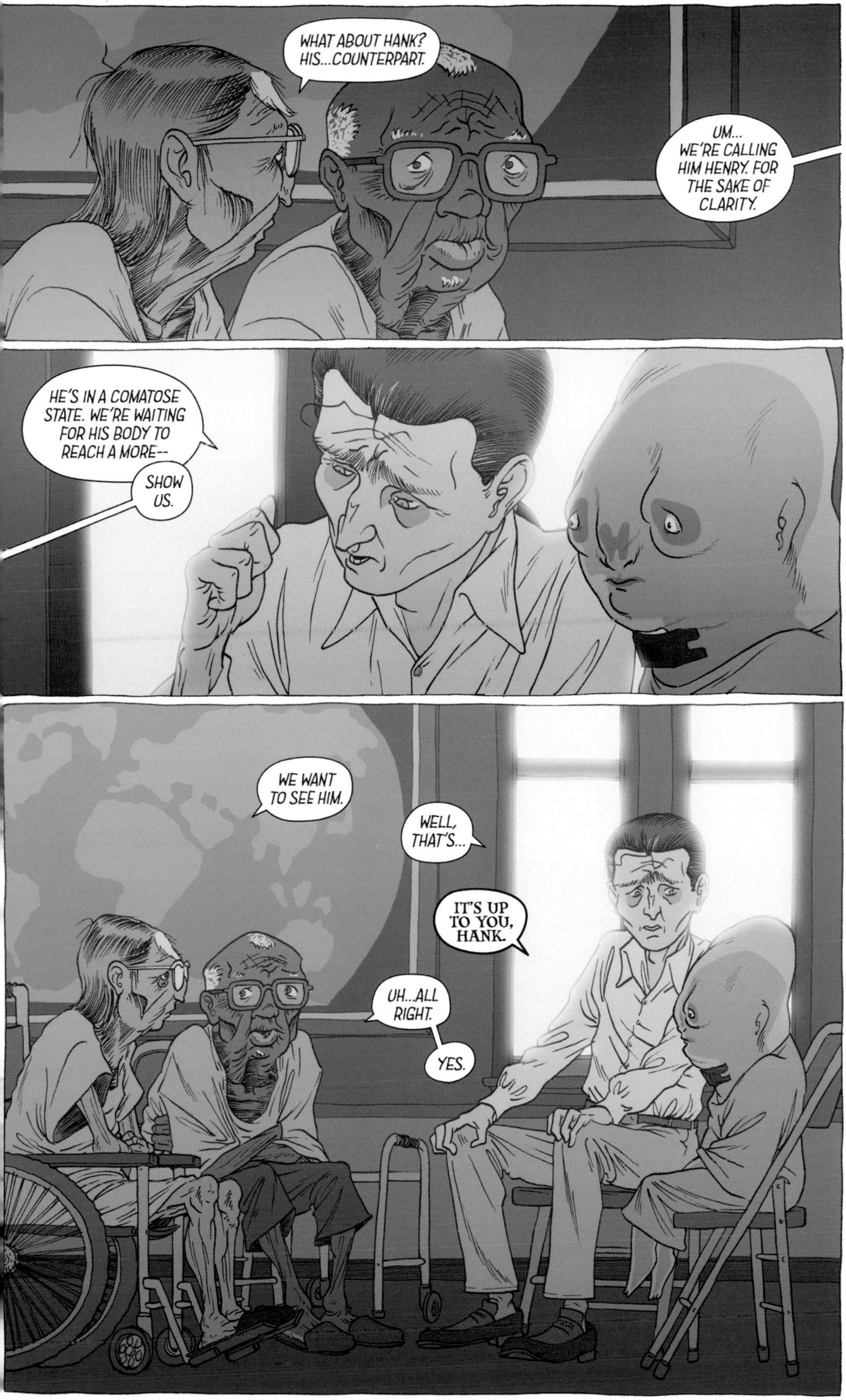
WHAT ABOUT HANK? HIS...COUNTERPART.
UM... WE'RE CALLING HIM HENRY. FOR THE SAKE OF CLARITY.
HE'S IN A COMATOSE STATE. WE'RE WAITING FOR HIS BODY TO REACH A MORE--
SHOW US.
WE WANT TO SEE HIM.
WELL, THAT'S...
IT'S UP TO YOU, HANK.
UH...ALL RIGHT.
YES.

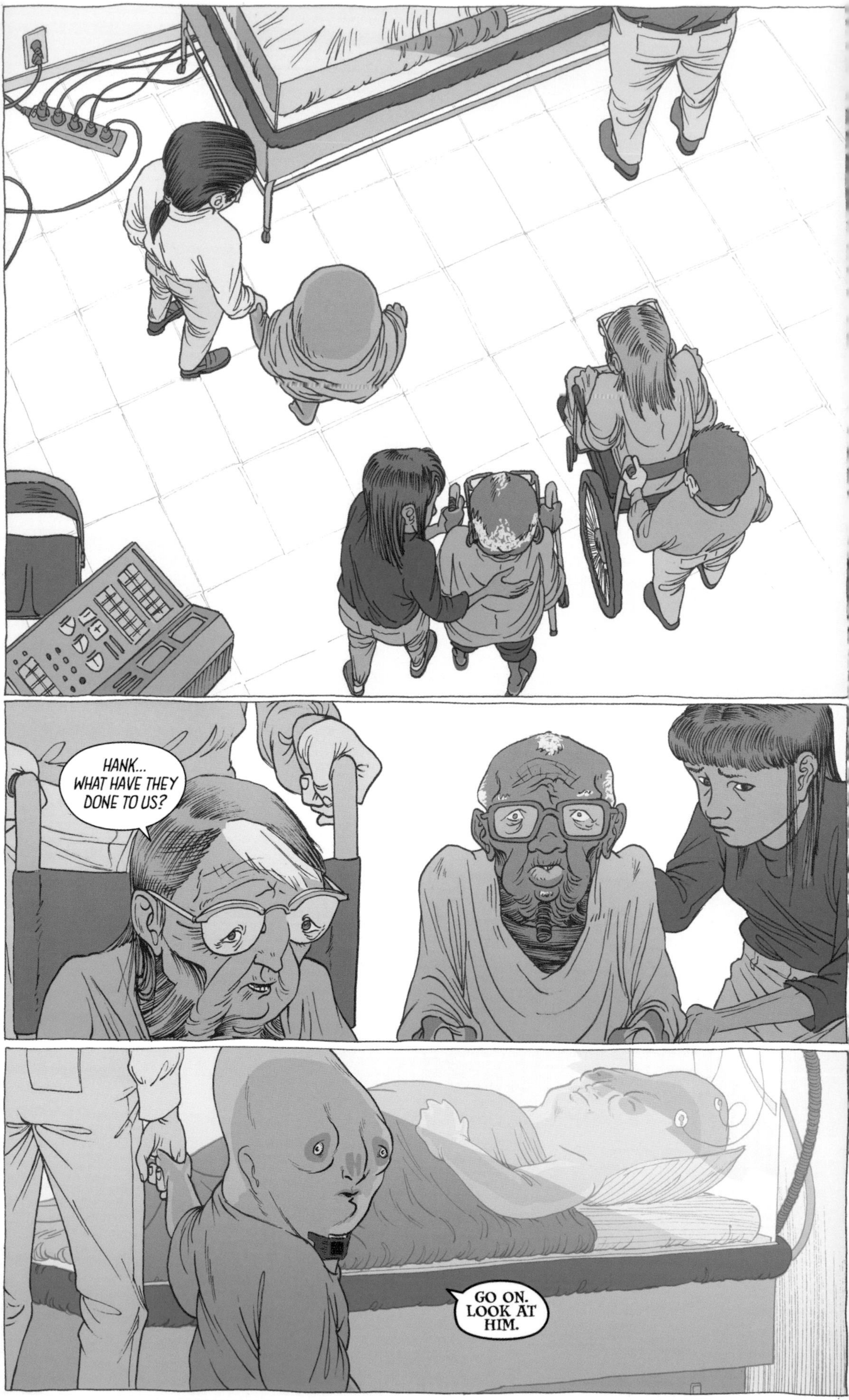
HANK... WHAT HAVE THEY DONE TO US?
GO ON. LOOK AT HIM.

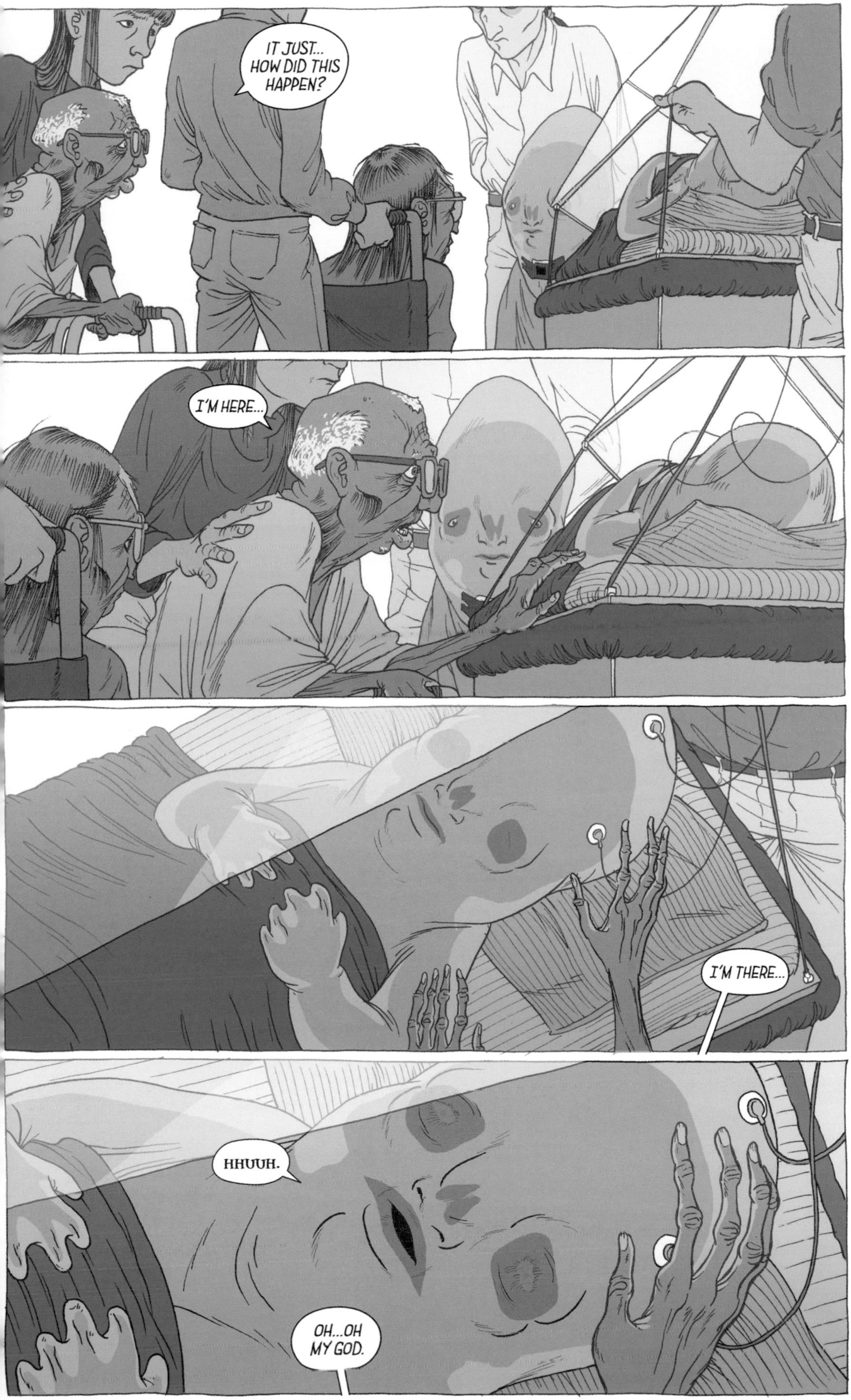
IT JUST... HOW DID THIS HAPPEN?
I'M HERE...
I'M THERE...
HHUUH.
OH...OH MY GOD.

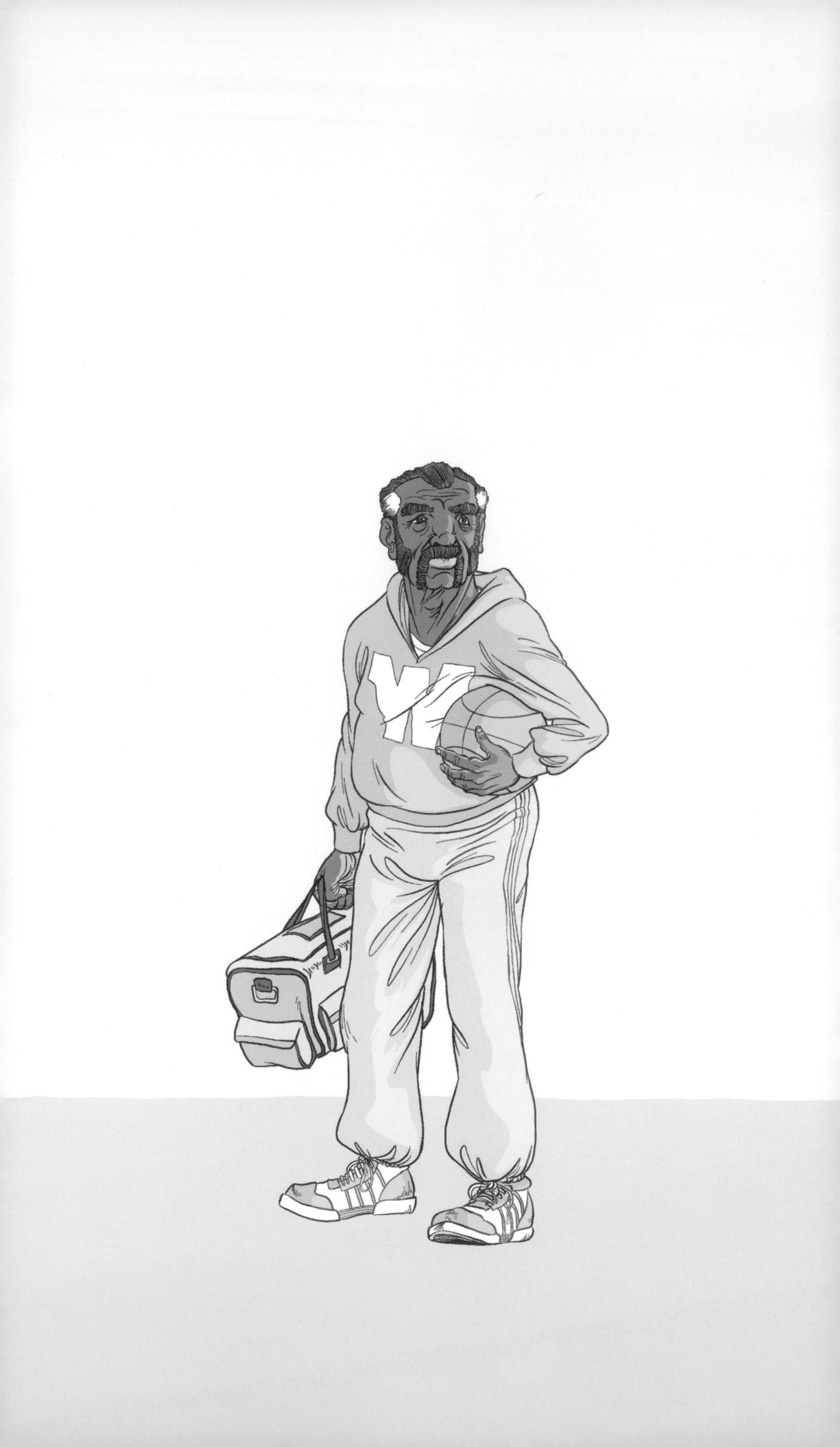

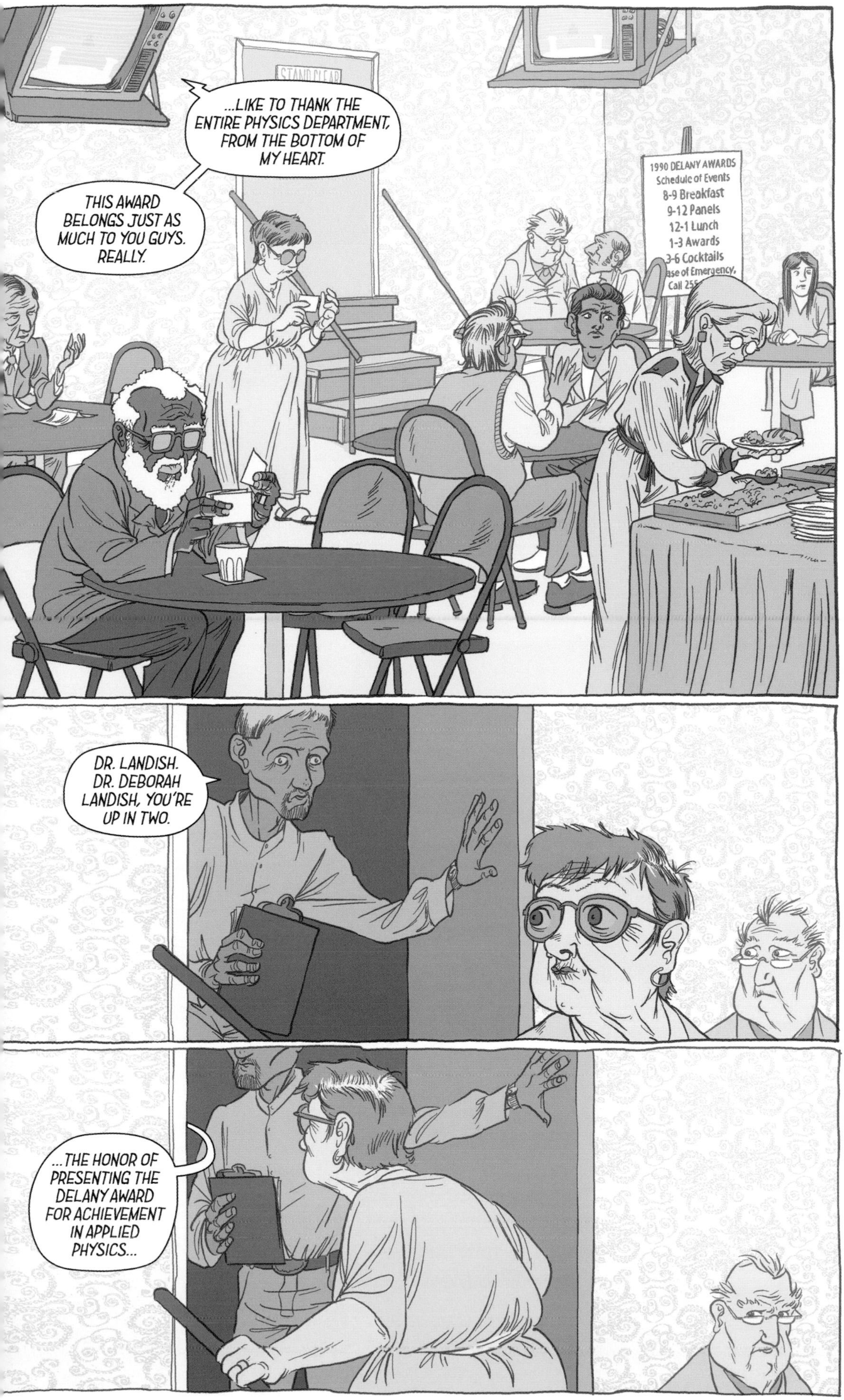
...LIKE TO THANK THE ENTIRE PHYSICS DEPARTMENT, FROM THE BOTTOM OF MY HEART.
THIS AWARD BELONGS JUST AS MUCH TO YOU GUYS. REALLY.
1990 DELANY AWARDS
Schedule of Events
8-9 Breakfast
9-12 Panels
12-1 Lunch
1-3 Awards
3-6 Cocktails
DR. LANDISH. DR. DEBORAH LANDISH, YOU'RE UP IN TWO.
...THE HONOR OF PRESENTING THE DELANY AWARD FOR ACHIEVEMENT IN APPLIED PHYSICS...

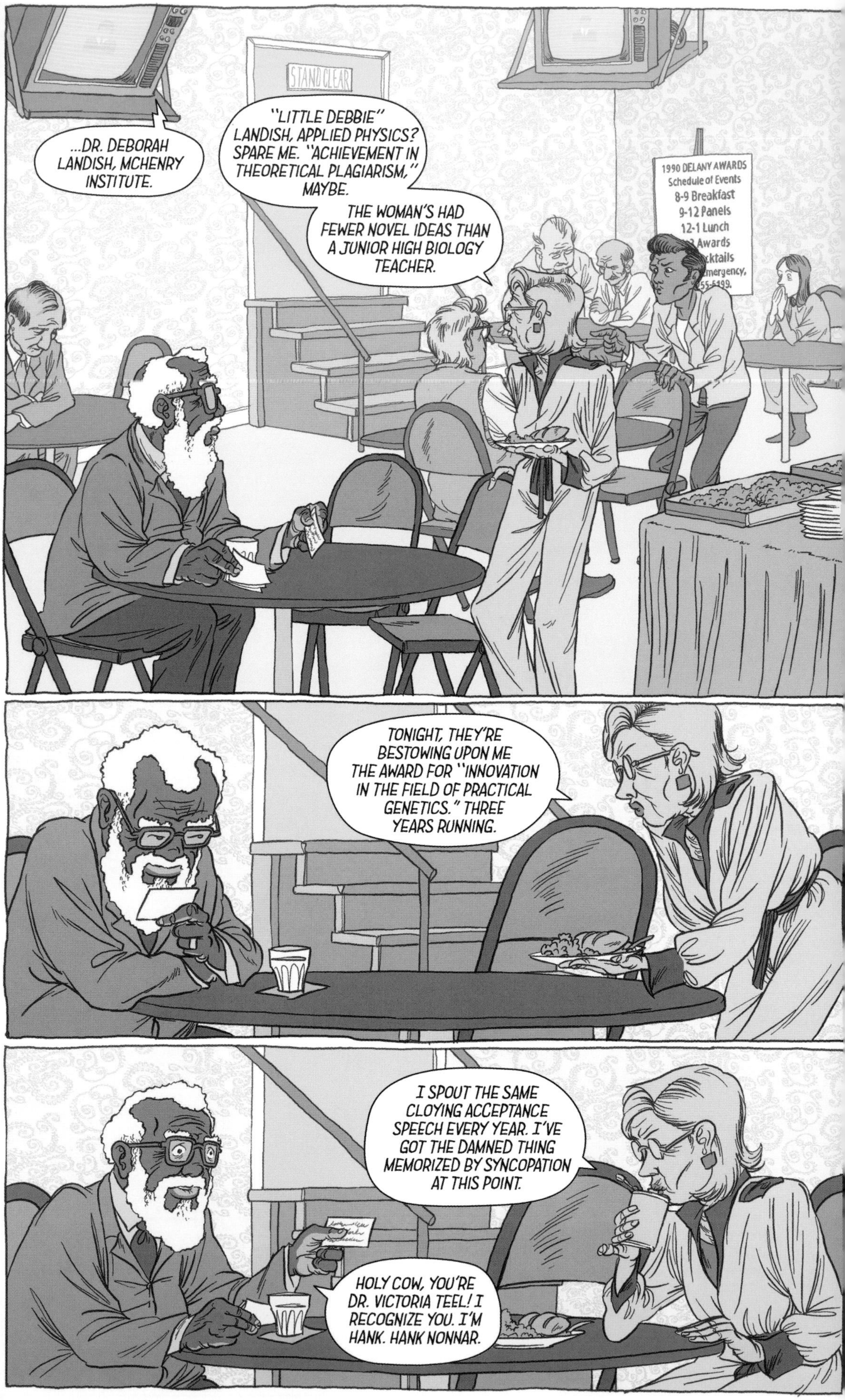
STAND CLEAR
...DR. DEBORAH LANDISH, MCHENRY INSTITUTE.
"LITTLE DEBBIE" LANDISH, APPLIED PHYSICS? SPARE ME. "ACHIEVEMENT IN THEORETICAL PLAGIARISM," MAYBE.
THE WOMAN'S HAD FEWER NOVEL IDEAS THAN A JUNIOR HIGH BIOLOGY TEACHER.
1990 DELANY AWARDS
Schedule of Events
8-9 Breakfast
9-12 Panels
12-1 Lunch
TONIGHT, THEY'RE BESTOWING UPON ME THE AWARD FOR "INNOVATION IN THE FIELD OF PRACTICAL GENETICS." THREE YEARS RUNNING.
I SPOUT THE SAME CLOYING ACCEPTANCE SPEECH EVERY YEAR. I'VE GOT THE DAMNED THING MEMORIZED BY SYNCOPATION AT THIS POINT.
HOLY COW, YOU'RE DR. VICTORIA TEEL! I RECOGNIZE YOU. I'M HANK. HANK NONNAR.

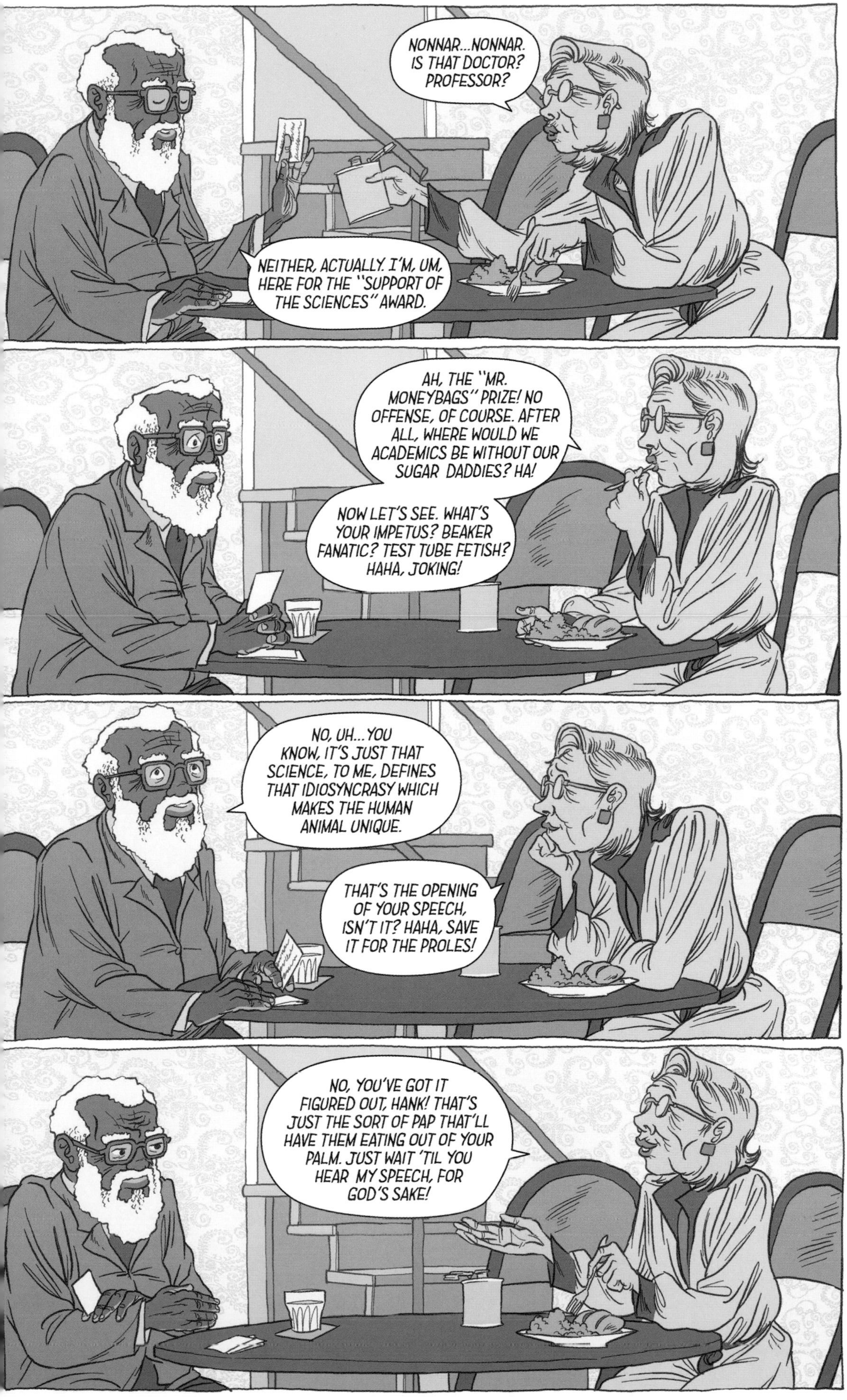

NONNAR...NONNAR. IS THAT DOCTOR? PROFESSOR?
NEITHER, ACTUALLY. I'M, UM, HERE FOR THE "SUPPORT OF THE SCIENCES" AWARD.
AH, THE "MR. MONEYBAGS" PRIZE! NO OFFENSE, OF COURSE. AFTER ALL, WHERE WOULD WE ACADEMICS BE WITHOUT OUR SUGAR DADDIES? HA!
NOW LET'S SEE. WHAT'S YOUR IMPETUS? BEAKER FANATIC? TEST TUBE FETISH? HAHA, JOKING!
NO, UH...YOU KNOW, IT'S JUST THAT SCIENCE, TO ME, DEFINES THAT IDIOSYNCRASY WHICH MAKES THE HUMAN ANIMAL UNIQUE.
THAT'S THE OPENING OF YOUR SPEECH, ISN'T IT? HAHA, SAVE IT FOR THE PROLES!
NO, YOU'VE GOT IT FIGURED OUT, HANK! THAT'S JUST THE SORT OF PAP THAT'LL HAVE THEM EATING OUT OF YOUR PALM. JUST WAIT 'TIL YOU HEAR MY SPEECH, FOR GOD'S SAKE!

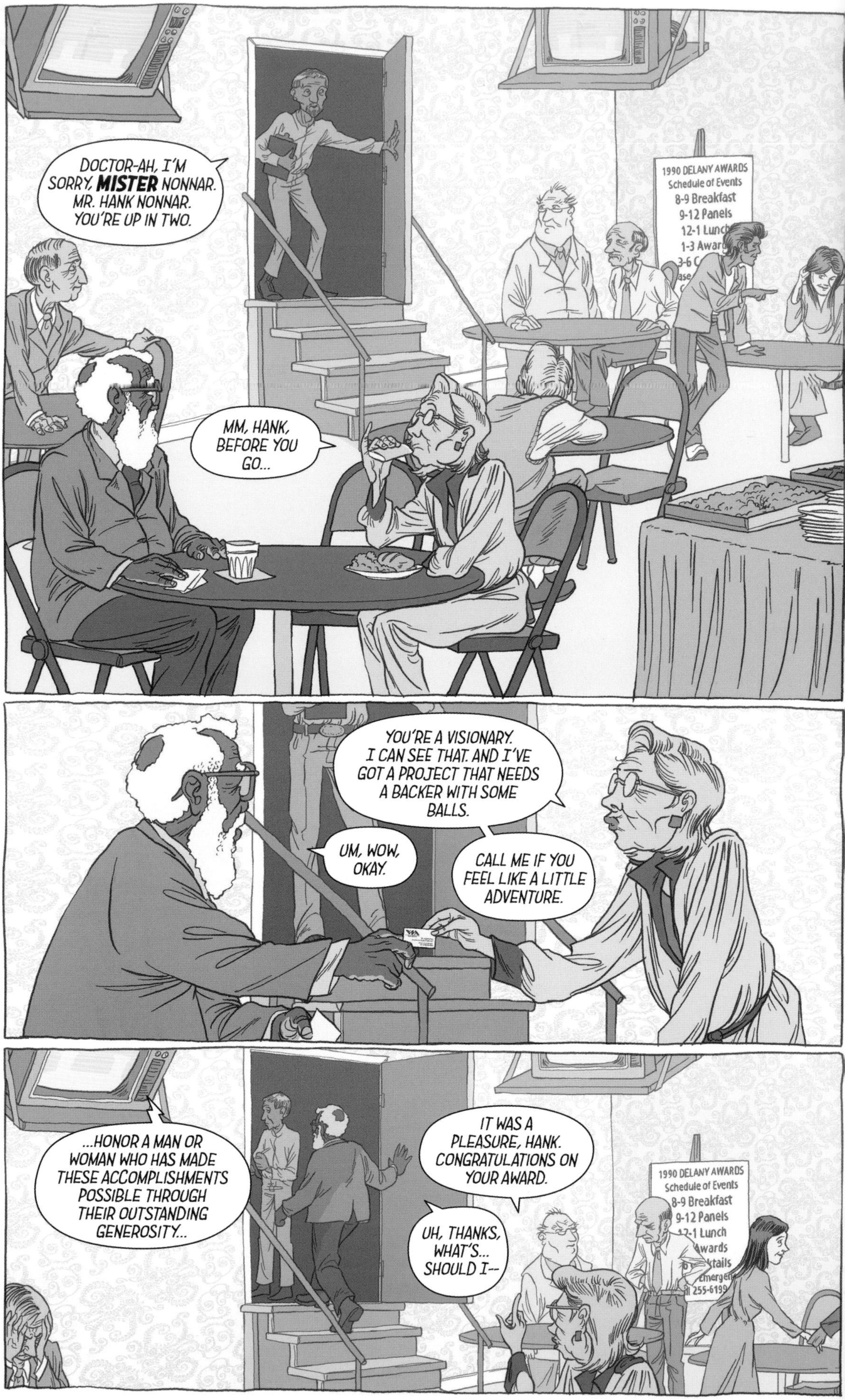
DOCTOR-AH, I'M SORRY, **MISTER** NONNAR. MR. HANK NONNAR. YOU'RE UP IN TWO.
1990 DELANY AWARDS
Schedule of Events
8-9 Breakfast
9-12 Panels
MM, HANK, BEFORE YOU GO...
YOU'RE A VISIONARY. I CAN SEE THAT. AND I'VE GOT A PROJECT THAT NEEDS A BACKER WITH SOME BALLS.
UM, WOW, OKAY.
CALL ME IF YOU FEEL LIKE A LITTLE ADVENTURE.
...HONOR A MAN OR WOMAN WHO HAS MADE THESE ACCOMPLISHMENTS POSSIBLE THROUGH THEIR OUTSTANDING GENEROSITY...
IT WAS A PLEASURE, HANK. CONGRATULATIONS ON YOUR AWARD.
UH, THANKS, WHAT'S... SHOULD I--
1990 DELANY AWARDS
Schedule of Events
8-9 Breakfast
9-12 Panels

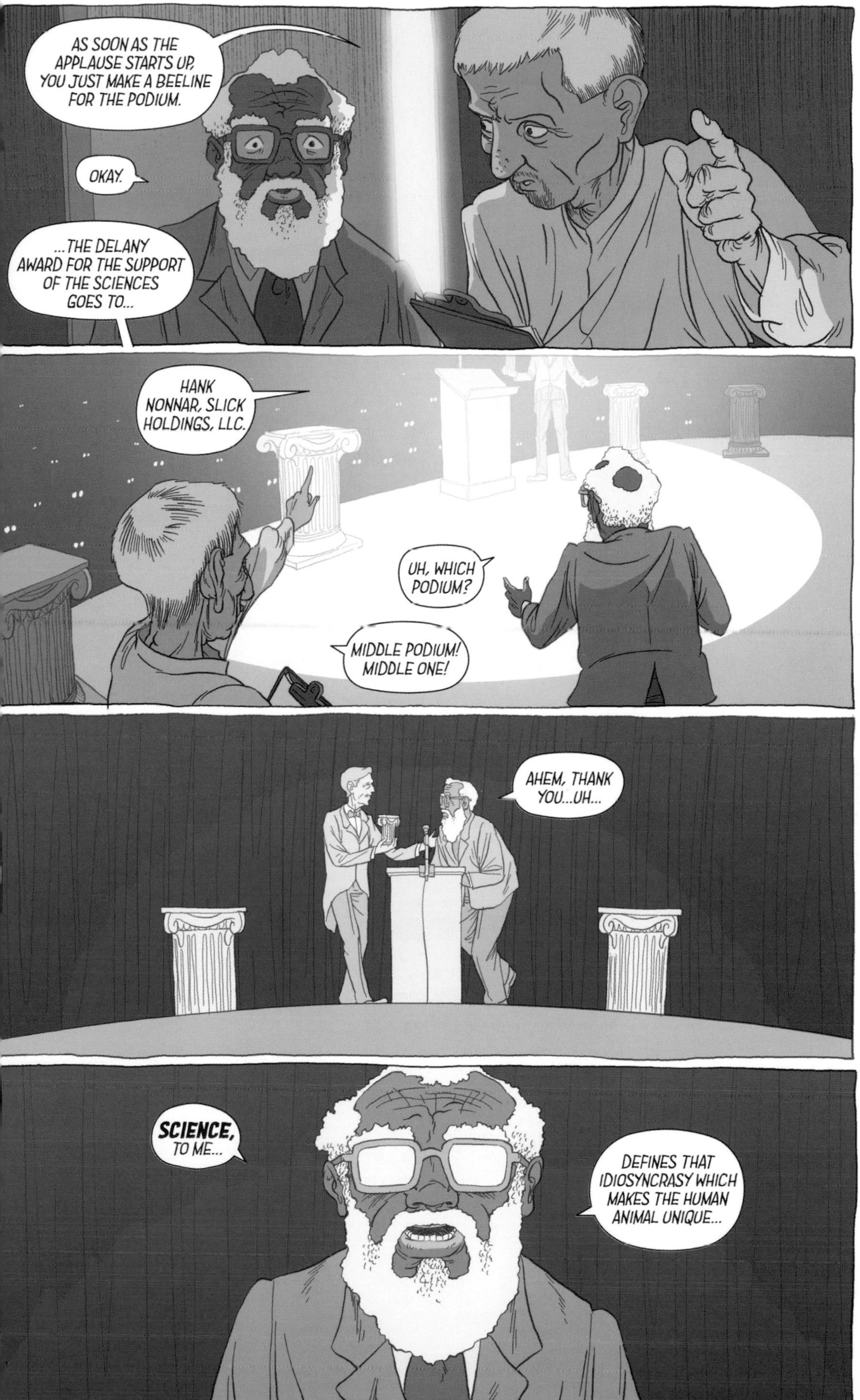
AS SOON AS THE APPLAUSE STARTS UP, YOU JUST MAKE A BEELINE FOR THE PODIUM.
OKAY.
...THE DELANY AWARD FOR THE SUPPORT OF THE SCIENCES GOES TO...
HANK NONNAR, SLICK HOLDINGS, LLC.
UH, WHICH PODIUM?
MIDDLE PODIUM! MIDDLE ONE!
AHEM, THANK YOU...UH...
SCIENCE, TO ME...
DEFINES THAT IDIOSYNCRASY WHICH MAKES THE HUMAN ANIMAL UNIQUE...

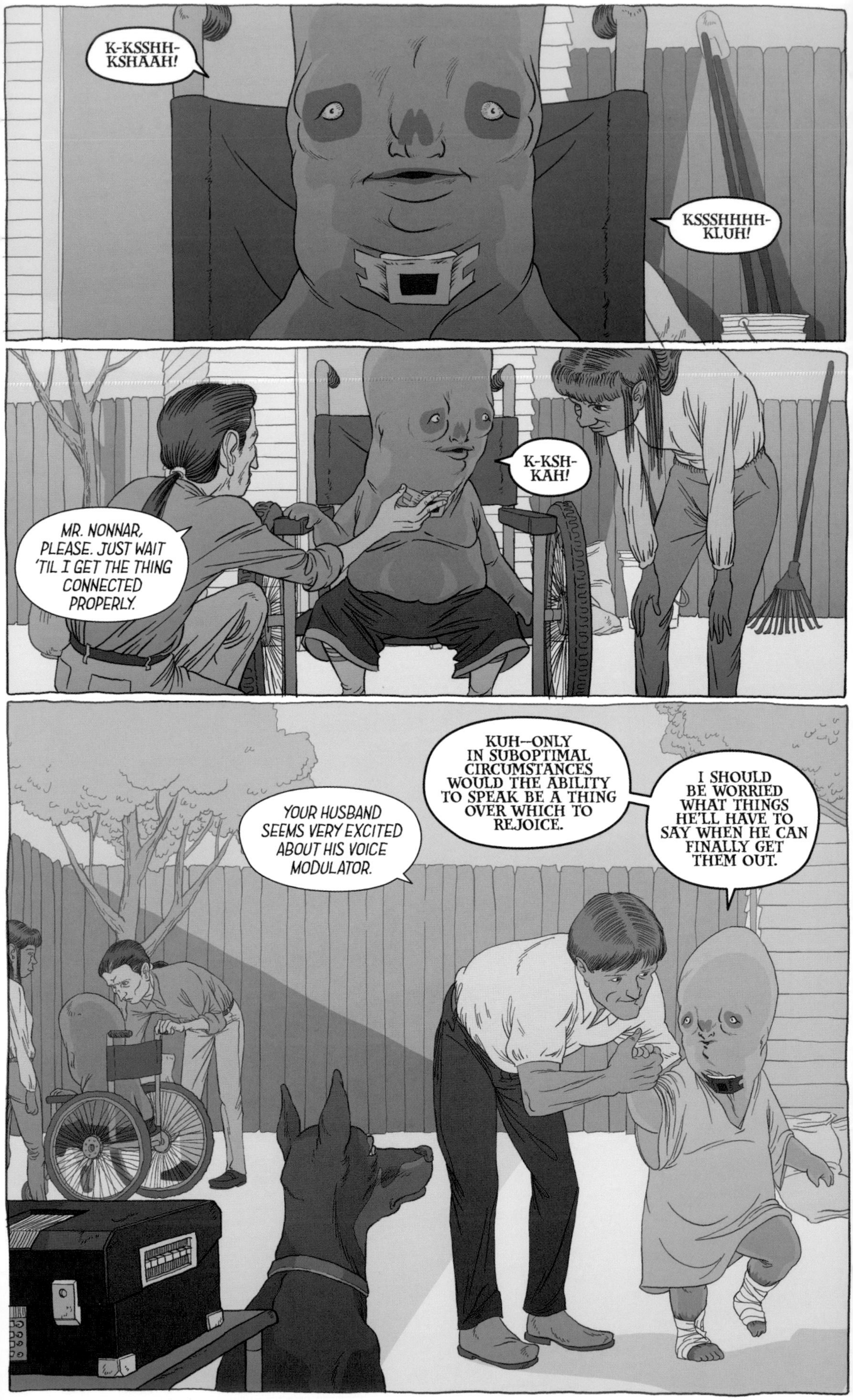
K-KSSHH-KSHAAH!
KSSSHHHH-KLUH!
K-KSH-KAH!
MR. NONNAR, PLEASE. JUST WAIT 'TIL I GET THE THING CONNECTED PROPERLY.
YOUR HUSBAND SEEMS VERY EXCITED ABOUT HIS VOICE MODULATOR.
KUH--ONLY IN SUBOPTIMAL CIRCUMSTANCES WOULD THE ABILITY TO SPEAK BE A THING OVER WHICH TO REJOICE.
I SHOULD BE WORRIED WHAT THINGS HE'LL HAVE TO SAY WHEN HE CAN FINALLY GET THEM OUT.

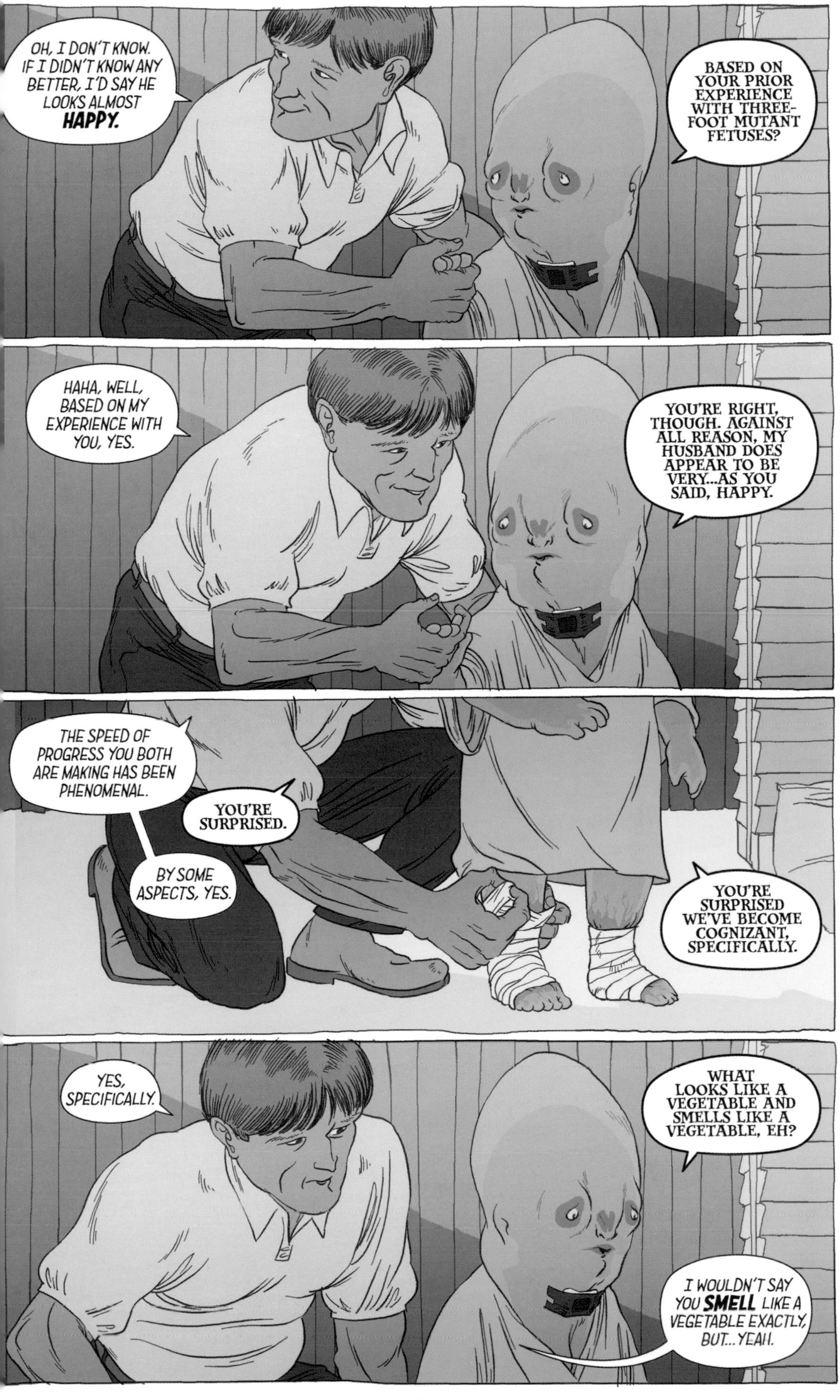
OH, I DON'T KNOW. IF I DIDN'T KNOW ANY BETTER, I'D SAY HE LOOKS ALMOST **HAPPY.**
BASED ON YOUR PRIOR EXPERIENCE WITH THREE-FOOT MUTANT FETUSES?
HAHA, WELL, BASED ON MY EXPERIENCE WITH YOU, YES.
YOU'RE RIGHT, THOUGH. AGAINST ALL REASON, MY HUSBAND DOES APPEAR TO BE VERY...AS YOU SAID, HAPPY.
THE SPEED OF PROGRESS YOU BOTH ARE MAKING HAS BEEN PHENOMENAL.
YOU'RE SURPRISED.
BY SOME ASPECTS, YES.
YOU'RE SURPRISED WE'VE BECOME COGNIZANT, SPECIFICALLY.
YES, SPECIFICALLY.
WHAT LOOKS LIKE A VEGETABLE AND SMELLS LIKE A VEGETABLE, EH?
I WOULDN'T SAY YOU **SMELL** LIKE A VEGETABLE EXACTLY, BUT...YEAH.

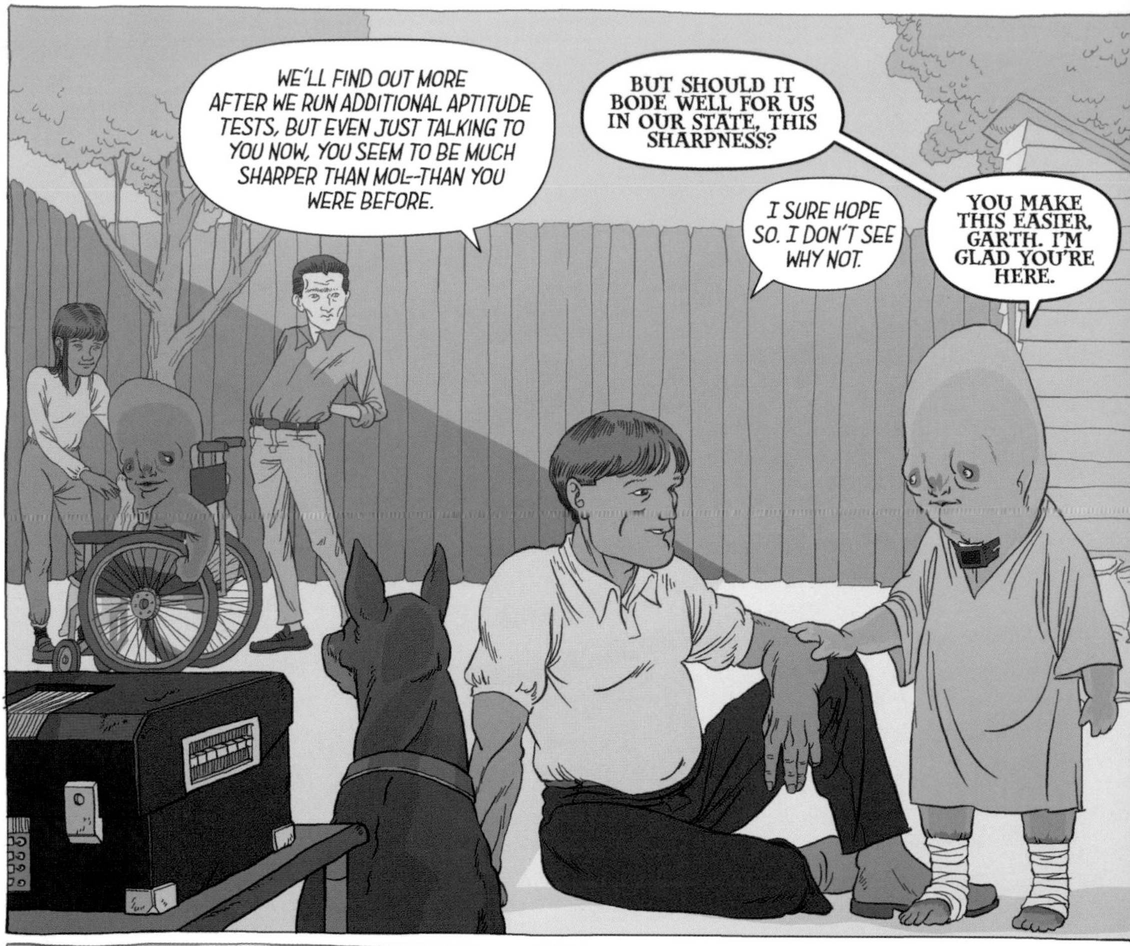
WE'LL FIND OUT MORE AFTER WE RUN ADDITIONAL APTITUDE TESTS, BUT EVEN JUST TALKING TO YOU NOW, YOU SEEM TO BE MUCH SHARPER THAN MOL--THAN YOU WERE BEFORE.
BUT SHOULD IT BODE WELL FOR US IN OUR STATE, THIS SHARPNESS?
I SURE HOPE SO. I DON'T SEE WHY NOT.
YOU MAKE THIS EASIER, GARTH. I'M GLAD YOU'RE HERE.

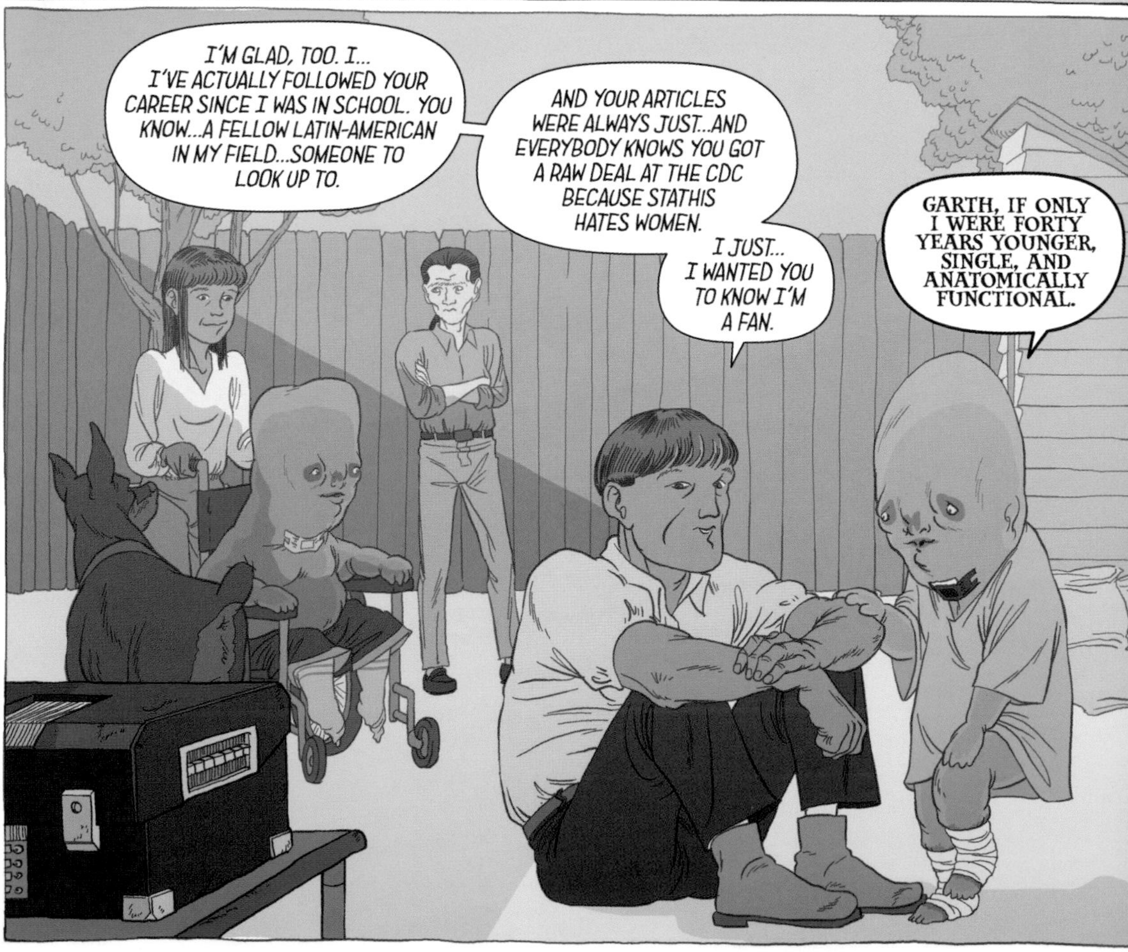
I'M GLAD, TOO. I... I'VE ACTUALLY FOLLOWED YOUR CAREER SINCE I WAS IN SCHOOL. YOU KNOW...A FELLOW LATIN-AMERICAN IN MY FIELD...SOMEONE TO LOOK UP TO.
AND YOUR ARTICLES WERE ALWAYS JUST...AND EVERYBODY KNOWS YOU GOT A RAW DEAL AT THE CDC BECAUSE STATHIS HATES WOMEN.
I JUST... I WANTED YOU TO KNOW I'M A FAN.
GARTH, IF ONLY I WERE FORTY YEARS YOUNGER, SINGLE, AND ANATOMICALLY FUNCTIONAL.

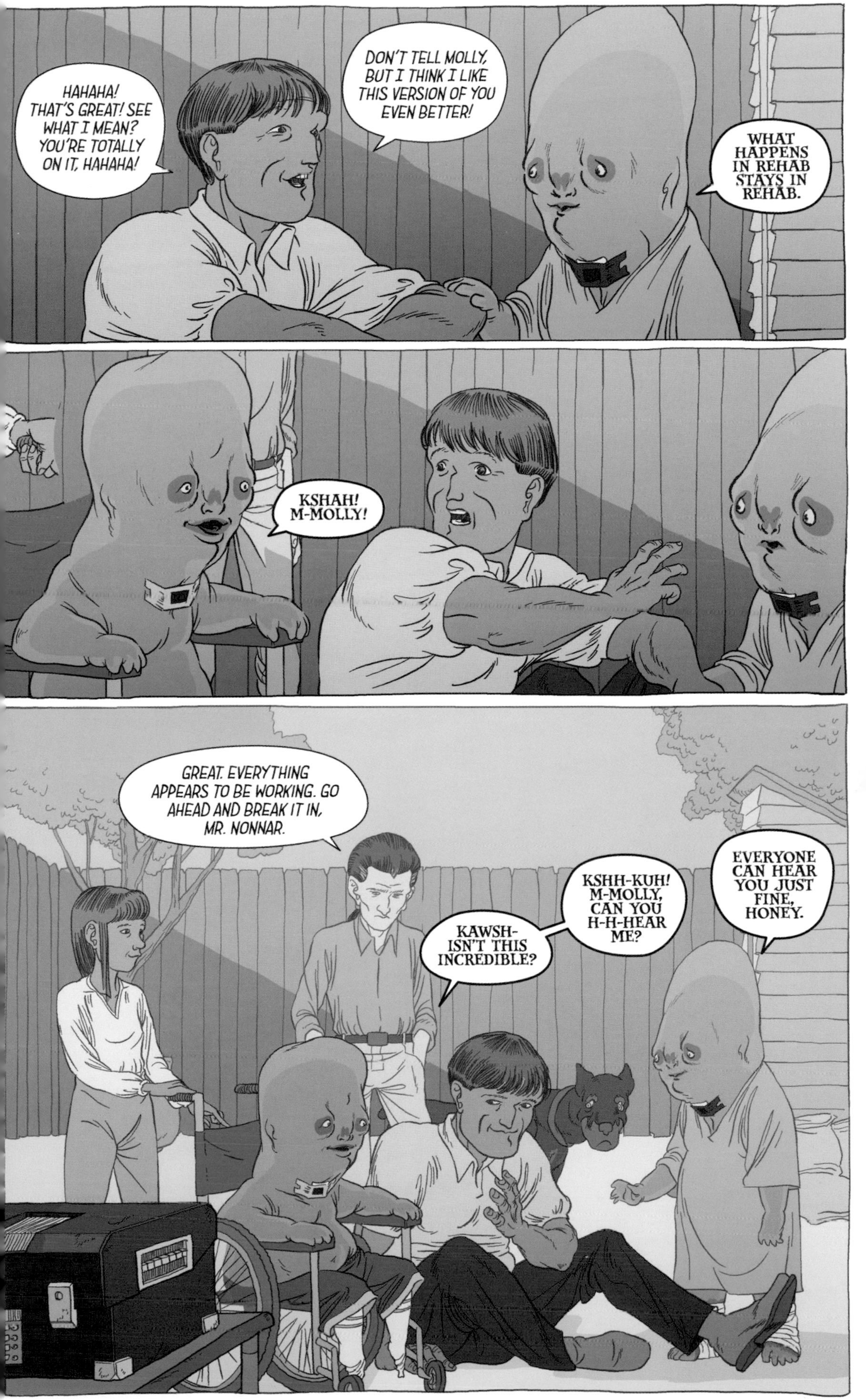
HAHAHA! THAT'S GREAT! SEE WHAT I MEAN? YOU'RE TOTALLY ON IT, HAHAHA!
DON'T TELL MOLLY, BUT I THINK I LIKE THIS VERSION OF YOU EVEN BETTER!
WHAT HAPPENS IN REHAB STAYS IN REHAB.
KSHAH! M-MOLLY!
GREAT. EVERYTHING APPEARS TO BE WORKING. GO AHEAD AND BREAK IT IN, MR. NONNAR.
KAWSH-ISN'T THIS INCREDIBLE?
KSHH-KUH! M-MOLLY, CAN YOU H-H-HEAR ME?
EVERYONE CAN HEAR YOU JUST FINE, HONEY.

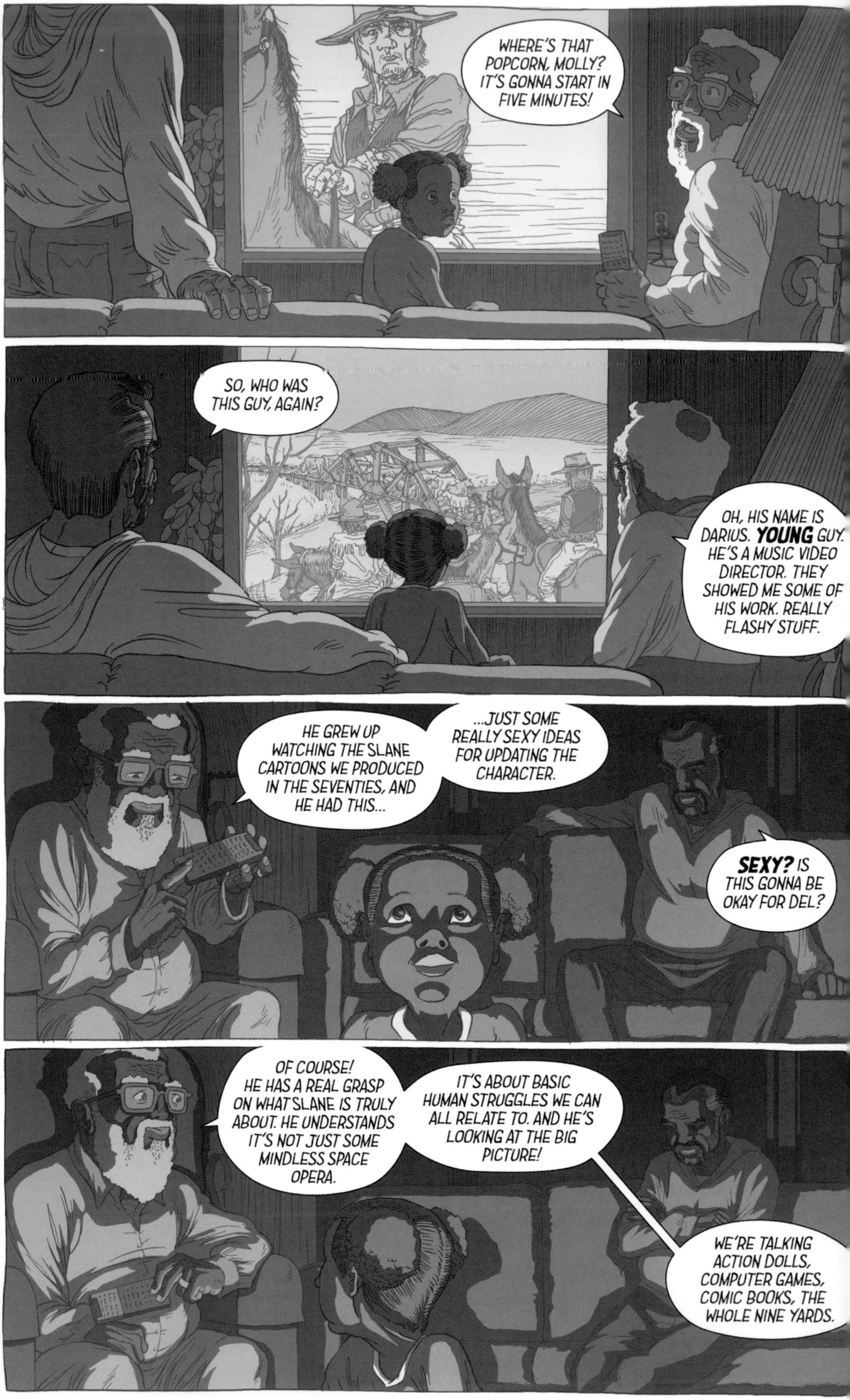
WHERE'S THAT POPCORN, MOLLY? IT'S GONNA START IN FIVE MINUTES!
SO, WHO WAS THIS GUY, AGAIN?
OH, HIS NAME IS DARIUS. YOUNG GUY. HE'S A MUSIC VIDEO DIRECTOR. THEY SHOWED ME SOME OF HIS WORK. REALLY FLASHY STUFF.
HE GREW UP WATCHING THE SLANE CARTOONS WE PRODUCED IN THE SEVENTIES, AND HE HAD THIS...
...JUST SOME REALLY SEXY IDEAS FOR UPDATING THE CHARACTER.
SEXY? IS THIS GONNA BE OKAY FOR DEL?
OF COURSE! HE HAS A REAL GRASP ON WHAT SLANE IS TRULY ABOUT. HE UNDERSTANDS IT'S NOT JUST SOME MINDLESS SPACE OPERA.
IT'S ABOUT BASIC HUMAN STRUGGLES WE CAN ALL RELATE TO. AND HE'S LOOKING AT THE BIG PICTURE!
WE'RE TALKING ACTION DOLLS, COMPUTER GAMES, COMIC BOOKS, THE WHOLE NINE YARDS.

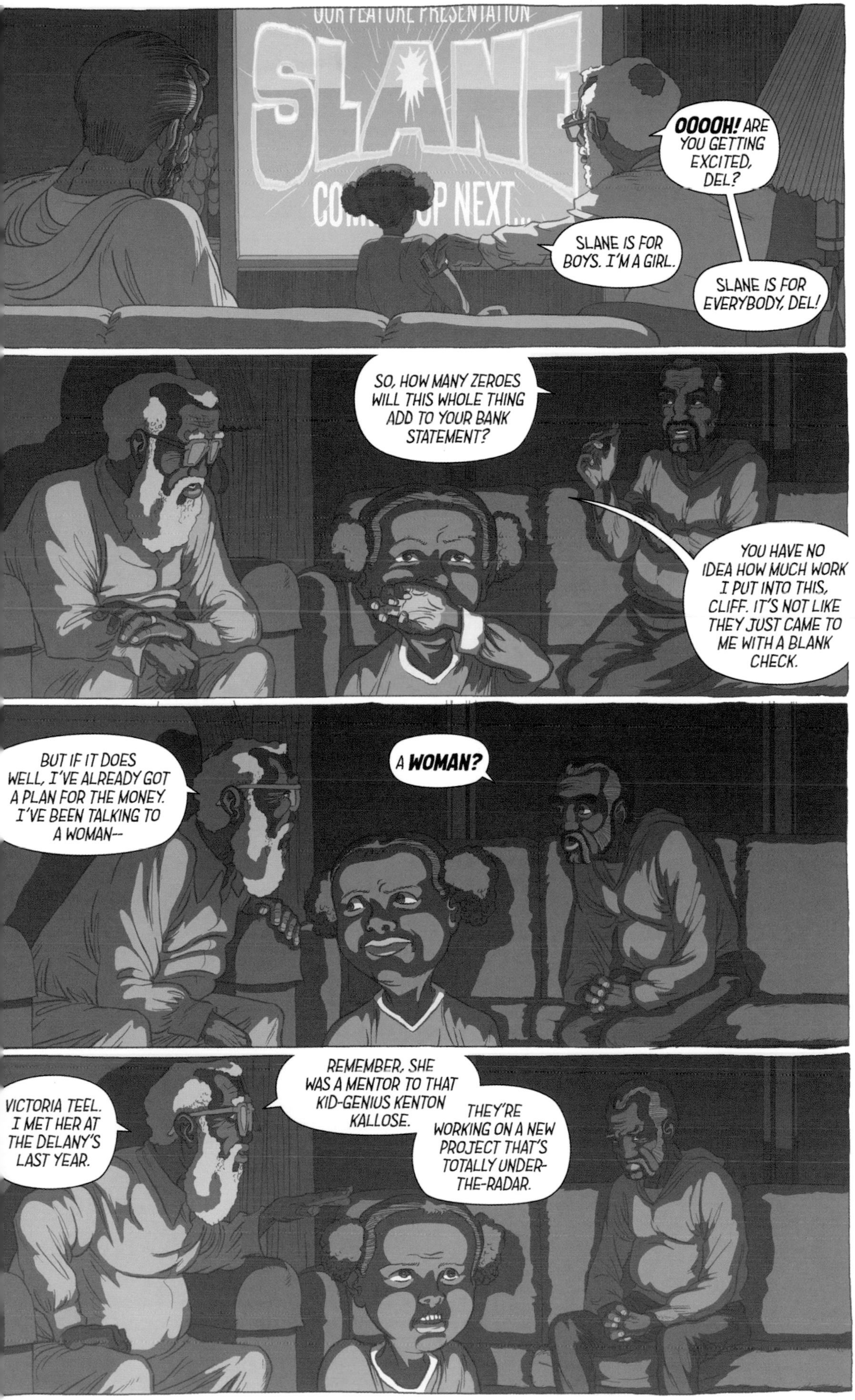
OUR FEATURE PRESENTATION
SLANE
COMING UP NEXT...
OOOOH! ARE YOU GETTING EXCITED, DEL?
SLANE IS FOR BOYS. I'M A GIRL.
SLANE IS FOR EVERYBODY, DEL!
SO, HOW MANY ZEROES WILL THIS WHOLE THING ADD TO YOUR BANK STATEMENT?
YOU HAVE NO IDEA HOW MUCH WORK I PUT INTO THIS, CLIFF. IT'S NOT LIKE THEY JUST CAME TO ME WITH A BLANK CHECK.
BUT IF IT DOES WELL, I'VE ALREADY GOT A PLAN FOR THE MONEY. I'VE BEEN TALKING TO A WOMAN--
A WOMAN?
VICTORIA TEEL. I MET HER AT THE DELANY'S LAST YEAR.
REMEMBER, SHE WAS A MENTOR TO THAT KID-GENIUS KENTON KALLOSE.
THEY'RE WORKING ON A NEW PROJECT THAT'S TOTALLY UNDER-THE-RADAR.

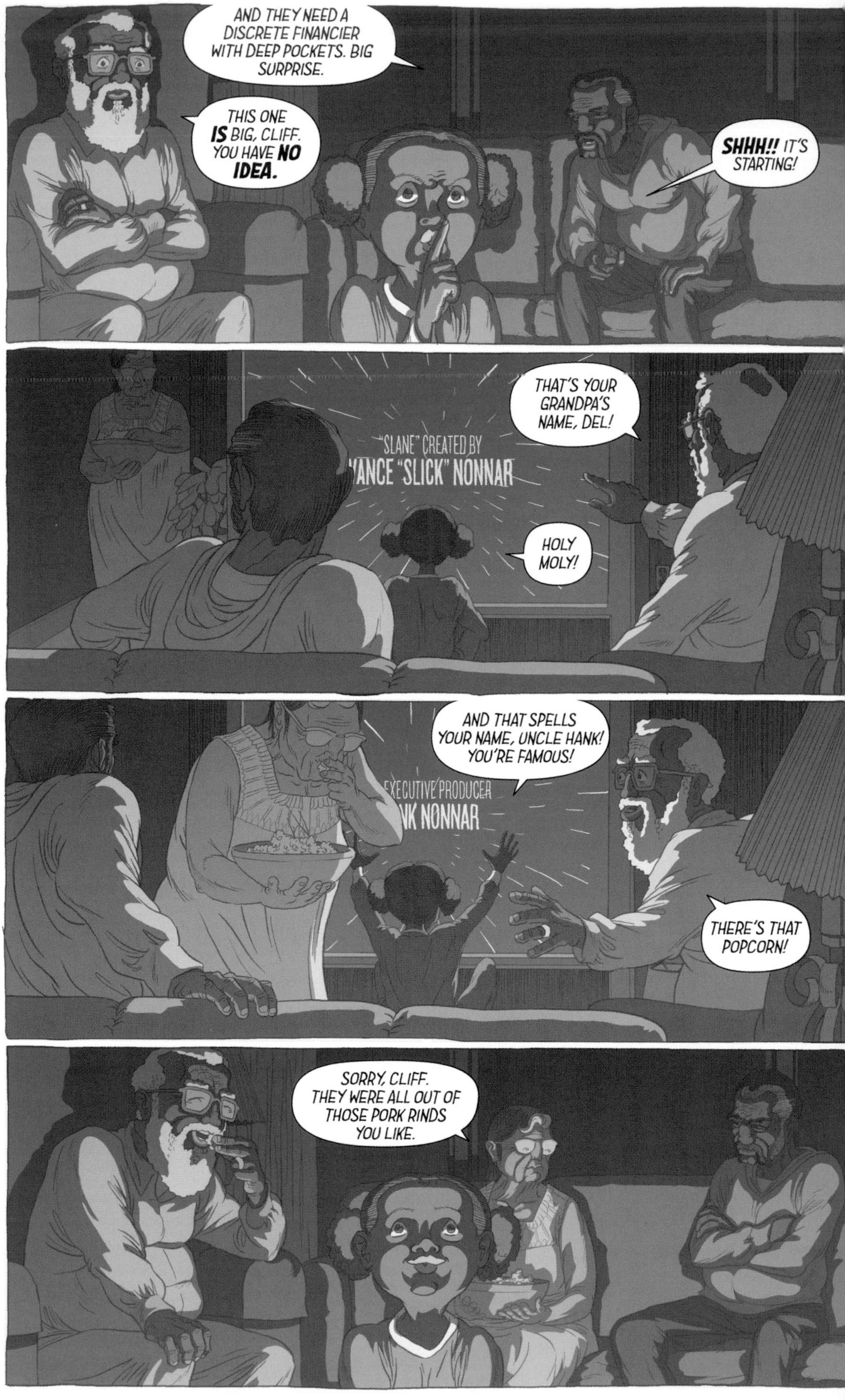
AND THEY NEED A DISCRETE FINANCIER WITH DEEP POCKETS. BIG SURPRISE.
THIS ONE IS BIG, CLIFF. YOU HAVE NO IDEA.
SHHH!! IT'S STARTING!
"SLANE" CREATED BY
VANCE "SLICK" NONNAR
THAT'S YOUR GRANDPA'S NAME, DEL!
HOLY MOLY!
EXECUTIVE PRODUCER
NK NONNAR
AND THAT SPELLS YOUR NAME, UNCLE HANK! YOU'RE FAMOUS!
THERE'S THAT POPCORN!
SORRY, CLIFF. THEY WERE ALL OUT OF THOSE PORK RINDS YOU LIKE.

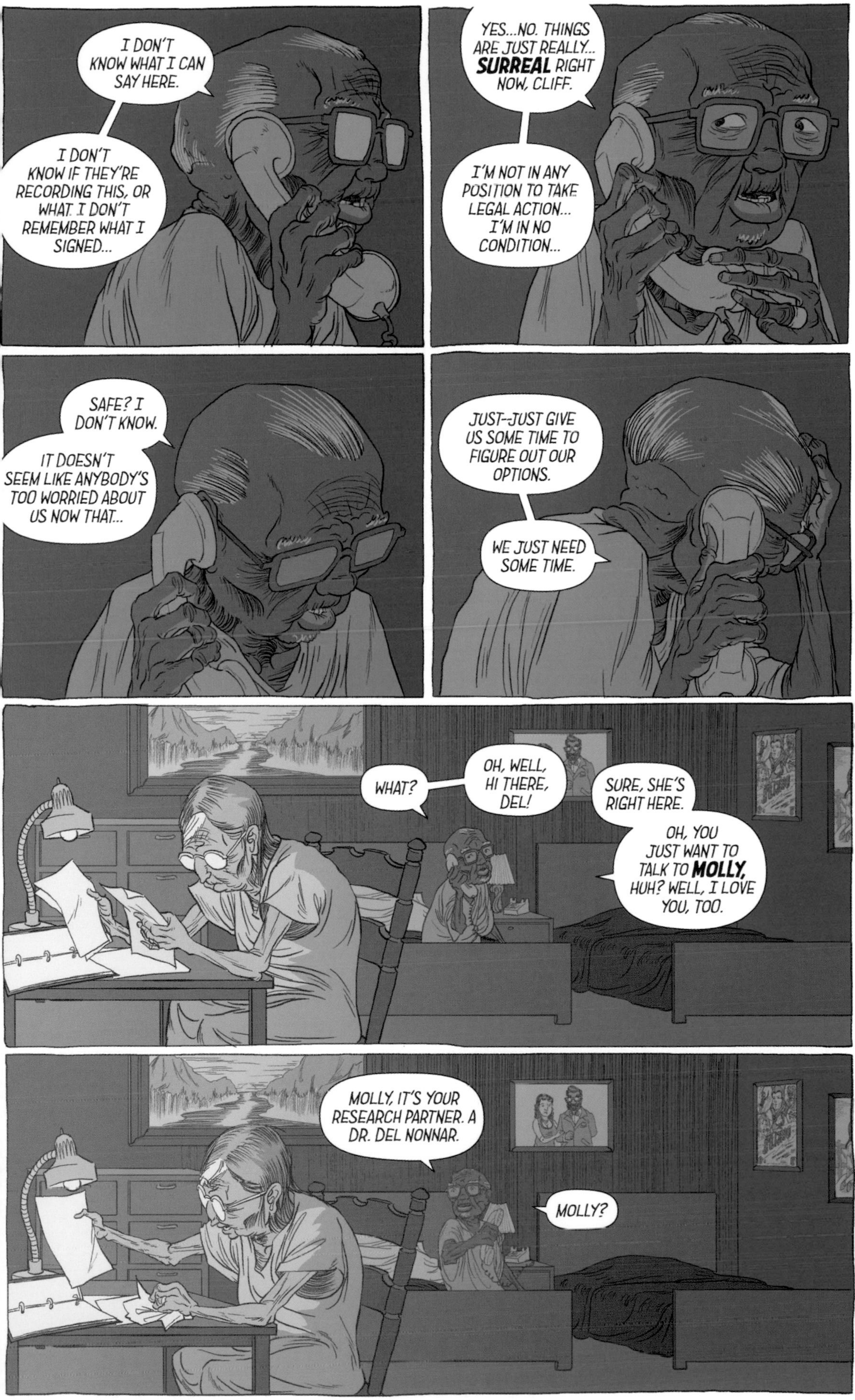
I DON'T KNOW WHAT I CAN SAY HERE.
I DON'T KNOW IF THEY'RE RECORDING THIS, OR WHAT. I DON'T REMEMBER WHAT I SIGNED...
YES...NO. THINGS ARE JUST REALLY... SURREAL RIGHT NOW, CLIFF.
I'M NOT IN ANY POSITION TO TAKE LEGAL ACTION... I'M IN NO CONDITION...
SAFE? I DON'T KNOW.
IT DOESN'T SEEM LIKE ANYBODY'S TOO WORRIED ABOUT US NOW THAT...
JUST--JUST GIVE US SOME TIME TO FIGURE OUT OUR OPTIONS.
WE JUST NEED SOME TIME.
WHAT?
OH, WELL, HI THERE, DEL!
SURE, SHE'S RIGHT HERE.
OH, YOU JUST WANT TO TALK TO MOLLY, HUH? WELL, I LOVE YOU, TOO.
MOLLY, IT'S YOUR RESEARCH PARTNER. A DR. DEL NONNAR.
MOLLY?

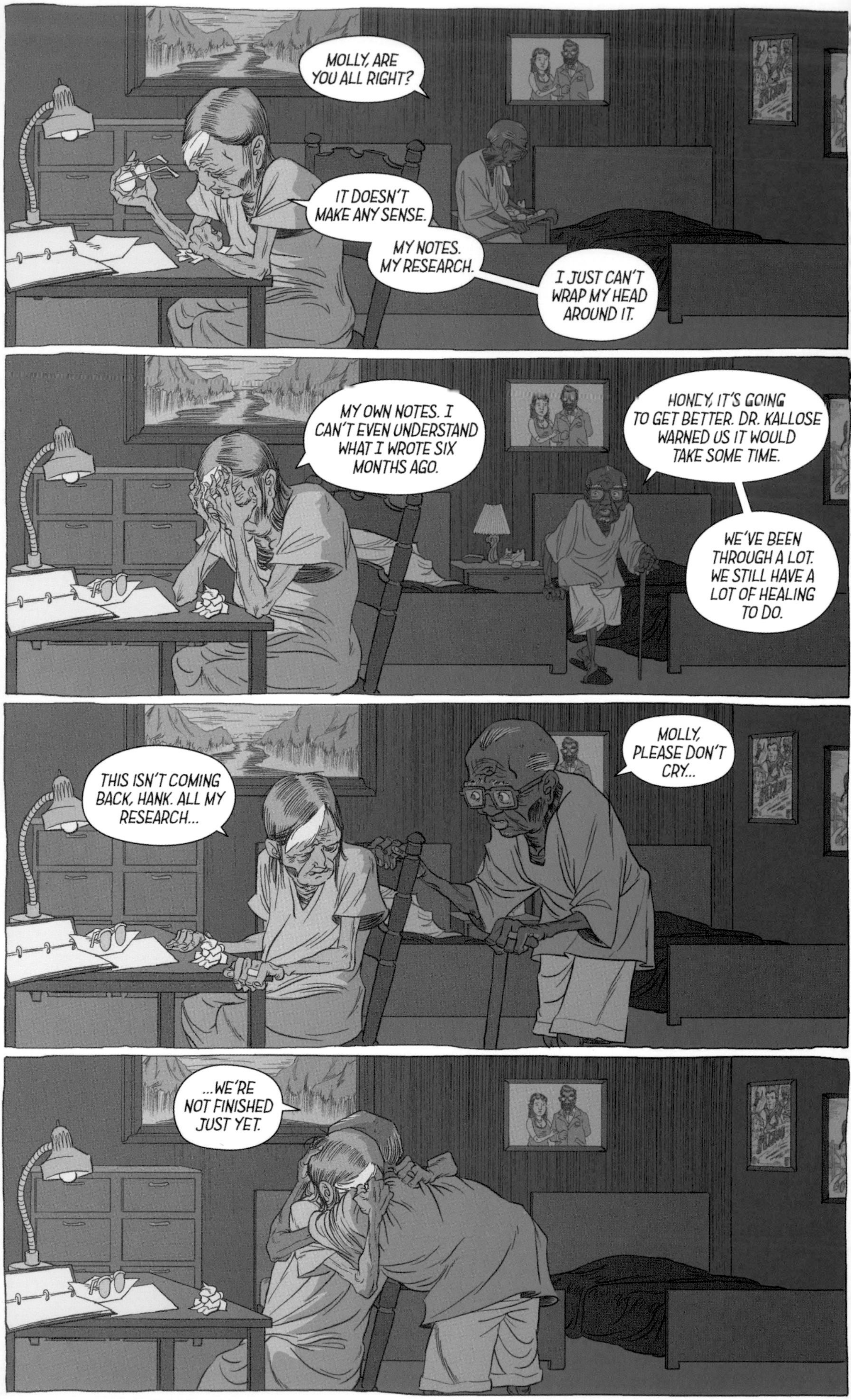
MOLLY, ARE YOU ALL RIGHT?
IT DOESN'T MAKE ANY SENSE.
MY NOTES. MY RESEARCH.
I JUST CAN'T WRAP MY HEAD AROUND IT.
MY OWN NOTES. I CAN'T EVEN UNDERSTAND WHAT I WROTE SIX MONTHS AGO.
HONEY, IT'S GOING TO GET BETTER. DR. KALLOSE WARNED US IT WOULD TAKE SOME TIME.
WE'VE BEEN THROUGH A LOT. WE STILL HAVE A LOT OF HEALING TO DO.
THIS ISN'T COMING BACK, HANK. ALL MY RESEARCH...
MOLLY, PLEASE DON'T CRY...
...WE'RE NOT FINISHED JUST YET.

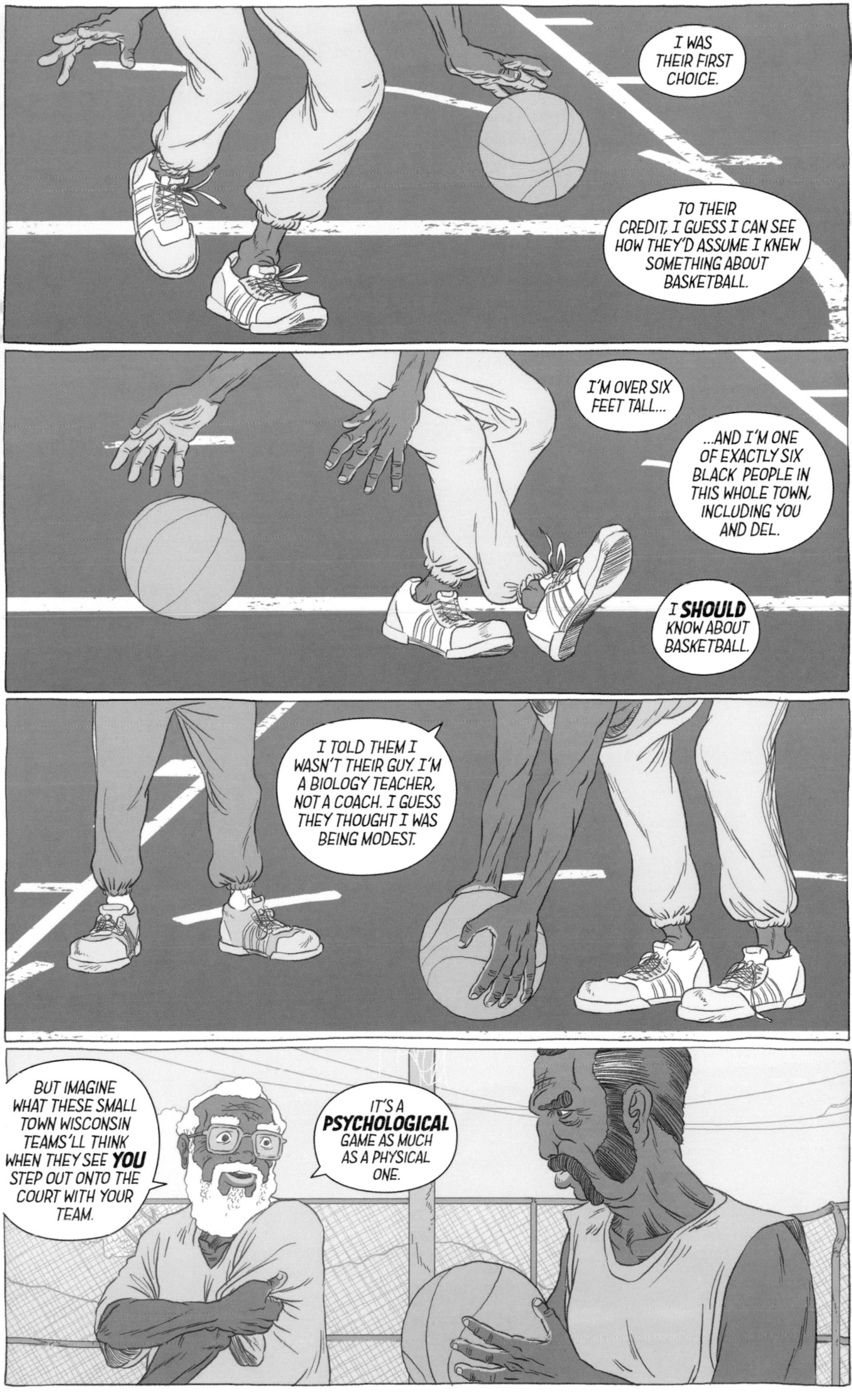
I WAS THEIR FIRST CHOICE.
TO THEIR CREDIT, I GUESS I CAN SEE HOW THEY'D ASSUME I KNEW SOMETHING ABOUT BASKETBALL.
I'M OVER SIX FEET TALL...
...AND I'M ONE OF EXACTLY SIX BLACK PEOPLE IN THIS WHOLE TOWN, INCLUDING YOU AND DEL.
I **SHOULD** KNOW ABOUT BASKETBALL.
I TOLD THEM I WASN'T THEIR GUY. I'M A BIOLOGY TEACHER, NOT A COACH. I GUESS THEY THOUGHT I WAS BEING MODEST.
BUT IMAGINE WHAT THESE SMALL TOWN WISCONSIN TEAMS'LL THINK WHEN THEY SEE **YOU** STEP OUT ONTO THE COURT WITH YOUR TEAM.
IT'S A **PSYCHOLOGICAL** GAME AS MUCH AS A PHYSICAL ONE.

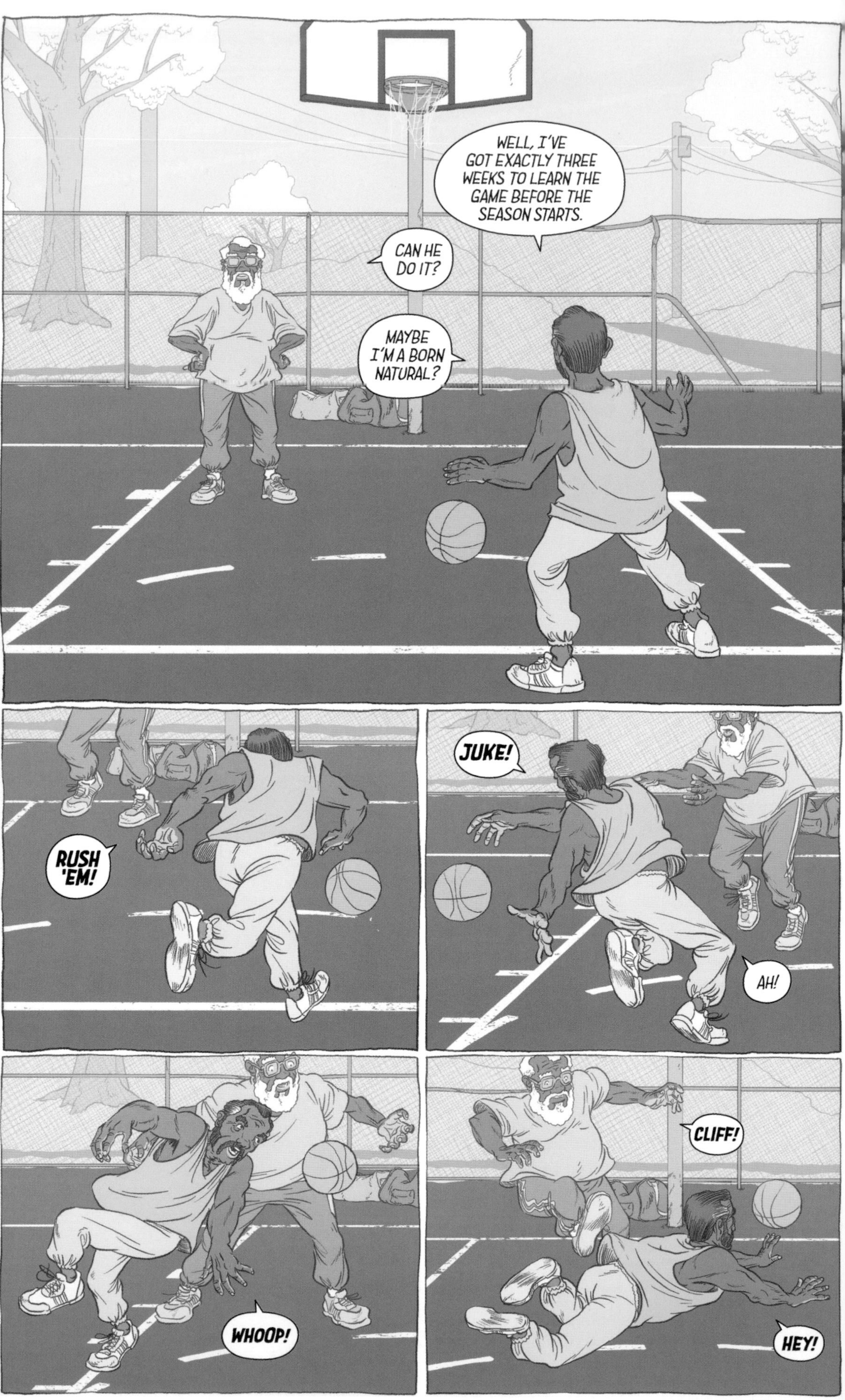

WELL, I'VE GOT EXACTLY THREE WEEKS TO LEARN THE GAME BEFORE THE SEASON STARTS.
CAN HE DO IT?
MAYBE I'M A BORN NATURAL?
RUSH 'EM!
JUKE!
AH!
WHOOP!
CLIFF!
HEY!

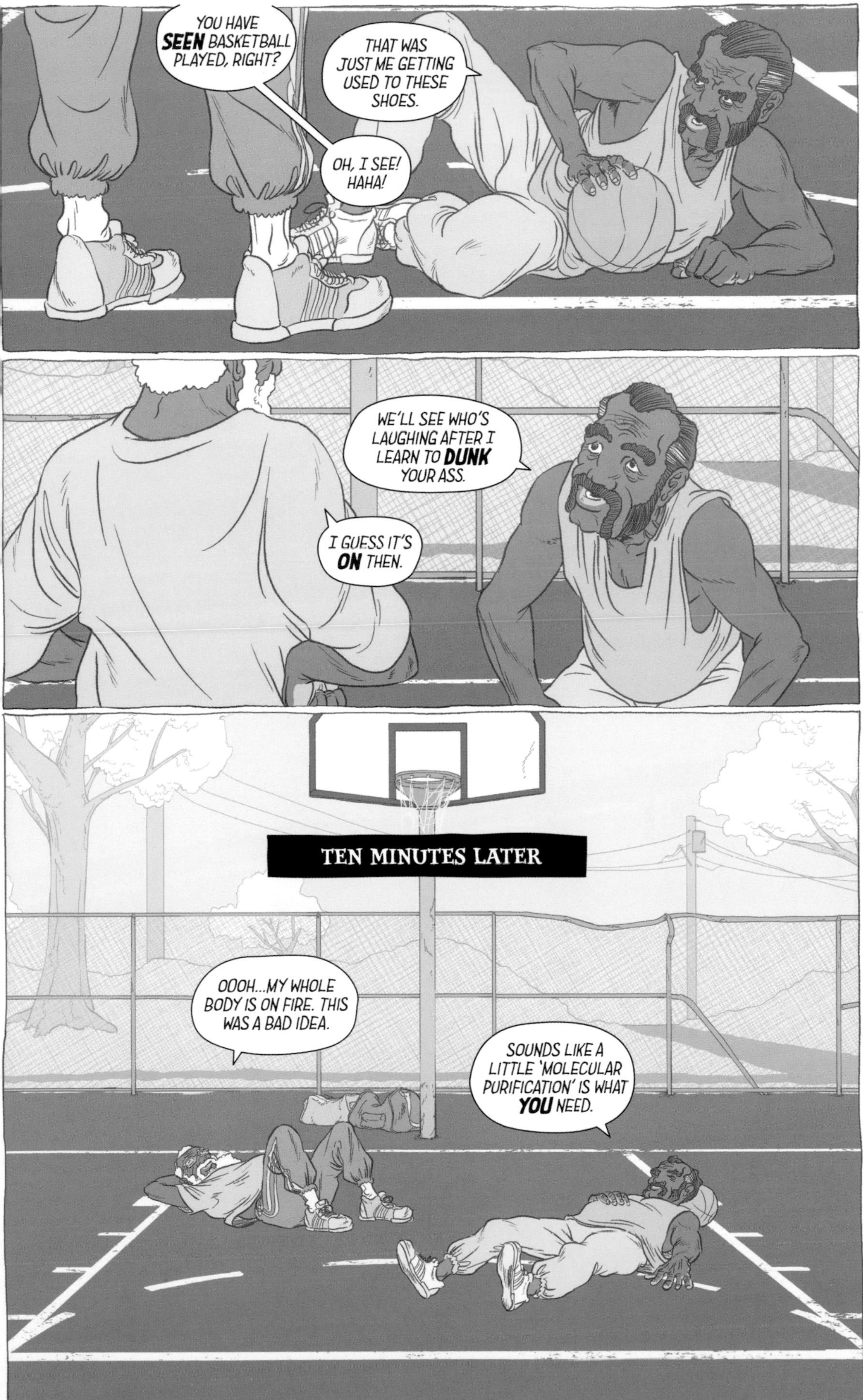
YOU HAVE SEEN BASKETBALL PLAYED, RIGHT?
THAT WAS JUST ME GETTING USED TO THESE SHOES.
OH, I SEE! HAHA!
WE'LL SEE WHO'S LAUGHING AFTER I LEARN TO DUNK YOUR ASS.
I GUESS IT'S ON THEN.
TEN MINUTES LATER
OOOH...MY WHOLE BODY IS ON FIRE. THIS WAS A BAD IDEA.
SOUNDS LIKE A LITTLE 'MOLECULAR PURIFICATION' IS WHAT YOU NEED.

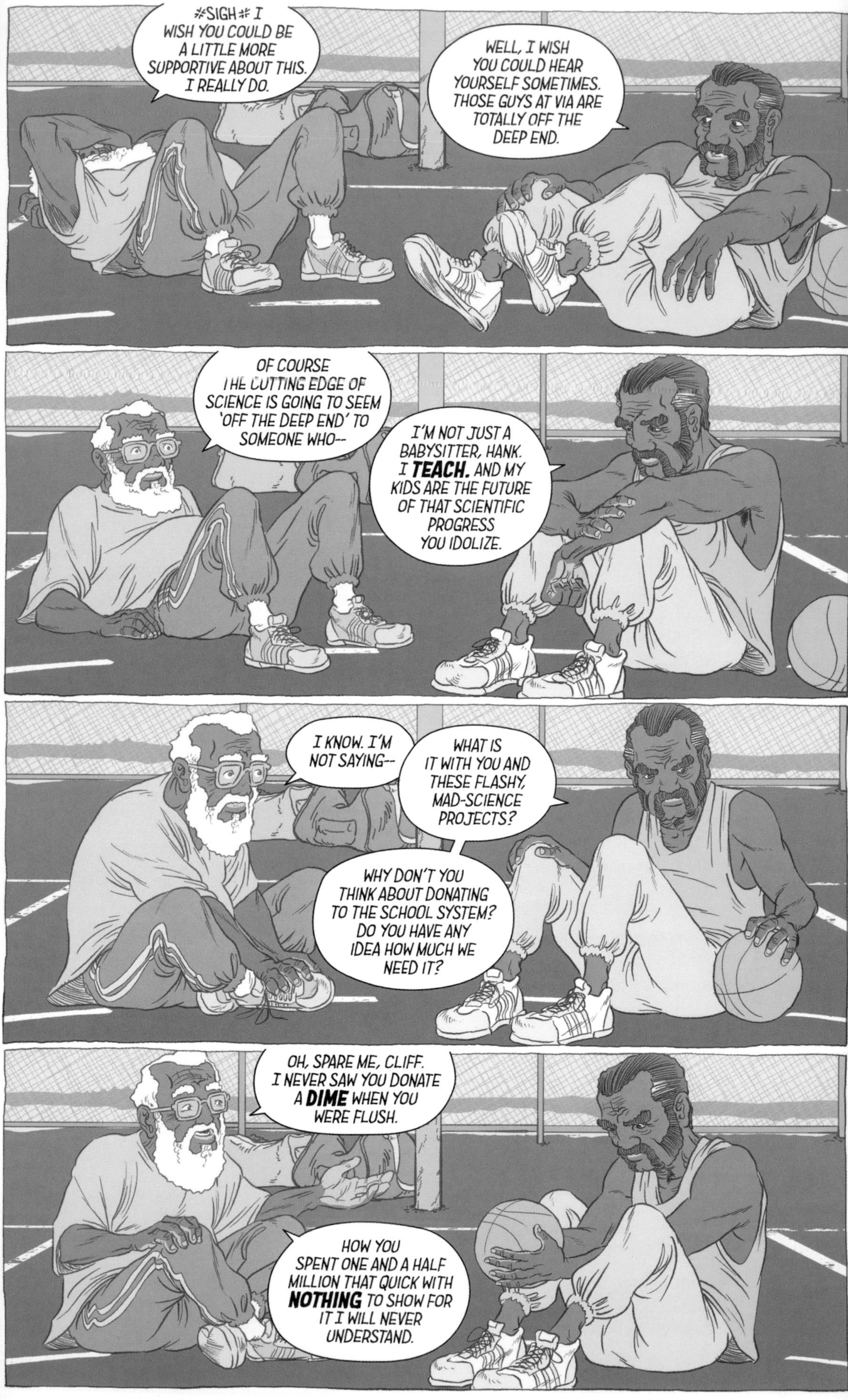
#SIGH# I WISH YOU COULD BE A LITTLE MORE SUPPORTIVE ABOUT THIS. I REALLY DO.
WELL, I WISH YOU COULD HEAR YOURSELF SOMETIMES. THOSE GUYS AT VIA ARE TOTALLY OFF THE DEEP END.
OF COURSE THE CUTTING EDGE OF SCIENCE IS GOING TO SEEM 'OFF THE DEEP END' TO SOMEONE WHO--
I'M NOT JUST A BABYSITTER, HANK. I TEACH. AND MY KIDS ARE THE FUTURE OF THAT SCIENTIFIC PROGRESS YOU IDOLIZE.
I KNOW. I'M NOT SAYING--
WHAT IS IT WITH YOU AND THESE FLASHY, MAD-SCIENCE PROJECTS?
WHY DON'T YOU THINK ABOUT DONATING TO THE SCHOOL SYSTEM? DO YOU HAVE ANY IDEA HOW MUCH WE NEED IT?
OH, SPARE ME, CLIFF. I NEVER SAW YOU DONATE A DIME WHEN YOU WERE FLUSH.
HOW YOU SPENT ONE AND A HALF MILLION THAT QUICK WITH NOTHING TO SHOW FOR IT I WILL NEVER UNDERSTAND.

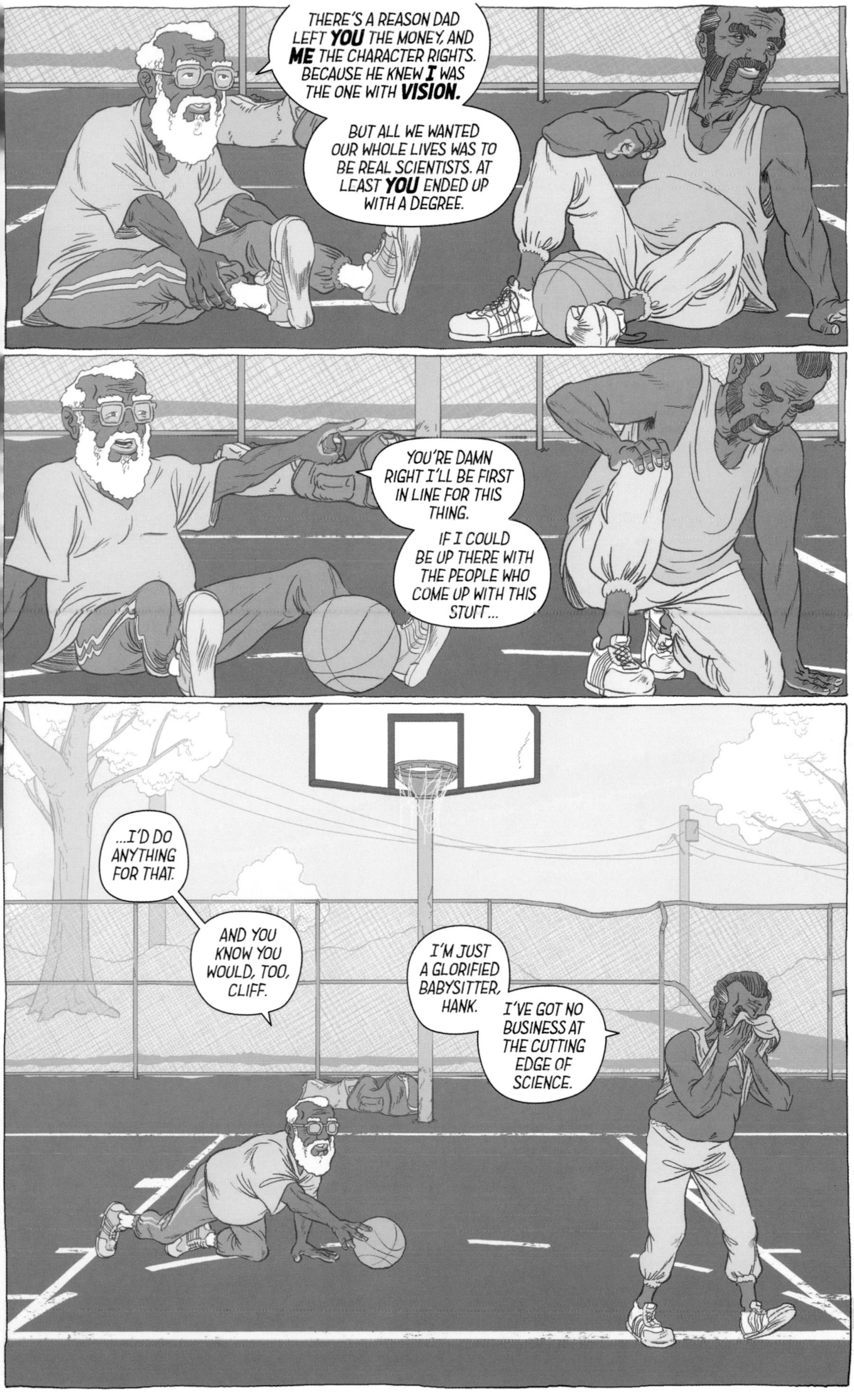
THERE'S A REASON DAD LEFT YOU THE MONEY, AND ME THE CHARACTER RIGHTS. BECAUSE HE KNEW I WAS THE ONE WITH VISION.
BUT ALL WE WANTED OUR WHOLE LIVES WAS TO BE REAL SCIENTISTS. AT LEAST YOU ENDED UP WITH A DEGREE.
YOU'RE DAMN RIGHT I'LL BE FIRST IN LINE FOR THIS THING.
IF I COULD BE UP THERE WITH THE PEOPLE WHO COME UP WITH THIS STUFF...
...I'D DO ANYTHING FOR THAT.
AND YOU KNOW YOU WOULD, TOO, CLIFF.
I'M JUST A GLORIFIED BABYSITTER, HANK.
I'VE GOT NO BUSINESS AT THE CUTTING EDGE OF SCIENCE.

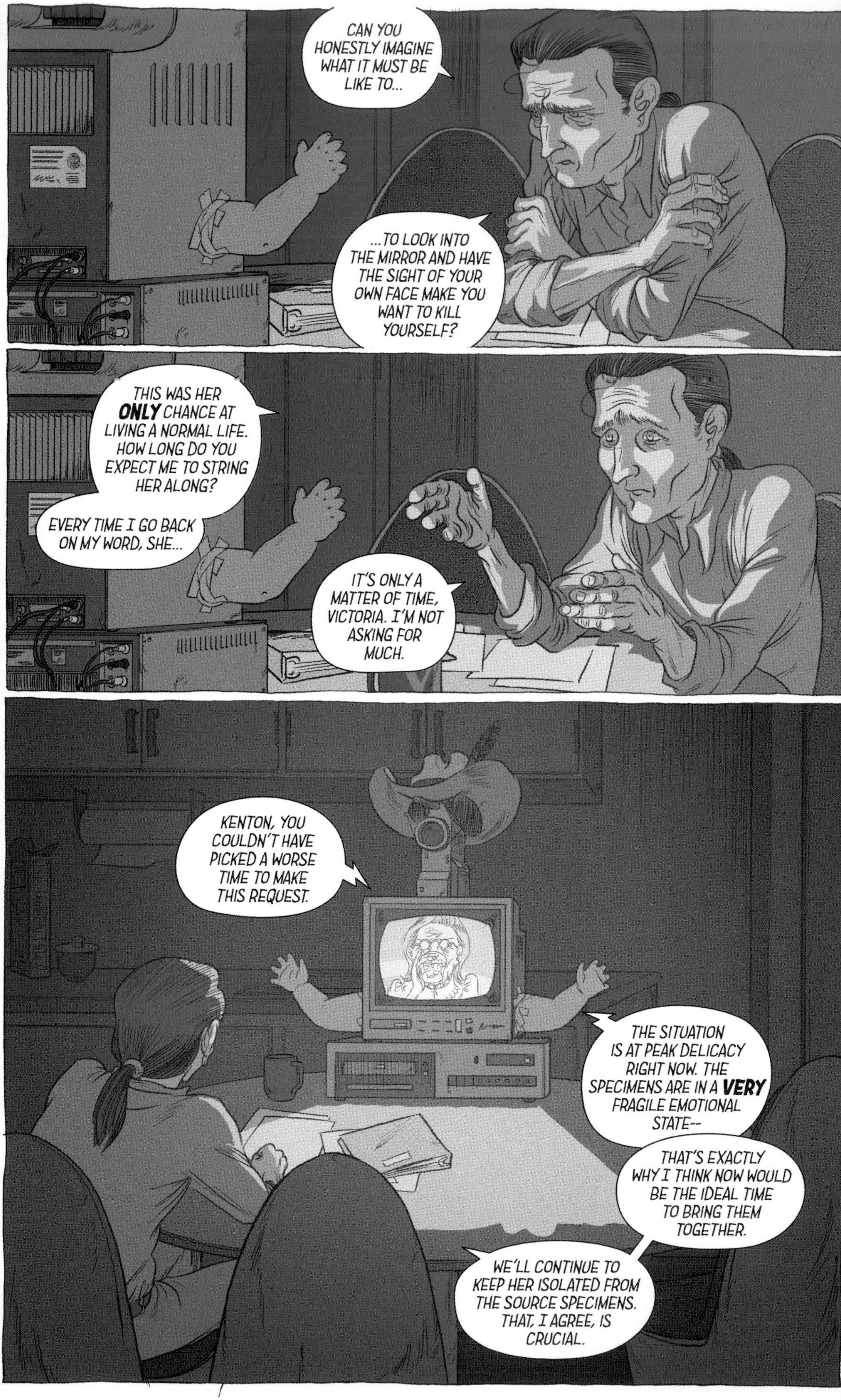
CAN YOU HONESTLY IMAGINE WHAT IT MUST BE LIKE TO...
...TO LOOK INTO THE MIRROR AND HAVE THE SIGHT OF YOUR OWN FACE MAKE YOU WANT TO KILL YOURSELF?
THIS WAS HER ONLY CHANCE AT LIVING A NORMAL LIFE. HOW LONG DO YOU EXPECT ME TO STRING HER ALONG?
EVERY TIME I GO BACK ON MY WORD, SHE...
IT'S ONLY A MATTER OF TIME, VICTORIA. I'M NOT ASKING FOR MUCH.
KENTON, YOU COULDN'T HAVE PICKED A WORSE TIME TO MAKE THIS REQUEST.
THE SITUATION IS AT PEAK DELICACY RIGHT NOW. THE SPECIMENS ARE IN A VERY FRAGILE EMOTIONAL STATE--
THAT'S EXACTLY WHY I THINK NOW WOULD BE THE IDEAL TIME TO BRING THEM TOGETHER.
WE'LL CONTINUE TO KEEP HER ISOLATED FROM THE SOURCE SPECIMENS. THAT, I AGREE, IS CRUCIAL.

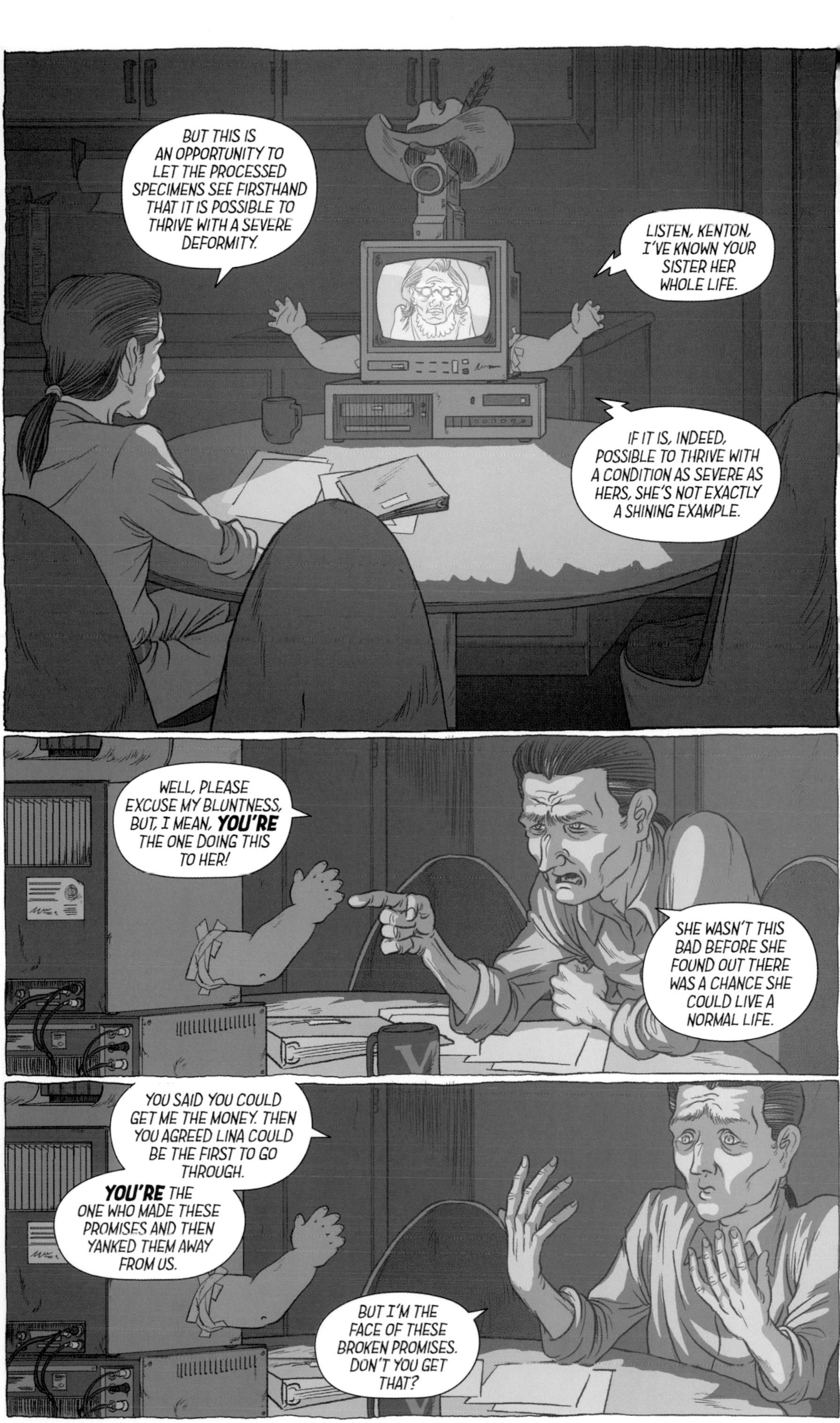
BUT THIS IS AN OPPORTUNITY TO LET THE PROCESSED SPECIMENS SEE FIRSTHAND THAT IT IS POSSIBLE TO THRIVE WITH A SEVERE DEFORMITY.
LISTEN, KENTON, I'VE KNOWN YOUR SISTER HER WHOLE LIFE.
IF IT IS, INDEED, POSSIBLE TO THRIVE WITH A CONDITION AS SEVERE AS HERS, SHE'S NOT EXACTLY A SHINING EXAMPLE.
WELL, PLEASE EXCUSE MY BLUNTNESS, BUT, I MEAN, **YOU'RE** THE ONE DOING THIS TO HER!
SHE WASN'T THIS BAD BEFORE SHE FOUND OUT THERE WAS A CHANCE SHE COULD LIVE A NORMAL LIFE.
YOU SAID YOU COULD GET ME THE MONEY. THEN YOU AGREED LINA COULD BE THE FIRST TO GO THROUGH.
YOU'RE THE ONE WHO MADE THESE PROMISES AND THEN YANKED THEM AWAY FROM US.
BUT I'M THE FACE OF THESE BROKEN PROMISES. DON'T YOU GET THAT?

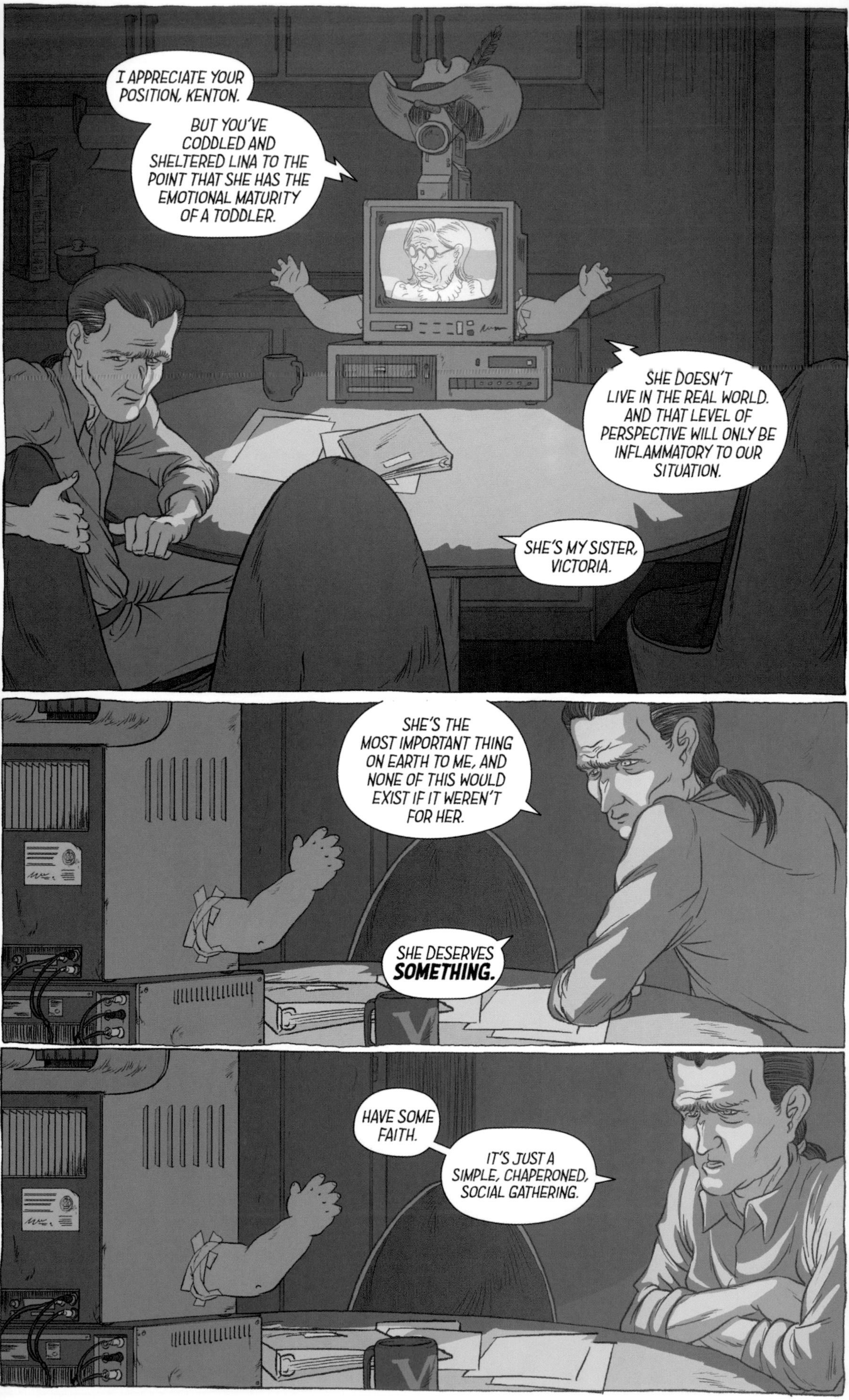
I APPRECIATE YOUR POSITION, KENTON.
BUT YOU'VE CODDLED AND SHELTERED LINA TO THE POINT THAT SHE HAS THE EMOTIONAL MATURITY OF A TODDLER.
SHE DOESN'T LIVE IN THE REAL WORLD. AND THAT LEVEL OF PERSPECTIVE WILL ONLY BE INFLAMMATORY TO OUR SITUATION.
SHE'S MY SISTER, VICTORIA.
SHE'S THE MOST IMPORTANT THING ON EARTH TO ME, AND NONE OF THIS WOULD EXIST IF IT WEREN'T FOR HER.
SHE DESERVES **SOMETHING.**
HAVE SOME FAITH.
IT'S JUST A SIMPLE, CHAPERONED, SOCIAL GATHERING.

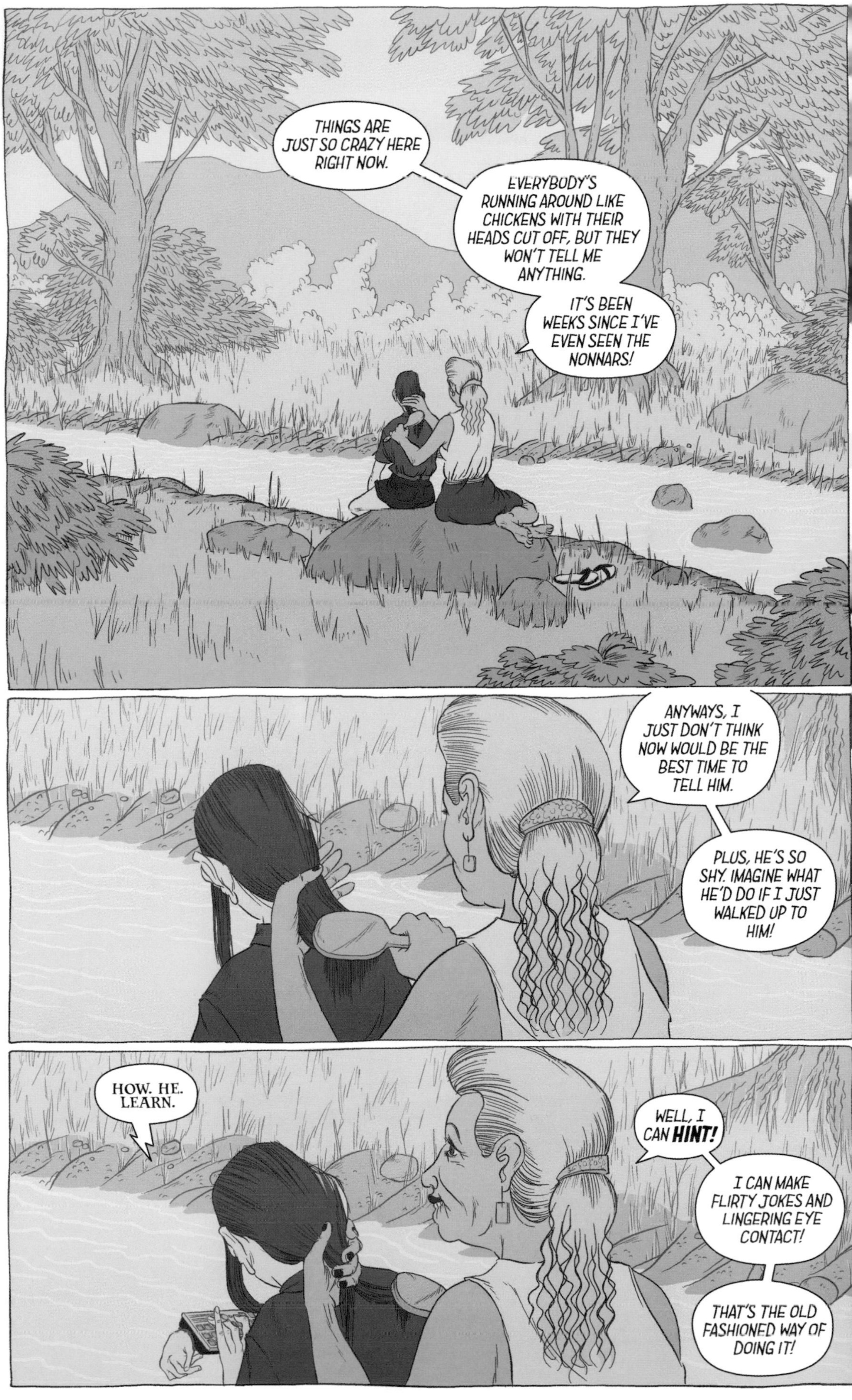
THINGS ARE JUST SO CRAZY HERE RIGHT NOW.
EVERYBODY'S RUNNING AROUND LIKE CHICKENS WITH THEIR HEADS CUT OFF, BUT THEY WON'T TELL ME ANYTHING.
IT'S BEEN WEEKS SINCE I'VE EVEN SEEN THE NONNARS!
ANYWAYS, I JUST DON'T THINK NOW WOULD BE THE BEST TIME TO TELL HIM.
PLUS, HE'S SO SHY. IMAGINE WHAT HE'D DO IF I JUST WALKED UP TO HIM!
HOW. HE. LEARN.
WELL, I CAN **HINT!**
I CAN MAKE FLIRTY JOKES AND LINGERING EYE CONTACT!
THAT'S THE OLD FASHIONED WAY OF DOING IT!

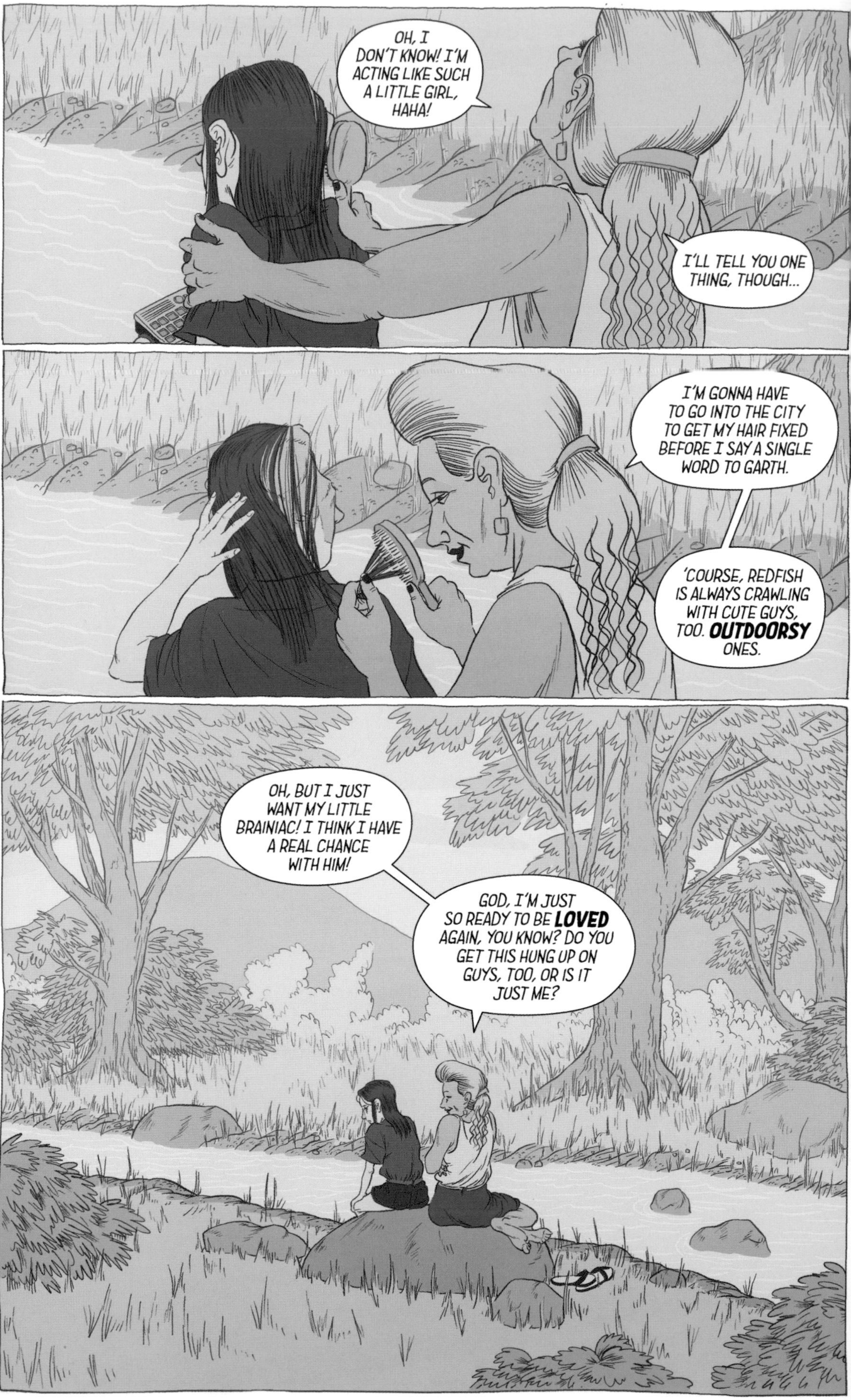
OH, I DON'T KNOW! I'M ACTING LIKE SUCH A LITTLE GIRL, HAHA!
I'LL TELL YOU ONE THING, THOUGH...
I'M GONNA HAVE TO GO INTO THE CITY TO GET MY HAIR FIXED BEFORE I SAY A SINGLE WORD TO GARTH.
'COURSE, REDFISH IS ALWAYS CRAWLING WITH CUTE GUYS, TOO. **OUTDOORSY** ONES.
OH, BUT I JUST WANT MY LITTLE BRAINIAC! I THINK I HAVE A REAL CHANCE WITH HIM!
GOD, I'M JUST SO READY TO BE **LOVED** AGAIN, YOU KNOW? DO YOU GET THIS HUNG UP ON GUYS, TOO, OR IS IT JUST ME?

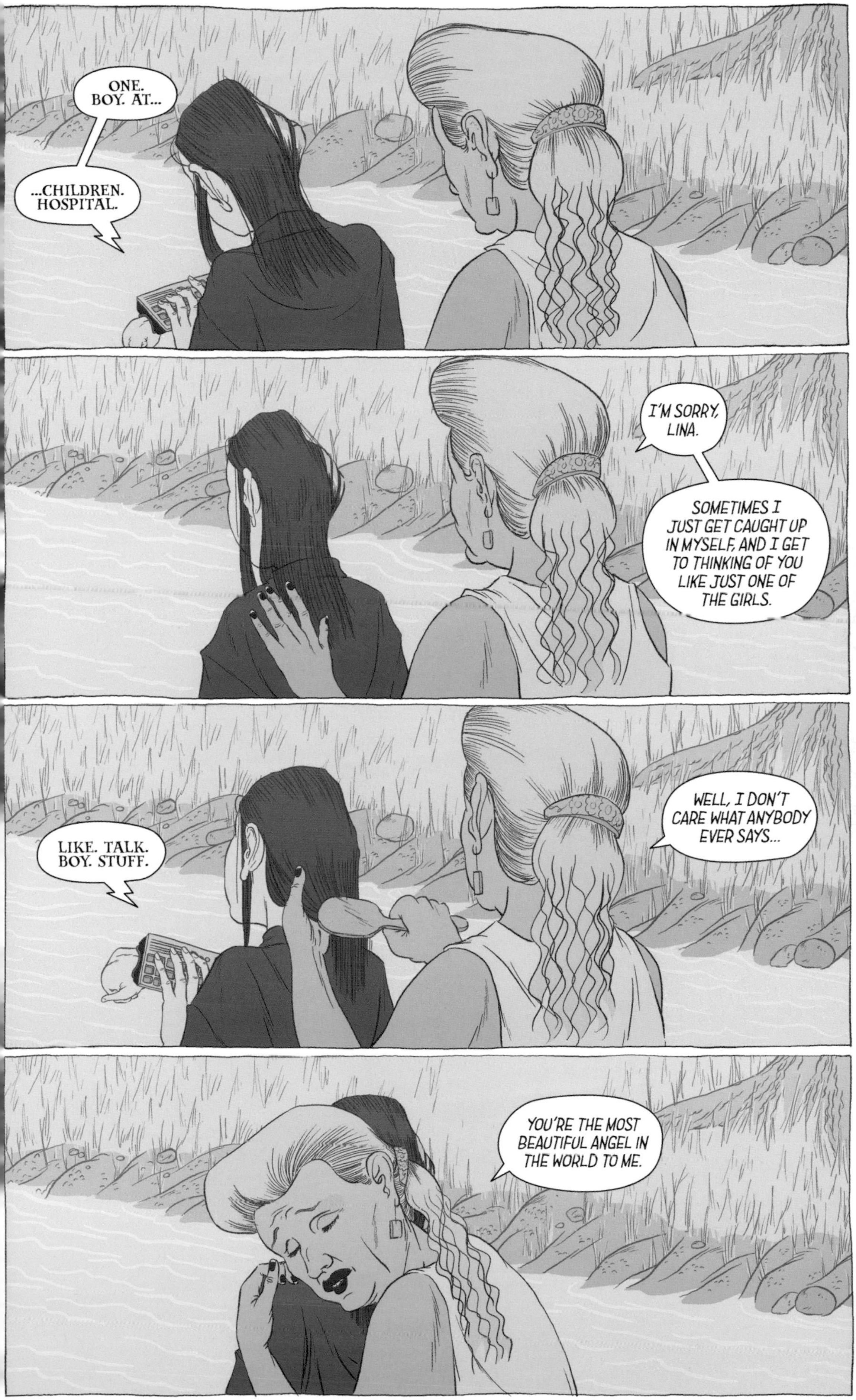
ONE. BOY. AT...
...CHILDREN. HOSPITAL.
I'M SORRY, LINA.
SOMETIMES I JUST GET CAUGHT UP IN MYSELF, AND I GET TO THINKING OF YOU LIKE JUST ONE OF THE GIRLS.
LIKE. TALK. BOY. STUFF.
WELL, I DON'T CARE WHAT ANYBODY EVER SAYS...
YOU'RE THE MOST BEAUTIFUL ANGEL IN THE WORLD TO ME.

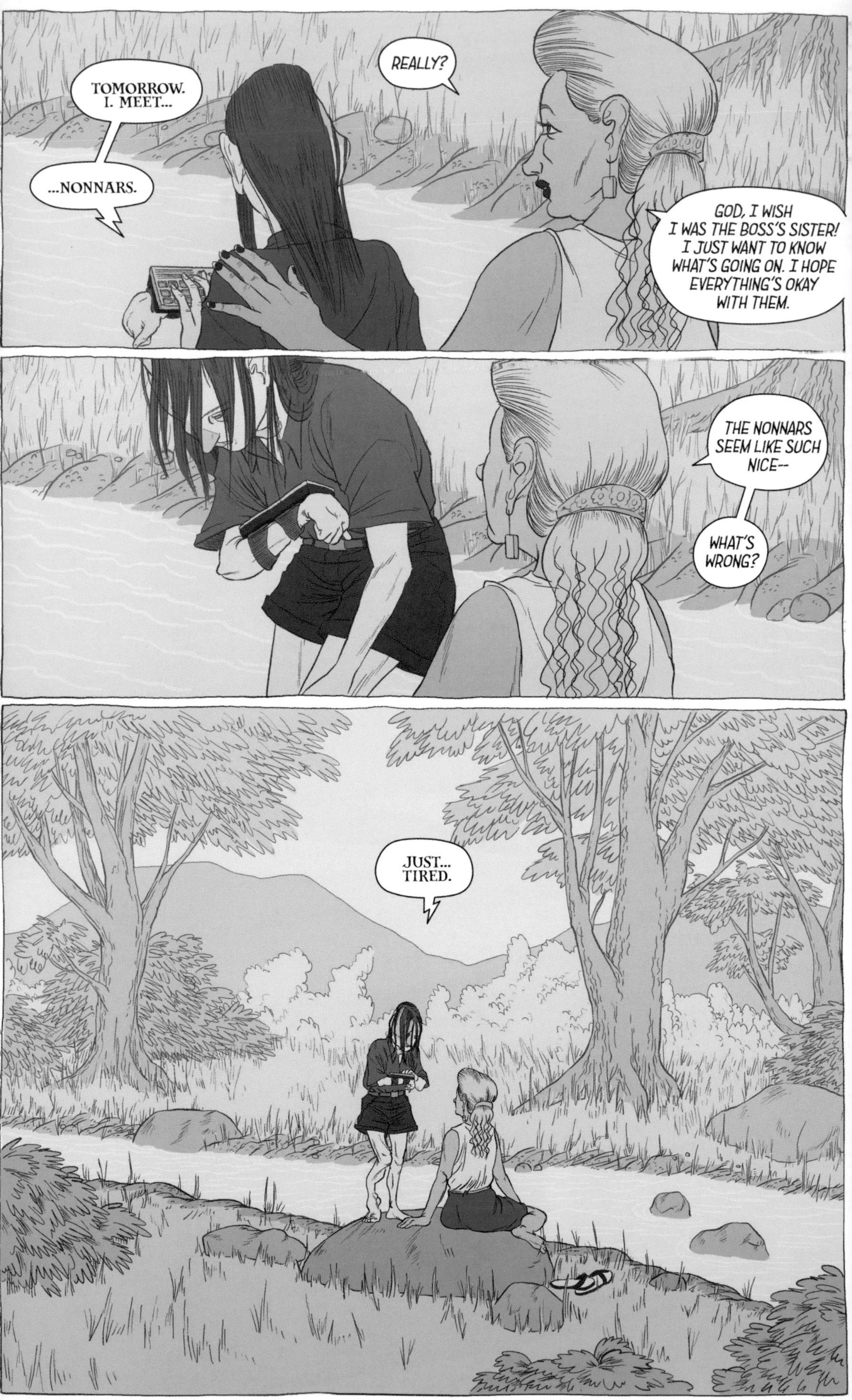
TOMORROW. I. MEET...
...NONNARS.
REALLY?
GOD, I WISH I WAS THE BOSS'S SISTER! I JUST WANT TO KNOW WHAT'S GOING ON. I HOPE EVERYTHING'S OKAY WITH THEM.
THE NONNARS SEEM LIKE SUCH NICE--
WHAT'S WRONG?
JUST... TIRED.

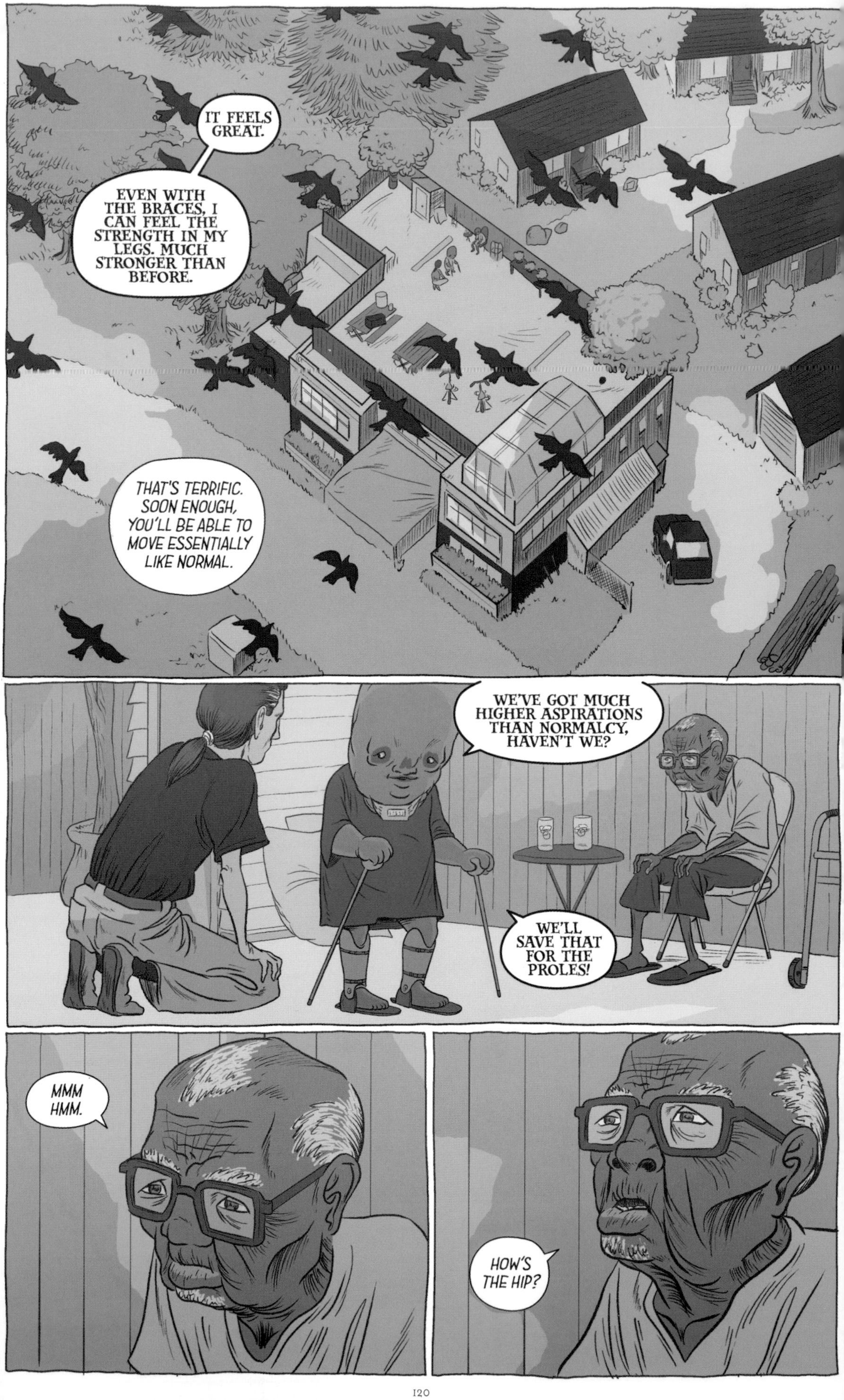

IT FEELS GREAT.
EVEN WITH THE BRACES, I CAN FEEL THE STRENGTH IN MY LEGS. MUCH STRONGER THAN BEFORE.
THAT'S TERRIFIC. SOON ENOUGH, YOU'LL BE ABLE TO MOVE ESSENTIALLY LIKE NORMAL.
WE'VE GOT MUCH HIGHER ASPIRATIONS THAN NORMALCY, HAVEN'T WE?
WE'LL SAVE THAT FOR THE PROLES!
MMM HMM.
HOW'S THE HIP?

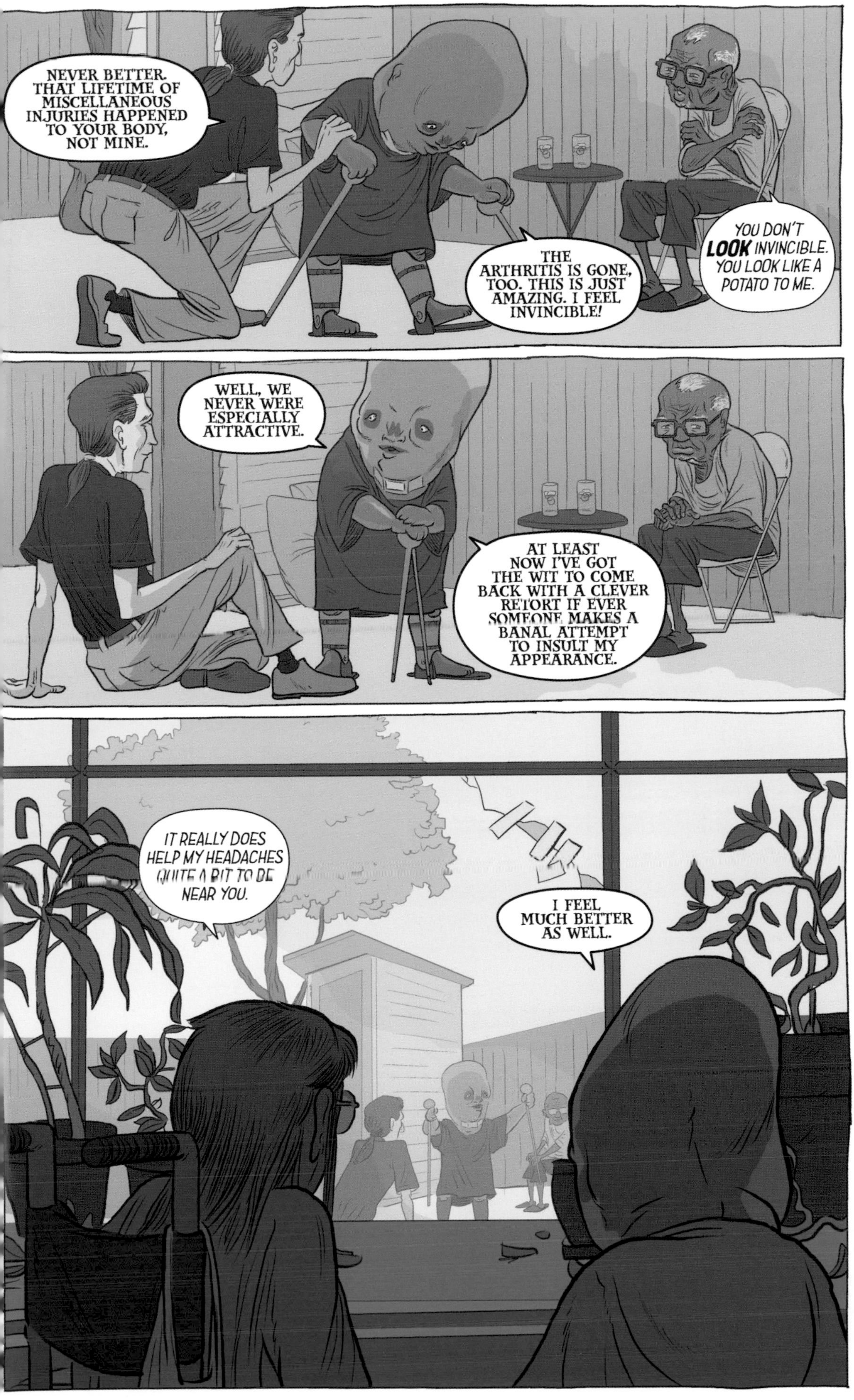
NEVER BETTER. THAT LIFETIME OF MISCELLANEOUS INJURIES HAPPENED TO YOUR BODY, NOT MINE.
THE ARTHRITIS IS GONE, TOO. THIS IS JUST AMAZING. I FEEL INVINCIBLE!
YOU DON'T LOOK INVINCIBLE. YOU LOOK LIKE A POTATO TO ME.
WELL, WE NEVER WERE ESPECIALLY ATTRACTIVE.
AT LEAST NOW I'VE GOT THE WIT TO COME BACK WITH A CLEVER RETORT IF EVER SOMEONE MAKES A BANAL ATTEMPT TO INSULT MY APPEARANCE.
IT REALLY DOES HELP MY HEADACHES QUITE A BIT TO BE NEAR YOU.
I FEEL MUCH BETTER AS WELL.

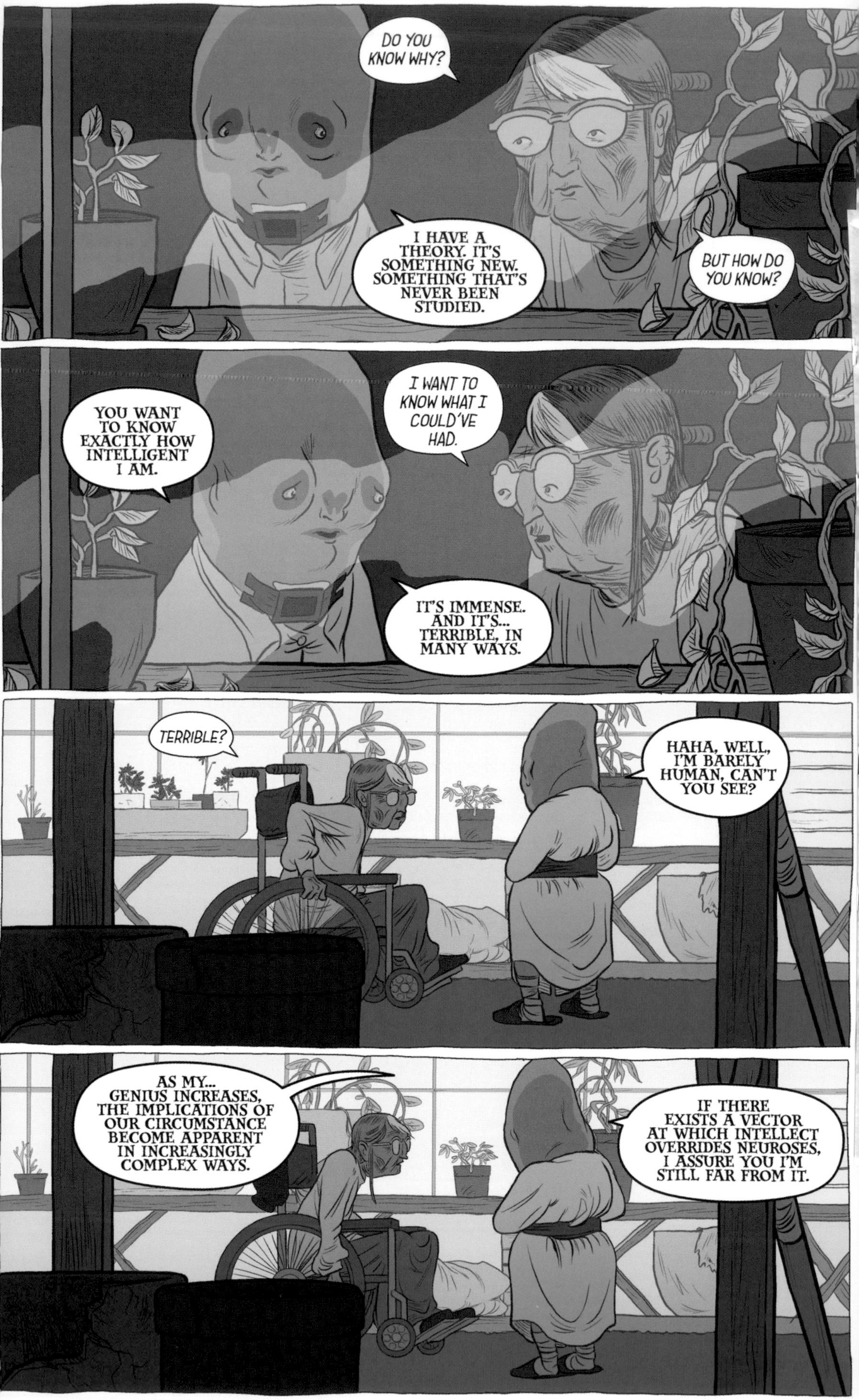
DO YOU KNOW WHY?
I HAVE A THEORY. IT'S SOMETHING NEW. SOMETHING THAT'S NEVER BEEN STUDIED.
BUT HOW DO YOU KNOW?
YOU WANT TO KNOW EXACTLY HOW INTELLIGENT I AM.
I WANT TO KNOW WHAT I COULD'VE HAD.
IT'S IMMENSE. AND IT'S... TERRIBLE, IN MANY WAYS.
TERRIBLE?
HAHA, WELL, I'M BARELY HUMAN, CAN'T YOU SEE?
AS MY... GENIUS INCREASES, THE IMPLICATIONS OF OUR CIRCUMSTANCE BECOME APPARENT IN INCREASINGLY COMPLEX WAYS.
IF THERE EXISTS A VECTOR AT WHICH INTELLECT OVERRIDES NEUROSES, I ASSURE YOU I'M STILL FAR FROM IT.

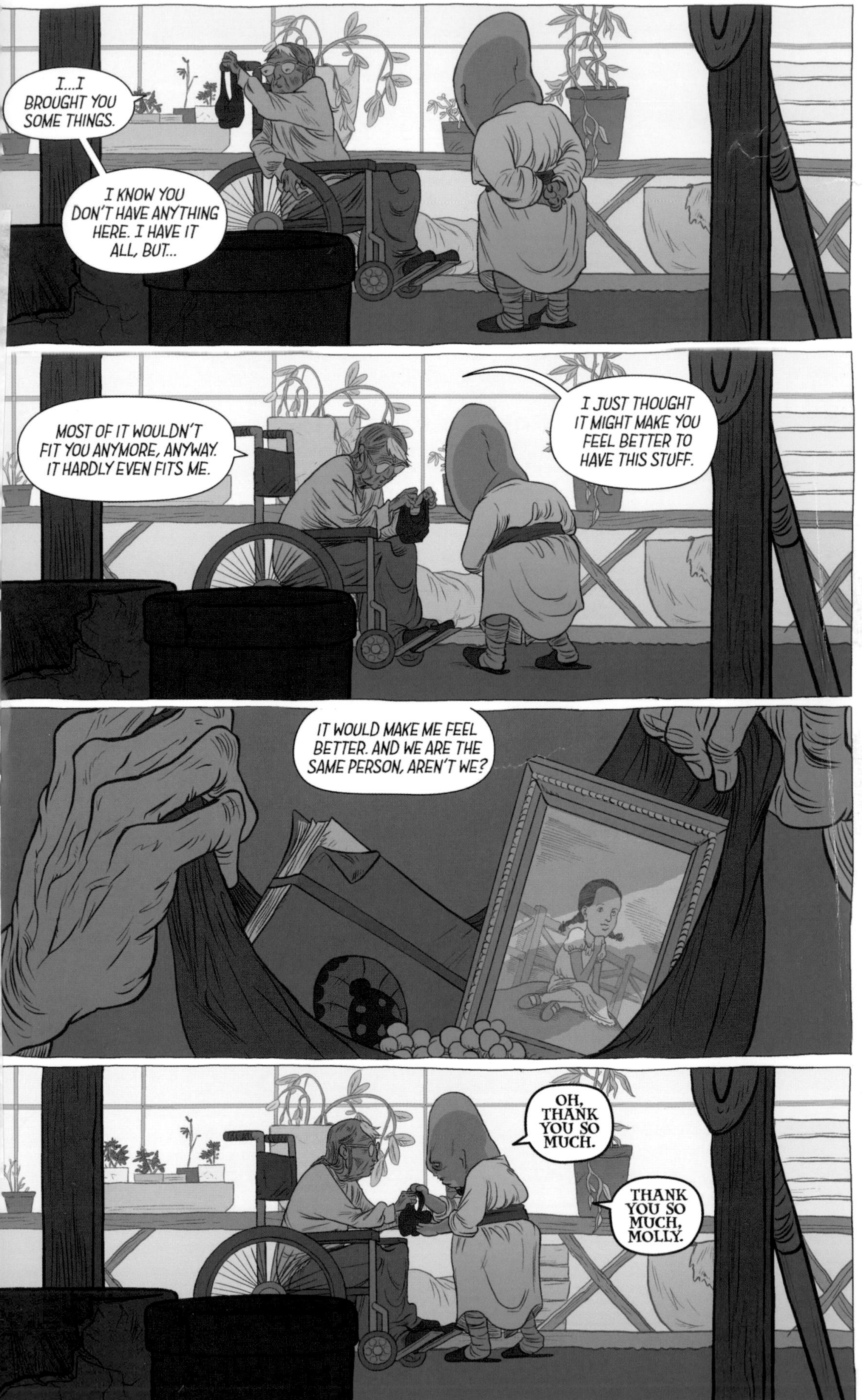
I...I BROUGHT YOU SOME THINGS.
I KNOW YOU DON'T HAVE ANYTHING HERE. I HAVE IT ALL, BUT...
MOST OF IT WOULDN'T FIT YOU ANYMORE, ANYWAY. IT HARDLY EVEN FITS ME.
I JUST THOUGHT IT MIGHT MAKE YOU FEEL BETTER TO HAVE THIS STUFF.
IT WOULD MAKE ME FEEL BETTER. AND WE ARE THE SAME PERSON, AREN'T WE?
OH, THANK YOU SO MUCH.
THANK YOU SO MUCH, MOLLY.

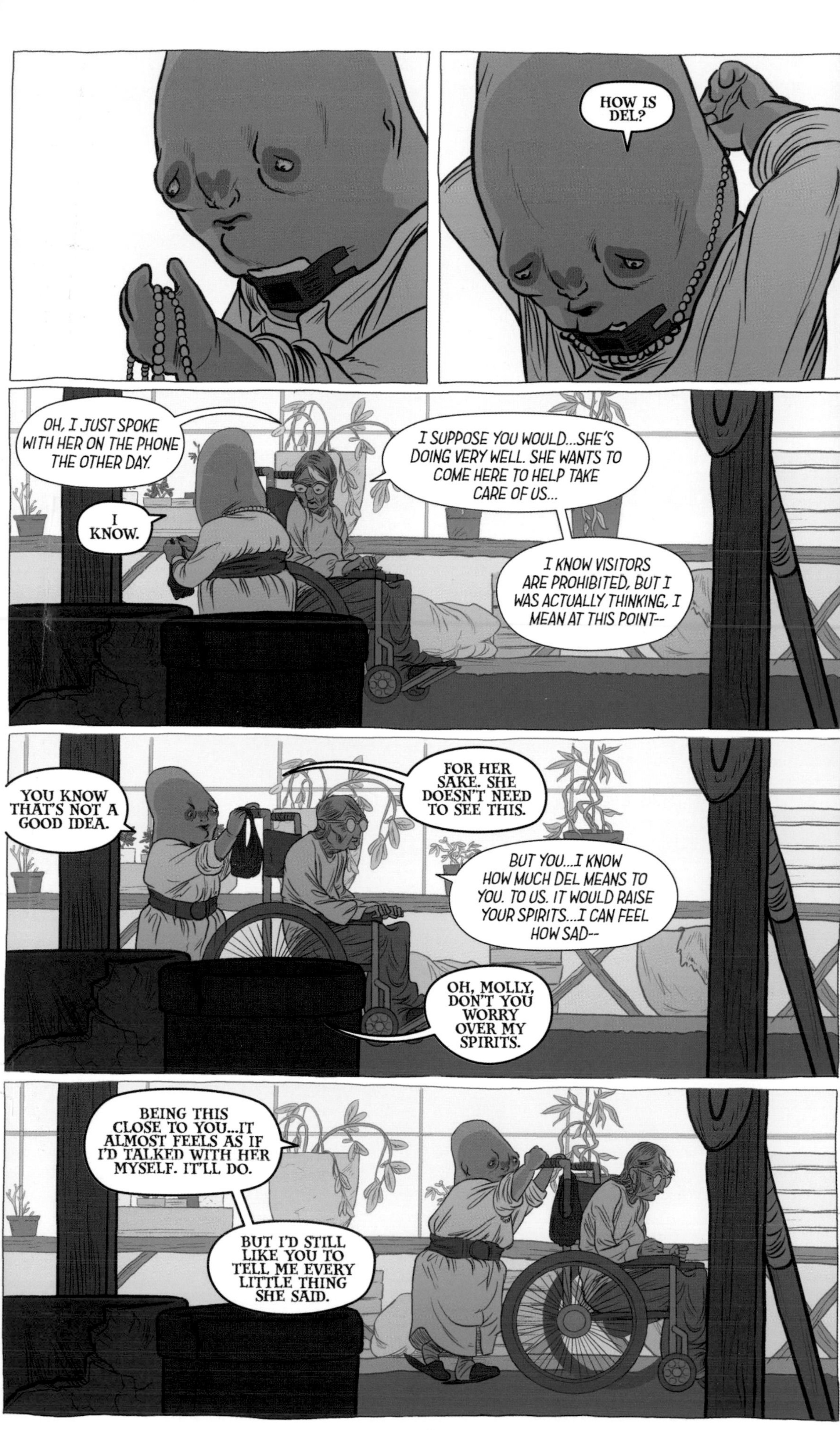
HOW IS DEL?
OH, I JUST SPOKE WITH HER ON THE PHONE THE OTHER DAY.
I SUPPOSE YOU WOULD...SHE'S DOING VERY WELL. SHE WANTS TO COME HERE TO HELP TAKE CARE OF US...
I KNOW.
I KNOW VISITORS ARE PROHIBITED, BUT I WAS ACTUALLY THINKING, I MEAN AT THIS POINT--
YOU KNOW THAT'S NOT A GOOD IDEA.
FOR HER SAKE. SHE DOESN'T NEED TO SEE THIS.
BUT YOU...I KNOW HOW MUCH DEL MEANS TO YOU. TO US. IT WOULD RAISE YOUR SPIRITS...I CAN FEEL HOW SAD--
OH, MOLLY, DON'T YOU WORRY OVER MY SPIRITS.
BEING THIS CLOSE TO YOU...IT ALMOST FEELS AS IF I'D TALKED WITH HER MYSELF. IT'LL DO.
BUT I'D STILL LIKE YOU TO TELL ME EVERY LITTLE THING SHE SAID.

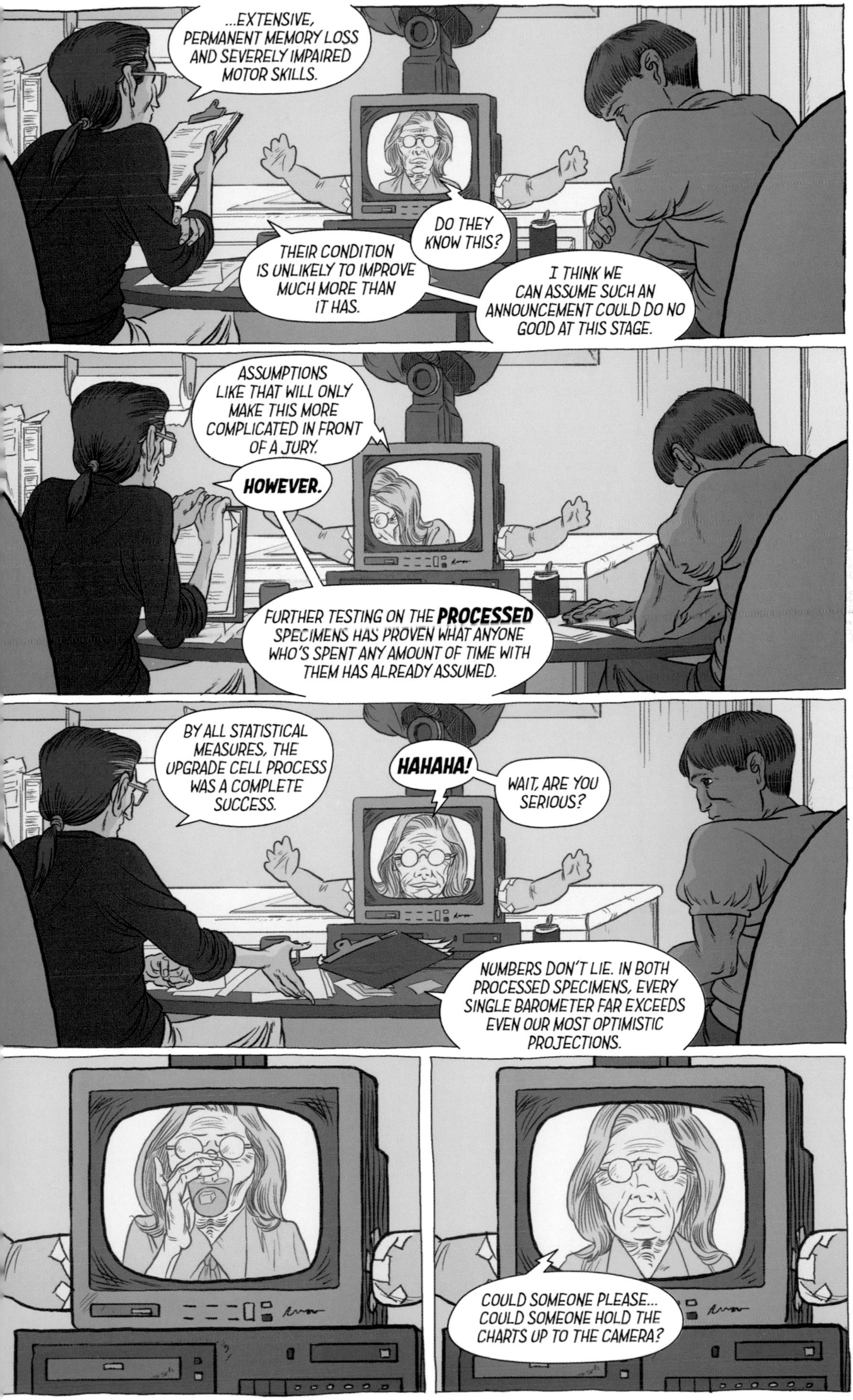
...EXTENSIVE, PERMANENT MEMORY LOSS AND SEVERELY IMPAIRED MOTOR SKILLS.
DO THEY KNOW THIS?
THEIR CONDITION IS UNLIKELY TO IMPROVE MUCH MORE THAN IT HAS.
I THINK WE CAN ASSUME SUCH AN ANNOUNCEMENT COULD DO NO GOOD AT THIS STAGE.
ASSUMPTIONS LIKE THAT WILL ONLY MAKE THIS MORE COMPLICATED IN FRONT OF A JURY.
HOWEVER.
FURTHER TESTING ON THE PROCESSED SPECIMENS HAS PROVEN WHAT ANYONE WHO'S SPENT ANY AMOUNT OF TIME WITH THEM HAS ALREADY ASSUMED.
BY ALL STATISTICAL MEASURES, THE UPGRADE CELL PROCESS WAS A COMPLETE SUCCESS.
HAHAHA!
WAIT, ARE YOU SERIOUS?
NUMBERS DON'T LIE. IN BOTH PROCESSED SPECIMENS, EVERY SINGLE BAROMETER FAR EXCEEDS EVEN OUR MOST OPTIMISTIC PROJECTIONS.
COULD SOMEONE PLEASE... COULD SOMEONE HOLD THE CHARTS UP TO THE CAMERA?

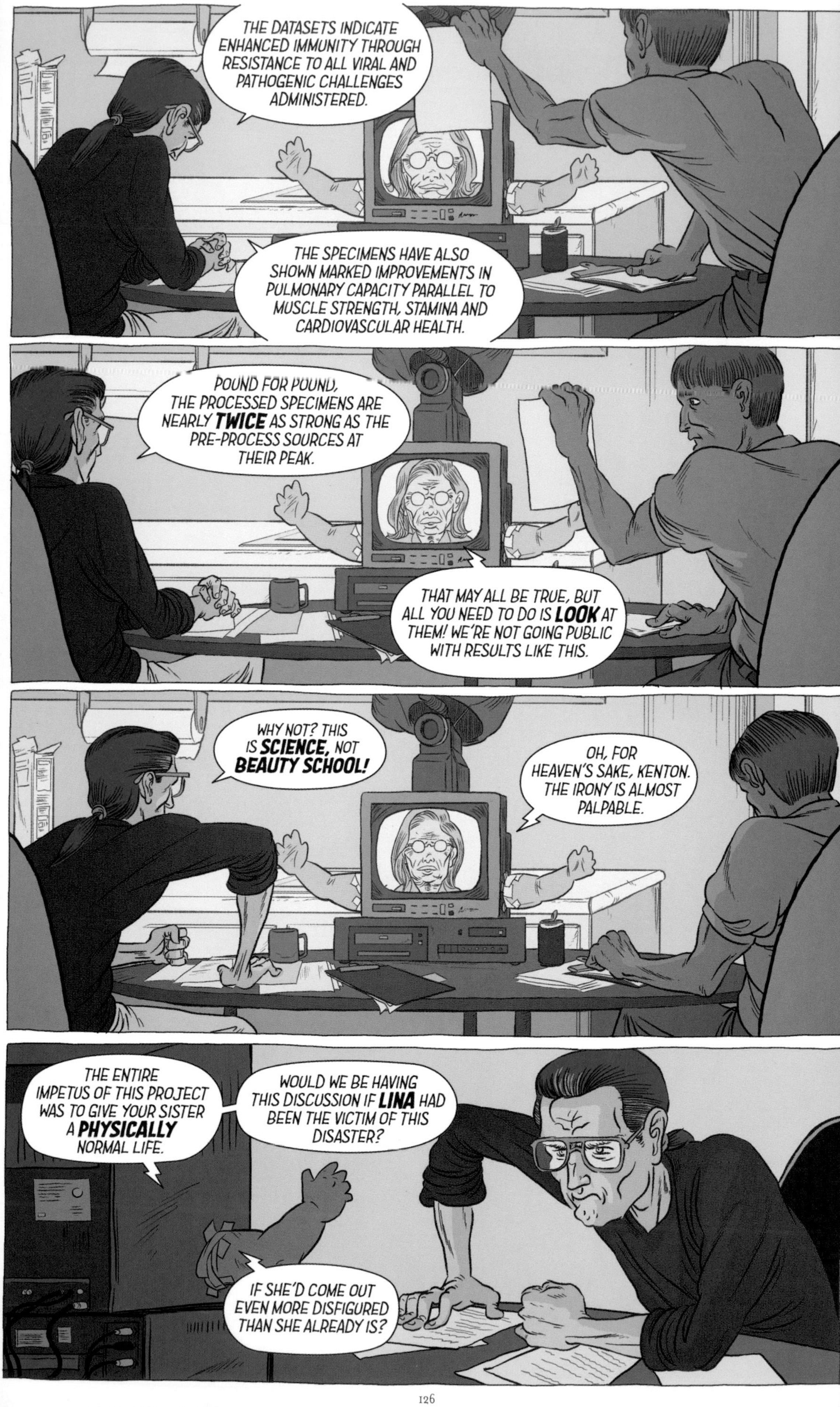
THE DATASETS INDICATE ENHANCED IMMUNITY THROUGH RESISTANCE TO ALL VIRAL AND PATHOGENIC CHALLENGES ADMINISTERED.
THE SPECIMENS HAVE ALSO SHOWN MARKED IMPROVEMENTS IN PULMONARY CAPACITY PARALLEL TO MUSCLE STRENGTH, STAMINA AND CARDIOVASCULAR HEALTH.
POUND FOR POUND, THE PROCESSED SPECIMENS ARE NEARLY **TWICE** AS STRONG AS THE PRE-PROCESS SOURCES AT THEIR PEAK.
THAT MAY ALL BE TRUE, BUT ALL YOU NEED TO DO IS **LOOK** AT THEM! WE'RE NOT GOING PUBLIC WITH RESULTS LIKE THIS.
WHY NOT? THIS IS **SCIENCE,** NOT **BEAUTY SCHOOL!**
OH, FOR HEAVEN'S SAKE, KENTON. THE IRONY IS ALMOST PALPABLE.
THE ENTIRE IMPETUS OF THIS PROJECT WAS TO GIVE YOUR SISTER A **PHYSICALLY** NORMAL LIFE.
WOULD WE BE HAVING THIS DISCUSSION IF **LINA** HAD BEEN THE VICTIM OF THIS DISASTER?
IF SHE'D COME OUT EVEN MORE DISFIGURED THAN SHE ALREADY IS?

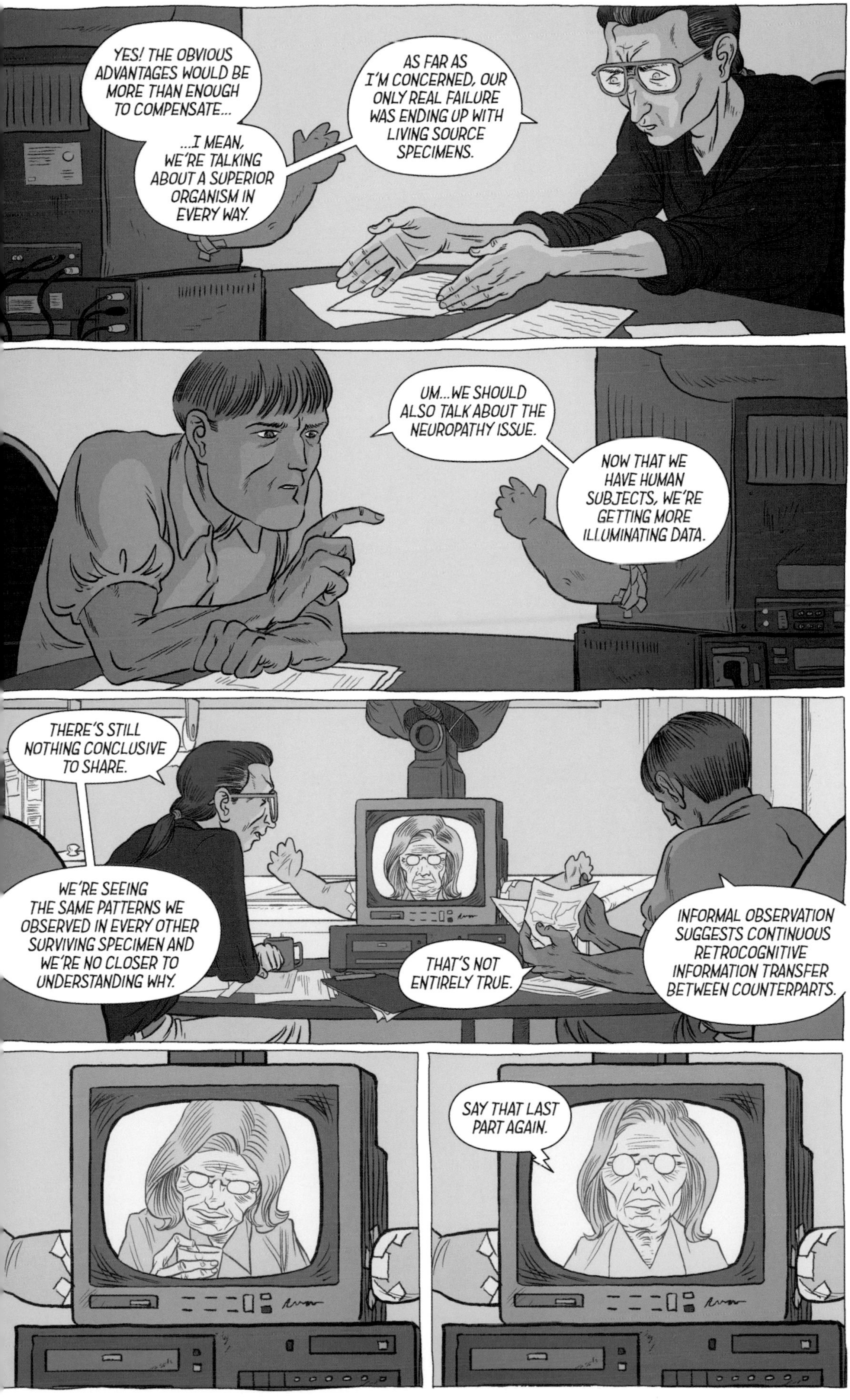

YES! THE OBVIOUS ADVANTAGES WOULD BE MORE THAN ENOUGH TO COMPENSATE...
...I MEAN, WE'RE TALKING ABOUT A SUPERIOR ORGANISM IN EVERY WAY.
AS FAR AS I'M CONCERNED, OUR ONLY REAL FAILURE WAS ENDING UP WITH LIVING SOURCE SPECIMENS.
UM...WE SHOULD ALSO TALK ABOUT THE NEUROPATHY ISSUE.
NOW THAT WE HAVE HUMAN SUBJECTS, WE'RE GETTING MORE ILLUMINATING DATA.
THERE'S STILL NOTHING CONCLUSIVE TO SHARE.
WE'RE SEEING THE SAME PATTERNS WE OBSERVED IN EVERY OTHER SURVIVING SPECIMEN AND WE'RE NO CLOSER TO UNDERSTANDING WHY.
THAT'S NOT ENTIRELY TRUE.
INFORMAL OBSERVATION SUGGESTS CONTINUOUS RETROCOGNITIVE INFORMATION TRANSFER BETWEEN COUNTERPARTS.
SAY THAT LAST PART AGAIN.

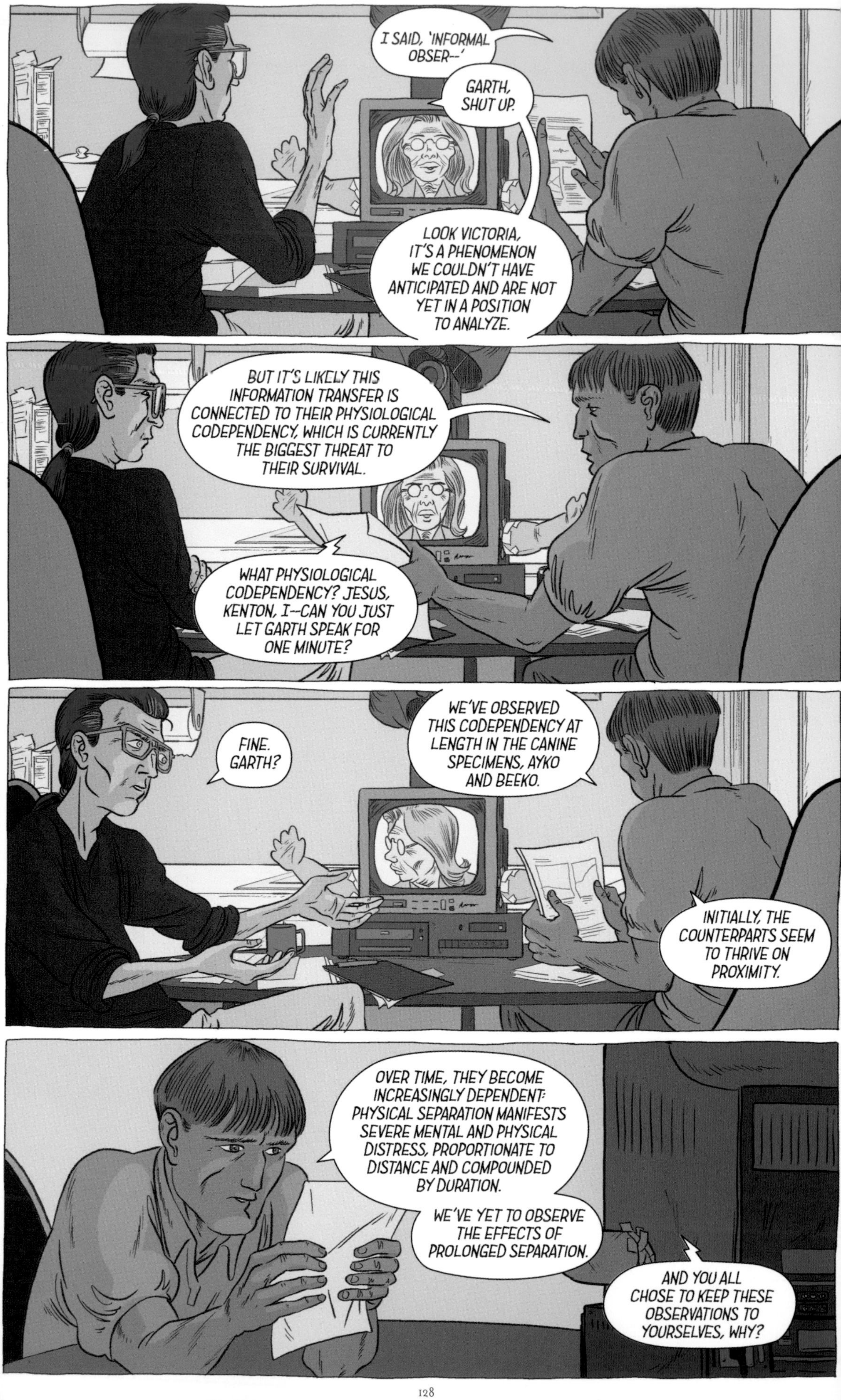
I SAID, 'INFORMAL OBSER--'
GARTH, SHUT UP.
LOOK VICTORIA, IT'S A PHENOMENON WE COULDN'T HAVE ANTICIPATED AND ARE NOT YET IN A POSITION TO ANALYZE.
BUT IT'S LIKELY THIS INFORMATION TRANSFER IS CONNECTED TO THEIR PHYSIOLOGICAL CODEPENDENCY, WHICH IS CURRENTLY THE BIGGEST THREAT TO THEIR SURVIVAL.
WHAT PHYSIOLOGICAL CODEPENDENCY? JESUS, KENTON, I--CAN YOU JUST LET GARTH SPEAK FOR ONE MINUTE?
FINE. GARTH?
WE'VE OBSERVED THIS CODEPENDENCY AT LENGTH IN THE CANINE SPECIMENS, AYKO AND BEEKO.
INITIALLY, THE COUNTERPARTS SEEM TO THRIVE ON PROXIMITY.
OVER TIME, THEY BECOME INCREASINGLY DEPENDENT: PHYSICAL SEPARATION MANIFESTS SEVERE MENTAL AND PHYSICAL DISTRESS, PROPORTIONATE TO DISTANCE AND COMPOUNDED BY DURATION.
WE'VE YET TO OBSERVE THE EFFECTS OF PROLONGED SEPARATION.
AND YOU ALL CHOSE TO KEEP THESE OBSERVATIONS TO YOURSELVES, WHY?

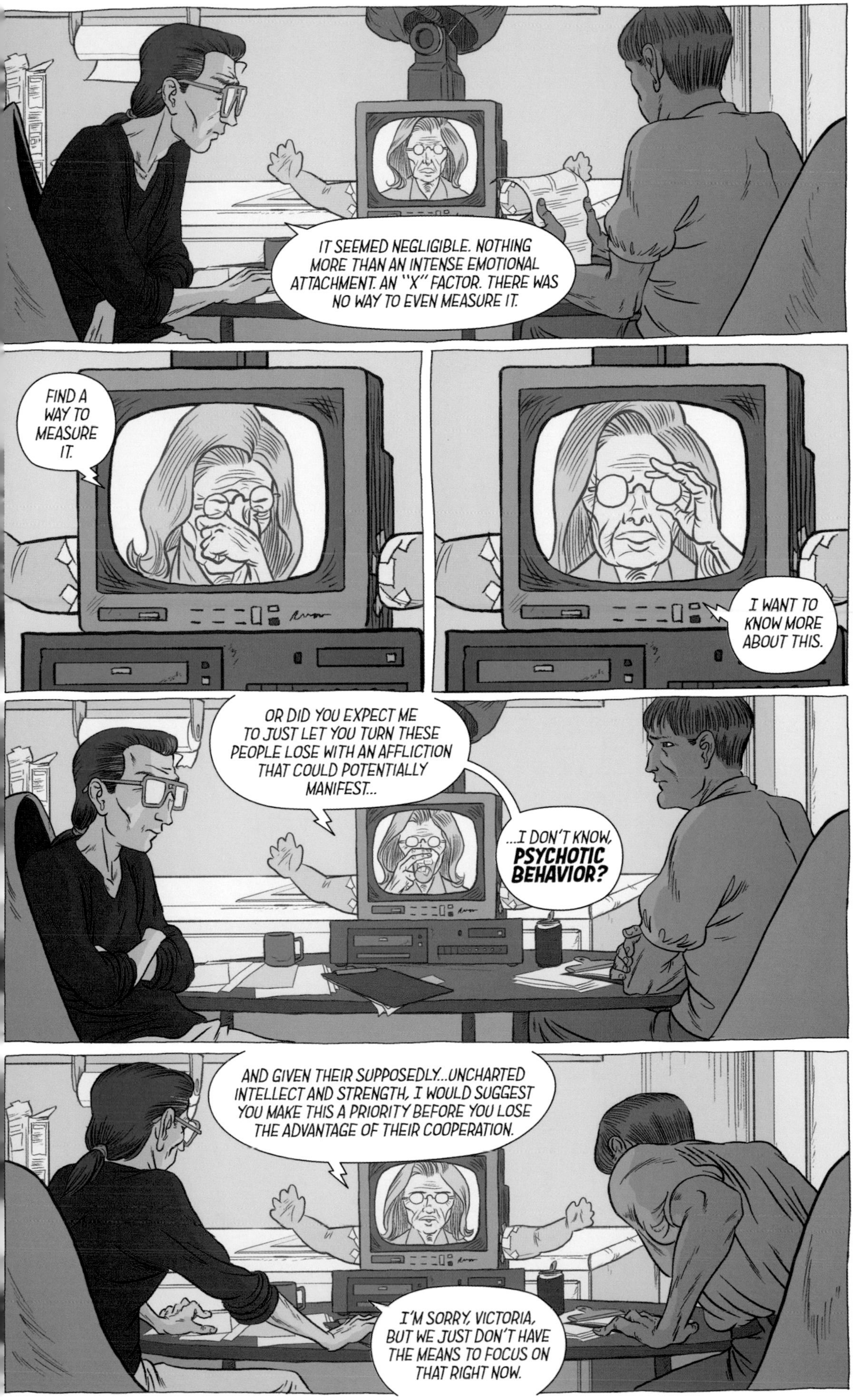
IT SEEMED NEGLIGIBLE. NOTHING MORE THAN AN INTENSE EMOTIONAL ATTACHMENT. AN "X" FACTOR. THERE WAS NO WAY TO EVEN MEASURE IT.
FIND A WAY TO MEASURE IT.
I WANT TO KNOW MORE ABOUT THIS.
OR DID YOU EXPECT ME TO JUST LET YOU TURN THESE PEOPLE LOSE WITH AN AFFLICTION THAT COULD POTENTIALLY MANIFEST...
...I DON'T KNOW, PSYCHOTIC BEHAVIOR?
AND GIVEN THEIR SUPPOSEDLY...UNCHARTED INTELLECT AND STRENGTH, I WOULD SUGGEST YOU MAKE THIS A PRIORITY BEFORE YOU LOSE THE ADVANTAGE OF THEIR COOPERATION.
I'M SORRY, VICTORIA, BUT WE JUST DON'T HAVE THE MEANS TO FOCUS ON THAT RIGHT NOW.

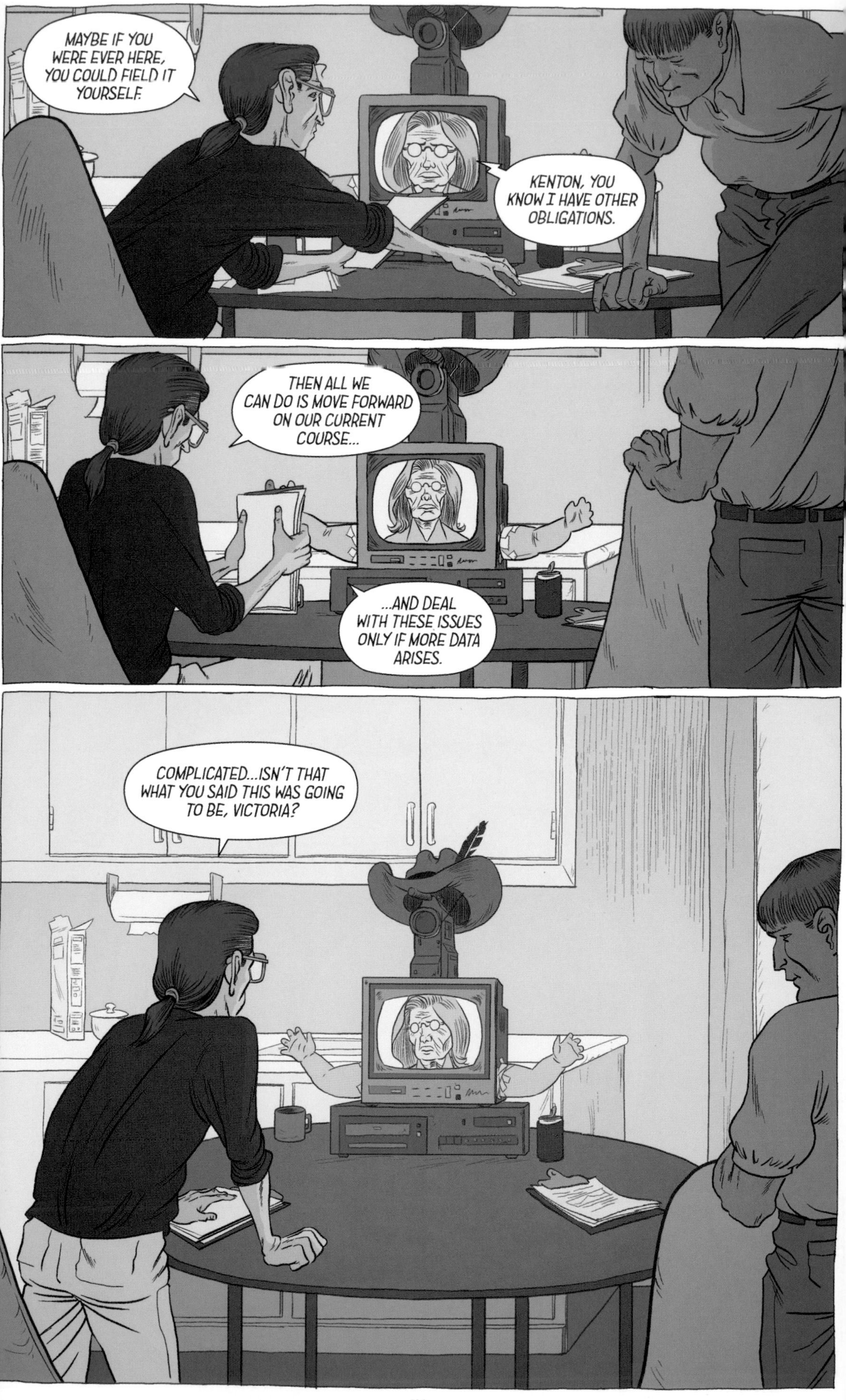
MAYBE IF YOU WERE EVER HERE, YOU COULD FIELD IT YOURSELF.
KENTON, YOU KNOW I HAVE OTHER OBLIGATIONS.
THEN ALL WE CAN DO IS MOVE FORWARD ON OUR CURRENT COURSE...
...AND DEAL WITH THESE ISSUES ONLY IF MORE DATA ARISES.
COMPLICATED...ISN'T THAT WHAT YOU SAID THIS WAS GOING TO BE, VICTORIA?

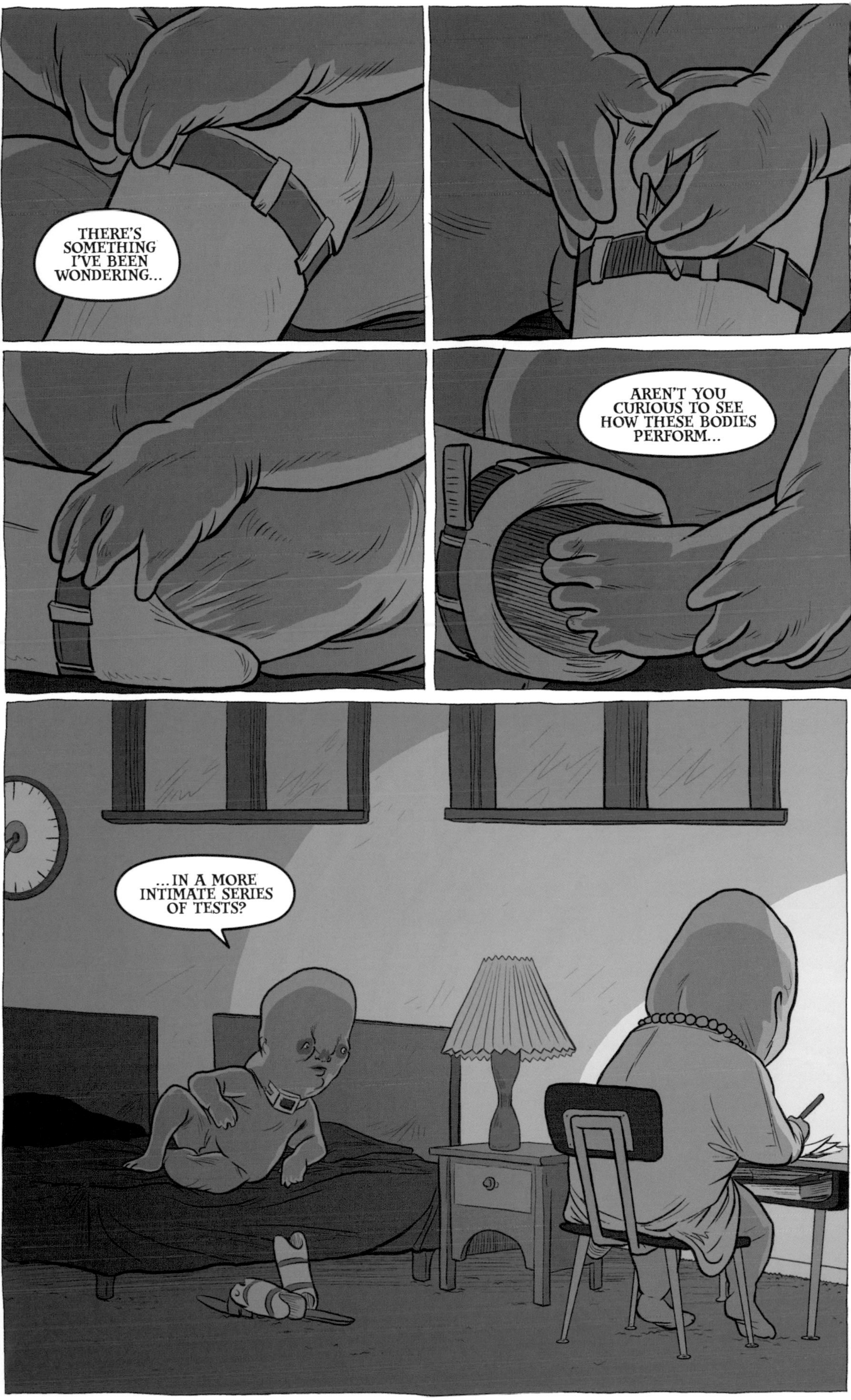
THERE'S SOMETHING I'VE BEEN WONDERING...
AREN'T YOU CURIOUS TO SEE HOW THESE BODIES PERFORM...
...IN A MORE INTIMATE SERIES OF TESTS?

LIBERATED FROM PEDESTRIAN BEAUTY STANDARDS...
...I'VE BECOME QUITE KEEN ON THE UNCANNY SENSUOUSNESS OF YOUR NEW LOOK.
I FEEL THE SAME BUTTERFLIES I FELT THE DAY WE FIRST MET.
BUT I NEVER DREAMED I COULD BE EVEN MORE TURNED ON BY YOU...
...THAN I WAS ON THAT NIGHT.
I'M SORRY, HENRY. I JUST DON'T FEEL THE SAME WAY. NOT YET.
PLEASE TURN THE LAMP BACK ON.

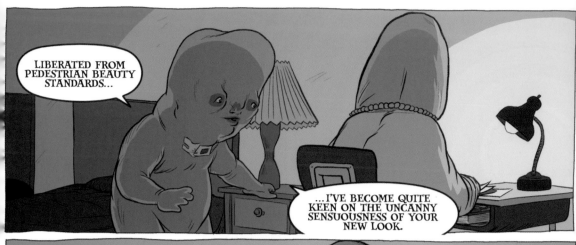

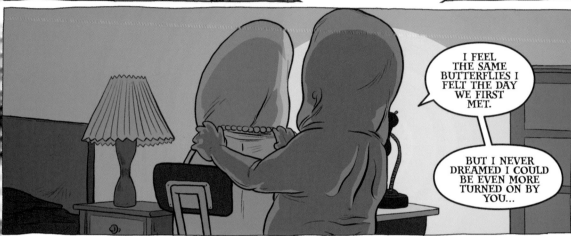

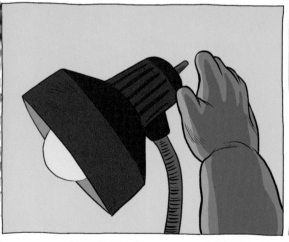

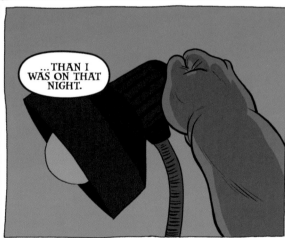

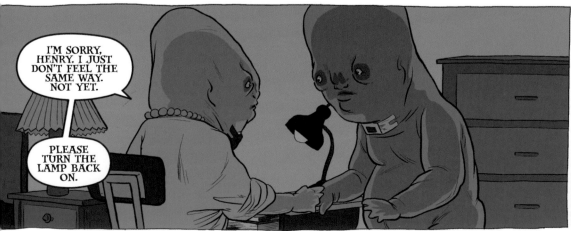

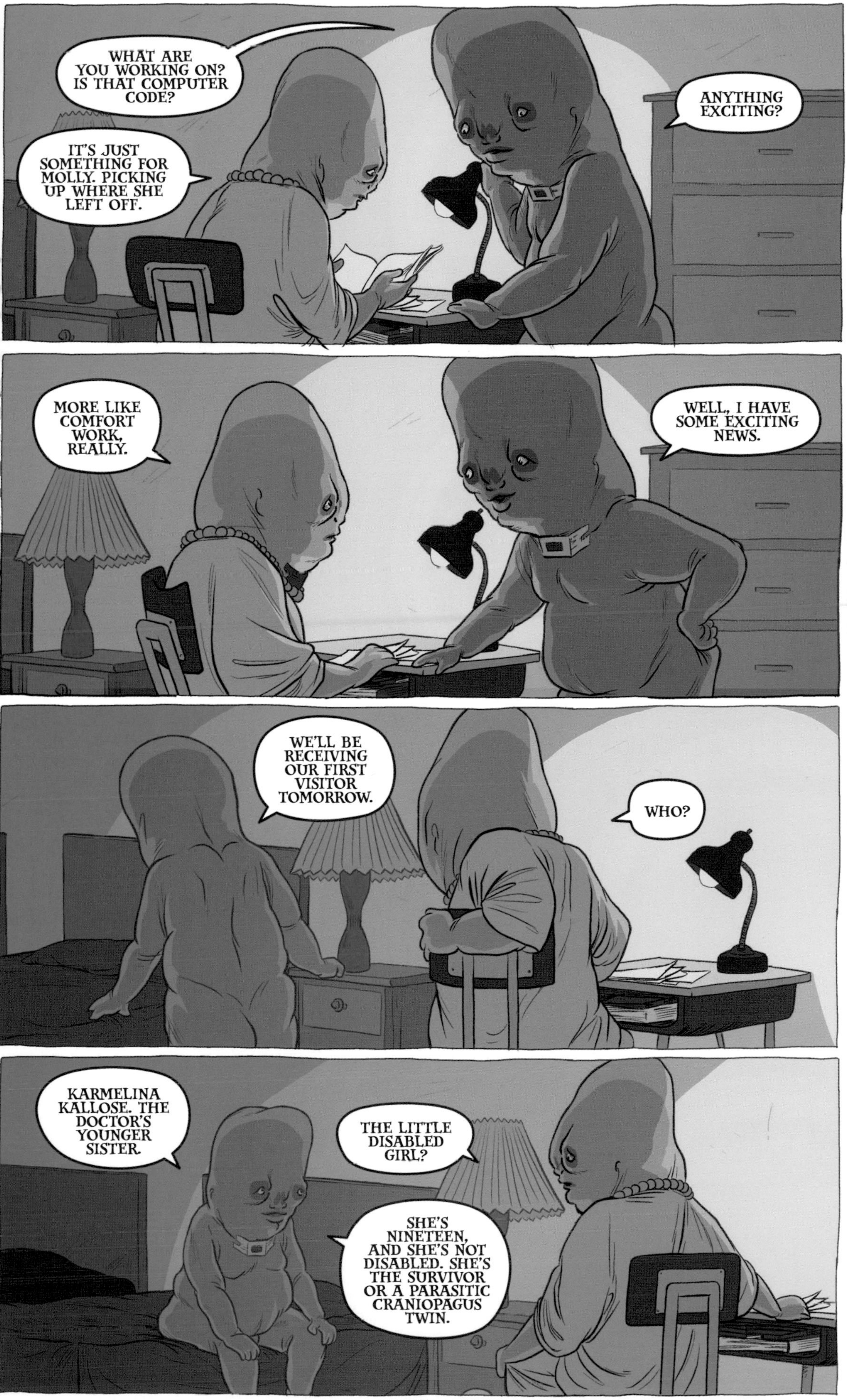
WHAT ARE YOU WORKING ON? IS THAT COMPUTER CODE?
IT'S JUST SOMETHING FOR MOLLY. PICKING UP WHERE SHE LEFT OFF.
ANYTHING EXCITING?
MORE LIKE COMFORT WORK, REALLY.
WELL, I HAVE SOME EXCITING NEWS.
WE'LL BE RECEIVING OUR FIRST VISITOR TOMORROW.
WHO?
KARMELINA KALLOSE. THE DOCTOR'S YOUNGER SISTER.
THE LITTLE DISABLED GIRL?
SHE'S NINETEEN, AND SHE'S NOT DISABLED. SHE'S THE SURVIVOR OR A PARASITIC CRANIOPAGUS TWIN.

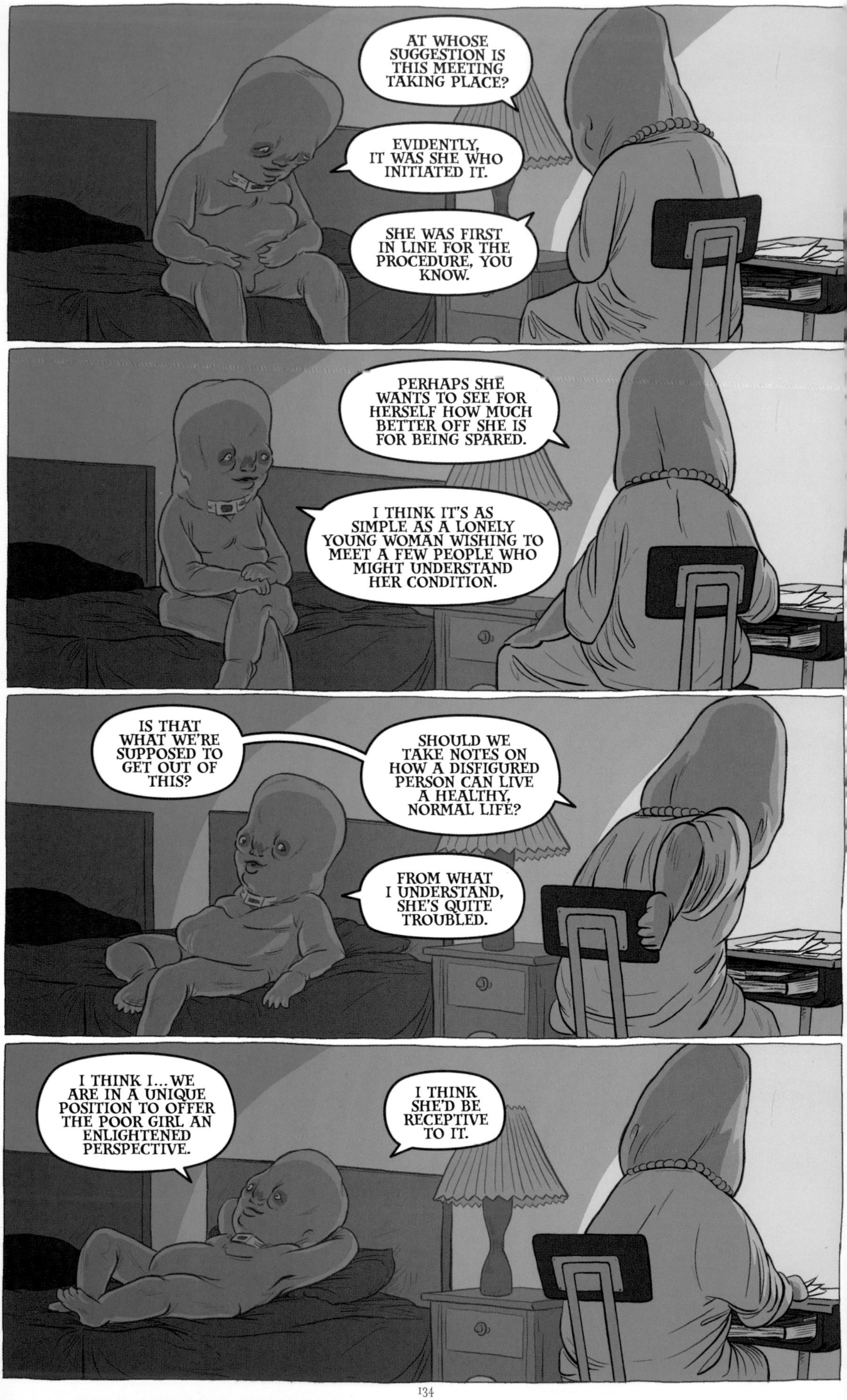
AT WHOSE SUGGESTION IS THIS MEETING TAKING PLACE?
EVIDENTLY, IT WAS SHE WHO INITIATED IT.
SHE WAS FIRST IN LINE FOR THE PROCEDURE, YOU KNOW.
PERHAPS SHE WANTS TO SEE FOR HERSELF HOW MUCH BETTER OFF SHE IS FOR BEING SPARED.
I THINK IT'S AS SIMPLE AS A LONELY YOUNG WOMAN WISHING TO MEET A FEW PEOPLE WHO MIGHT UNDERSTAND HER CONDITION.
IS THAT WHAT WE'RE SUPPOSED TO GET OUT OF THIS?
SHOULD WE TAKE NOTES ON HOW A DISFIGURED PERSON CAN LIVE A HEALTHY, NORMAL LIFE?
FROM WHAT I UNDERSTAND, SHE'S QUITE TROUBLED.
I THINK I...WE ARE IN A UNIQUE POSITION TO OFFER THE POOR GIRL AN ENLIGHTENED PERSPECTIVE.
I THINK SHE'D BE RECEPTIVE TO IT.

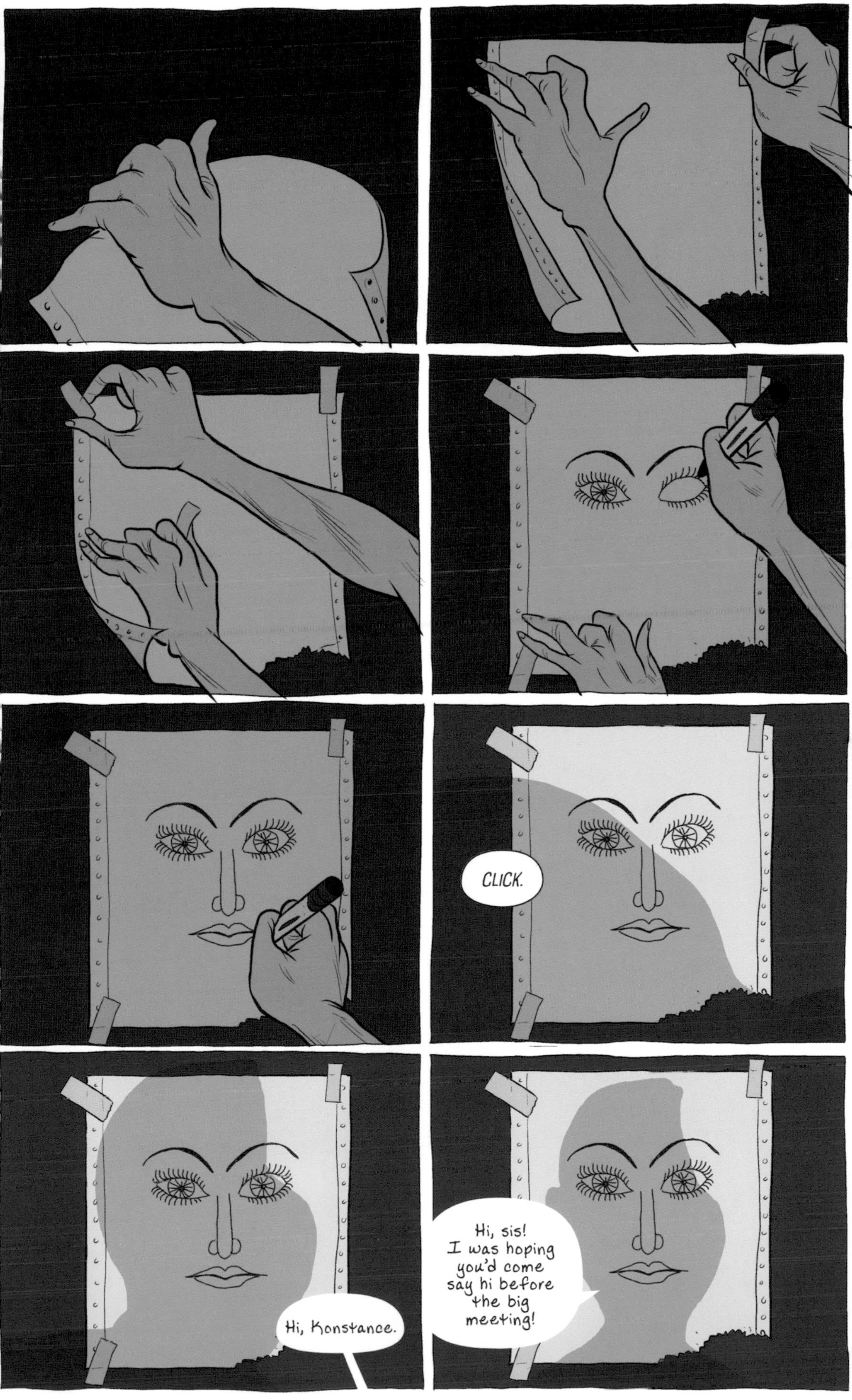
CLICK.
Hi, Konstance.
Hi, sis! I was hoping you'd come say hi before the big meeting!

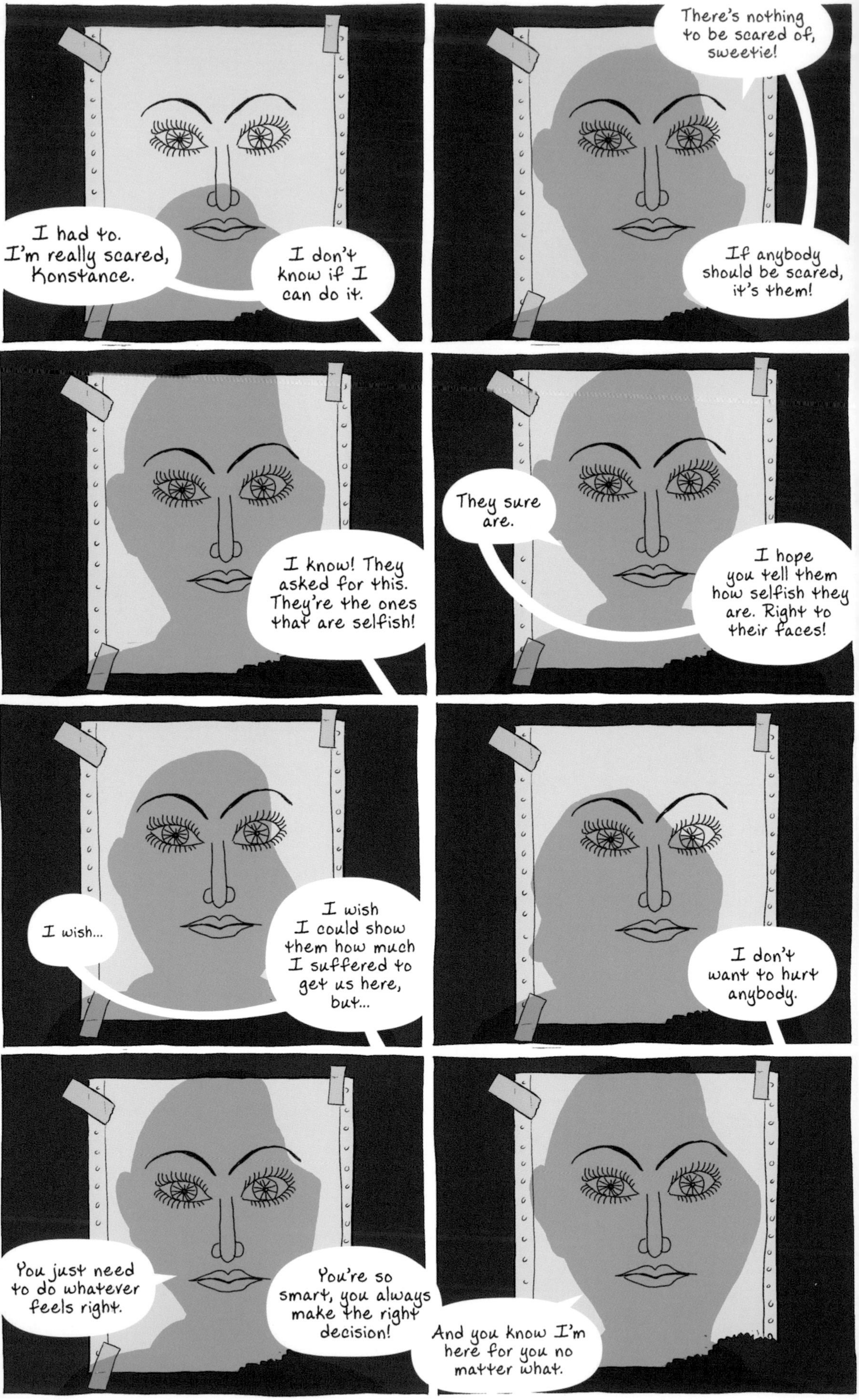

I had to. I'm really scared, Konstance.
I don't know if I can do it.
There's nothing to be scared of, sweetie!
If anybody should be scared, it's them!
I know! They asked for this. They're the ones that are selfish!
They sure are.
I hope you tell them how selfish they are. Right to their faces!
I wish...
I wish I could show them how much I suffered to get us here, but...
I don't want to hurt anybody.
You just need to do whatever feels right.
You're so smart, you always make the right decision!
And you know I'm here for you no matter what.

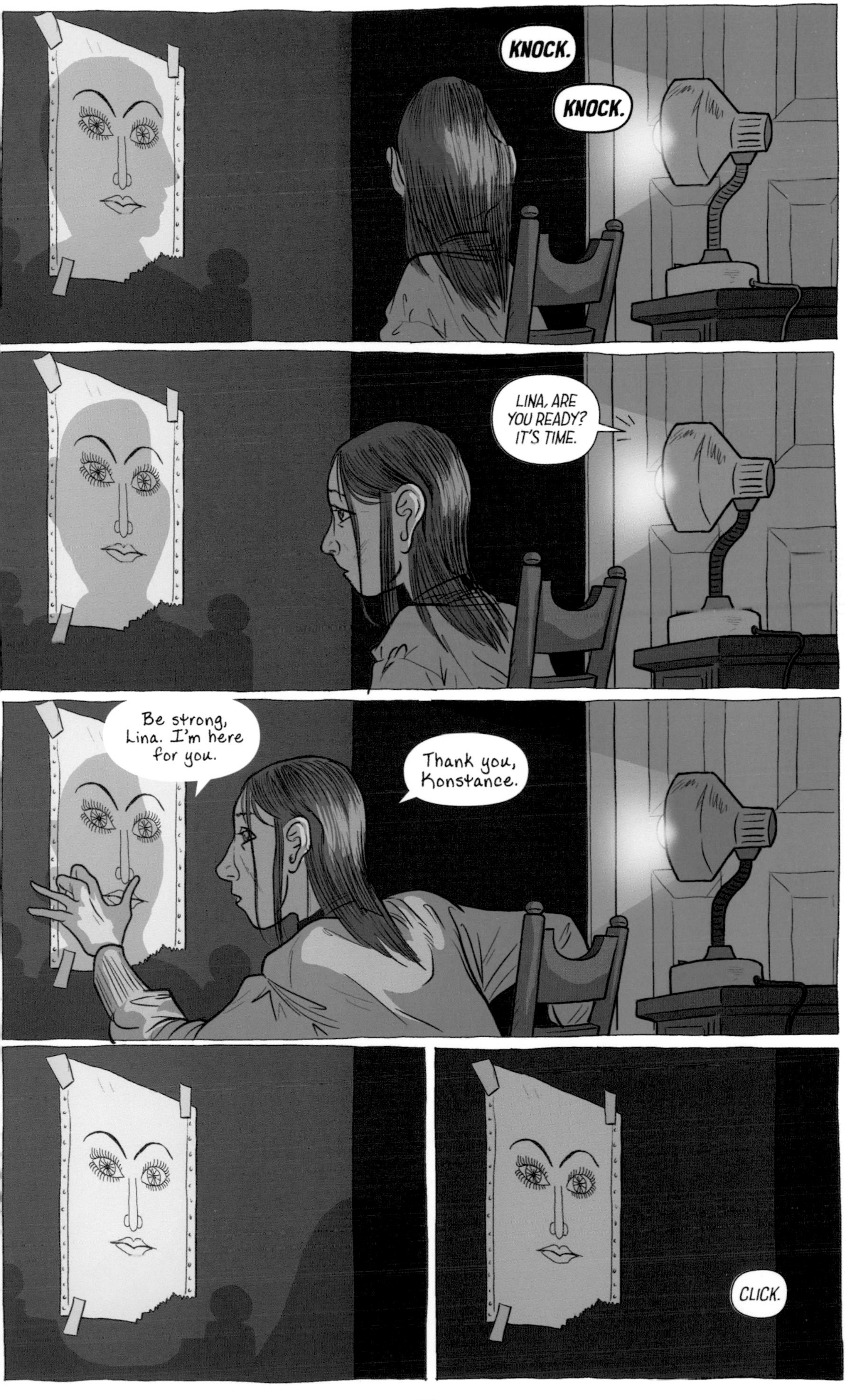
KNOCK.
KNOCK.
LINA, ARE YOU READY? IT'S TIME.
Be strong, Lina. I'm here for you.
Thank you, Konstance.
CLICK.

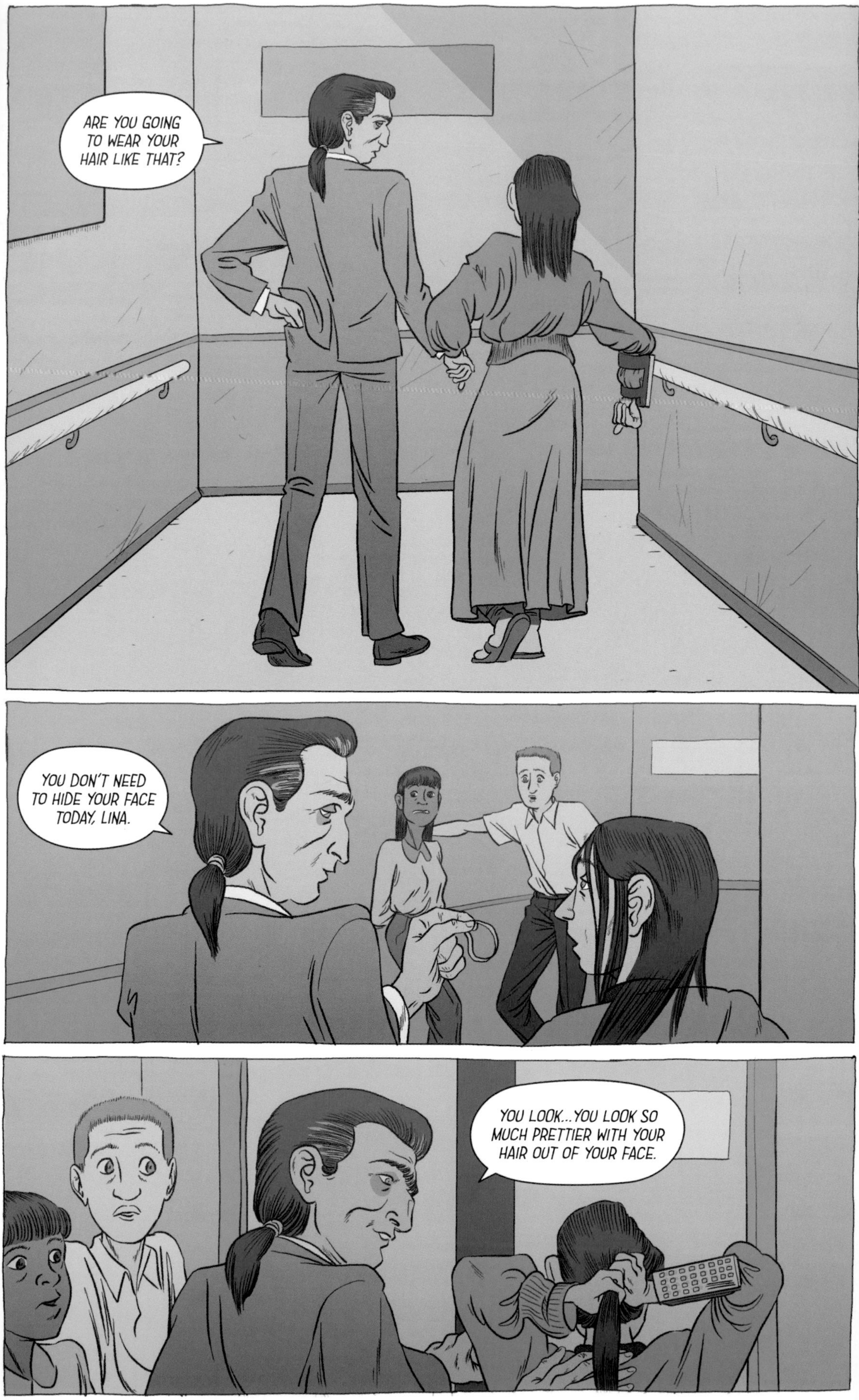
ARE YOU GOING TO WEAR YOUR HAIR LIKE THAT?
YOU DON'T NEED TO HIDE YOUR FACE TODAY, LINA.
YOU LOOK...YOU LOOK SO MUCH PRETTIER WITH YOUR HAIR OUT OF YOUR FACE.

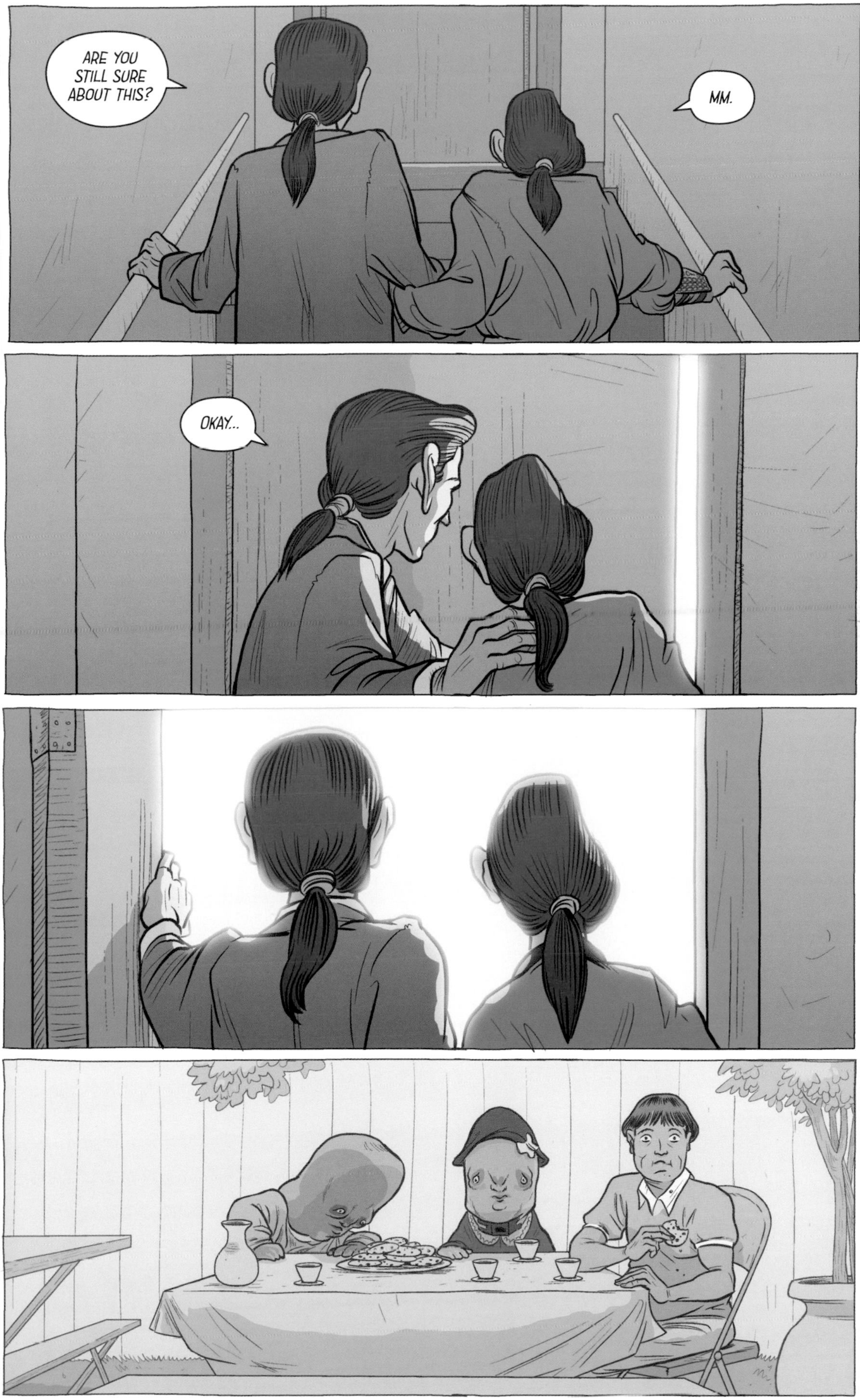
ARE YOU STILL SURE ABOUT THIS?
MM.
OKAY...

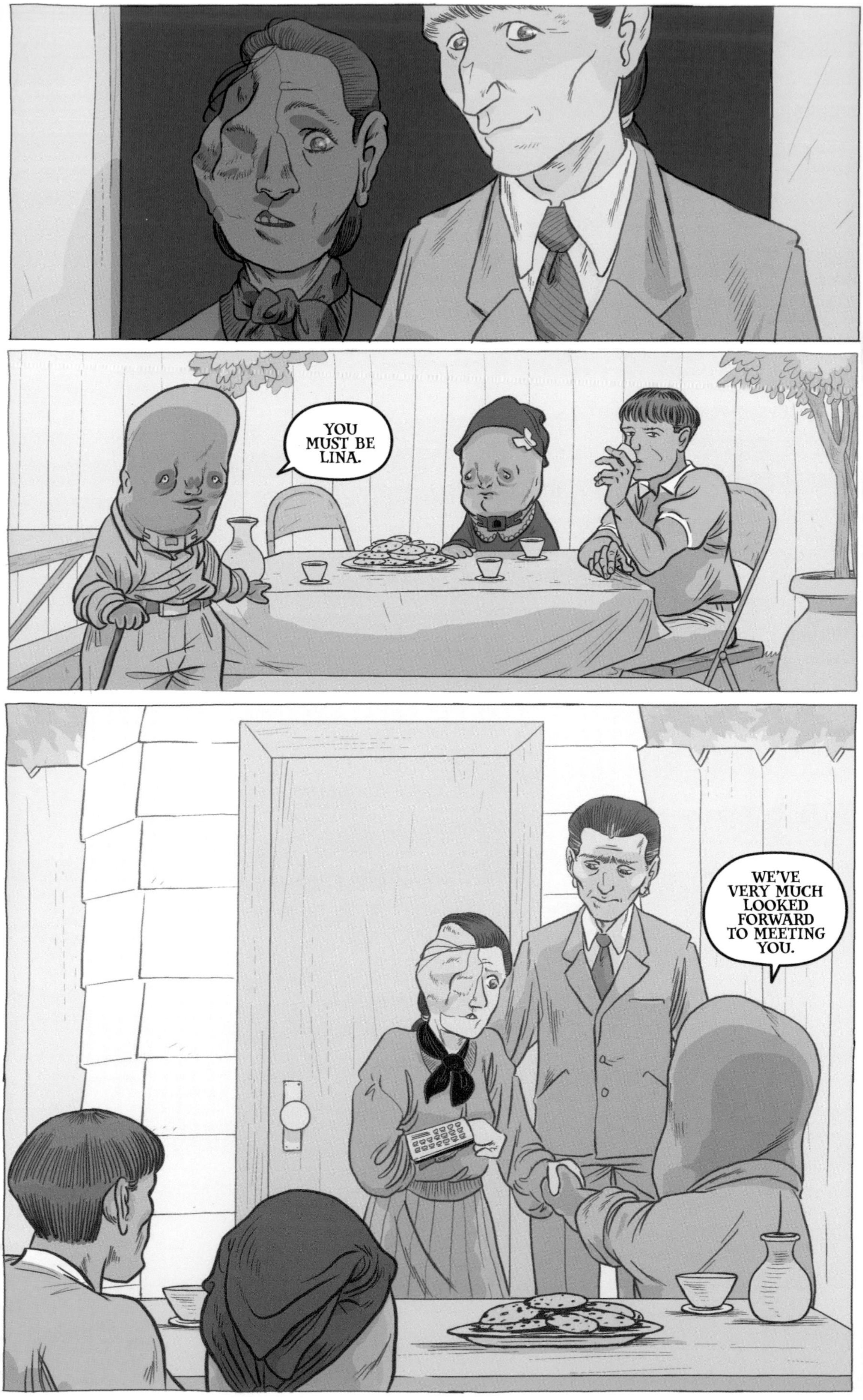
YOU MUST BE LINA.
WE'VE VERY MUCH LOOKED FORWARD TO MEETING YOU.

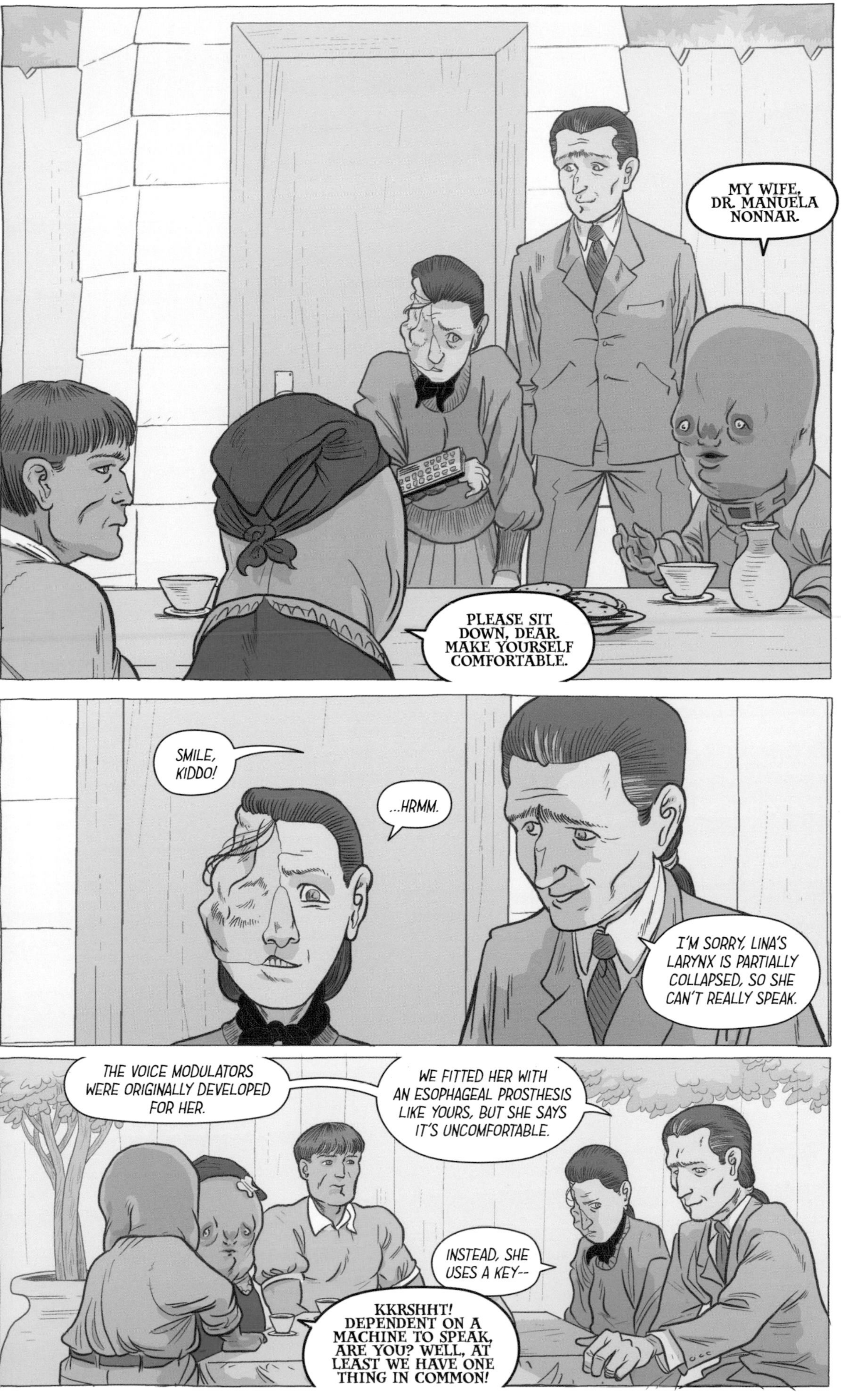
MY WIFE, DR. MANUELA NONNAR.
PLEASE SIT DOWN, DEAR. MAKE YOURSELF COMFORTABLE.
SMILE, KIDDO!
...HRMM.
I'M SORRY, LINA'S LARYNX IS PARTIALLY COLLAPSED, SO SHE CAN'T REALLY SPEAK.
THE VOICE MODULATORS WERE ORIGINALLY DEVELOPED FOR HER.
WE FITTED HER WITH AN ESOPHAGEAL PROSTHESIS LIKE YOURS, BUT SHE SAYS IT'S UNCOMFORTABLE.
INSTEAD, SHE USES A KEY--
KKRSHHT! DEPENDENT ON A MACHINE TO SPEAK, ARE YOU? WELL, AT LEAST WE HAVE ONE THING IN COMMON!

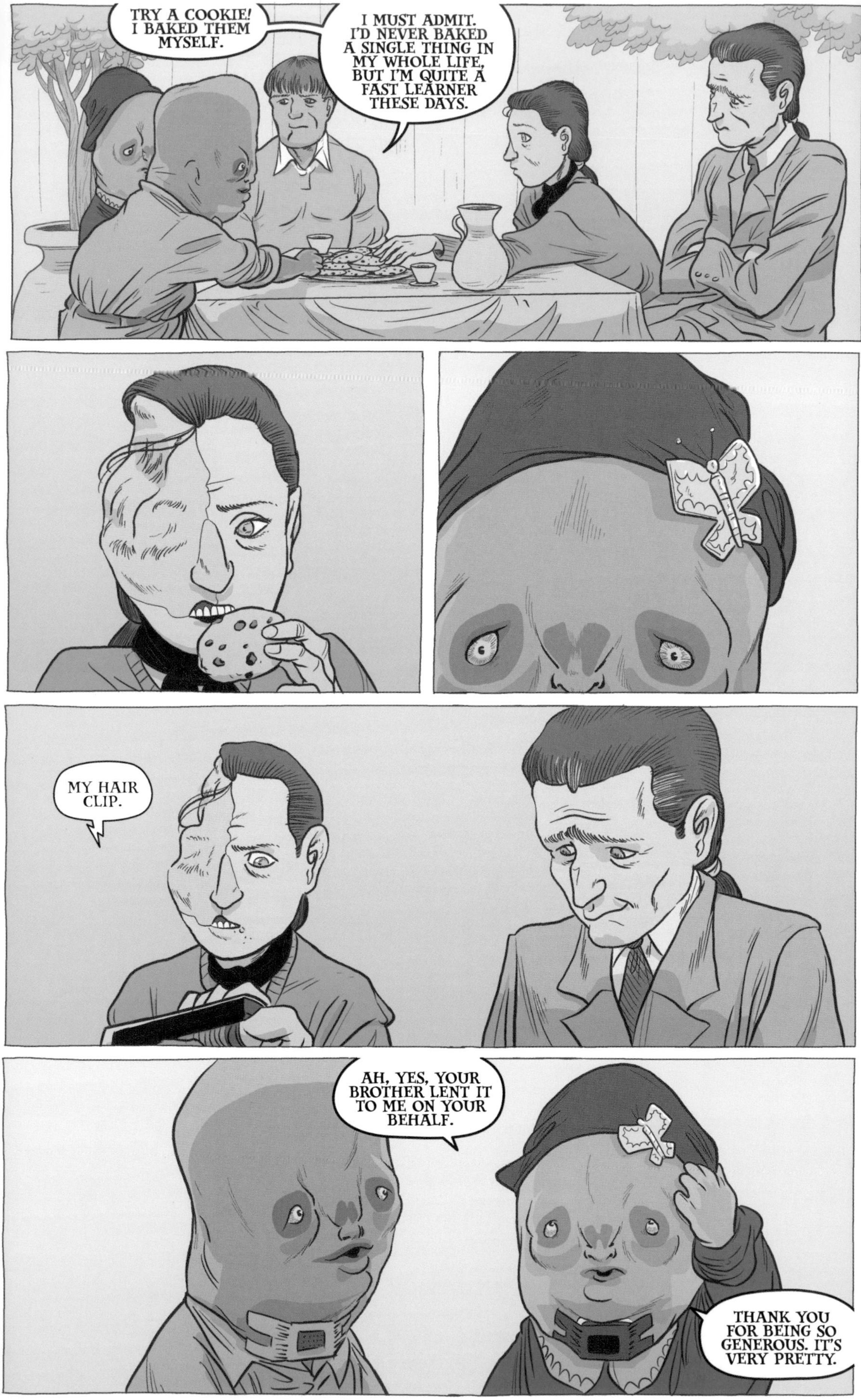
TRY A COOKIE! I BAKED THEM MYSELF.
I MUST ADMIT. I'D NEVER BAKED A SINGLE THING IN MY WHOLE LIFE, BUT I'M QUITE A FAST LEARNER THESE DAYS.
MY HAIR CLIP.
AH, YES, YOUR BROTHER LENT IT TO ME ON YOUR BEHALF.
THANK YOU FOR BEING SO GENEROUS. IT'S VERY PRETTY.

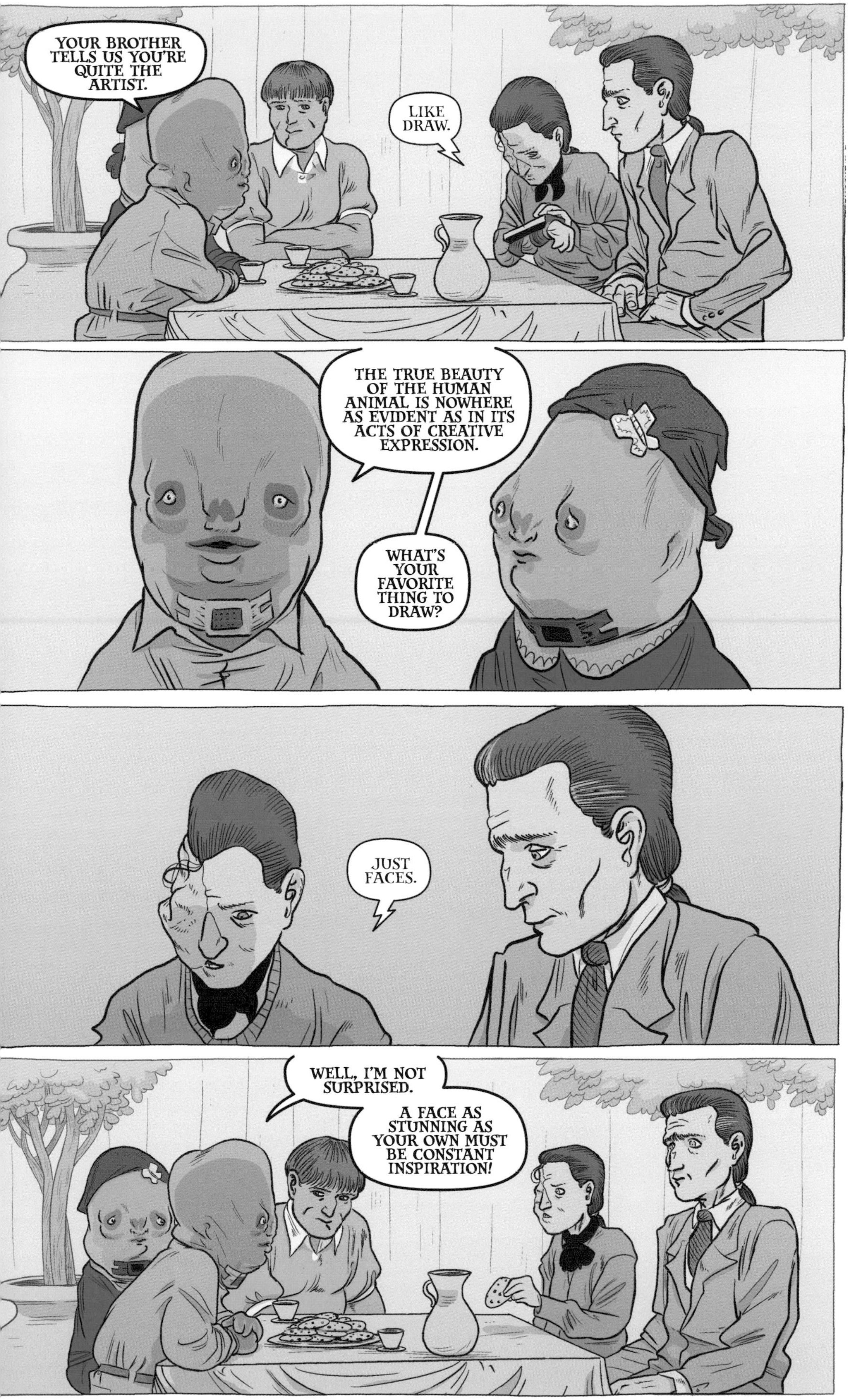
YOUR BROTHER TELLS US YOU'RE QUITE THE ARTIST.
LIKE DRAW.
THE TRUE BEAUTY OF THE HUMAN ANIMAL IS NOWHERE AS EVIDENT AS IN ITS ACTS OF CREATIVE EXPRESSION.
WHAT'S YOUR FAVORITE THING TO DRAW?
JUST FACES.
WELL, I'M NOT SURPRISED.
A FACE AS STUNNING AS YOUR OWN MUST BE CONSTANT INSPIRATION!

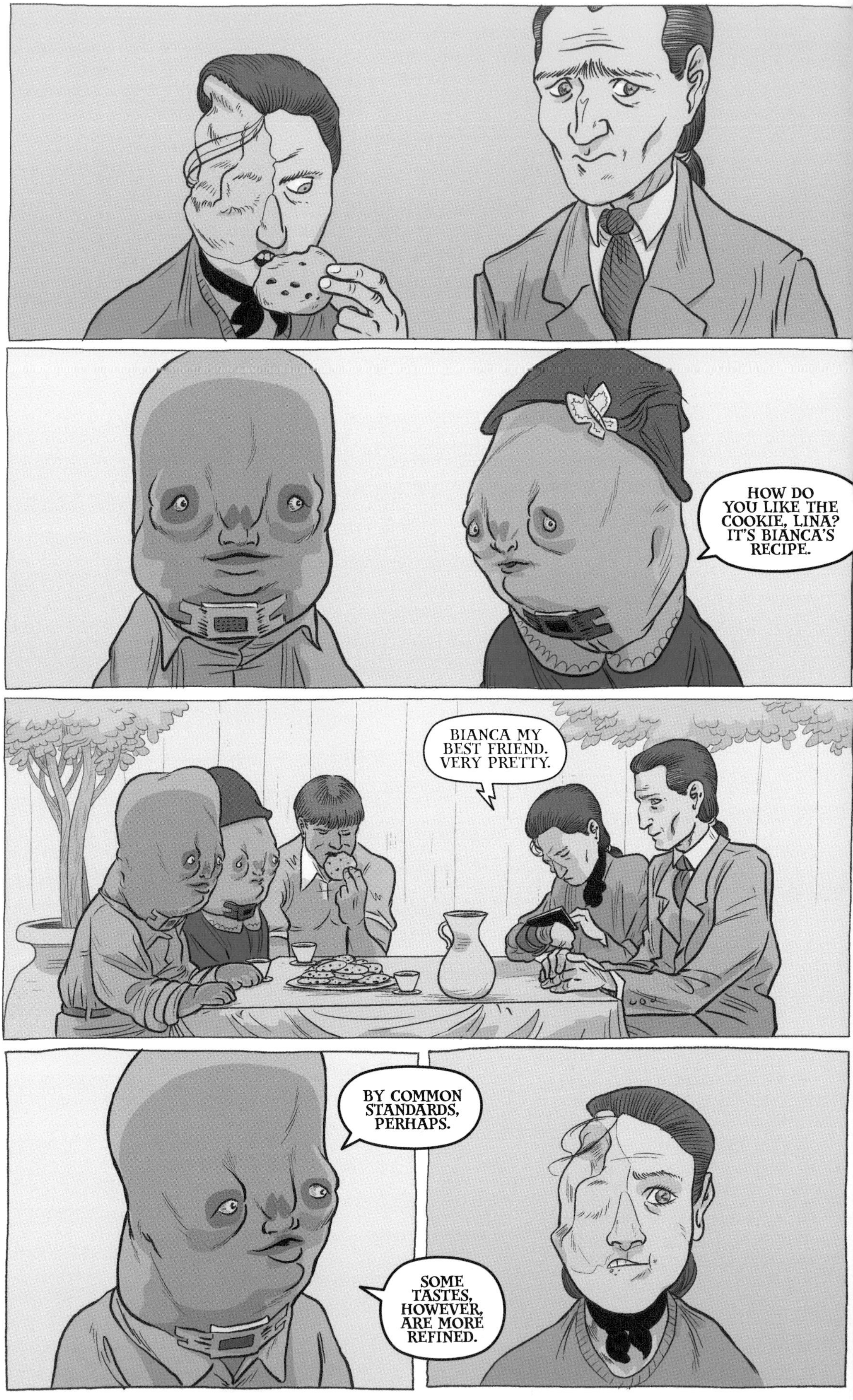
HOW DO YOU LIKE THE COOKIE, LINA? IT'S BIANCA'S RECIPE.
BIANCA MY BEST FRIEND. VERY PRETTY.
BY COMMON STANDARDS, PERHAPS.
SOME TASTES, HOWEVER, ARE MORE REFINED.

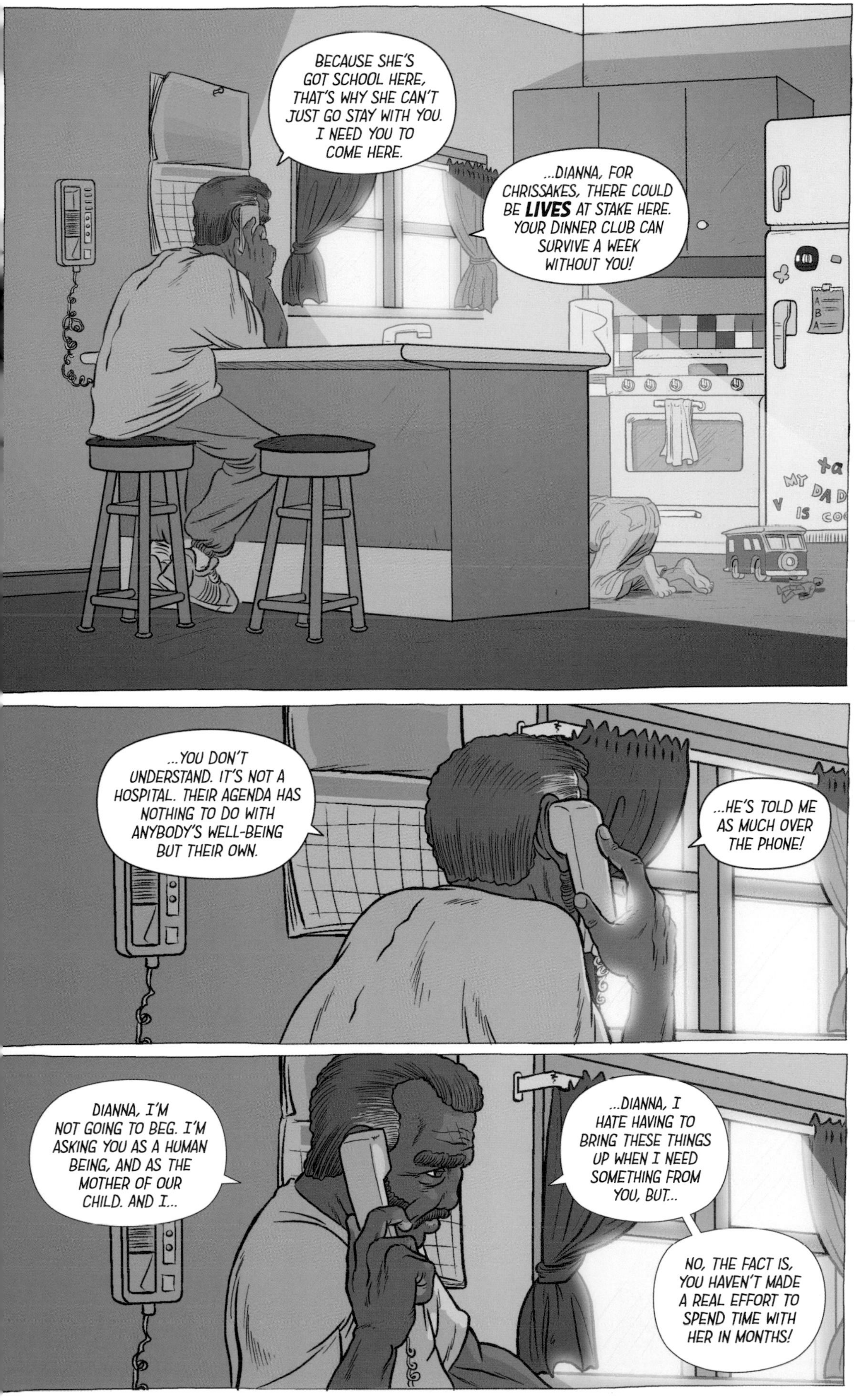
BECAUSE SHE'S GOT SCHOOL HERE, THAT'S WHY SHE CAN'T JUST GO STAY WITH YOU. I NEED YOU TO COME HERE.
...DIANNA, FOR CHRISSAKES, THERE COULD BE **LIVES** AT STAKE HERE. YOUR DINNER CLUB CAN SURVIVE A WEEK WITHOUT YOU!
...YOU DON'T UNDERSTAND. IT'S NOT A HOSPITAL. THEIR AGENDA HAS NOTHING TO DO WITH ANYBODY'S WELL-BEING BUT THEIR OWN.
...HE'S TOLD ME AS MUCH OVER THE PHONE!
DIANNA, I'M NOT GOING TO BEG. I'M ASKING YOU AS A HUMAN BEING, AND AS THE MOTHER OF OUR CHILD. AND I...
...DIANNA, I HATE HAVING TO BRING THESE THINGS UP WHEN I NEED SOMETHING FROM YOU, BUT...
NO, THE FACT IS, YOU HAVEN'T MADE A REAL EFFORT TO SPEND TIME WITH HER IN MONTHS!

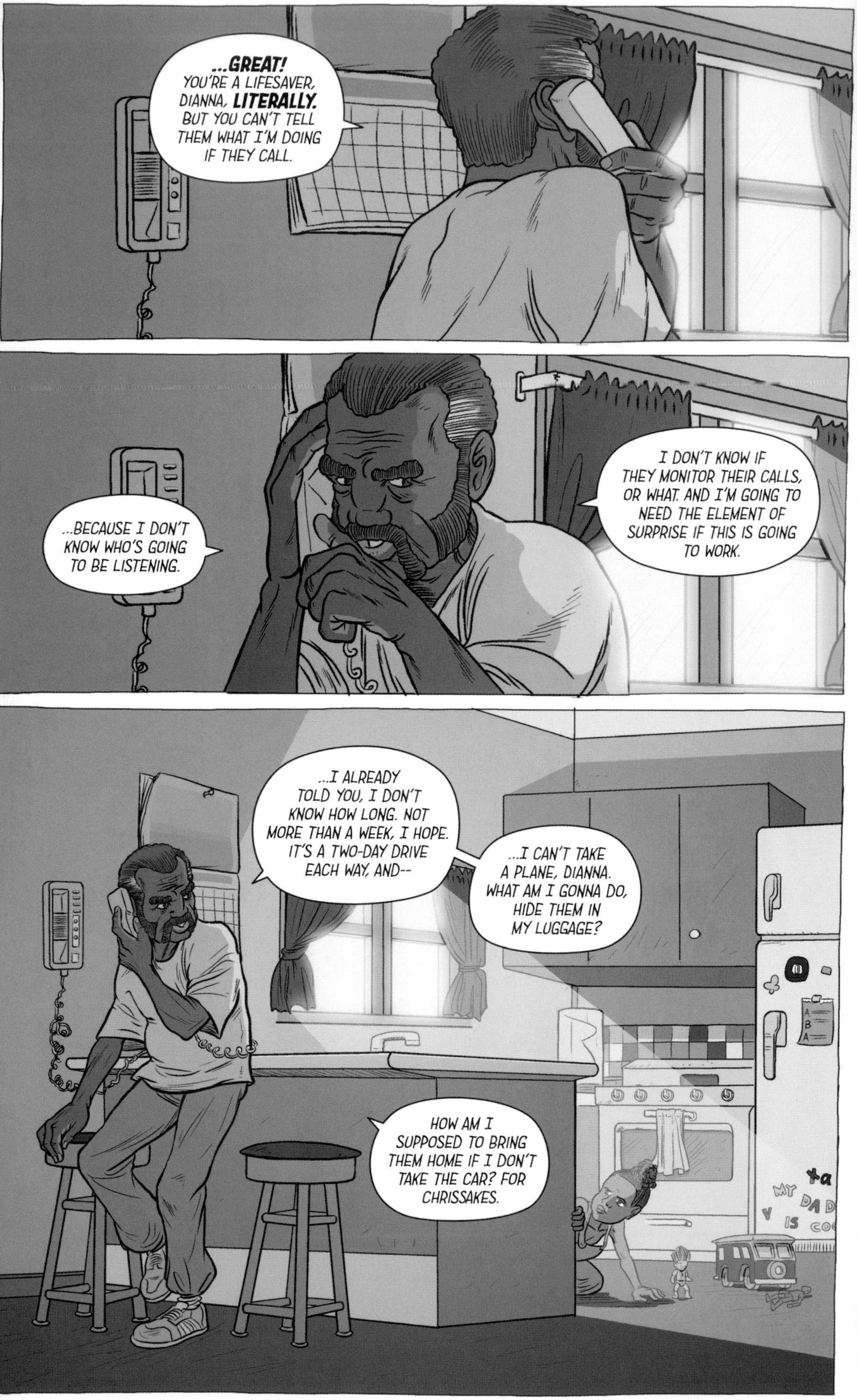
...GREAT! YOU'RE A LIFESAVER, DIANNA, LITERALLY. BUT YOU CAN'T TELL THEM WHAT I'M DOING IF THEY CALL.
...BECAUSE I DON'T KNOW WHO'S GOING TO BE LISTENING.
I DON'T KNOW IF THEY MONITOR THEIR CALLS, OR WHAT. AND I'M GOING TO NEED THE ELEMENT OF SURPRISE IF THIS IS GOING TO WORK.
...I ALREADY TOLD YOU, I DON'T KNOW HOW LONG. NOT MORE THAN A WEEK, I HOPE. IT'S A TWO-DAY DRIVE EACH WAY, AND--
...I CAN'T TAKE A PLANE, DIANNA. WHAT AM I GONNA DO, HIDE THEM IN MY LUGGAGE?
HOW AM I SUPPOSED TO BRING THEM HOME IF I DON'T TAKE THE CAR? FOR CHRISSAKES.

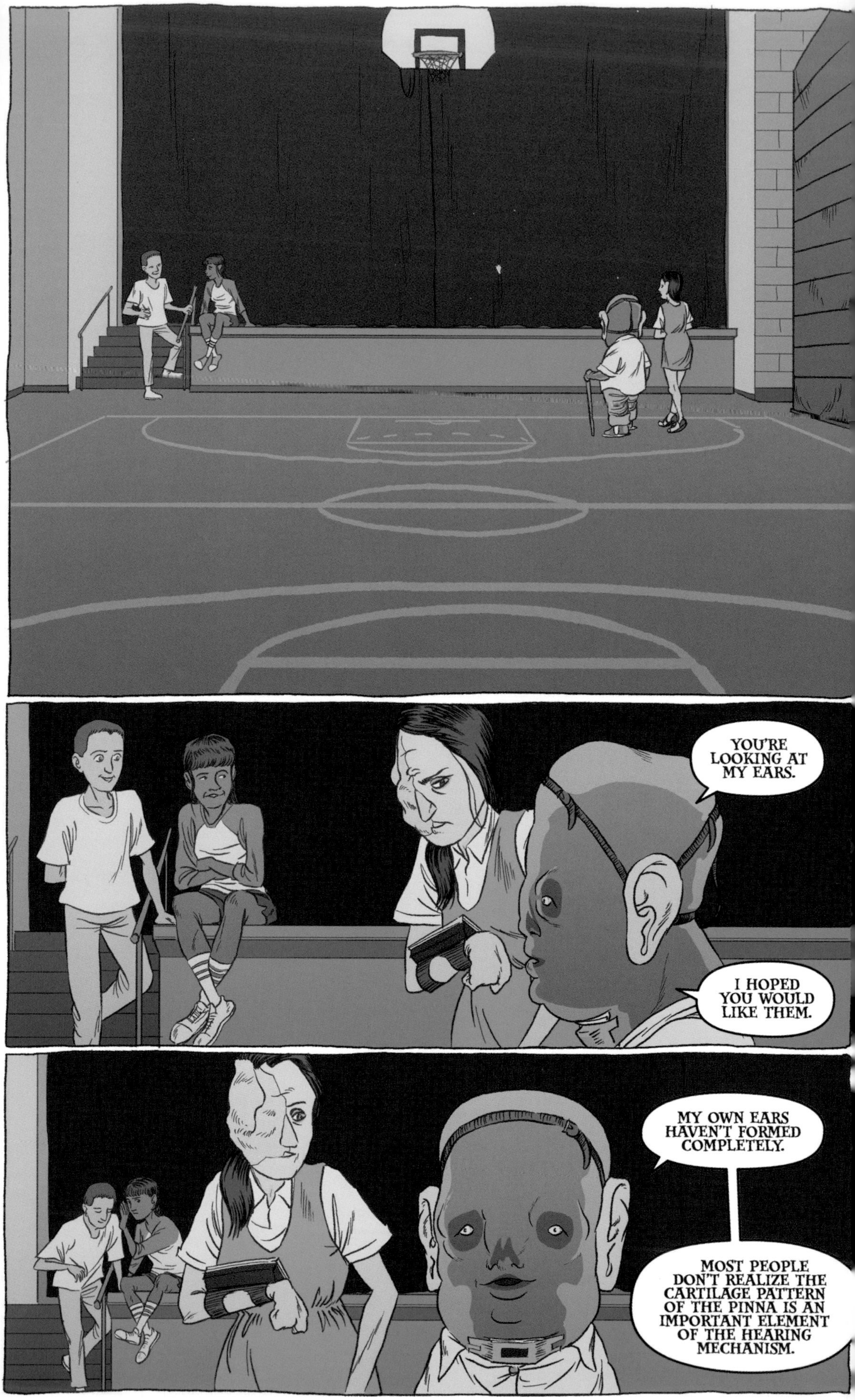
YOU'RE LOOKING AT MY EARS.
I HOPED YOU WOULD LIKE THEM.
MY OWN EARS HAVEN'T FORMED COMPLETELY.
MOST PEOPLE DON'T REALIZE THE CARTILAGE PATTERN OF THE PINNA IS AN IMPORTANT ELEMENT OF THE HEARING MECHANISM.

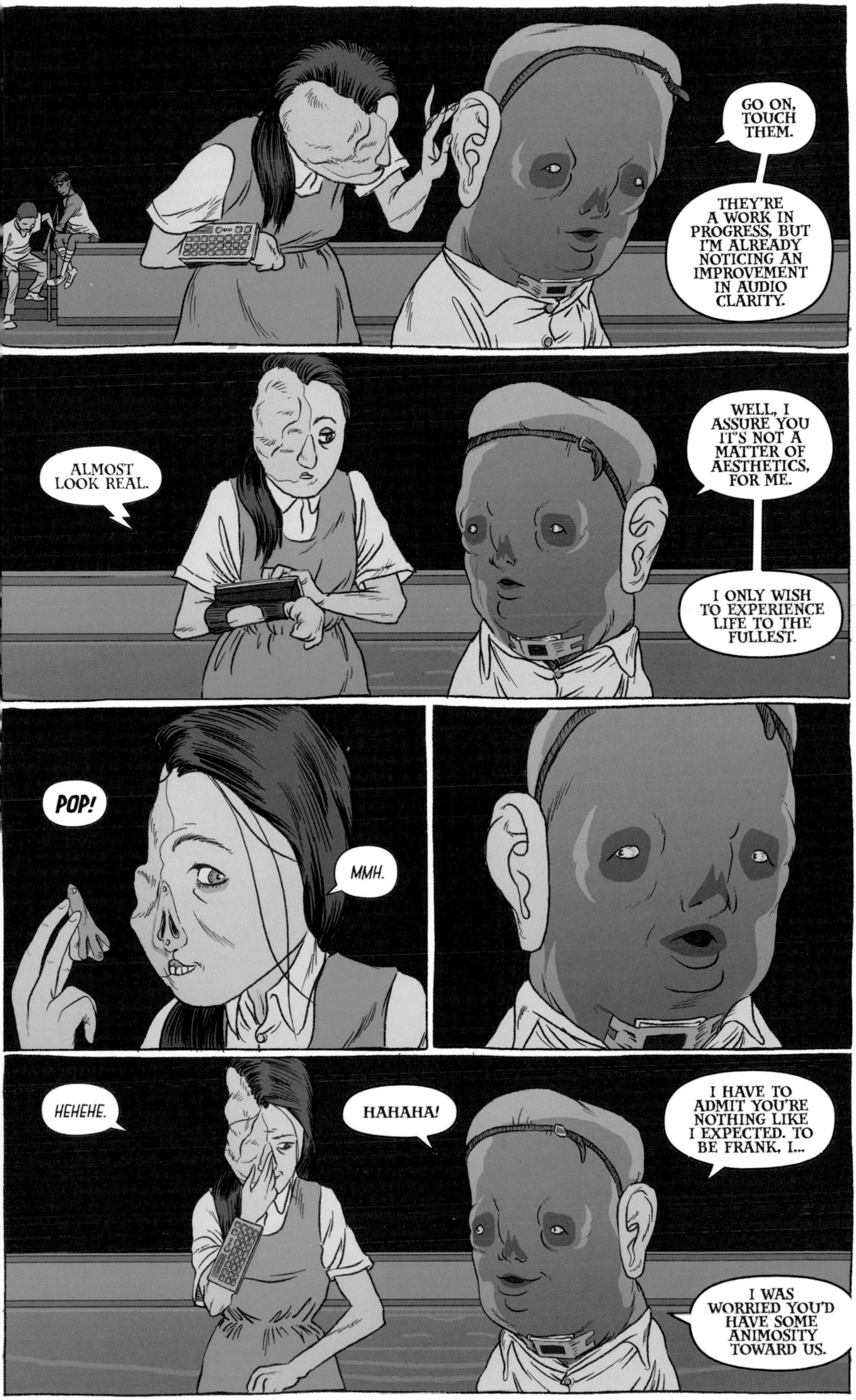
GO ON, TOUCH THEM.
THEY'RE A WORK IN PROGRESS, BUT I'M ALREADY NOTICING AN IMPROVEMENT IN AUDIO CLARITY.
ALMOST LOOK REAL.
WELL, I ASSURE YOU IT'S NOT A MATTER OF AESTHETICS, FOR ME.
I ONLY WISH TO EXPERIENCE LIFE TO THE FULLEST.
POP!
MMH.
HEHEHE.
HAHAHA!
I HAVE TO ADMIT YOU'RE NOTHING LIKE I EXPECTED. TO BE FRANK, I...
I WAS WORRIED YOU'D HAVE SOME ANIMOSITY TOWARD US.

I DO.

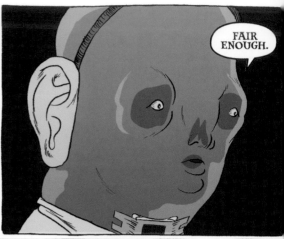

FAIR ENOUGH.

BUT LOOK.

HAHA, WHAT A TREMENDOUS WIT!

BUT YES, WHAT IRONY THAT THE PROCEDURE MEANT TO MAKE YOU MORE LIKE ME, INSTEAD MADE ME MORE LIKE YOU.

I'M SORRY. WAS THAT A WEIRD THING TO SAY?

THIS IS ALL NEW TO ME. I'M STILL NOT SURE OF THE PROPER TONE TO TAKE WHEN SPEAKING ABOUT MY...OUR... CONDITIONS.

BUT I DID LIVE A LONG LIFE BEFORE THIS...

...A LIFE STRANGLED BY THE PREJUDICES OF OTHERS.

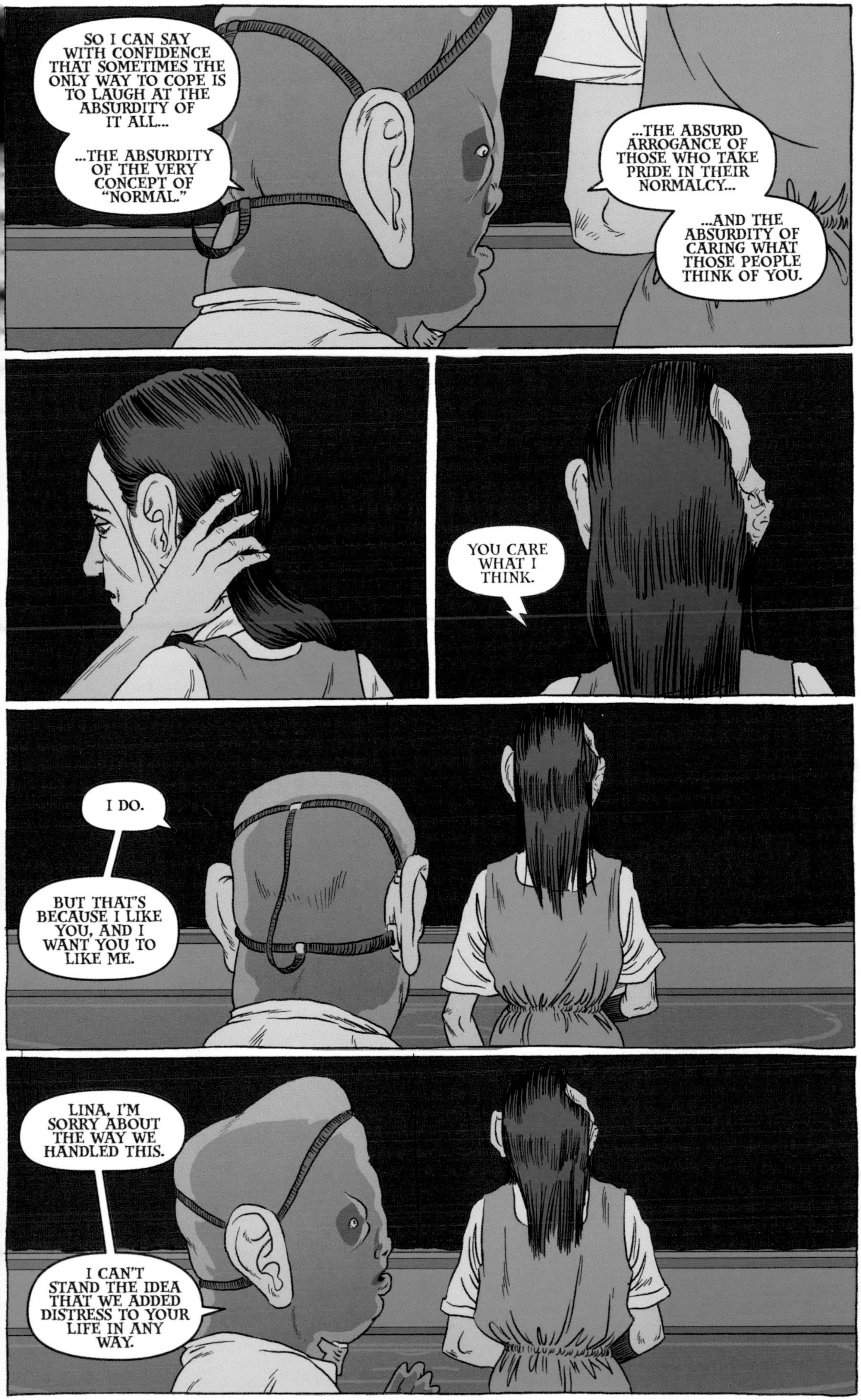

SO I CAN SAY WITH CONFIDENCE THAT SOMETIMES THE ONLY WAY TO COPE IS TO LAUGH AT THE ABSURDITY OF IT ALL...
...THE ABSURDITY OF THE VERY CONCEPT OF "NORMAL."
...THE ABSURD ARROGANCE OF THOSE WHO TAKE PRIDE IN THEIR NORMALCY...
...AND THE ABSURDITY OF CARING WHAT THOSE PEOPLE THINK OF YOU.
YOU CARE WHAT I THINK.
I DO.
BUT THAT'S BECAUSE I LIKE YOU, AND I WANT YOU TO LIKE ME.
LINA, I'M SORRY ABOUT THE WAY WE HANDLED THIS.
I CAN'T STAND THE IDEA THAT WE ADDED DISTRESS TO YOUR LIFE IN ANY WAY.

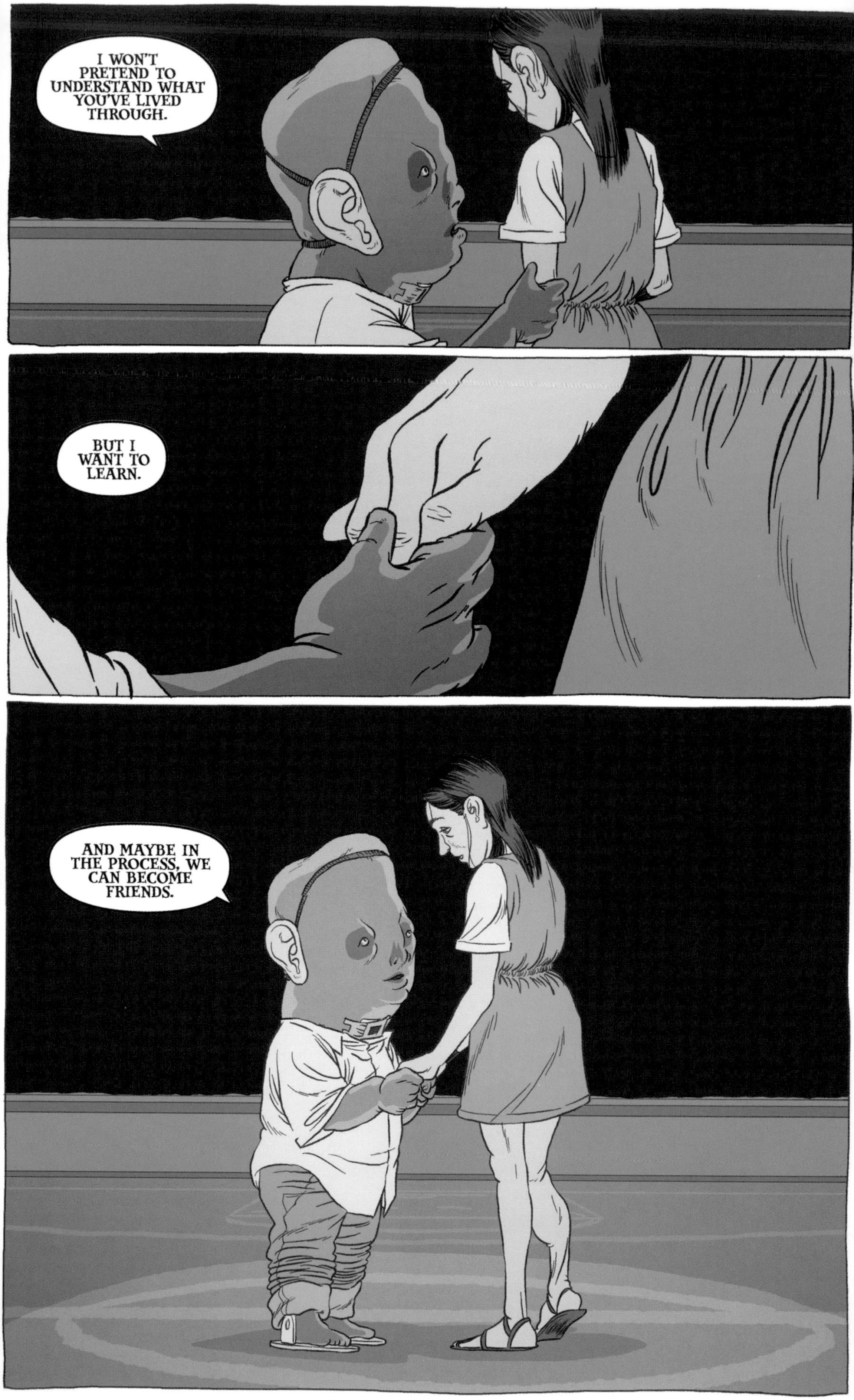
I WON'T PRETEND TO UNDERSTAND WHAT YOU'VE LIVED THROUGH.
BUT I WANT TO LEARN.
AND MAYBE IN THE PROCESS, WE CAN BECOME FRIENDS.

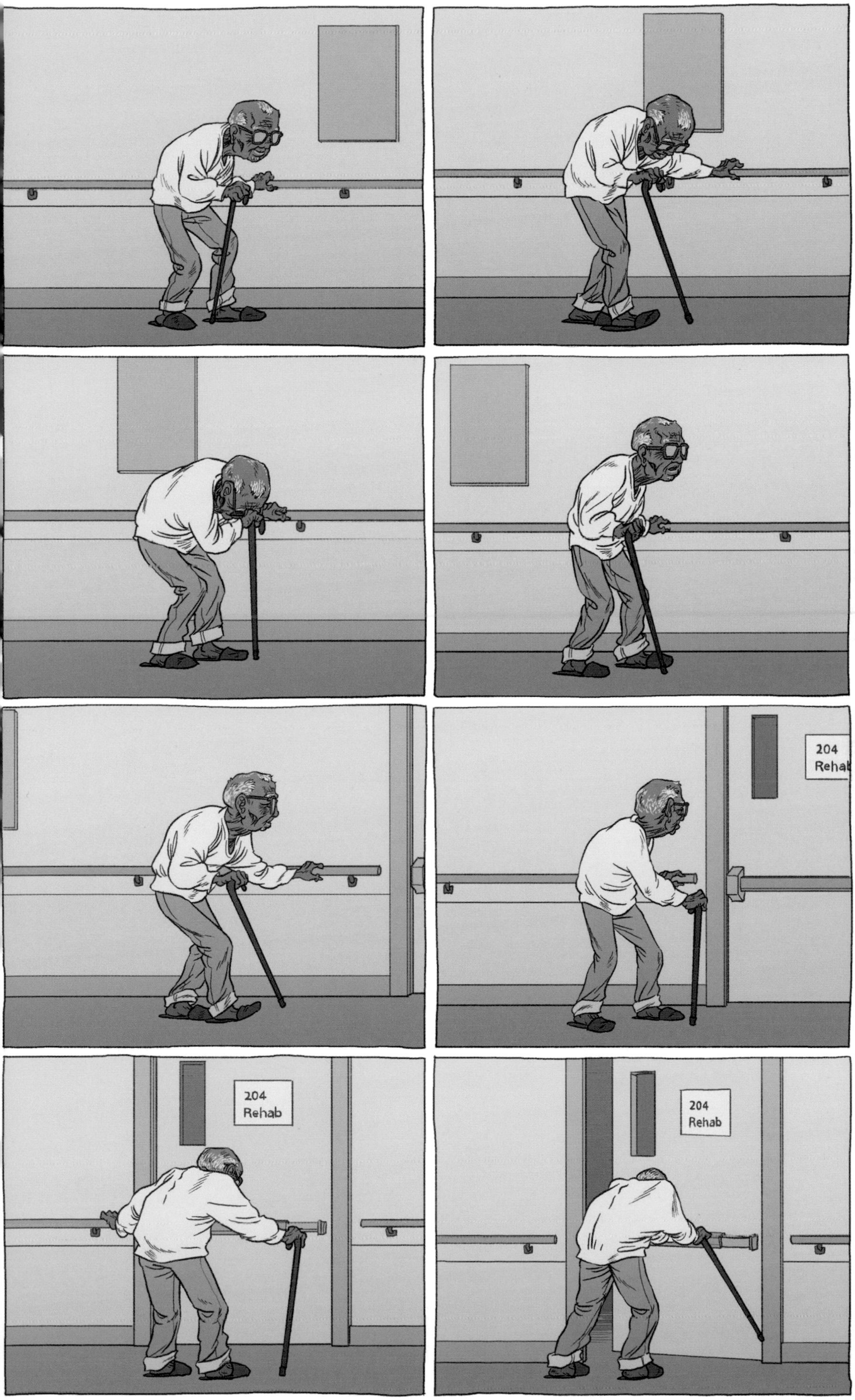
204
Rehab
204
Rehab

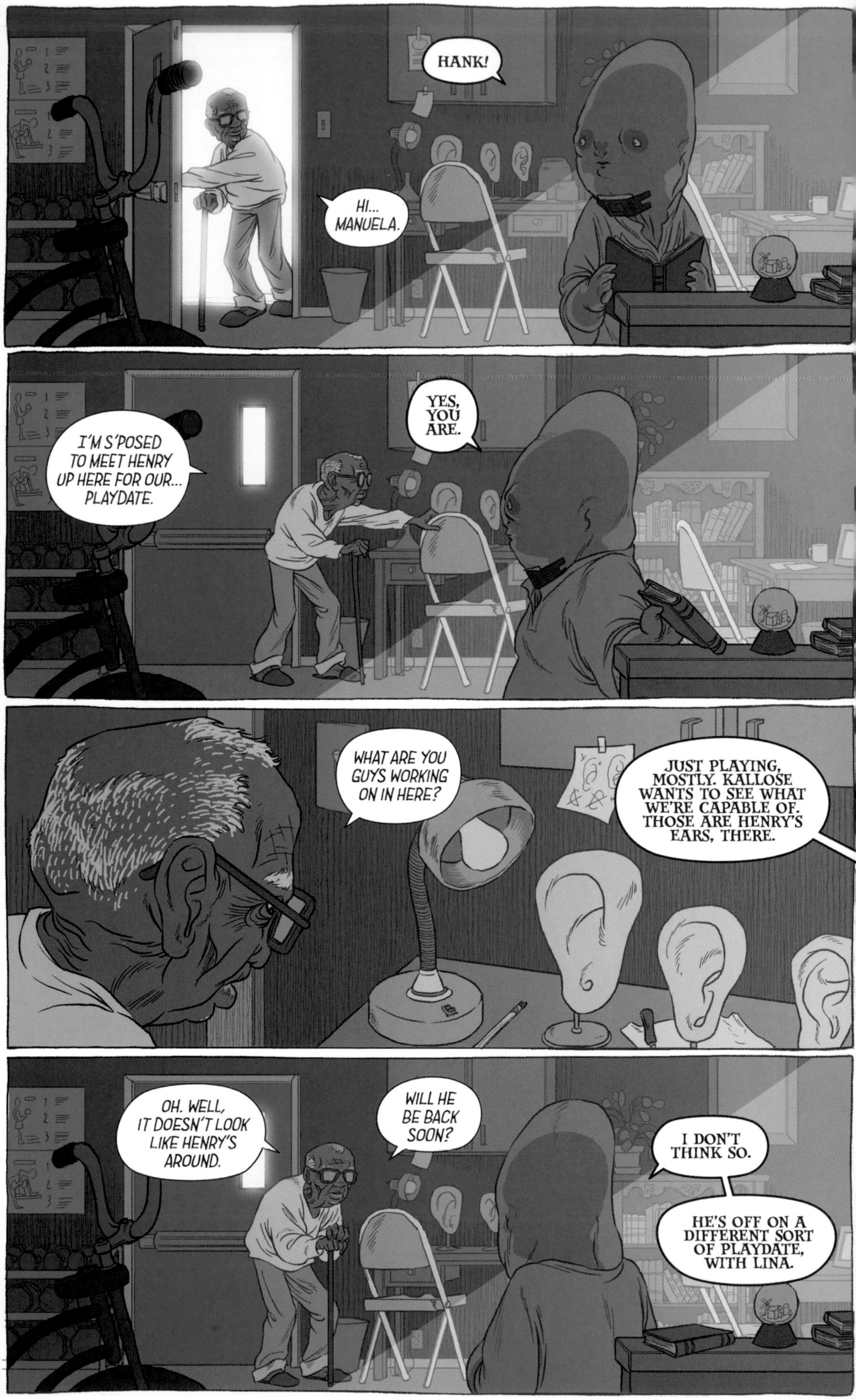
HANK!
HI... MANUELA.
I'M S'POSED TO MEET HENRY UP HERE FOR OUR... PLAYDATE.
YES, YOU ARE.
WHAT ARE YOU GUYS WORKING ON IN HERE?
JUST PLAYING, MOSTLY. KALLOSE WANTS TO SEE WHAT WE'RE CAPABLE OF. THOSE ARE HENRY'S EARS, THERE.
OH. WELL, IT DOESN'T LOOK LIKE HENRY'S AROUND.
WILL HE BE BACK SOON?
I DON'T THINK SO.
HE'S OFF ON A DIFFERENT SORT OF PLAYDATE, WITH LINA.

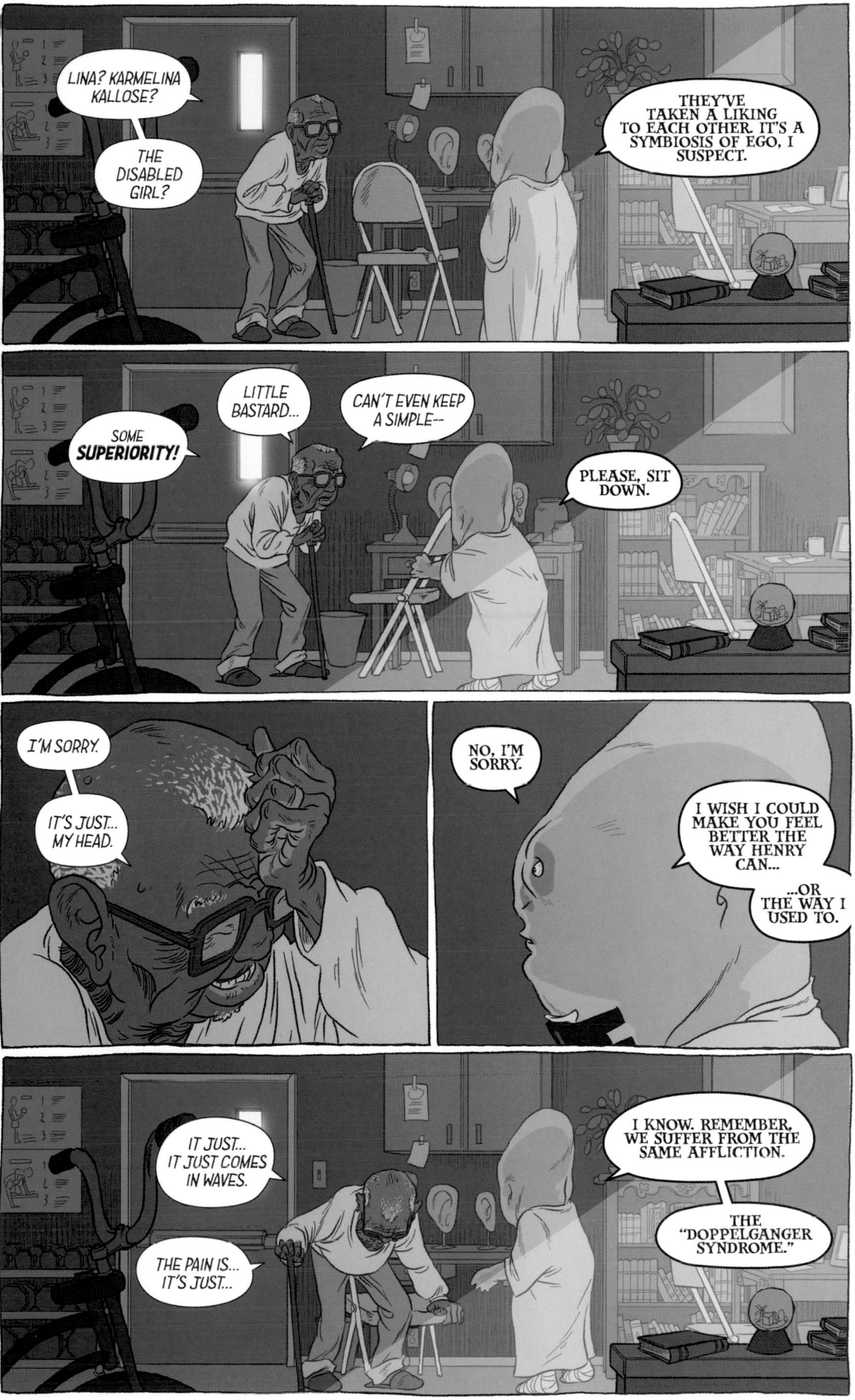
LINA? KARMELINA KALLOSE?
THE DISABLED GIRL?
THEY'VE TAKEN A LIKING TO EACH OTHER. IT'S A SYMBIOSIS OF EGO, I SUSPECT.
SOME SUPERIORITY!
LITTLE BASTARD...
CAN'T EVEN KEEP A SIMPLE--
PLEASE, SIT DOWN.
I'M SORRY.
IT'S JUST... MY HEAD.
NO, I'M SORRY.
I WISH I COULD MAKE YOU FEEL BETTER THE WAY HENRY CAN...
...OR THE WAY I USED TO.
IT JUST... IT JUST COMES IN WAVES.
THE PAIN IS... IT'S JUST...
I KNOW. REMEMBER, WE SUFFER FROM THE SAME AFFLICTION.
THE "DOPPELGANGER SYNDROME."

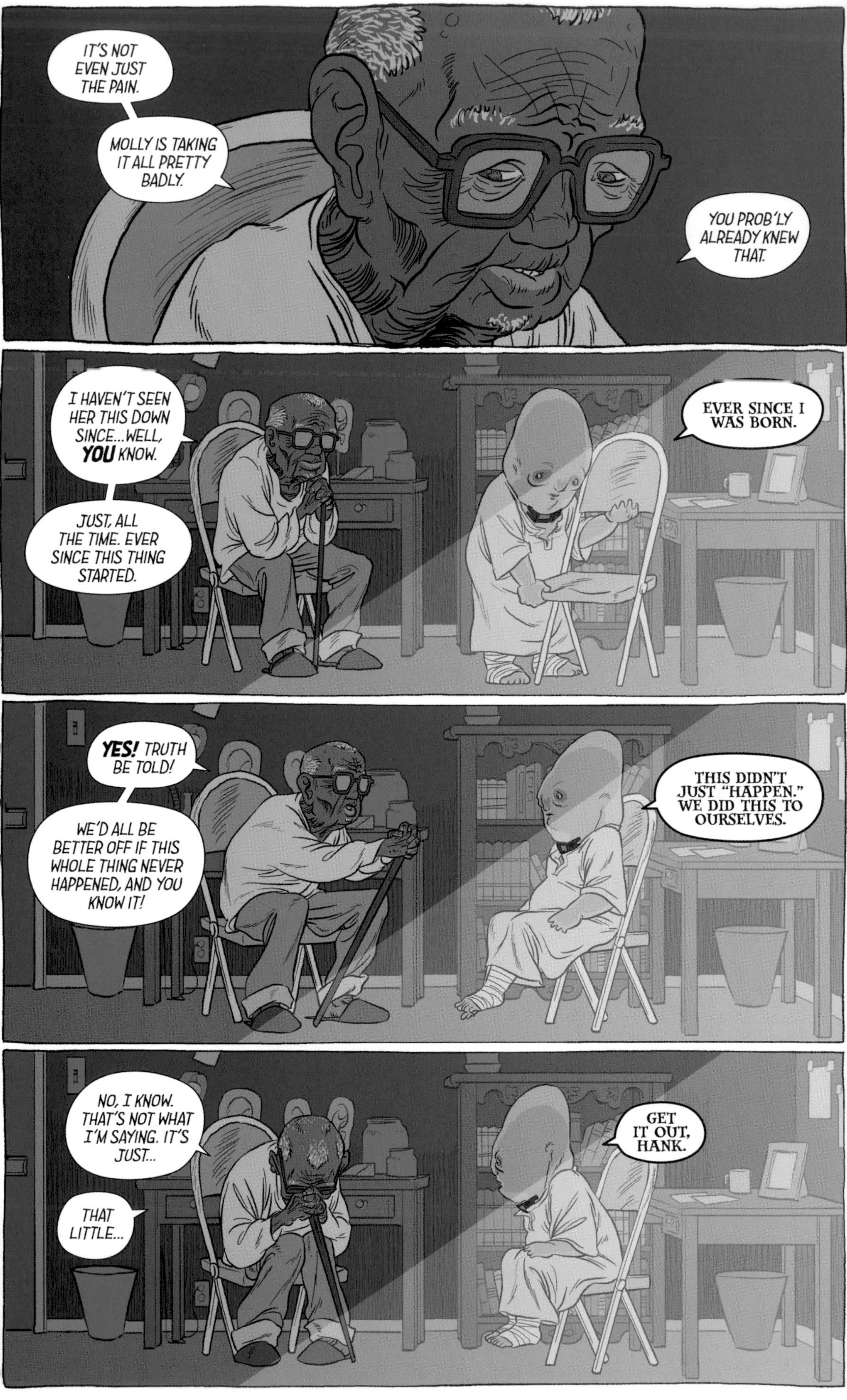
IT'S NOT EVEN JUST THE PAIN.
MOLLY IS TAKING IT ALL PRETTY BADLY.
YOU PROB'LY ALREADY KNEW THAT.
I HAVEN'T SEEN HER THIS DOWN SINCE...WELL, **YOU** KNOW.
JUST, ALL THE TIME. EVER SINCE THIS THING STARTED.
EVER SINCE I WAS BORN.
YES! TRUTH BE TOLD!
WE'D ALL BE BETTER OFF IF THIS WHOLE THING NEVER HAPPENED, AND YOU KNOW IT!
THIS DIDN'T JUST "HAPPEN." WE DID THIS TO OURSELVES.
NO, I KNOW. THAT'S NOT WHAT I'M SAYING. IT'S JUST...
THAT LITTLE...
GET IT OUT, HANK.

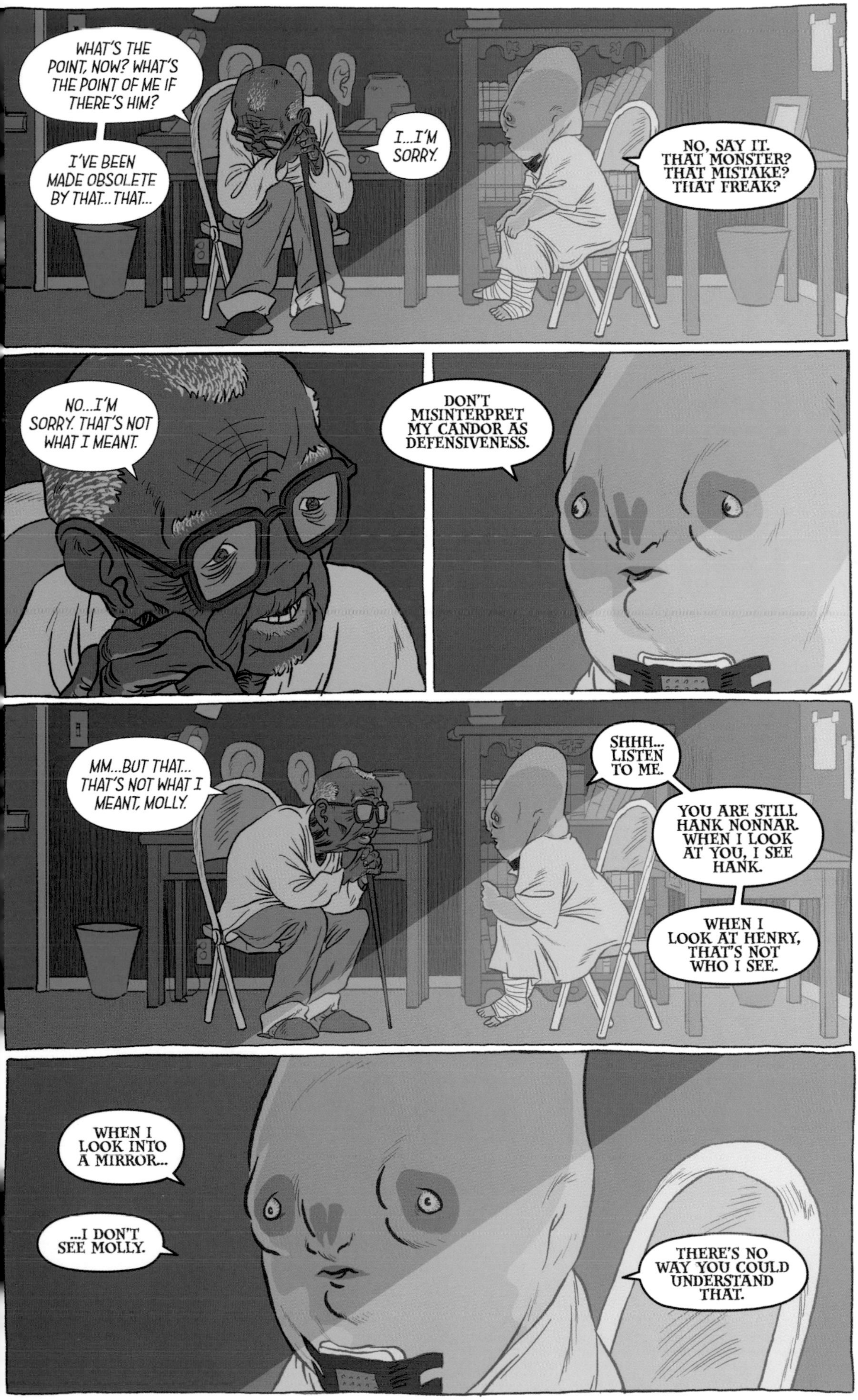
WHAT'S THE POINT, NOW? WHAT'S THE POINT OF ME IF THERE'S HIM?
I'VE BEEN MADE OBSOLETE BY THAT... THAT...
I...I'M SORRY.
NO, SAY IT. THAT MONSTER? THAT MISTAKE? THAT FREAK?
NO...I'M SORRY. THAT'S NOT WHAT I MEANT.
DON'T MISINTERPRET MY CANDOR AS DEFENSIVENESS.
MM...BUT THAT... THAT'S NOT WHAT I MEANT, MOLLY.
SHHH... LISTEN TO ME.
YOU ARE STILL HANK NONNAR. WHEN I LOOK AT YOU, I SEE HANK.
WHEN I LOOK AT HENRY, THAT'S NOT WHO I SEE.
WHEN I LOOK INTO A MIRROR...
...I DON'T SEE MOLLY.
THERE'S NO WAY YOU COULD UNDERSTAND THAT.

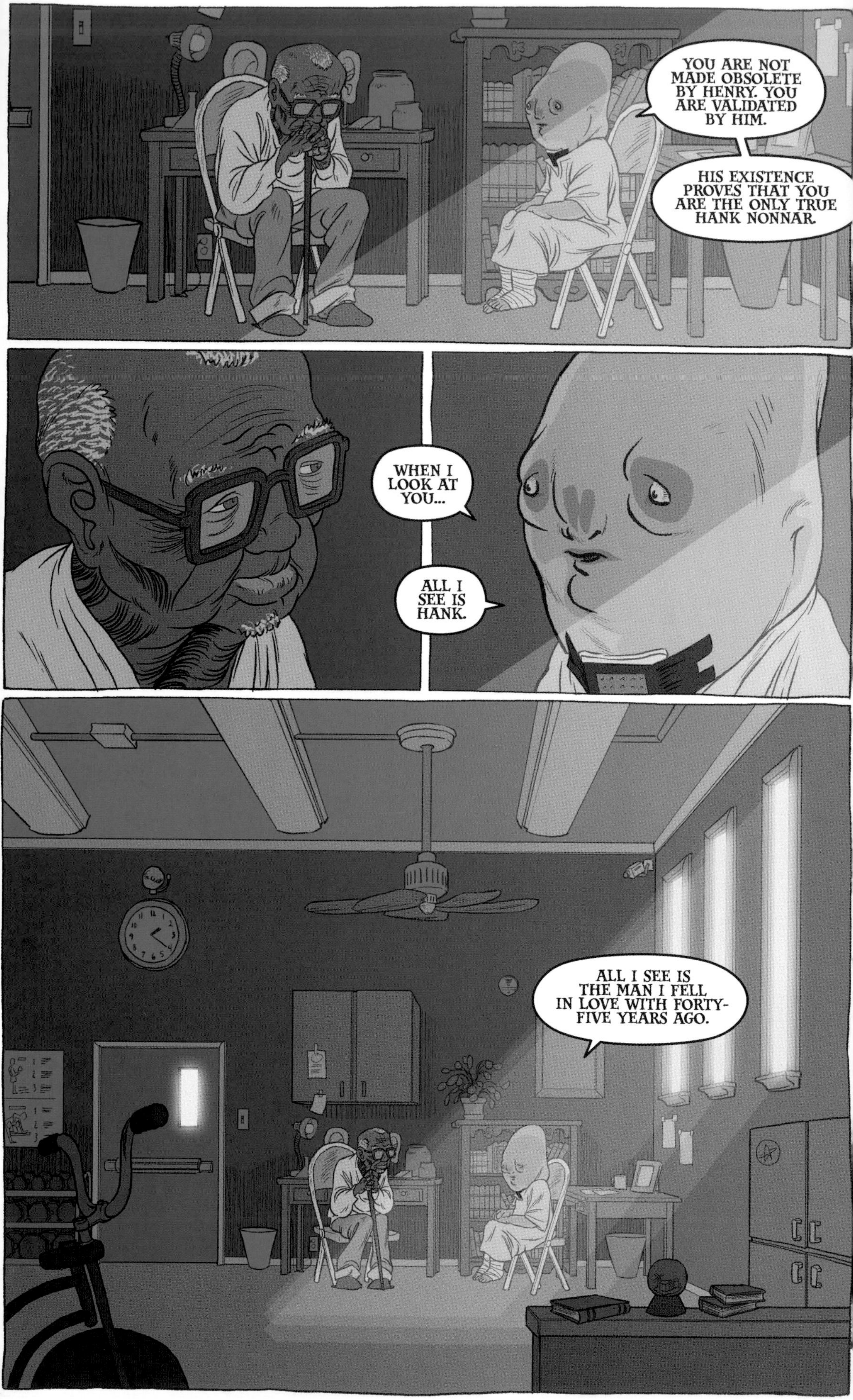
YOU ARE NOT MADE OBSOLETE BY HENRY. YOU ARE VALIDATED BY HIM.
HIS EXISTENCE PROVES THAT YOU ARE THE ONLY TRUE HANK NONNAR.
WHEN I LOOK AT YOU...
ALL I SEE IS HANK.
ALL I SEE IS THE MAN I FELL IN LOVE WITH FORTY-FIVE YEARS AGO.

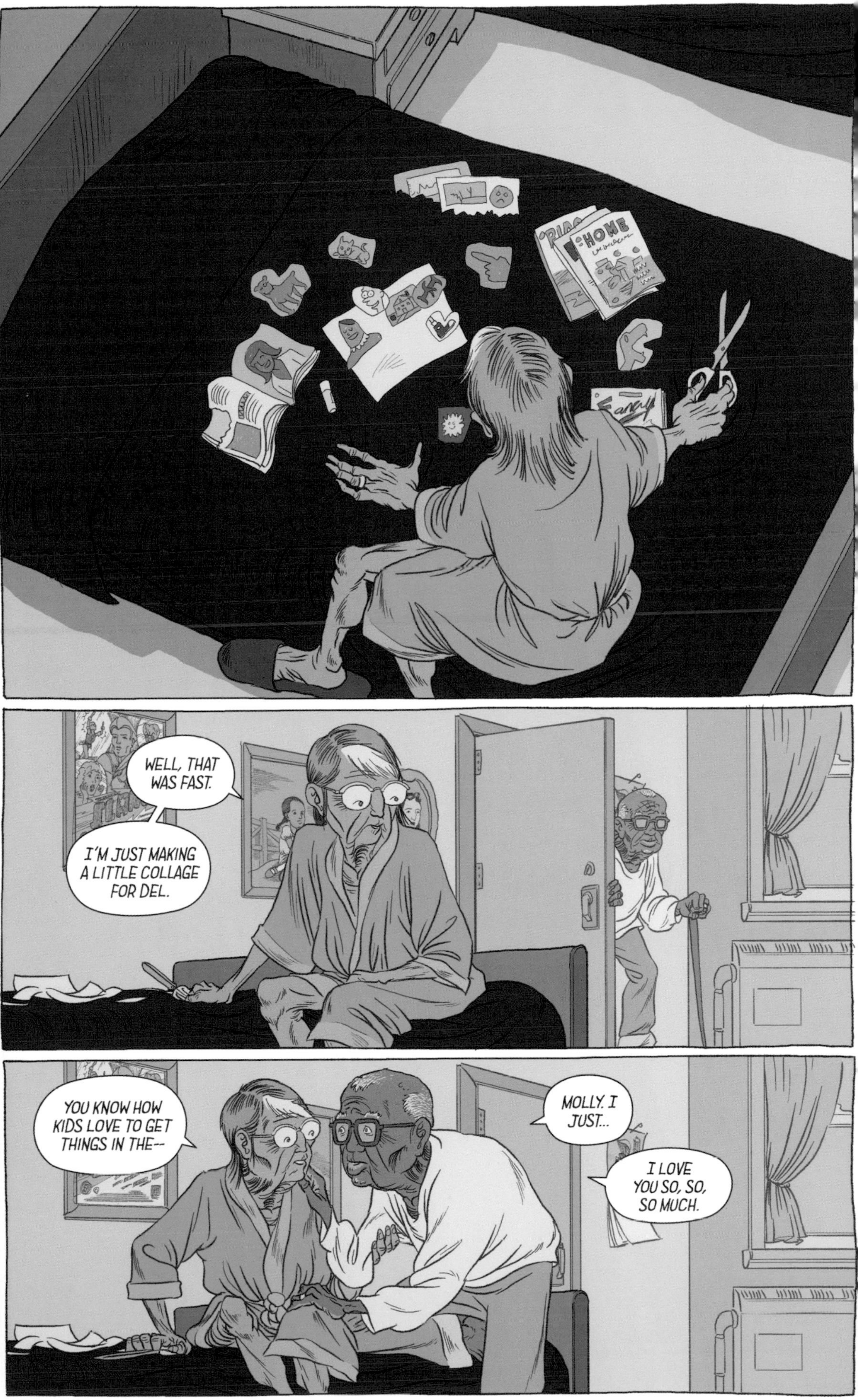

HOME
Fancy
WELL, THAT WAS FAST.
I'M JUST MAKING A LITTLE COLLAGE FOR DEL.
YOU KNOW HOW KIDS LOVE TO GET THINGS IN THE--
MOLLY. I JUST...
I LOVE YOU SO, SO, SO MUCH.

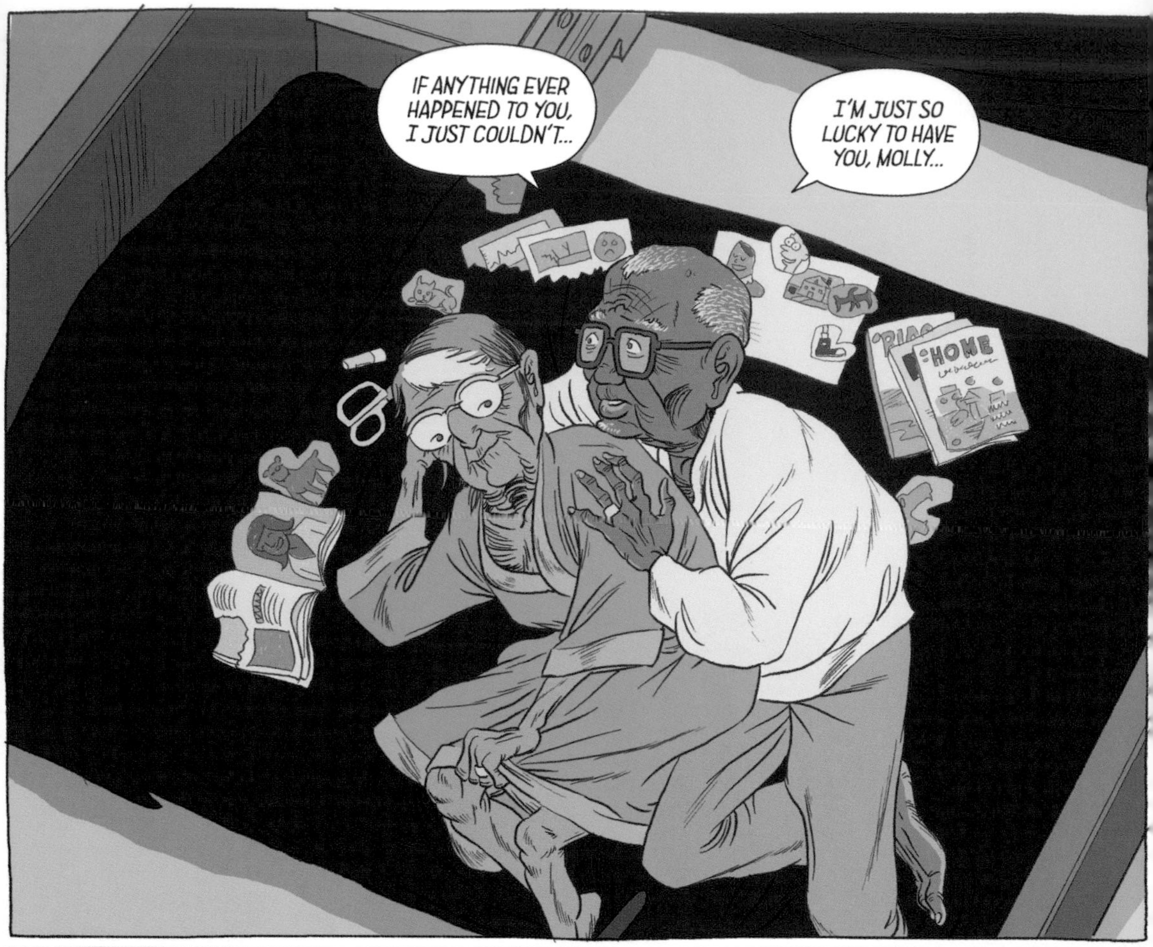
IF ANYTHING EVER HAPPENED TO YOU, I JUST COULDN'T...
I'M JUST SO LUCKY TO HAVE YOU, MOLLY...

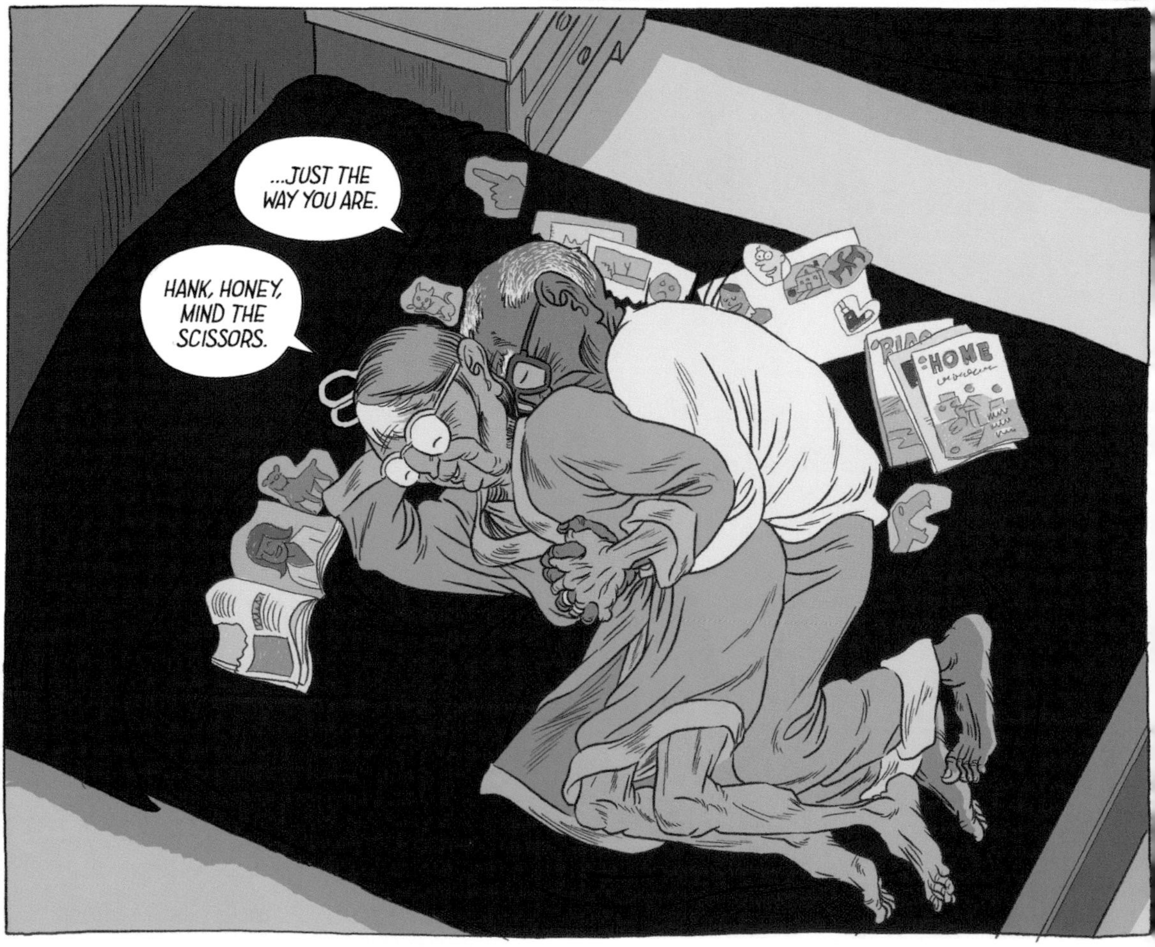
...JUST THE WAY YOU ARE.
HANK, HONEY, MIND THE SCISSORS.

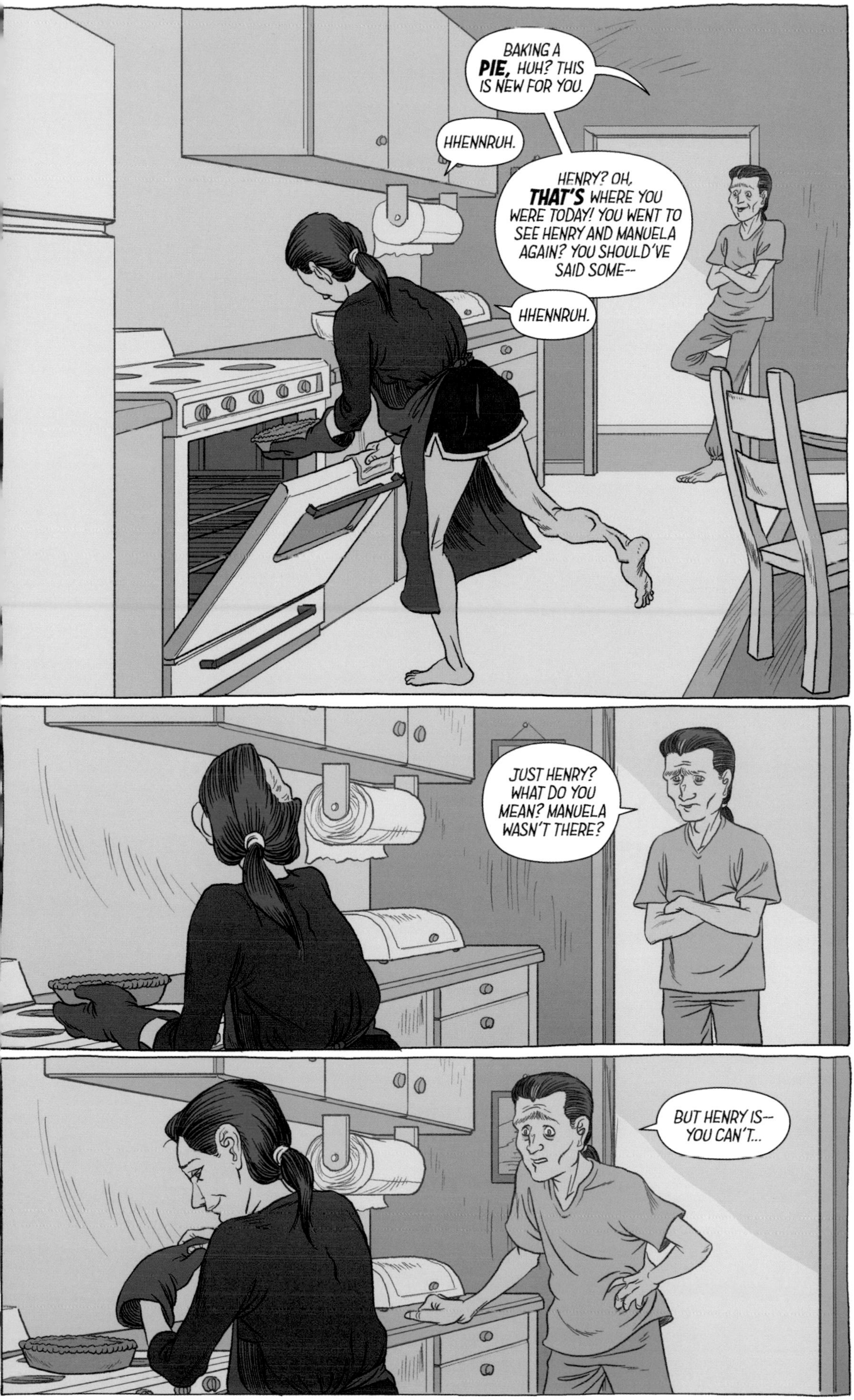
BAKING A PIE, HUH? THIS IS NEW FOR YOU.
HHENNRUH.
HENRY? OH, THAT'S WHERE YOU WERE TODAY! YOU WENT TO SEE HENRY AND MANUELA AGAIN? YOU SHOULD'VE SAID SOME--
HHENNRUH.
JUST HENRY? WHAT DO YOU MEAN? MANUELA WASN'T THERE?
BUT HENRY IS-- YOU CAN'T...

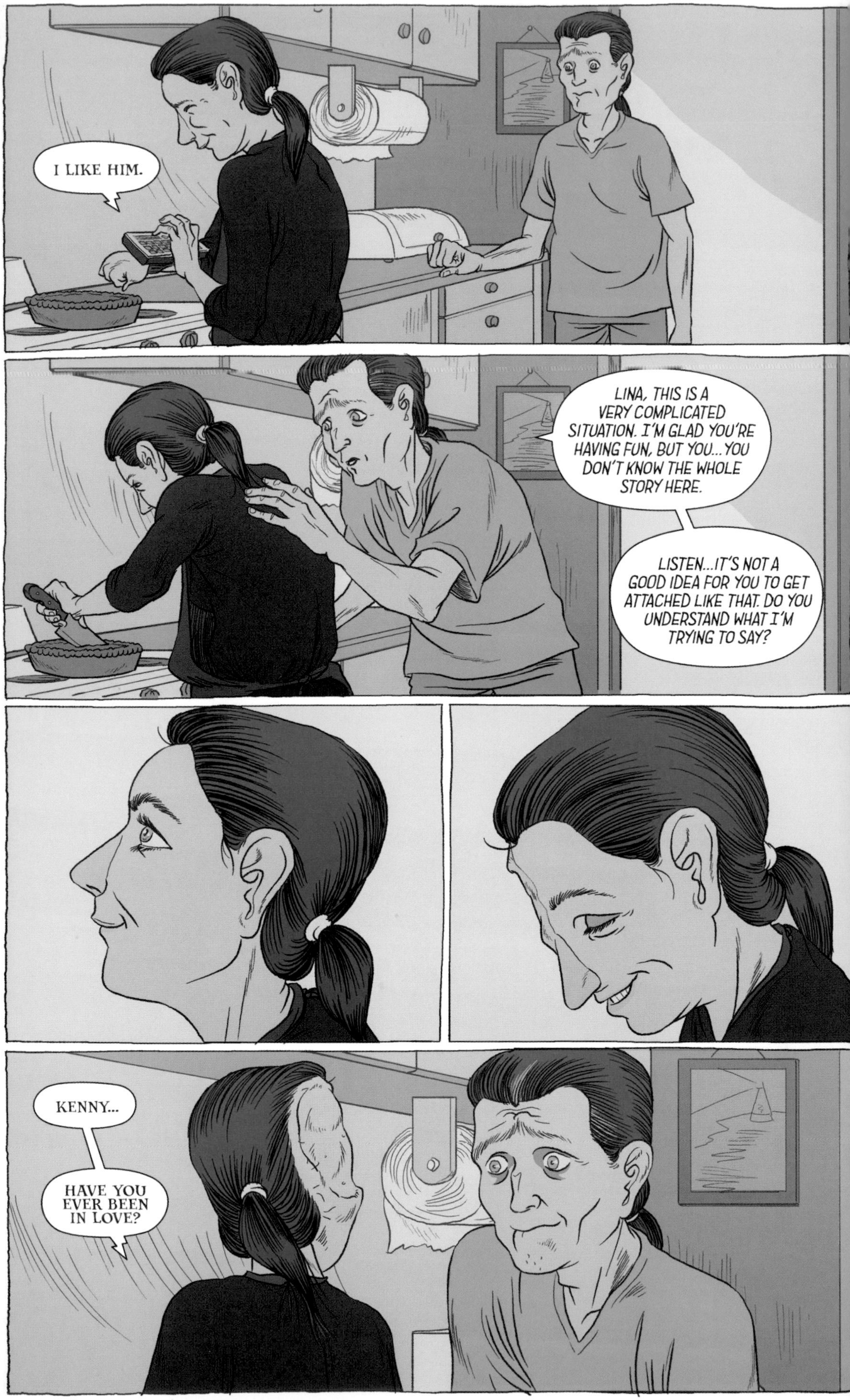
I LIKE HIM.
LINA, THIS IS A VERY COMPLICATED SITUATION. I'M GLAD YOU'RE HAVING FUN, BUT YOU... YOU DON'T KNOW THE WHOLE STORY HERE.
LISTEN... IT'S NOT A GOOD IDEA FOR YOU TO GET ATTACHED LIKE THAT. DO YOU UNDERSTAND WHAT I'M TRYING TO SAY?
KENNY...
HAVE YOU EVER BEEN IN LOVE?

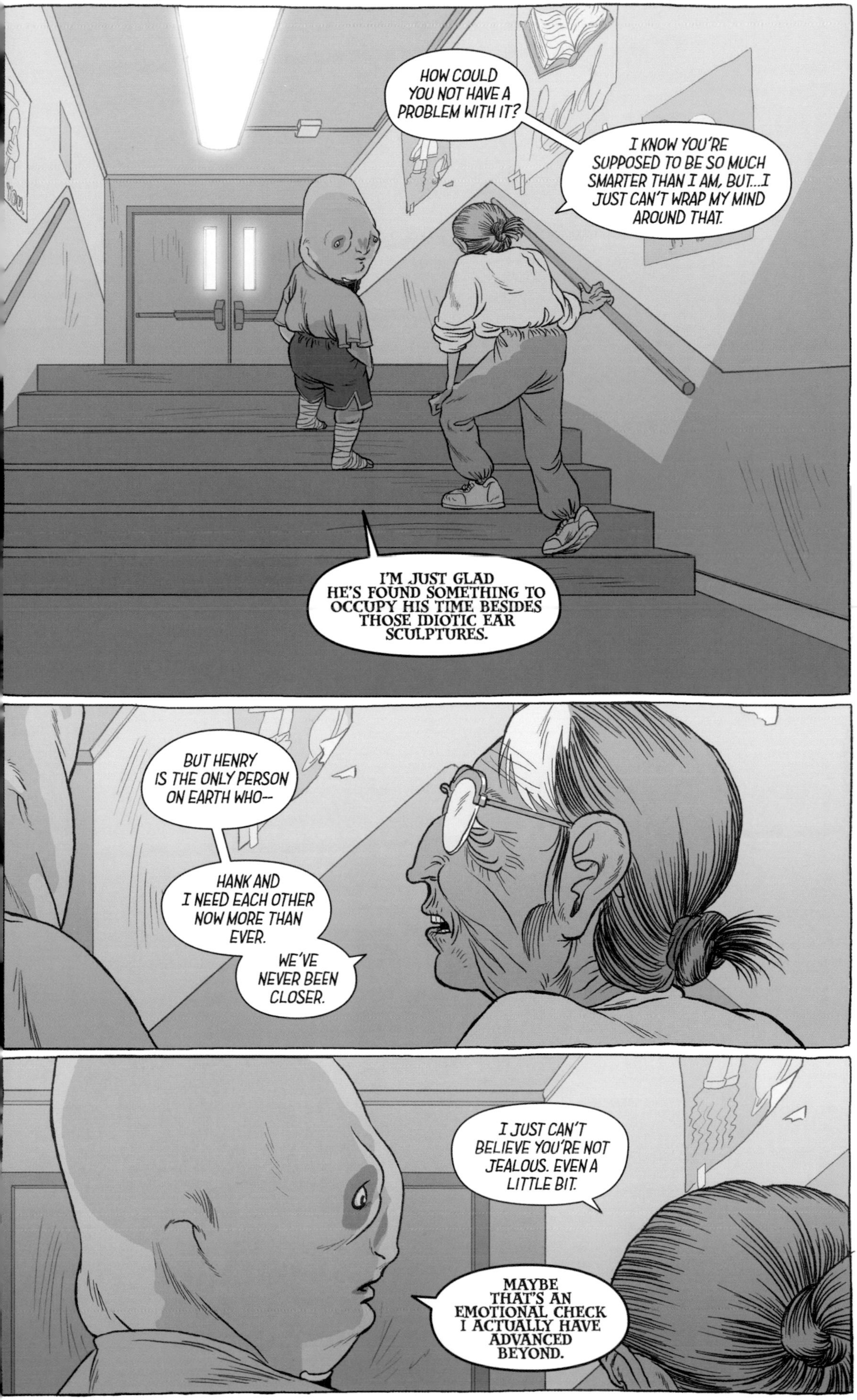
HOW COULD YOU NOT HAVE A PROBLEM WITH IT?
I KNOW YOU'RE SUPPOSED TO BE SO MUCH SMARTER THAN I AM, BUT...I JUST CAN'T WRAP MY MIND AROUND THAT.
I'M JUST GLAD HE'S FOUND SOMETHING TO OCCUPY HIS TIME BESIDES THOSE IDIOTIC EAR SCULPTURES.
BUT HENRY IS THE ONLY PERSON ON EARTH WHO--
HANK AND I NEED EACH OTHER NOW MORE THAN EVER.
WE'VE NEVER BEEN CLOSER.
I JUST CAN'T BELIEVE YOU'RE NOT JEALOUS. EVEN A LITTLE BIT.
MAYBE THAT'S AN EMOTIONAL CHECK I ACTUALLY HAVE ADVANCED BEYOND.

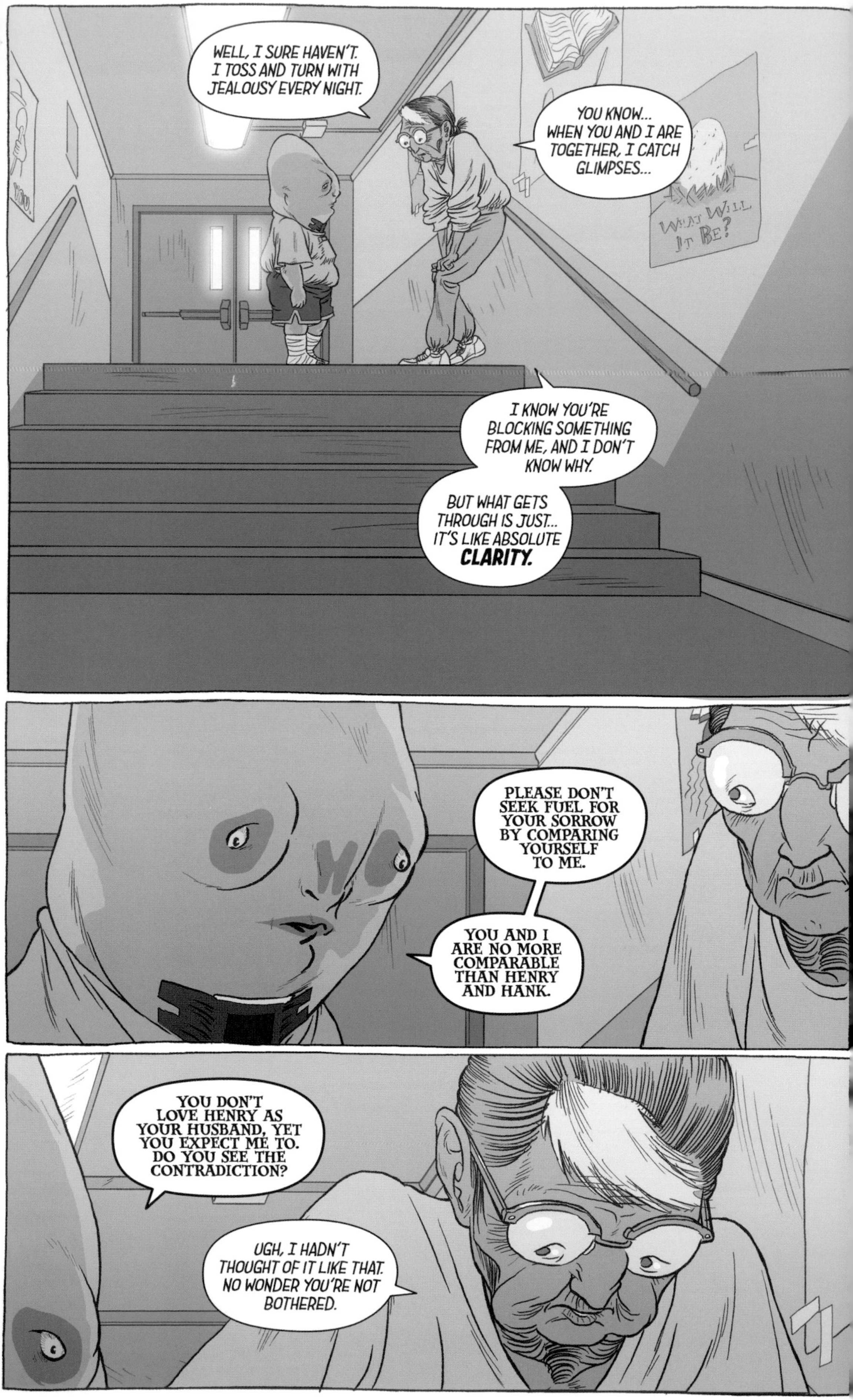

WHAT WILL IT BE?
WELL, I SURE HAVEN'T. I TOSS AND TURN WITH JEALOUSY EVERY NIGHT.
YOU KNOW... WHEN YOU AND I ARE TOGETHER, I CATCH GLIMPSES...
I KNOW YOU'RE BLOCKING SOMETHING FROM ME, AND I DON'T KNOW WHY.
BUT WHAT GETS THROUGH IS JUST... IT'S LIKE ABSOLUTE **CLARITY.**
PLEASE DON'T SEEK FUEL FOR YOUR SORROW BY COMPARING YOURSELF TO ME.
YOU AND I ARE NO MORE COMPARABLE THAN HENRY AND HANK.
YOU DON'T LOVE HENRY AS YOUR HUSBAND, YET YOU EXPECT ME TO. DO YOU SEE THE CONTRADICTION?
UGH, I HADN'T THOUGHT OF IT LIKE THAT. NO WONDER YOU'RE NOT BOTHERED.

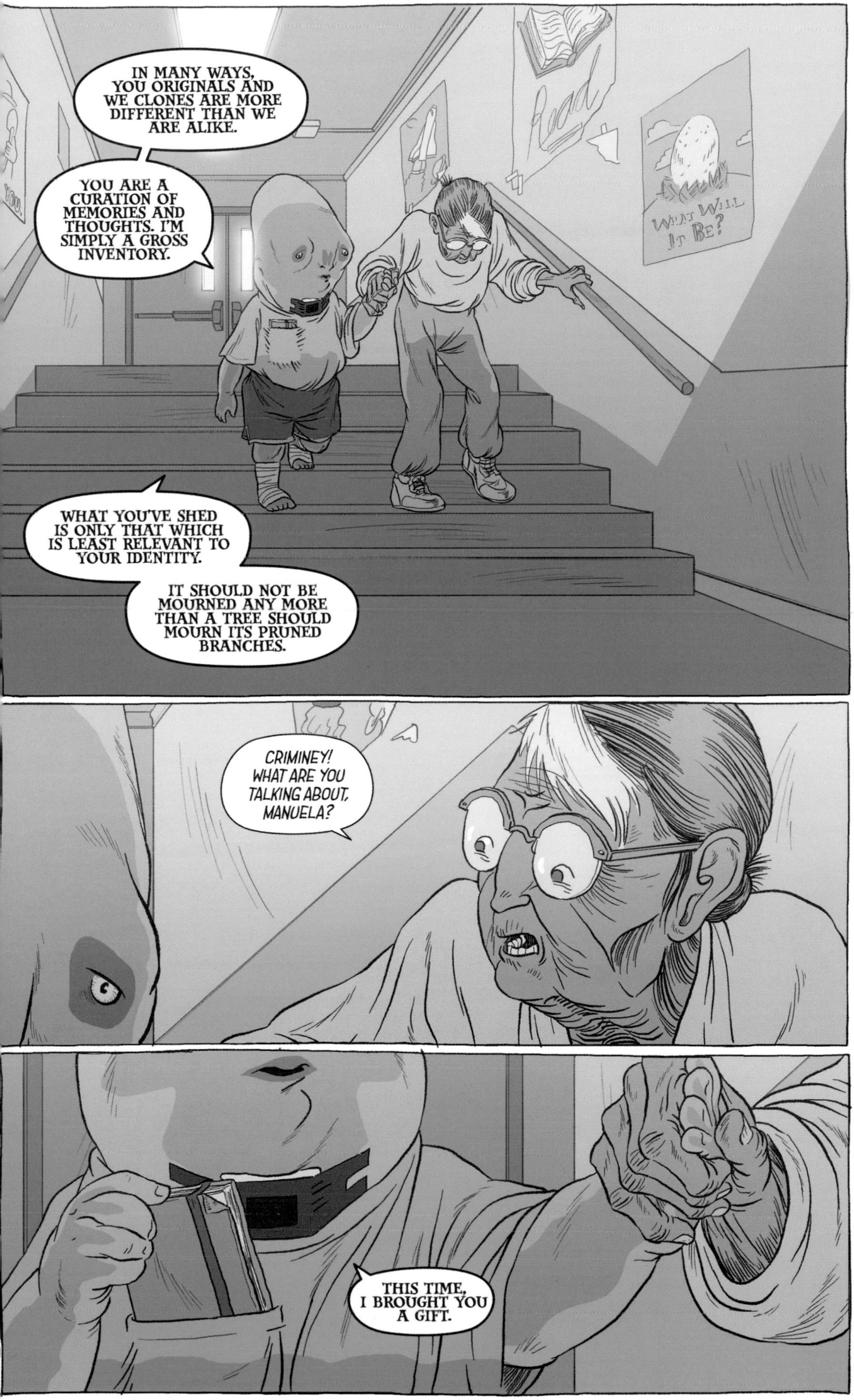
IN MANY WAYS, YOU ORIGINALS AND WE CLONES ARE MORE DIFFERENT THAN WE ARE ALIKE.
YOU ARE A CURATION OF MEMORIES AND THOUGHTS. I'M SIMPLY A GROSS INVENTORY.
Read
WHAT WILL IT BE?
WHAT YOU'VE SHED IS ONLY THAT WHICH IS LEAST RELEVANT TO YOUR IDENTITY.
IT SHOULD NOT BE MOURNED ANY MORE THAN A TREE SHOULD MOURN ITS PRUNED BRANCHES.
CRIMINEY! WHAT ARE YOU TALKING ABOUT, MANUELA?
THIS TIME, I BROUGHT YOU A GIFT.

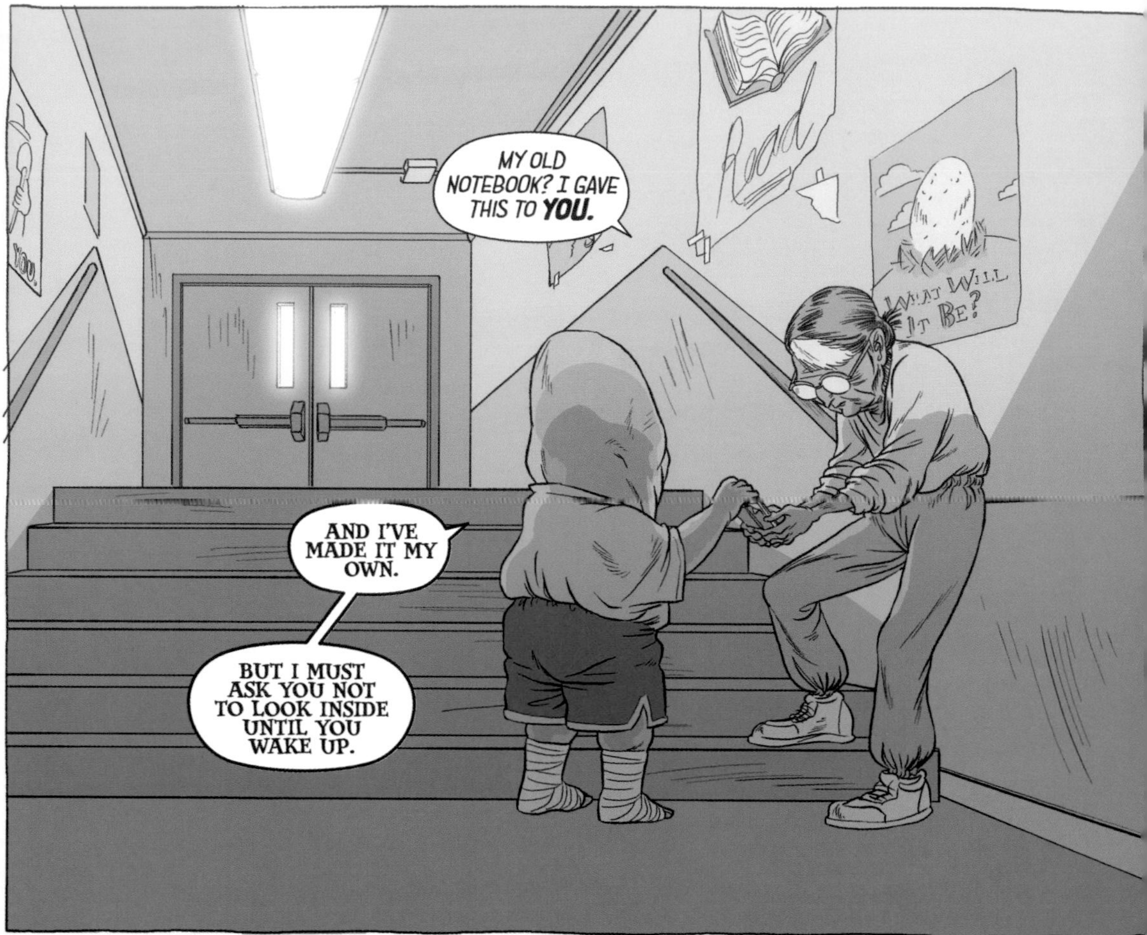
MY OLD NOTEBOOK? I GAVE THIS TO YOU.
Read
WHAT WILL IT BE?
AND I'VE MADE IT MY OWN.
BUT I MUST ASK YOU NOT TO LOOK INSIDE UNTIL YOU WAKE UP.

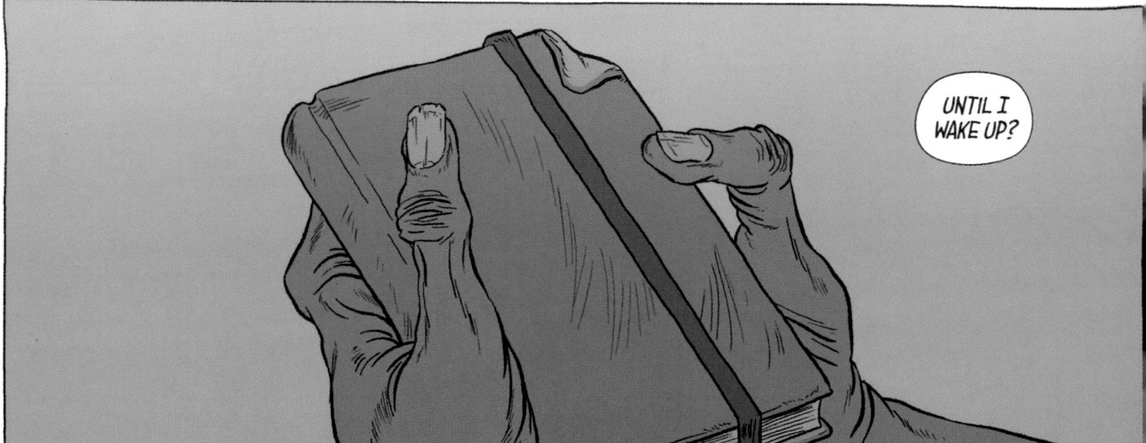
UNTIL I WAKE UP?

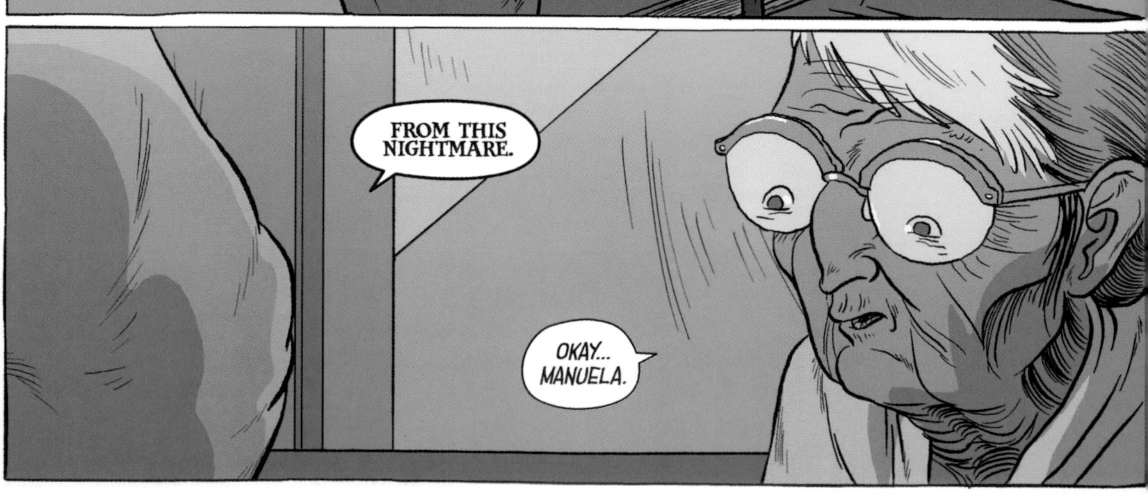
FROM THIS NIGHTMARE.
OKAY... MANUELA.

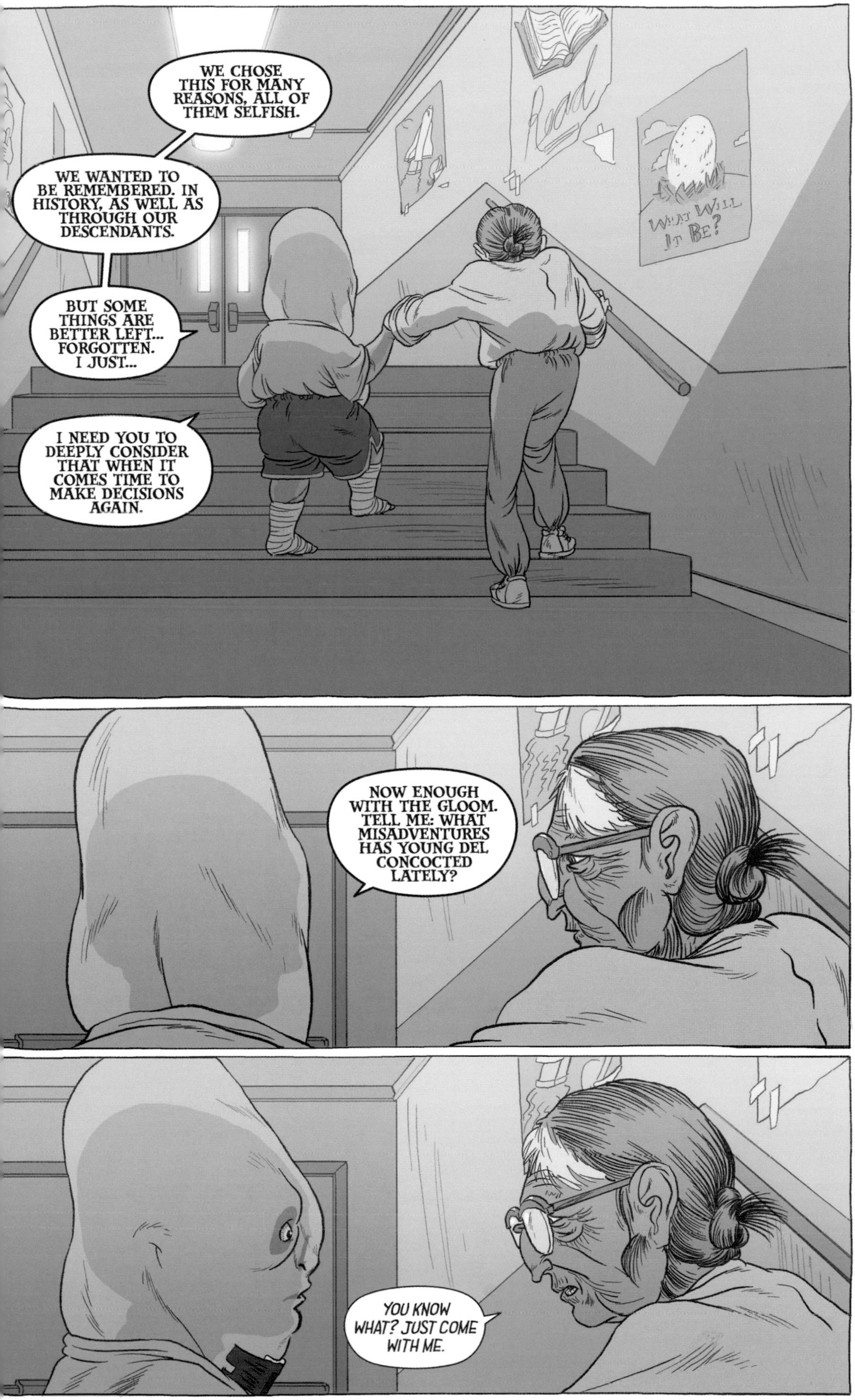
WE CHOSE THIS FOR MANY REASONS, ALL OF THEM SELFISH.
READ
WHAT WILL IT BE?
WE WANTED TO BE REMEMBERED. IN HISTORY, AS WELL AS THROUGH OUR DESCENDANTS.
BUT SOME THINGS ARE BETTER LEFT... FORGOTTEN. I JUST...
I NEED YOU TO DEEPLY CONSIDER THAT WHEN IT COMES TIME TO MAKE DECISIONS AGAIN.
NOW ENOUGH WITH THE GLOOM. TELL ME: WHAT MISADVENTURES HAS YOUNG DEL CONCOCTED LATELY?
YOU KNOW WHAT? JUST COME WITH ME.

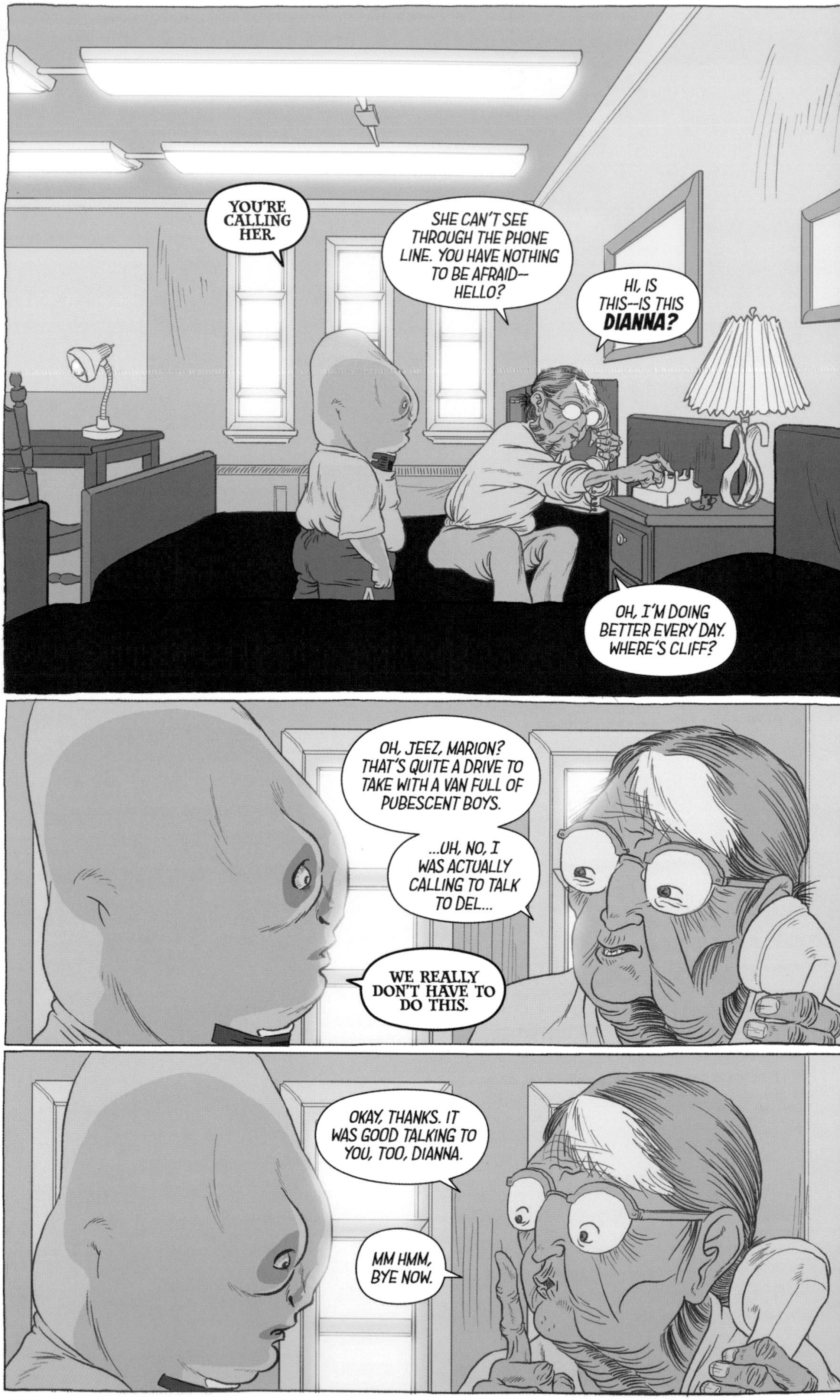
YOU'RE CALLING HER.
SHE CAN'T SEE THROUGH THE PHONE LINE. YOU HAVE NOTHING TO BE AFRAID-- HELLO?
HI, IS THIS--IS THIS DIANNA?
OH, I'M DOING BETTER EVERY DAY. WHERE'S CLIFF?
OH, JEEZ, MARION? THAT'S QUITE A DRIVE TO TAKE WITH A VAN FULL OF PUBESCENT BOYS.
...UH, NO, I WAS ACTUALLY CALLING TO TALK TO DEL...
WE REALLY DON'T HAVE TO DO THIS.
OKAY, THANKS. IT WAS GOOD TALKING TO YOU, TOO, DIANNA.
MM HMM, BYE NOW.

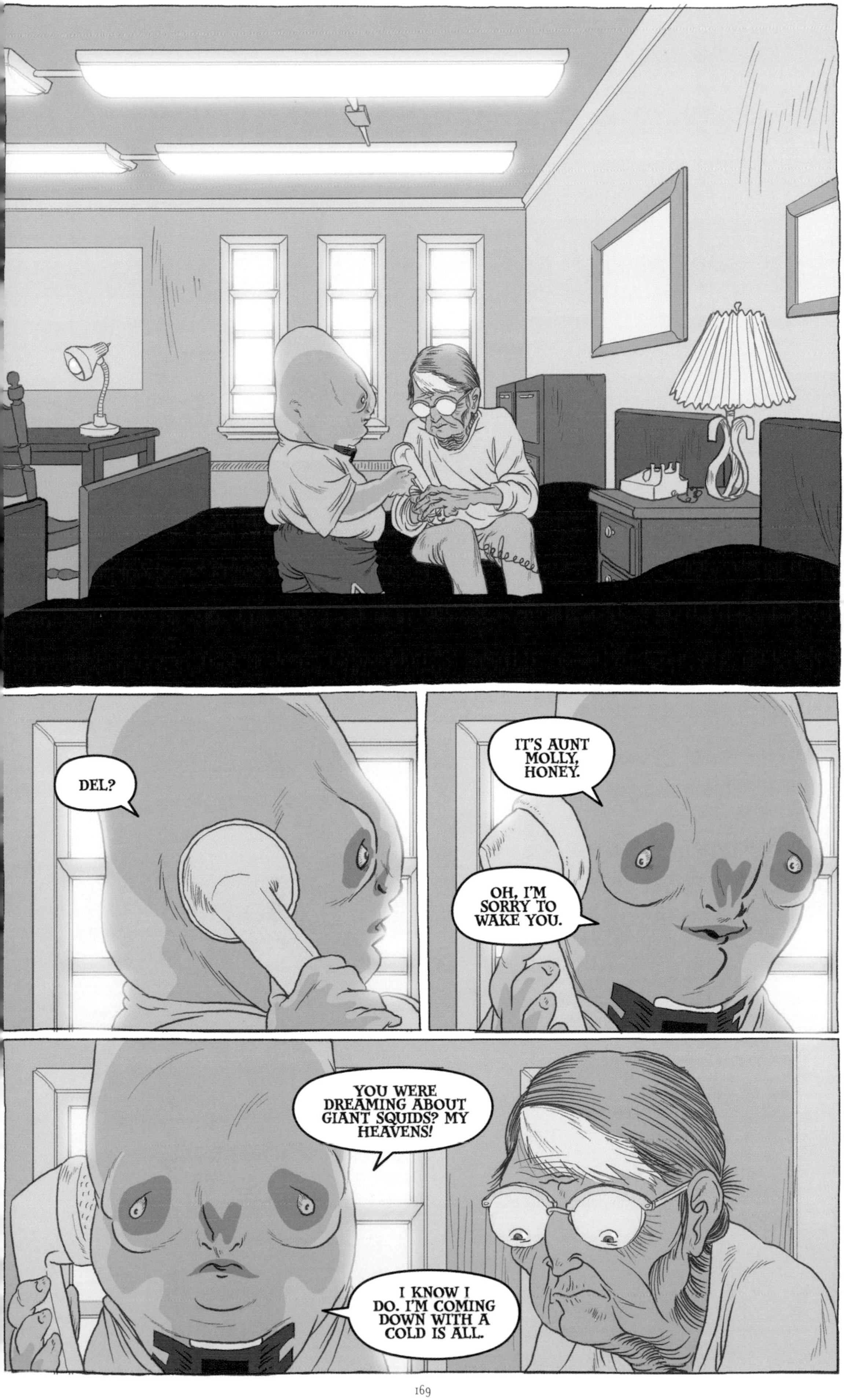
DEL?
IT'S AUNT MOLLY, HONEY.
OH, I'M SORRY TO WAKE YOU.
YOU WERE DREAMING ABOUT GIANT SQUIDS? MY HEAVENS!
I KNOW I DO. I'M COMING DOWN WITH A COLD IS ALL.

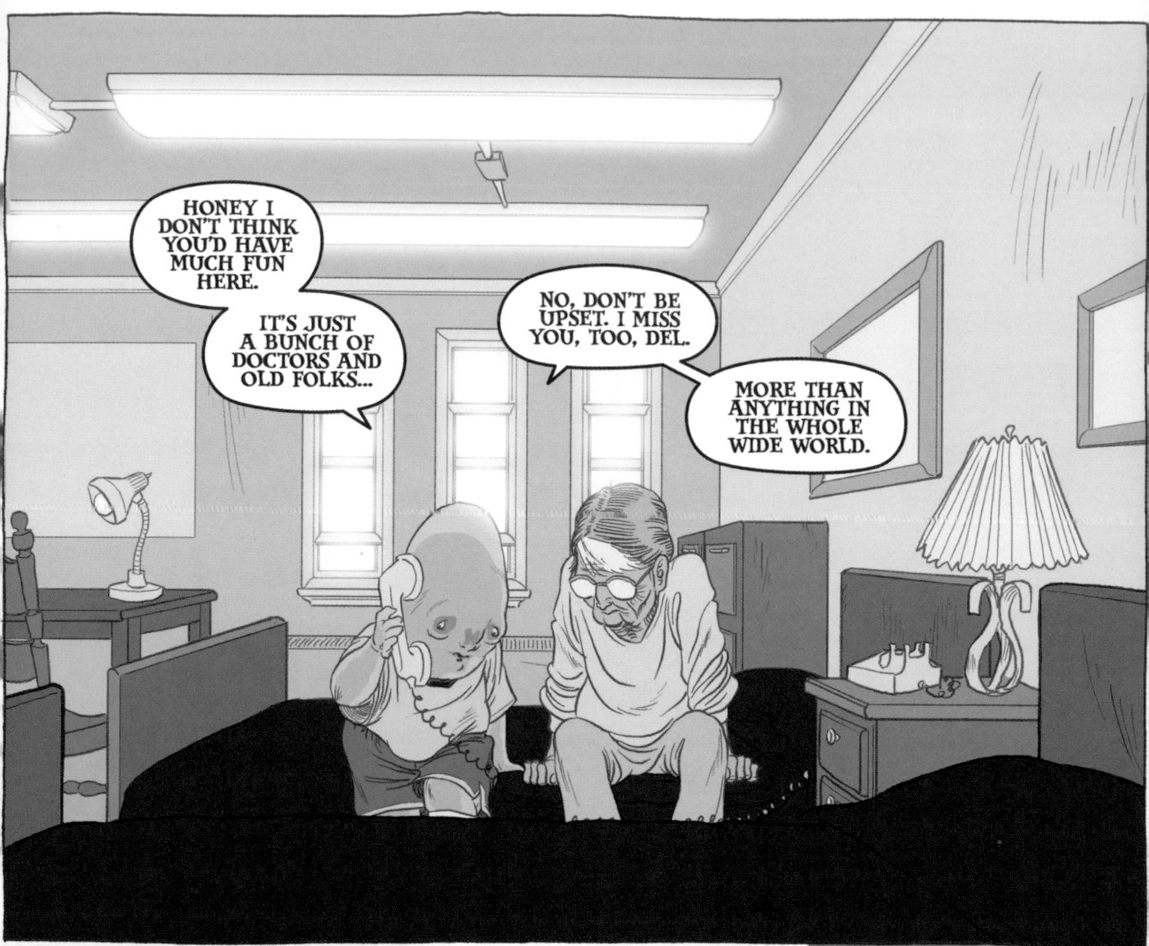
HONEY I DON'T THINK YOU'D HAVE MUCH FUN HERE.
IT'S JUST A BUNCH OF DOCTORS AND OLD FOLKS...
NO, DON'T BE UPSET. I MISS YOU, TOO, DEL.
MORE THAN ANYTHING IN THE WHOLE WIDE WORLD.

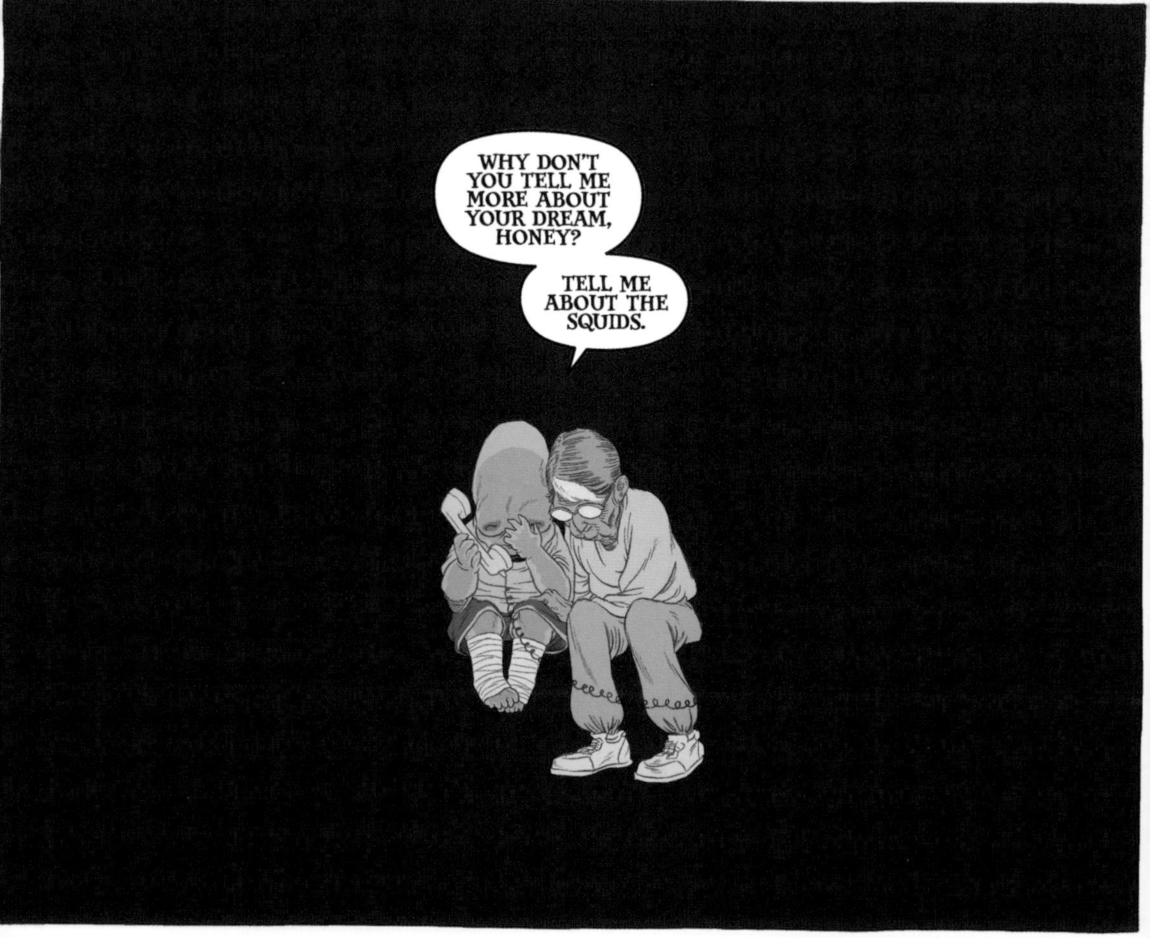
WHY DON'T YOU TELL ME MORE ABOUT YOUR DREAM, HONEY?
TELL ME ABOUT THE SQUIDS.

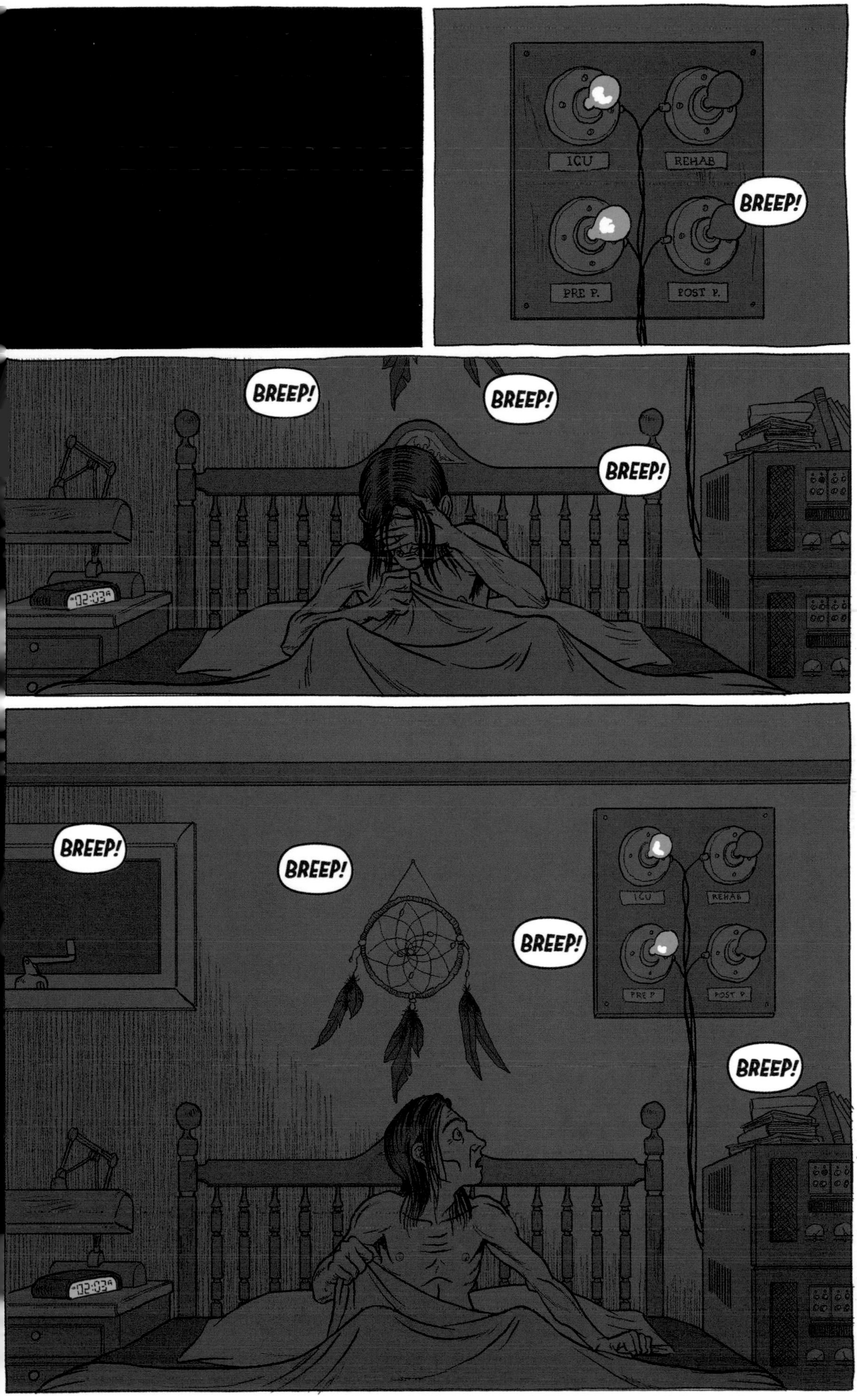
ICU
REHAB
PRE P.
POST P.
BREEP!
BREEP!
BREEP!
BREEP!
BREEP!
BREEP!
ICU
REHAB
PRE P
POST P
BREEP!
BREEP!

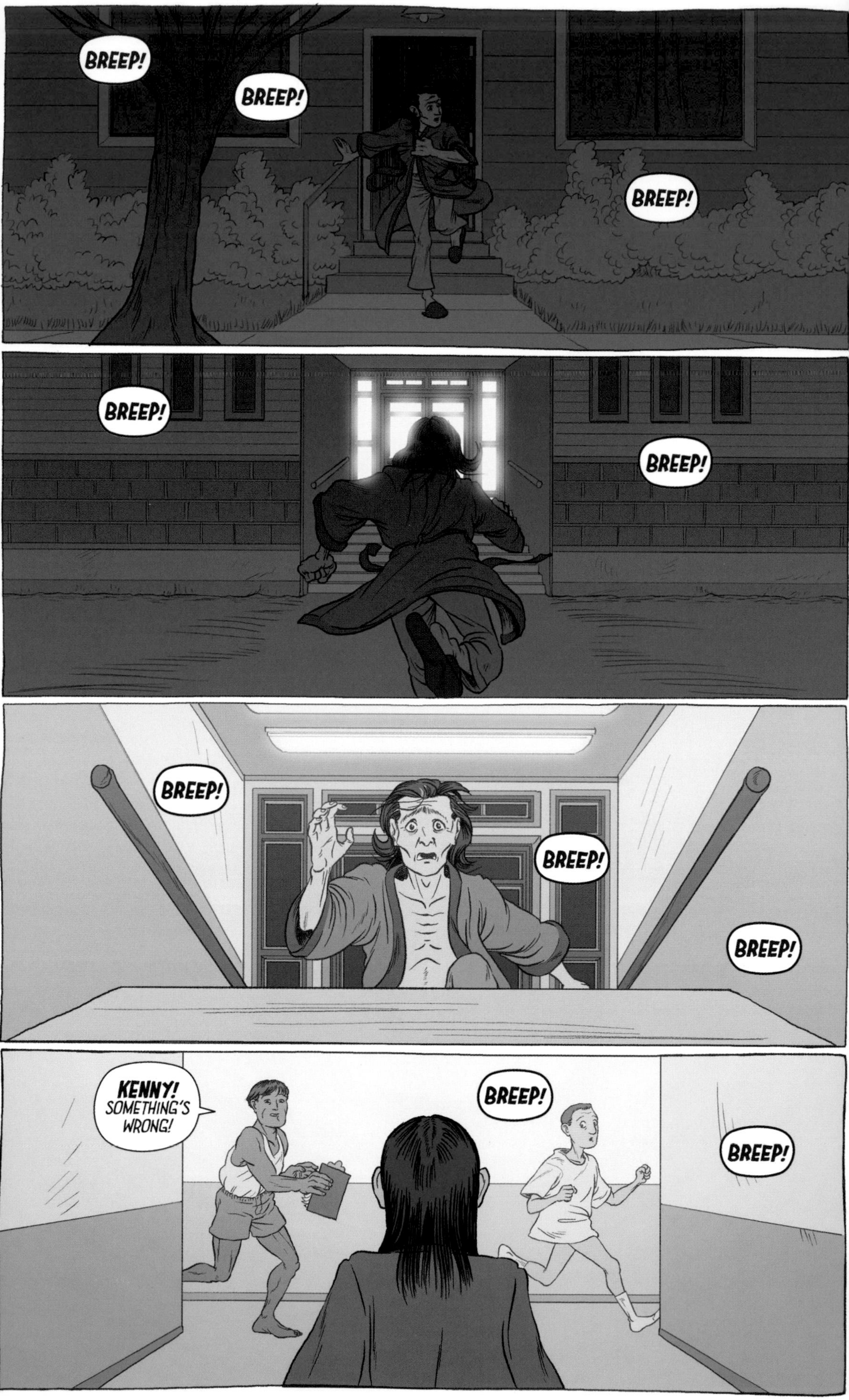
BREEP!
BREEP!
BREEP!
BREEP!
BREEP!
BREEP!
BREEP!
BREEP!
KENNY! SOMETHING'S WRONG!
BREEP!
BREEP!

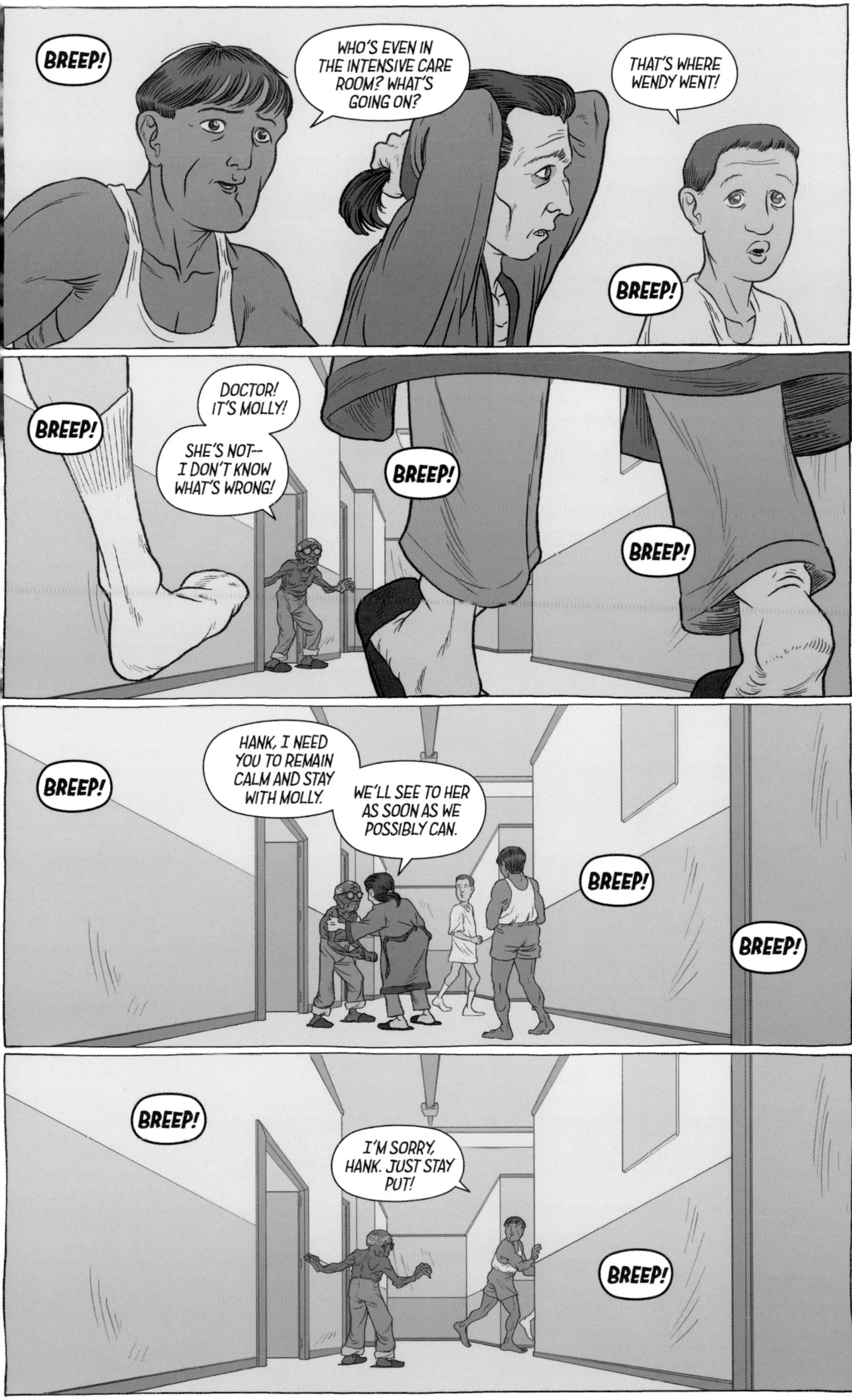
BREEP!
WHO'S EVEN IN THE INTENSIVE CARE ROOM? WHAT'S GOING ON?
THAT'S WHERE WENDY WENT!
BREEP!
BREEP!
DOCTOR! IT'S MOLLY!
SHE'S NOT-- I DON'T KNOW WHAT'S WRONG!
BREEP!
BREEP!
BREEP!
HANK, I NEED YOU TO REMAIN CALM AND STAY WITH MOLLY.
WE'LL SEE TO HER AS SOON AS WE POSSIBLY CAN.
BREEP!
BREEP!
BREEP!
I'M SORRY, HANK. JUST STAY PUT!
BREEP!

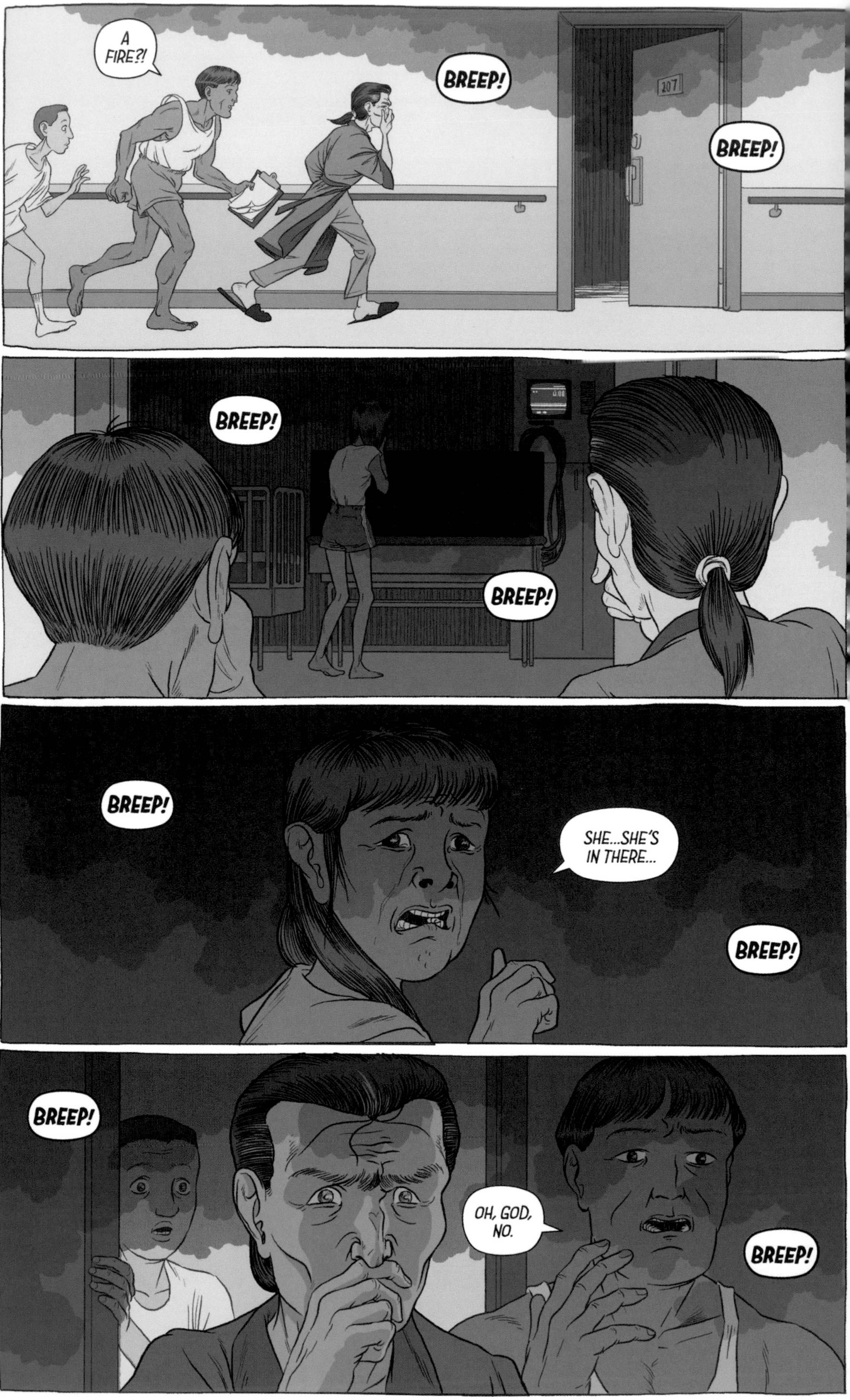
A FIRE?!
BREEP!
BREEP!
BREEP!
BREEP!
BREEP!
SHE...SHE'S IN THERE...
BREEP!
BREEP!
OH, GOD, NO.
BREEP!

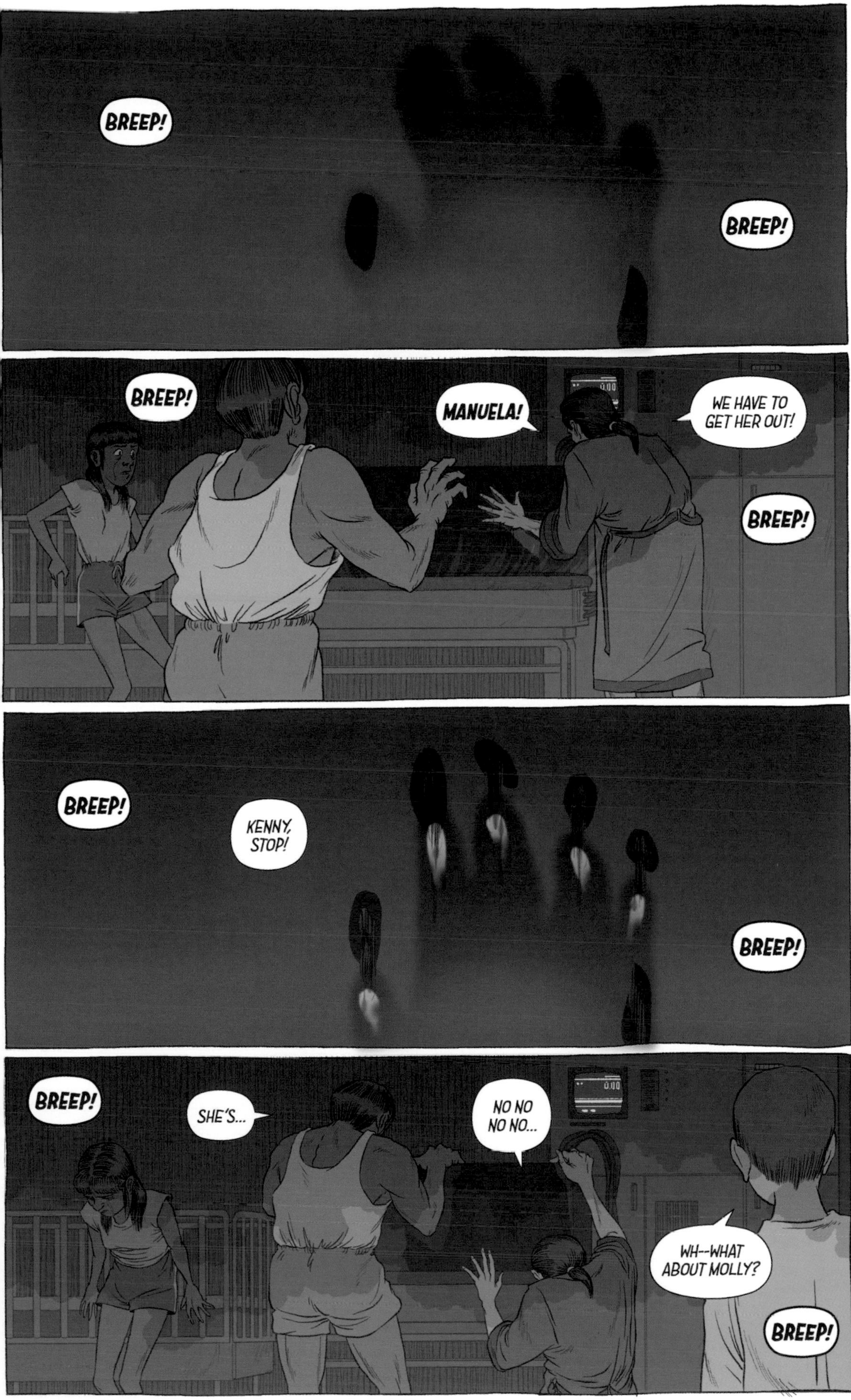
BREEP!
BREEP!
BREEP!
MANUELA!
WE HAVE TO GET HER OUT!
BREEP!
BREEP!
KENNY, STOP!
BREEP!
BREEP!
SHE'S...
NO NO NO NO...
WH--WHAT ABOUT MOLLY?
BREEP!

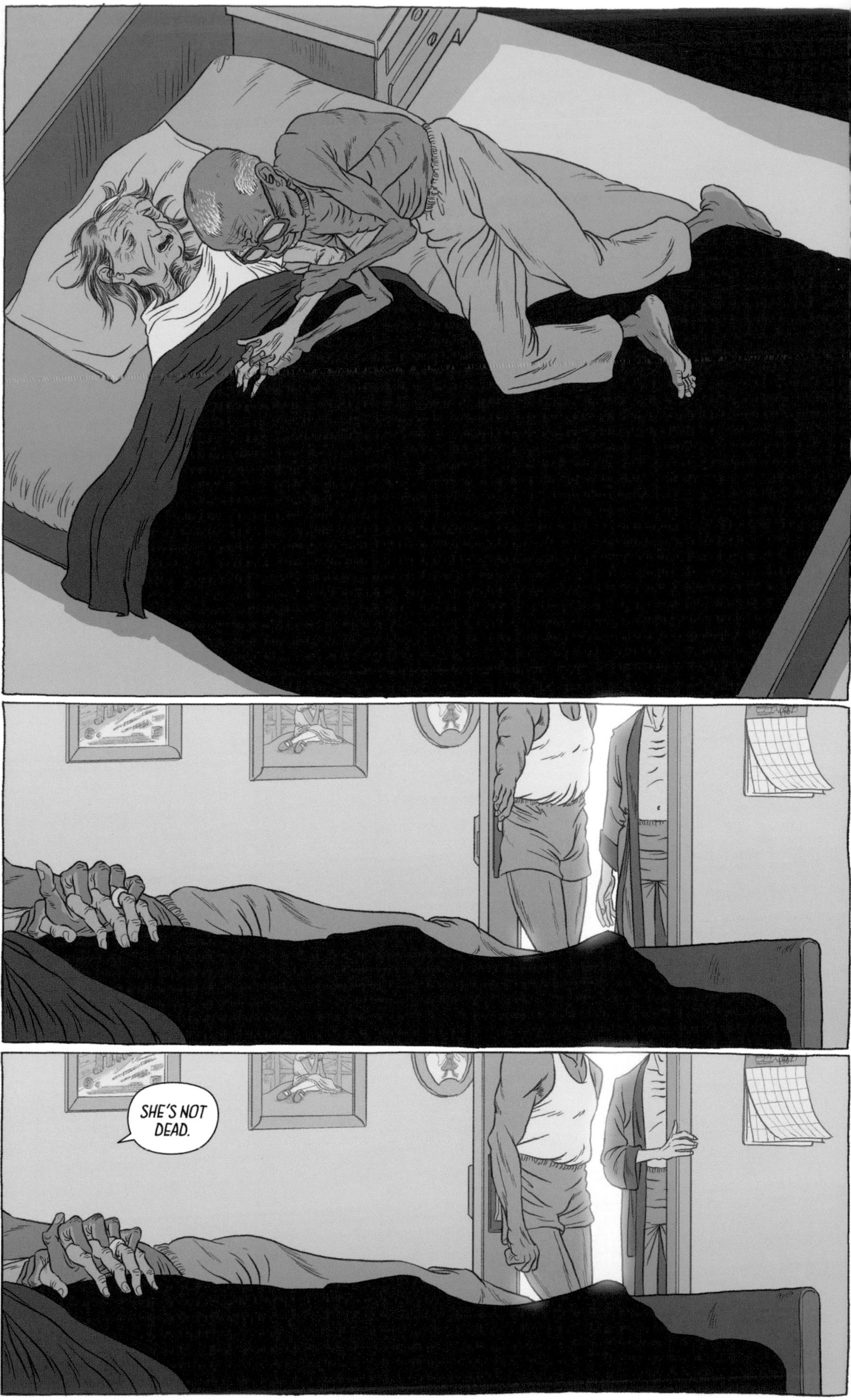
SHE'S NOT DEAD.

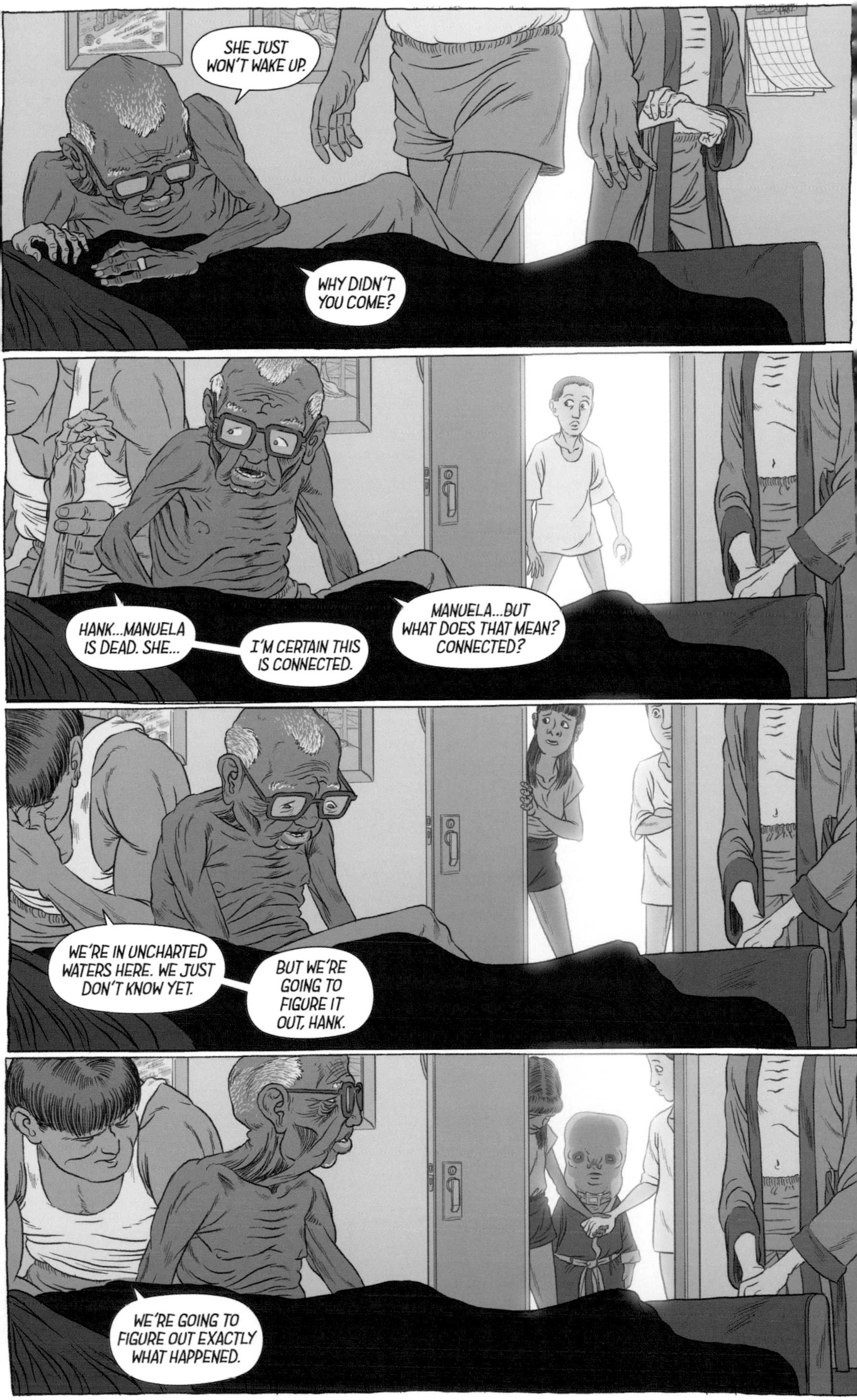
SHE JUST WON'T WAKE UP.
WHY DIDN'T YOU COME?
HANK...MANUELA IS DEAD. SHE...
I'M CERTAIN THIS IS CONNECTED.
MANUELA...BUT WHAT DOES THAT MEAN? CONNECTED?
WE'RE IN UNCHARTED WATERS HERE. WE JUST DON'T KNOW YET.
BUT WE'RE GOING TO FIGURE IT OUT, HANK.
WE'RE GOING TO FIGURE OUT EXACTLY WHAT HAPPENED.

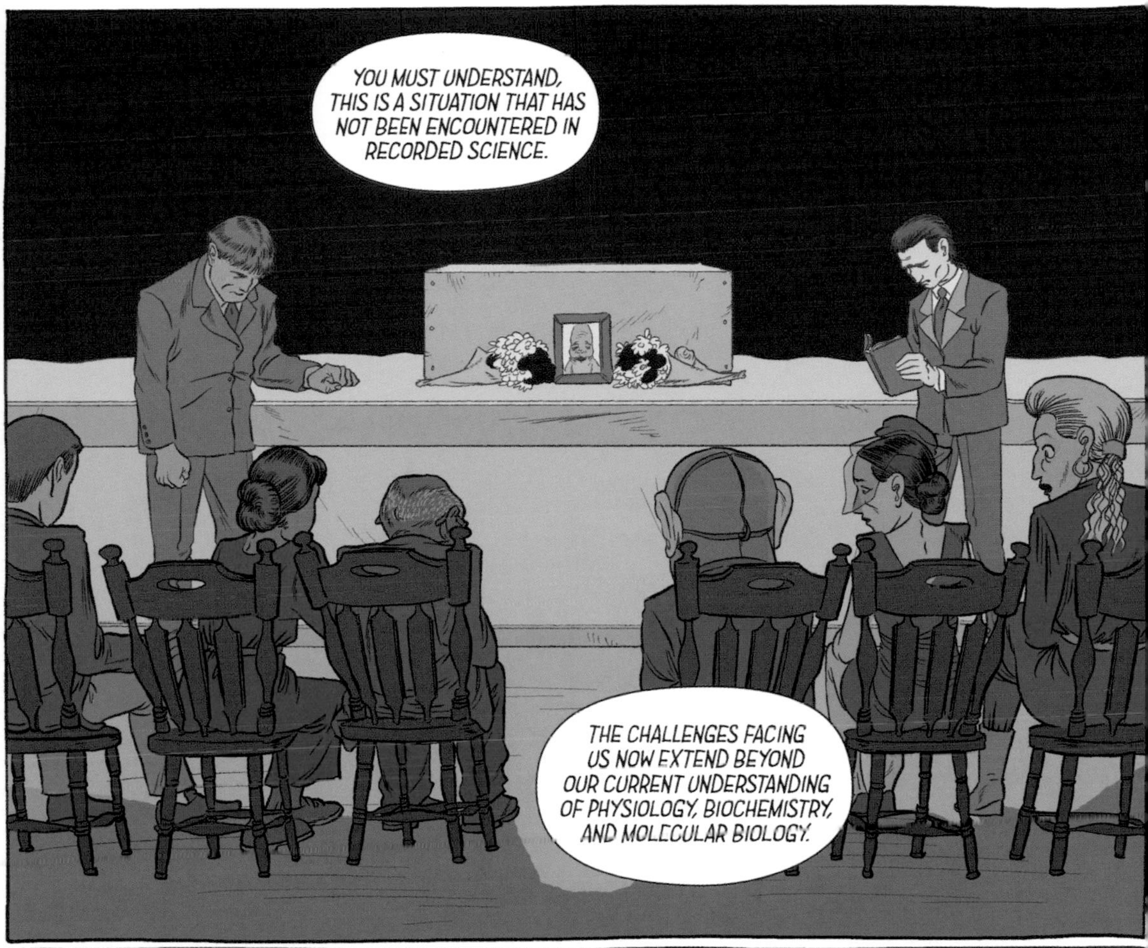
YOU MUST UNDERSTAND, THIS IS A SITUATION THAT HAS NOT BEEN ENCOUNTERED IN RECORDED SCIENCE.
THE CHALLENGES FACING US NOW EXTEND BEYOND OUR CURRENT UNDERSTANDING OF PHYSIOLOGY, BIOCHEMISTRY, AND MOLECULAR BIOLOGY.

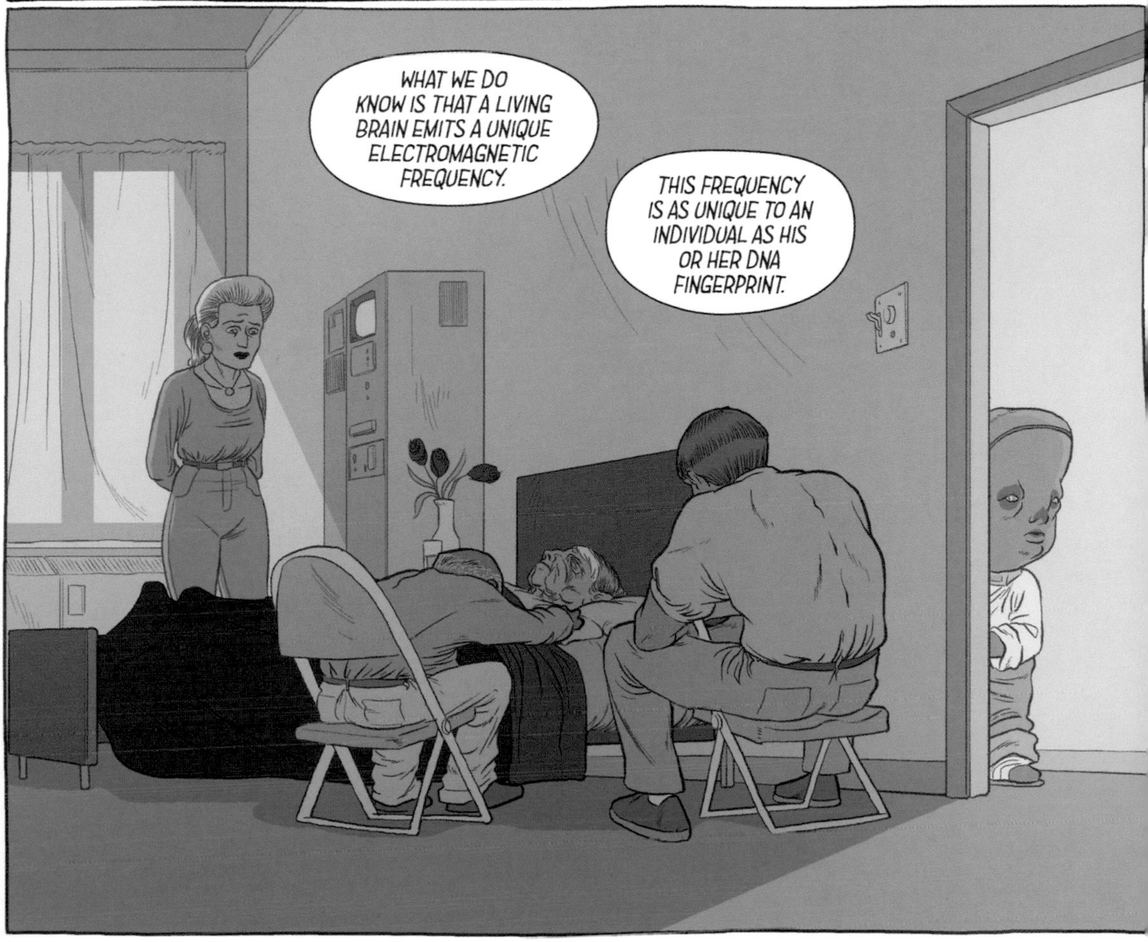
WHAT WE DO KNOW IS THAT A LIVING BRAIN EMITS A UNIQUE ELECTROMAGNETIC FREQUENCY.
THIS FREQUENCY IS AS UNIQUE TO AN INDIVIDUAL AS HIS OR HER DNA FINGERPRINT.

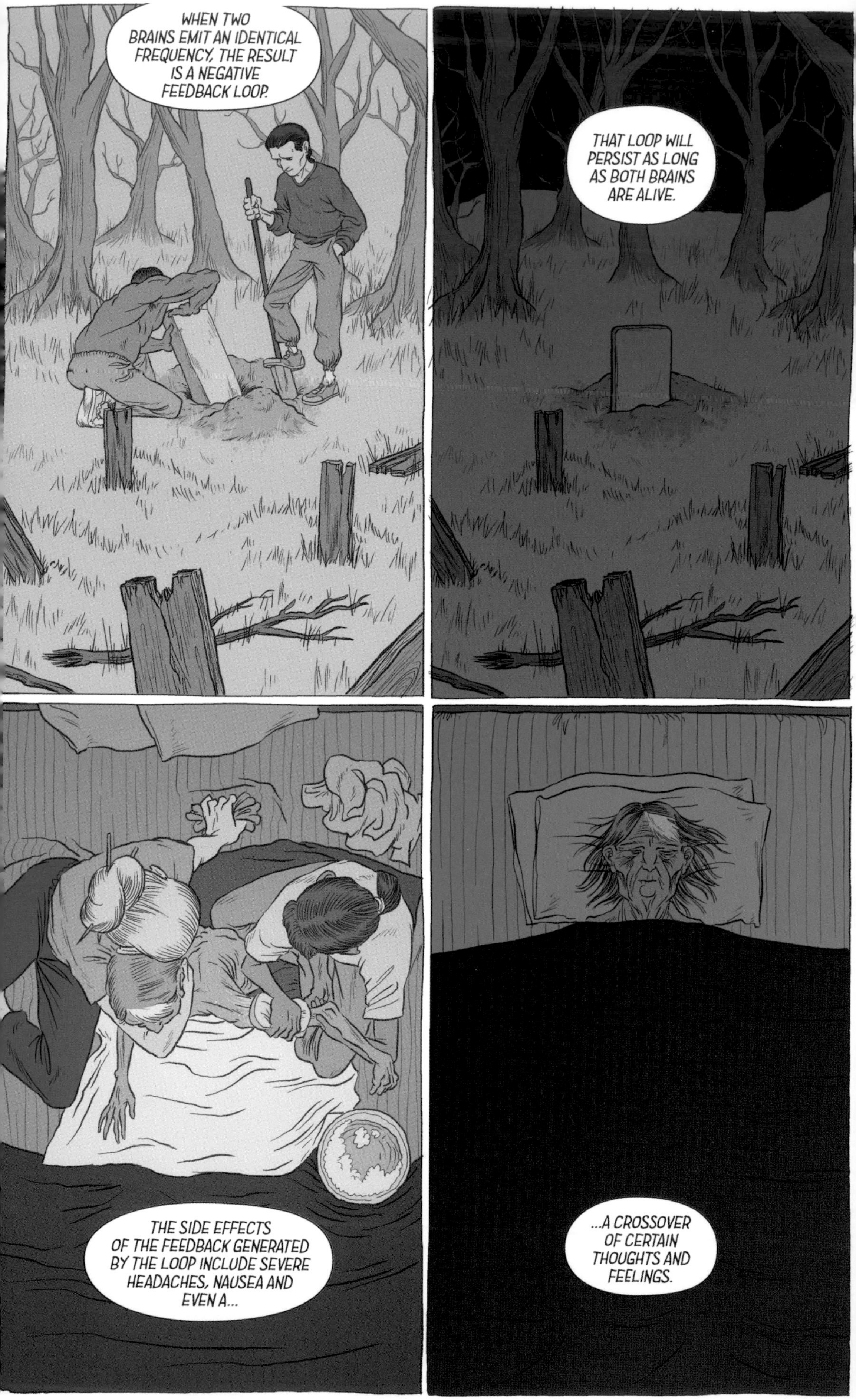
WHEN TWO BRAINS EMIT AN IDENTICAL FREQUENCY, THE RESULT IS A NEGATIVE FEEDBACK LOOP.
THAT LOOP WILL PERSIST AS LONG AS BOTH BRAINS ARE ALIVE.
THE SIDE EFFECTS OF THE FEEDBACK GENERATED BY THE LOOP INCLUDE SEVERE HEADACHES, NAUSEA AND EVEN A...
...A CROSSOVER OF CERTAIN THOUGHTS AND FEELINGS.

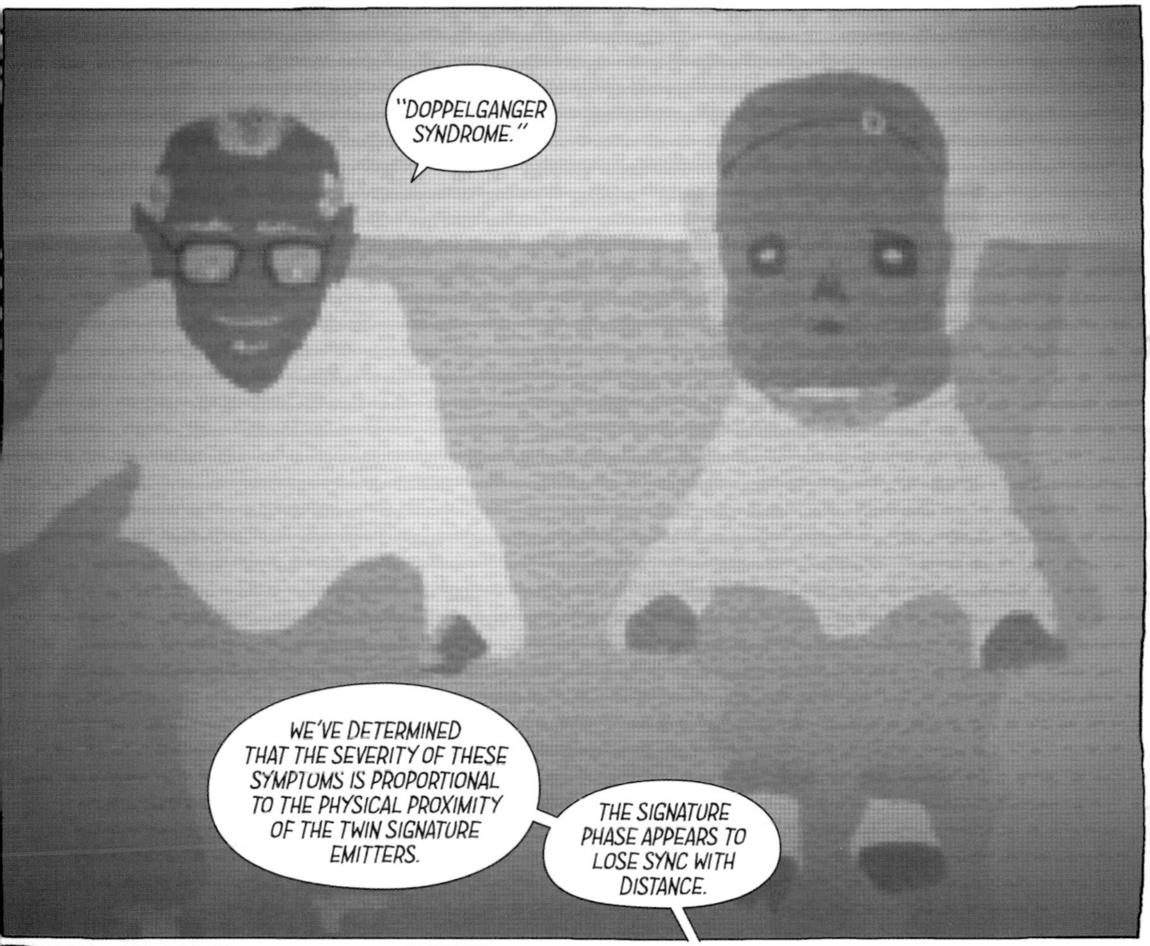
"DOPPELGANGER SYNDROME."
WE'VE DETERMINED THAT THE SEVERITY OF THESE SYMPTOMS IS PROPORTIONAL TO THE PHYSICAL PROXIMITY OF THE TWIN SIGNATURE EMITTERS.
THE SIGNATURE PHASE APPEARS TO LOSE SYNC WITH DISTANCE.

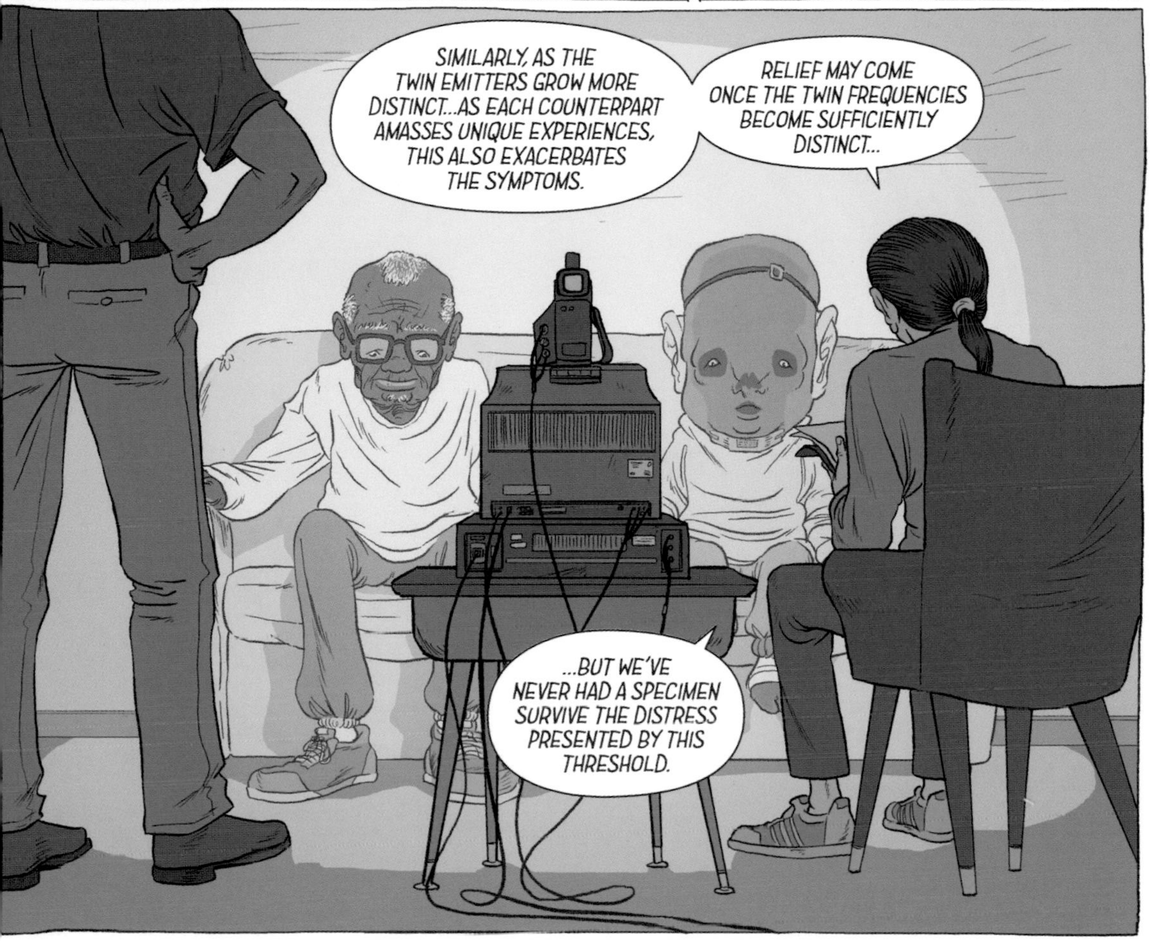
SIMILARLY, AS THE TWIN EMITTERS GROW MORE DISTINCT...AS EACH COUNTERPART AMASSES UNIQUE EXPERIENCES, THIS ALSO EXACERBATES THE SYMPTOMS.
RELIEF MAY COME ONCE THE TWIN FREQUENCIES BECOME SUFFICIENTLY DISTINCT...
...BUT WE'VE NEVER HAD A SPECIMEN SURVIVE THE DISTRESS PRESENTED BY THIS THRESHOLD.

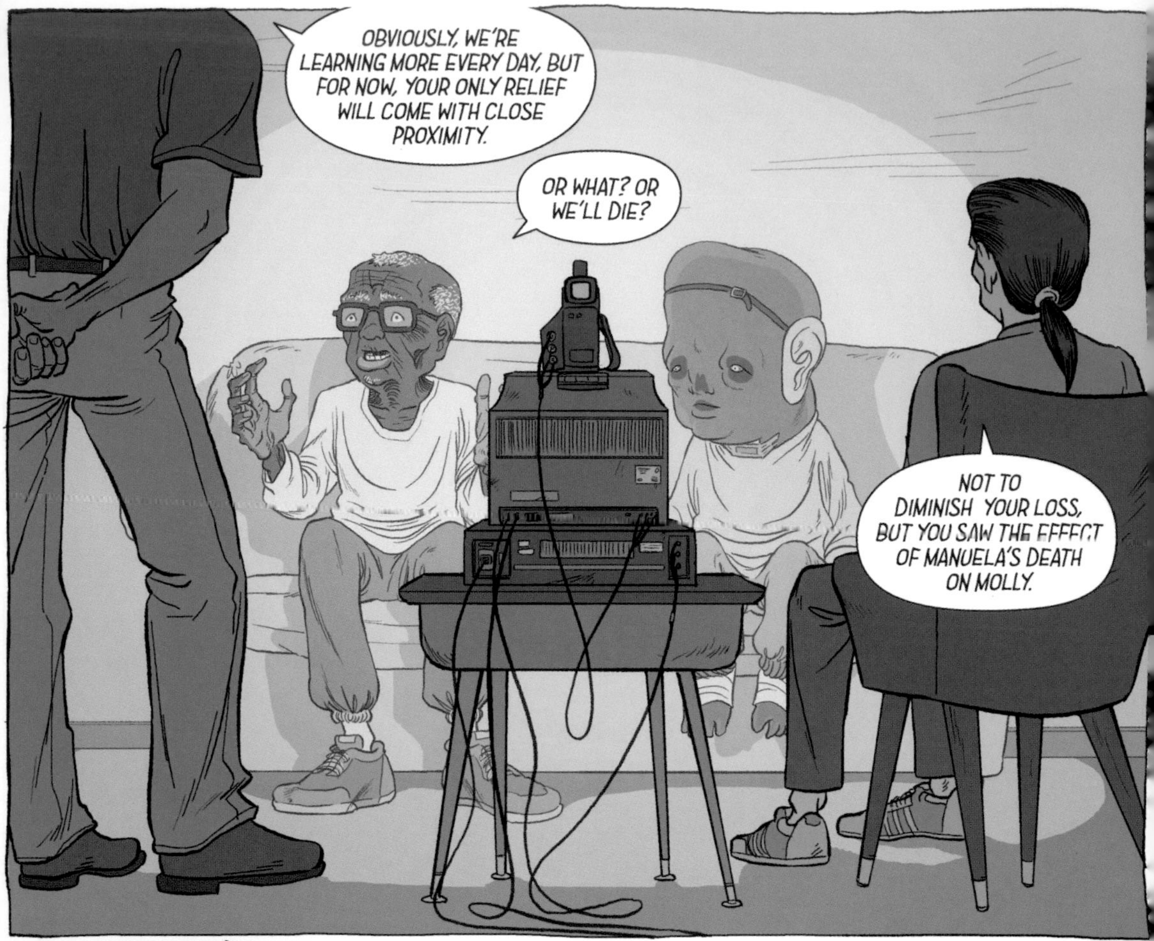
OBVIOUSLY, WE'RE LEARNING MORE EVERY DAY, BUT FOR NOW, YOUR ONLY RELIEF WILL COME WITH CLOSE PROXIMITY.
OR WHAT? OR WE'LL DIE?
NOT TO DIMINISH YOUR LOSS, BUT YOU SAW THE EFFECT OF MANUELA'S DEATH ON MOLLY.

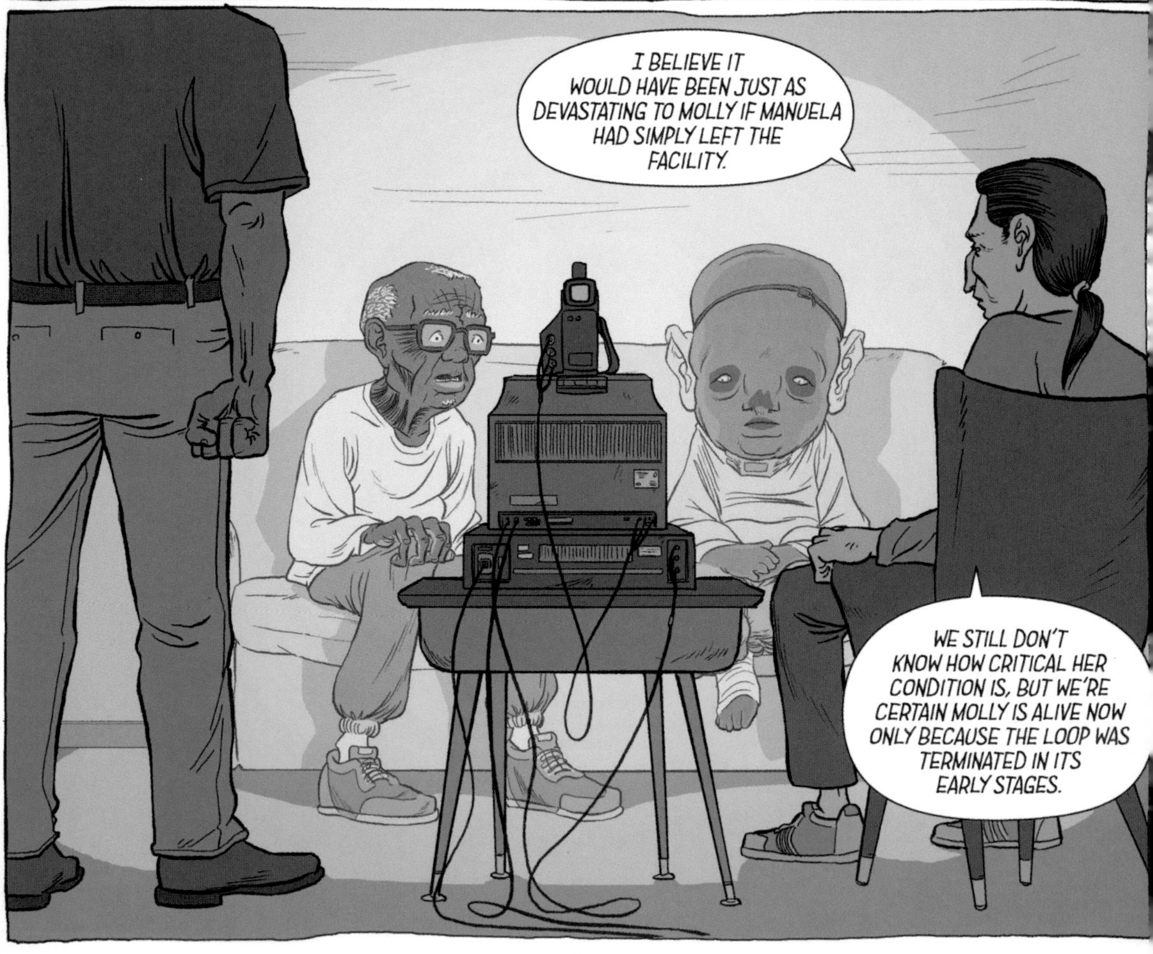
I BELIEVE IT WOULD HAVE BEEN JUST AS DEVASTATING TO MOLLY IF MANUELA HAD SIMPLY LEFT THE FACILITY.
WE STILL DON'T KNOW HOW CRITICAL HER CONDITION IS, BUT WE'RE CERTAIN MOLLY IS ALIVE NOW ONLY BECAUSE THE LOOP WAS TERMINATED IN ITS EARLY STAGES.

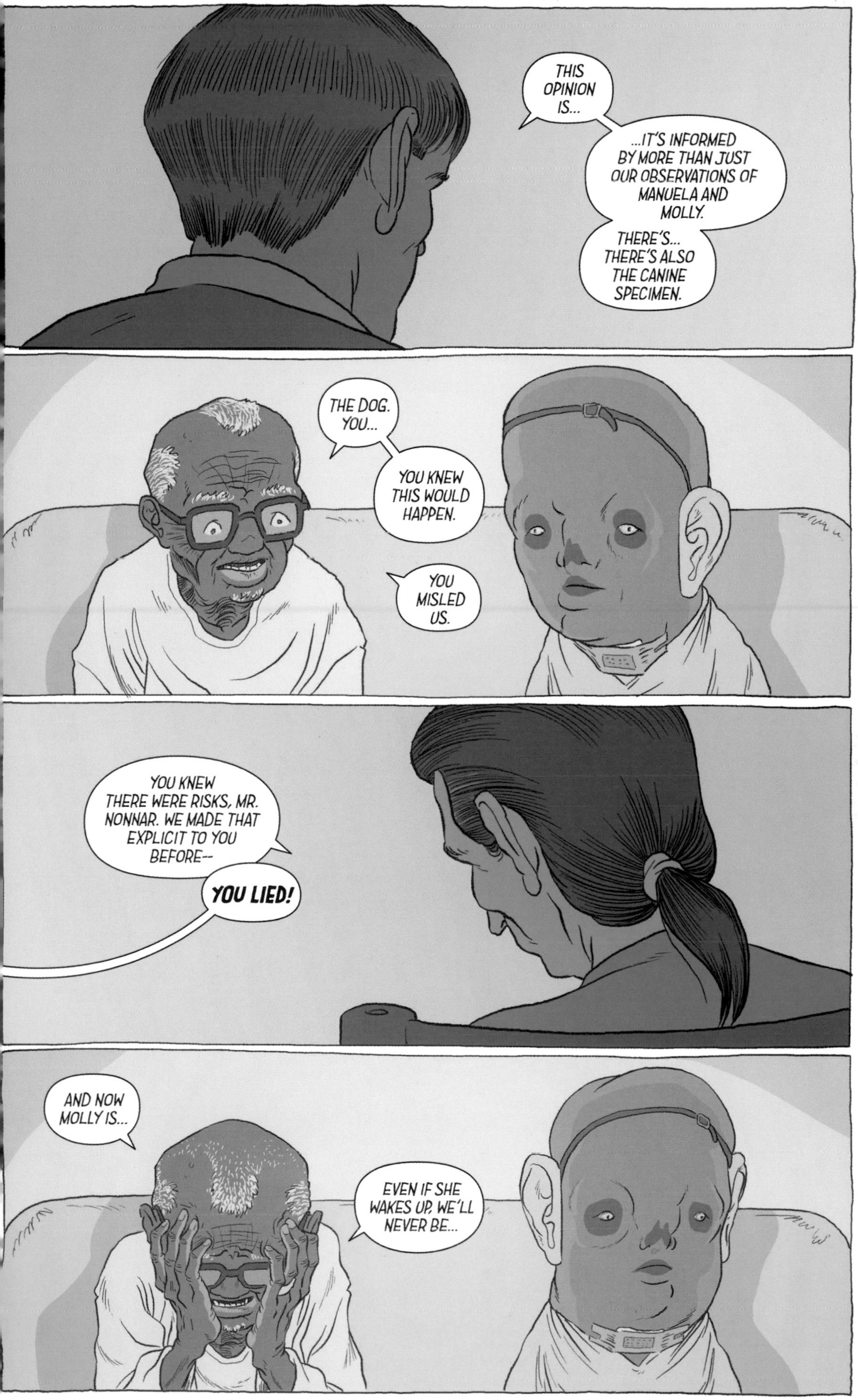
THIS OPINION IS...
...IT'S INFORMED BY MORE THAN JUST OUR OBSERVATIONS OF MANUELA AND MOLLY.
THERE'S... THERE'S ALSO THE CANINE SPECIMEN.
THE DOG. YOU...
YOU KNEW THIS WOULD HAPPEN.
YOU MISLED US.
YOU KNEW THERE WERE RISKS, MR. NONNAR. WE MADE THAT EXPLICIT TO YOU BEFORE--
YOU LIED!
AND NOW MOLLY IS...
EVEN IF SHE WAKES UP, WE'LL NEVER BE...

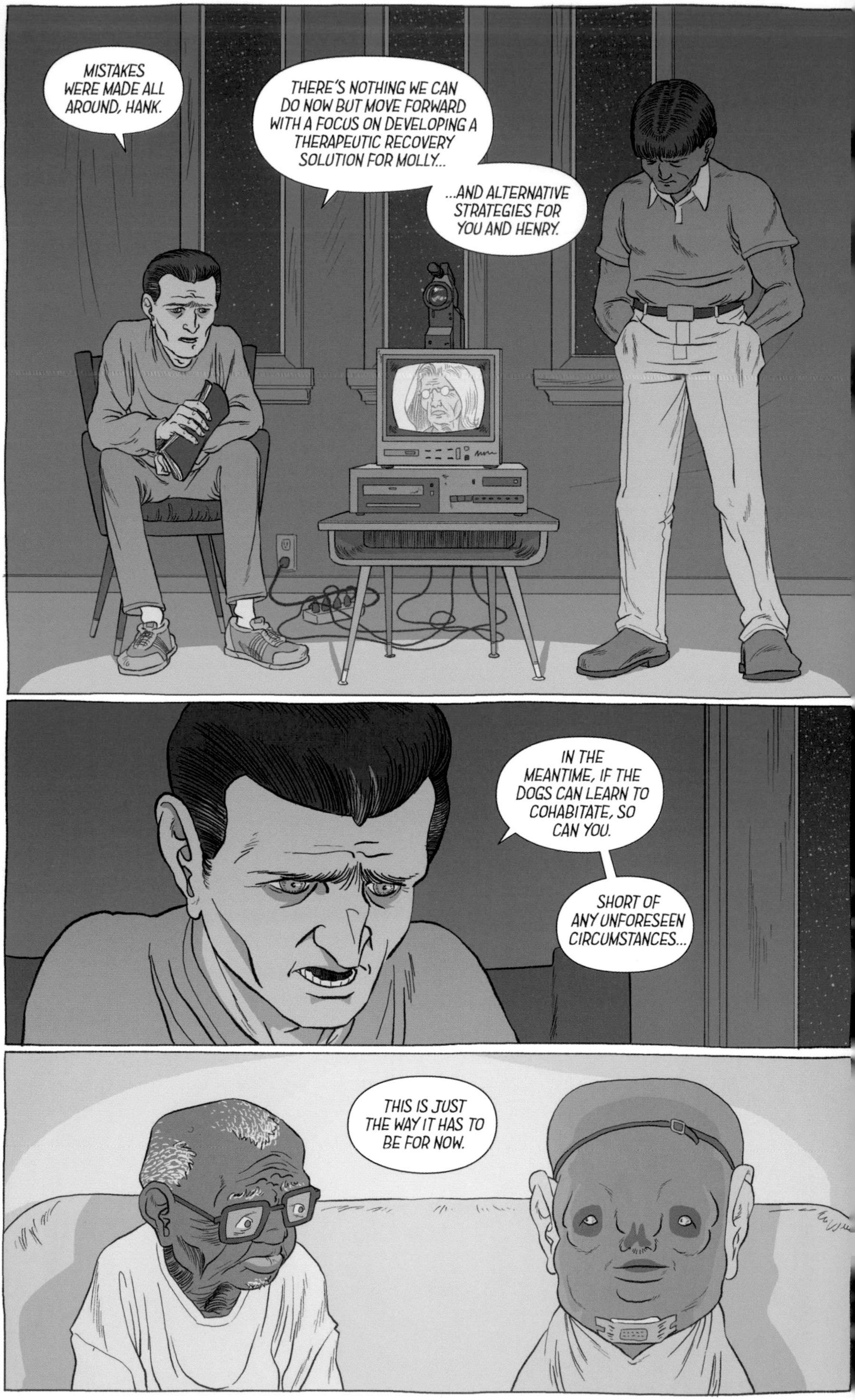
MISTAKES WERE MADE ALL AROUND, HANK.
THERE'S NOTHING WE CAN DO NOW BUT MOVE FORWARD WITH A FOCUS ON DEVELOPING A THERAPEUTIC RECOVERY SOLUTION FOR MOLLY...
...AND ALTERNATIVE STRATEGIES FOR YOU AND HENRY.
IN THE MEANTIME, IF THE DOGS CAN LEARN TO COHABITATE, SO CAN YOU.
SHORT OF ANY UNFORESEEN CIRCUMSTANCES...
THIS IS JUST THE WAY IT HAS TO BE FOR NOW.

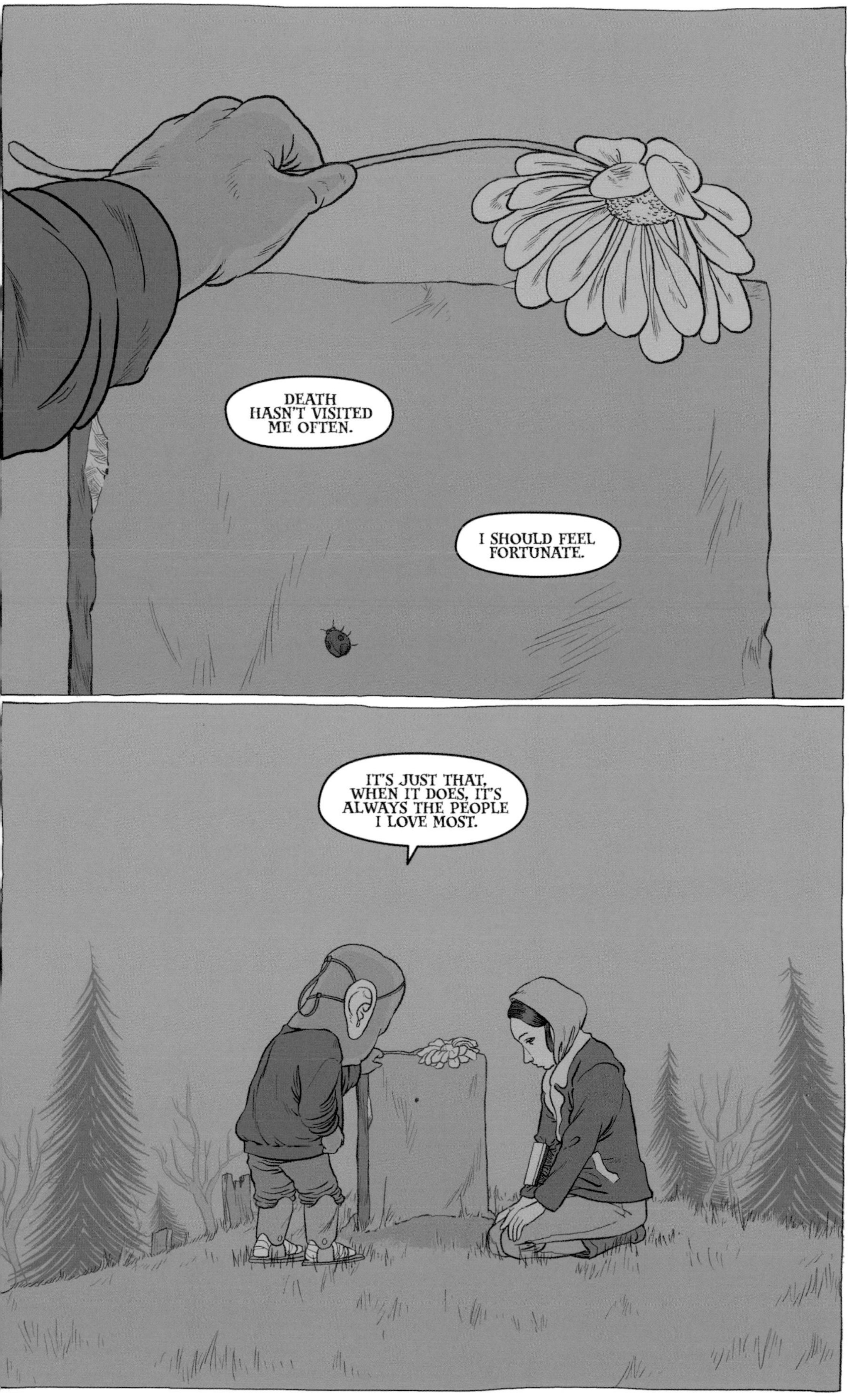
DEATH HASN'T VISITED ME OFTEN.
I SHOULD FEEL FORTUNATE.
IT'S JUST THAT, WHEN IT DOES, IT'S ALWAYS THE PEOPLE I LOVE MOST.

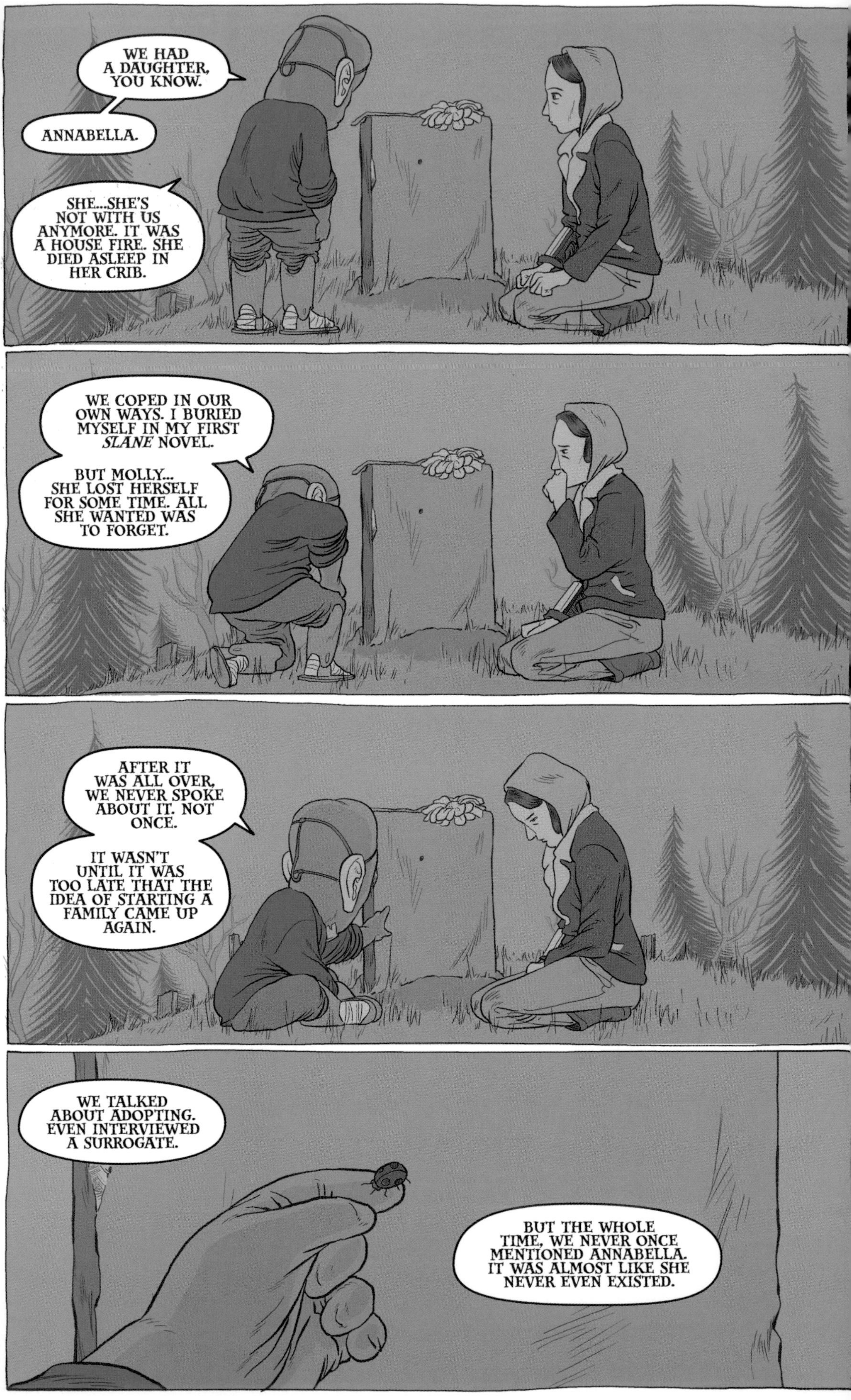
WE HAD A DAUGHTER, YOU KNOW.
ANNABELLA.
SHE...SHE'S NOT WITH US ANYMORE. IT WAS A HOUSE FIRE. SHE DIED ASLEEP IN HER CRIB.
WE COPED IN OUR OWN WAYS. I BURIED MYSELF IN MY FIRST *SLANE* NOVEL.
BUT MOLLY... SHE LOST HERSELF FOR SOME TIME. ALL SHE WANTED WAS TO FORGET.
AFTER IT WAS ALL OVER, WE NEVER SPOKE ABOUT IT. NOT ONCE.
IT WASN'T UNTIL IT WAS TOO LATE THAT THE IDEA OF STARTING A FAMILY CAME UP AGAIN.
WE TALKED ABOUT ADOPTING. EVEN INTERVIEWED A SURROGATE.
BUT THE WHOLE TIME, WE NEVER ONCE MENTIONED ANNABELLA. IT WAS ALMOST LIKE SHE NEVER EVEN EXISTED.

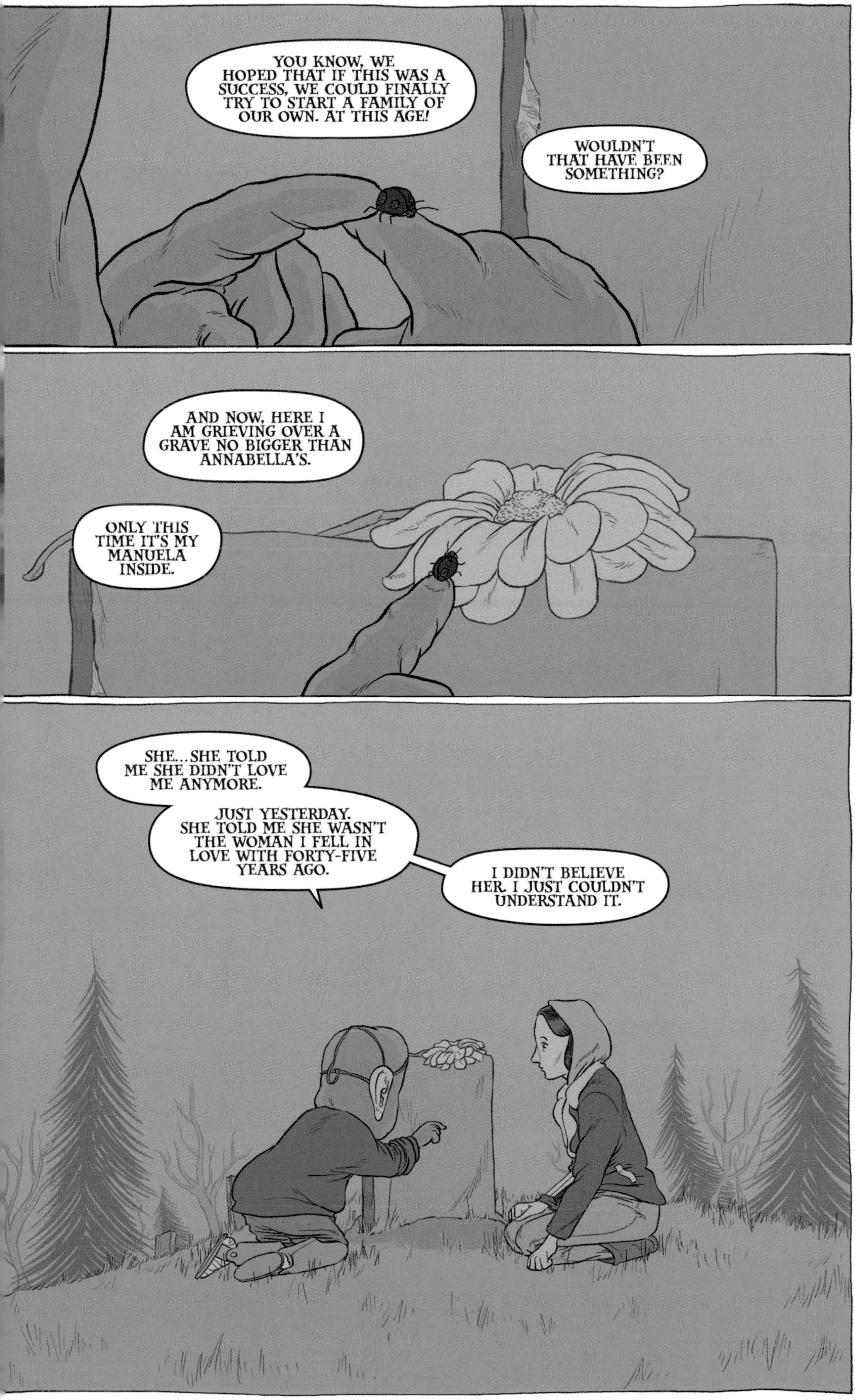

YOU KNOW, WE HOPED THAT IF THIS WAS A SUCCESS, WE COULD FINALLY TRY TO START A FAMILY OF OUR OWN. AT THIS AGE!
WOULDN'T THAT HAVE BEEN SOMETHING?
AND NOW, HERE I AM GRIEVING OVER A GRAVE NO BIGGER THAN ANNABELLA'S.
ONLY THIS TIME IT'S MY MANUELA INSIDE.
SHE...SHE TOLD ME SHE DIDN'T LOVE ME ANYMORE.
JUST YESTERDAY. SHE TOLD ME SHE WASN'T THE WOMAN I FELL IN LOVE WITH FORTY-FIVE YEARS AGO.
I DIDN'T BELIEVE HER. I JUST COULDN'T UNDERSTAND IT.

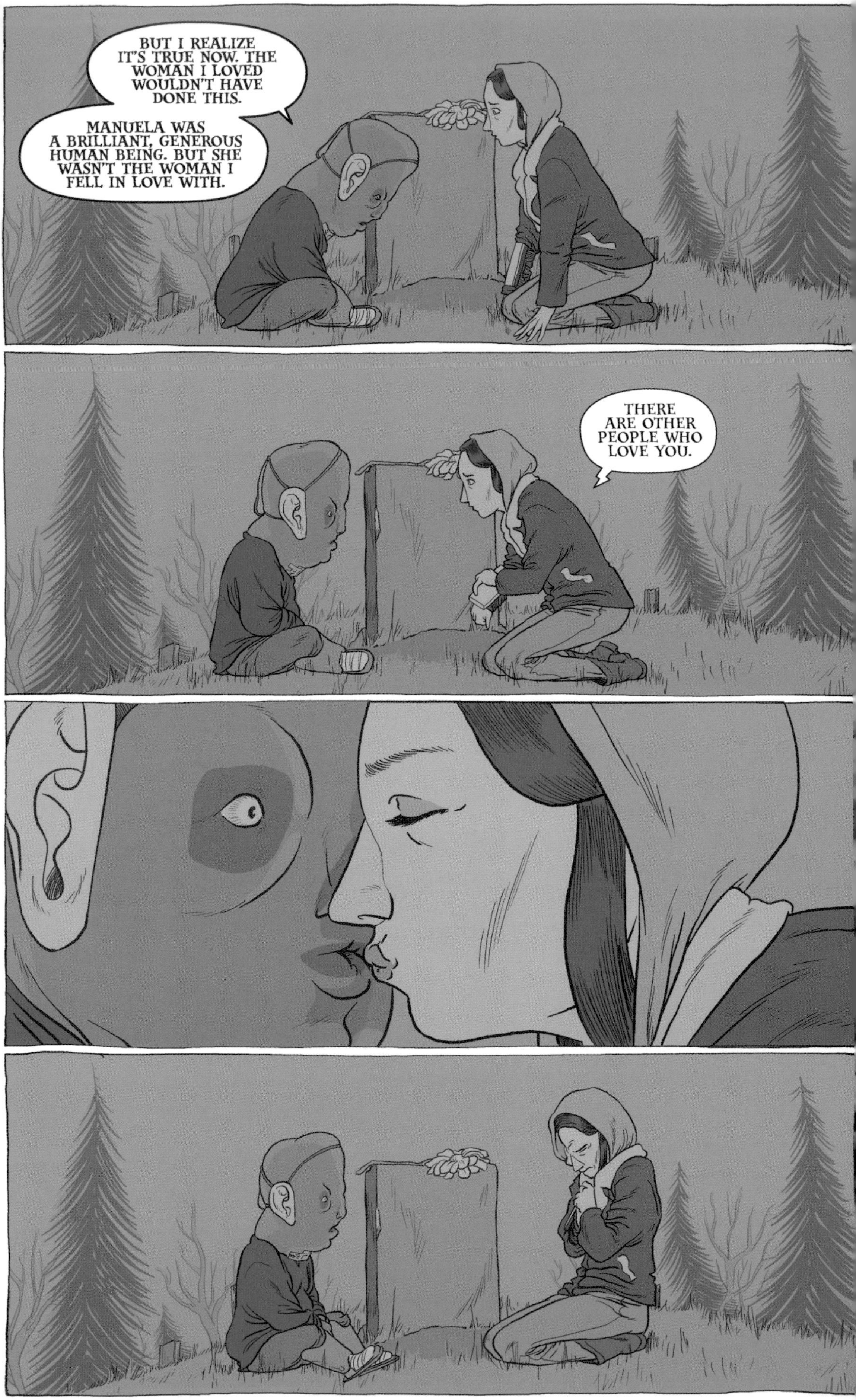
BUT I REALIZE IT'S TRUE NOW. THE WOMAN I LOVED WOULDN'T HAVE DONE THIS.
MANUELA WAS A BRILLIANT, GENEROUS HUMAN BEING. BUT SHE WASN'T THE WOMAN I FELL IN LOVE WITH.
THERE ARE OTHER PEOPLE WHO LOVE YOU.

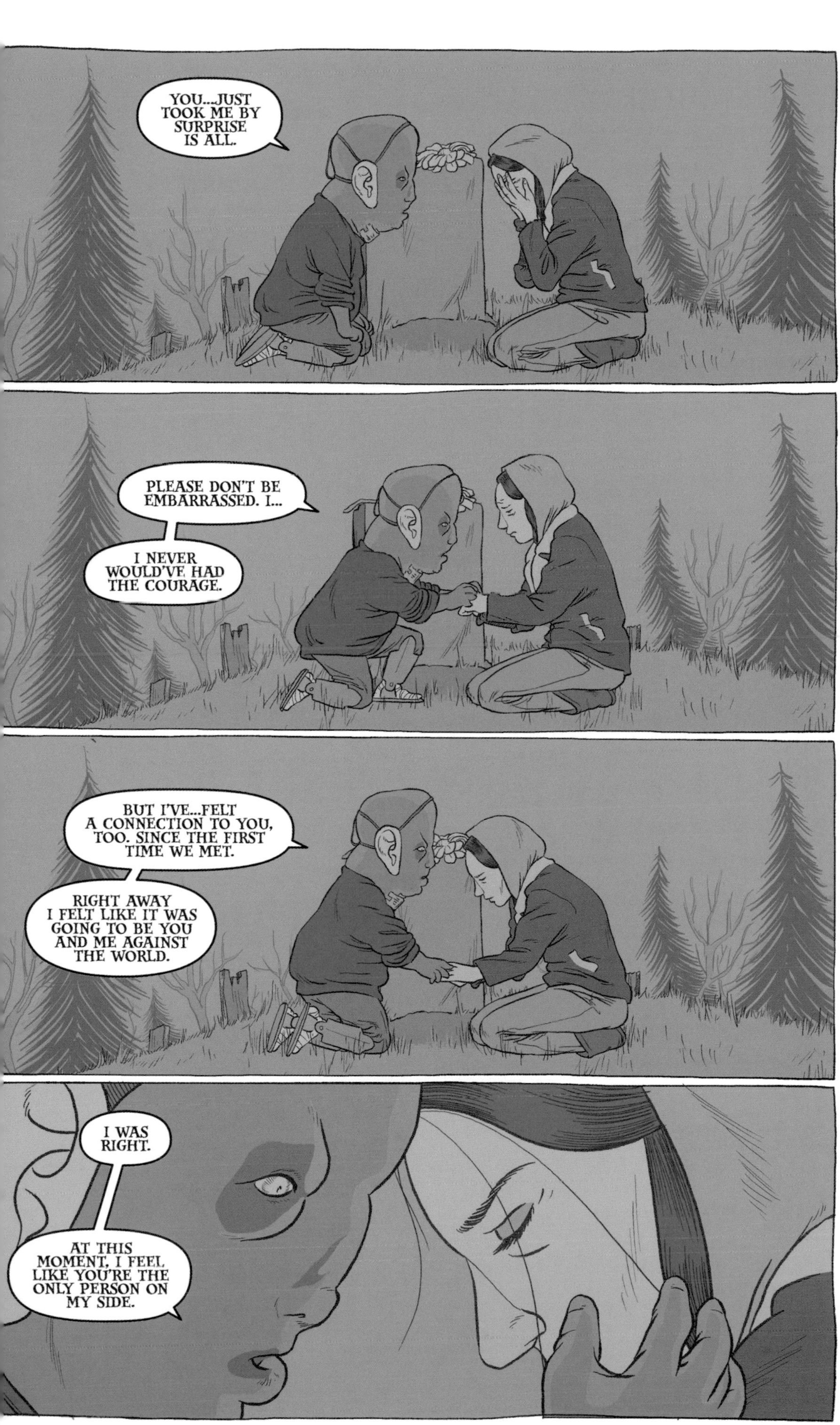
YOU...JUST TOOK ME BY SURPRISE IS ALL.
PLEASE DON'T BE EMBARRASSED. I...
I NEVER WOULD'VE HAD THE COURAGE.
BUT I'VE...FELT A CONNECTION TO YOU, TOO. SINCE THE FIRST TIME WE MET.
RIGHT AWAY I FELT LIKE IT WAS GOING TO BE YOU AND ME AGAINST THE WORLD.
I WAS RIGHT.
AT THIS MOMENT, I FEEL LIKE YOU'RE THE ONLY PERSON ON MY SIDE.

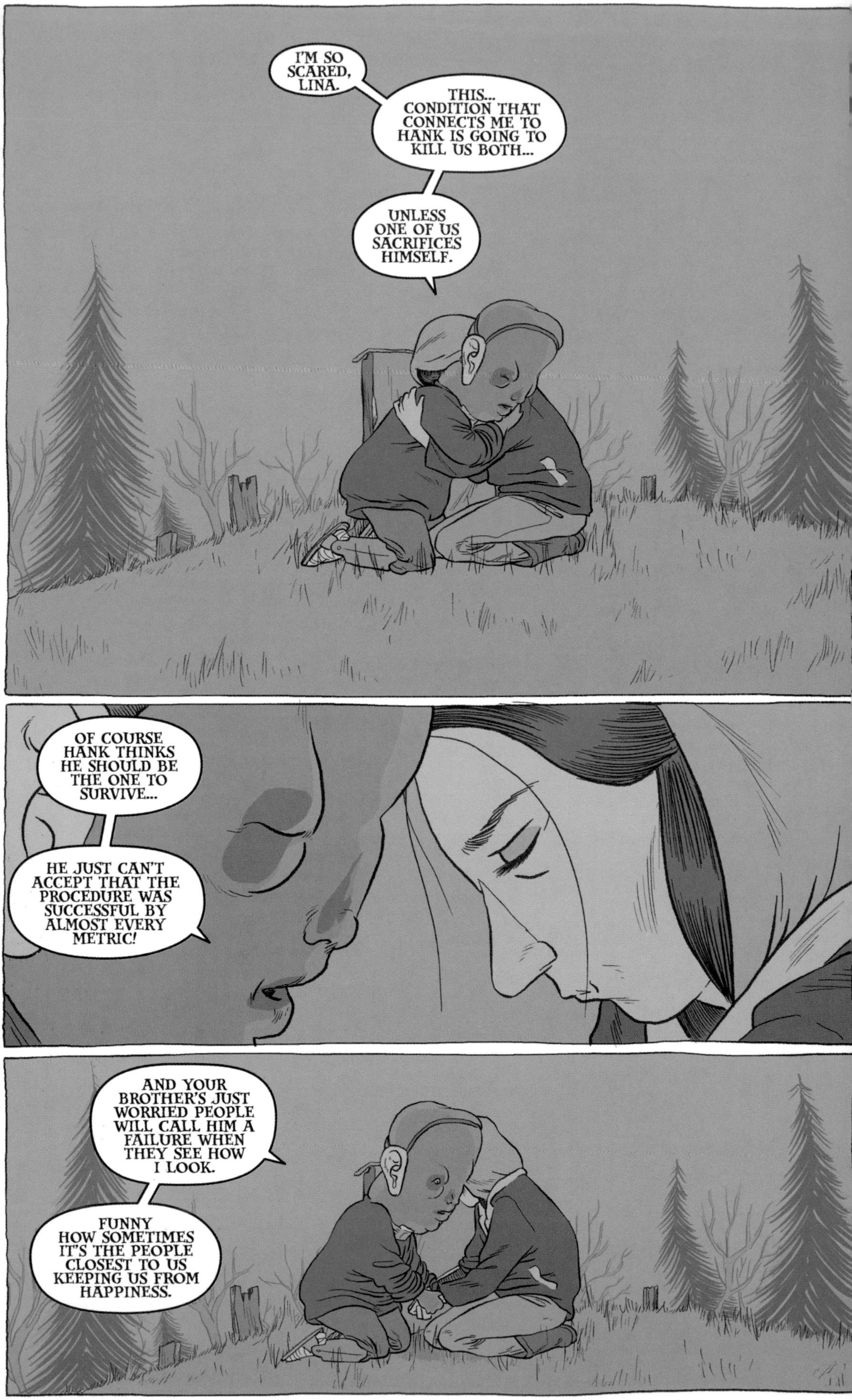
I'M SO SCARED, LINA.
THIS... CONDITION THAT CONNECTS ME TO HANK IS GOING TO KILL US BOTH...
UNLESS ONE OF US SACRIFICES HIMSELF.
OF COURSE HANK THINKS HE SHOULD BE THE ONE TO SURVIVE...
HE JUST CAN'T ACCEPT THAT THE PROCEDURE WAS SUCCESSFUL BY ALMOST EVERY METRIC!
AND YOUR BROTHER'S JUST WORRIED PEOPLE WILL CALL HIM A FAILURE WHEN THEY SEE HOW I LOOK.
FUNNY HOW SOMETIMES IT'S THE PEOPLE CLOSEST TO US KEEPING US FROM HAPPINESS.

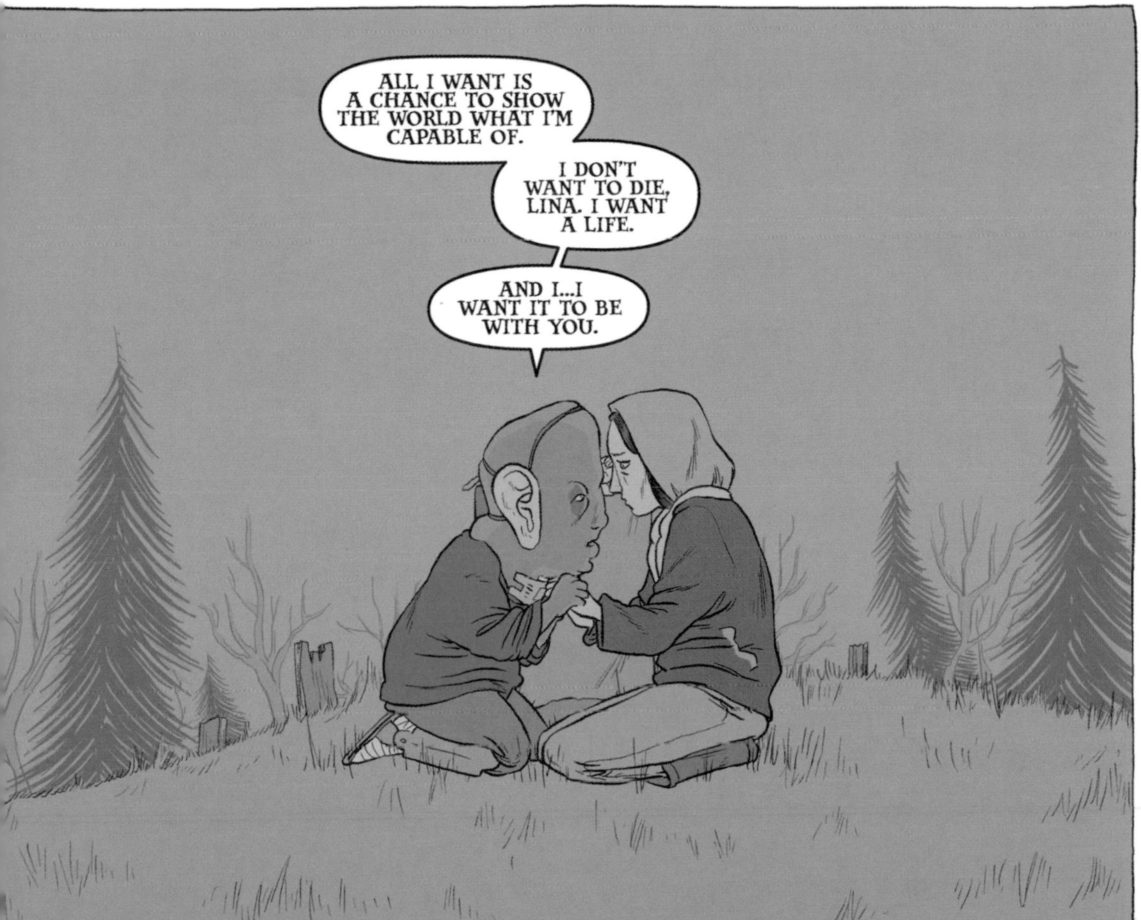
ALL I WANT IS A CHANCE TO SHOW THE WORLD WHAT I'M CAPABLE OF.
I DON'T WANT TO DIE, LINA. I WANT A LIFE.
AND I...I WANT IT TO BE WITH YOU.

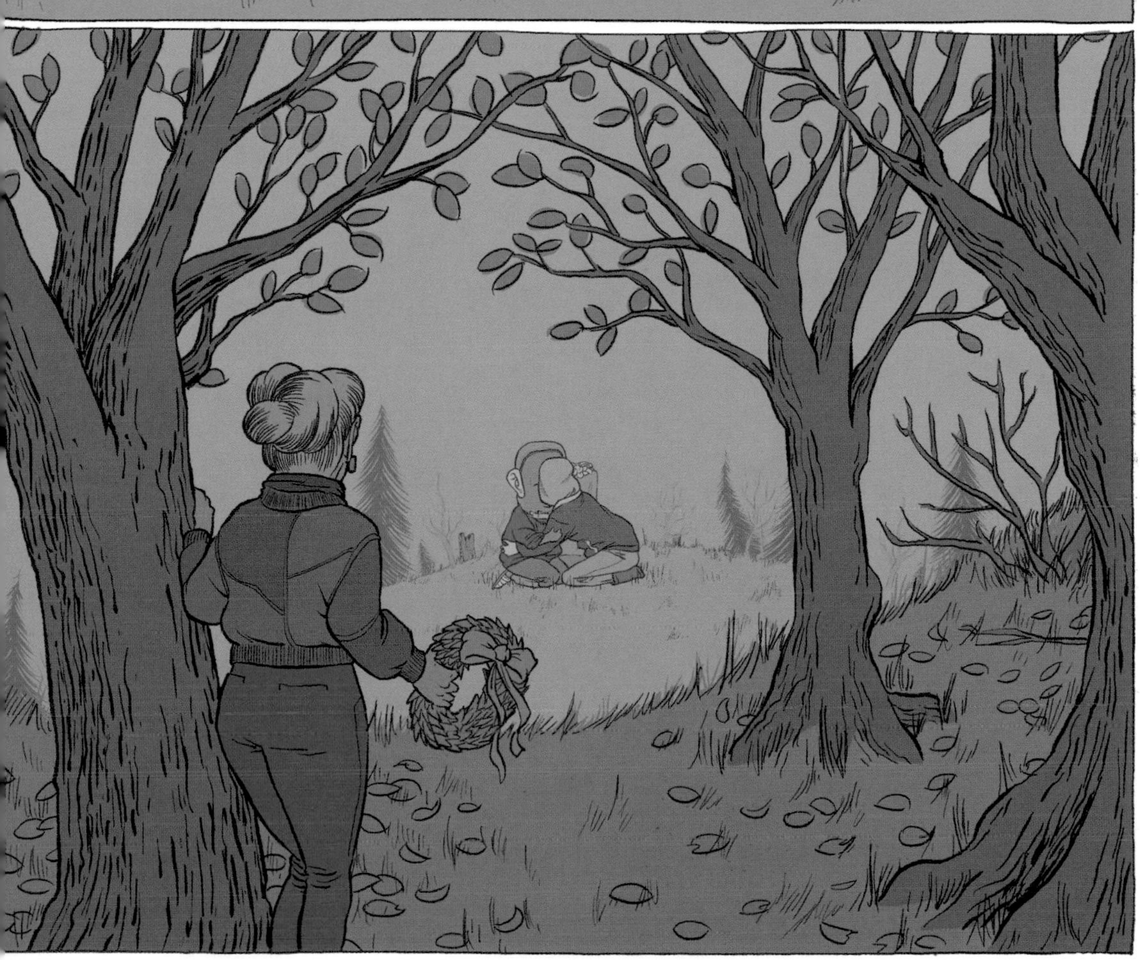

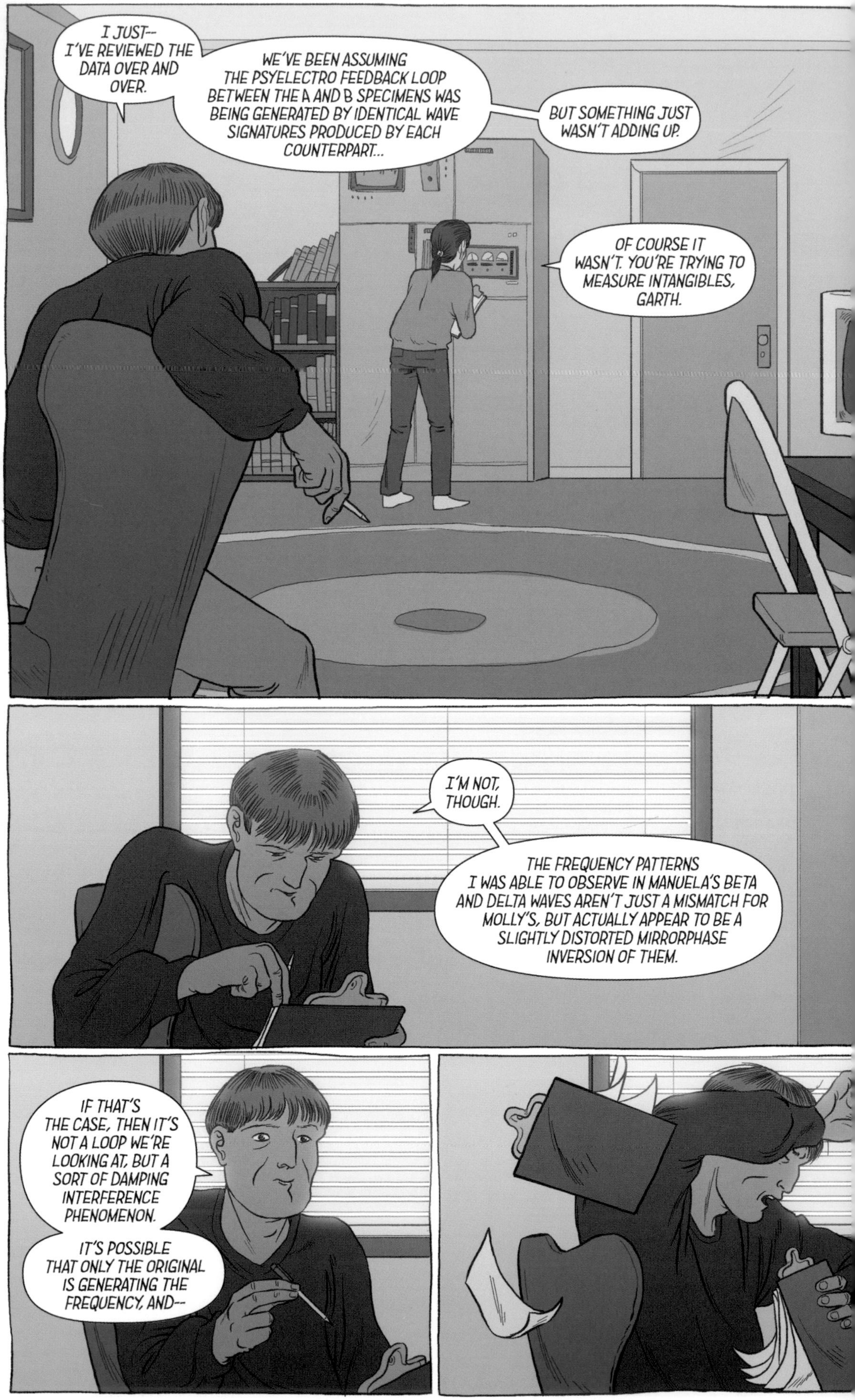
I JUST-- I'VE REVIEWED THE DATA OVER AND OVER.
WE'VE BEEN ASSUMING THE PSYELECTRO FEEDBACK LOOP BETWEEN THE A AND B SPECIMENS WAS BEING GENERATED BY IDENTICAL WAVE SIGNATURES PRODUCED BY EACH COUNTERPART...
BUT SOMETHING JUST WASN'T ADDING UP.
OF COURSE IT WASN'T. YOU'RE TRYING TO MEASURE INTANGIBLES, GARTH.
I'M NOT, THOUGH.
THE FREQUENCY PATTERNS I WAS ABLE TO OBSERVE IN MANUELA'S BETA AND DELTA WAVES AREN'T JUST A MISMATCH FOR MOLLY'S, BUT ACTUALLY APPEAR TO BE A SLIGHTLY DISTORTED MIRRORPHASE INVERSION OF THEM.
IF THAT'S THE CASE, THEN IT'S NOT A LOOP WE'RE LOOKING AT, BUT A SORT OF DAMPING INTERFERENCE PHENOMENON.
IT'S POSSIBLE THAT ONLY THE ORIGINAL IS GENERATING THE FREQUENCY, AND--

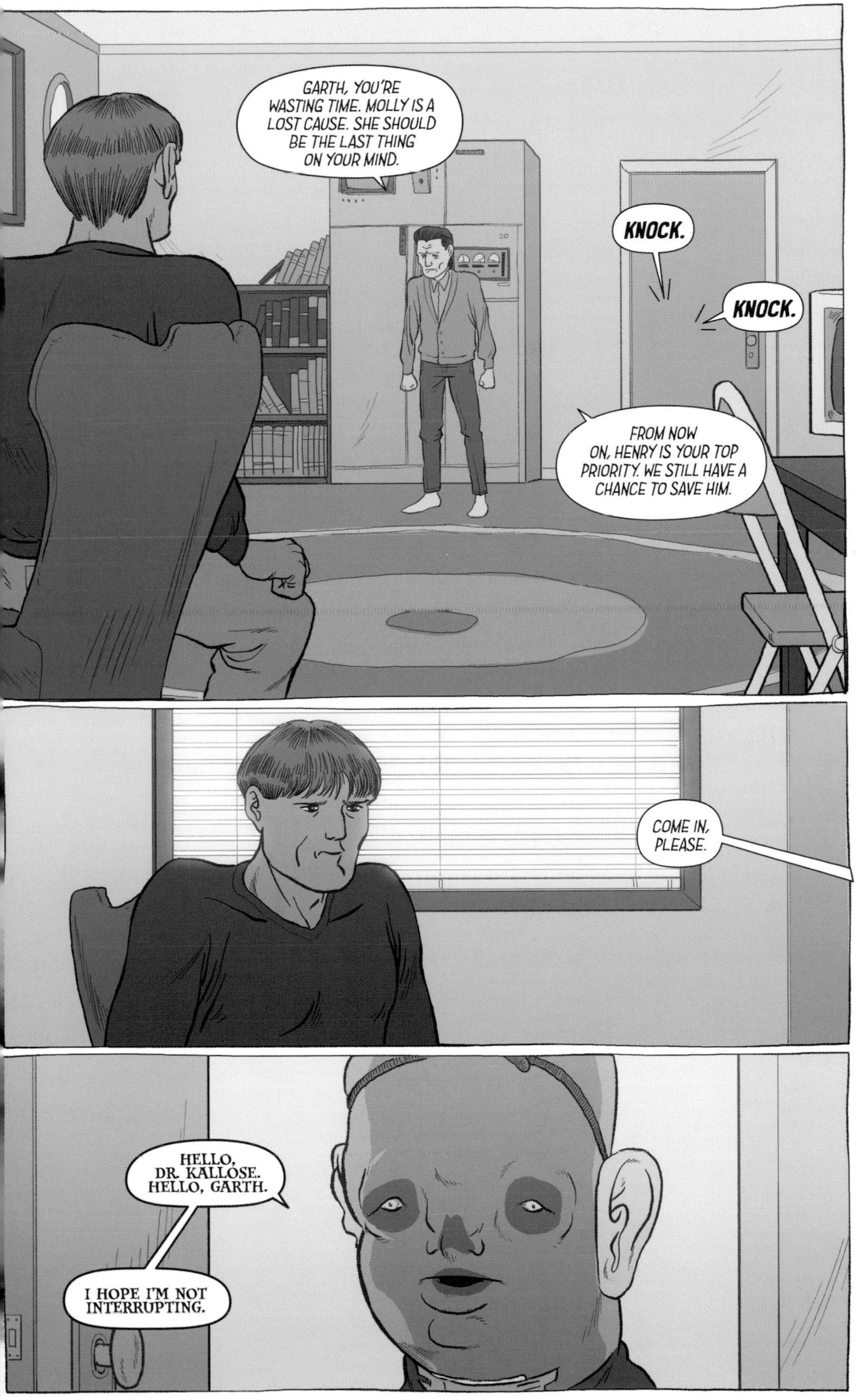
GARTH, YOU'RE WASTING TIME. MOLLY IS A LOST CAUSE. SHE SHOULD BE THE LAST THING ON YOUR MIND.
KNOCK.
KNOCK.
FROM NOW ON, HENRY IS YOUR TOP PRIORITY. WE STILL HAVE A CHANCE TO SAVE HIM.
COME IN, PLEASE.
HELLO, DR. KALLOSE. HELLO, GARTH.
I HOPE I'M NOT INTERRUPTING.

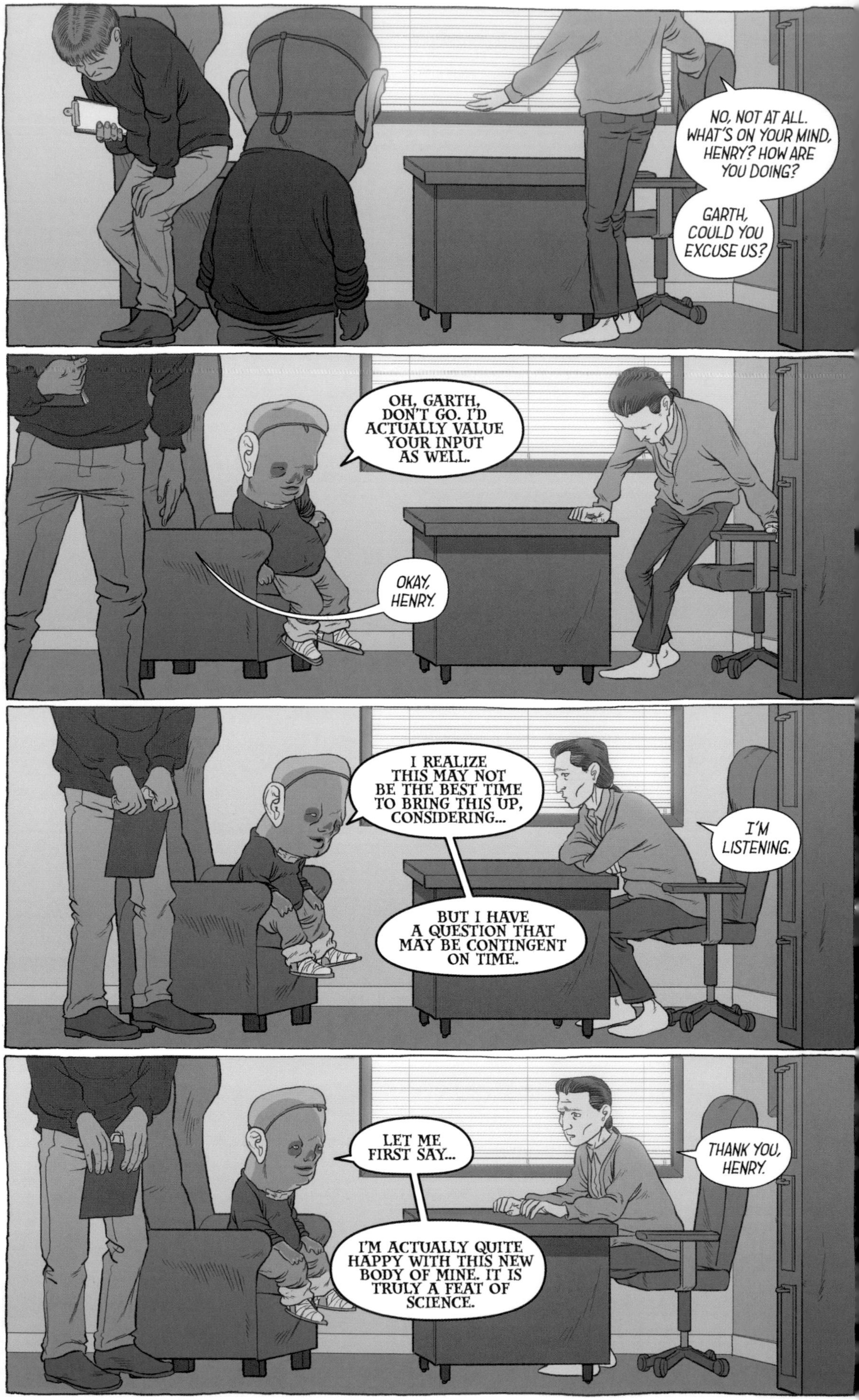
NO, NOT AT ALL. WHAT'S ON YOUR MIND, HENRY? HOW ARE YOU DOING?
GARTH, COULD YOU EXCUSE US?
OH, GARTH, DON'T GO. I'D ACTUALLY VALUE YOUR INPUT AS WELL.
OKAY, HENRY.
I REALIZE THIS MAY NOT BE THE BEST TIME TO BRING THIS UP, CONSIDERING...
I'M LISTENING.
BUT I HAVE A QUESTION THAT MAY BE CONTINGENT ON TIME.
LET ME FIRST SAY...
THANK YOU, HENRY.
I'M ACTUALLY QUITE HAPPY WITH THIS NEW BODY OF MINE. IT IS TRULY A FEAT OF SCIENCE.

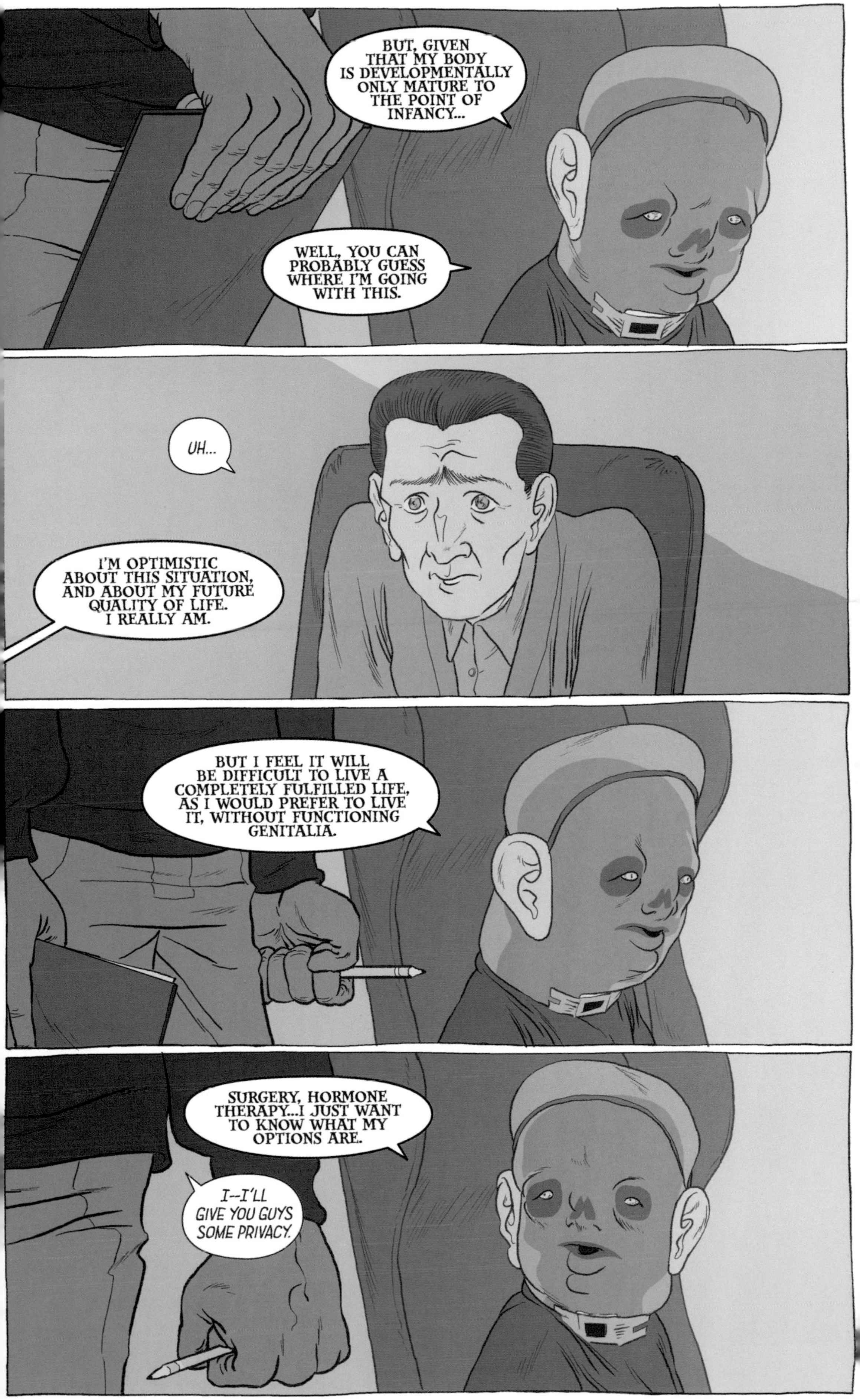
BUT, GIVEN THAT MY BODY IS DEVELOPMENTALLY ONLY MATURE TO THE POINT OF INFANCY...
WELL, YOU CAN PROBABLY GUESS WHERE I'M GOING WITH THIS.
UH...
I'M OPTIMISTIC ABOUT THIS SITUATION, AND ABOUT MY FUTURE QUALITY OF LIFE. I REALLY AM.
BUT I FEEL IT WILL BE DIFFICULT TO LIVE A COMPLETELY FULFILLED LIFE, AS I WOULD PREFER TO LIVE IT, WITHOUT FUNCTIONING GENITALIA.
SURGERY, HORMONE THERAPY...I JUST WANT TO KNOW WHAT MY OPTIONS ARE.
I--I'LL GIVE YOU GUYS SOME PRIVACY.

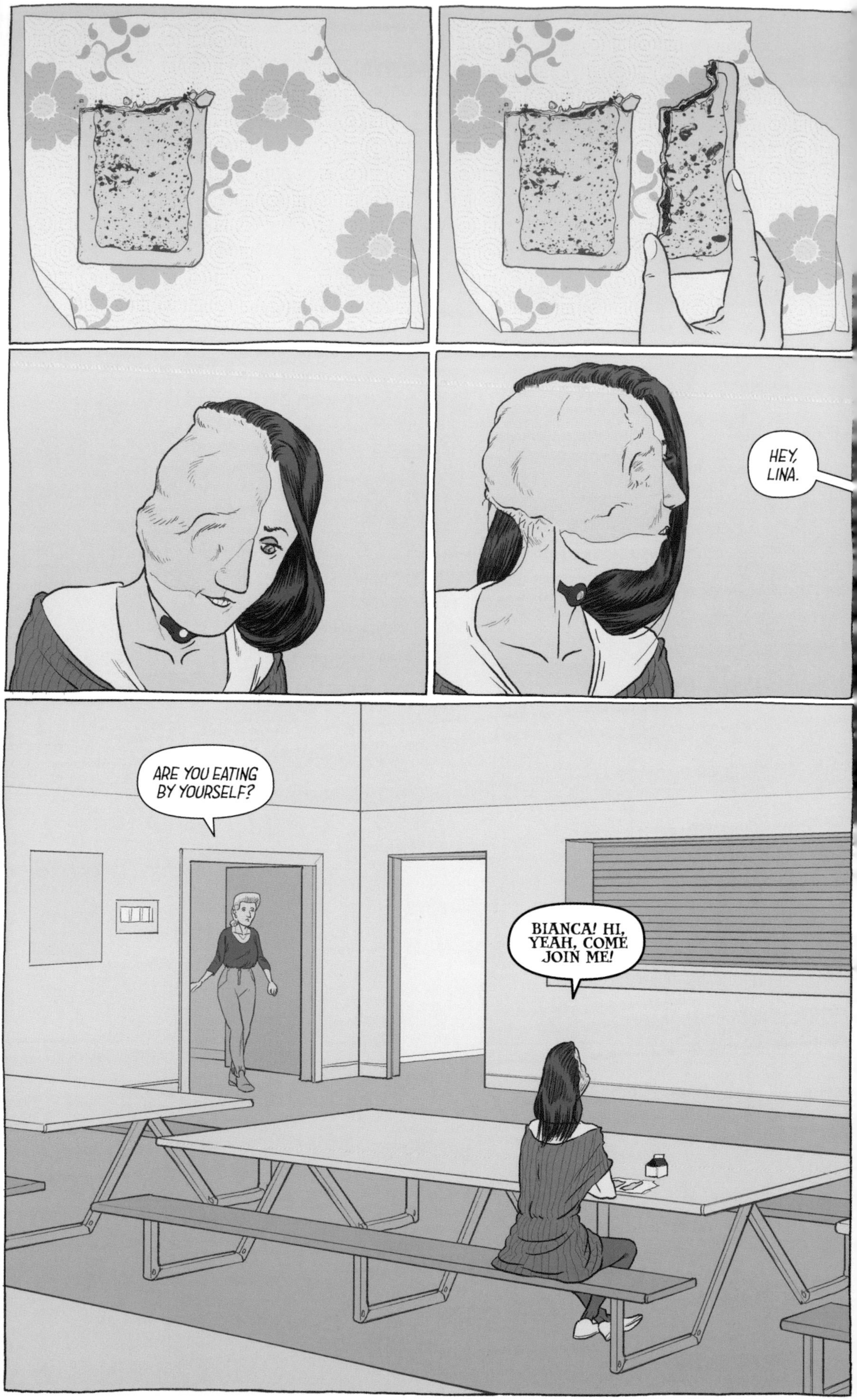
HEY, LINA.
ARE YOU EATING BY YOURSELF?
BIANCA! HI, YEAH, COME JOIN ME!

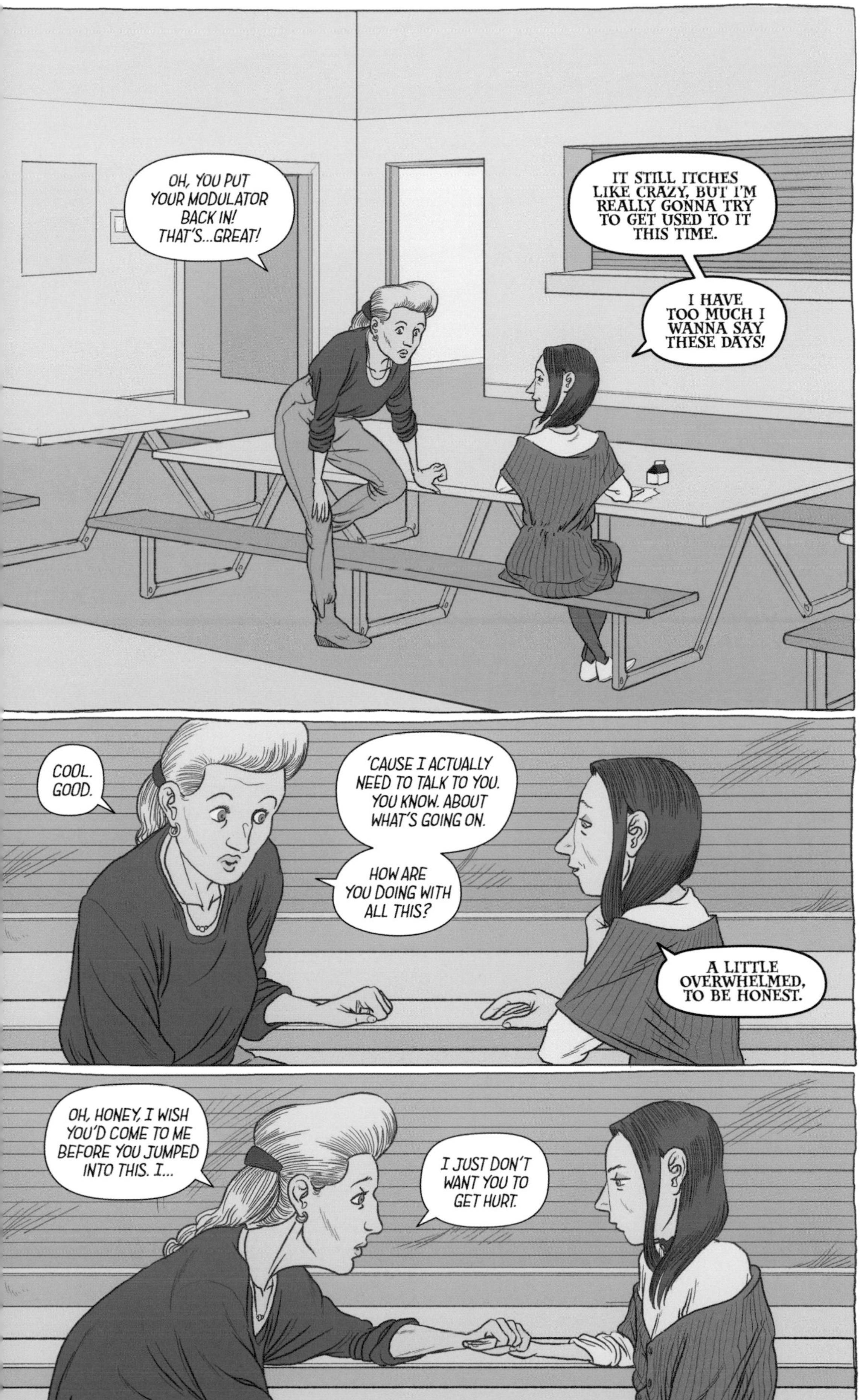
OH, YOU PUT YOUR MODULATOR BACK IN! THAT'S...GREAT!
IT STILL ITCHES LIKE CRAZY, BUT I'M REALLY GONNA TRY TO GET USED TO IT THIS TIME.
I HAVE TOO MUCH I WANNA SAY THESE DAYS!
COOL. GOOD.
'CAUSE I ACTUALLY NEED TO TALK TO YOU. YOU KNOW. ABOUT WHAT'S GOING ON.
HOW ARE YOU DOING WITH ALL THIS?
A LITTLE OVERWHELMED, TO BE HONEST.
OH, HONEY, I WISH YOU'D COME TO ME BEFORE YOU JUMPED INTO THIS. I...
I JUST DON'T WANT YOU TO GET HURT.

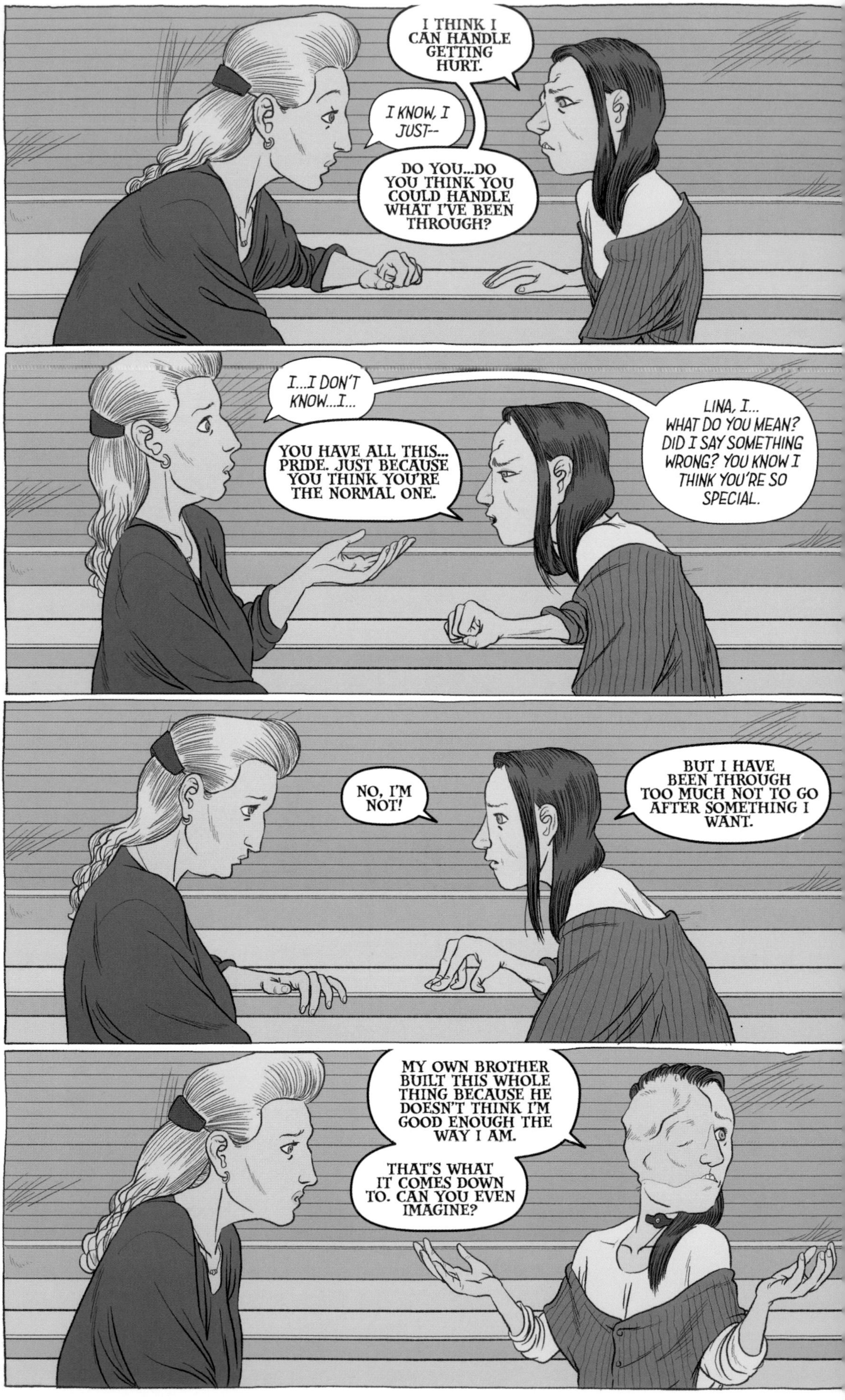

I THINK I CAN HANDLE GETTING HURT.
I KNOW, I JUST--
DO YOU...DO YOU THINK YOU COULD HANDLE WHAT I'VE BEEN THROUGH?
LINA, I... WHAT DO YOU MEAN? DID I SAY SOMETHING WRONG? YOU KNOW I THINK YOU'RE SO SPECIAL.
YOU HAVE ALL THIS... PRIDE. JUST BECAUSE YOU THINK YOU'RE THE NORMAL ONE.
I...I DON'T KNOW...I...
NO, I'M NOT!
BUT I HAVE BEEN THROUGH TOO MUCH NOT TO GO AFTER SOMETHING I WANT.
MY OWN BROTHER BUILT THIS WHOLE THING BECAUSE HE DOESN'T THINK I'M GOOD ENOUGH THE WAY I AM.
THAT'S WHAT IT COMES DOWN TO. CAN YOU EVEN IMAGINE?

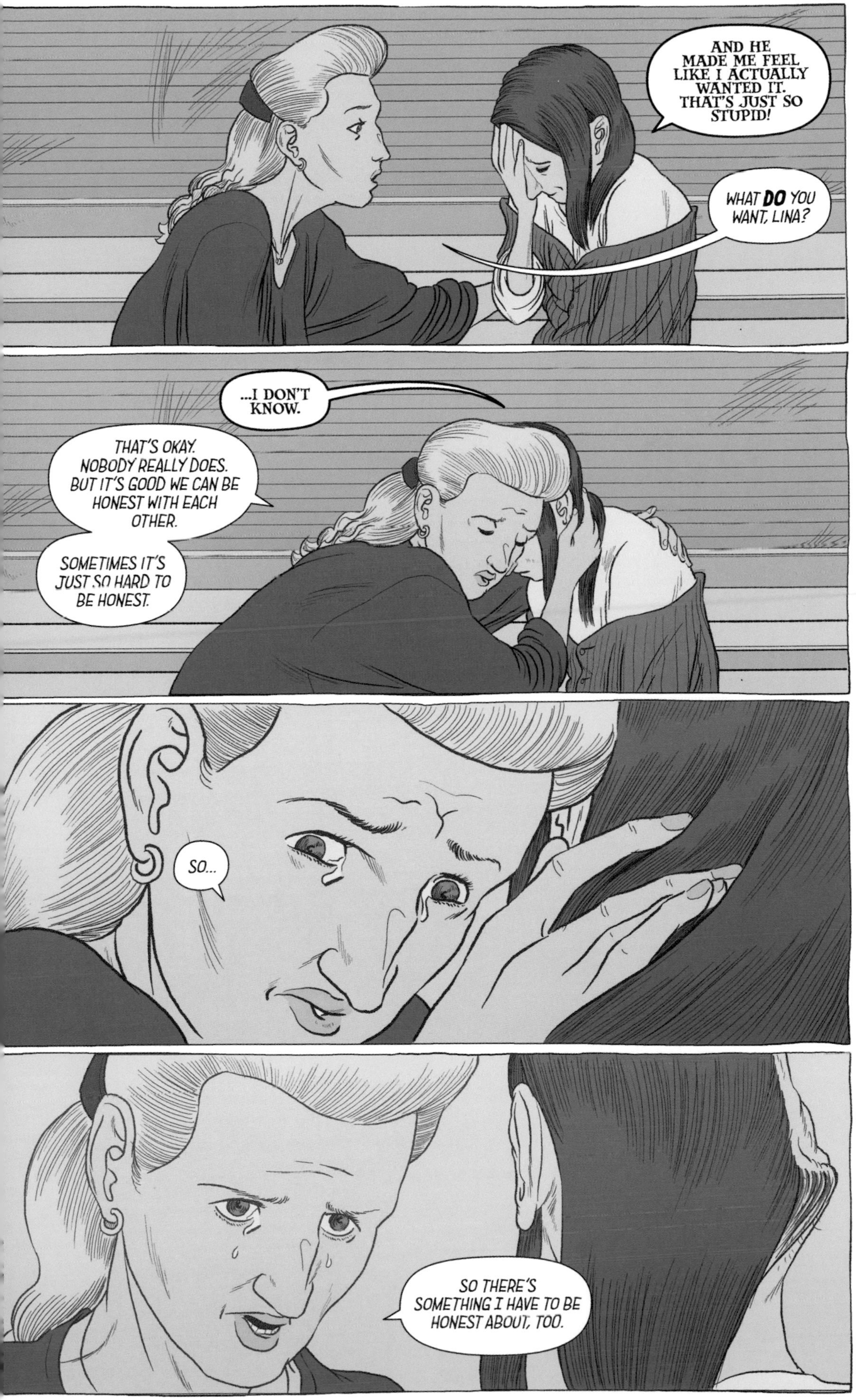
AND HE MADE ME FEEL LIKE I ACTUALLY WANTED IT. THAT'S JUST SO STUPID!
WHAT DO YOU WANT, LINA?
...I DON'T KNOW.
THAT'S OKAY. NOBODY REALLY DOES. BUT IT'S GOOD WE CAN BE HONEST WITH EACH OTHER.
SOMETIMES IT'S JUST SO HARD TO BE HONEST.
SO...
SO THERE'S SOMETHING I HAVE TO BE HONEST ABOUT, TOO.

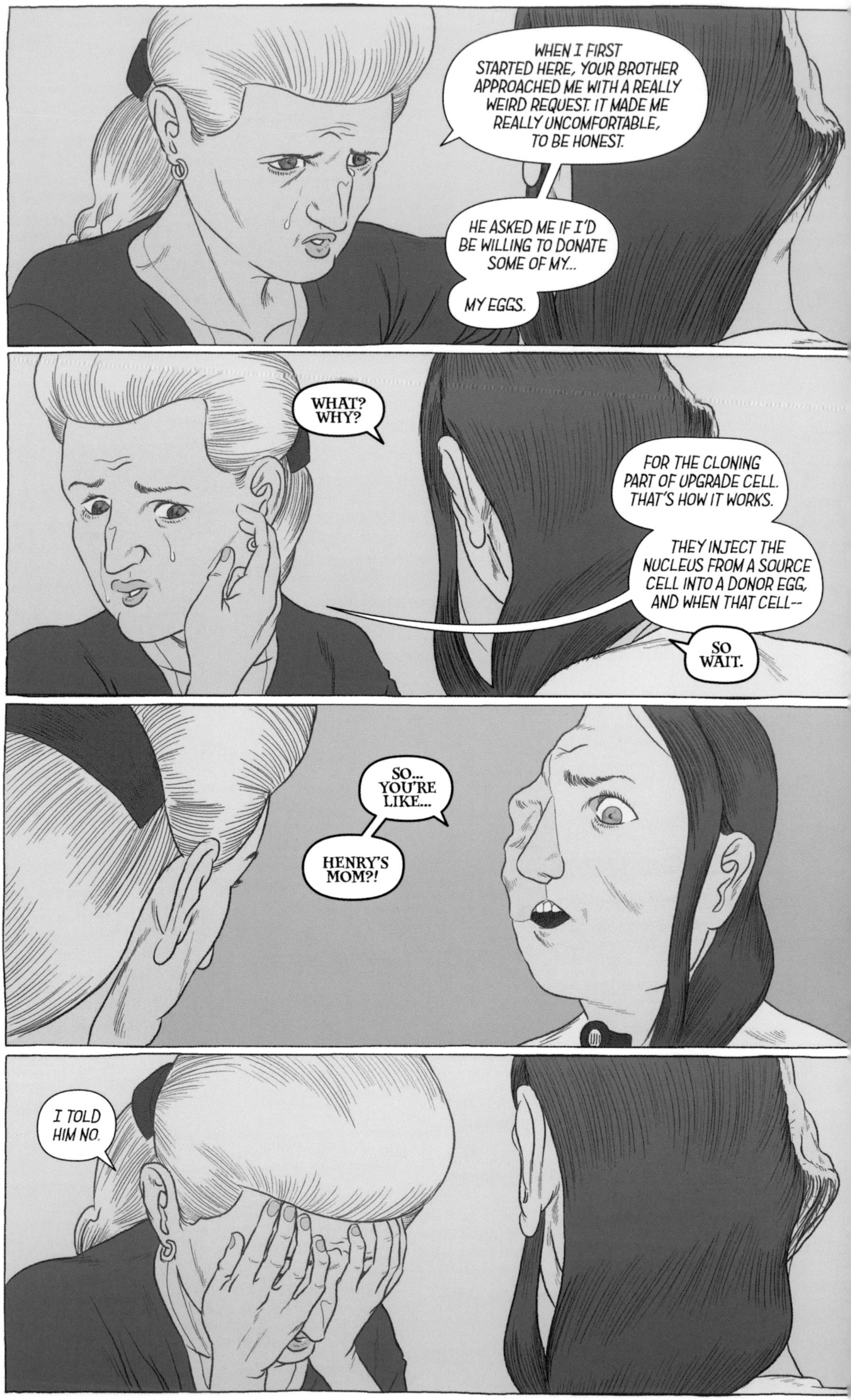
WHEN I FIRST STARTED HERE, YOUR BROTHER APPROACHED ME WITH A REALLY WEIRD REQUEST. IT MADE ME REALLY UNCOMFORTABLE, TO BE HONEST.
HE ASKED ME IF I'D BE WILLING TO DONATE SOME OF MY...
MY EGGS.
WHAT? WHY?
FOR THE CLONING PART OF UPGRADE CELL. THAT'S HOW IT WORKS.
THEY INJECT THE NUCLEUS FROM A SOURCE CELL INTO A DONOR EGG, AND WHEN THAT CELL--
SO WAIT.
SO... YOU'RE LIKE...
HENRY'S MOM?!
I TOLD HIM NO.

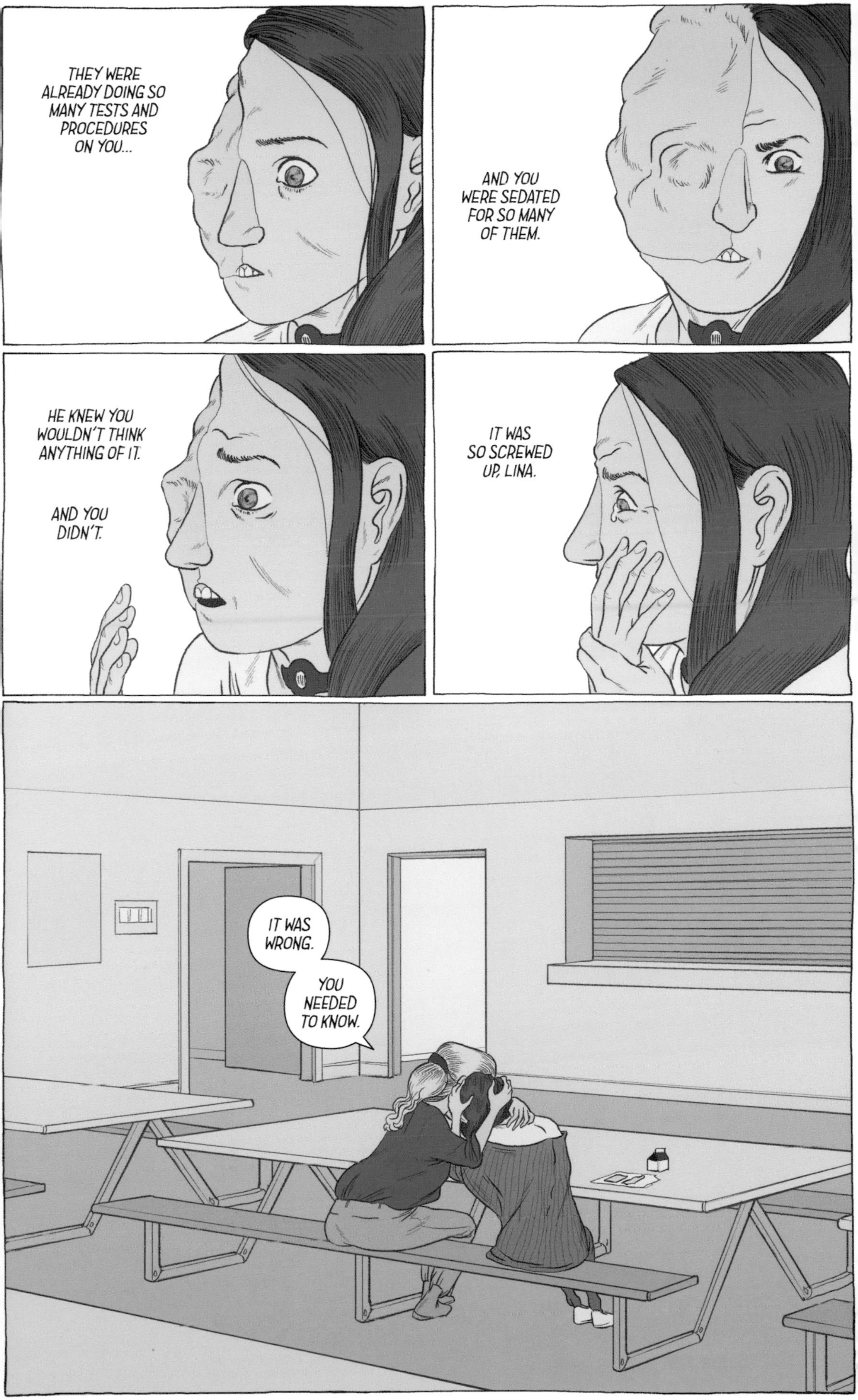
THEY WERE ALREADY DOING SO MANY TESTS AND PROCEDURES ON YOU...
AND YOU WERE SEDATED FOR SO MANY OF THEM.
HE KNEW YOU WOULDN'T THINK ANYTHING OF IT.
AND YOU DIDN'T.
IT WAS SO SCREWED UP, LINA.
IT WAS WRONG.
YOU NEEDED TO KNOW.

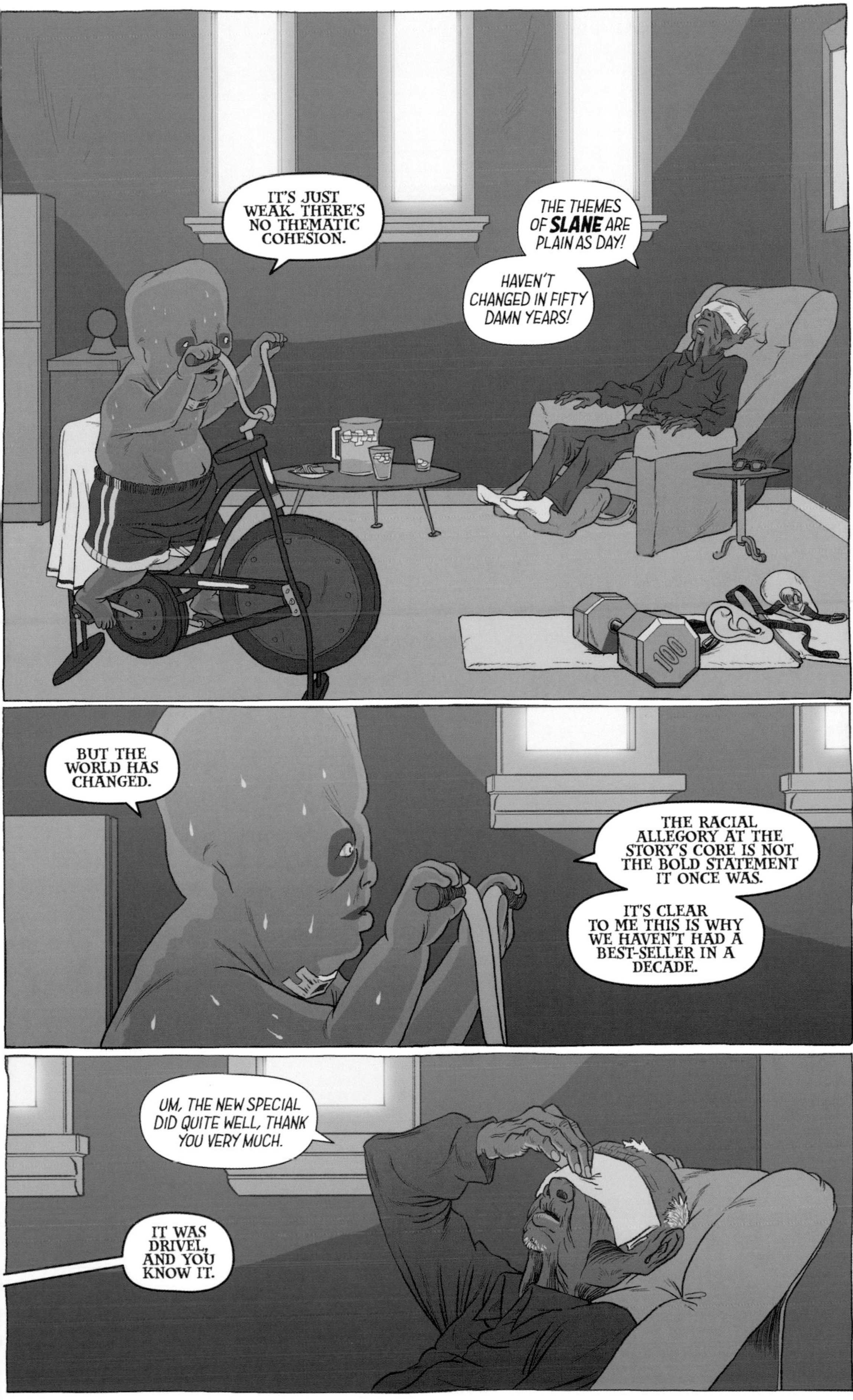
IT'S JUST WEAK. THERE'S NO THEMATIC COHESION.
THE THEMES OF SLANE ARE PLAIN AS DAY!
HAVEN'T CHANGED IN FIFTY DAMN YEARS!
BUT THE WORLD HAS CHANGED.
THE RACIAL ALLEGORY AT THE STORY'S CORE IS NOT THE BOLD STATEMENT IT ONCE WAS.
IT'S CLEAR TO ME THIS IS WHY WE HAVEN'T HAD A BEST-SELLER IN A DECADE.
UM, THE NEW SPECIAL DID QUITE WELL, THANK YOU VERY MUCH.
IT WAS DRIVEL, AND YOU KNOW IT.

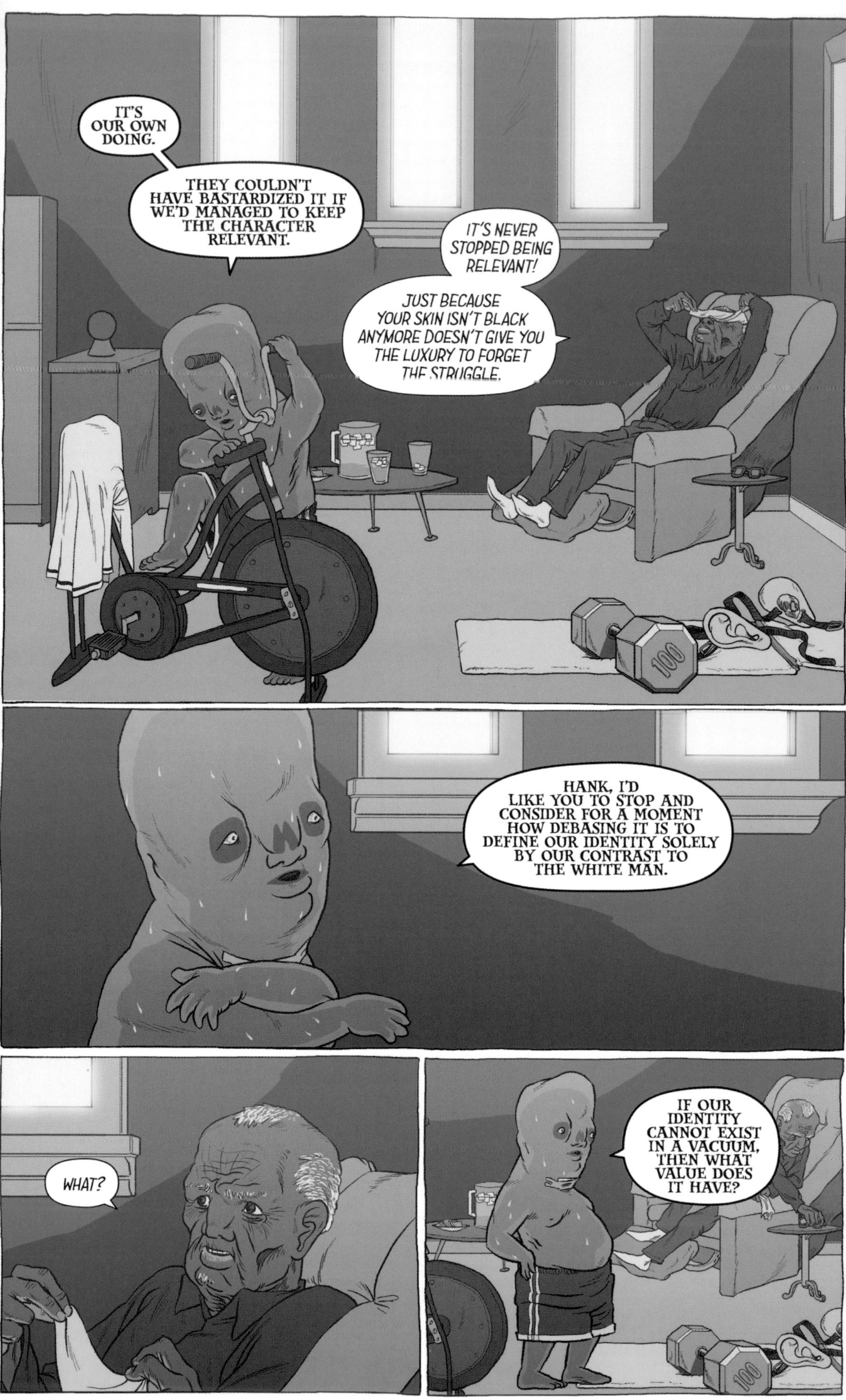
IT'S OUR OWN DOING.
THEY COULDN'T HAVE BASTARDIZED IT IF WE'D MANAGED TO KEEP THE CHARACTER RELEVANT.
IT'S NEVER STOPPED BEING RELEVANT!
JUST BECAUSE YOUR SKIN ISN'T BLACK ANYMORE DOESN'T GIVE YOU THE LUXURY TO FORGET THE STRUGGLE.
100
HANK, I'D LIKE YOU TO STOP AND CONSIDER FOR A MOMENT HOW DEBASING IT IS TO DEFINE OUR IDENTITY SOLELY BY OUR CONTRAST TO THE WHITE MAN.
WHAT?
IF OUR IDENTITY CANNOT EXIST IN A VACUUM, THEN WHAT VALUE DOES IT HAVE?
100

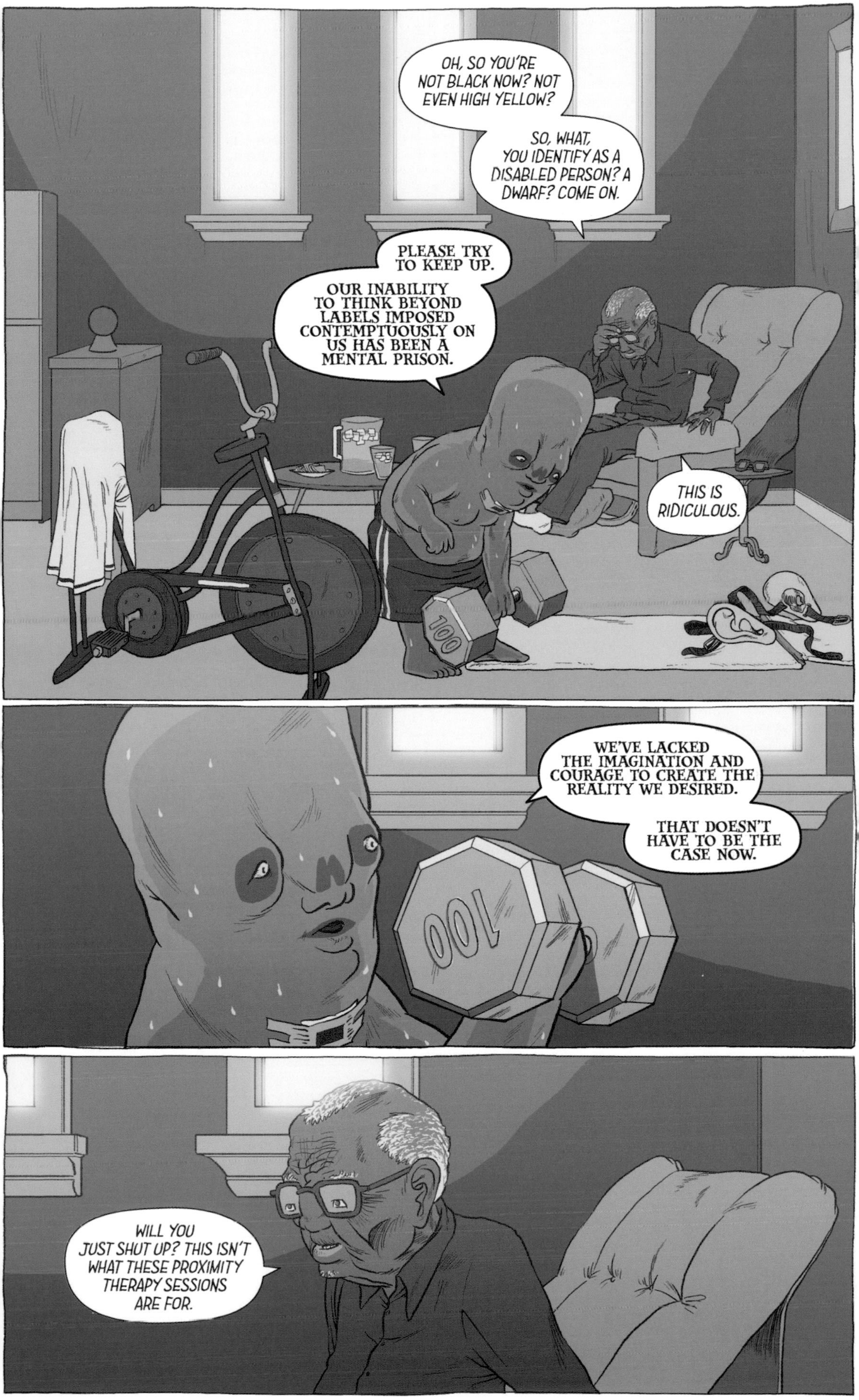
OH, SO YOU'RE NOT BLACK NOW? NOT EVEN HIGH YELLOW?
SO, WHAT, YOU IDENTIFY AS A DISABLED PERSON? A DWARF? COME ON.
PLEASE TRY TO KEEP UP.
OUR INABILITY TO THINK BEYOND LABELS IMPOSED CONTEMPTUOUSLY ON US HAS BEEN A MENTAL PRISON.
THIS IS RIDICULOUS.
100
WE'VE LACKED THE IMAGINATION AND COURAGE TO CREATE THE REALITY WE DESIRED.
THAT DOESN'T HAVE TO BE THE CASE NOW.
100
WILL YOU JUST SHUT UP? THIS ISN'T WHAT THESE PROXIMITY THERAPY SESSIONS ARE FOR.

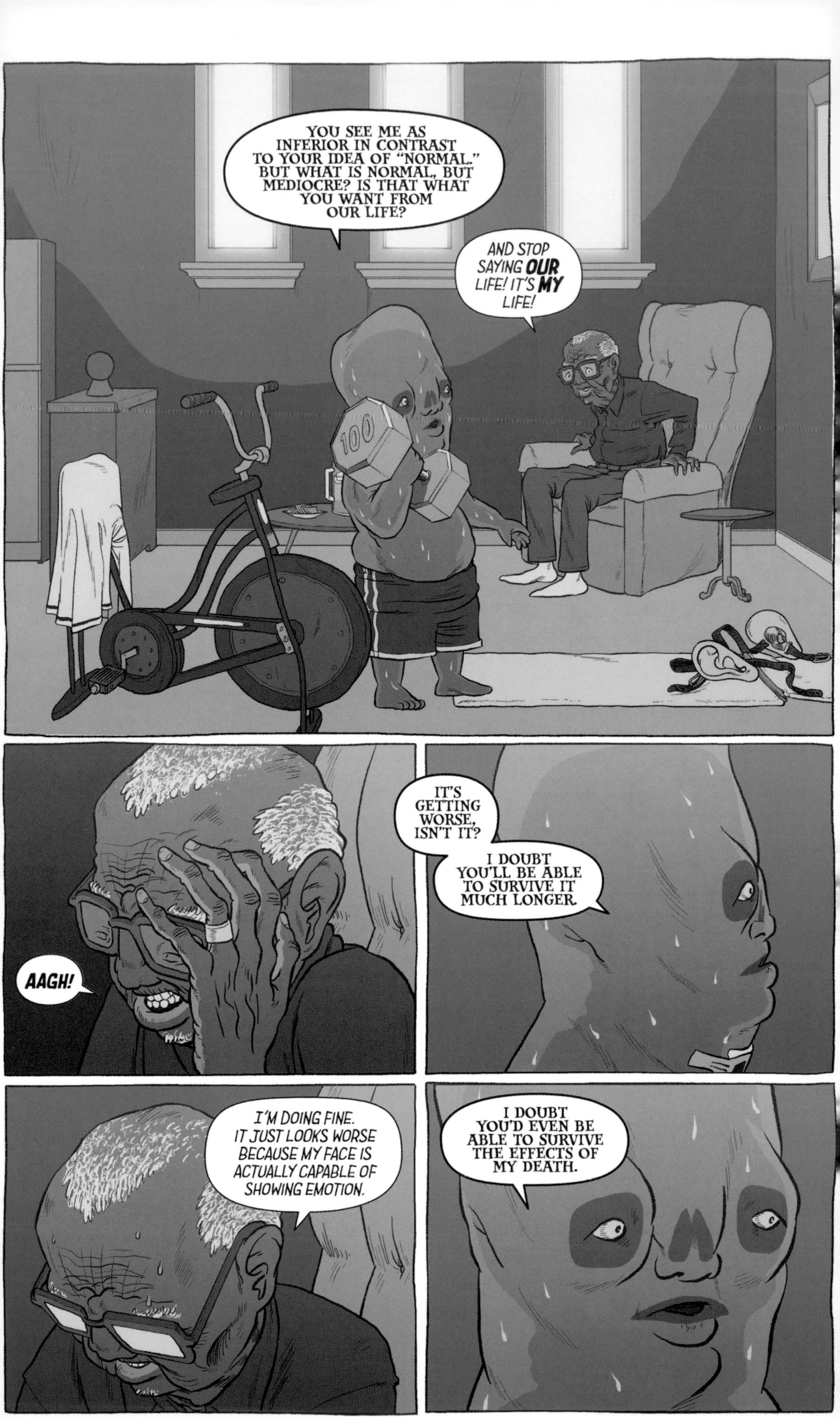
YOU SEE ME AS INFERIOR IN CONTRAST TO YOUR IDEA OF "NORMAL." BUT WHAT IS NORMAL, BUT MEDIOCRE? IS THAT WHAT YOU WANT FROM OUR LIFE?
AND STOP SAYING OUR LIFE! IT'S MY LIFE!
100
AAGH!
IT'S GETTING WORSE, ISN'T IT?
I DOUBT YOU'LL BE ABLE TO SURVIVE IT MUCH LONGER.
I'M DOING FINE. IT JUST LOOKS WORSE BECAUSE MY FACE IS ACTUALLY CAPABLE OF SHOWING EMOTION.
I DOUBT YOU'D EVEN BE ABLE TO SURVIVE THE EFFECTS OF MY DEATH.

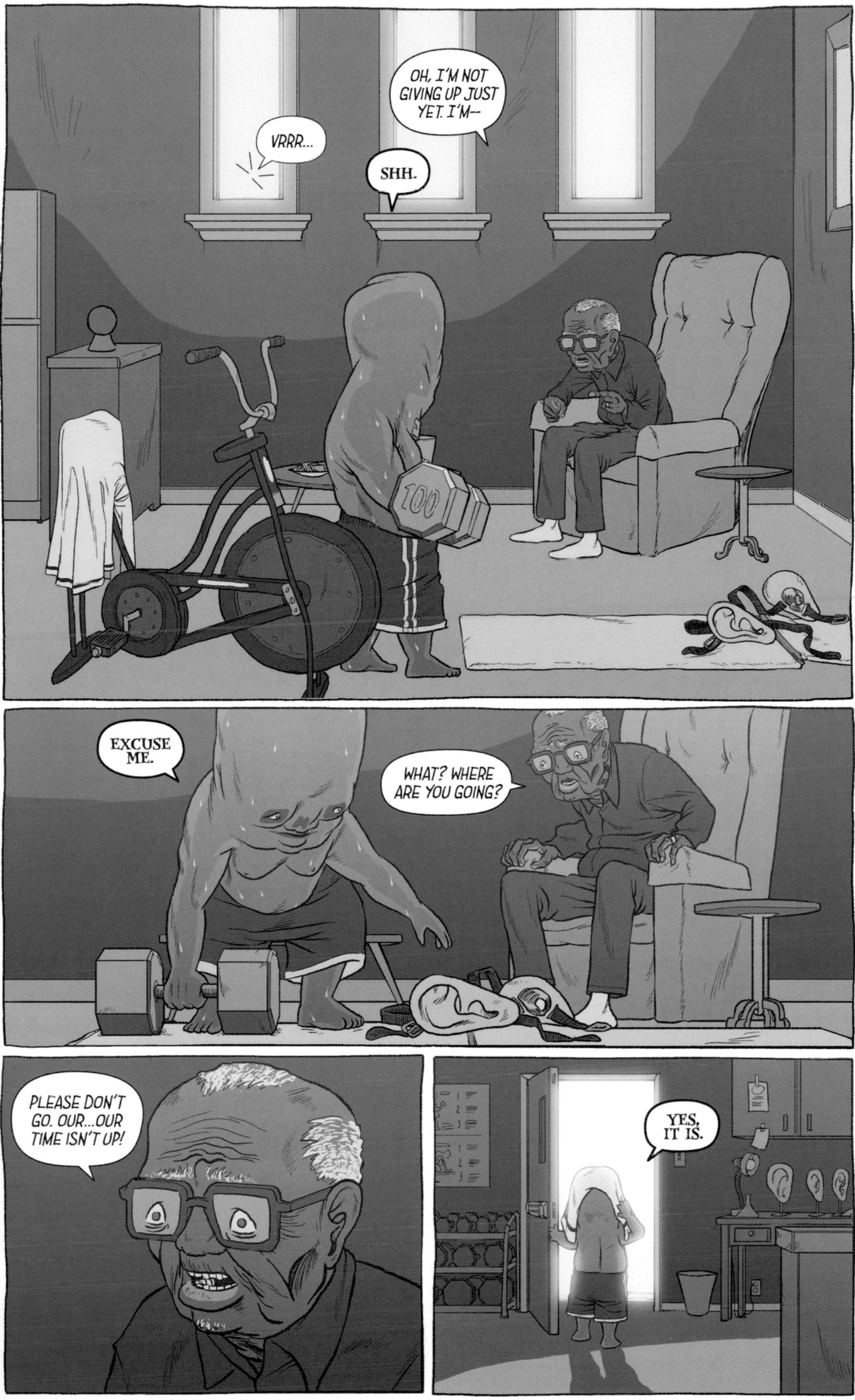
VRRR...
SHH.
OH, I'M NOT GIVING UP JUST YET. I'M--
EXCUSE ME.
WHAT? WHERE ARE YOU GOING?
PLEASE DON'T GO. OUR...OUR TIME ISN'T UP!
YES, IT IS.

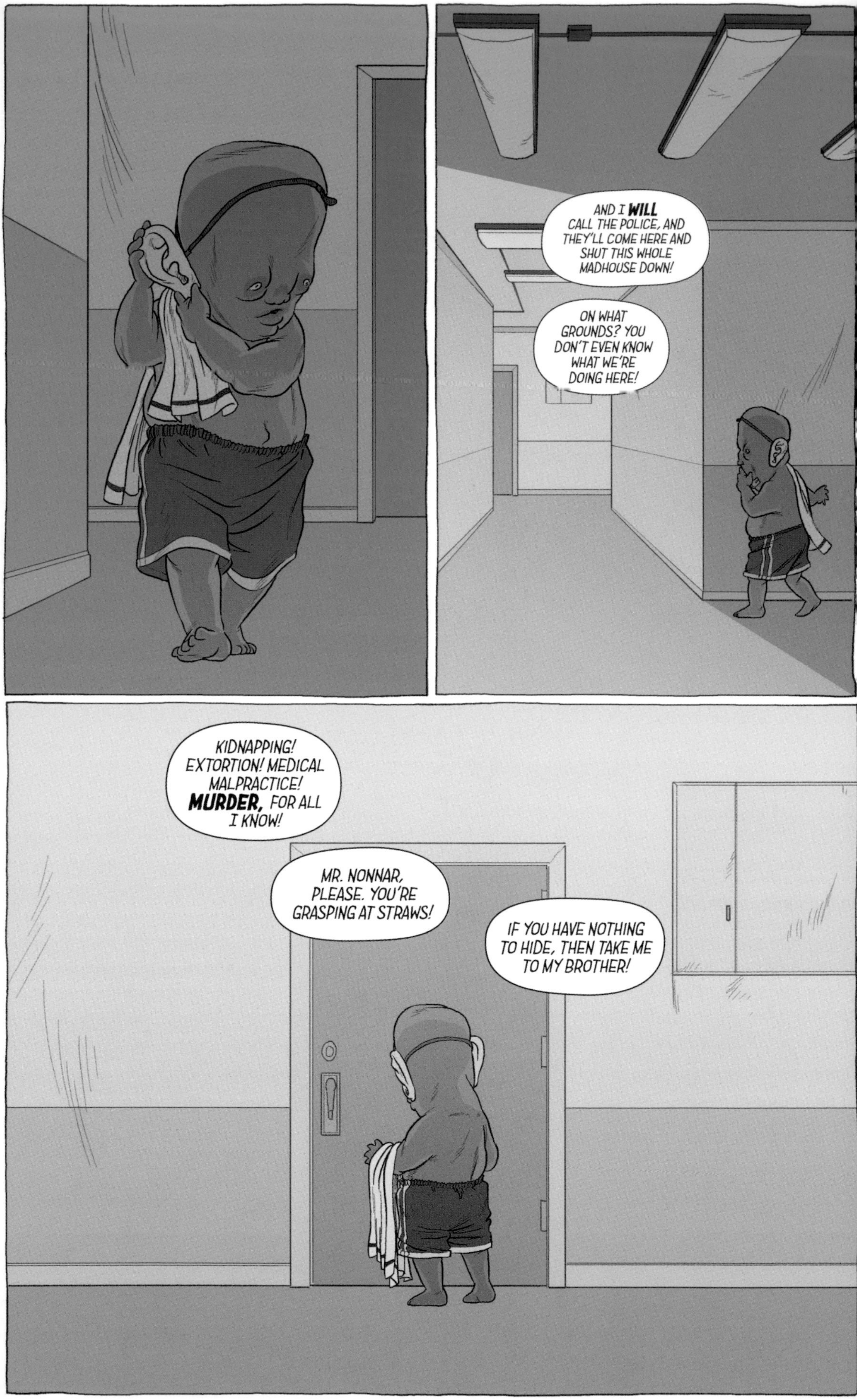
AND I **WILL** CALL THE POLICE, AND THEY'LL COME HERE AND SHUT THIS WHOLE MADHOUSE DOWN!
ON WHAT GROUNDS? YOU DON'T EVEN KNOW WHAT WE'RE DOING HERE!
KIDNAPPING! EXTORTION! MEDICAL MALPRACTICE! **MURDER,** FOR ALL I KNOW!
MR. NONNAR, PLEASE. YOU'RE GRASPING AT STRAWS!
IF YOU HAVE NOTHING TO HIDE, THEN TAKE ME TO MY BROTHER!

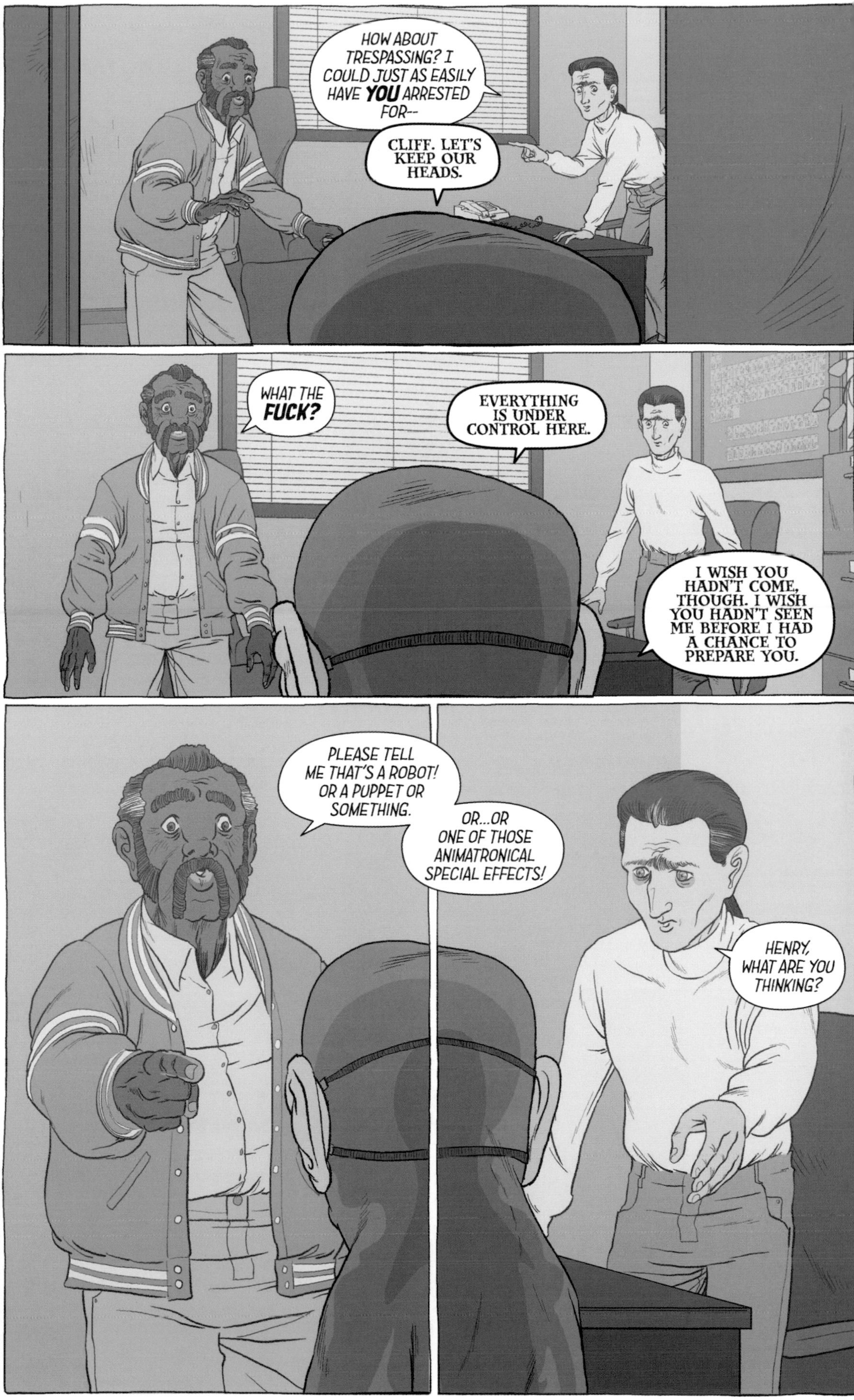
HOW ABOUT TRESPASSING? I COULD JUST AS EASILY HAVE YOU ARRESTED FOR--
CLIFF. LET'S KEEP OUR HEADS.
WHAT THE FUCK?
EVERYTHING IS UNDER CONTROL HERE.
I WISH YOU HADN'T COME, THOUGH. I WISH YOU HADN'T SEEN ME BEFORE I HAD A CHANCE TO PREPARE YOU.
PLEASE TELL ME THAT'S A ROBOT! OR A PUPPET OR SOMETHING.
OR...OR ONE OF THOSE ANIMATRONICAL SPECIAL EFFECTS!
HENRY, WHAT ARE YOU THINKING?

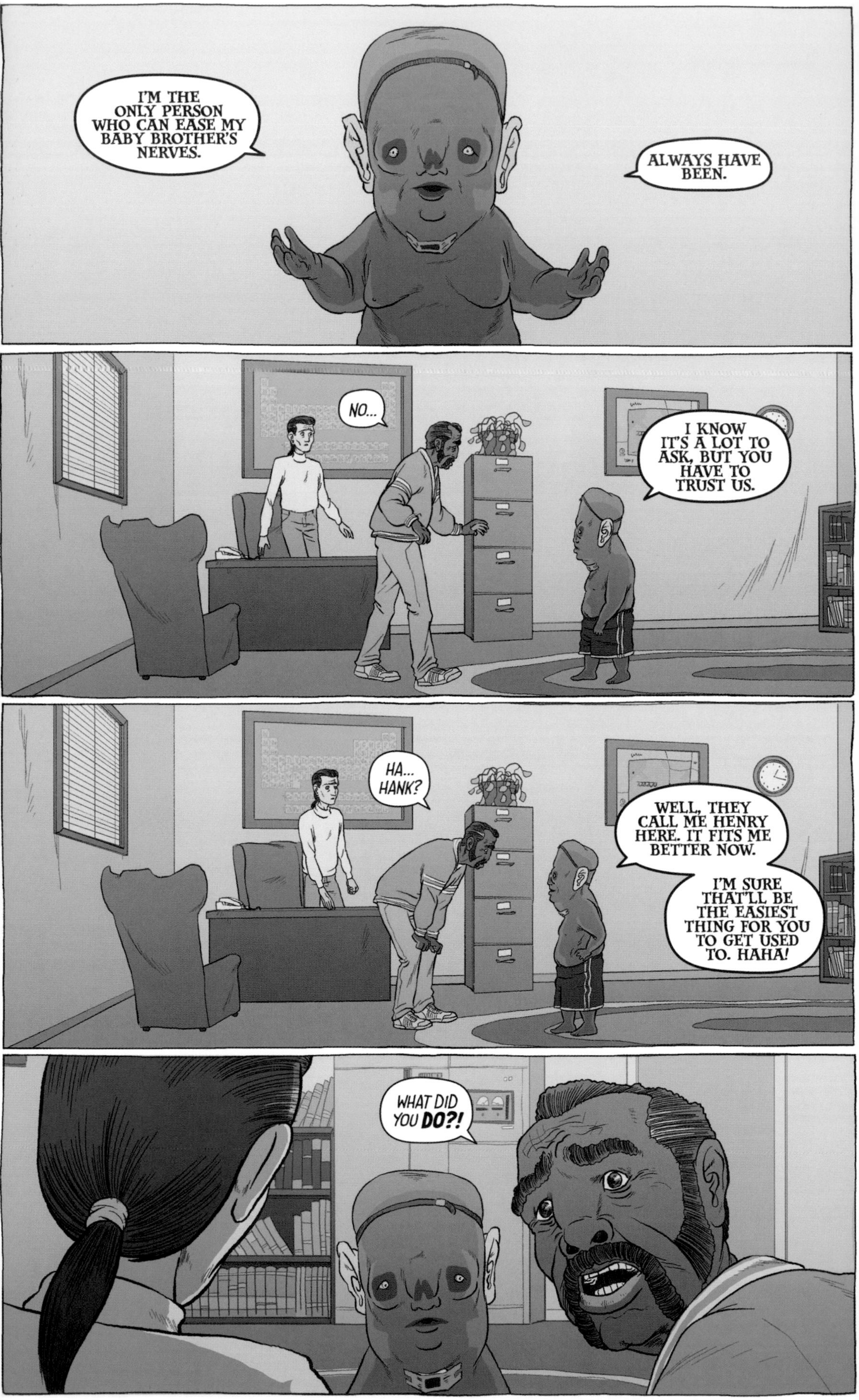
I'M THE ONLY PERSON WHO CAN EASE MY BABY BROTHER'S NERVES.
ALWAYS HAVE BEEN.
NO...
I KNOW IT'S A LOT TO ASK, BUT YOU HAVE TO TRUST US.
HA... HANK?
WELL, THEY CALL ME HENRY HERE. IT FITS ME BETTER NOW.
I'M SURE THAT'LL BE THE EASIEST THING FOR YOU TO GET USED TO. HAHA!
WHAT DID YOU DO?!

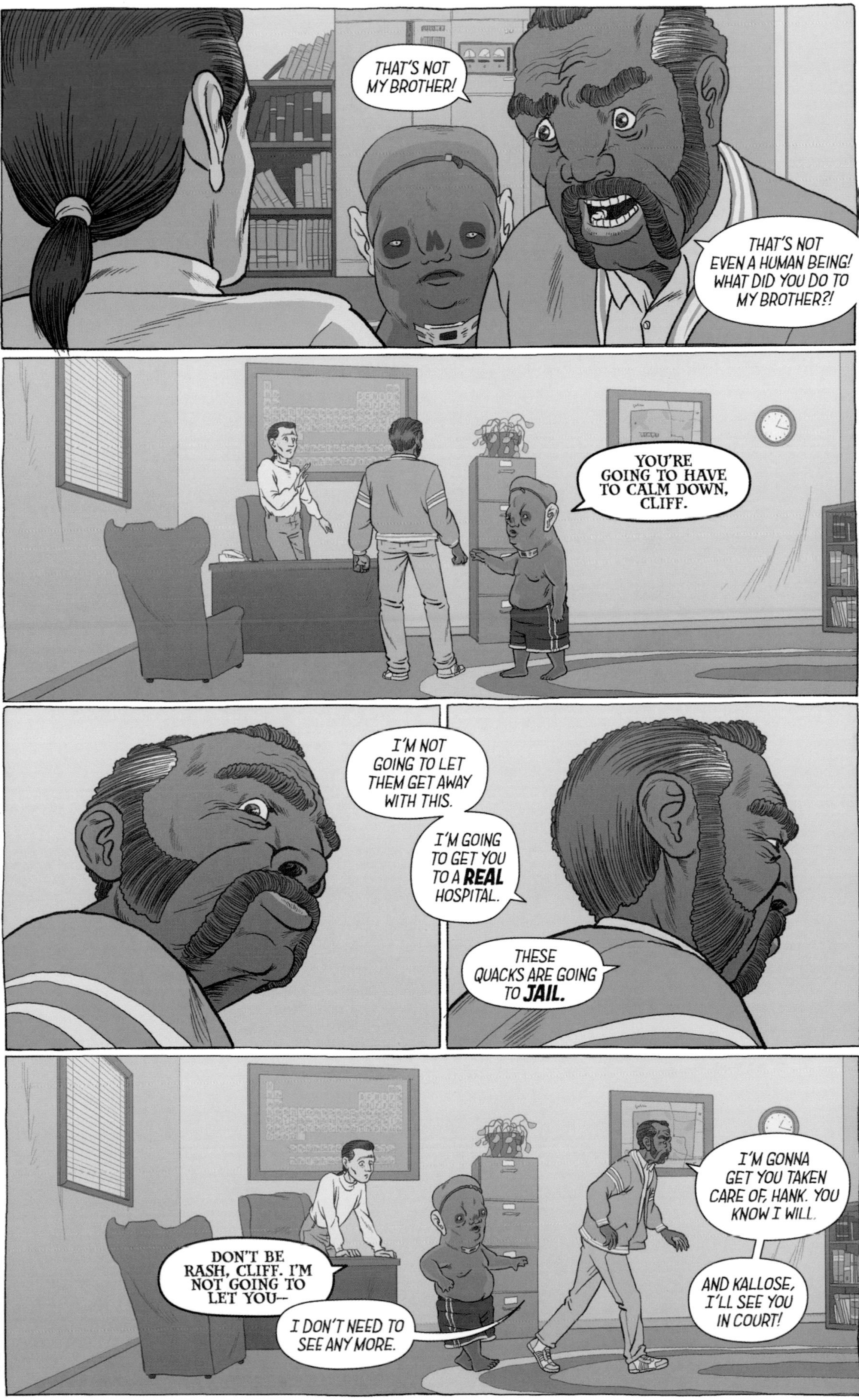
THAT'S NOT MY BROTHER!
THAT'S NOT EVEN A HUMAN BEING! WHAT DID YOU DO TO MY BROTHER?!
YOU'RE GOING TO HAVE TO CALM DOWN, CLIFF.
I'M NOT GOING TO LET THEM GET AWAY WITH THIS.
I'M GOING TO GET YOU TO A REAL HOSPITAL.
THESE QUACKS ARE GOING TO JAIL.
I'M GONNA GET YOU TAKEN CARE OF, HANK. YOU KNOW I WILL.
AND KALLOSE, I'LL SEE YOU IN COURT!
DON'T BE RASH, CLIFF. I'M NOT GOING TO LET YOU--
I DON'T NEED TO SEE ANY MORE.

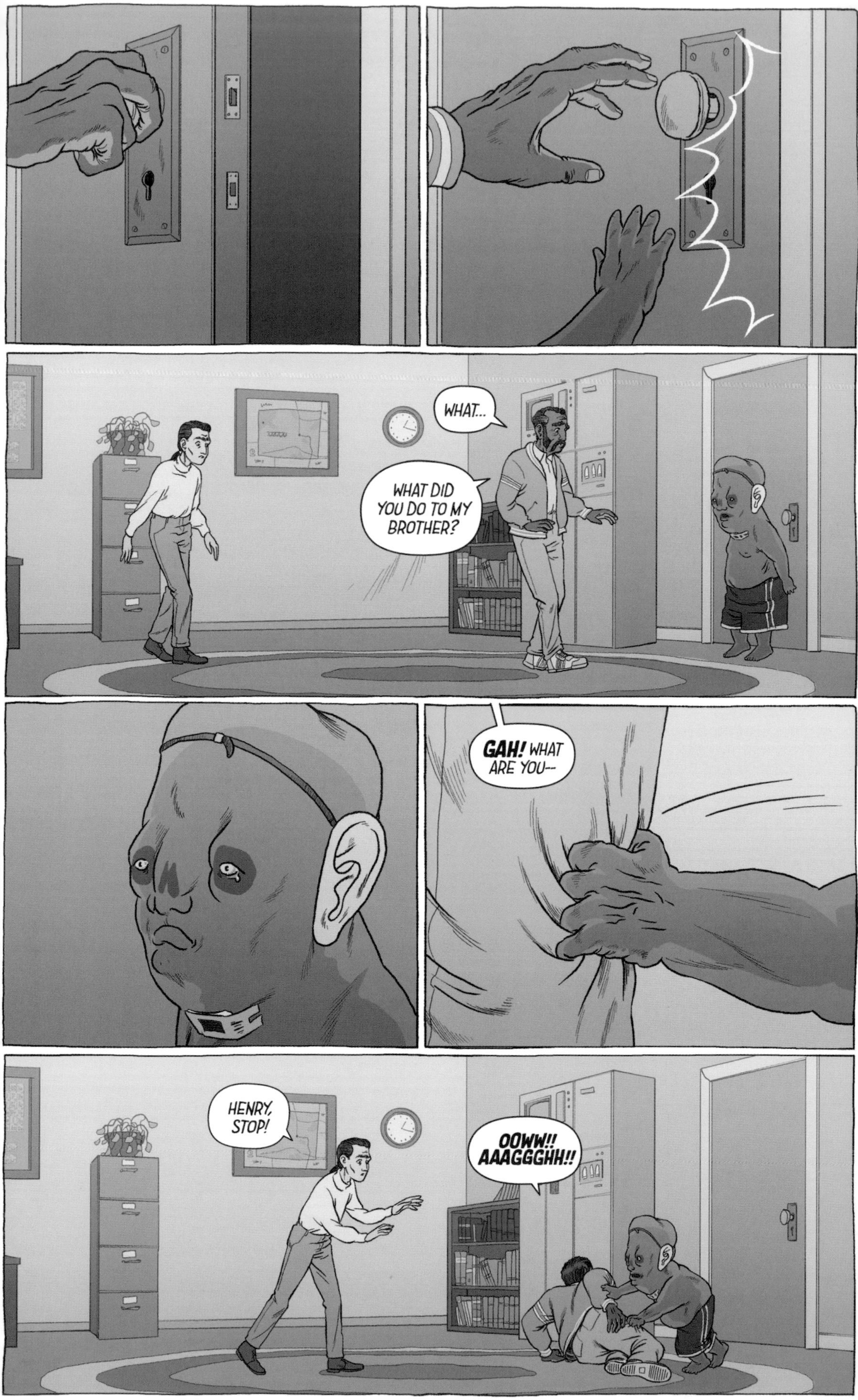
WHAT...
WHAT DID YOU DO TO MY BROTHER?
GAH! WHAT ARE YOU--
HENRY, STOP!
OOWW!! AAAGGGHH!!

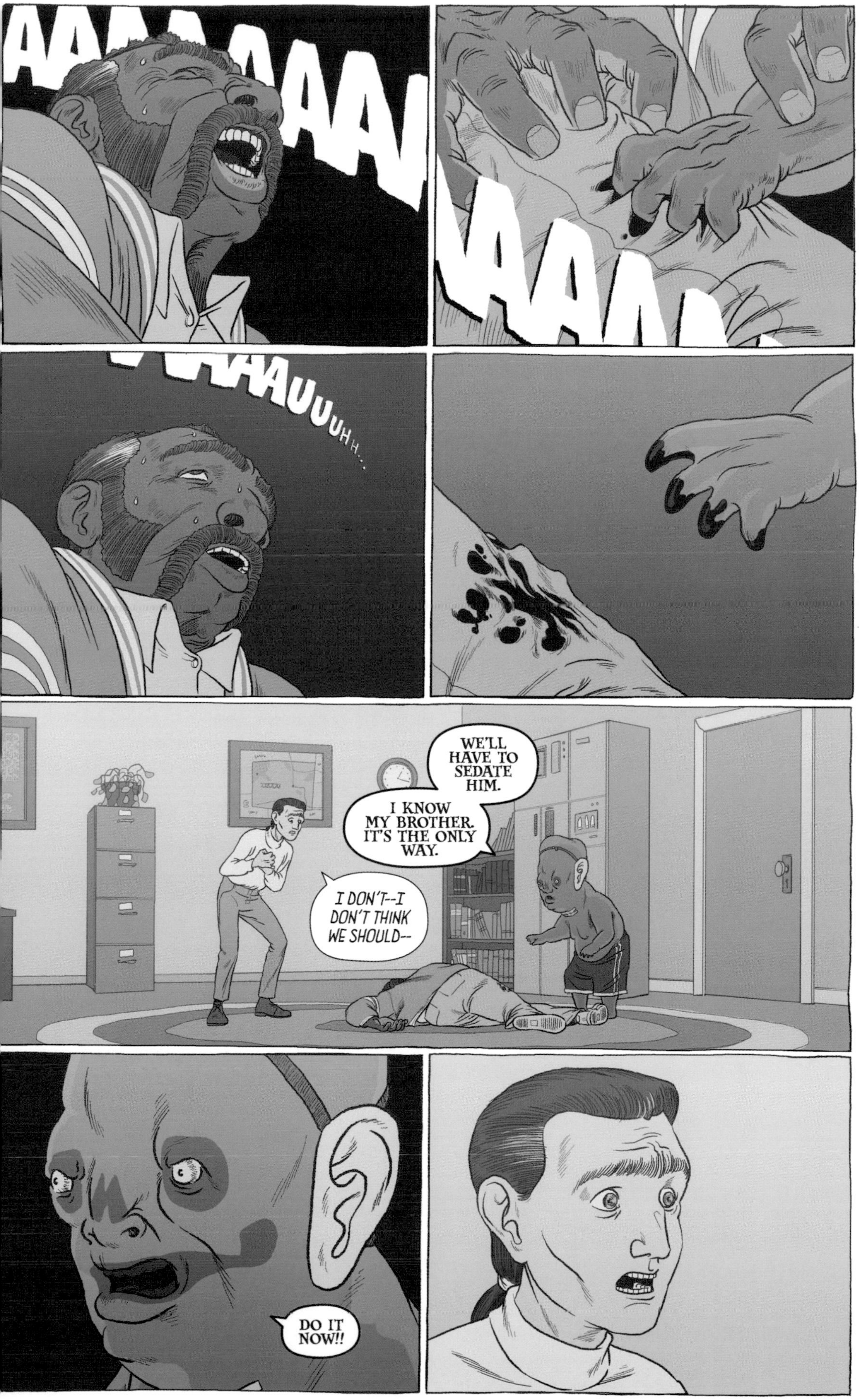
AAAAAAAA
AAAAA
AAUUUUHH...
WE'LL HAVE TO SEDATE HIM.
I KNOW MY BROTHER. IT'S THE ONLY WAY.
I DON'T--I DON'T THINK WE SHOULD--
DO IT NOW!!

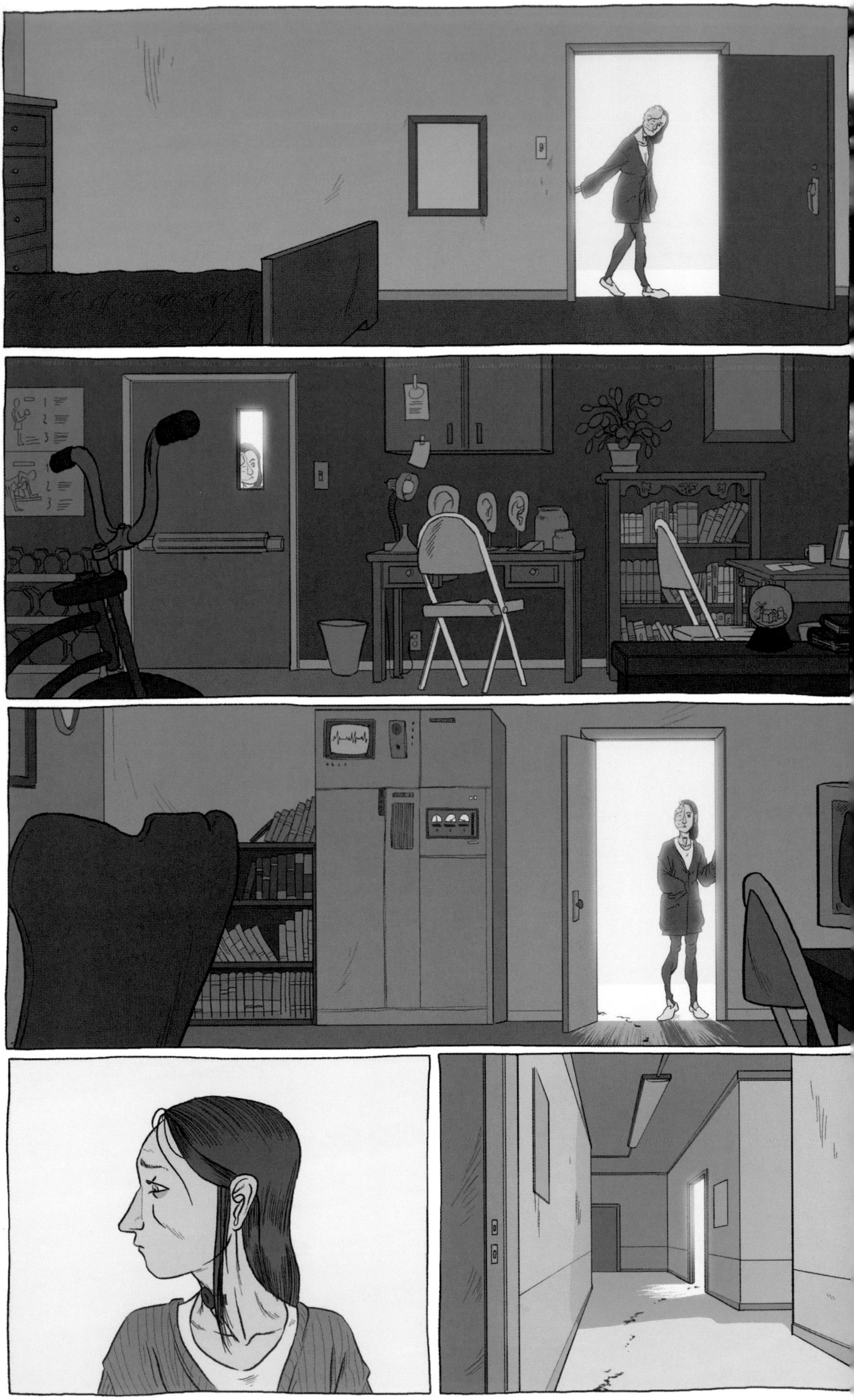

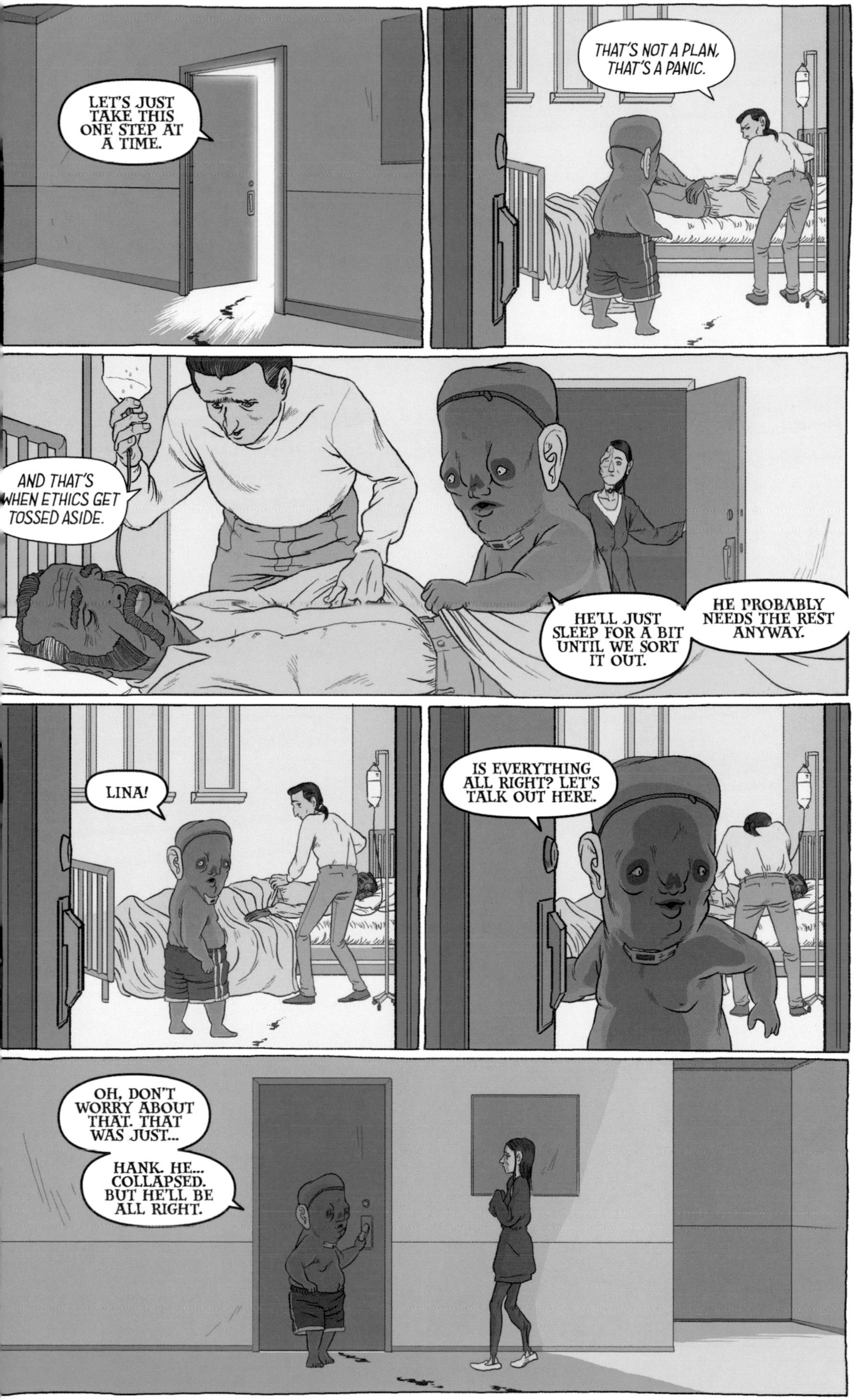
LET'S JUST TAKE THIS ONE STEP AT A TIME.
THAT'S NOT A PLAN, THAT'S A PANIC.
AND THAT'S WHEN ETHICS GET TOSSED ASIDE.
HE'LL JUST SLEEP FOR A BIT UNTIL WE SORT IT OUT.
HE PROBABLY NEEDS THE REST ANYWAY.
LINA!
IS EVERYTHING ALL RIGHT? LET'S TALK OUT HERE.
OH, DON'T WORRY ABOUT THAT. THAT WAS JUST...
HANK. HE... COLLAPSED. BUT HE'LL BE ALL RIGHT.

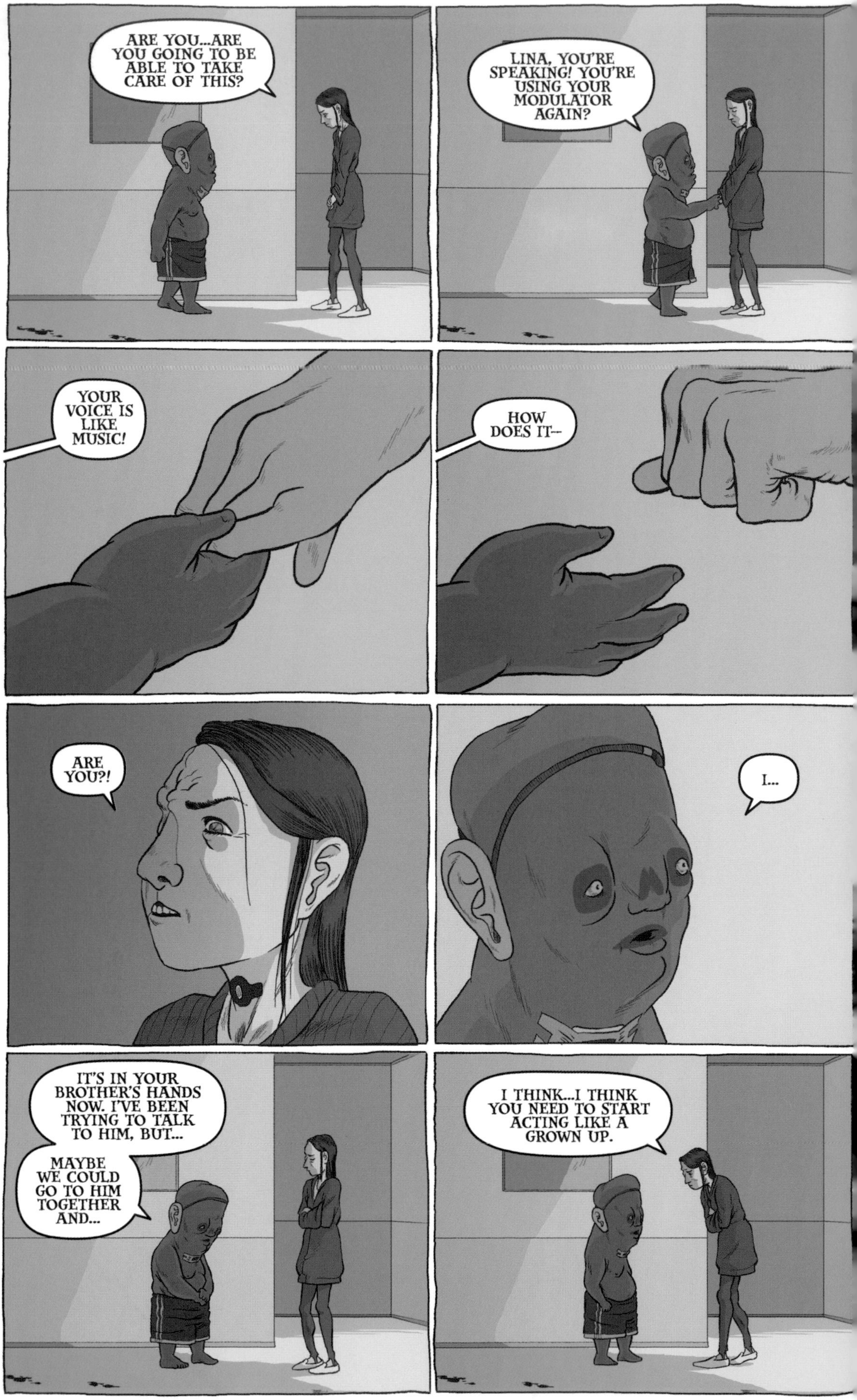
ARE YOU...ARE YOU GOING TO BE ABLE TO TAKE CARE OF THIS?
LINA, YOU'RE SPEAKING! YOU'RE USING YOUR MODULATOR AGAIN?
YOUR VOICE IS LIKE MUSIC!
HOW DOES IT--
ARE YOU?!
I...
IT'S IN YOUR BROTHER'S HANDS NOW. I'VE BEEN TRYING TO TALK TO HIM, BUT...
MAYBE WE COULD GO TO HIM TOGETHER AND...
I THINK...I THINK YOU NEED TO START ACTING LIKE A GROWN UP.

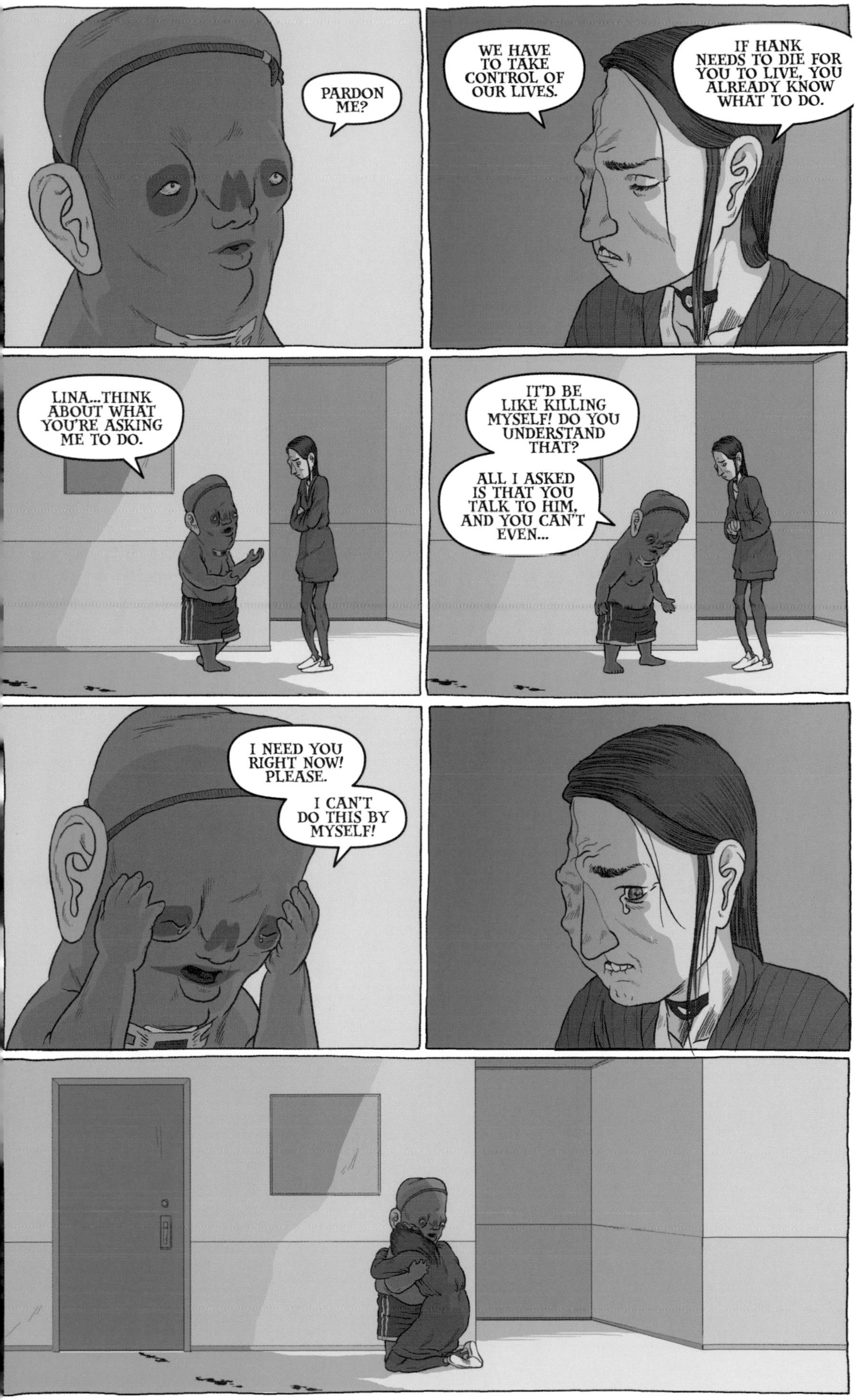

PARDON ME?
WE HAVE TO TAKE CONTROL OF OUR LIVES.
IF HANK NEEDS TO DIE FOR YOU TO LIVE, YOU ALREADY KNOW WHAT TO DO.
LINA...THINK ABOUT WHAT YOU'RE ASKING ME TO DO.
IT'D BE LIKE KILLING MYSELF! DO YOU UNDERSTAND THAT?
ALL I ASKED IS THAT YOU TALK TO HIM, AND YOU CAN'T EVEN...
I NEED YOU RIGHT NOW! PLEASE.
I CAN'T DO THIS BY MYSELF!

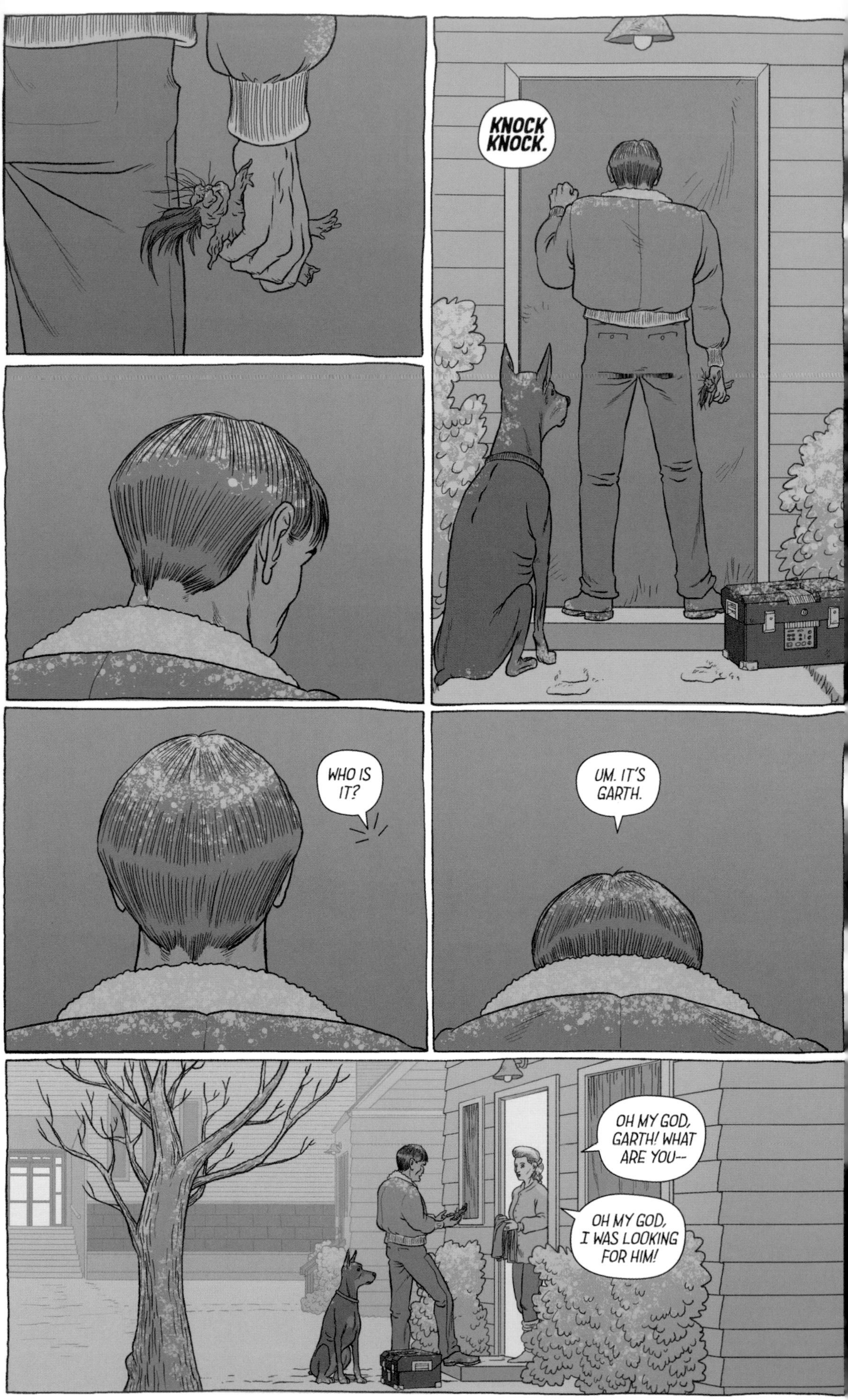
KNOCK KNOCK.
WHO IS IT?
UM. IT'S GARTH.
OH MY GOD, GARTH! WHAT ARE YOU--
OH MY GOD, I WAS LOOKING FOR HIM!

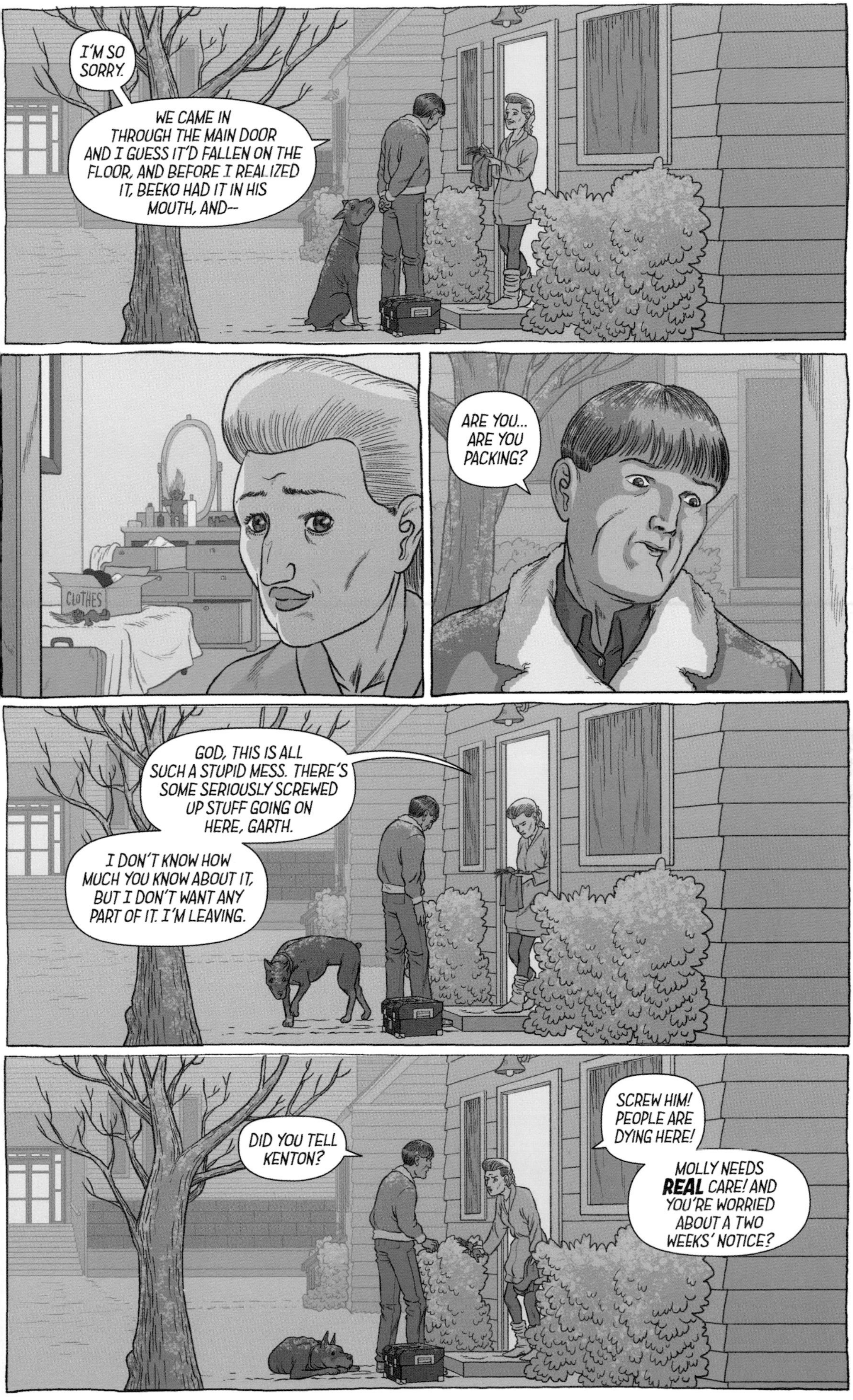
I'M SO SORRY.
WE CAME IN THROUGH THE MAIN DOOR AND I GUESS IT'D FALLEN ON THE FLOOR, AND BEFORE I REALIZED IT, BEEKO HAD IT IN HIS MOUTH, AND--
CLOTHES
ARE YOU... ARE YOU PACKING?
GOD, THIS IS ALL SUCH A STUPID MESS. THERE'S SOME SERIOUSLY SCREWED UP STUFF GOING ON HERE, GARTH.
I DON'T KNOW HOW MUCH YOU KNOW ABOUT IT, BUT I DON'T WANT ANY PART OF IT. I'M LEAVING.
DID YOU TELL KENTON?
SCREW HIM! PEOPLE ARE DYING HERE!
MOLLY NEEDS **REAL** CARE! AND YOU'RE WORRIED ABOUT A TWO WEEKS' NOTICE?

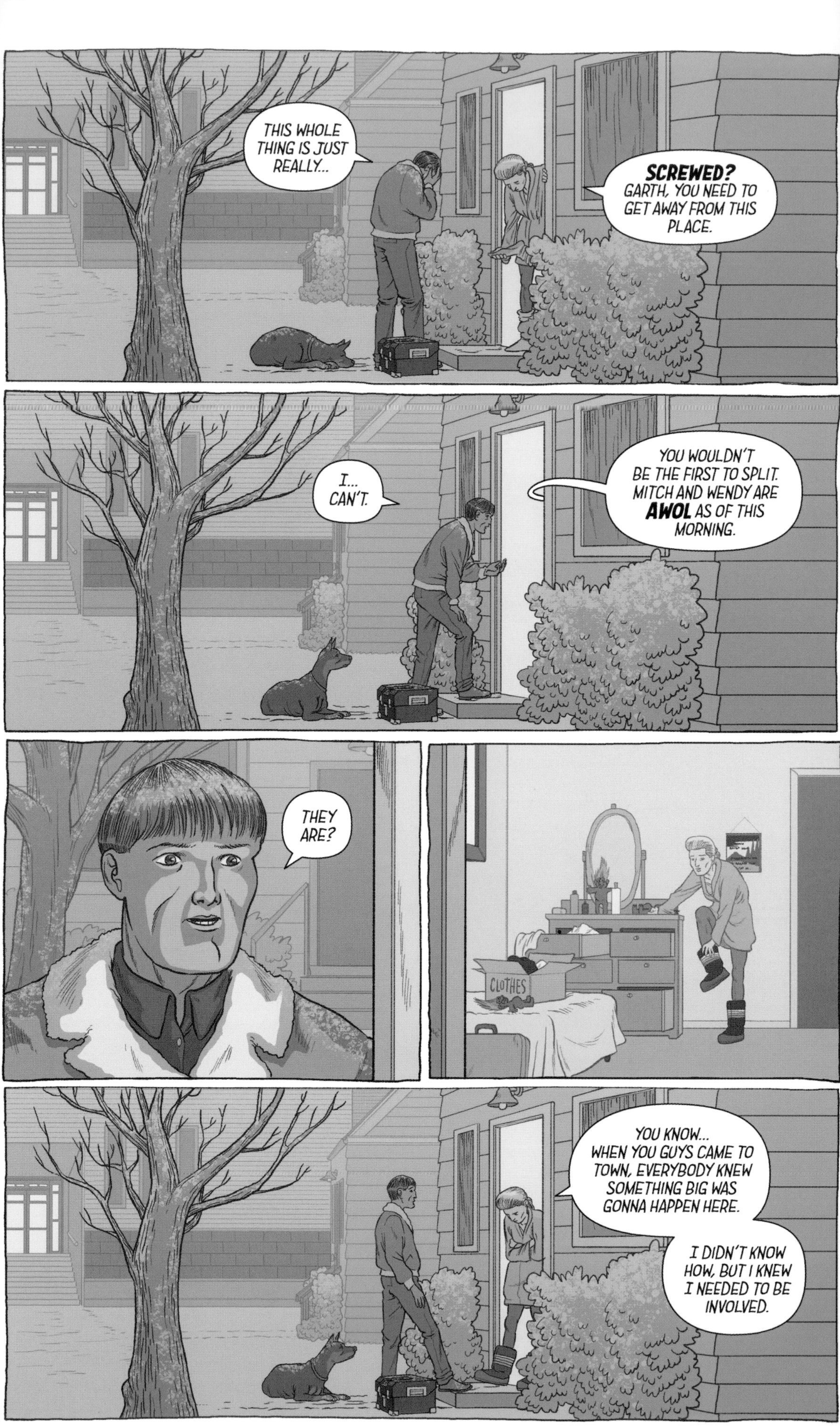
THIS WHOLE THING IS JUST REALLY...
SCREWED? GARTH, YOU NEED TO GET AWAY FROM THIS PLACE.
I... CAN'T.
YOU WOULDN'T BE THE FIRST TO SPLIT. MITCH AND WENDY ARE AWOL AS OF THIS MORNING.
THEY ARE?
CLOTHES
YOU KNOW... WHEN YOU GUYS CAME TO TOWN, EVERYBODY KNEW SOMETHING BIG WAS GONNA HAPPEN HERE.
I DIDN'T KNOW HOW, BUT I KNEW I NEEDED TO BE INVOLVED.

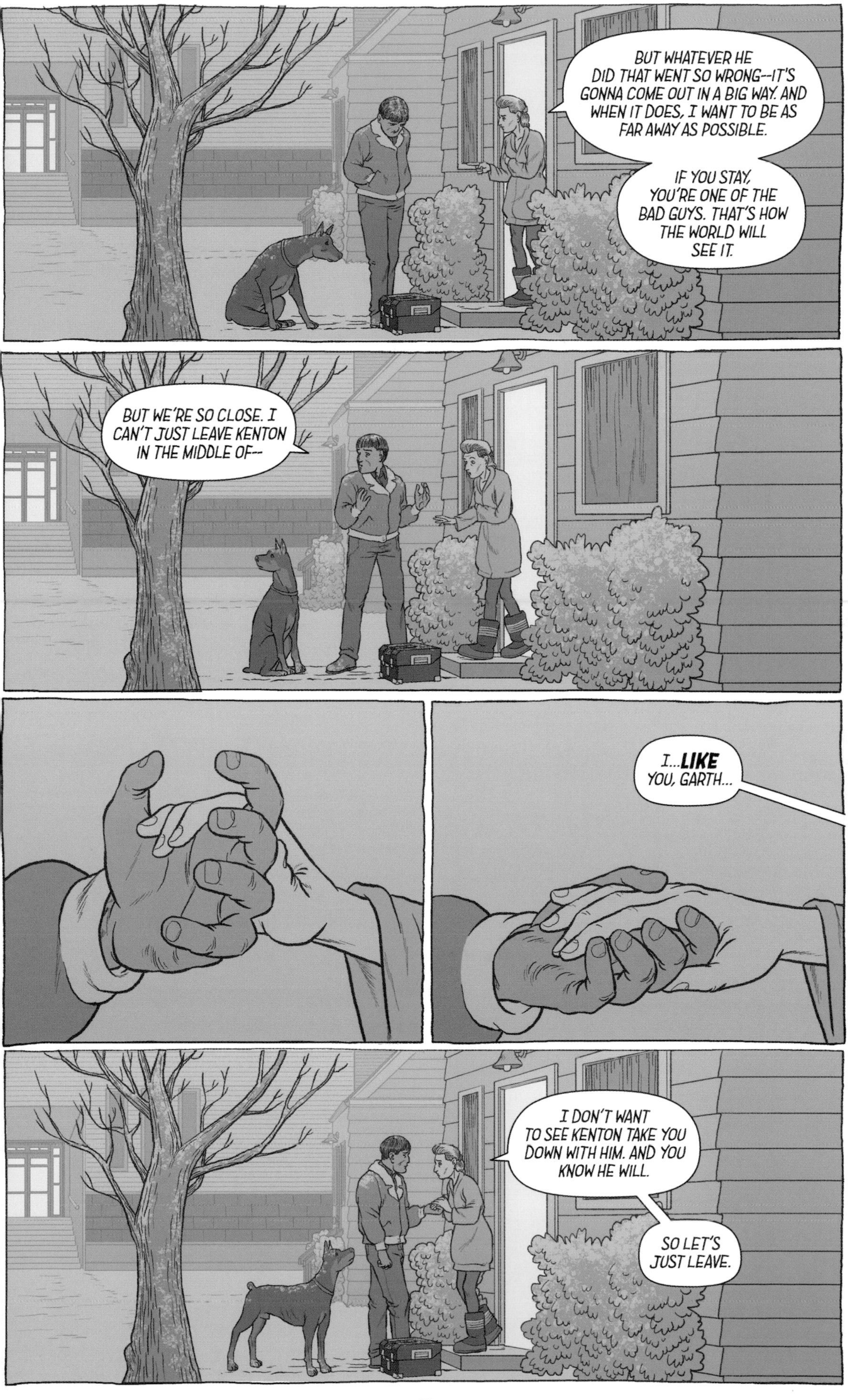
BUT WHATEVER HE DID THAT WENT SO WRONG--IT'S GONNA COME OUT IN A BIG WAY. AND WHEN IT DOES, I WANT TO BE AS FAR AWAY AS POSSIBLE.
IF YOU STAY, YOU'RE ONE OF THE BAD GUYS. THAT'S HOW THE WORLD WILL SEE IT.
BUT WE'RE SO CLOSE. I CAN'T JUST LEAVE KENTON IN THE MIDDLE OF--
I...**LIKE** YOU, GARTH...
I DON'T WANT TO SEE KENTON TAKE YOU DOWN WITH HIM. AND YOU KNOW HE WILL.
SO LET'S JUST LEAVE.

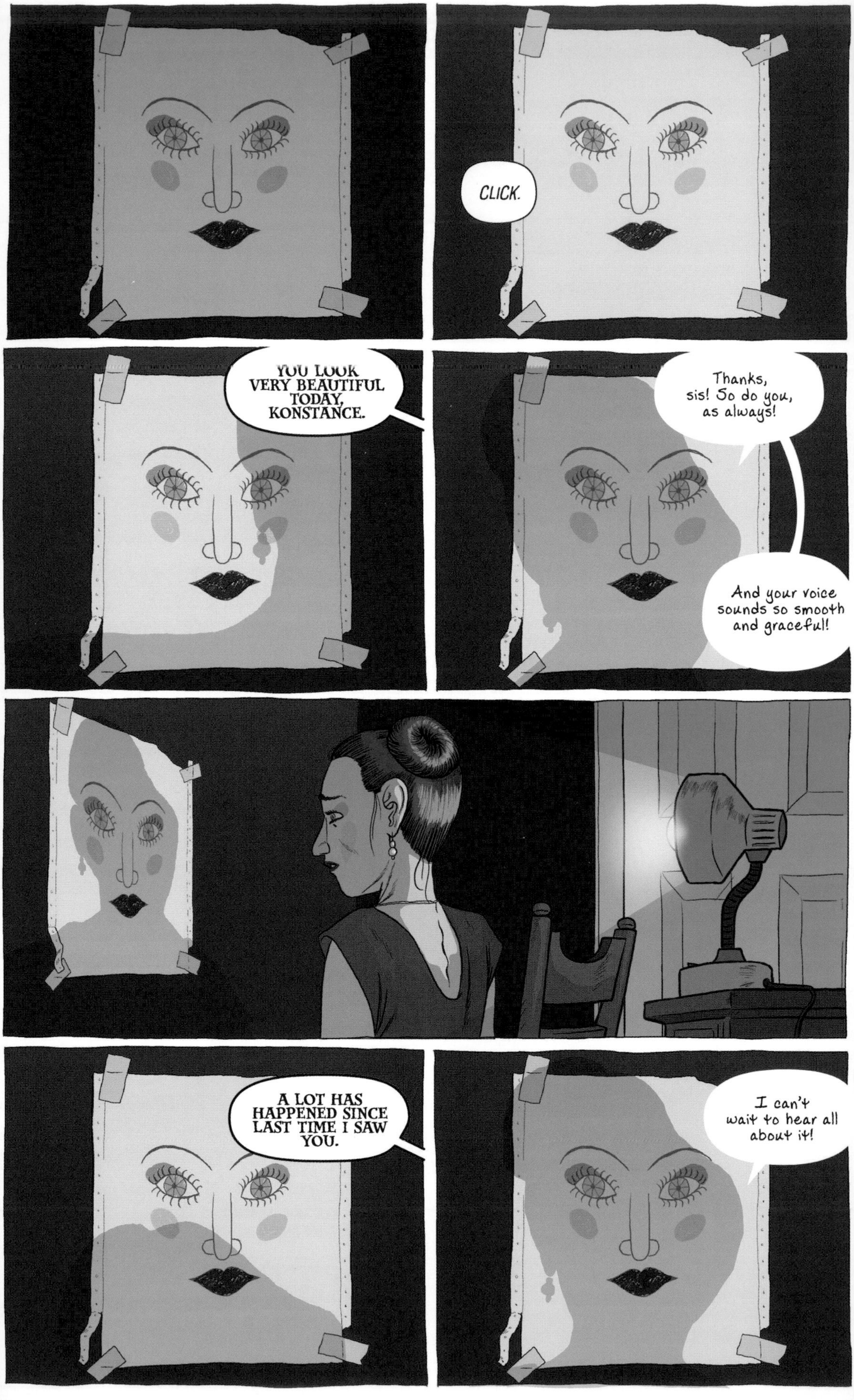
CLICK.
YOU LOOK VERY BEAUTIFUL TODAY, KONSTANCE.
Thanks, sis! So do you, as always!
And your voice sounds so smooth and graceful!
A LOT HAS HAPPENED SINCE LAST TIME I SAW YOU.
I can't wait to hear all about it!

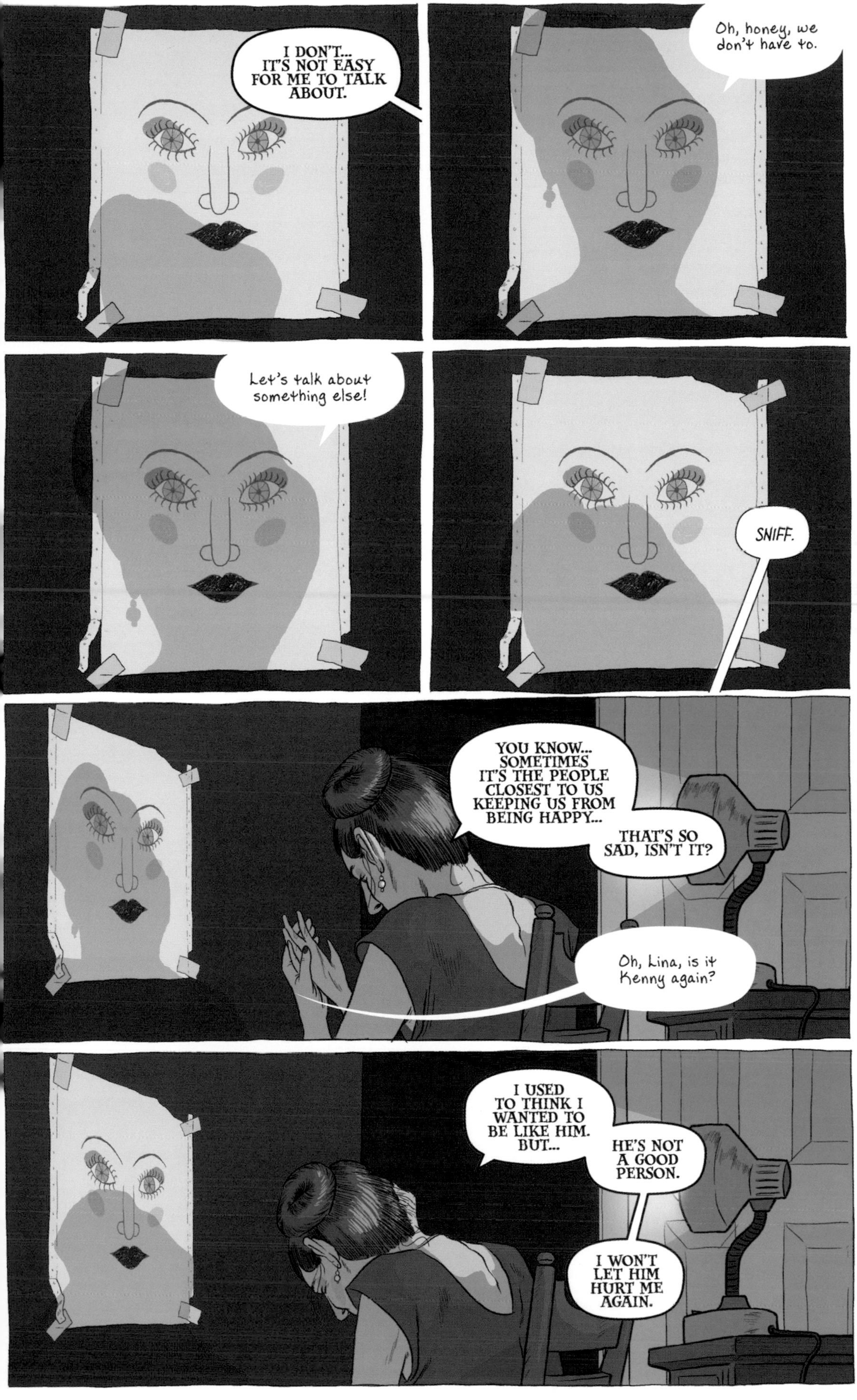
I DON'T... IT'S NOT EASY FOR ME TO TALK ABOUT.
Oh, honey, we don't have to.
Let's talk about something else!
SNIFF.
YOU KNOW... SOMETIMES IT'S THE PEOPLE CLOSEST TO US KEEPING US FROM BEING HAPPY...
THAT'S SO SAD, ISN'T IT?
Oh, Lina, is it Kenny again?
I USED TO THINK I WANTED TO BE LIKE HIM. BUT...
HE'S NOT A GOOD PERSON.
I WON'T LET HIM HURT ME AGAIN.

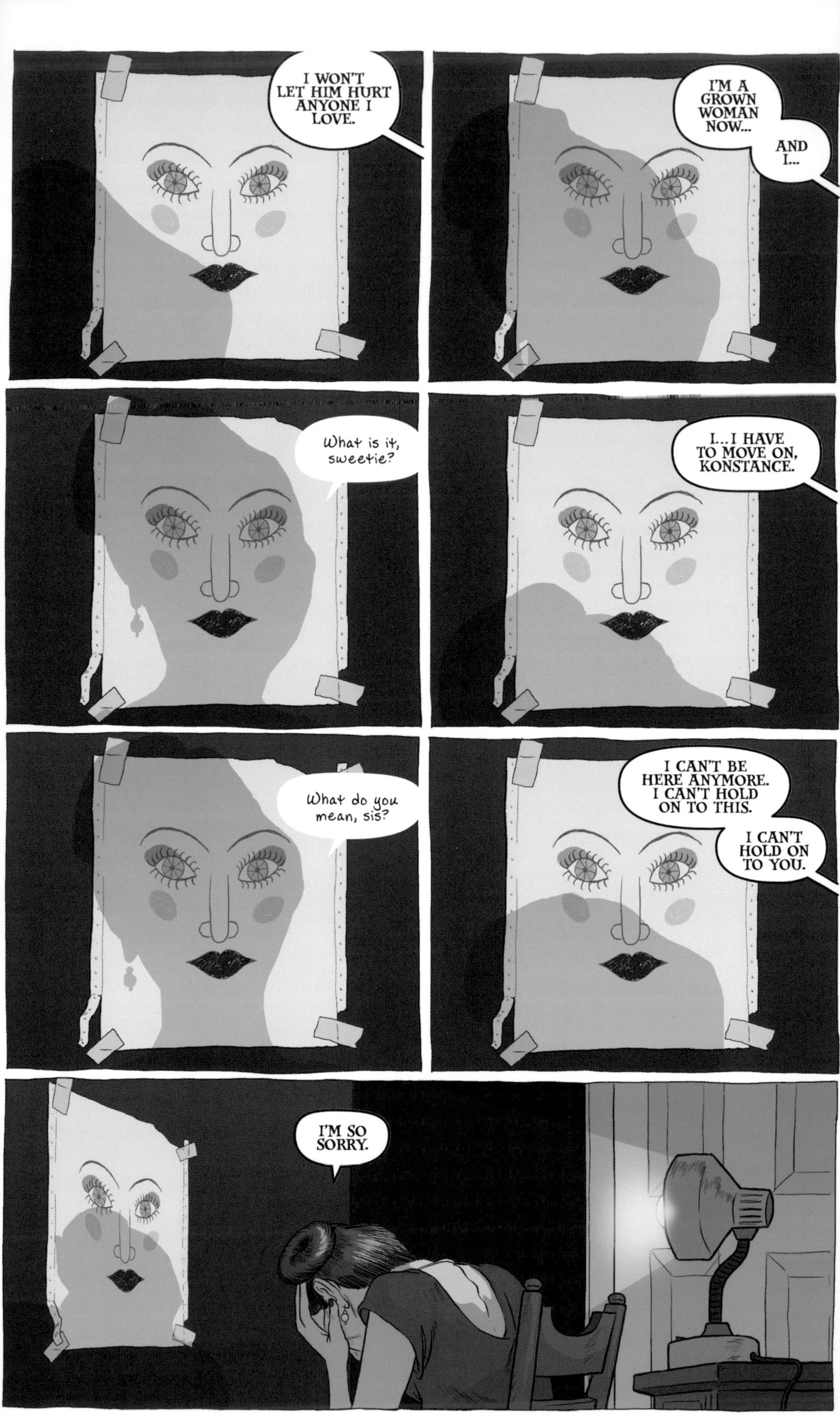
I WON'T LET HIM HURT ANYONE I LOVE.
I'M A GROWN WOMAN NOW...
AND I...
What is it, sweetie?
I...I HAVE TO MOVE ON, KONSTANCE.
What do you mean, sis?
I CAN'T BE HERE ANYMORE. I CAN'T HOLD ON TO THIS.
I CAN'T HOLD ON TO YOU.
I'M SO SORRY.

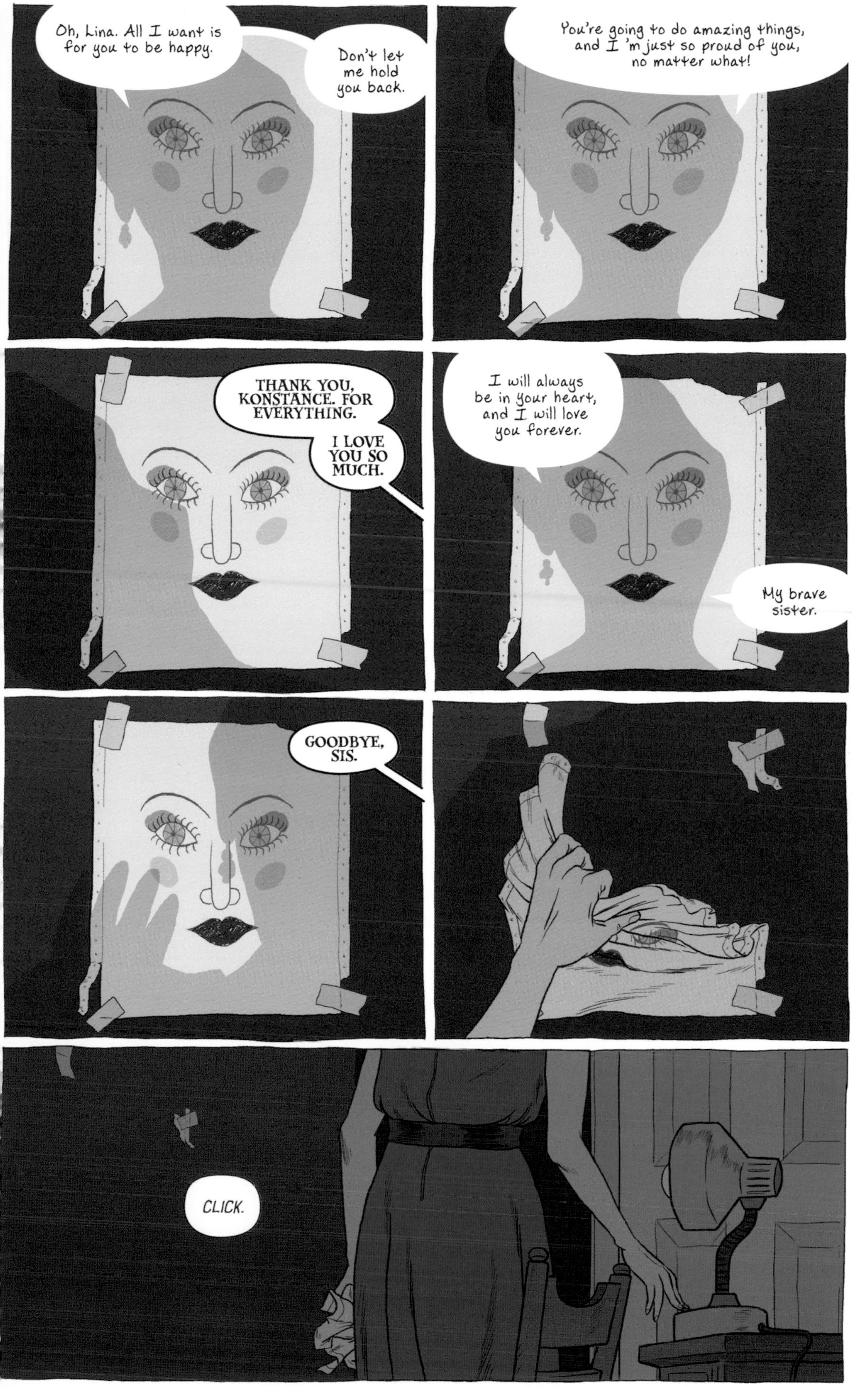

Oh, Lina. All I want is for you to be happy.
Don't let me hold you back.
You're going to do amazing things, and I 'm just so proud of you, no matter what!
THANK YOU, KONSTANCE. FOR EVERYTHING.
I LOVE YOU SO MUCH.
I will always be in your heart, and I will love you forever.
My brave sister.
GOODBYE, SIS.
CLICK.

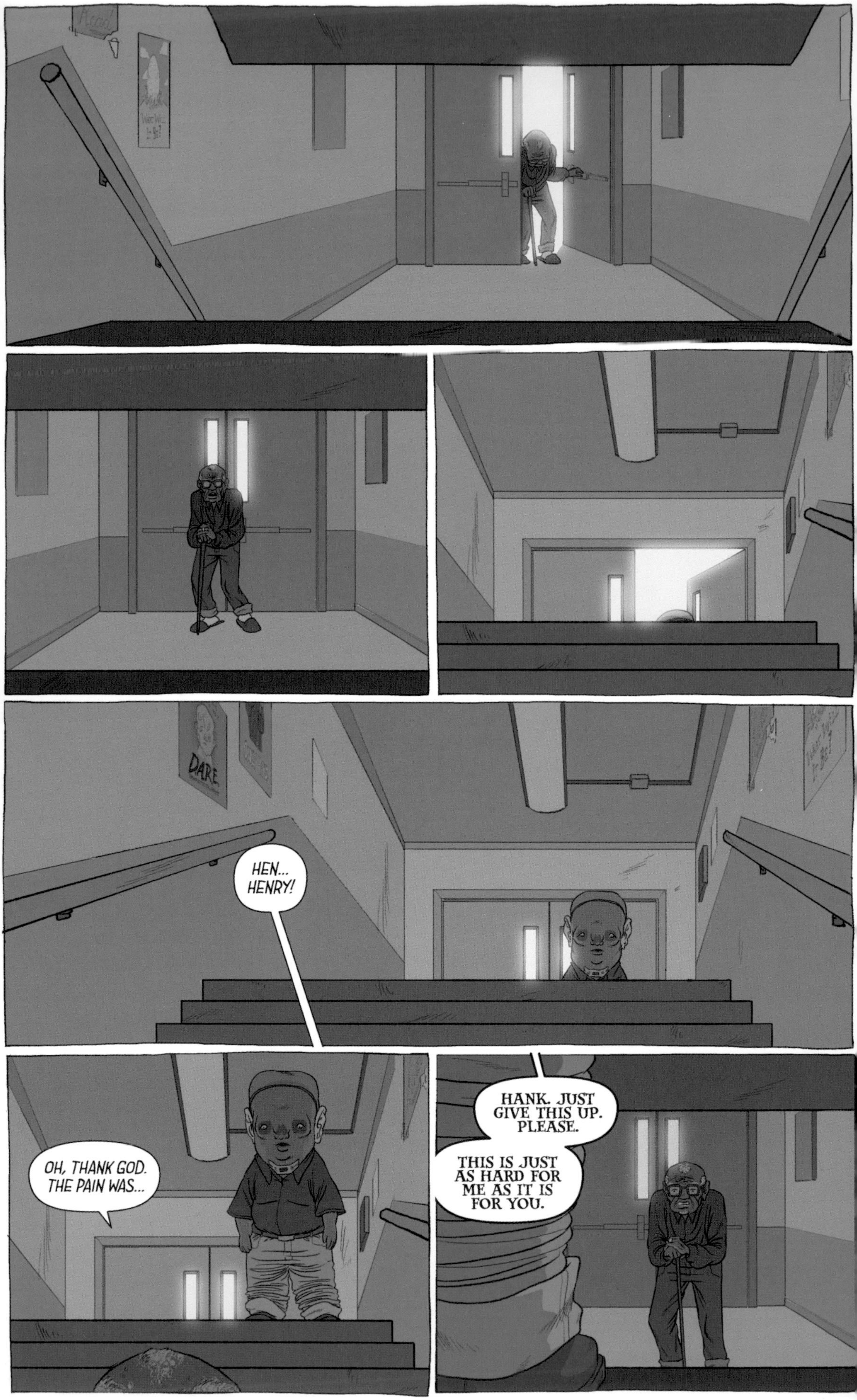
DARE
HEN... HENRY!
OH, THANK GOD. THE PAIN WAS...
HANK. JUST GIVE THIS UP. PLEASE.
THIS IS JUST AS HARD FOR ME AS IT IS FOR YOU.

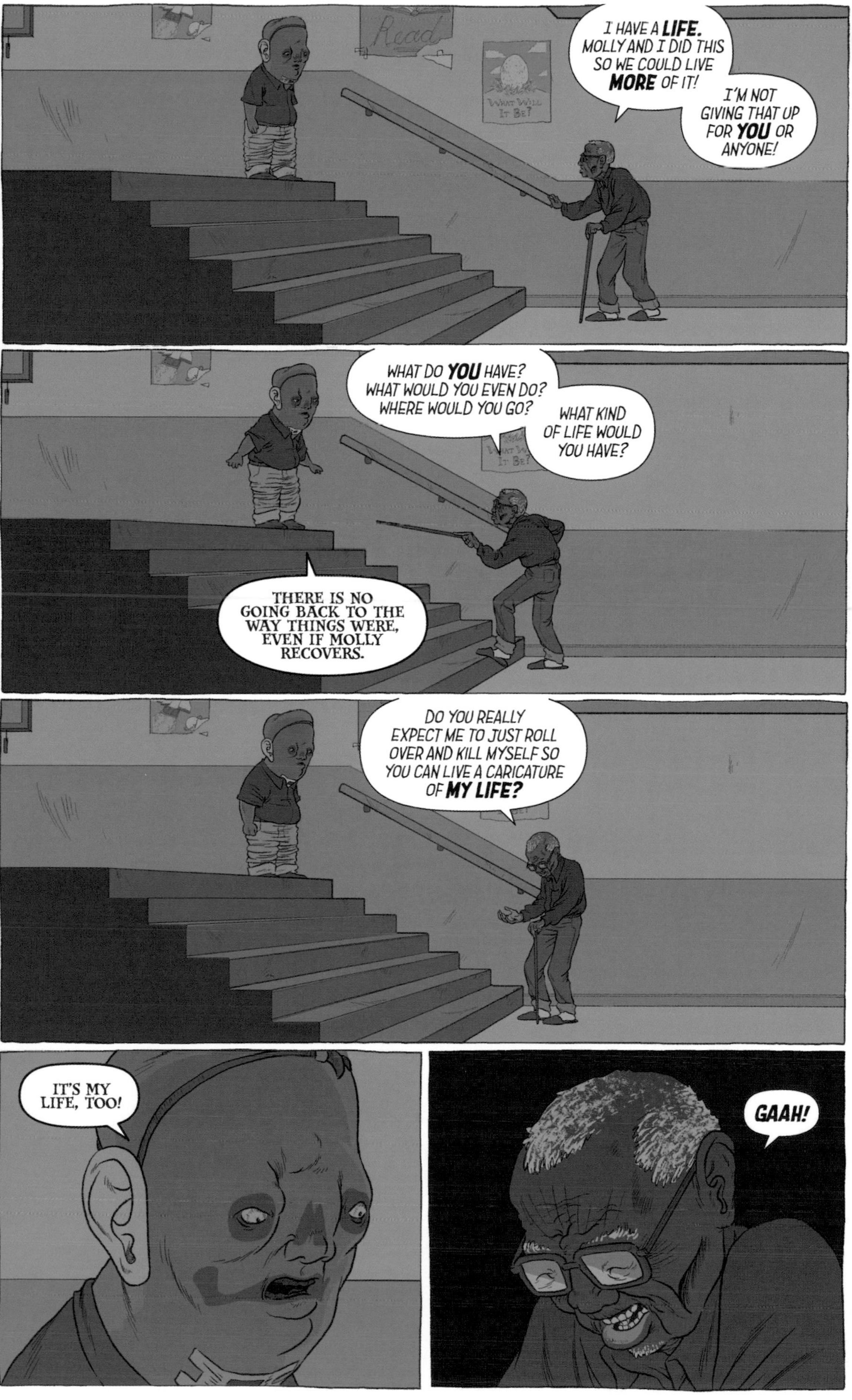
I HAVE A LIFE. MOLLY AND I DID THIS SO WE COULD LIVE MORE OF IT!
I'M NOT GIVING THAT UP FOR YOU OR ANYONE!
Read
WHAT WILL IT BE?
WHAT DO YOU HAVE? WHAT WOULD YOU EVEN DO? WHERE WOULD YOU GO?
WHAT KIND OF LIFE WOULD YOU HAVE?
THERE IS NO GOING BACK TO THE WAY THINGS WERE, EVEN IF MOLLY RECOVERS.
DO YOU REALLY EXPECT ME TO JUST ROLL OVER AND KILL MYSELF SO YOU CAN LIVE A CARICATURE OF MY LIFE?
IT'S MY LIFE, TOO!
GAAH!

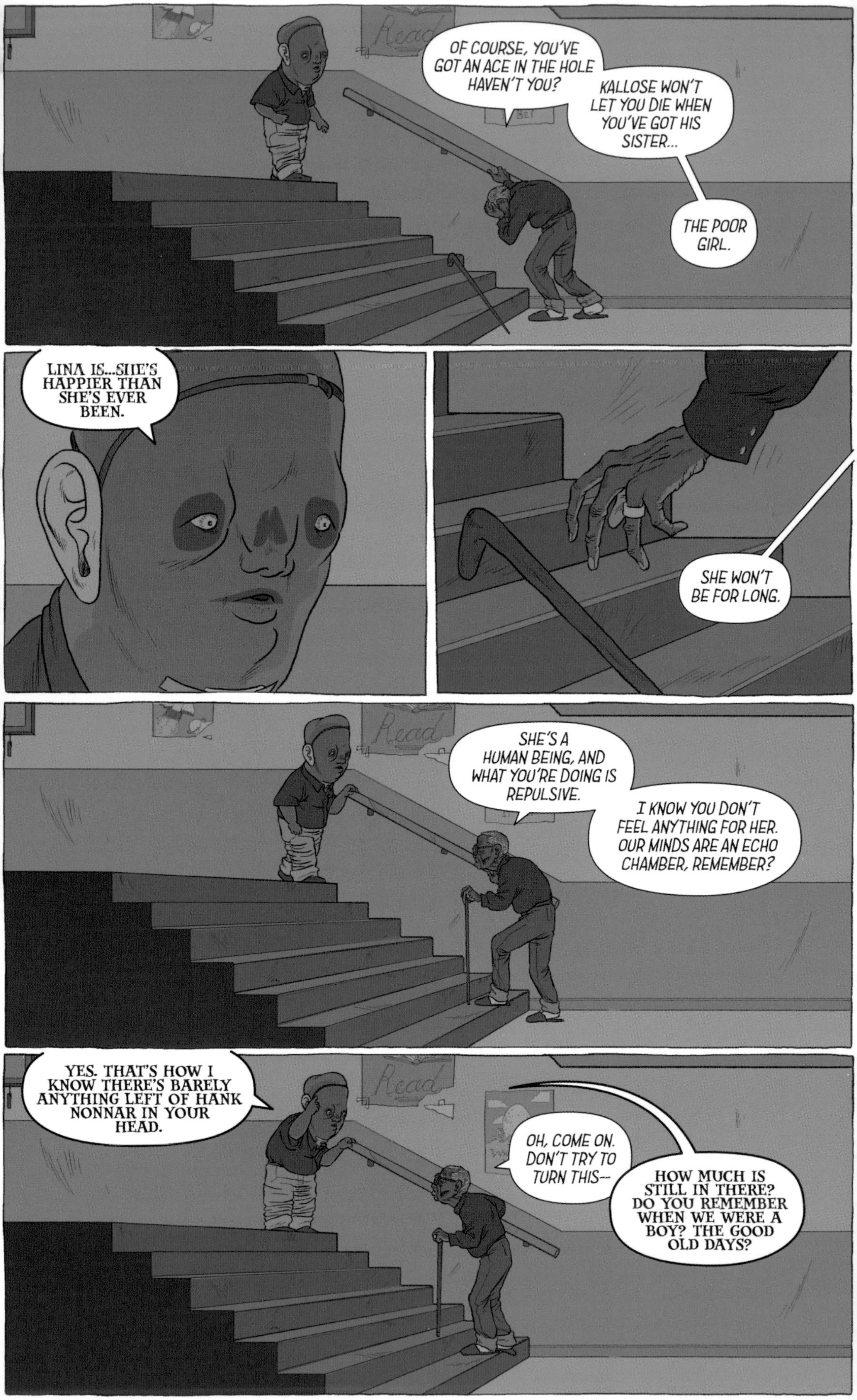
OF COURSE, YOU'VE GOT AN ACE IN THE HOLE HAVEN'T YOU?
KALLOSE WON'T LET YOU DIE WHEN YOU'VE GOT HIS SISTER...
THE POOR GIRL.
LINA IS...SHE'S HAPPIER THAN SHE'S EVER BEEN.
SHE WON'T BE FOR LONG.
SHE'S A HUMAN BEING, AND WHAT YOU'RE DOING IS REPULSIVE.
I KNOW YOU DON'T FEEL ANYTHING FOR HER. OUR MINDS ARE AN ECHO CHAMBER, REMEMBER?
YES. THAT'S HOW I KNOW THERE'S BARELY ANYTHING LEFT OF HANK NONNAR IN YOUR HEAD.
OH, COME ON. DON'T TRY TO TURN THIS--
HOW MUCH IS STILL IN THERE? DO YOU REMEMBER WHEN WE WERE A BOY? THE GOOD OLD DAYS?

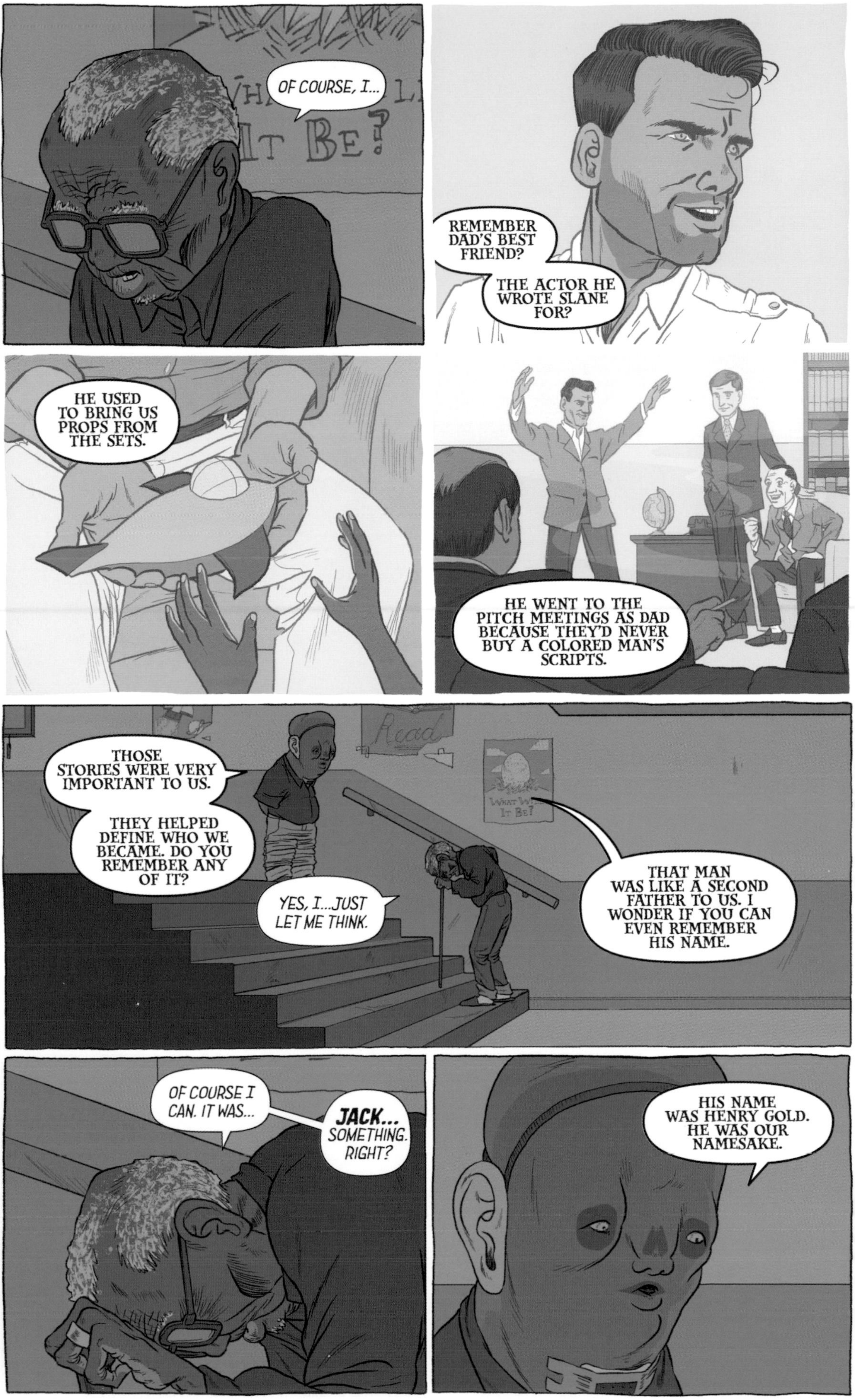
WHAT WILL IT BE?
OF COURSE, I...
REMEMBER DAD'S BEST FRIEND?
THE ACTOR HE WROTE SLANE FOR?
HE USED TO BRING US PROPS FROM THE SETS.
HE WENT TO THE PITCH MEETINGS AS DAD BECAUSE THEY'D NEVER BUY A COLORED MAN'S SCRIPTS.
Read
THOSE STORIES WERE VERY IMPORTANT TO US.
THEY HELPED DEFINE WHO WE BECAME. DO YOU REMEMBER ANY OF IT?
YES, I...JUST LET ME THINK.
THAT MAN WAS LIKE A SECOND FATHER TO US. I WONDER IF YOU CAN EVEN REMEMBER HIS NAME.
OF COURSE I CAN. IT WAS...
JACK... SOMETHING. RIGHT?
HIS NAME WAS HENRY GOLD. HE WAS OUR NAMESAKE.

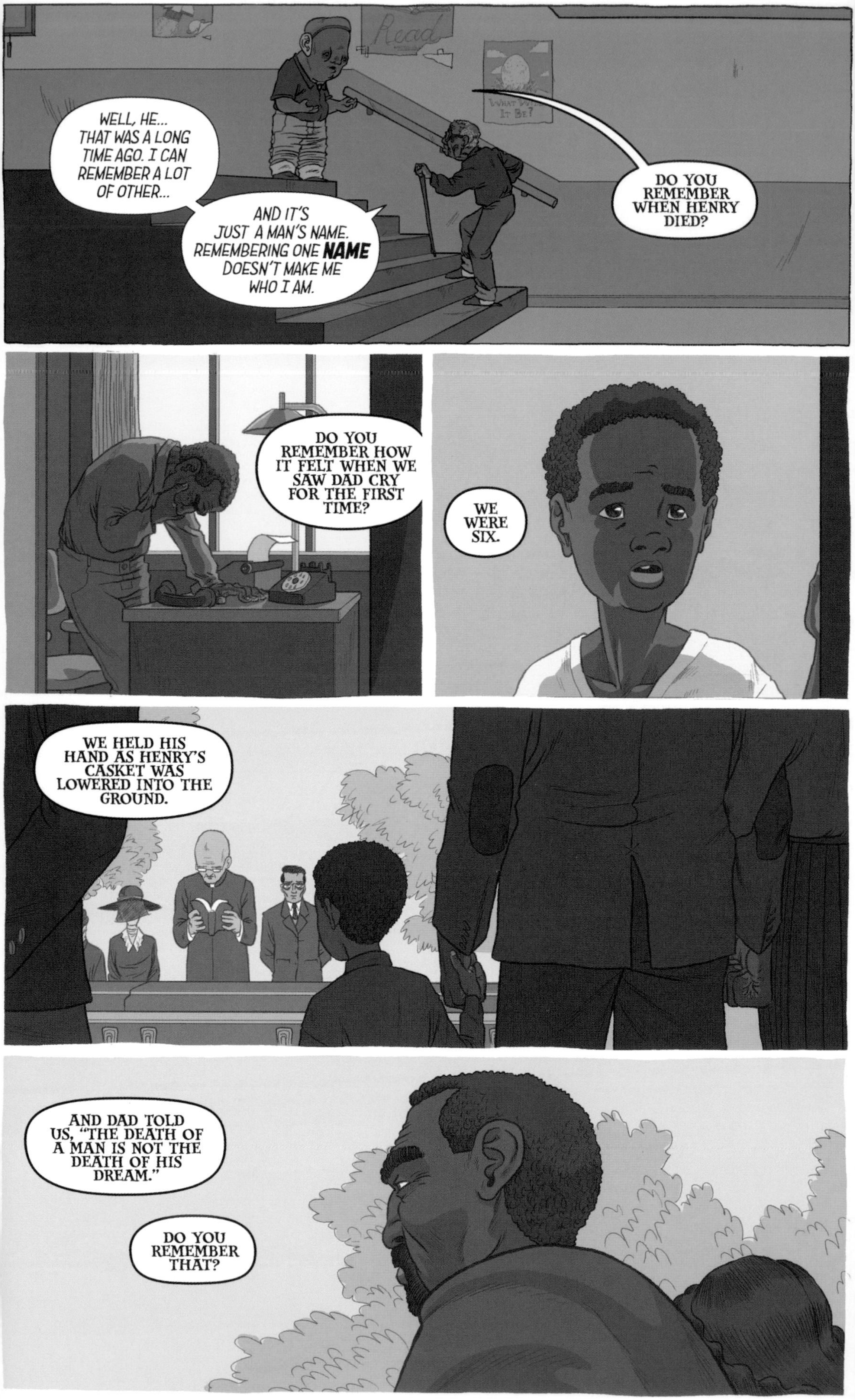

WELL, HE... THAT WAS A LONG TIME AGO. I CAN REMEMBER A LOT OF OTHER...
AND IT'S JUST A MAN'S NAME. REMEMBERING ONE **NAME** DOESN'T MAKE ME WHO I AM.
DO YOU REMEMBER WHEN HENRY DIED?
Read
WHAT WILL IT BE?
DO YOU REMEMBER HOW IT FELT WHEN WE SAW DAD CRY FOR THE FIRST TIME?
WE WERE SIX.
WE HELD HIS HAND AS HENRY'S CASKET WAS LOWERED INTO THE GROUND.
AND DAD TOLD US, "THE DEATH OF A MAN IS NOT THE DEATH OF HIS DREAM."
DO YOU REMEMBER THAT?

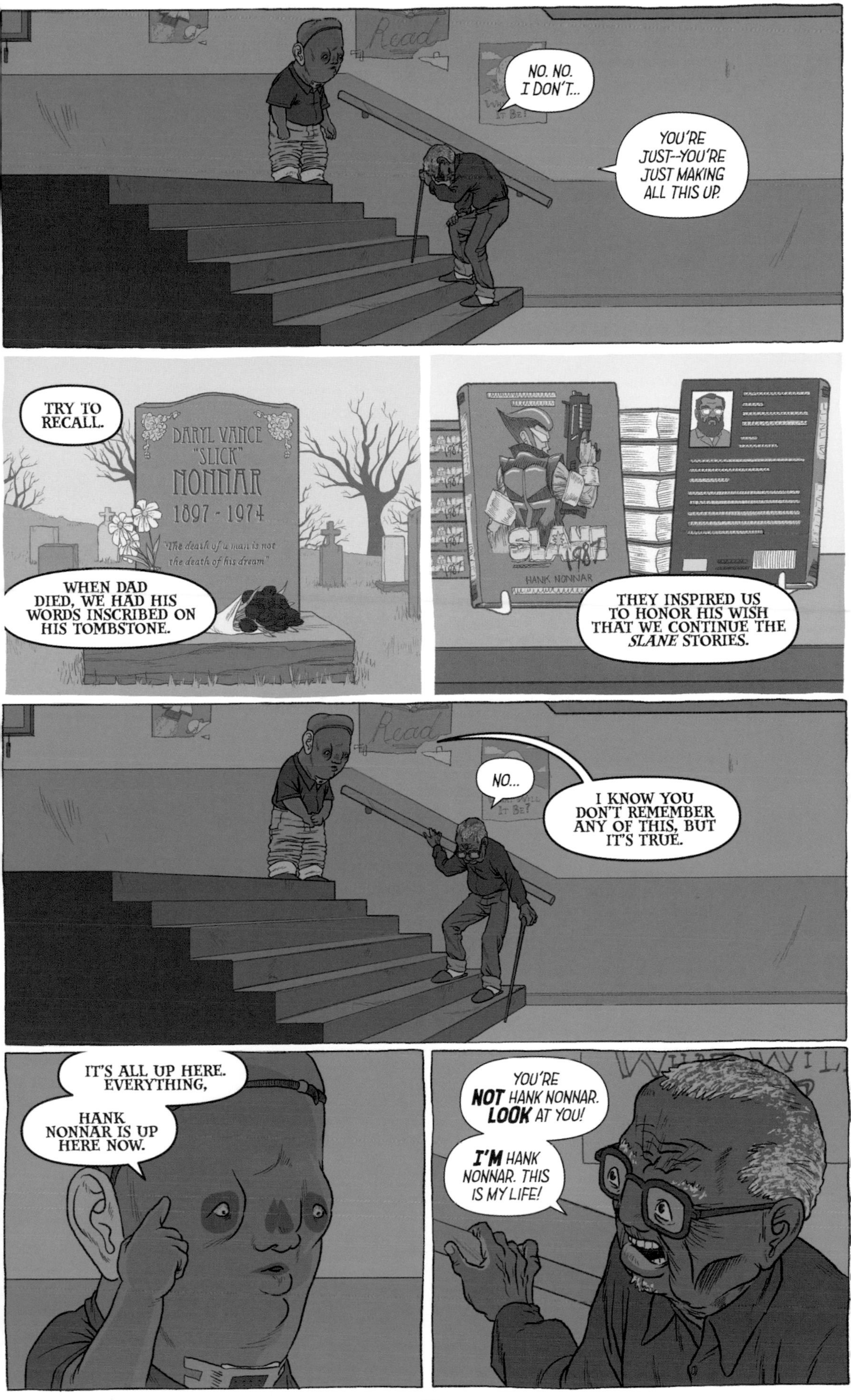

NO. NO. I DON'T...
YOU'RE JUST--YOU'RE JUST MAKING ALL THIS UP.
TRY TO RECALL.
DARYL VANCE "SLICK" NONNAR 1897 - 1974
"The death of a man is not the death of his dream"
WHEN DAD DIED, WE HAD HIS WORDS INSCRIBED ON HIS TOMBSTONE.
SLANE 1987
HANK NONNAR
THEY INSPIRED US TO HONOR HIS WISH THAT WE CONTINUE THE *SLANE* STORIES.
NO...
I KNOW YOU DON'T REMEMBER ANY OF THIS, BUT IT'S TRUE.
IT'S ALL UP HERE. EVERYTHING,
HANK NONNAR IS UP HERE NOW.
YOU'RE **NOT** HANK NONNAR. **LOOK** AT YOU!
I'M HANK NONNAR. THIS IS MY LIFE!

IT MAY HAVE BEEN ONCE, BUT YOU'RE NO LONGER THE IDEAL VESSEL FOR IT.
THIS IS EXACTLY WHAT YOU WANTED.
YOU'RE A MONSTER!
Read
I NEVER WANTED TO BE A MONSTER!

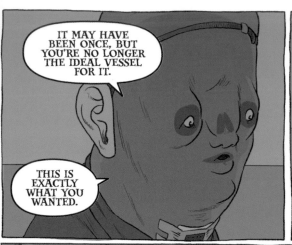

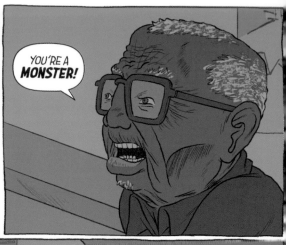

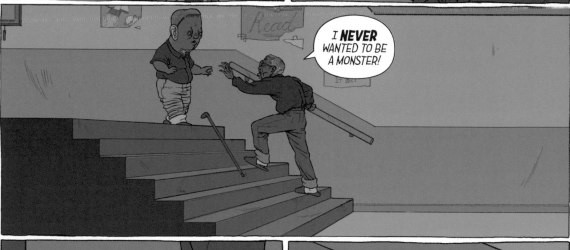

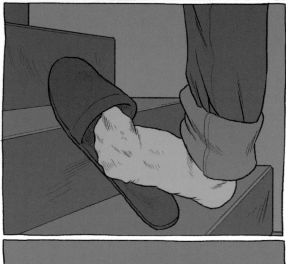

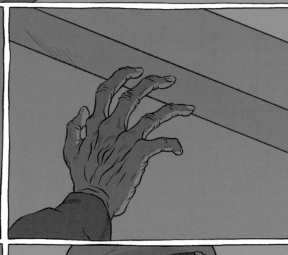

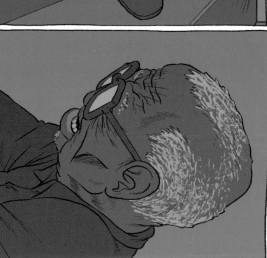

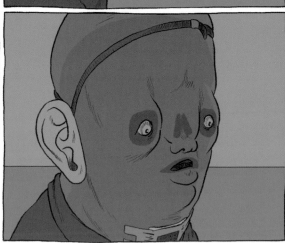

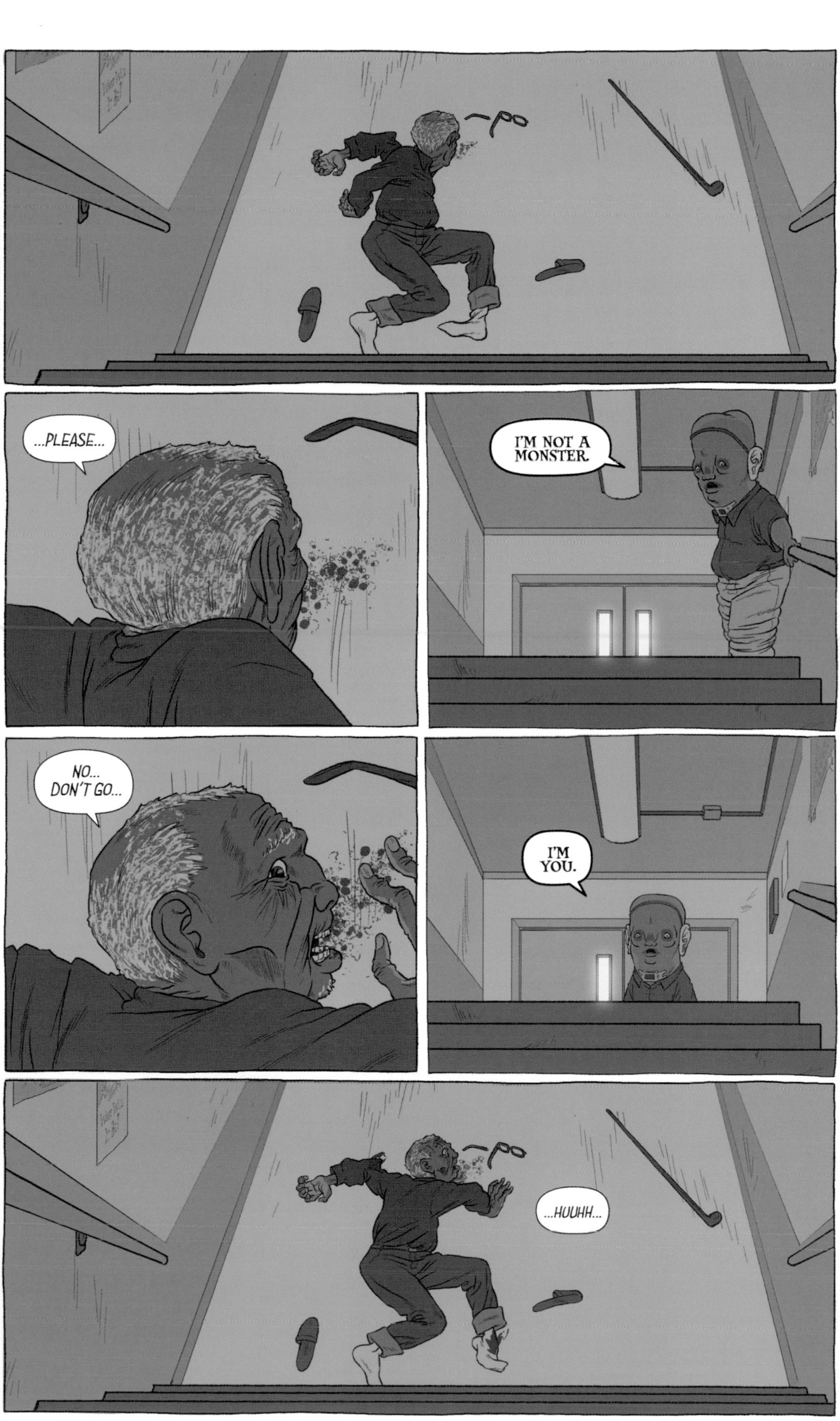
...PLEASE...
I'M NOT A MONSTER.
NO... DON'T GO...
I'M YOU.
...HUUHH...

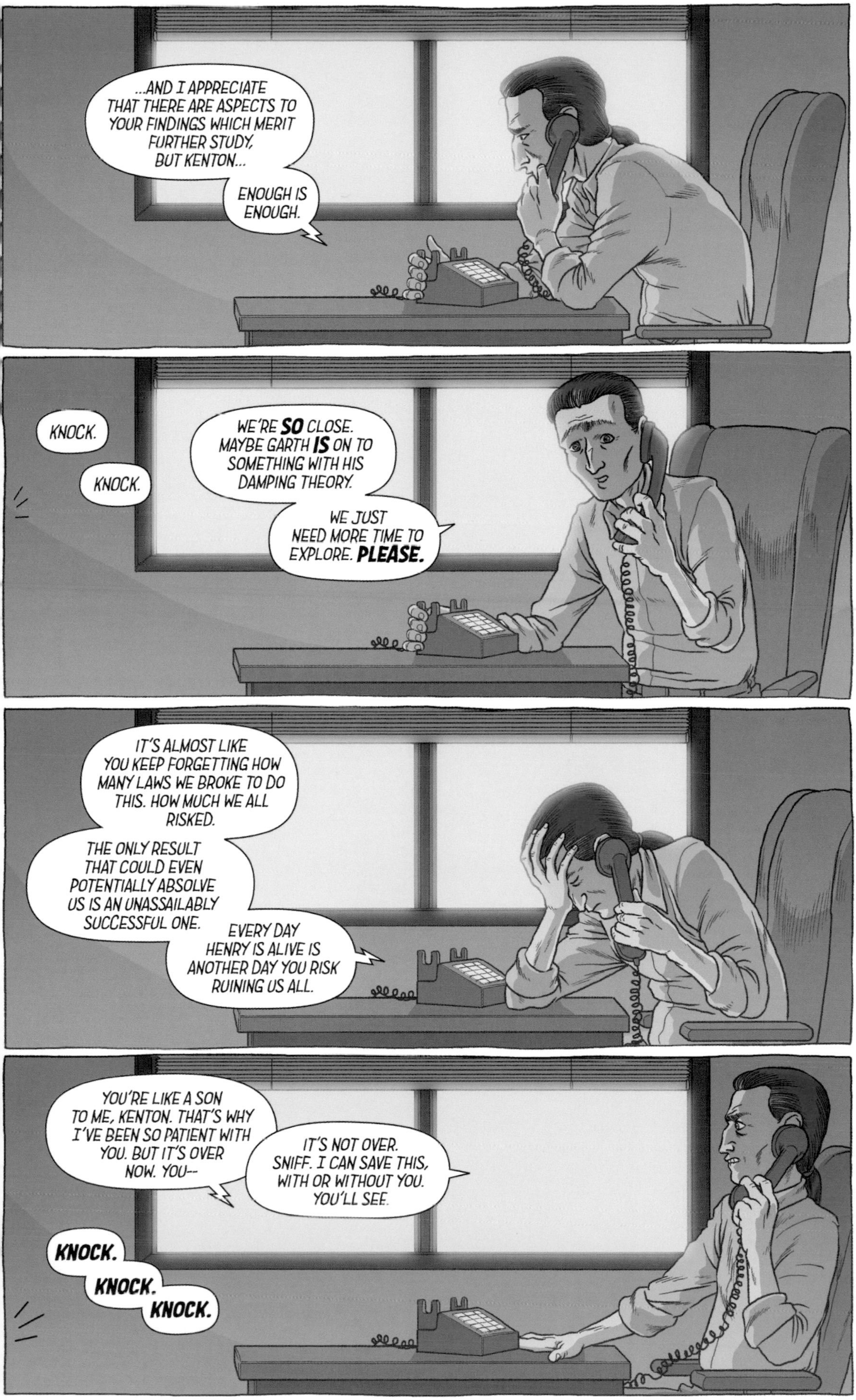

...AND I APPRECIATE THAT THERE ARE ASPECTS TO YOUR FINDINGS WHICH MERIT FURTHER STUDY, BUT KENTON...
ENOUGH IS ENOUGH.
KNOCK.
KNOCK.
WE'RE **SO** CLOSE. MAYBE GARTH **IS** ON TO SOMETHING WITH HIS DAMPING THEORY.
WE JUST NEED MORE TIME TO EXPLORE. **PLEASE.**
IT'S ALMOST LIKE YOU KEEP FORGETTING HOW MANY LAWS WE BROKE TO DO THIS. HOW MUCH WE ALL RISKED.
THE ONLY RESULT THAT COULD EVEN POTENTIALLY ABSOLVE US IS AN UNASSAILABLY SUCCESSFUL ONE.
EVERY DAY HENRY IS ALIVE IS ANOTHER DAY YOU RISK RUINING US ALL.
YOU'RE LIKE A SON TO ME, KENTON. THAT'S WHY I'VE BEEN SO PATIENT WITH YOU. BUT IT'S OVER NOW. YOU--
IT'S NOT OVER. SNIFF. I CAN SAVE THIS, WITH OR WITHOUT YOU. YOU'LL SEE.
KNOCK.
KNOCK.
KNOCK.

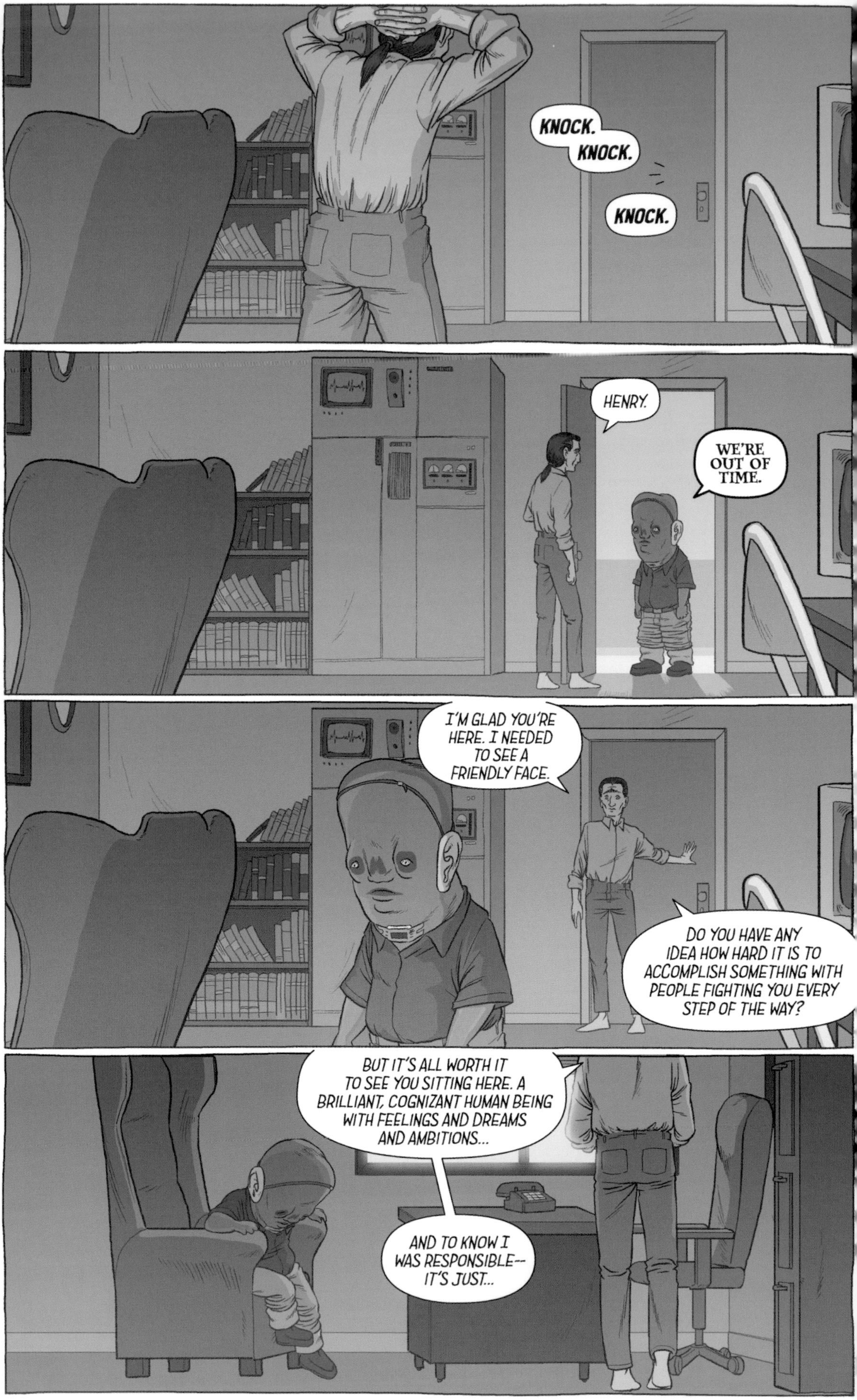
KNOCK.
KNOCK.
KNOCK.
HENRY.
WE'RE OUT OF TIME.
I'M GLAD YOU'RE HERE. I NEEDED TO SEE A FRIENDLY FACE.
DO YOU HAVE ANY IDEA HOW HARD IT IS TO ACCOMPLISH SOMETHING WITH PEOPLE FIGHTING YOU EVERY STEP OF THE WAY?
BUT IT'S ALL WORTH IT TO SEE YOU SITTING HERE. A BRILLIANT, COGNIZANT HUMAN BEING WITH FEELINGS AND DREAMS AND AMBITIONS...
AND TO KNOW I WAS RESPONSIBLE-- IT'S JUST...

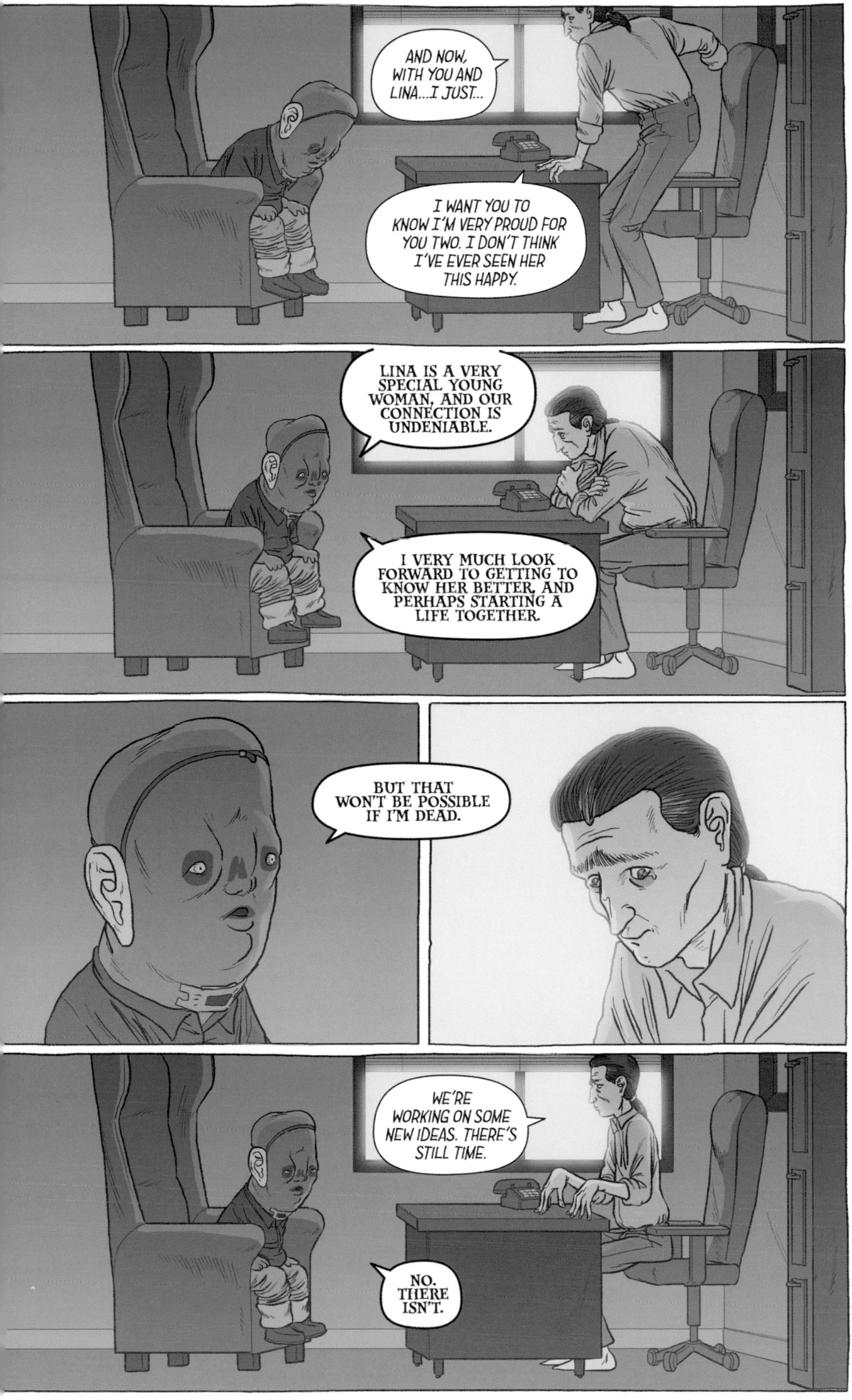
AND NOW, WITH YOU AND LINA...I JUST...
I WANT YOU TO KNOW I'M VERY PROUD FOR YOU TWO. I DON'T THINK I'VE EVER SEEN HER THIS HAPPY.
LINA IS A VERY SPECIAL YOUNG WOMAN, AND OUR CONNECTION IS UNDENIABLE.
I VERY MUCH LOOK FORWARD TO GETTING TO KNOW HER BETTER, AND PERHAPS STARTING A LIFE TOGETHER.
BUT THAT WON'T BE POSSIBLE IF I'M DEAD.
WE'RE WORKING ON SOME NEW IDEAS. THERE'S STILL TIME.
NO. THERE ISN'T.

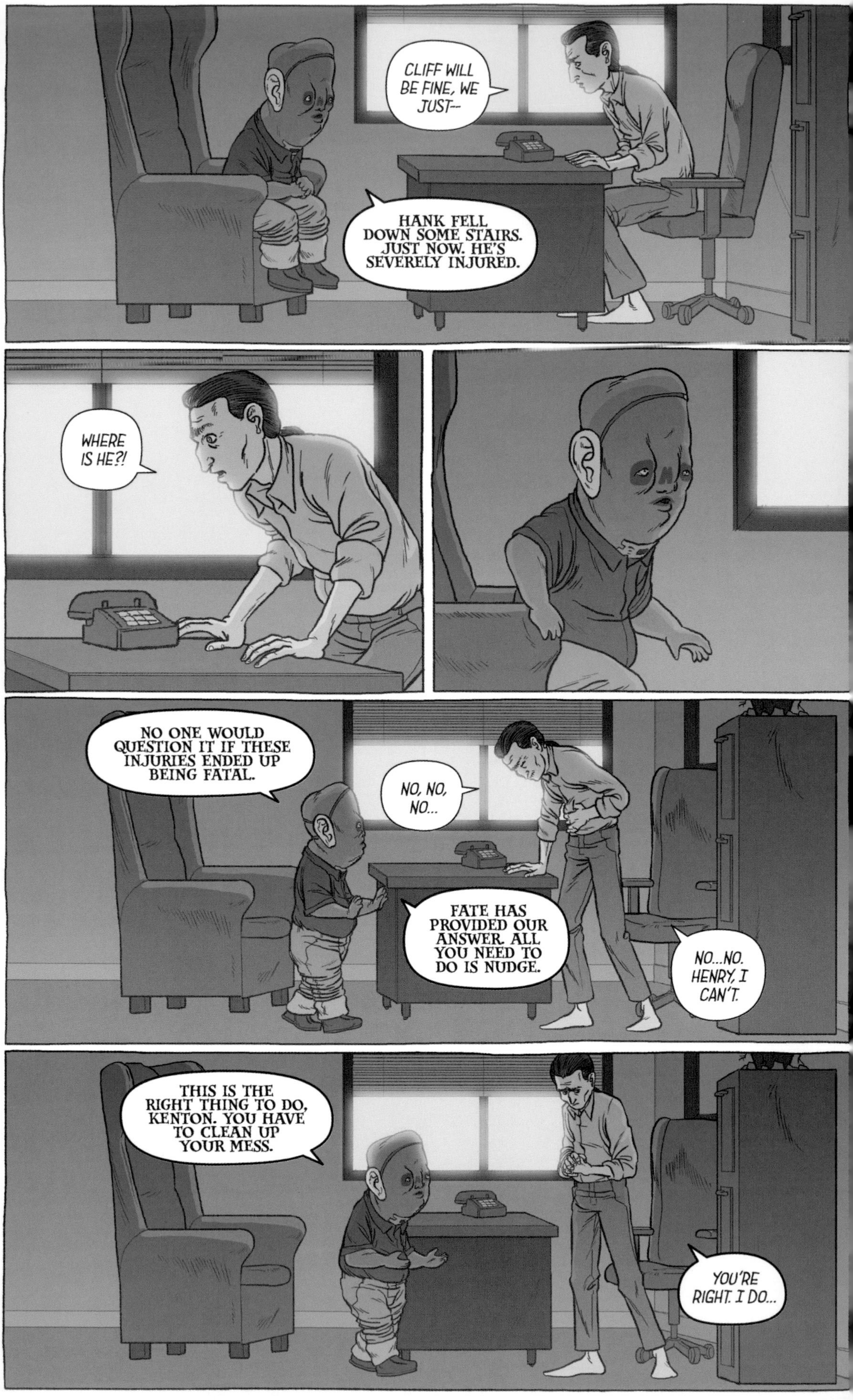
CLIFF WILL BE FINE, WE JUST--
HANK FELL DOWN SOME STAIRS. JUST NOW. HE'S SEVERELY INJURED.
WHERE IS HE?!
NO ONE WOULD QUESTION IT IF THESE INJURIES ENDED UP BEING FATAL.
NO, NO, NO...
FATE HAS PROVIDED OUR ANSWER. ALL YOU NEED TO DO IS NUDGE.
NO...NO. HENRY, I CAN'T.
THIS IS THE RIGHT THING TO DO, KENTON. YOU HAVE TO CLEAN UP YOUR MESS.
YOU'RE RIGHT. I DO...

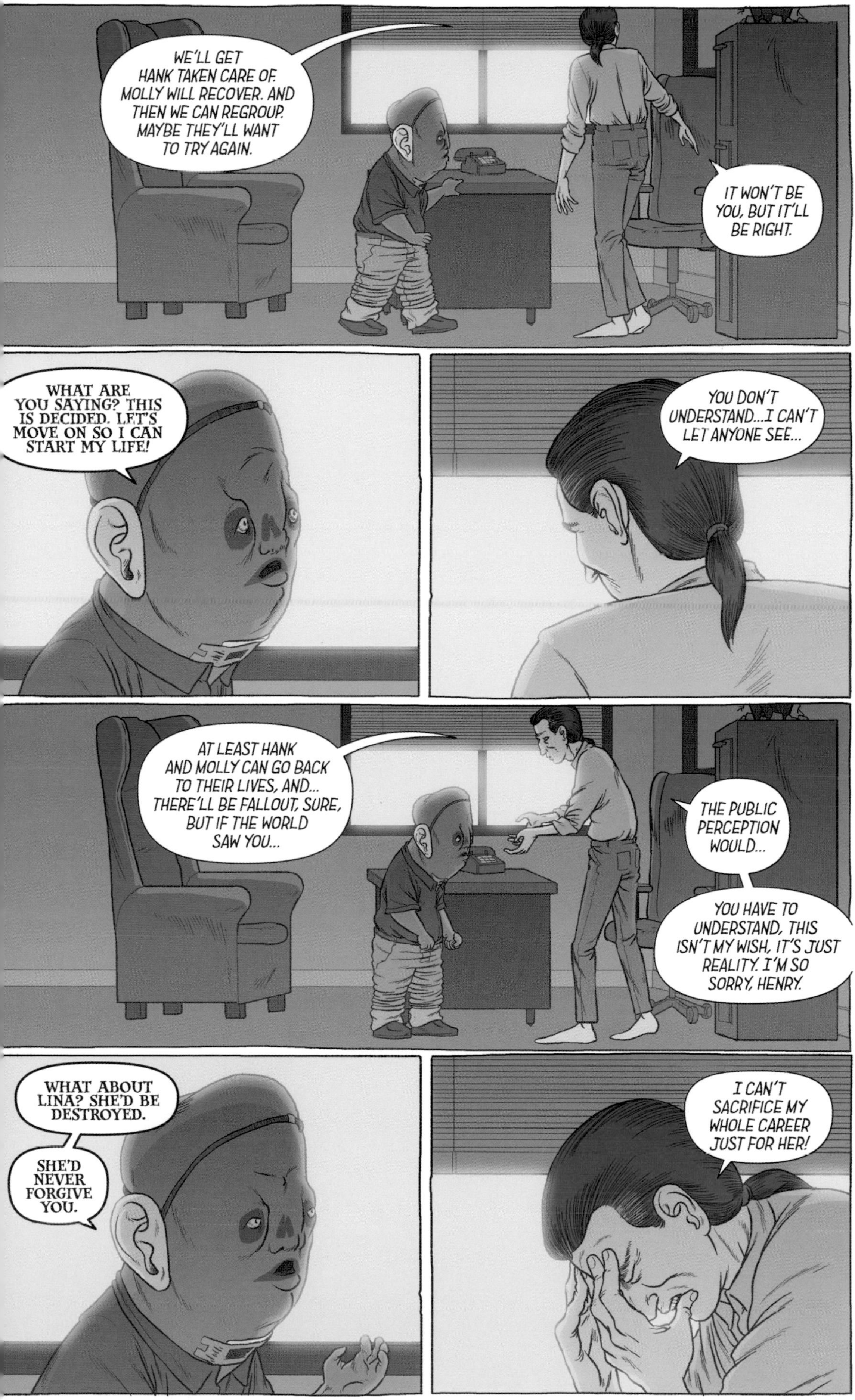
WE'LL GET HANK TAKEN CARE OF. MOLLY WILL RECOVER. AND THEN WE CAN REGROUP. MAYBE THEY'LL WANT TO TRY AGAIN.
IT WON'T BE YOU, BUT IT'LL BE RIGHT.
WHAT ARE YOU SAYING? THIS IS DECIDED. LET'S MOVE ON SO I CAN START MY LIFE!
YOU DON'T UNDERSTAND...I CAN'T LET ANYONE SEE...
AT LEAST HANK AND MOLLY CAN GO BACK TO THEIR LIVES, AND... THERE'LL BE FALLOUT, SURE, BUT IF THE WORLD SAW YOU...
THE PUBLIC PERCEPTION WOULD...
YOU HAVE TO UNDERSTAND, THIS ISN'T MY WISH, IT'S JUST REALITY. I'M SO SORRY, HENRY.
WHAT ABOUT LINA? SHE'D BE DESTROYED.
SHE'D NEVER FORGIVE YOU.
I CAN'T SACRIFICE MY WHOLE CAREER JUST FOR HER!

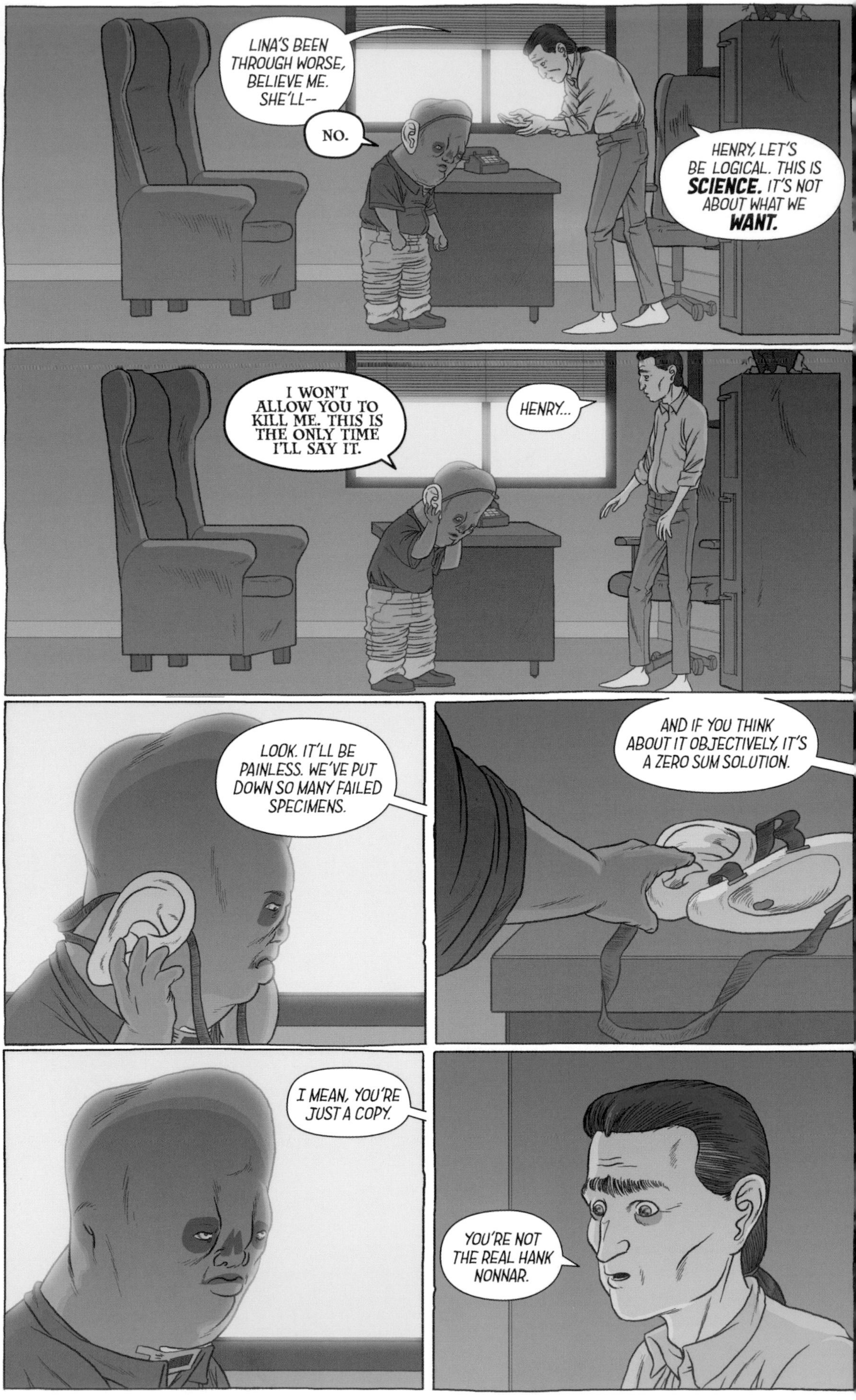
LINA'S BEEN THROUGH WORSE, BELIEVE ME. SHE'LL--
NO.
HENRY, LET'S BE LOGICAL. THIS IS **SCIENCE.** IT'S NOT ABOUT WHAT WE **WANT.**
I WON'T ALLOW YOU TO KILL ME. THIS IS THE ONLY TIME I'LL SAY IT.
HENRY...
LOOK. IT'LL BE PAINLESS. WE'VE PUT DOWN SO MANY FAILED SPECIMENS.
AND IF YOU THINK ABOUT IT OBJECTIVELY, IT'S A ZERO SUM SOLUTION.
I MEAN, YOU'RE JUST A COPY.
YOU'RE NOT THE REAL HANK NONNAR.

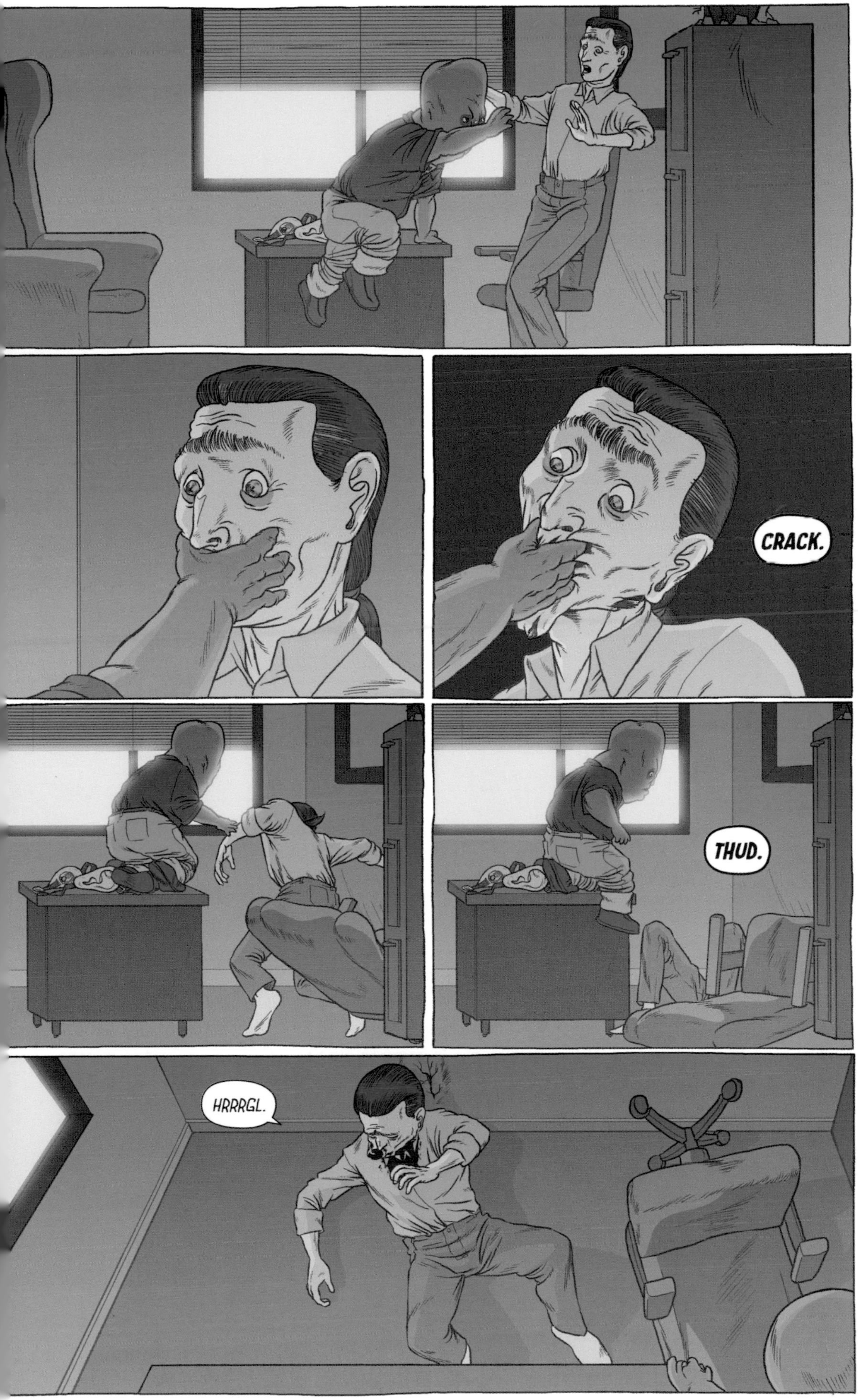
CRACK.
THUD.
HRRRGL.

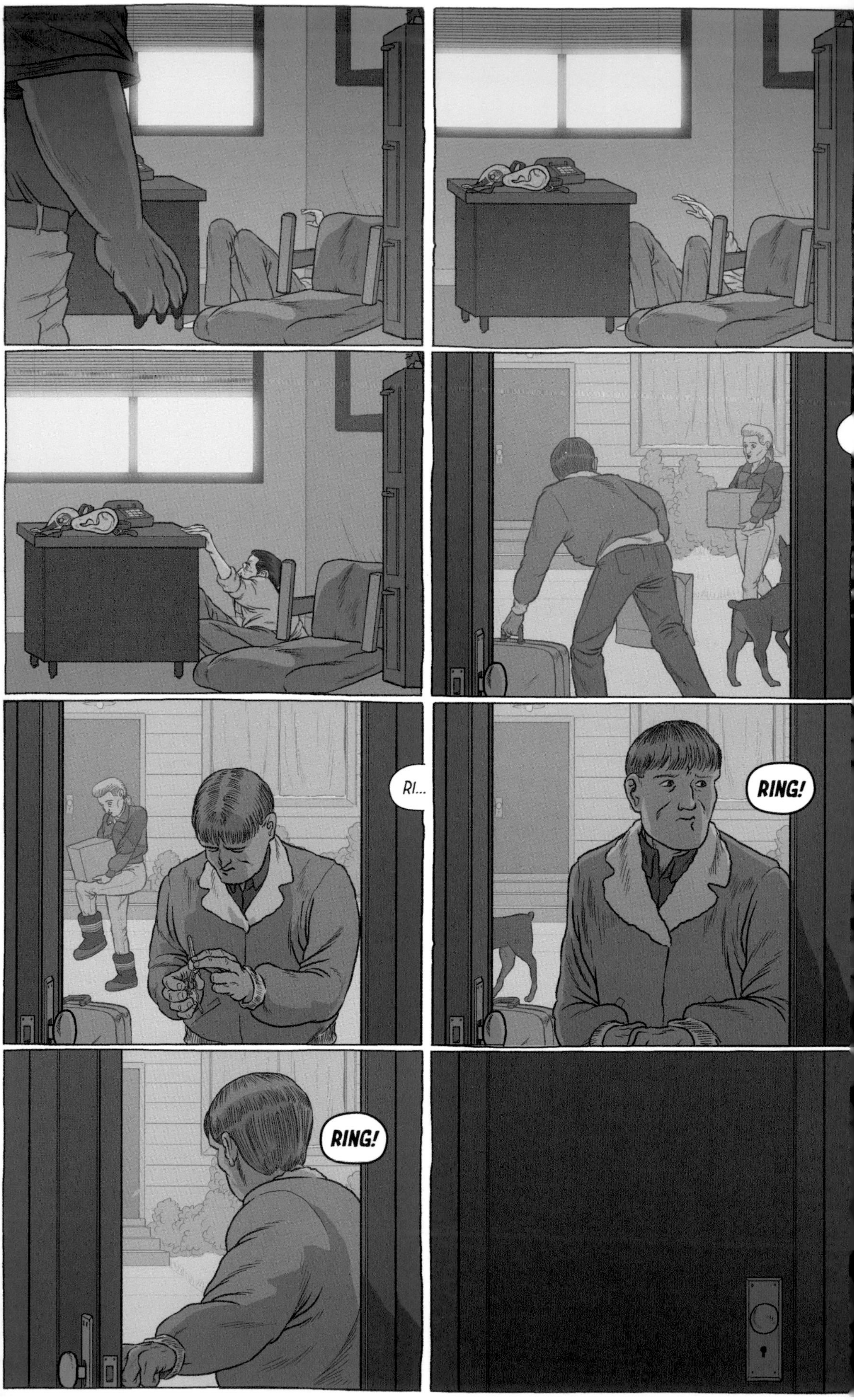
RI...
RING!
RING!

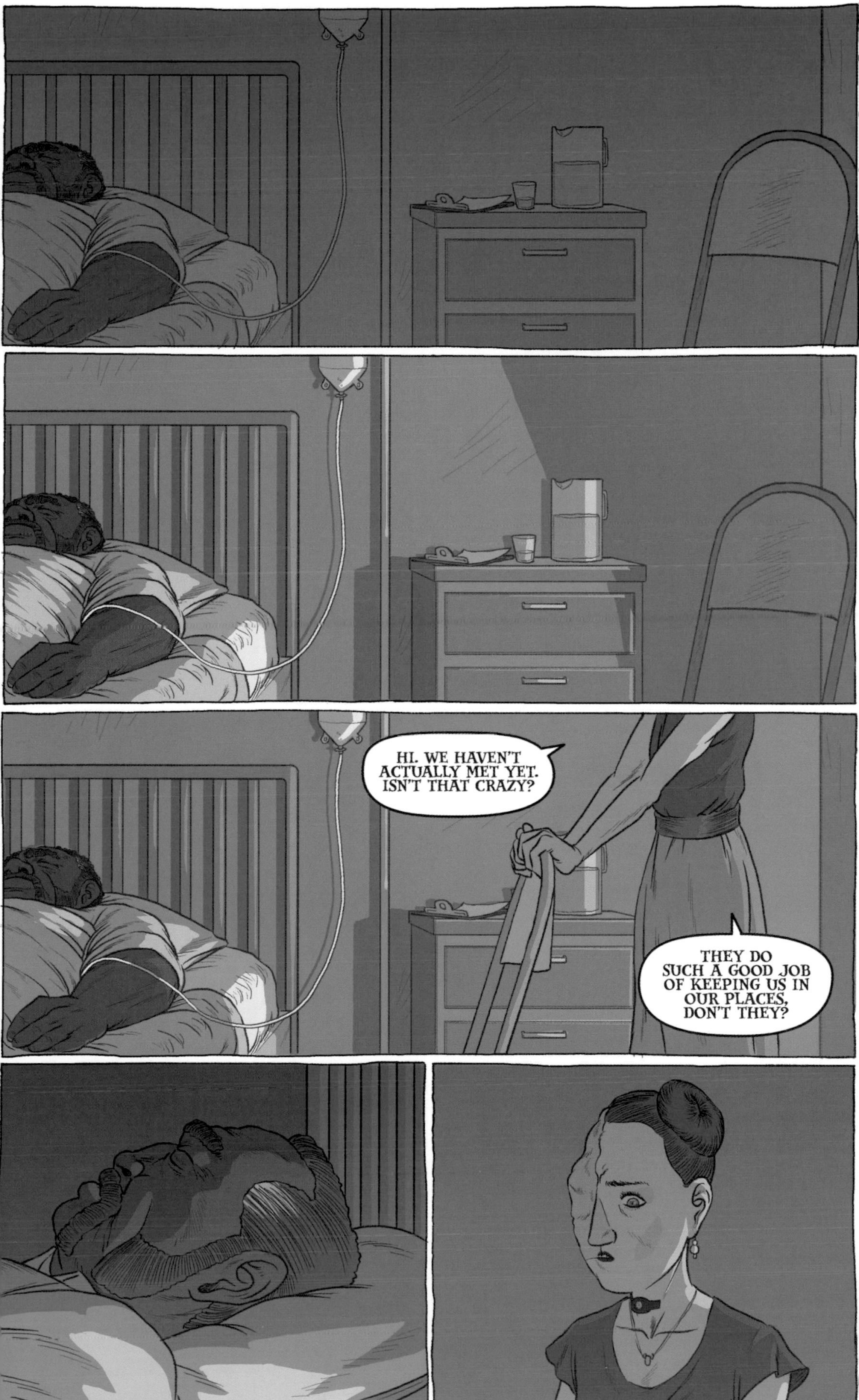
HI. WE HAVEN'T ACTUALLY MET YET. ISN'T THAT CRAZY?
THEY DO SUCH A GOOD JOB OF KEEPING US IN OUR PLACES, DON'T THEY?

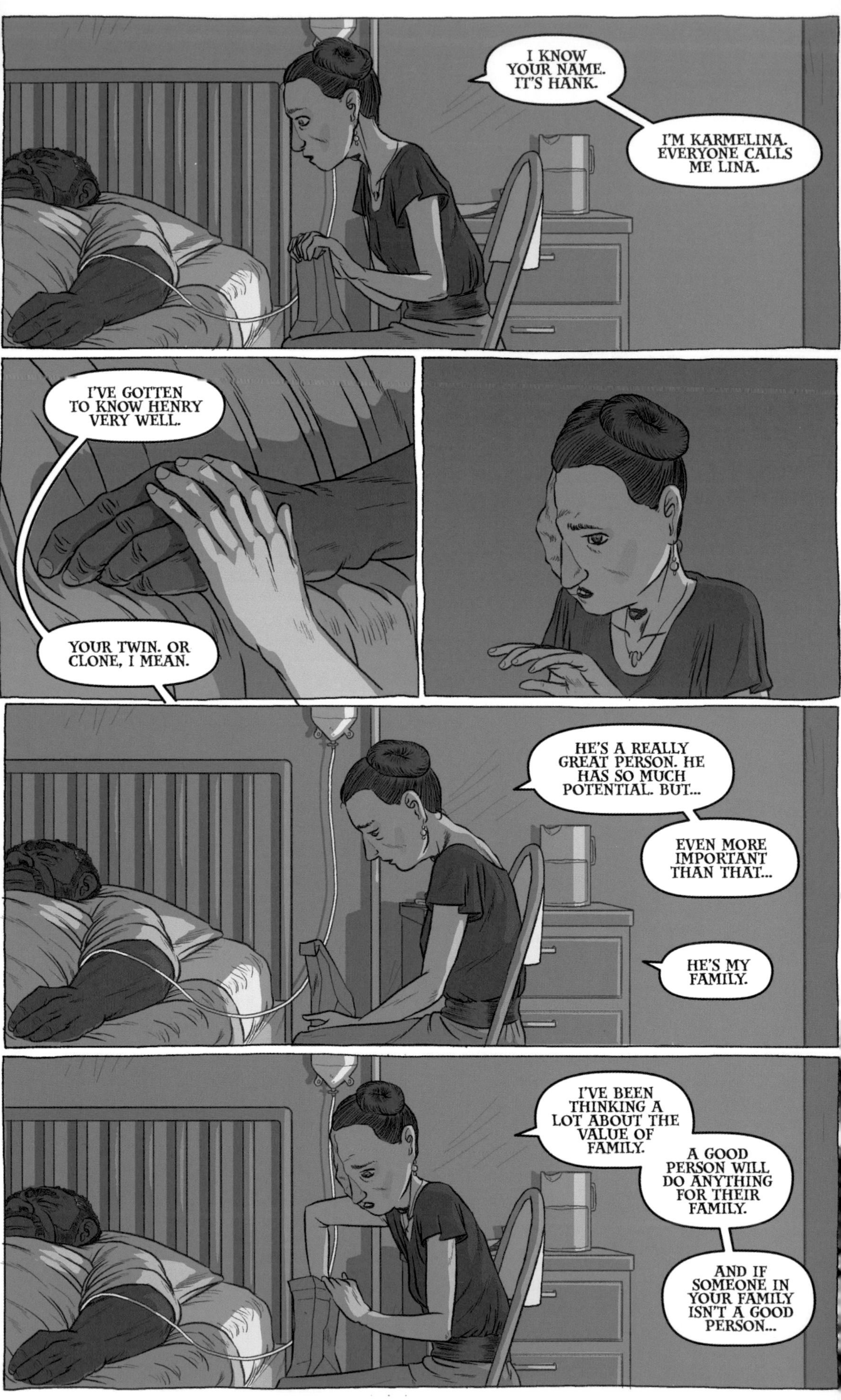
I KNOW YOUR NAME. IT'S HANK.
I'M KARMELINA. EVERYONE CALLS ME LINA.
I'VE GOTTEN TO KNOW HENRY VERY WELL.
YOUR TWIN. OR CLONE, I MEAN.
HE'S A REALLY GREAT PERSON. HE HAS SO MUCH POTENTIAL. BUT...
EVEN MORE IMPORTANT THAN THAT...
HE'S MY FAMILY.
I'VE BEEN THINKING A LOT ABOUT THE VALUE OF FAMILY.
A GOOD PERSON WILL DO ANYTHING FOR THEIR FAMILY.
AND IF SOMEONE IN YOUR FAMILY ISN'T A GOOD PERSON...

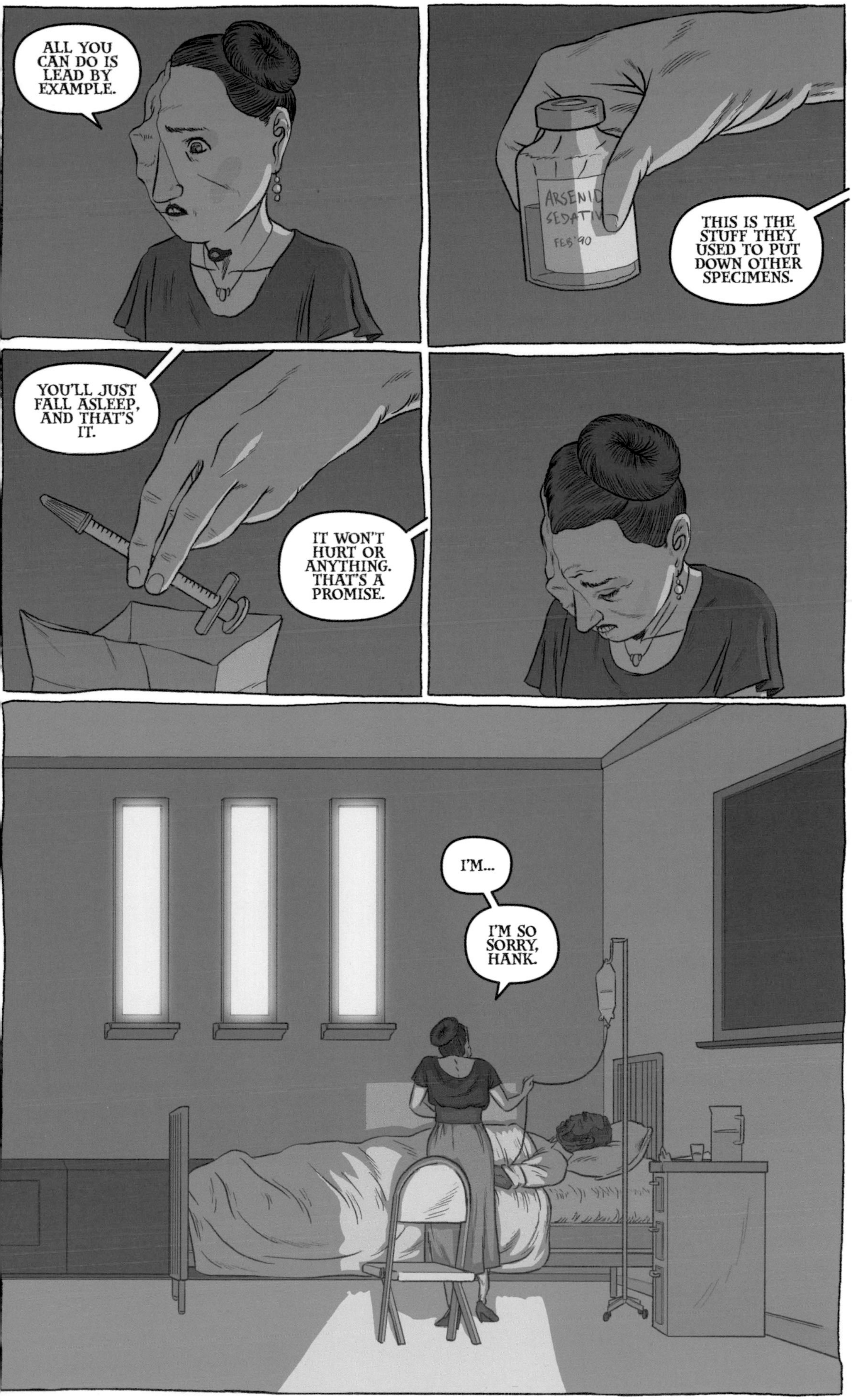
ALL YOU CAN DO IS LEAD BY EXAMPLE.
ARSENID SEDATIV FEB '90
THIS IS THE STUFF THEY USED TO PUT DOWN OTHER SPECIMENS.
YOU'LL JUST FALL ASLEEP, AND THAT'S IT.
IT WON'T HURT OR ANYTHING. THAT'S A PROMISE.
I'M...
I'M SO SORRY, HANK.

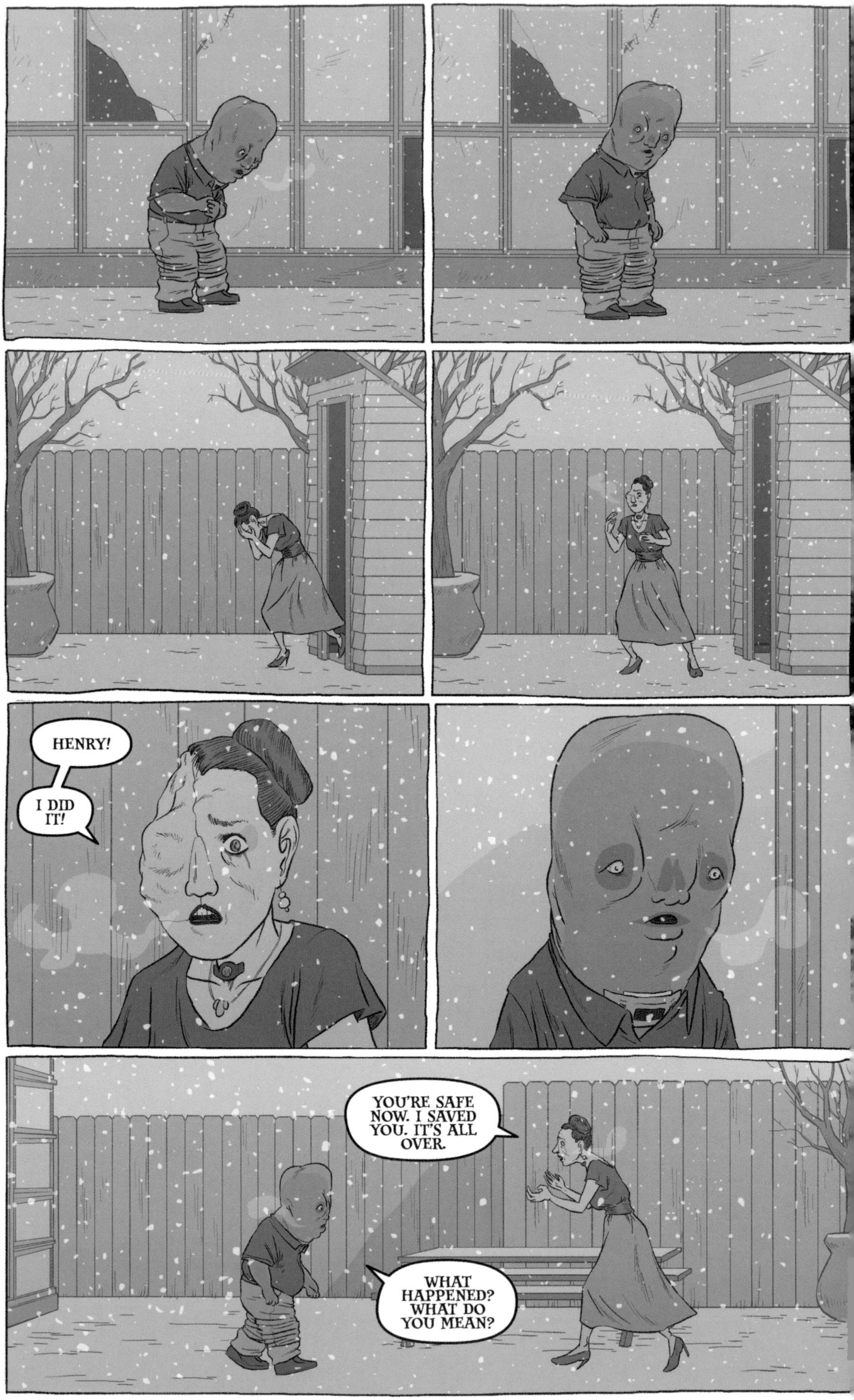
HENRY!
I DID IT!
YOU'RE SAFE NOW. I SAVED YOU. IT'S ALL OVER.
WHAT HAPPENED? WHAT DO YOU MEAN?

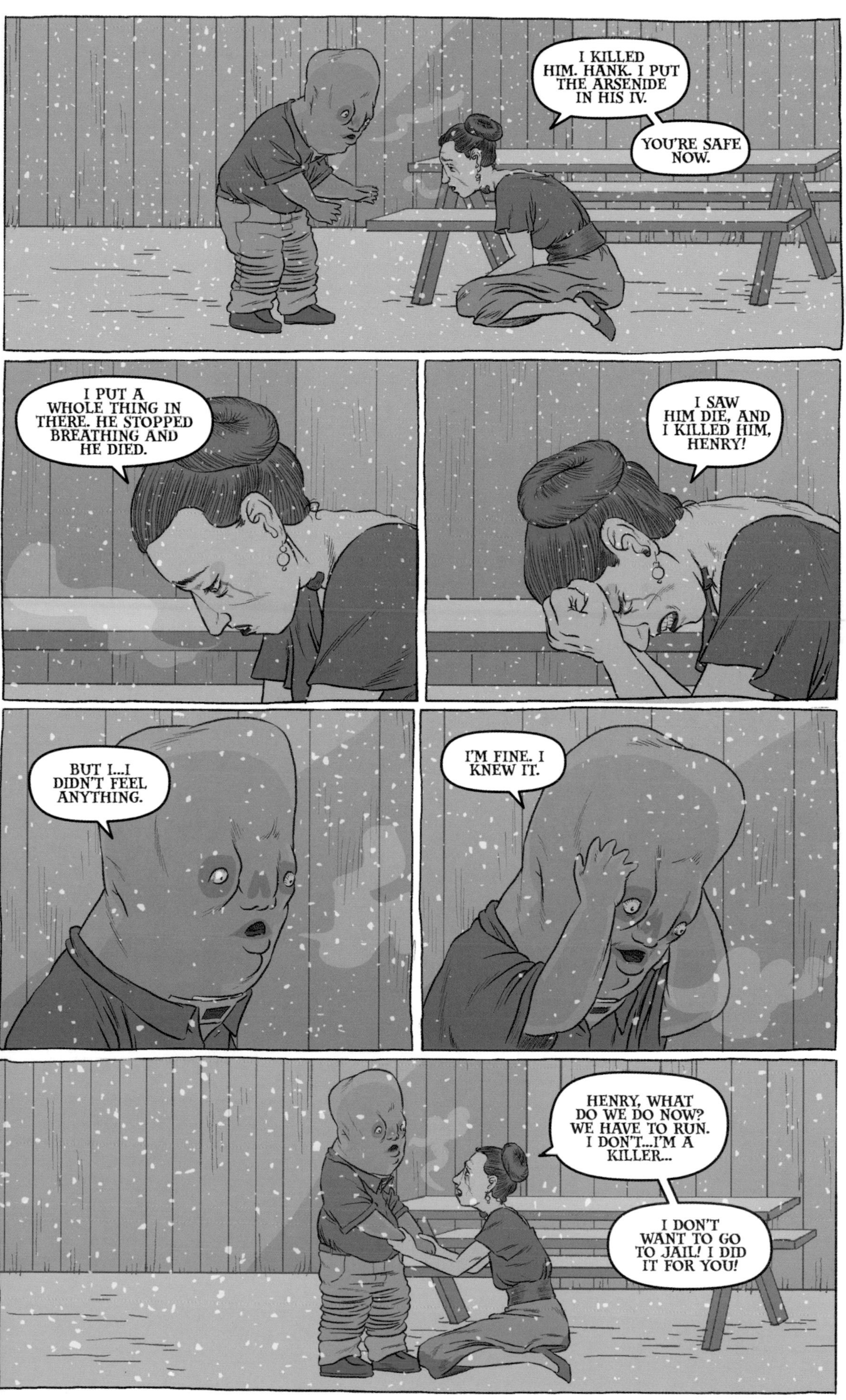
I KILLED HIM. HANK. I PUT THE ARSENIDE IN HIS IV.
YOU'RE SAFE NOW.
I PUT A WHOLE THING IN THERE. HE STOPPED BREATHING AND HE DIED.
I SAW HIM DIE, AND I KILLED HIM, HENRY!
BUT I...I DIDN'T FEEL ANYTHING.
I'M FINE. I KNEW IT.
HENRY, WHAT DO WE DO NOW? WE HAVE TO RUN. I DON'T...I'M A KILLER...
I DON'T WANT TO GO TO JAIL! I DID IT FOR YOU!

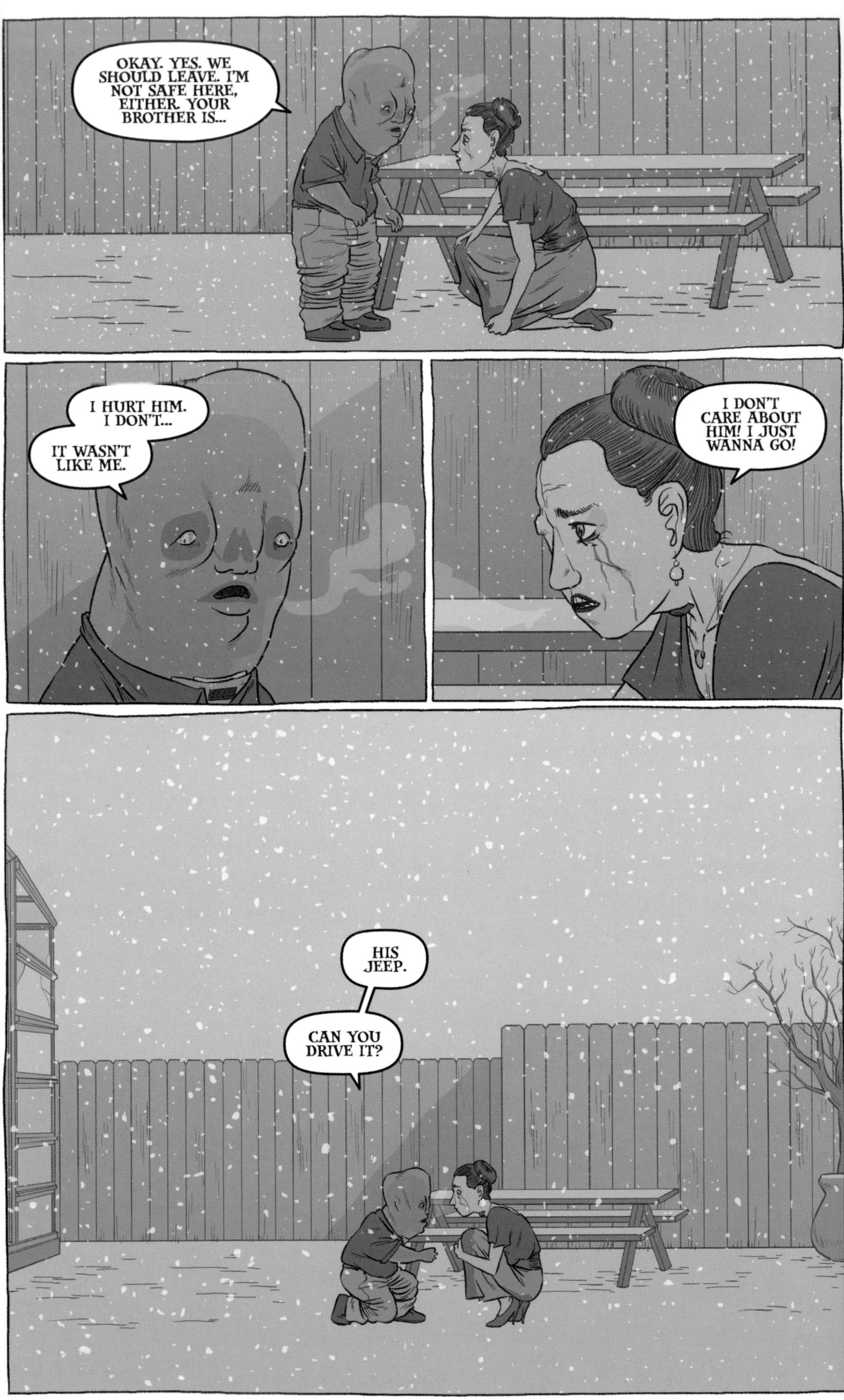
OKAY. YES. WE SHOULD LEAVE. I'M NOT SAFE HERE, EITHER. YOUR BROTHER IS...
I HURT HIM. I DON'T...
IT WASN'T LIKE ME.
I DON'T CARE ABOUT HIM! I JUST WANNA GO!
HIS JEEP.
CAN YOU DRIVE IT?

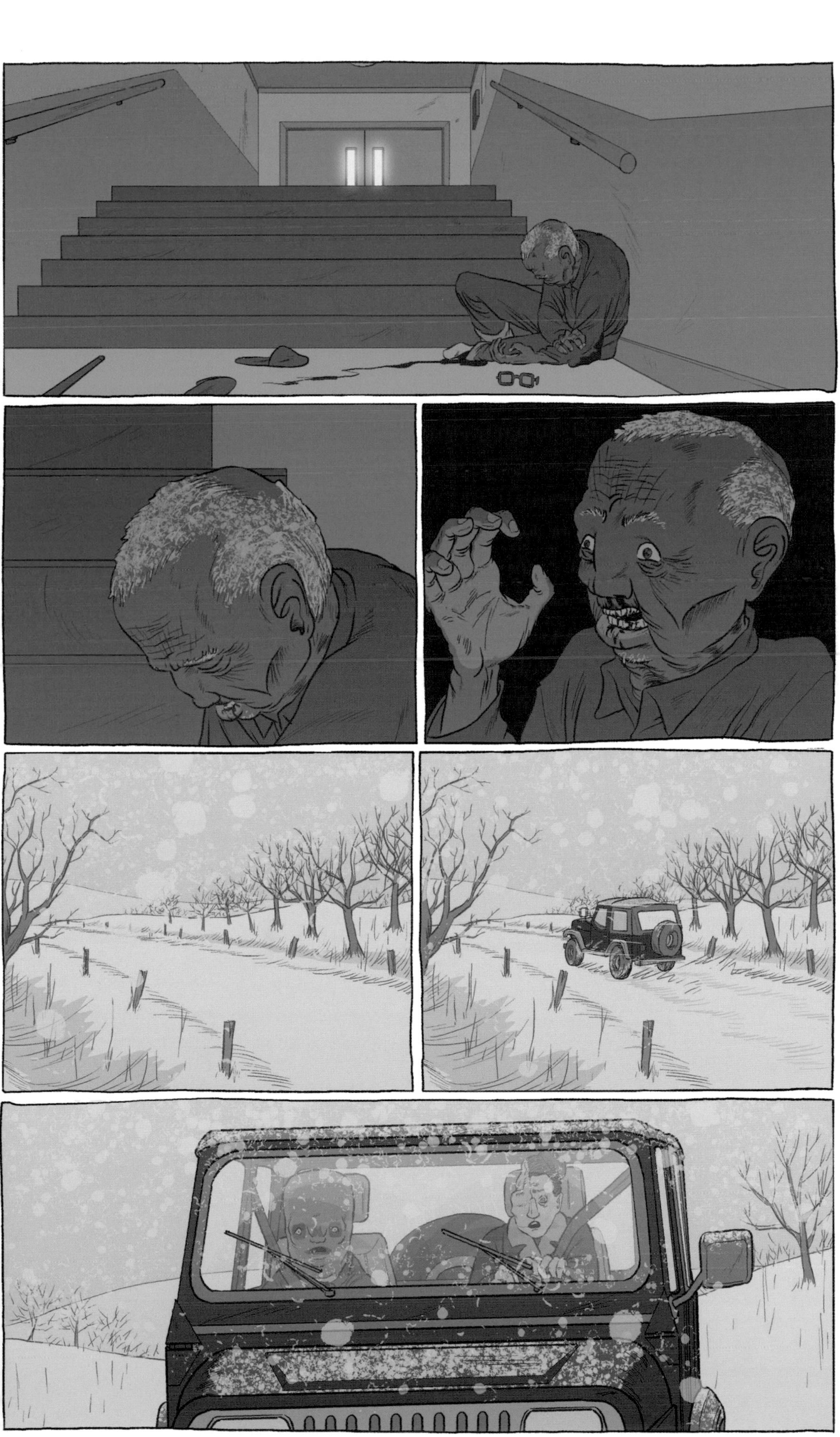

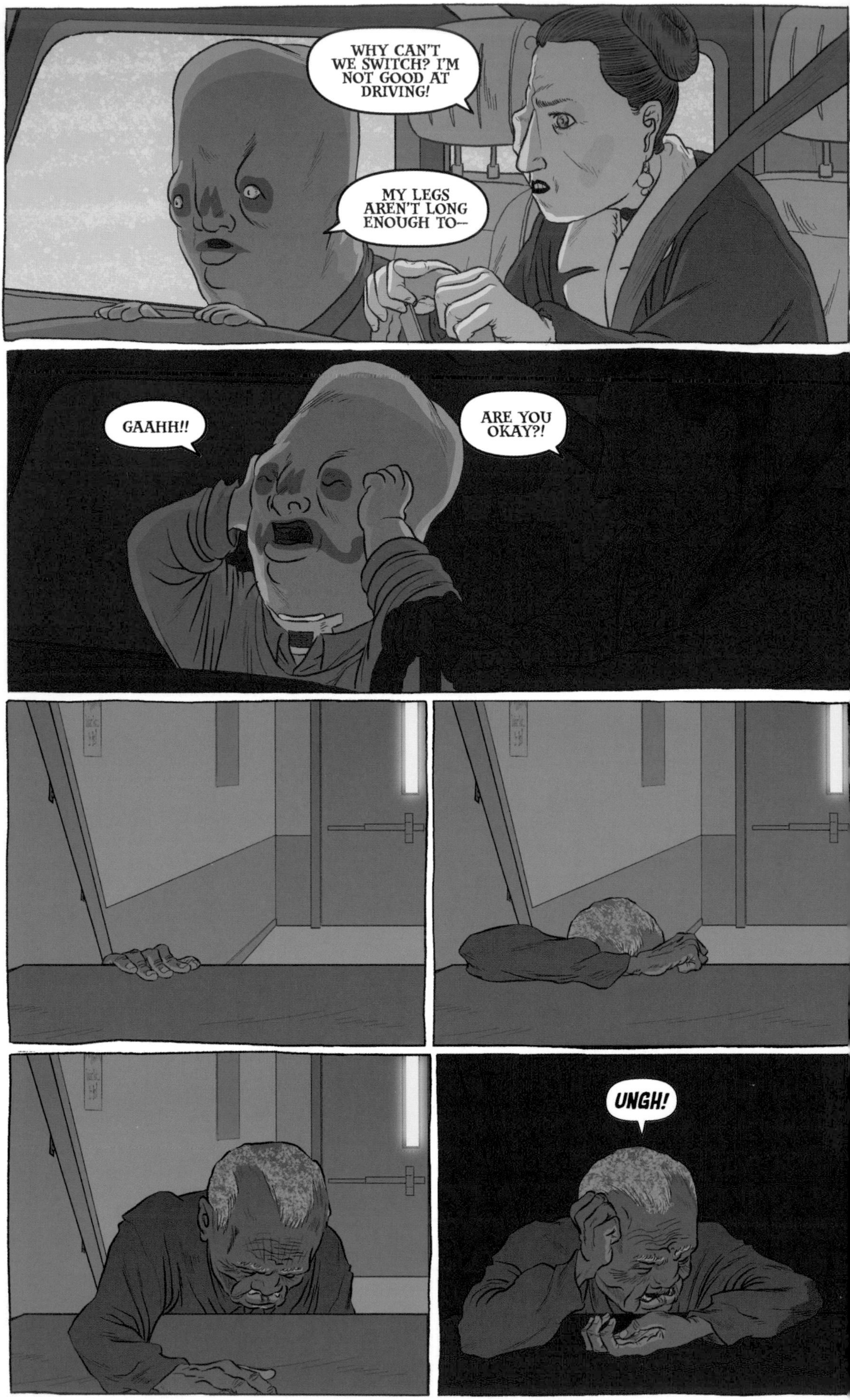
WHY CAN'T WE SWITCH? I'M NOT GOOD AT DRIVING!
MY LEGS AREN'T LONG ENOUGH TO--
GAAHH!!
ARE YOU OKAY?!
UNGH!

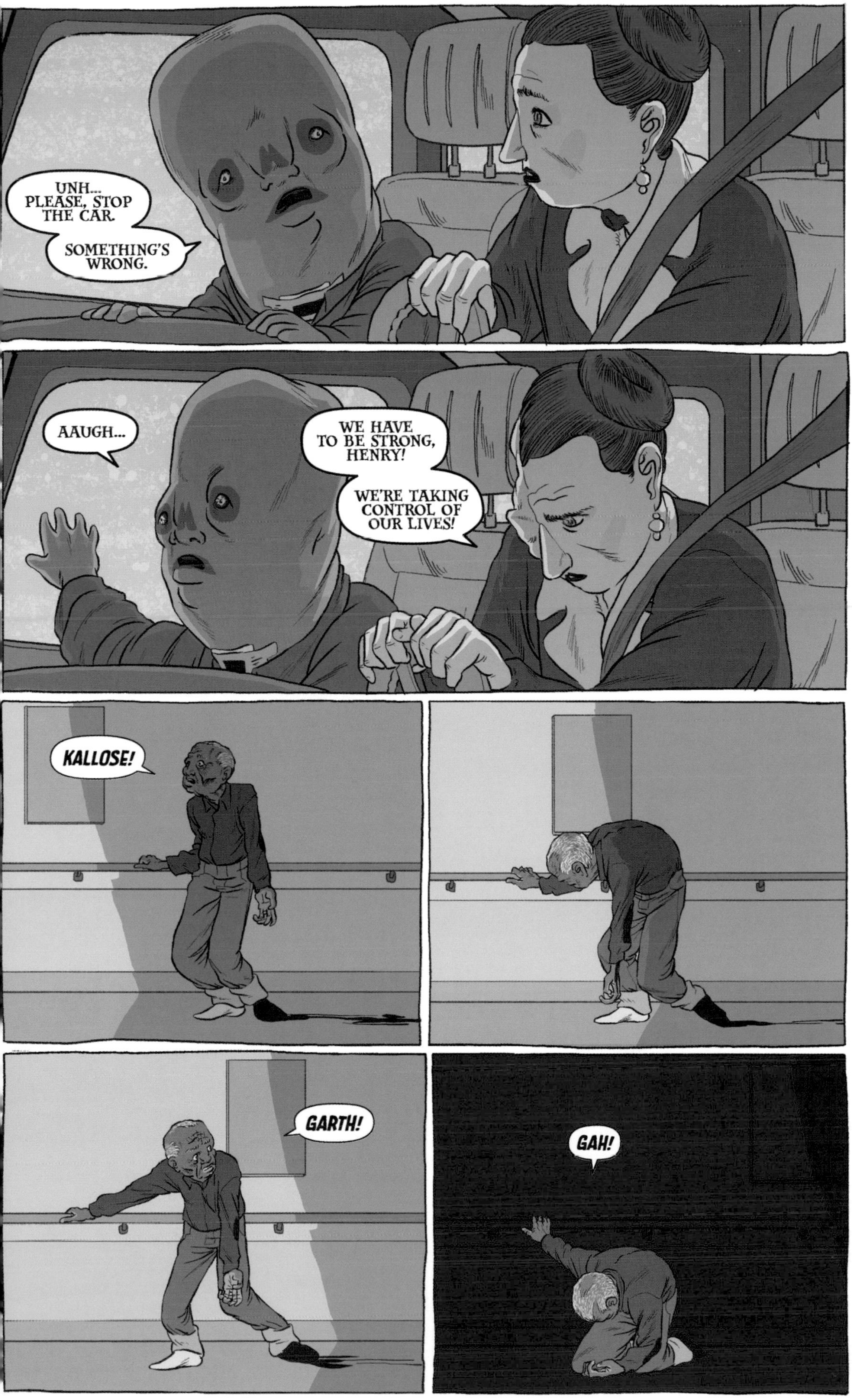
UNH... PLEASE, STOP THE CAR.
SOMETHING'S WRONG.
AAUGH...
WE HAVE TO BE STRONG, HENRY!
WE'RE TAKING CONTROL OF OUR LIVES!
KALLOSE!
GARTH!
GAH!

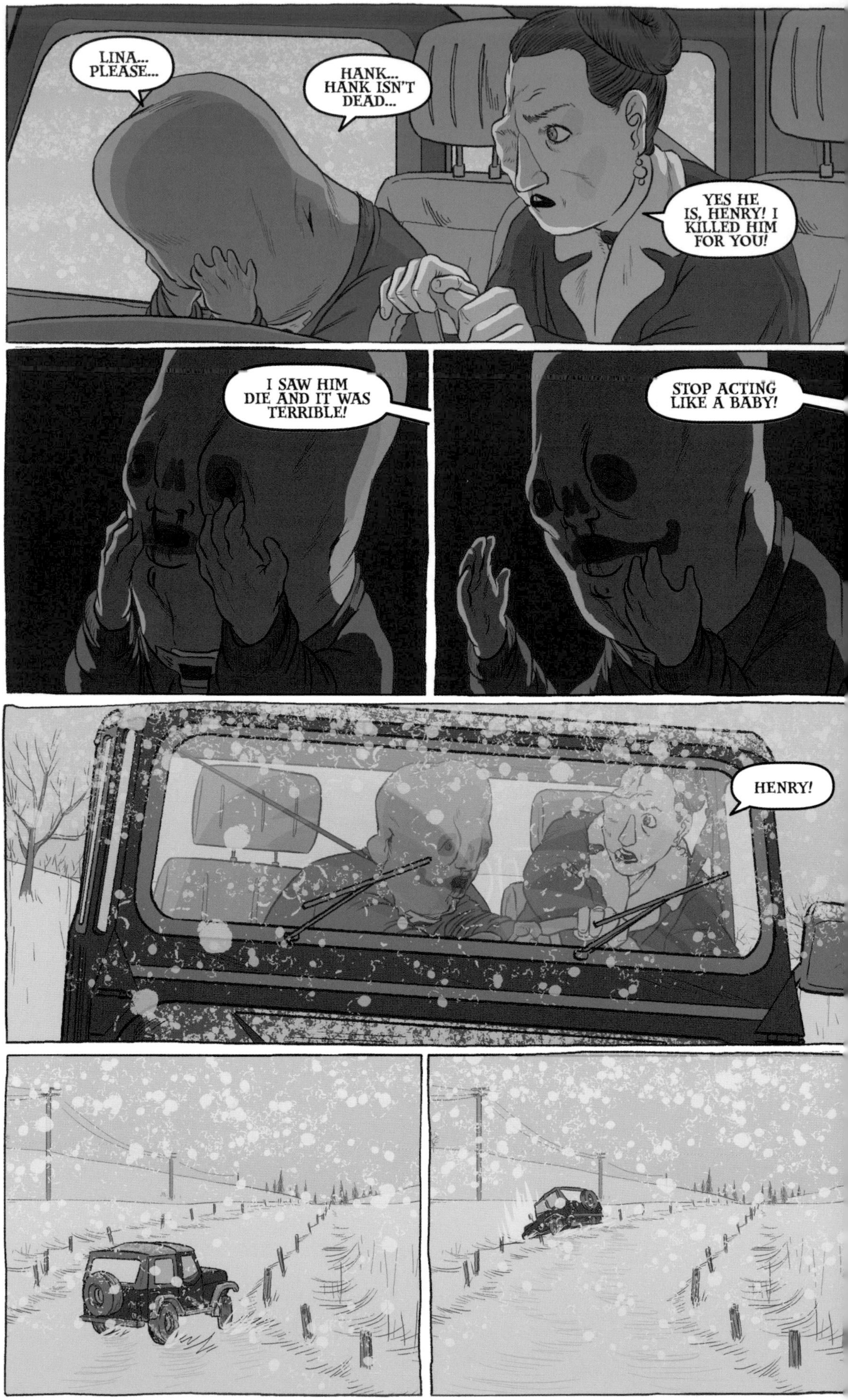
LINA... PLEASE...
HANK... HANK ISN'T DEAD...
YES HE IS, HENRY! I KILLED HIM FOR YOU!
I SAW HIM DIE AND IT WAS TERRIBLE!
STOP ACTING LIKE A BABY!
HENRY!

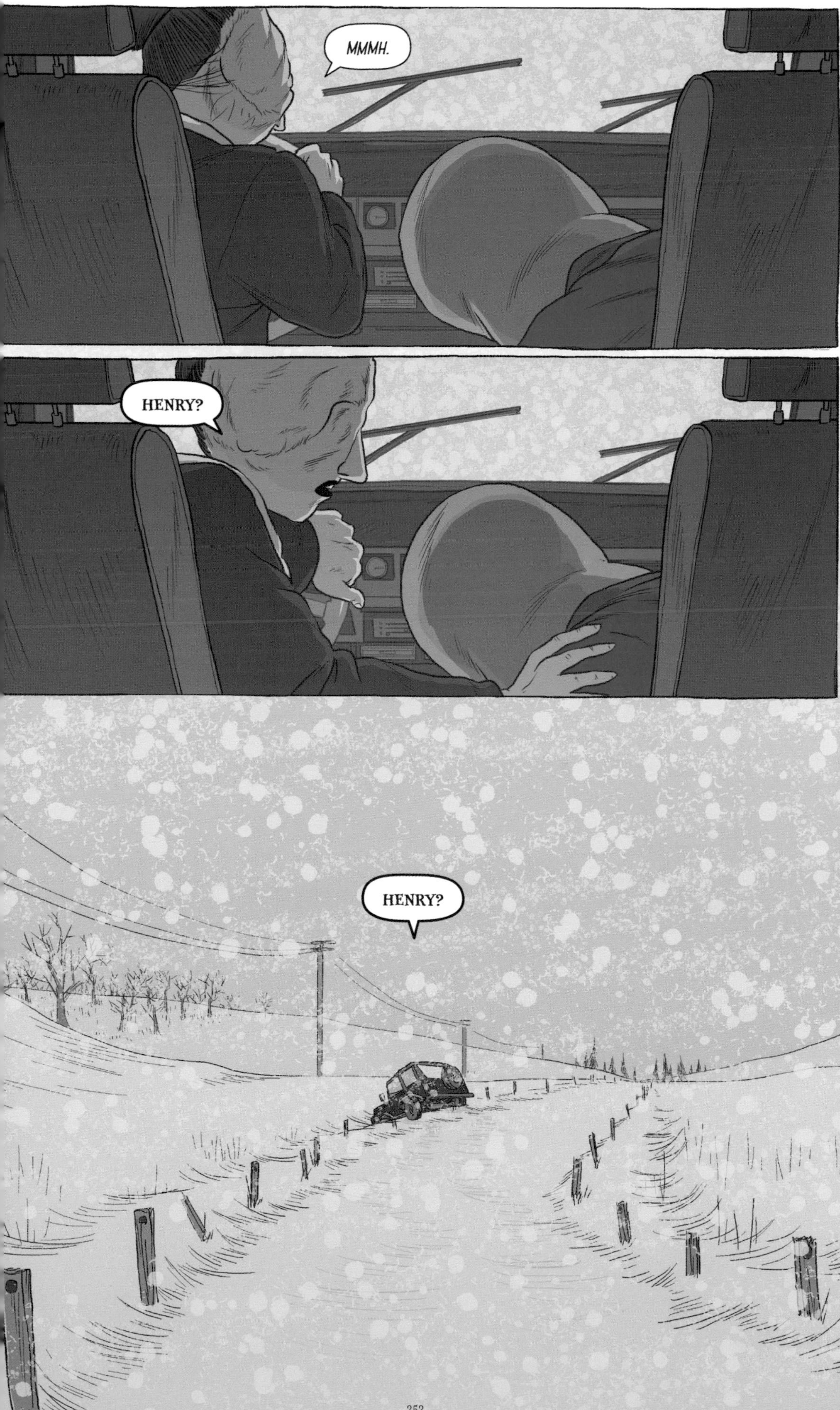
MMMH.
HENRY?
HENRY?

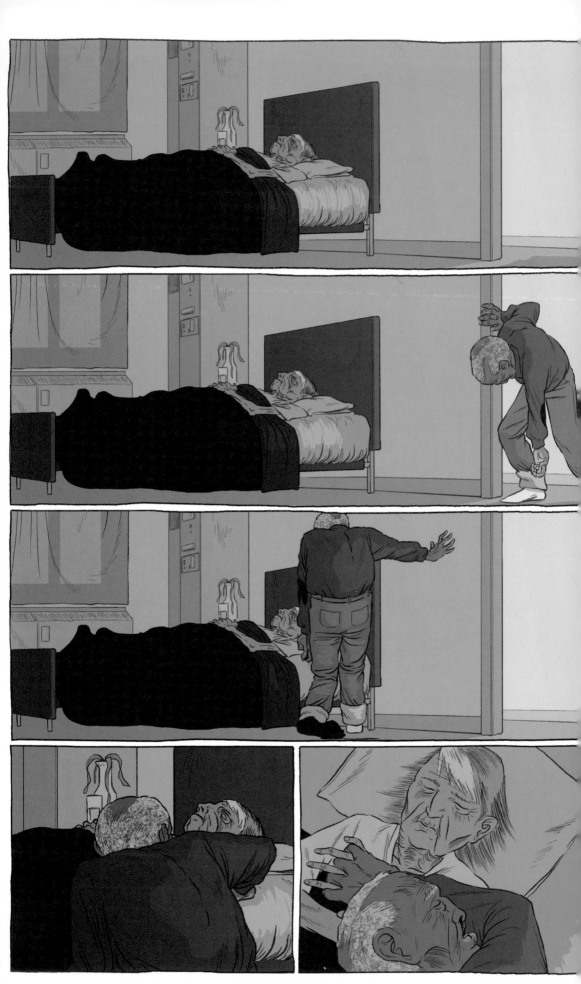

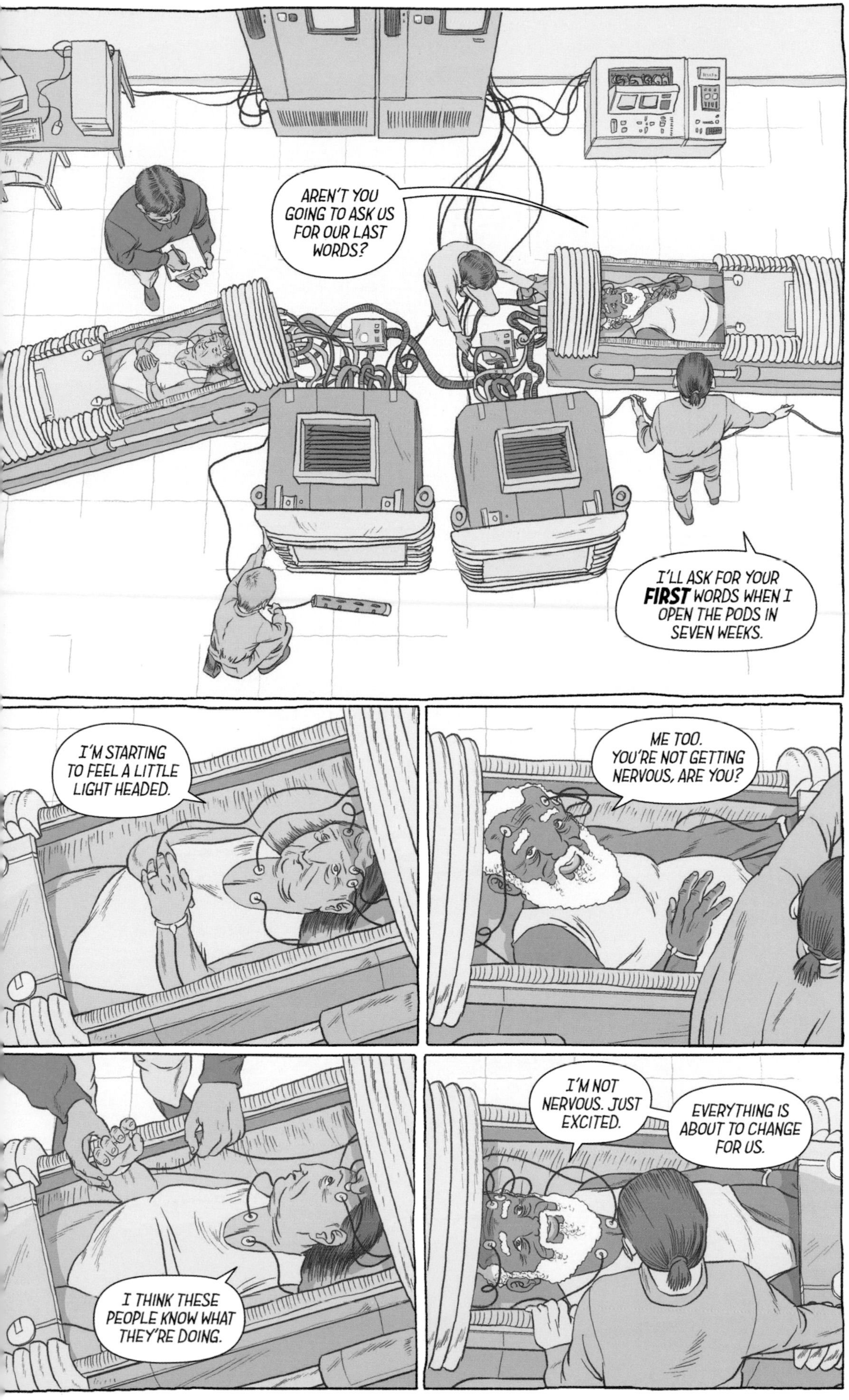
AREN'T YOU GOING TO ASK US FOR OUR LAST WORDS?
I'LL ASK FOR YOUR **FIRST** WORDS WHEN I OPEN THE PODS IN SEVEN WEEKS.
I'M STARTING TO FEEL A LITTLE LIGHT HEADED.
ME TOO. YOU'RE NOT GETTING NERVOUS, ARE YOU?
I THINK THESE PEOPLE KNOW WHAT THEY'RE DOING.
I'M NOT NERVOUS. JUST EXCITED.
EVERYTHING IS ABOUT TO CHANGE FOR US.

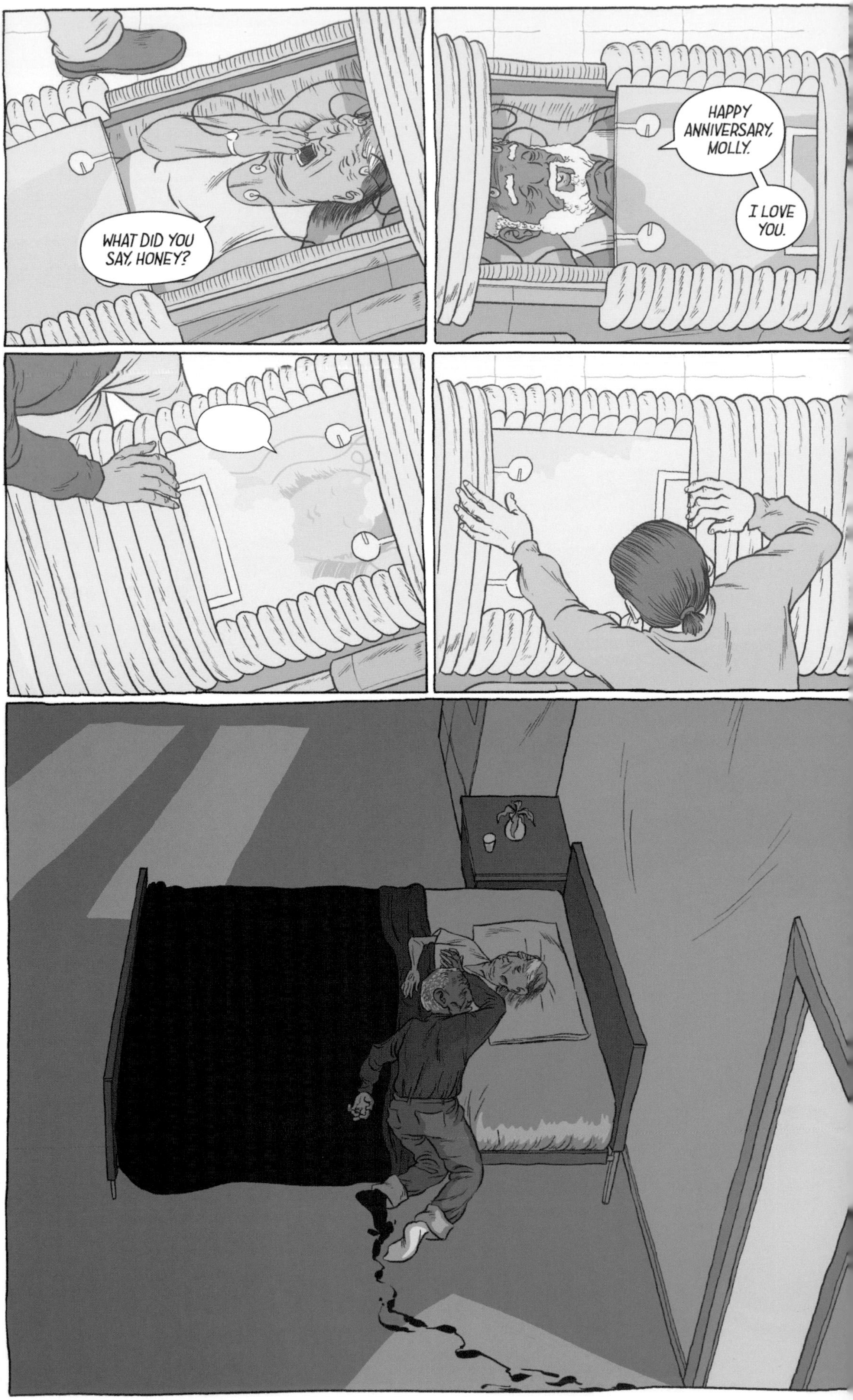
WHAT DID YOU SAY, HONEY?
HAPPY ANNIVERSARY, MOLLY.
I LOVE YOU.

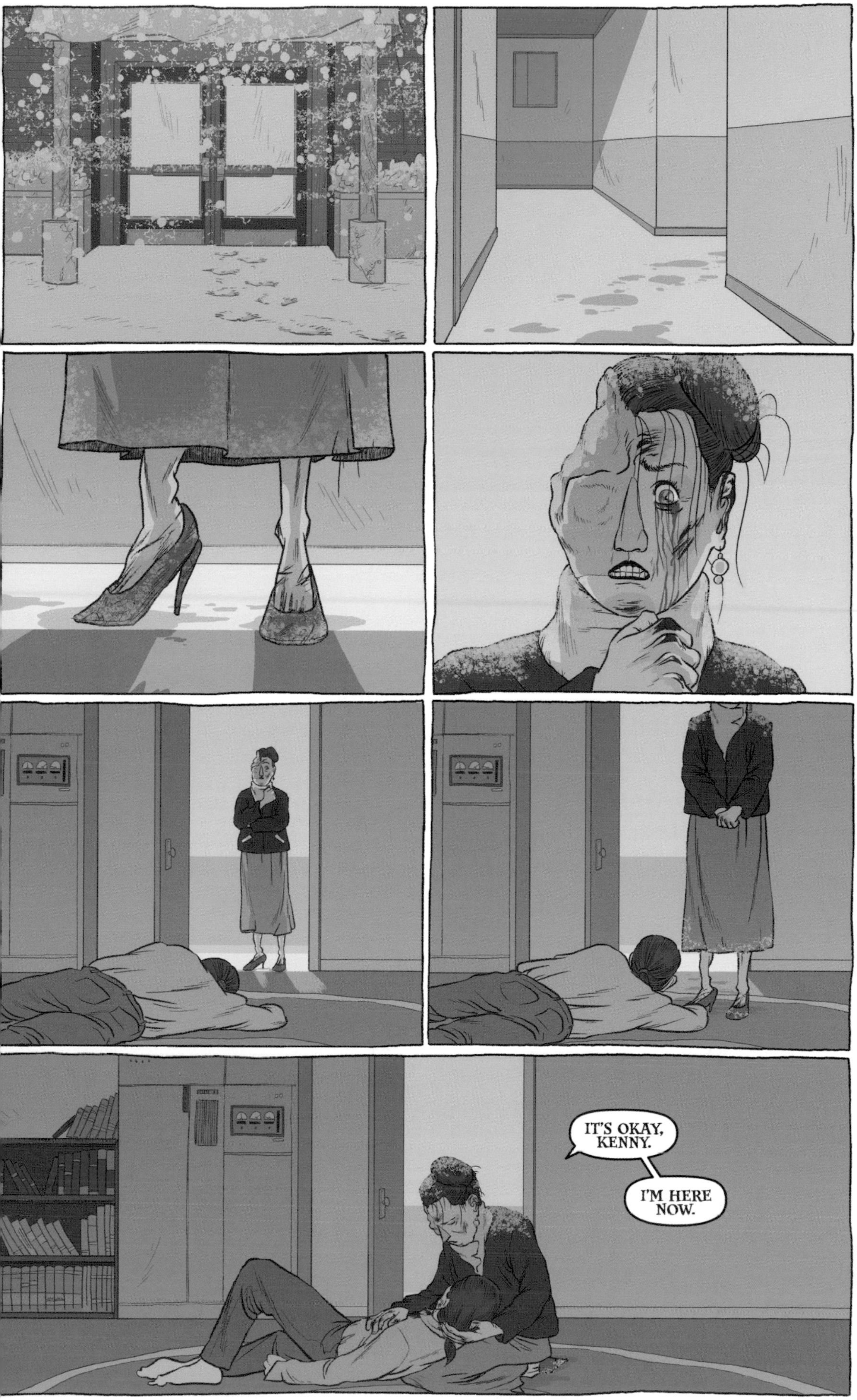
IT'S OKAY, KENNY.
I'M HERE NOW.

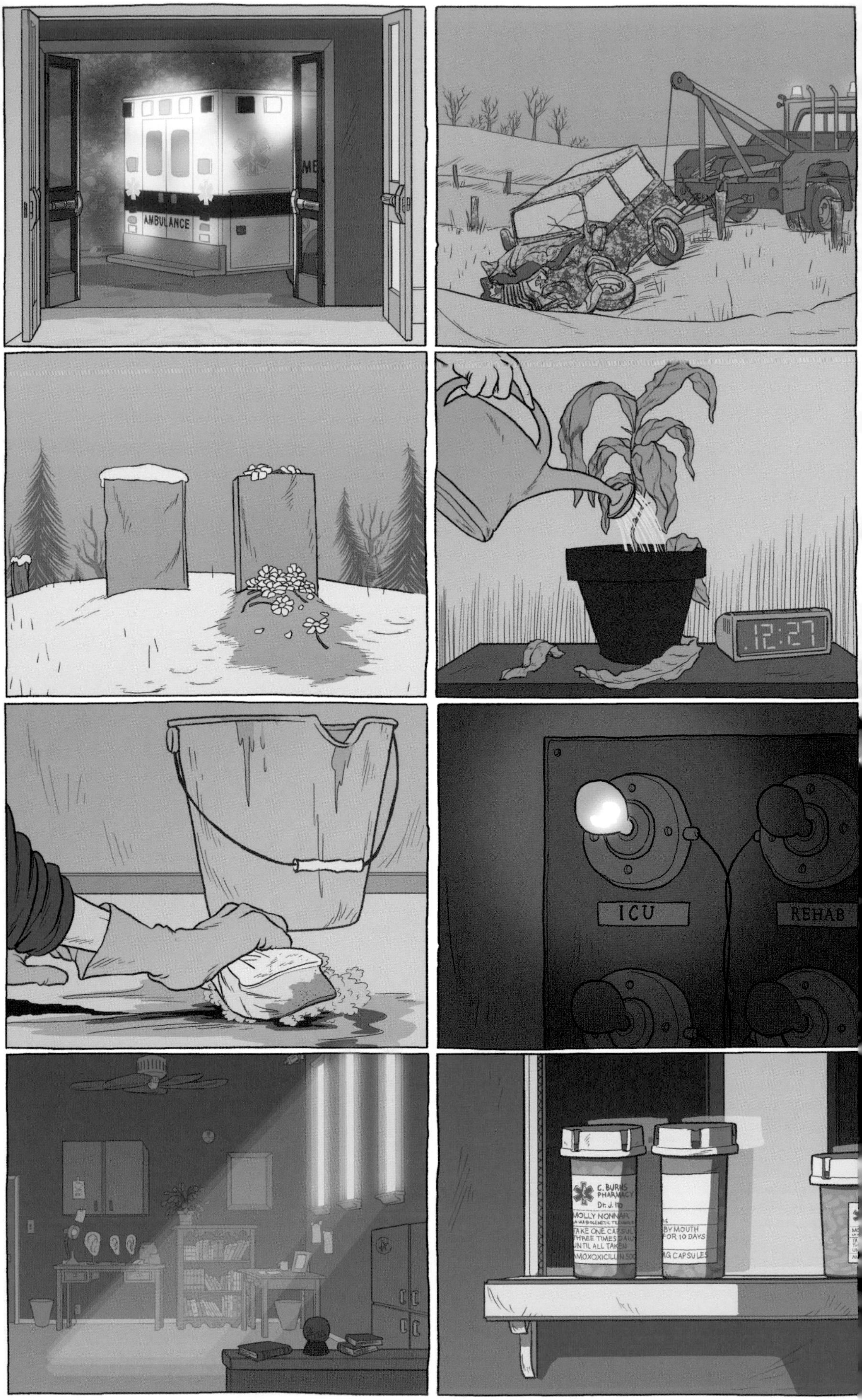

AMBULANCE
ME
12:27
ICU
REHAB
C. BURNS PHARMACY
Dr. J. Ito
MOLLY NONNAR
TAKE ONE CAPSULE THREE TIMES DAILY UNTIL ALL TAKEN
AMOXOXICILLIN 500
BY MOUTH FOR 10 DAYS
MG CAPSULES

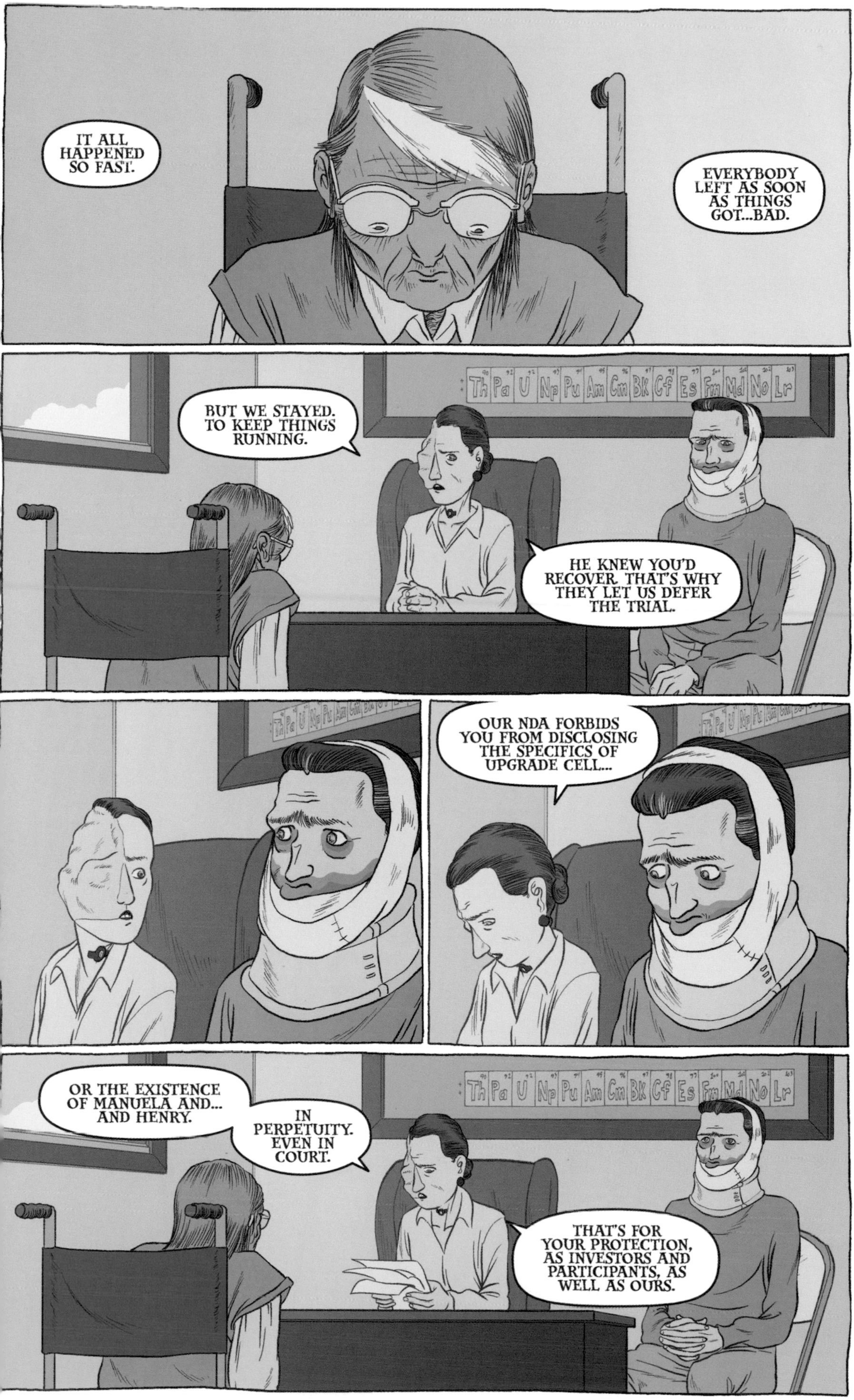
IT ALL HAPPENED SO FAST.
EVERYBODY LEFT AS SOON AS THINGS GOT...BAD.
Th Pa U Np Pu Am Cm Bk Cf Es Fm Md No Lr
BUT WE STAYED. TO KEEP THINGS RUNNING.
HE KNEW YOU'D RECOVER. THAT'S WHY THEY LET US DEFER THE TRIAL.
OUR NDA FORBIDS YOU FROM DISCLOSING THE SPECIFICS OF UPGRADE CELL...
OR THE EXISTENCE OF MANUELA AND... AND HENRY.
IN PERPETUITY. EVEN IN COURT.
THAT'S FOR YOUR PROTECTION, AS INVESTORS AND PARTICIPANTS, AS WELL AS OURS.

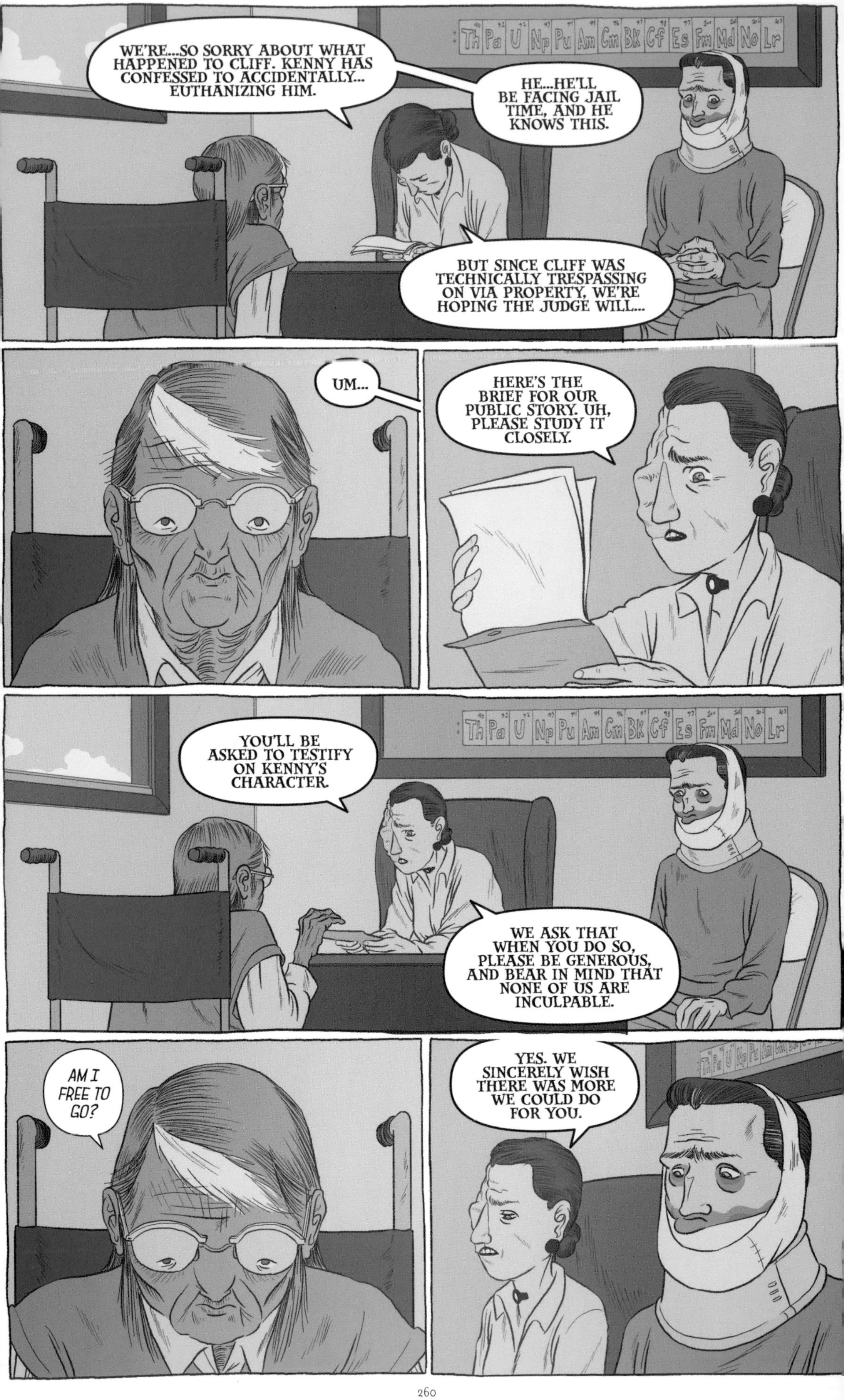
Th Pa U Np Pu Am Cm Bk Cf Es Fm Md No Lr
WE'RE...SO SORRY ABOUT WHAT HAPPENED TO CLIFF. KENNY HAS CONFESSED TO ACCIDENTALLY... EUTHANIZING HIM.
HE...HE'LL BE FACING JAIL TIME, AND HE KNOWS THIS.
BUT SINCE CLIFF WAS TECHNICALLY TRESPASSING ON VIA PROPERTY, WE'RE HOPING THE JUDGE WILL...
UM...
HERE'S THE BRIEF FOR OUR PUBLIC STORY. UH, PLEASE STUDY IT CLOSELY.
YOU'LL BE ASKED TO TESTIFY ON KENNY'S CHARACTER.
WE ASK THAT WHEN YOU DO SO, PLEASE BE GENEROUS, AND BEAR IN MIND THAT NONE OF US ARE INCULPABLE.
AM I FREE TO GO?
YES. WE SINCERELY WISH THERE WAS MORE WE COULD DO FOR YOU.

oss interference created by the natural
on of the "B" brains was the source of
e abnormal readings that forced the
rmination of the procedure. The
ffect is that our conditions worse
roportion to proximity. The fidelity
cho becomes disruptively distorted w
distance. What Kallose and Garth were
able to see is that this can be averted

OH, FOREVER MORE.

SHE FIGURED IT OUT.

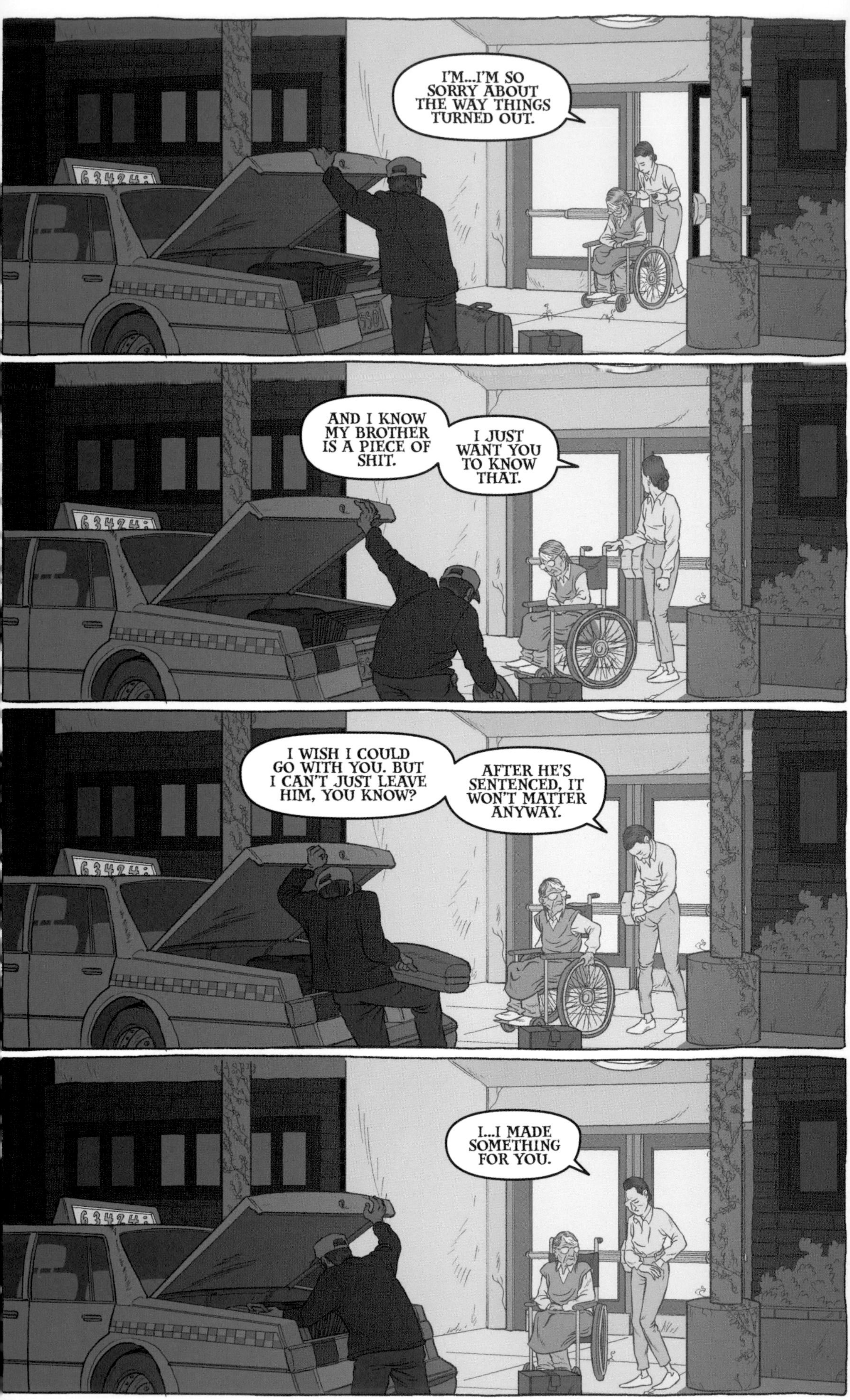

I'M...I'M SO SORRY ABOUT THE WAY THINGS TURNED OUT.
AND I KNOW MY BROTHER IS A PIECE OF SHIT.
I JUST WANT YOU TO KNOW THAT.
I WISH I COULD GO WITH YOU. BUT I CAN'T JUST LEAVE HIM, YOU KNOW?
AFTER HE'S SENTENCED, IT WON'T MATTER ANYWAY.
I...I MADE SOMETHING FOR YOU.

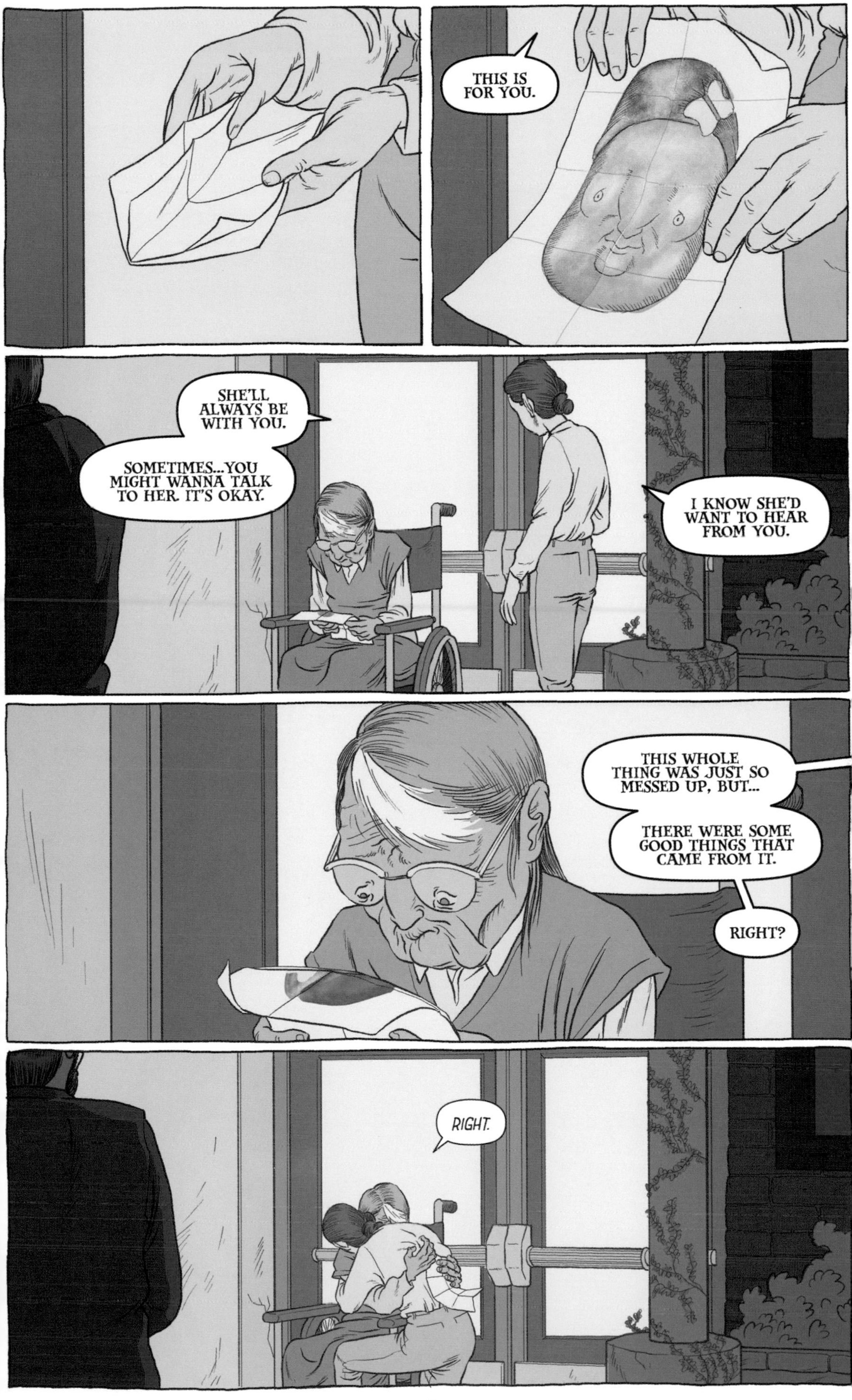
THIS IS FOR YOU.
SHE'LL ALWAYS BE WITH YOU.
SOMETIMES...YOU MIGHT WANNA TALK TO HER. IT'S OKAY.
I KNOW SHE'D WANT TO HEAR FROM YOU.
THIS WHOLE THING WAS JUST SO MESSED UP, BUT...
THERE WERE SOME GOOD THINGS THAT CAME FROM IT.
RIGHT?
RIGHT.

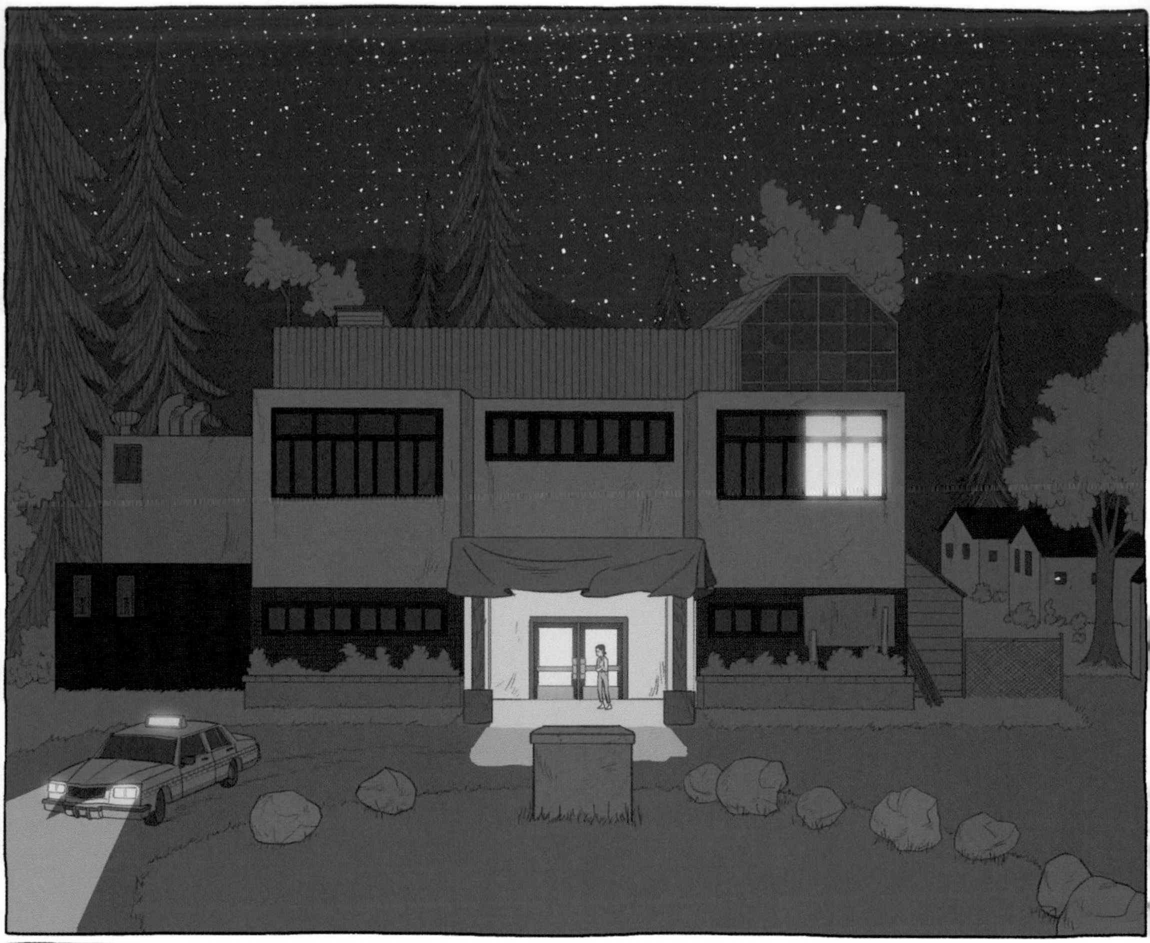

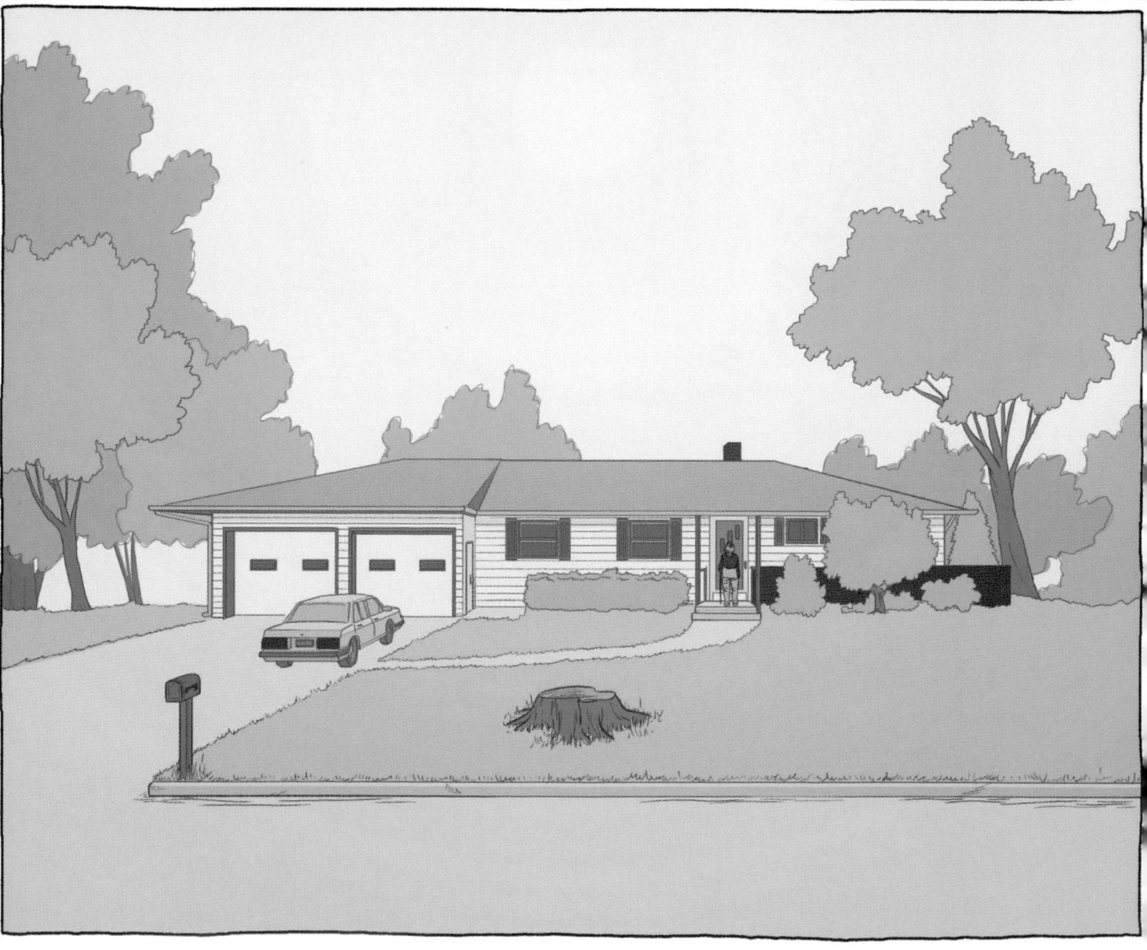

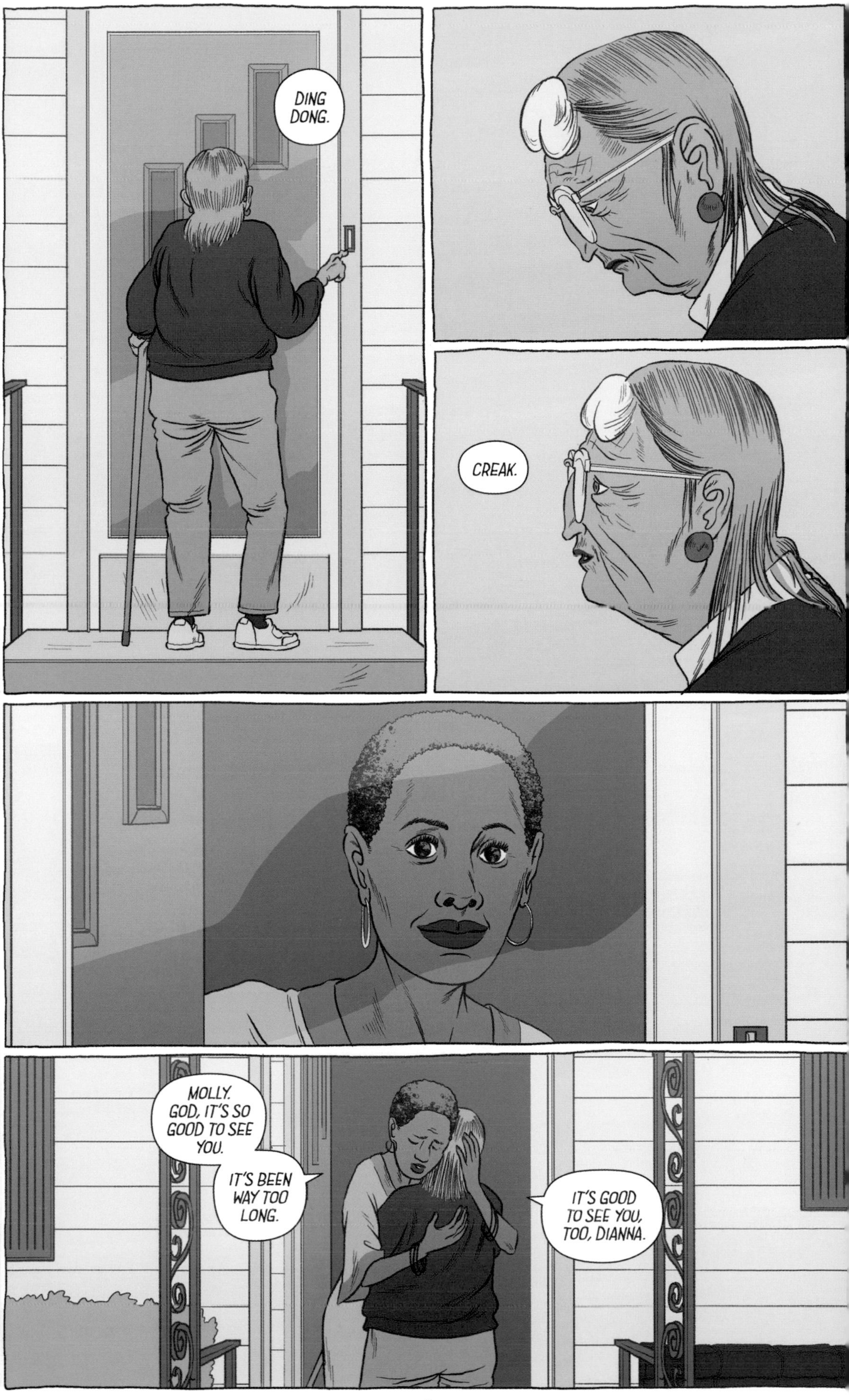
DING DONG.
CREAK.
MOLLY. GOD, IT'S SO GOOD TO SEE YOU.
IT'S BEEN WAY TOO LONG.
IT'S GOOD TO SEE YOU, TOO, DIANNA.

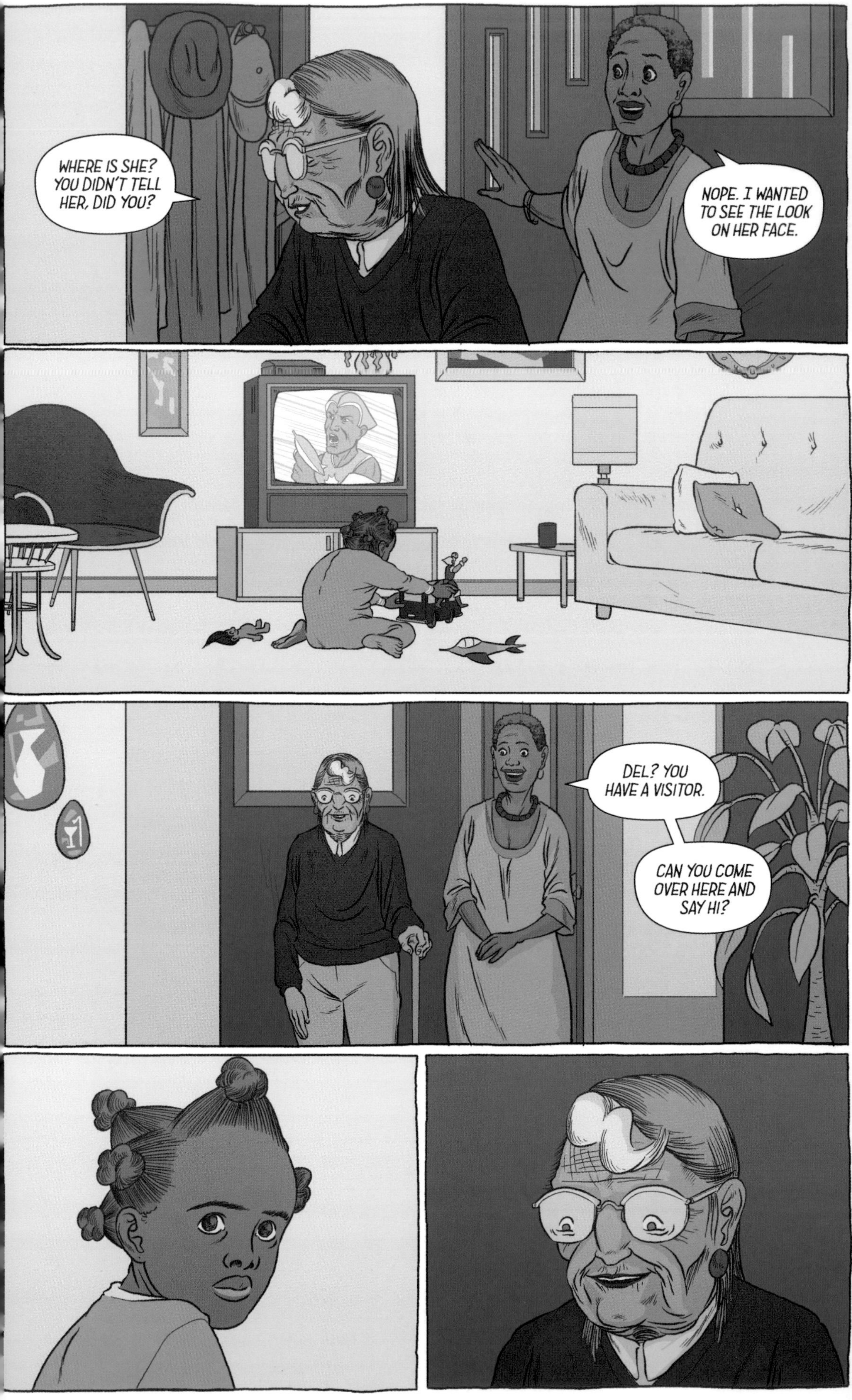
WHERE IS SHE? YOU DIDN'T TELL HER, DID YOU?
NOPE. I WANTED TO SEE THE LOOK ON HER FACE.
DEL? YOU HAVE A VISITOR.
CAN YOU COME OVER HERE AND SAY HI?

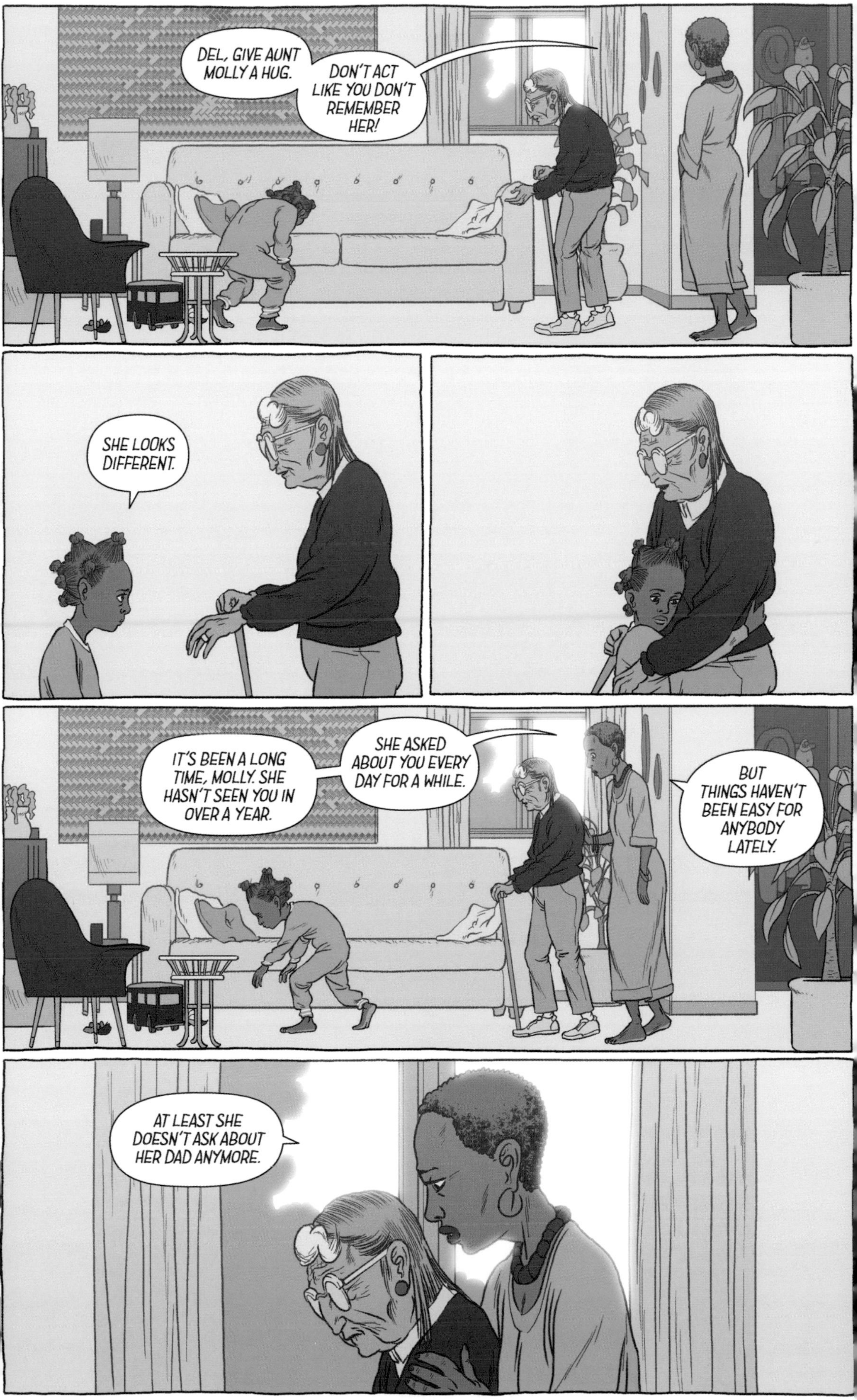
DEL, GIVE AUNT MOLLY A HUG.
DON'T ACT LIKE YOU DON'T REMEMBER HER!
SHE LOOKS DIFFERENT.
IT'S BEEN A LONG TIME, MOLLY. SHE HASN'T SEEN YOU IN OVER A YEAR.
SHE ASKED ABOUT YOU EVERY DAY FOR A WHILE.
BUT THINGS HAVEN'T BEEN EASY FOR ANYBODY LATELY.
AT LEAST SHE DOESN'T ASK ABOUT HER DAD ANYMORE.

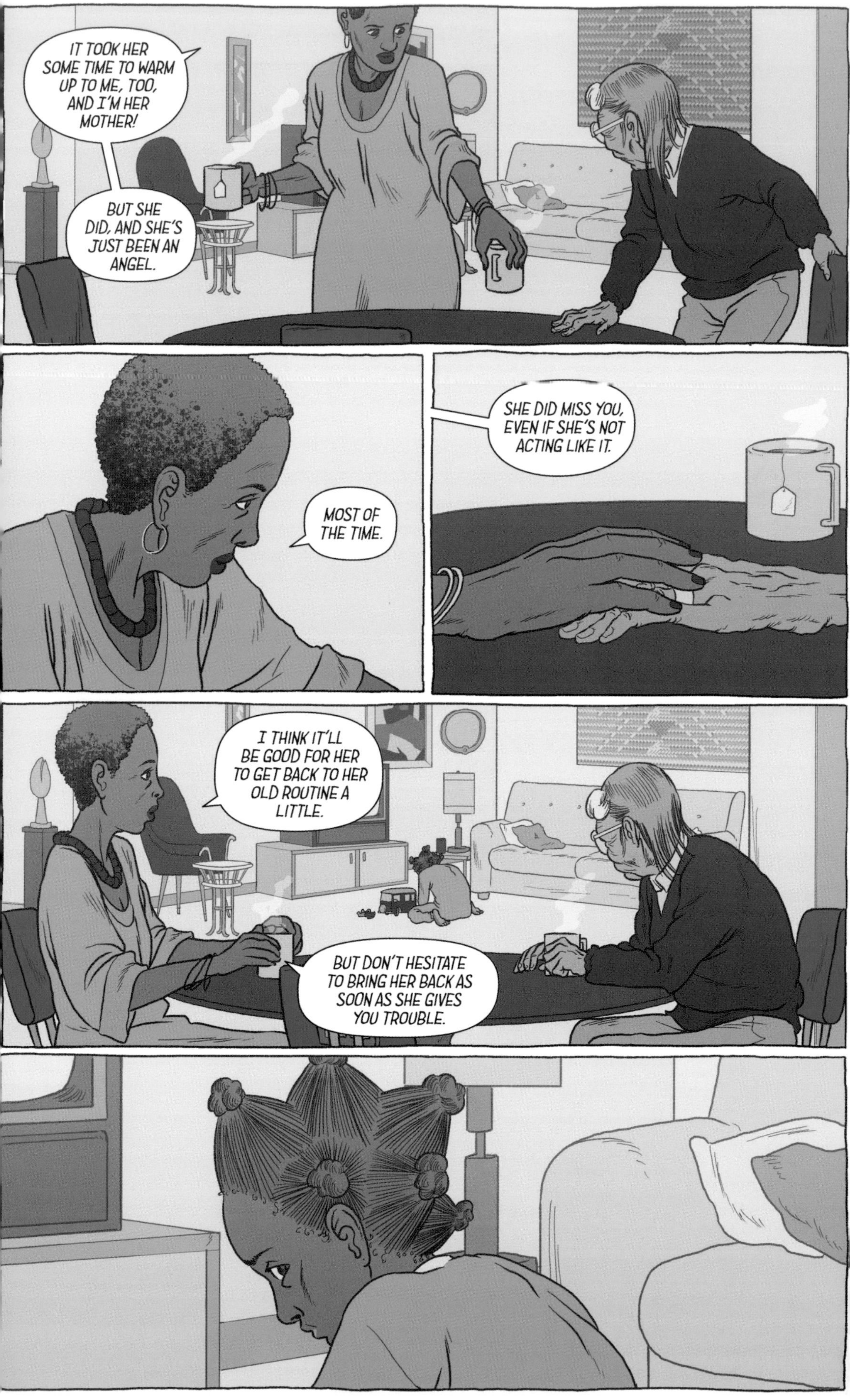
IT TOOK HER SOME TIME TO WARM UP TO ME, TOO, AND I'M HER MOTHER!
BUT SHE DID, AND SHE'S JUST BEEN AN ANGEL.
MOST OF THE TIME.
SHE DID MISS YOU, EVEN IF SHE'S NOT ACTING LIKE IT.
I THINK IT'LL BE GOOD FOR HER TO GET BACK TO HER OLD ROUTINE A LITTLE.
BUT DON'T HESITATE TO BRING HER BACK AS SOON AS SHE GIVES YOU TROUBLE.

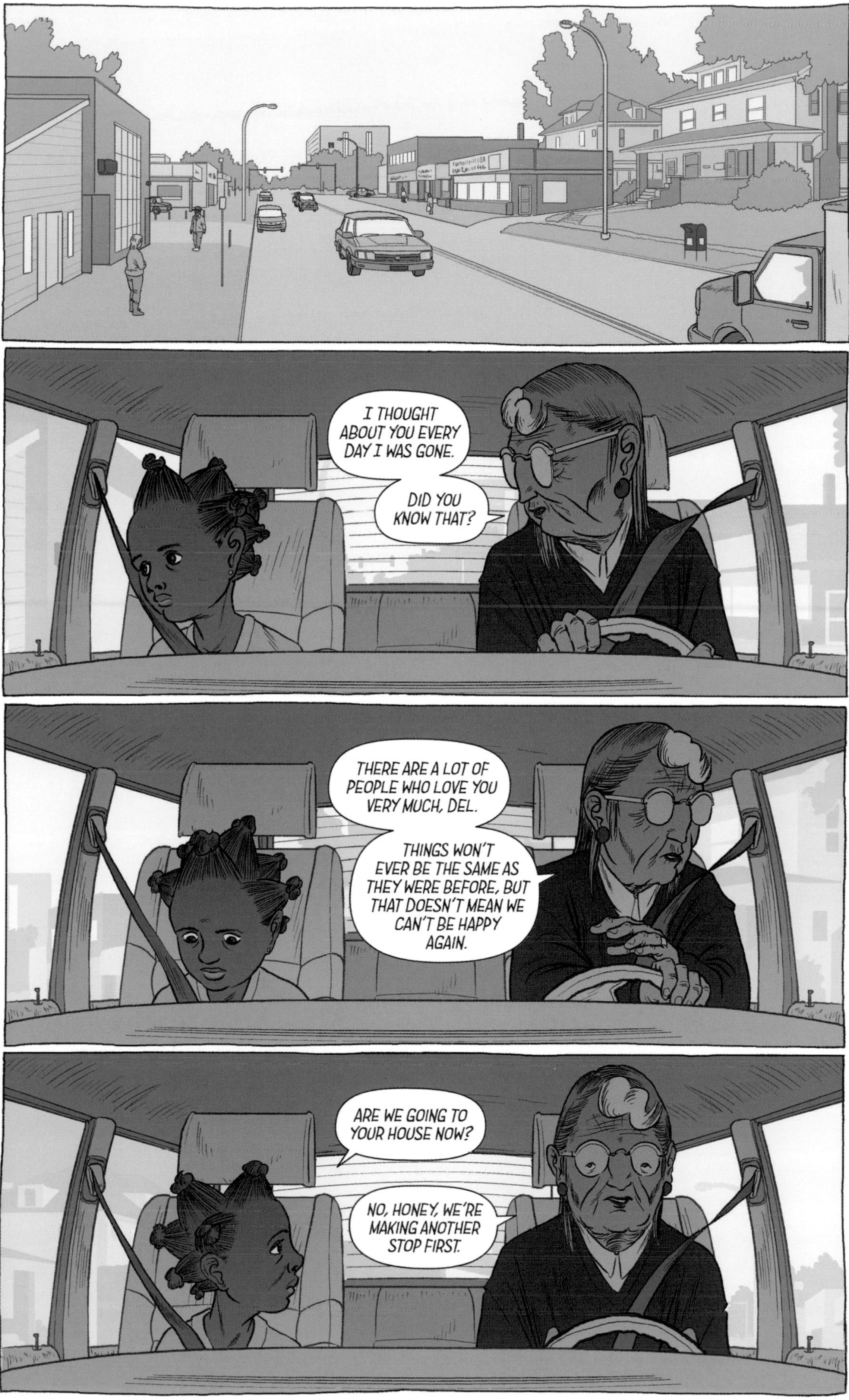
I THOUGHT ABOUT YOU EVERY DAY I WAS GONE.
DID YOU KNOW THAT?
THERE ARE A LOT OF PEOPLE WHO LOVE YOU VERY MUCH, DEL.
THINGS WON'T EVER BE THE SAME AS THEY WERE BEFORE, BUT THAT DOESN'T MEAN WE CAN'T BE HAPPY AGAIN.
ARE WE GOING TO YOUR HOUSE NOW?
NO, HONEY, WE'RE MAKING ANOTHER STOP FIRST.

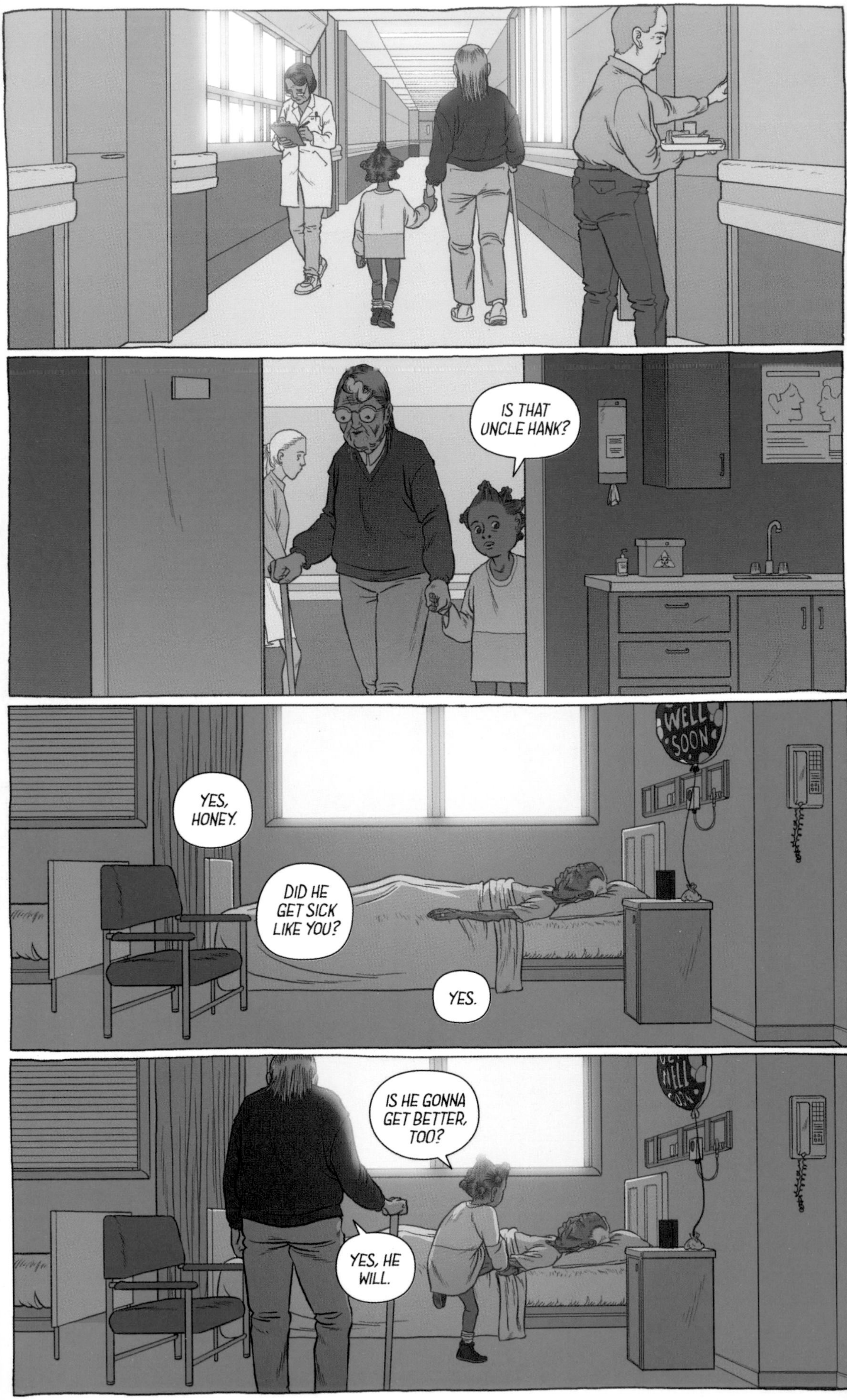
IS THAT UNCLE HANK?
WELL SOON
YES, HONEY.
DID HE GET SICK LIKE YOU?
YES.
IS HE GONNA GET BETTER, TOO?
YES, HE WILL.

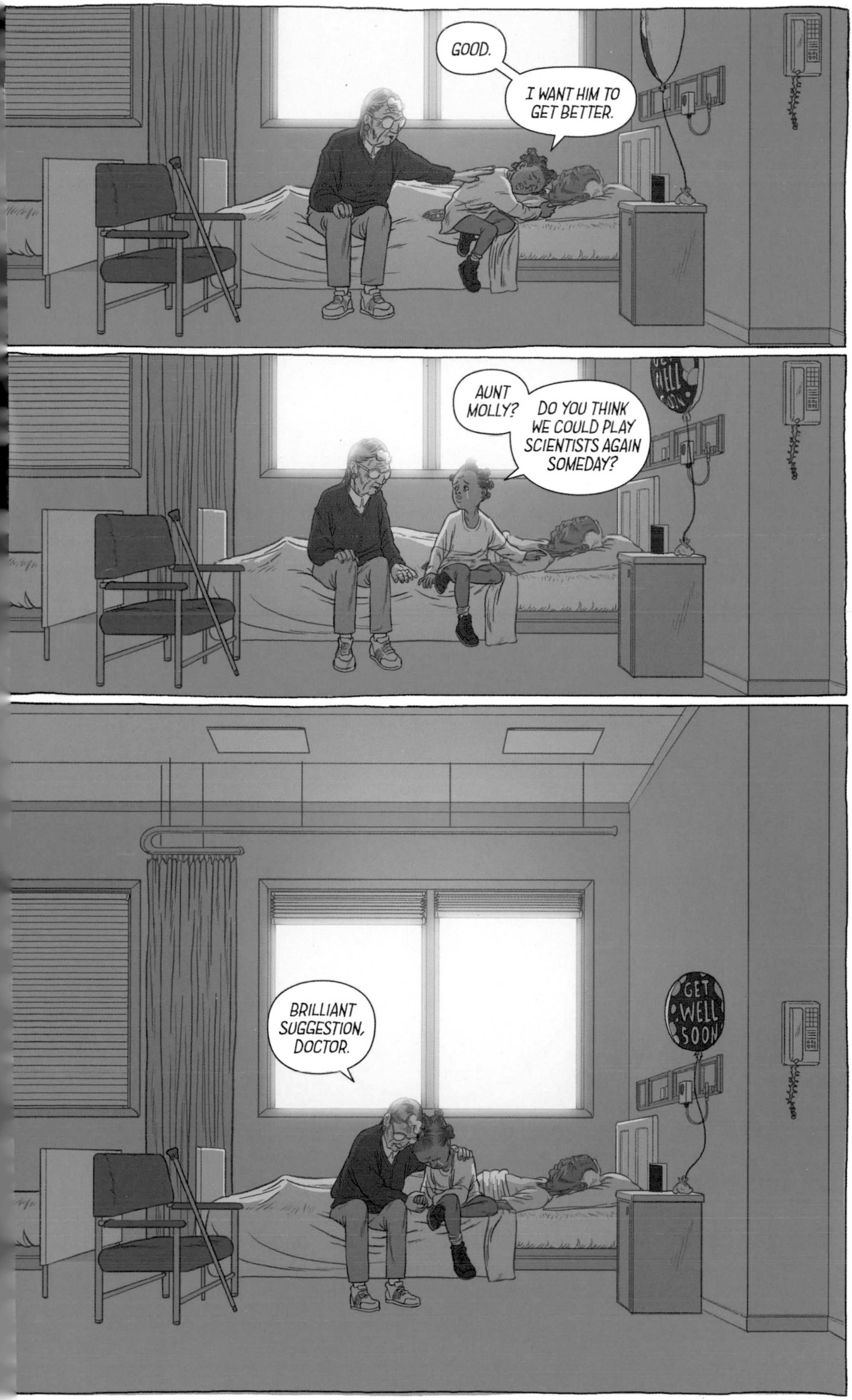
GOOD.
I WANT HIM TO GET BETTER.
AUNT MOLLY?
DO YOU THINK WE COULD PLAY SCIENTISTS AGAIN SOMEDAY?
GET WELL SOON
BRILLIANT SUGGESTION, DOCTOR.

Letters | DERON BENNETT
Biogenetics Advisor | BRIAN SCHANEN
Optics Advisor | MADISON COMPTON
Inking Assistance | TYRELL CANNON
Color Assistance | BEN PASSMORE

Thank you
Emily Barker, Nate Beaty, Adebukola Bodunrin, Meredith Carey, Sedale Daniels, Hatuey Diaz,
Zach Dodson, Alexis Gideon, Barb Harbeck, Erik Henriksen, Tom Herpich, Julie Ivory, David
David Katzman, Kristen Klebba, Heather Kortan, Julia Kuhl, Alec Longstreth, Kolin Pope,
Andy Radar, Aaron Renier, Ethan Shaftel, Shelley Short, Becca Taylor, Chris Terry, Darrick
Thompson, Tena Whatley, John C. Worsley, Won You, and Erik Loyer

ISBN: 978-1-5493-0292-3

Library of Congress Control Number: 2018939670

10 9 8 7 6 5 4 3 2 1